Impressionist &
Post-Impressionist
Drawings

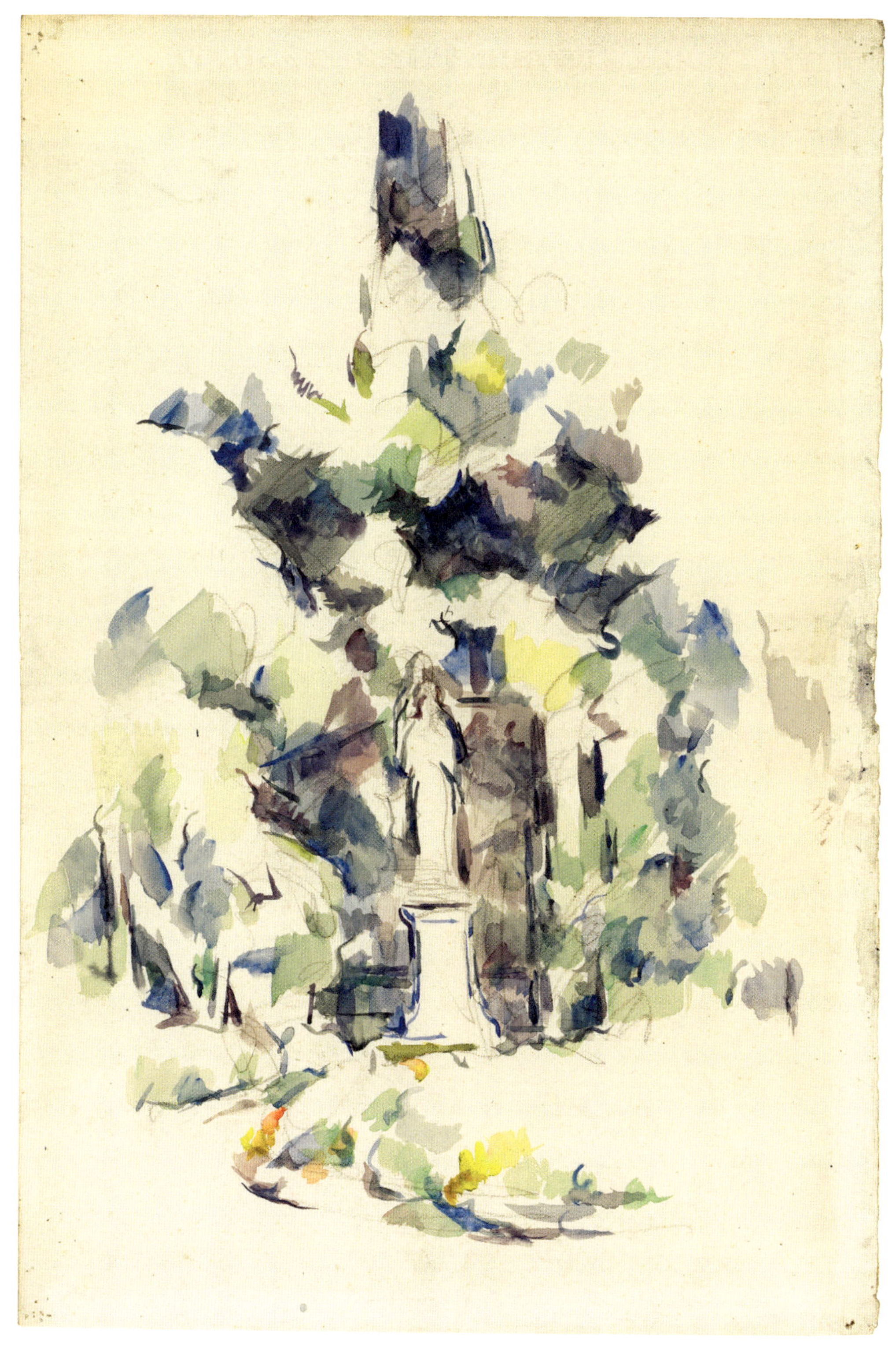

Christopher Lloyd

Impressionist &
Post-Impressionist
Drawings

with 224 illustrations

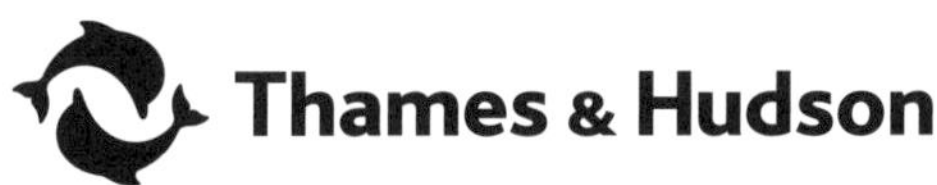

Thames & Hudson

For Alexander, Benedict, Oliver and Rupert
who in their different ways have opened my eyes to the world

On the cover, front: Edgar Degas, *The Dance Examination, c.* 1879. Denver Art Museum/akg-images; back, top: Paul Cézanne, *Still Life with Blue Pot, c.* 1900–06. J. Paul Getty Museum, Los Angeles; right: Henri de Toulouse-Lautrec, *Monsieur Boileau at the Café, c.* 1893. Cleveland Museum of Art; bottom: Vincent van Gogh, *Souvenir of Saintes-Maries on the Mediterranean: Boats on the Beach,* Saintes-Maries-de-la-Mer, *c.* 4 June 1888. Private Collection. Photo © Christie's Images/Bridgeman Images.

Frontispiece: Paul Cézanne, *Statue under Trees,* 1898–1900. Pencil and watercolour, 48.2 × 31.3 cm (19 × 12⅜ in.). The Courtauld Gallery, London

First published in the United Kingdom in 2019 by Thames & Hudson Ltd, 181A High Holborn, London WC1V 7QX

This paperback edition published in 2025

Impressionist and Post-Impressionist Drawings
© 2019 and 2025 Thames & Hudson Ltd, London
Text © 2019 Christopher Lloyd

British Library Cataloguing-in-Publication Data
A catalogue record for this book is available from the British Library

ISBN 978-0-500-29821-3

Printed and bound in China by C&C Offset Printing Co. Ltd

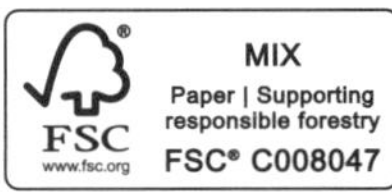

' *[Delacroix] once said to a young man of my acquaintance: "If you have not sufficient skill to make a sketch of a man throwing himself out of a window, in the time that it takes him to fall from the fourth floor to the ground, you will never be capable of producing great machines [grand painting]."* '
Charles Baudelaire, 1863

'*A back should reveal temperament, age and social position, a pair of hands should reveal the magistrate or the merchant, and a gesture should reveal an entire range of feelings. Physiognomy will tell us with certainty that one man is dry, orderly and meticulous, while another is the epitome of carelessness and disorder. Attitude will reveal to us whether a person is going to a business meeting, or is returning from a tryst.*'
Edmond Duranty, 1876

'*Drawings don't close down with age: they're always open to rediscovery.*'
Deanna Petherbridge, 2017

Contents

Introduction
The Triumph of Drawing

The passing of time and ever-increasing popularity have engendered a number of myths about Impressionist and Post-Impressionist art. Both movements were associated with the avant-garde in Paris during the second half of the nineteenth century. The Impressionists, who were active for at least a decade before the eight exhibitions held between 1874 and 1886 that defined them, chose to depict scenes from everyday life, as opposed to historical, religious or mythological subjects. In order to do this they devised a new style that was dominated by bravura brushwork and strong colour. Their pictures were controversial and had a direct and unsettling impact on the viewer. The Post-Impressionists mainly belonged to the younger generation, who began to exhibit together in the mid-1880s. They were less concerned with a literal transcription of reality. Consequently, they originated styles – pointillism and cloisonnism among them – that interpreted everyday life in a more imaginative way. Their work veered towards symbolism and idealism: its effect was hermetic and its mood one of reverie.

The division between the Impressionists and the Post-Impressionists was by no means clear cut. Initially, there was mutual respect over professional matters and any influences were reciprocal and openly acknowledged. Several of the Post-Impressionists – Paul Gauguin, Georges Seurat, Vincent van Gogh – knew the Impressionists and so can be said to have emerged directly from Impressionism. On the other hand, some of the Impressionists themselves – Edgar Degas, Claude Monet, Auguste Renoir – outlived the younger Post-Impressionists by many years. Both movements had sufficient cohesion to be separately identifiable, but even before the Impressionist exhibitions had run their course divisions were occurring over who should be included or excluded, revealing tensions between figurative painters and landscapists. Similarly, the Post-Impressionists could be said only to have been united for a short time while based at Pont-Aven in Brittany during the late 1880s before going their separate ways.

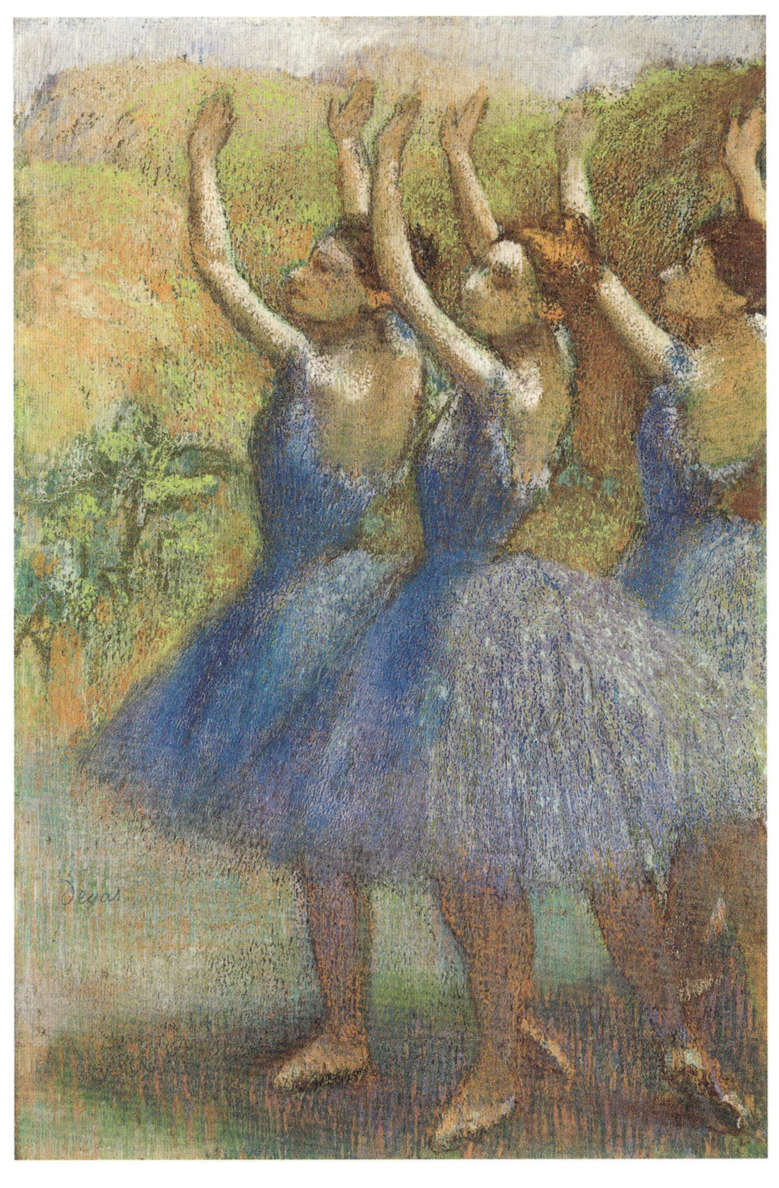

1. Edgar Degas
Three Dancers in Violet Tutus, c. 1895–99
Pastel, 73.2 × 49 cm (28⅞ × 19¼ in.). Signed.
PRIVATE COLLECTION ON LOAN TO THE NATIONAL GALLERY, LONDON

There has been a tendency to discuss Impressionism and Post-Impressionism in isolation as though divorced from the rest of nineteenth-century French art. As a result, the disruptive aspects of their work that so upset the official body governing French art and sections of the public have been diluted as opposed to being reinforced. It is apparent, however, that the changes and innovations that were so deliberately and tirelessly sought by avant-garde artists were unlikely to have been made *ex nihil*. The context of Impressionist and Post-Impressionist art, both its roots in the past and its relationship with the art of its own time, is essential for a proper appreciation of the achievements of these two movements that stand at the threshold of modern art. As Paul Cézanne succinctly expressed it in a letter of 23 January 1905 to the critic Roger Marx, 'In my opinion, one does not replace the past, one only adds a new link'.

One of the statements most frequently made about Impressionism and Post-Impressionism is that this art was made directly in front of nature. Renoir's well-known work *Monet Painting in his Garden at Argenteuil* of 1873 (Wadsworth Atheneum, Hartford, Connecticut) undoubtedly suggests that this was the case. Certainly, Camille Pissarro and Cézanne, in addition to Monet and Renoir, as well as Gauguin and Van Gogh, made it clear in statements that they believed their art was in some ways a record of the sensations they experienced at first hand before nature and a considerable amount of their work was indeed done *en plein air*. Others though, such as Degas, Seurat and Henri de Toulouse-Lautrec, had diametrically opposed views. They preferred to explore themes found in domestic interiors or places of urban public entertainment. Degas laconically records in one of his early notebooks that, 'Boredom soon overcomes me when I am contemplating nature'. On balance, though, it is now acknowledged that whatever the subject, most of the work was progressed in the studios of Impressionist and Post-Impressionist artists rather than *sur le motif*. Undeniably, the abundance of sketchbooks shows that both landscape and figurative painters did gather their visual evidence at source outside the studio, but then much of the ensuing work was undertaken indoors on the basis of oil-sketches and drawings made at an earlier stage and, if necessary, with the help of models. As Degas told the Irish novelist George Moore, '...I assure you no art was ever less spontaneous than mine. What I do is the result of reflection and study of the great masters; of inspiration, spontaneity, temperament – temperament is the word – I know nothing.'

The numerous drawings made by Impressionist and Post-Impressionist painters constitute vitally significant evidence for an understanding of the working practices of avant-garde artists in late nineteenth-century France. In short, drawing was an essential component in the revolutionary art that they produced. Added to this is the indisputable fact that Degas, Cézanne, Seurat, Van Gogh and Toulouse-Lautrec are

among the greatest draughtsmen who have ever lived, and it would be perilous to be
dismissive of the efforts of others such as Édouard Manet, Pissarro, Renoir, Gauguin,
Mary Cassatt, Monet and Odilon Redon. Although never totally ignored, but unlike
the extensive literature on the paintings, there have been few attempts to assess
the true relevance of the drawings made by these and related artists in the overall
development of Impressionism and Post-Impressionism. Drawings continued to be
made in the traditional way as preparation for finished paintings, but they were also
made for exhibition as works of art in their own right in a variety of media – chalk,
charcoal, conté crayon, watercolour, pastel, tempera, gouache, and *peinture à l'essence*
(oil paint diluted with turpentine). The average number of drawings included in
the eight Impressionist exhibitions amounts to 20 per cent of the total works shown:
the highest representation was in 1879 (30 per cent) and in 1886 (26 per cent).
Degas showed more drawings in these exhibitions than anyone else (67), followed
by Pissarro (50), Henri Rouart (49), Berthe Morisot (40) and Jean-Louis Forain (39).
Drawings were also included at the Société des Artistes Indépendants in Paris, where
the Post-Impressionists exhibited from 1884, and at Les Vingt in Brussels beginning
in the same year.*

There had been a mounting interest in the art of drawing during the nineteenth
century in France. The annual Salon at the Palais des Champs-Elysées regularly
accepted large numbers of drawings (over 10,000 between 1860 and 1881) of different
types and displayed them separately from the paintings. On a smaller scale,
specialist groups such as the Société des Aquarellistes (1879–96), the Société des
Pastellistes (1885–1928), the Noir et Blanc (1876 and 1881) and Blanc et Noir (1885–92)
demonstrated a more discerning enthusiasm. Exhibitions of old master drawings and
retrospective exhibitions of recently deceased artists of distinction were organized by
the Musée du Louvre and the École des Beaux-Arts (administered by the Académie
des Beaux-Arts), as well as at the international World's Fairs held in Paris in 1867,
1878 and 1889. Dealers, such as Paul Durand-Ruel and Georges Petit, also showed a
greater interest in displaying drawings, and major journals, notably *La Vie Moderne*,
La Plume and *L'Art*, not only commissioned drawings and promoted exhibitions but
also organized them on their own premises. Later, at the turn of the nineteenth and
twentieth centuries, Ambroise Vollard and the Galerie Bernheim-Jeune mounted
exhibitions of Cézanne's watercolours that were instrumental in establishing
his reputation. Auction houses held sales of drawings and private collectors
flourished. Monographs on artists referred to drawings; exhibitions were reviewed
by knowledgeable critics in influential journals such as the *Gazette des Beaux-Arts*;
and publications (often short-lived) devoted to technical aspects of the subject
(*Le Fusain, Le Dessin, Le Blanc & Noir: Revue des Beaux-Arts et de l'Enseignement
des Arts du Dessin*) were launched and usually underwritten by publishers.

* The information in this paragraph and the following one is from Debra J. DeWitte, 'Drawings on View in
State-funded Venues and Artists' Societies in Paris, 1860–90: A Data-driven Study', *Master Drawings*, 55:2 (2017),
pp. 225–48. An earlier statistical breakdown can be found in Christopher Lloyd and Richard Thomson, *Impressionist
Drawings from British Public and Private Collections* (The Arts Council of Great Britain, 1986), p. 50 n. 35.

Such developments form the background to the interest taken by the
Impressionists and Post-Impressionists in drawing. They were intent on breaking
down existing hierarchies, and the subservience of drawing to painting was a
precedent that they felt impelled to challenge. This they were able to do, since
there was now a greater unity between their styles of painting and drawing due
to the rapidity of execution and the adoption of freer, more varied techniques.
The surfaces of pictures were no longer highly finished and so the gap in physical
appearance between a painting and a drawing was narrowed. There was also an
economic advantage in the production of drawings for exhibition and sale. It was
technically quicker to make a drawing than a painting, whatever the scale, and this
accelerated turnover. Dealers saw this as an advantage and encouraged their artists
to concentrate more on this aspect of their work. Degas, Pissarro, Cézanne and
Toulouse-Lautrec, for example, were given and accepted such advice.

That the Impressionists and Post-Impressionists found themselves in this
position was due not just to a change in their sense of purpose, but also to certain
practical measures that proved to be advantageous. Artists now had a wider choice
of materials that they could use in new contexts and without any obligation to follow
established practices. This was particularly the case as regards the softer media such
as chalk, charcoal, conté crayon, lithographic crayon, pastel, watercolour, tempera
and gouache, which were also now all more easily obtainable either in natural or
manufactured forms. There was, too, greater open-mindedness in the use of more
traditional instruments such as pencil, pen and brushes: Van Gogh, for example,
liked carpenters' pencils, reed pens and quills. Complementing these choices was
a greater willingness to experiment, so that many drawings were executed in mixed
media that can be extremely complex to analyse and did not exclude oil, which
was normally reserved for painting. Improvisation allowed for various forms of
manipulation of the surface: smudging, stumping, lifting, rubbing out, scraping and
wetting or fixing – some of which drawing shared with printmaking. As a result of
these developments, line and colour in avant-garde art converged and so in effect
drawing became indistinguishable from painting.

Artists continued to favour good quality papers such as the brand known as
'Ingres', but coloured and prepared papers, some of lesser quality, were also in
circulation. For Cézanne and Seurat in particular, the choice of paper was closely
related to their techniques. On a more practical basis, Degas's use of tracing paper
made it possible for him to transfer figures or reverse them in order to facilitate new
compositions sometimes conceived in series. Sketchbooks came in various sizes, as
did sketching pads, which became part of an artist's equipment while on the move.
Specially textured Gillot papers enabled drawings to be reproduced more easily
in journals. Supports other than paper were now being selected by artists: canvas,

linen, silk, cardboard and wood panels, each of which had a different absorbency
and was therefore important for determining the degree of finish. The scale of
the supports was no longer restricted to standard sizes and indeed several artists,
notably Degas and Toulouse-Lautrec, enlarged their compositions by adding extra
strips while work was in progress and then added another backing as reinforcement.
For exhibition purposes such drawings would be framed, which had the effect of
making drawings resemble paintings even more closely, and, indeed, no distinction
was made between them on the walls.

By such means avant-garde artists narrowed the technical distinctions between
painting and drawing. There was now little to distinguish between such works
either aesthetically or practically. Furthermore, the change in the status of drawing
presented it with an autonomy that it had never previously been granted. Although
it would seem that the immediate beneficiaries of this development in France might
be the Nabis and the Fauves followed by Henri Matisse and Pablo Picasso, there were
longer-term consequences. For it is difficult to envisage the work of the Abstract
Expressionists and many other modern art movements without the fusion of painting
and drawing brought about by the Impressionists and Post-Impressionists. In this
respect, there is a definite visual correlation between works by Degas [1] and Willem
de Kooning, between Seurat [2] and Mark Rothko or Barnett Newman, and between
Van Gogh [3] and Jackson Pollock.

II

The art of drawing is an activity central to European painting, and it is important
to recognize the degree to which the Impressionists and Post-Impressionists were
the heirs to a widely acknowledged tradition. Pliny the Elder, in his *Natural History*
written in the first century AD, wrote, 'All...agree that painting began with the
outlining of a man's shadow'. Until the Renaissance, drawing meant no more than
a means to an end, as in Cennino Cennini's handbook *The Book of Art*, written
towards the end of the fourteenth century. But a change of emphasis occurred in
sixteenth-century Italy. Giorgio Vasari's *Lives of the Artists* (second edition 1568)
invested the Italian word for drawing ('*disegno*') with a deeper meaning, whereby
it denoted more the idea behind a work of art than any practical considerations as
to how it might be made.

The first academies for teaching the art of drawing were founded in Italy: the
Accademia del Disegno in Florence in 1563, the Accademia di San Luca in Rome
and the Accademia degli Incamminati in Bologna, both in 1577. These institutions
enshrined a code of practice for the training of young artists combining intellectual

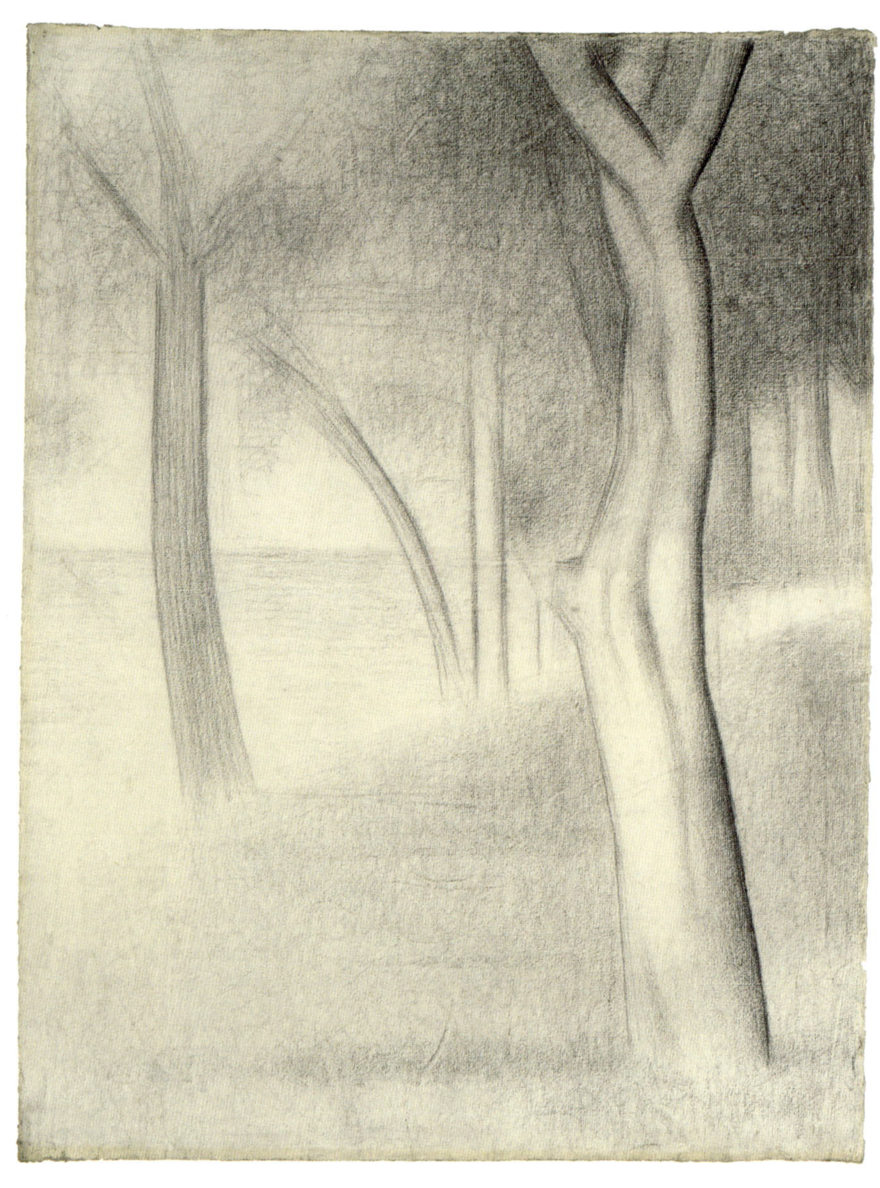

2. Georges Seurat
Trees (study for 'A Sunday on the Island of La Grande Jatte'), 1884
Conté crayon, 62 × 47.5 cm (24½ × 18¾ in.).
THE ART INSTITUTE OF CHICAGO

     Introduction

principles with manual skills. Theoretical treatises began to be published at the same time and helped to disseminate these new ideas about the importance of drawing.

The legacy of classical sculpture and the achievements of the leading Renaissance painters made Rome the indisputable centre for art in Europe – a position it held for several centuries. Seventeenth-century French artists such as Claude Lorrain and Nicolas Poussin spent a great part of their working lives in the city, but ironically it was not in Rome but in Paris that the most influential academy in Europe was established. The Académie de Peinture et de Sculpture was a royal foundation dating from 1648. It became the official body for the training of artists in France and, through the municipal academies that it controlled in the *départements*, also the chief proponent of artistic practice in the country. The

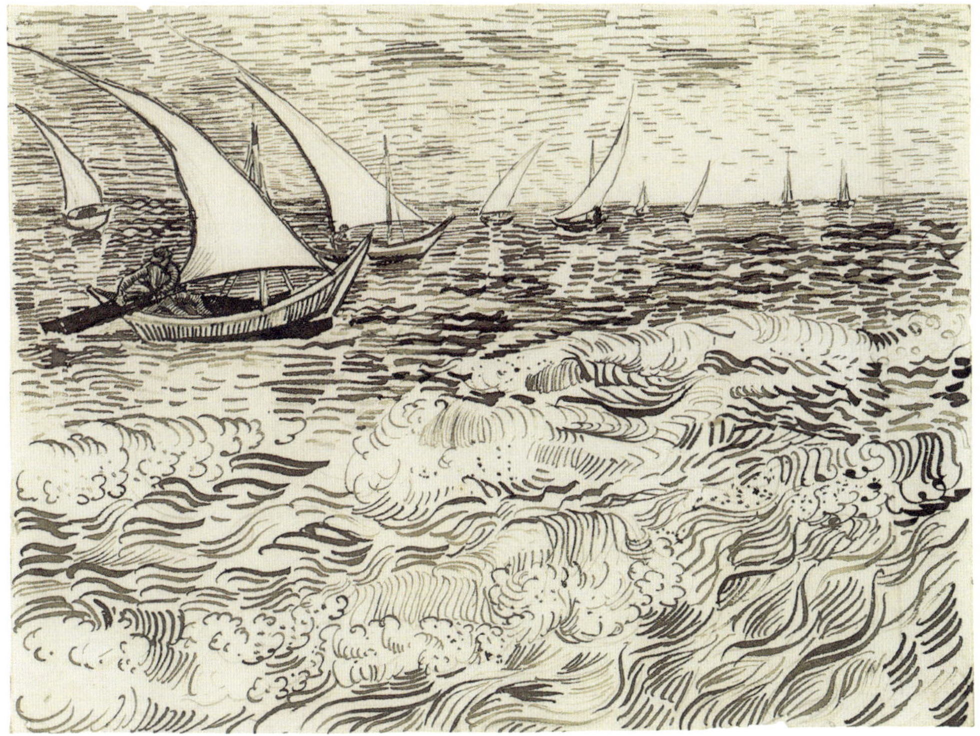

3. Vincent van Gogh
Boats at Sea: Saintes-Maries-de-la-Mer, mid-July 1888
Reed pen and ink over pencil, 24 × 32 cm (9½ × 14⅝ in.).

Académie in Paris was followed in 1666 by the foundation of an outpost in Rome – the Académie de France – where those students who won the prestigious Prix de Rome for history painting were based for three or more years. The Directors of these institutions in Paris and Rome were highly influential appointments.

The learning process at the Académie was organized hierarchically [4]. Students began by copying parts or whole works of art from prints or drawings and progressed to making copies after three-dimensional works, usually plaster casts after antique sculpture. The final stage of the process involved making drawings from live models, often posed in accordance with classical taste. This closely monitored system inculcated strict discipline and respect for tradition as well as equating correct drawing with moral rectitude. Drawings made from live models formed a special category known as *académies*, which were admired for their skill but limited in terms of interpretation. An exception at the beginning of the nineteenth century was Pierre-Paul Prud'hon, court artist to Napoleon I, who was an outstanding specialist in highly finished life drawings. Using blue-grey paper as a mid-tone, he created a velvety texture and a glowing luminosity that helped to translate a static pose into a moment of individual consequence [5].

Apart from practical instruction, teaching took the form of lectures or discussions published as *Conférences* or manuals amounting to the official doctrine of the Académie. The most famous of these were *Proportions du Corps Humain Mesurées sur les Plus Belles Figures de l'Antiquité* (1683) by Gérard Audran and *Conférence sur l'Expression Générale et Particulière* (1698) by Charles Le Brun, one of the most distinguished of the earlier Directors of the Académie. Both publications were frequently republished and proved to be deeply influential throughout Europe for a considerable time.

The main shortcoming of the Académie's system was that although it helped young artists to be skilful draughtsmen, it stifled creativity and individuality. But, nonetheless, from the second half of the seventeenth century it was these same artists who won official commissions from church and state and whose work was regularly exhibited at the Salon exhibitions that dictated taste. The Académie was denounced at the time of the French Revolution, but was afterwards reinstated as the Académie des Beaux-Arts. Teaching was the responsibility of the affiliated École des Beaux-Arts, to which admission was gained by examination and where success was measured by competitions in various aspects of drawing. The École itself, however, was reformed by government decree in 1863. Admission then became more open, proper studio facilities were provided on site, and new techniques and ideas were encouraged. These changes allowed for a greater freedom of expression and widened the appeal of the École, where the teaching was done by some of the leading masters of the day. They also encouraged open ateliers that aspiring

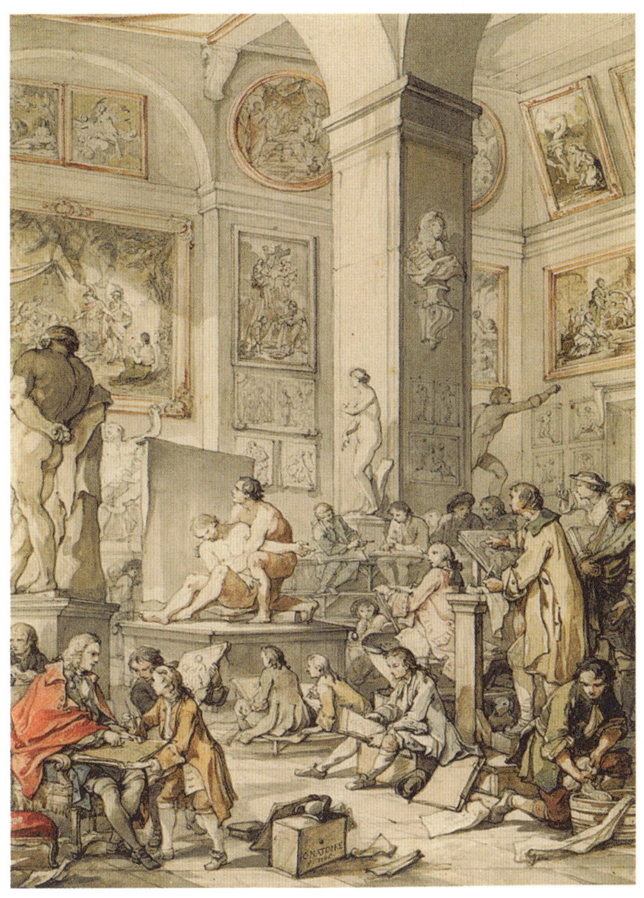

4. **Charles-Joseph Natoire**
Life Class at the Royal Academy of Painting and Sculpture, 1746
Pen, black and brown ink, grey wash and watercolour and
traces of pencil over black chalk, 45.3 × 32.3 cm (17⅞ × 12¾ in.).
Signed and dated.

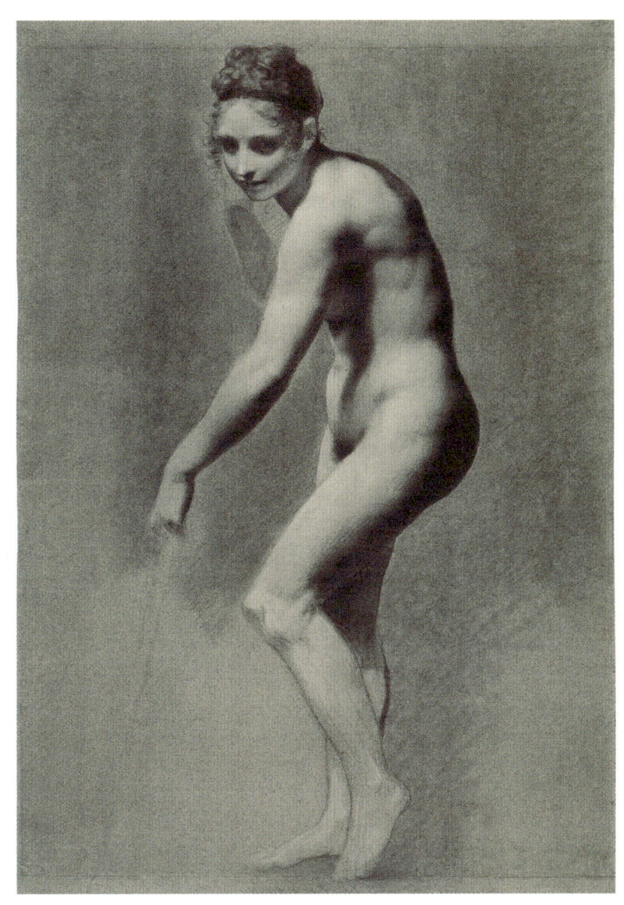

5. **Pierre-Paul Prud'hon**
Standing Female Nude, c. 1810–20
Black and white chalk on blue-grey paper,
62.5 × 41.5 cm (24⅝ × 16⅜ in.).

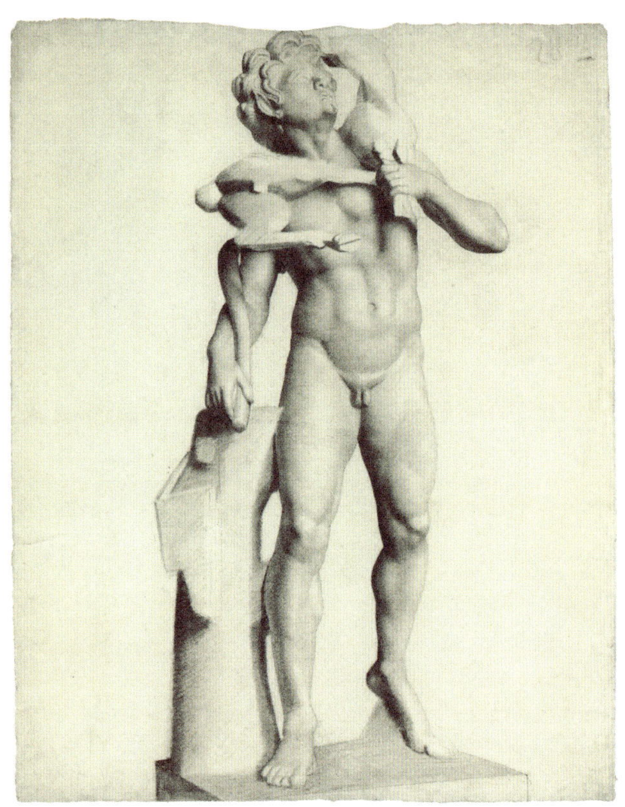

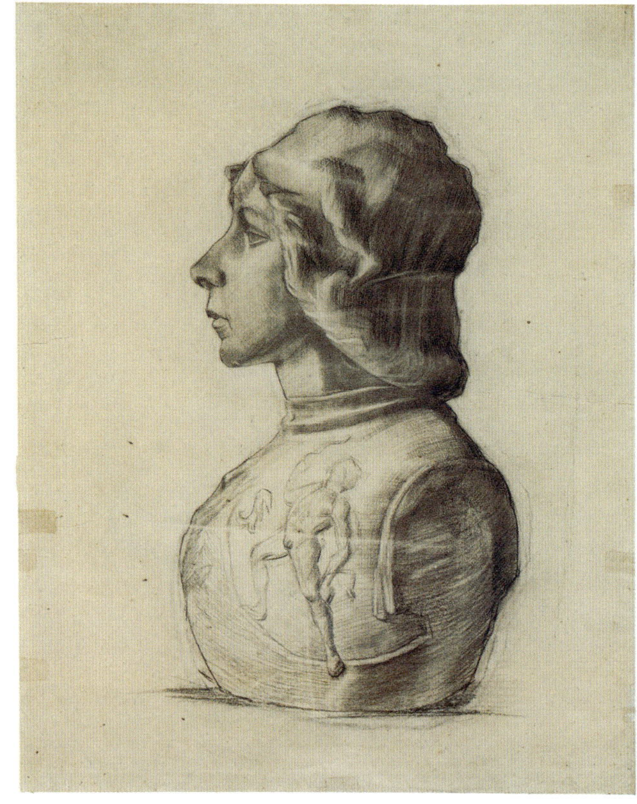

6. Georges Seurat
Satyr and Goat (after the Antique), c. 1877–79
Black chalk and pencil, 63.6 × 48.4 cm (25 × 19 in.).
PRIVATE COLLECTION

7. Vincent van Gogh
Bust of a Young Warrior (after Antonio Pollaiuolo), 1886
Charcoal and chalk, 61.7 × 48.2 cm (24 × 19 in.).
VAN GOGH MUSEUM, AMSTERDAM

16   *Introduction*

students could attend before admission to gain the skills required to pass the entrance examination. Several Impressionists and Post-Impressionists took advantage of joining these ateliers. Manet worked with Thomas Couture; Degas with Félix Barrias; Monet, Frédéric Bazille, Alfred Sisley and Renoir with Charles Gleyre; Seurat [6] with Henri Lehmann; and Van Gogh [7] and Toulouse-Lautrec [8] with Fernand Cormon.

In the event of failing to obtain a place at the École, other opportunities for learning to draw were available. There were private academies such as the Académie Suisse on the Île de la Cité where the rules were more relaxed, the models struck less formal poses and a more open attitude to techniques and materials prevailed. Pissarro, Cézanne [9], Monet and Armand Guillaumin all used the Académie Suisse, whose owner was a former model. Of greater renown was the Académie Julian, which was founded in 1868, admitted women and was run on a more commercial basis. Pierre Bonnard, Édouard Vuillard, André Derain, Fernand Léger and Matisse can be counted among the Académie Julian's protégés. These independent academies had greater appeal for avant-garde artists, especially those who failed to gain admission to the École des Beaux-Arts or, having done so, found the teaching uninspiring.

For the enterprising young artist a further initiative was to register as a copyist at the Musée du Louvre or the Cabinet des Estampes at the Bibliothèque Nationale, as Degas did in 1853 [10]. Similarly, Cézanne made copies in the Musée du Louvre [11] and the Musée de Sculpture Comparée in the Palais du Trocadéro, which opened in 1882. Both Degas and Cézanne were prolific copyists, making several hundred each, and in Cézanne's case he retained the habit of copying throughout his life. Further opportunities for making copies presented themselves when artists had the means to travel abroad, as both Manet [12] and Degas did during the 1850s.

Additional sources were provided by published material extending from the illustrated compendium

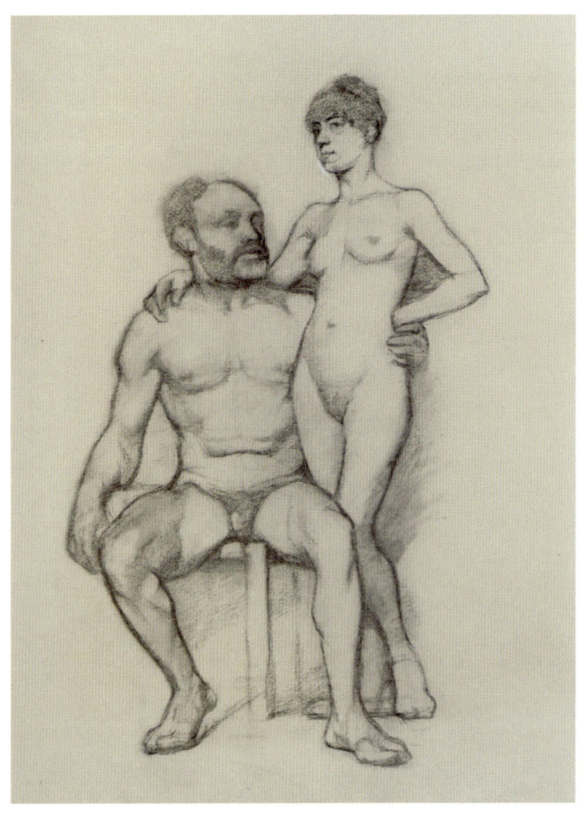

8. Henri de Toulouse-Lautrec
Seated Male Nude: Standing Female Nude, c. 1883–87
Charcoal, 69 × 54 cm (27¼ × 21⅜ in.).
MUSÉE TOULOUSE-LAUTREC, ALBI

in fourteen volumes by Charles Blanc, *Histoire des Peintres de Toutes les Écoles* (1845–76), to journals such as *L'Artiste*, *L'Illustration*, *Le Magasin Pittoresque* and beyond these fashion magazines. A profusion of drawing manuals also existed and these were frequently reissued. Those by Charles Bargue and Armand Cassagne, for instance, which taught the basic principles for different types of drawing, were consulted by Van Gogh. Of greater significance was Blanc's *Grammaire des Arts du Dessin* (1867), which was an authoritative but by no means retardataire text by one of the most influential figures in nineteenth-century French art. Seurat developed

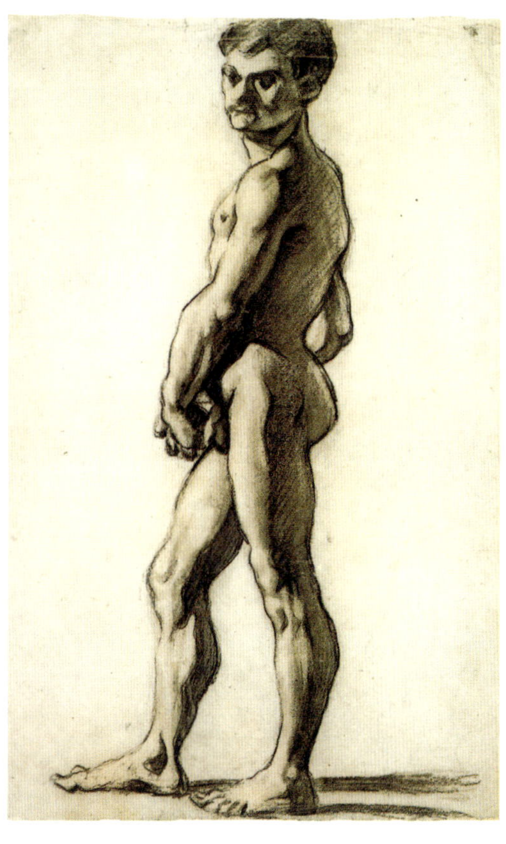

9. Paul Cézanne
Male Nude, c. 1865
Charcoal heightened with white,
49 × 31 cm (19¼ × 12¼ in.).
FITZWILLIAM MUSEUM, CAMBRIDGE

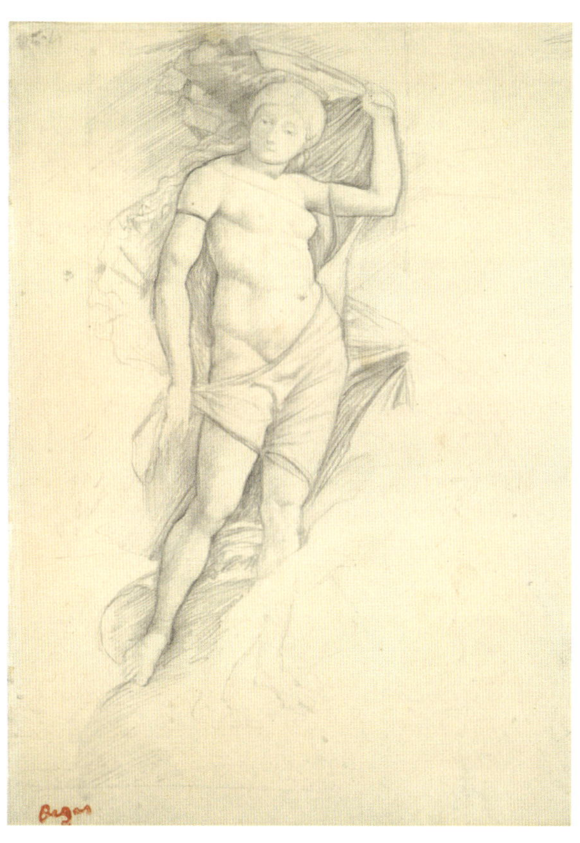

10. Edgar Degas
Copy after Andrea Mantegna ('Pallas Expelling the Vices from the Garden of Virtue'), c. 1855
Pencil, 29.1 × 20.2 cm (11½ × 8 in.). Artist's stamp.
ASHMOLEAN MUSEUM, OXFORD

his theories of pointillism by reading Blanc's *Grammaire*. Similarly, Horace Lecoq de Boisbaudran's *L'Education de la Mémoire Pittoresque* (1848) had a wide readership. The author was on the staff of the École Royale Gratuite de Dessin (known as the Petite École). He advocated drawing and copying from memory and suggested posing models in the open air rather than the studio. Most avant-garde artists followed his precepts and practices, as drawing from memory encouraged close visual analysis and the retention of images while also promoting direct application and release of the imagination.

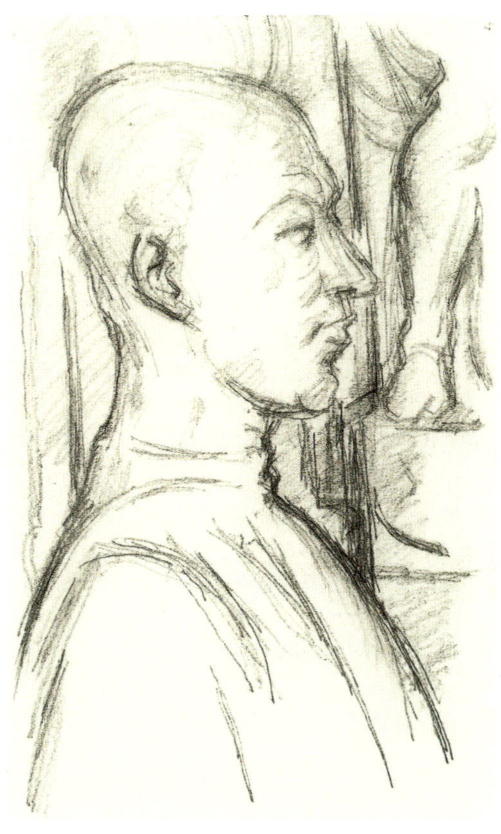

11. Paul Cézanne
Filippo Strozzi (after Benedetto da Maiano), 1881–84
Pencil, 21.4 × 13.1 cm (8⅜ × 5⅛ in.).
KUPFERSTICHKABINETT, KUNSTMUSEUM, BASEL

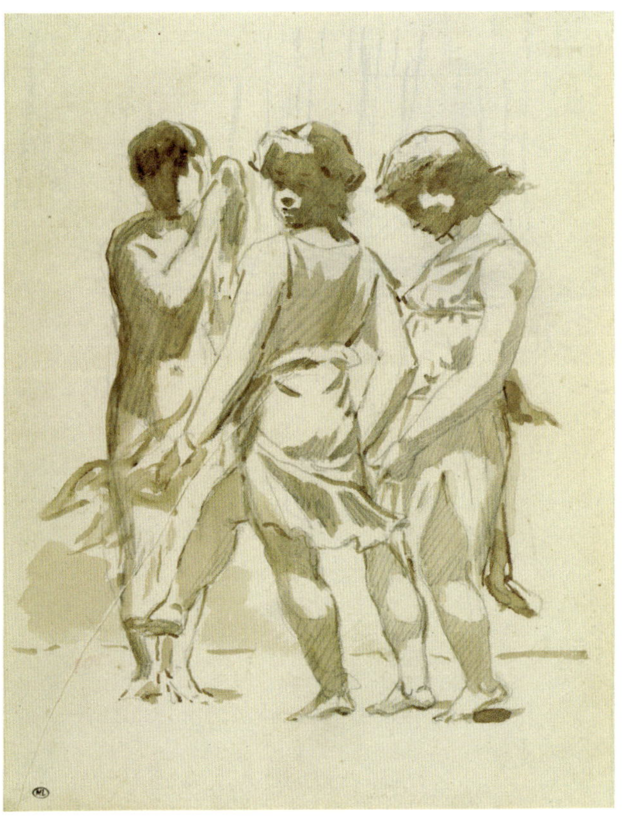

12. Édouard Manet
Copy after the 'Cantoria' by Luca della Robbia formerly in the Duomo, Florence, 1853 or 1857
Pencil and sepia wash, 28.4 × 21.8 cm (11¼ × 8⅝ in.).
MUSÉE DU LOUVRE (COLLECTION MUSÉE D'ORSAY), PARIS

III

One of the writers who defended the avant-garde in France was Edmond Duranty. His thirty-eight-page pamphlet, *La Nouvelle Peinture*, was published in 1876 coinciding with the second Impressionist exhibition of that year. A section of the essay discusses the relevance of drawing in avant-garde art:

> *Farewell to the human body treated like a vase, with an eye for the decorative curve. Farewell to the uniform monotony of bone structure, to the anatomical model beneath the nude. What we need are the special characteristics of the modern individual – in his clothing, in social situations, at home, or on the street.*

The implication in this passage is that the teaching offered by the École des Beaux-Arts had so far failed to produce artists who in their work could 'reflect the inexhaustible diversity of character' in modern life. Duranty's claim was that by contrast the Impressionists had developed a style that could express 'the essence of life'. Significantly, though, in order to find a way of depicting the contemporary scene convincingly, avant-garde artists had had to find different sources of inspiration outside academic circles, and in doing this they were searching for what may be called an alternative tradition.

The two key figures in French art during the first half of the nineteenth century were Jean-Auguste-Dominique Ingres (1780–1867) and Eugène Delacroix (1798–1863). It is customary to regard these artists as the leaders of different factions – Ingres of the Neoclassicists and Delacroix of the Romantics. Yet, somewhat surprisingly, their personalities ran counter to their art. Ingres, who in his work seemed so rational and conformist, was a man of deep emotions, whereas Delacroix, who appeared so vital and impetuous, was often calculating and reclusive. Ingres idolized Raphael and spent many years in Rome; Delacroix admired Rubens and travelled in North Africa. The poet and critic Charles Baudelaire wrote that Ingres had a 'relentless and searching talent', while Delacroix enjoyed 'covering paper with dreams, ideas, figures half-glimpsed amid the random accidents of life'. Ingres's drawings are part of a process of disclosure; Delacroix's are incremental. Both artists drew compulsively and both, although nurtured within the academic system and to a certain extent beneficiaries of it as regards their success at the Salon, in the end had ambivalent relationships with the official bodies of French art. Such dichotomies were recognized by the Impressionists and Post-Impressionists and turned to creative advantage.

Paintings by Ingres are notable for their lucid compositions and high finish. The artist achieved this by careful preparation in numerous drawings amounting to a process of distillation [13]. The precision and accuracy demonstrated in his history paintings is matched by the refinement of his portraits, of which so many were made as drawings. For Ingres drawing was an intensely disciplined exercise resulting from consistency of purpose and single-mindedness. More significant was the emphasis he placed on the purpose of drawing. For him it was the major constituent element of a painting. It was 'not just reproducing contours, it is not just the line; drawing is also the expression, the inner form, the composition, the modelling. See what is left after that. Drawing is seven-eighths of what makes up a painting.'

If for Ingres drawing was almost an act of contrition, for Delacroix it was sheer exultation expressed most tellingly in his instinctive use of watercolour and pastel. His drawings reflect an urgent, unabashed, almost naïve curiosity about the world; the hand is restless, the eye omniscient and the energy unflagging [14]. This virtuosic dynamism is present in the explosive quality of Delacroix's use of line – leaping, flowing, agitated, curling, broken – and matched in the freedom of his watercolours and the intensity of colour in his pastels. Of his drawings the artist himself declared that the 'contour should come last, only a very experienced eye can place it rightly'. Ideas are stretched across the paper like a river in spate, but always with a sense of purpose. The skill lay in controlling a mass of material that was carefully accumulated and almost continually revised. As Baudelaire wrote, 'Delacroix was passionately in love with passion and coldly determined to seek the means of expressing it in the most visible way.' The artist's virtuosity was such that he was perpetually searching for new solutions. As he himself wrote, 'One must be bold to *extremity*; without daring, and even extreme daring, there is no beauty.'

For the Impressionists and Post-Impressionists, Ingres and Delacroix offered conflicting examples, but both were formative influences. The refinement of Ingres inspired Degas, Renoir and Morisot; the abandon of Delacroix appealed to Gauguin, Cézanne and Redon. Two other French artists working in the mid-nineteenth century provided an additional sense of direction. The reputations of Honoré Daumier (1808–1879) and Constantin Guys

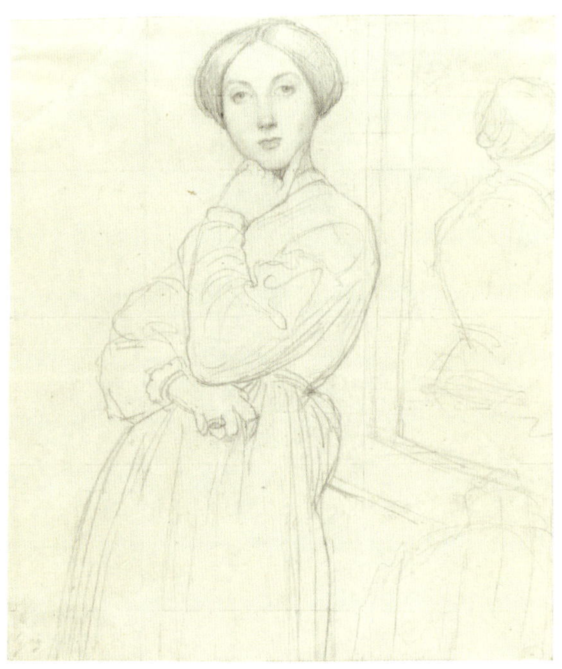

13. Jean-Auguste-Dominique Ingres
Study for the 'Portrait of Comtesse Louise d'Haussonville', 1842–45
Pencil, 23.4 × 19.6 cm (9¼ × 7¾ in.).
Harvard Art Museums (Fogg Museum), Cambridge, Massachusetts

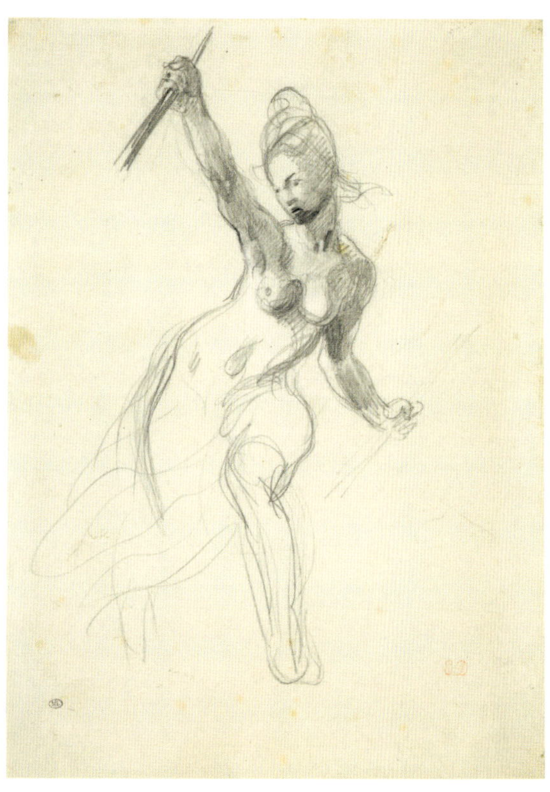

14. Eugène Delacroix
Study of a Half-Naked Woman for 'Liberty Guiding the People', 1831
Pencil with white highlights, 32.4 × 22.8 cm (12⅞ × 9 in.).
MUSÉE DU LOUVRE, PARIS

(1802–1892) rested on their graphic illustrations. Daumier trained as a lithographic draughtsman contributing tirelessly and almost exclusively to journals such as *Le Charivari*, founded in 1832. He was immensely prolific, eventually adding painting and sculpture to his *oeuvre*. At the same time he was remarkably versatile, as the range of his subjects from contemporary life shows, in addition to which were scenes from the theatre and the circus, as well as literature. He drew from memory and inclined towards caricature. An ardent Republican, he found that in order to avoid censorship he needed to widen his targets to include the pretensions and injustices of the whole of French society under changing systems of government, rather than just political commentary. As Baudelaire wrote of Daumier in an essay entitled 'Some French Caricaturists',

Look through his works, and you will see parading before your eyes all that a great city contains of living monstrosities, in all their fantastic and thrilling reality. There can be no item of the fearful, the grotesque, the sinister or the farcical in its treasury, but Daumier knows it.

The style of Daumier's drawings is lyrical. There is a rhythm to the outlines that seem to bend so easily to his every whim, and the washes are applied with a rhapsodic flourish that recalls rococo art. The finished drawings are usually in mixed media – pen and ink with wash, watercolour and gouache highlights [15]. This technique consciously matches the elaborate content of much of Daumier's work, the meaning of which he nonetheless endeavoured to convey to the viewer instantly as though the captions, which he never wrote himself, did not exist. His paintings and sculpture were more experimental, but no less penetrating and hard-hitting than his prints and drawings. Although he died in relative obscurity, Daumier was greatly revered by his fellow artists because of his concern for the human condition and his desire to correct society's wrongs.

Where Daumier's range extended from the heroic to the pitiful, the tragic to the comic and the allegorical to the caricatural, Guys was more restricted in scope even though he had travelled widely. After becoming an artist fairly late in life, Guys was employed as an official illustrator for *The Illustrated London News* and *Le Figaro*. He was used to working at speed in changing circumstances and in far-flung places including a theatre of war. His style is one of total commitment characterized by spirited pen work combined with flurries of abundant wash [16]. Lines are short and pithy, but they pulsate with rhythm. No moralist, Guys shows the world in a state of flux observed at random and taken on its own terms. What he relished was the angle of a top hat, the swing of a crinoline, the cut of a uniform, the curve of a nimble foot, the curl of a moustache, the prance of a horse and the sway of a carriage.

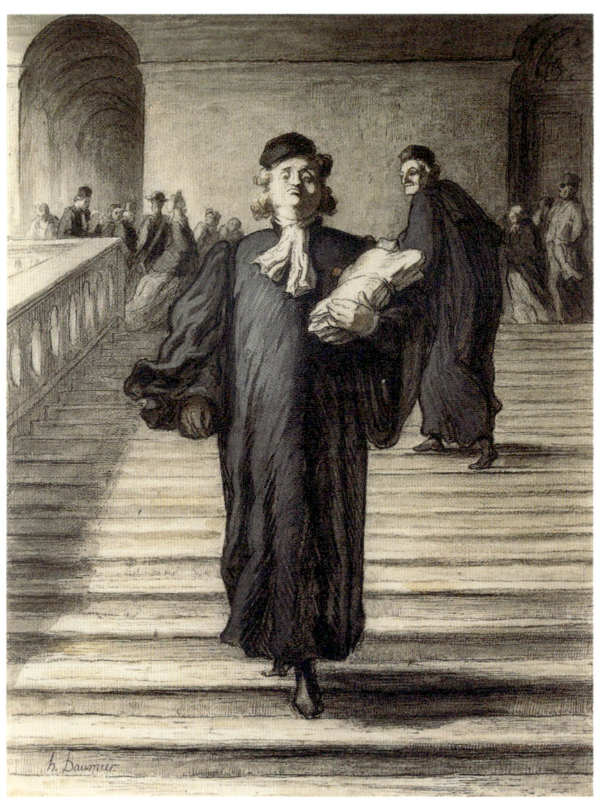

15. Honoré Daumier
The Grand Staircase of the Palais de Justice, c. 1864
Charcoal, conté crayon, watercolour, pen and ink, wash,
35.9 × 26.7 cm (14⅛ × 10½ in.). Signed.

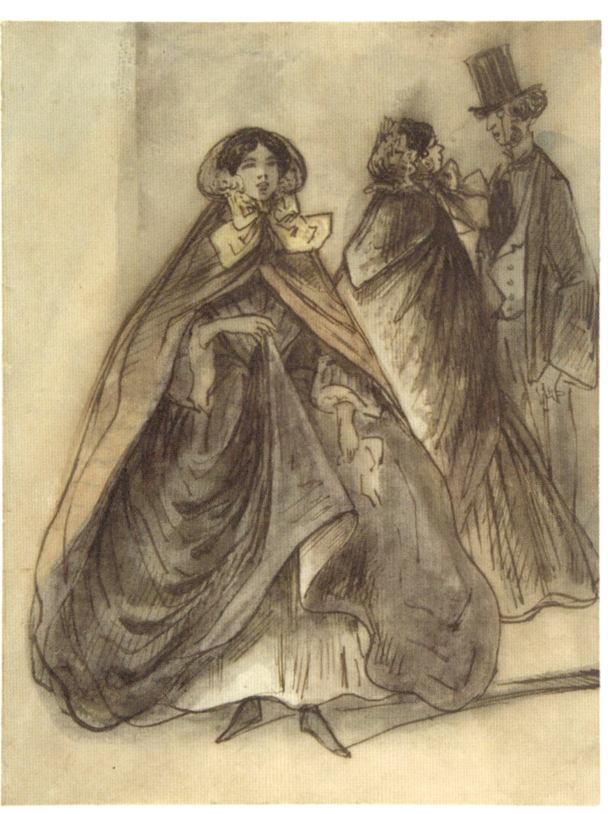

16. Constantin Guys
Two Women and a Man with a Top Hat and a Monocle, c. 1860
Pen and brown ink, brown wash, with touches of pale blue, orange
and yellow washes, 21.1 × 16 cm (8⅝ × 6⅜ in.).

Baudelaire made Guys the sole subject of one of his most influential essays, entitled 'The Painter of Modern Life', published in *Le Figaro* in 1863, where he states that the artist 'has contrived to concentrate in his drawings the acrid or heady bouquet of the wine of life'. According to Baudelaire, Guys spent the day observing in the street or in the park, but as darkness fell 'when the curtains of heaven are drawn and cities light up' he withdrew to his studio and began 'skirmishing with his pencil, his pen, his brush, splashing his glass of water up to the ceiling, wiping his pen on his shirt, in a ferment of violent activity, as though afraid that the image might escape him, cantankerous though alone, elbowing himself on'. Clearly Baudelaire chose Guys as his exemplar of modern painting because of the subject matter, but it is significant that the artist in question is principally a draughtsman as opposed to a painter. For Baudelaire fluidity and immediacy were seen as the important components of the modern style.

Ingres, Delacroix, Daumier and Guys all had distinctive and highly individual styles of drawing, but each had elements that appealed to younger artists. What members of the emerging avant-garde realized was that by studying these important forerunners they could discover more effective ways of depicting the contemporary world than the rigid academic system allowed. Where Ingres purifies and Delacroix engorges, Daumier scoffs and Guys smirks – all of which amounted to a welcome spirit of rebellion. As such, these disparate and greatly respected artists constituted an alternative tradition that may have lacked cohesion but was certainly not without conviction.

IV

The artists with whom many of the Impressionists and Post-Impressionists felt the closest affinities were those associated with the Barbizon School. Barbizon is a small village situated on the edge of the Forest of Fontainebleau some thirty-five miles to the southeast of Paris. The area covered by the Forest is extensive and the terrain varied – valleys, outcrops of rock, boulders and wooded areas. Small villages such as Marlotte, Chailly, and Barbizon itself had by the mid-nineteenth century become centres of artistic activity and indeed feature in the early work of Monet, Renoir, Pissarro and Sisley. The Forest was part of the national patrimony: it was accurately mapped, frequently illustrated in topographical prints and had begun to be modernized with macadamized roads and access by railway.

The leading artists of the Barbizon School – Jean-Baptiste-Camille Corot, Charles François Daubigny, Jean-François Millet, Narcisse-Virgile Diaz de la Peña, Charles Jacque, Théodore Rousseau, Constant Troyon – were attracted to the Forest of Fontainebleau on account of the landscape, but allied to this was their interest in depicting rural activities both in paintings and drawings. By embracing such themes from the 1830s onwards the Barbizon School artists were distancing themselves from the hierarchical preferences of the Académie des Beaux-Arts, where biblical, historical and mythological subjects were preferred to genre or landscape. During previous centuries pure landscape painting, as pursued in seventeenth-century Holland or eighteenth-century Britain, was mistrusted in France as it did not in itself provide suitably edifying subject matter and encouraged different degrees of finish. Not only, therefore, did it undermine the intellectual content of painting, it also encouraged slipshod methods. Furthermore, by the end of the nineteenth century, rural subject matter could be interpreted politically, with the overworked and downtrodden peasant representing a threat to the social order.

Neoclassical landscapes dating from the late eighteenth and early nineteenth centuries hark back to works by Claude and Poussin. The compositions are characterized by balance, harmony and a carefully calculated set of tonal values in accordance with treatises such as *Éléments de Perspective Pratique à l'Usage des Artistes* (1800) by Pierre-Henri Valenciennes. Direct observation of nature recording the movement of clouds and trees, or the effects of changing light, combined with the spontaneous application of paint was permitted in oil studies made in front of the motif, but needed to be edited for use in the final painting. The Impressionists, however, particularly during the late 1860s and early 1870s, wanted to make those practices associated with oil studies the very basis of their art and it was the Barbizon School who showed them the way.

Of the leading Barbizon artists, Corot (1796–1875) was a seminal figure in the development of landscape painting in mid-nineteenth-century France. His application of the Neoclassical principles of landscape painting is most evident in the pictures he made while in Italy and Switzerland, but by the end of his career he produced pastoral themes with sylvan settings painted in a broader manner closer to Romanticism and on occasion anticipating Symbolism. Although he undertook religious, mythological and allegorical subjects for exhibition in the Salon, as well as portraits, it is Corot's depiction of the landscape of northern France that influenced the Impressionists to whom he acted as a father-figure.

Living at Ville-d'Avray, a village on the southwest side of Paris close to Versailles, Corot spent hours in the countryside making quantities of drawings. For most of his life he drew with pencil or pen and ink. He believed in capturing the outline of a motif seen as a whole before filling in more detailed aspects of individual forms and indicating tonal values [17]. The drawings comprise a combination of loose lines with sudden bursts of hatching that stand out darkly against the white of the paper. The amount of detail serves almost literally as an index to the content of a particular landscape, but it also reveals its rich diversity – movements of foliage, patterns of branches, contours of land. Many of the later drawings are in charcoal and often on coloured papers. They are broadly handled with strong tonal values and full of atmosphere.

Even more influential as a draughtsman than the gentle Corot was Millet (1814–1875), who was born near Cherbourg on the coast of northern France. He studied at the École des Beaux-Arts for two years (1837–39) and began a career as a portrait painter before specializing in pastoral idylls and rural subjects in a naturalist style. These last pictures, which include such famous images as *The Angelus* (1855–57) and *The Gleaners* (1857), both in the Musée d'Orsay in Paris, show peasant life in heroic terms and were open to political interpretation. During the artist's lifetime many such depictions of peasant life were thought to be infused with radicalism and threatening to the status quo, whereas following his death they were interpreted as being conservative and sentimental. Pure landscapes only occur towards the end of his life.

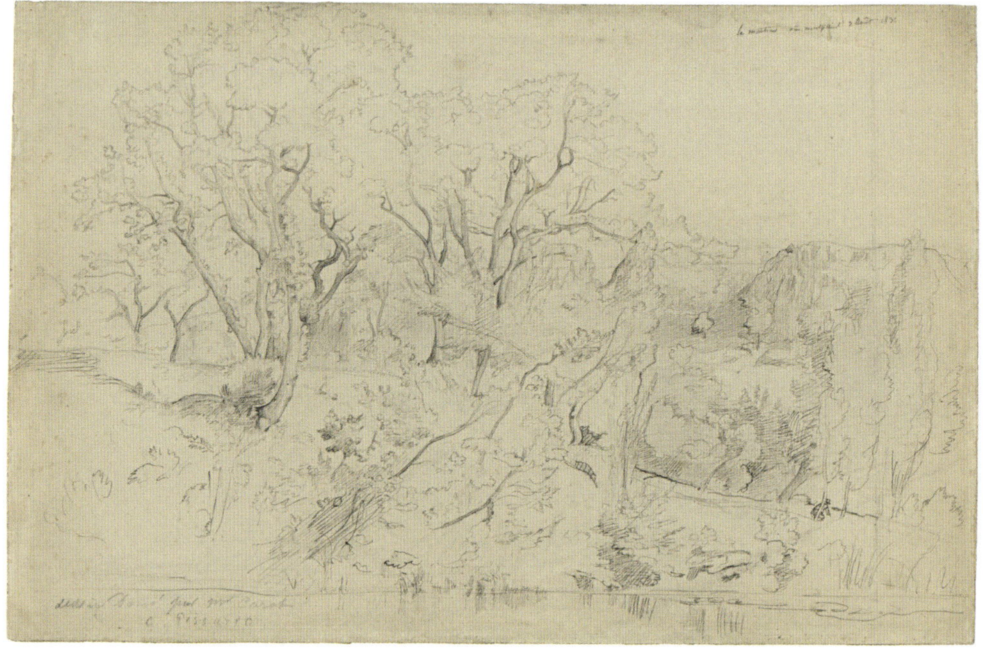

17. Jean-Baptiste-Camille Corot
Le Martinet near Montpellier, 1836
Pen and ink over pencil on light blue paper, 33.7 × 50.2 cm (13¼ × 19¾ in.).
Inscribed by the artist with the title and dated.
METROPOLITAN MUSEUM OF ART, NEW YORK

Millet's style was based on a close study of Michelangelo, Poussin and French eighteenth-century art, to which should be added his appreciation of European literature (Homer, Virgil, Shakespeare, Milton, Hugo, Chateaubriand, La Fontaine). Such eclectic sources imbue his work with a rarefied air and encouraged him to address all-embracing themes – the cyclical pattern in nature or the place of man in the universe. However, if Millet's paintings were controversial, his drawings were truly influential. He was the most significant draughtsman in mid-nineteenth-century France. Drawings by him were specially commissioned, eagerly collected and widely published during his lifetime. Immediately after his death they were included in exhibitions and sales, as well as being reproduced in the important monograph by Alfred Sensier (1881).

Essentially, Millet was an outstanding figure draughtsman. Nude or otherwise, the figures are solid and statuesque, bounded by firm contours and filled out with confident modelling [18]. Invariably in black chalk or its derivatives, nearly all of Millet's figures have a majestic, sculptural bearing and perhaps no artist since the Renaissance has been so concerned with portraying the dignity of man. Drawings of figures seen in movement or performing vigorous tasks are also eloquent [19]. The lines simulate the rhythm of the action itself, thereby giving the images an inner dynamism. Pen and ink was often preferred for depictions of the landscape.

Apart from those drawings made in preparation for paintings, Millet produced a large number of finished drawings especially for exhibition or sale. The finest of these are tenebrist in style, depending on subtle gradations of tone, which create a mood of reflection or reverie with forms dissolved in the dying light [20]. Such examples inspired highly finished charcoal drawings known as *fusains*. This type of work was widespread in the mid-nineteenth century, both in France and Britain. Societies were formed to cultivate the taste for such a specialized type of drawing and many artists practised it – Gustave Courbet, François Bonvin, Léon Lhermitte, Henri Fantin-Latour. Albert Lebourg exhibited examples in the fourth and fifth Impressionist exhibitions of 1879 and 1880 respectively. Of the younger generation it was Seurat, Redon and Eugène Carrière who benefited from Millet's successful advocacy of tenebrism.

Even more significant were the artist's pastels and drawings in coloured chalks. At first he chose these media as a system of highlighting, but during the 1860s he began to use them in their own right in conjunction with coloured papers. The scale of these drawings is often dramatically large [21]. The subjects range from figure compositions in specific settings to pure landscapes. As so often with Millet, the viewer is often conscious in these images of the season or the time of day. The surface is built up carefully with a series of gentle striations or soft dabs, as though the artist has yet to discover the full dramatic potential of the medium. One of Millet's patrons,

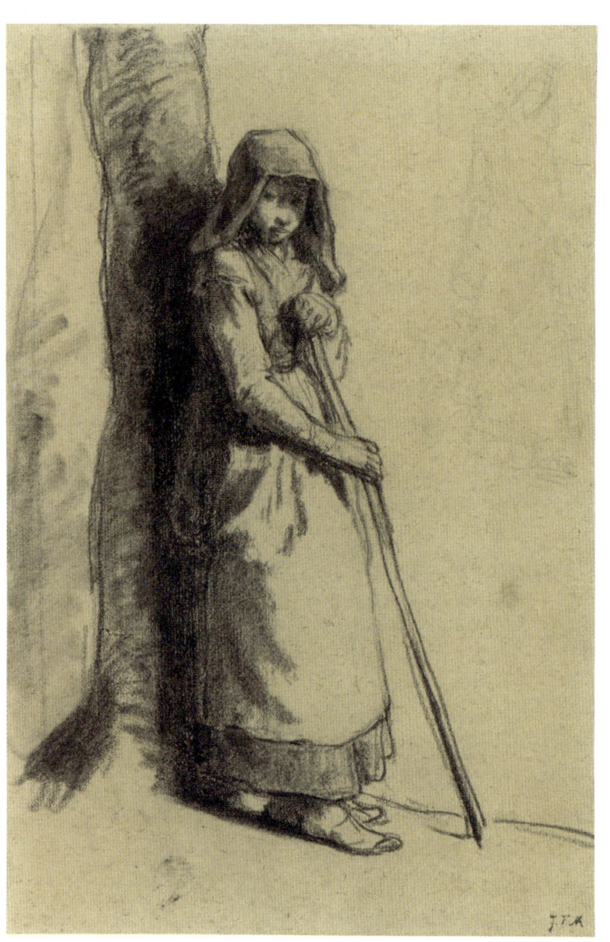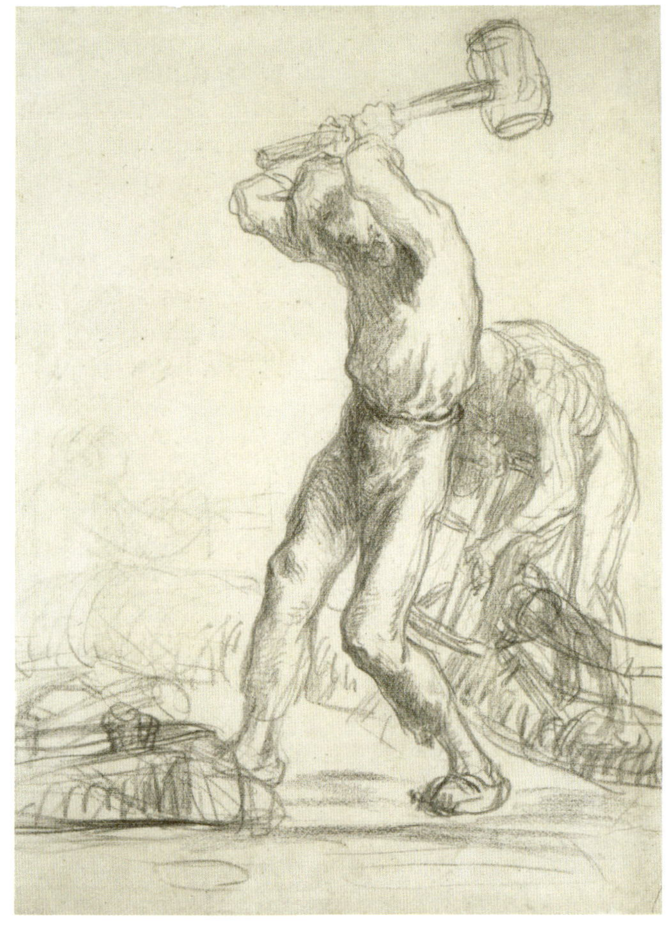

18. Jean-François Millet
Study for 'Bergère au repos', 1849
Black crayon on brownish paper, 29.8 × 19.2 cm
(11¾ × 7⅝ in.). Artist's stamp.
FITZWILLIAM MUSEUM, CAMBRIDGE

19. Jean-François Millet
Two Peasants Sawing and Splitting Wood, 1850–51
Black chalk, 40 × 27.9 cm (15¾ × 11 in.).
ASHMOLEAN MUSEUM, OXFORD

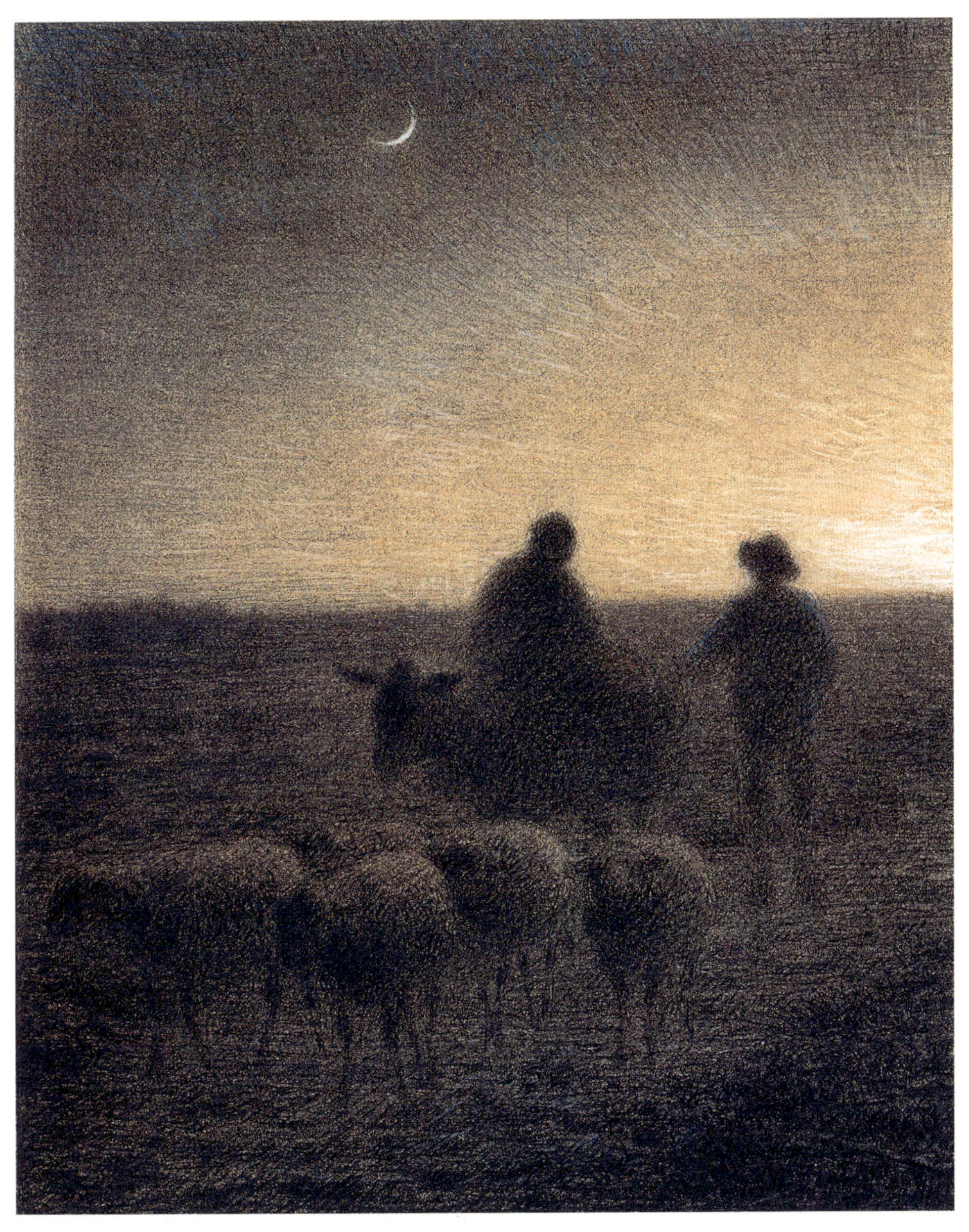

20. Jean-François Millet
Twilight, c. 1859–63
Conté crayon and pastel on buff paper,
50.5 × 38.9 cm (19⅞ × 15⅜ in.). Signed.

the Parisian architect Emile Gavet, commissioned many of these pastels and indeed
ninety-five of them were sold at auction in June 1875 following Gavet's death.
Among those who saw the drawings before the sale was Van Gogh, who in a letter
of 29 June 1875 described the experience in religious terms, 'I felt something
akin to: Put off thy shoes from off thy feet for the place whereon thou standest
is holy ground'.

Indeed, of those Impressionist and Post-Impressionist artists who looked
at Millet, it is Van Gogh who demonstrated his debt most keenly. He made
'improvisations' and colour 'translations' of works that he knew only from black-and-
white prints. Pissarro, who painted a number of rural subjects, also admired Millet,
but found his work to be 'just a bit too biblical' to satisfy his anarchist views. The
emphasis placed by Millet on his graphic work, however, was the bedrock on which
the changes in drawing that occurred towards the end of the century were based.

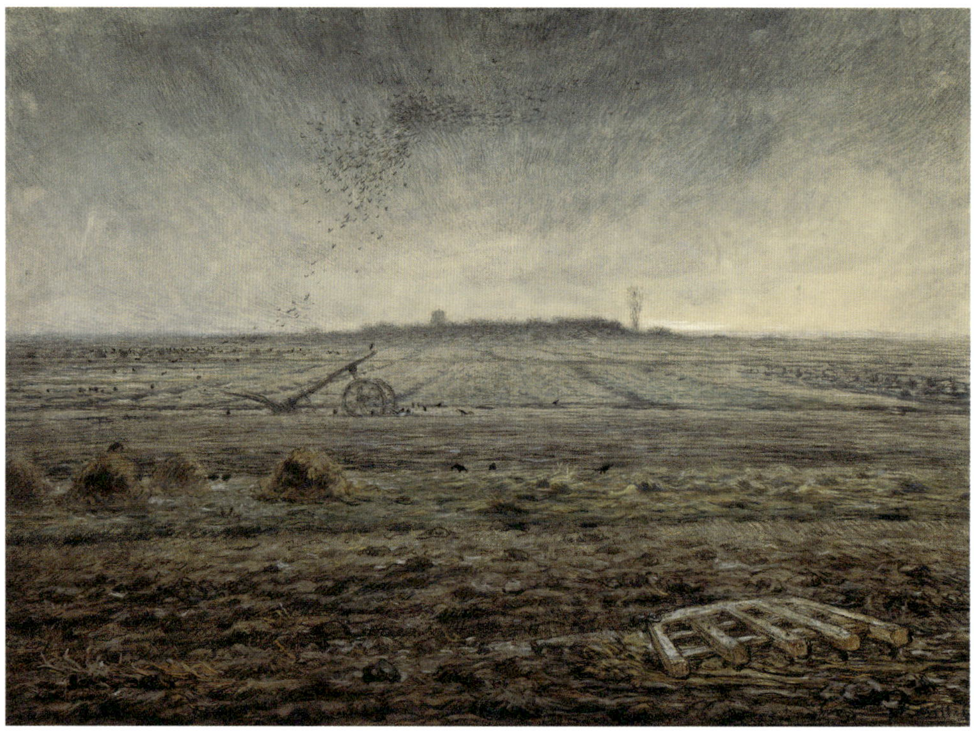

21. Jean-François Millet
Winter, the Plain of Chailly, c. 1862–63
Pastel on buff paper, 72.4 × 95.9 cm (28⅝ × 37⅞ in.). Signed.
BURRELL COLLECTION, GLASGOW

V

From the wide range of artists associated with Impressionism and Post-Impressionism whose work is illustrated in this book, three in particular pushed the art of drawing to its limits during the final decades of the nineteenth century – Degas, Van Gogh and Cézanne. Drawings were no longer kept hidden from view within the privacy of the studio as part of the preparatory process or considered to be expendable. Now they were recognized as autonomous compositions worthy of exhibition in their own right. As a result, the aesthetic differences between painting and drawing, formerly thought to be distinct, narrowed to the extent that stylistically and practically painting and drawing were no longer separate activities but interchangeable ones. The materials and methods of application were shared, creating new effects that were welcomed by exhibition organizers, dealers, critics and collectors. Yet, even if this breakthrough was made by avant-garde artists in France and Belgium, the advantages were by no means limited to them. Giuseppe de Nittis, for example, whose work was in the first Impressionist exhibition (1874), held a successful exhibition of eighteen pastels (including the vast triptych *At the Racetrack in Auteuil*; Galleria Nazionale d'Arte Moderna, Rome) at the Cercle de l'Union Artistique in 1881, which pandered to popular taste and was thought by some to betray the principles of the 'new painting'. Other mainstream artists more acceptable to the Salon also benefited from the change in status of drawing – Henri Gervex, James Jacques Joseph Tissot, Ernest-Ange Duez, Paul-Albert Besnard, Pierre Carrier-Belleuse, Emile Lévy – as well as the *belle époque* artists working at the turn of the century such as Paul César Helleu, Jacques-Emile Blanche and Giovanni Boldini, who all produced pastels in large formats.

Degas elected to use pastel when he undertook his most audacious drawings during the second half of his life. Gradually, he retreated into his studio and relied more on models and on making improvisations based on earlier studies. Pastel appealed to him because it was in effect drawing in colour and therefore combined the chief components of painting, which by the end of his life he was finding laborious and time-consuming as a medium. His pastels concentrated on three subjects – the female nude, the ballet and horse-racing. It is significant that by choosing pastel he was extending a well-founded tradition of French eighteenth-century art, which Edmond and Jules de Goncourt had drawn attention to in a series of fascicles published between 1859 and 1875 and later grouped together in a single volume entitled *L'Art du Dix-huitième Siècle*. These fascicles were devoted to Jean-Antoine Watteau, François Boucher, Jean-Baptiste-Siméon Chardin, Maurice-Quentin de la Tour and Jean-Baptiste Perronneau, among others, and inspired a revival of interest in their work. The composition of many of Degas's

ballet scenes of the 1870s can be seen in the light of
Watteau's *fêtes galantes*, just as the earlier artist's use
of *trois crayons* and repeated figures on single sheets
anticipate Degas's own studies of ballet dancers. The leap
from the formal portraits of La Tour and Perronneau, or
even the self-portraits by Chardin, to Degas's treatment
of the female nude is a considerable one. As the critic
Théodore Duret wrote in 1894, Degas shows 'woman as
she is, occupied with her ordinary habits of life or of the
toilette, exhibiting all the peculiarities – and one could say
all the defects – of a body unhealthily paled by town life'.
The application of such a delicate medium in the context of
the toilette, the dance or the horse was indeed far removed
from eighteenth-century sensibilities. Others participated
in what might be called the democratization of the pastel,
demonstrating at the same time a wide range of technical
skill: delicacy in the case of James Abbott McNeill Whistler
[22], vibrancy in Armand Guillaumin [23] and smooth
finish in Eva Gonzalès [24].

Van Gogh, too, was looking to the past in his pen-
and-ink drawings. The inspiration in this respect was
Rembrandt, whom he called in a letter of 28 December 1885
'the magician of magicians'. What Van Gogh most admired
in Rembrandt was the narrative power of his compositions
and the ability throughout his work to identify with the
human predicament. The earliest pen-and-ink drawings by
Van Gogh before he went to Paris late in 1885 are tautly and
heavily worked with an abundance of short lines and areas
of dense cross-hatching. The effect is like looking through
a wire mesh. All this changed when he travelled to Provence
early in 1888. Here he dramatically increased his output of
drawings and developed a more expressive style. There is
now complete stylistic unity between the paintings and the
drawings, with the brush alternating with the pen. Instead
of quill pens, his preference now was for specially cut reed
pens with which he could make drawings that are 'more
spontaneous, more exaggerated'. The flexibility of reed
pens allowed for a greater variety of line, extending from
strong and broad to fine and sharp. They also had to be

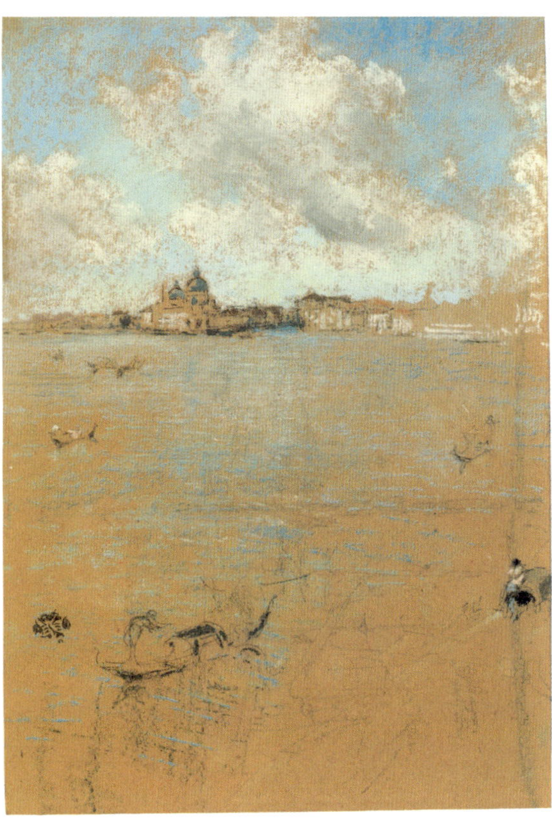

22. James Abbott McNeill Whistler
Venetian Scene, c. 1880
Pastel on brown paper, 27.9 × 19.1 cm
(11 × 7½ in.). Signed.
New Britain Museum of American Art, Connecticut

    Introduction

constantly recharged with ink so that the act of drawing itself had to be immediate. The freedom and fluidity of Van Gogh's drawings done in the south in 1888–89, as well as the wide range of marks spread across the whole sheet of paper, gave drawing a pre-eminence that even Rembrandt failed to achieve for it during his lifetime [3].

Where Degas succeeded in making a breakthrough with pastel and Van Gogh with pen and ink, Cézanne did with watercolour. This was a medium that was never central to the French tradition as it was in Britain. During the 1820s and 1830s French artists became conscious of the important role it played in the work of J. M. W. Turner, John Constable, David Wilkie and Richard Parkes Bonington. Even so, in France watercolour was regarded principally as a topographical exercise exemplified by elaborate collaborative publications such as Baron Isidore Taylor's *Voyages Pittoresques et Romantiques dans l'Ancienne France* (1820–78). Later artists, including Henri Harpignies and Johan Barthold Jongkind, who were both connected with Impressionism, tended to work in the same vein, and a more novel and creative

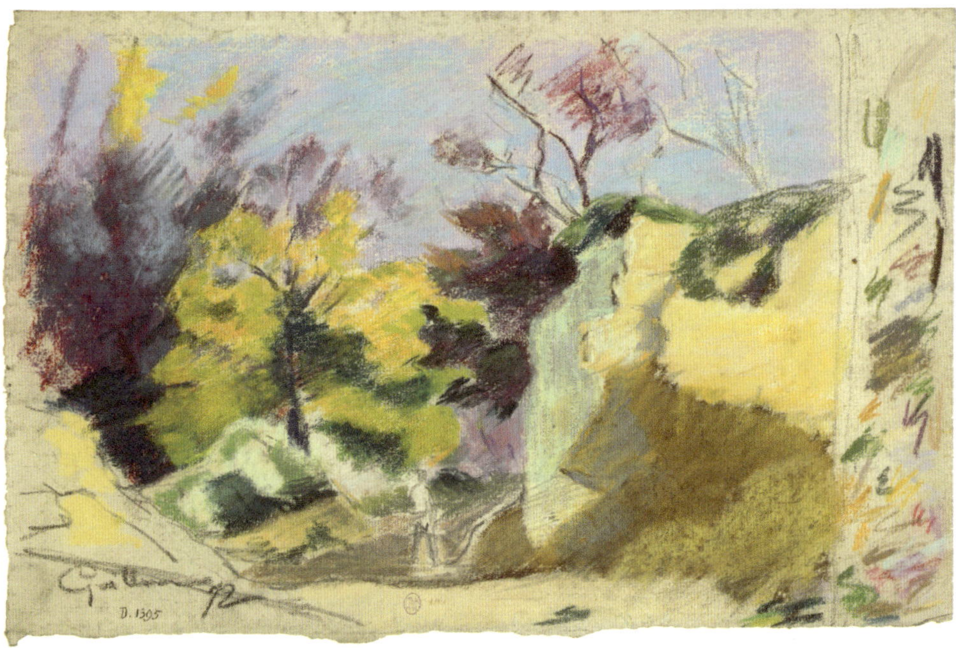

23. Armand Guillaumin
Landscape with Trees and Rocks with Colour Tests, 1872
Pastel, 25.9 × 39.2 cm (10¼ × 15½ in.). Signed and dated.
PETIT PALAIS, MUSÉE DES BEAUX-ARTS DE LA VILLE DE PARIS

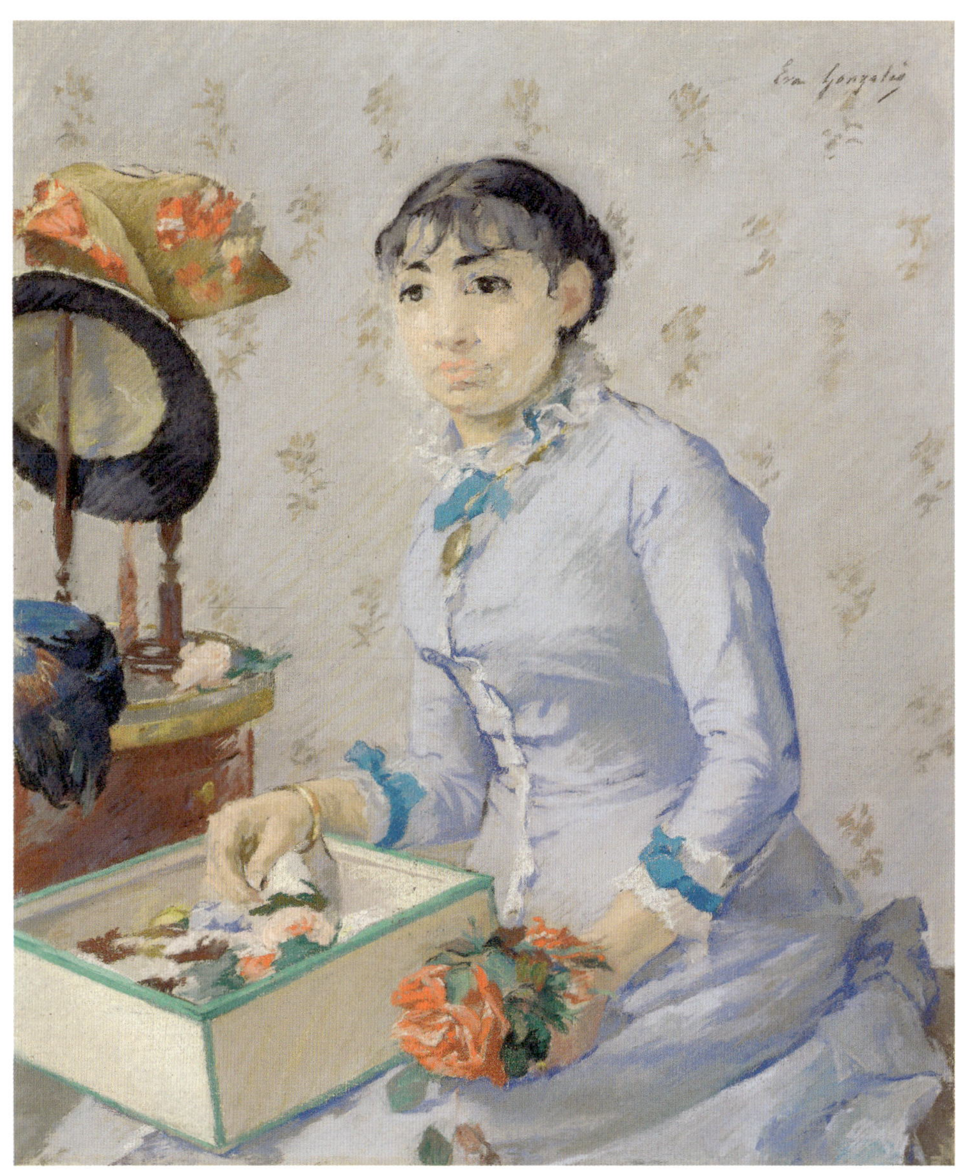

24. Eva Gonzalès

The Milliner, *c.* 1877
Pastel and watercolour on canvas,
45 × 37 cm (17¾ × 14⅝ in.). Signed.
THE ART INSTITUTE OF CHICAGO

approach could only be found in works by Victor Hugo, François-Marius Granet, Théodore Géricault and Delacroix.

By contrast, Cézanne attached great importance to his watercolours; it was a medium he made use of throughout his life. During the 1890s the watercolours serve as a complement to his paintings. Although other Impressionists and Post-Impressionists drew in watercolour, none gave it as much credence as Cézanne, who recognized it as a medium that was not only wholly appropriate for his purpose, which was to record the sensations he experienced before nature, but could in the process also become a vehicle for changing the direction of art.

Cézanne exhibited three early watercolours in the third Impressionist exhibition (1877), and his mature watercolours were only made known at exhibitions held towards the end of his life or immediately after his death. His method was to apply watercolour in conjunction with pencil, but by the 1890s the pencil lines only provided an armature. Dabs of watercolour were then applied over or around those pencil marks, creating interlocking rhythms and establishing spatial intervals. The careful placement of each brushstroke seen against blank areas of paper creates a sense of recession and a feeling of atmosphere. Landscape motifs are modelled in colour that seems to melt into the surrounding space (frontispiece). The architectonic quality of the compositions is such that if one poor decision is made the whole structure is in danger of collapsing. There is also variety in the way in which Cézanne applies the watercolour – sometimes it is diluted and at others several colours are overlaid in patches. The brushstrokes are occasionally so transparent that they seem to float on the surface of the paper. It is all magnificently grandiloquent, but at the same time emphatically economical. Nothing is overstated, and neither is anything understated.

Cézanne worked hard to acquire this level of skill as well as to sustain it. There is almost a baroque splendour to these watercolours however humble the subject. The artist strove to fix nature definitively on paper without denying its vibrancy. This, he realized, was almost impossible since nature constantly changes and therefore defies permanence, just as his chosen medium – watercolour – was the most fugitive.

Drawings by Degas, Van Gogh and Cézanne had a decisive influence on later artists. The technical experiments they undertook, the innovations they sought and the advances they made liberated art and created opportunities for others in a spirit of laissez-faire. The elevation of drawing during the second half of the nineteenth century to a level equal to painting proved to be a vital catalyst. Artists now had choice, greater freedom and endless possibilities. Drawing helped to show the way towards modernity.

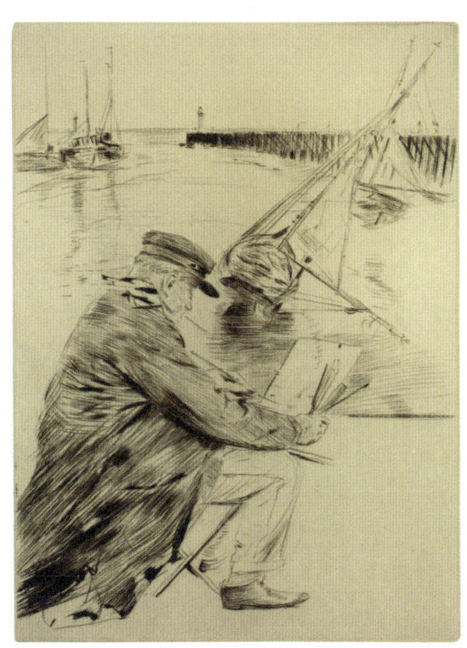

Eugène Boudin
1824–1898

Paintings, pastels and watercolours by Eugène Boudin were included in the first Impressionist exhibition held in 1874. He was 50 years old and after a long struggle had at last reached the point where he was considered an established artist. His participation was in many ways in recognition of his contribution to the inception of Impressionism. This was not limited to the personal encouragement that he had given to the young Monet, whom he met in Le Havre in 1856–57, but more importantly, it related to the example he set in his choice of subject matter and working practices. By no means an avant-garde artist himself, it was, nonetheless, his methods, priorities and ideas that gave younger artists the confidence to realize the artistic freedoms that they so ardently sought. Boudin is, in effect, the Palinurus of Impressionism, although, unlike the helmsman who in Virgil's *Aeneid* guided Aeneas across the Aegean, he was blessed with longevity. Born in the port of Honfleur in Normandy and educated in Le Havre, Boudin described himself as 'a man who only likes salt water'. His father was

Paul César Helleu
Boudin Painting on the Jetty at Trouville, 1894
Drypoint, 28.1 × 20 cm (11⅛ × 7⅞ in.).
DETROIT INSTITUTE OF ARTS

a mariner and his mother also worked on the steamers plying their trade between the ports on the coast of northern France. He did not become an artist immediately, and after spending a short time at sea went into partnership running a stationer's business, which also supplied materials for artists and occasionally displayed works of art. Although he first went to Paris in 1847 and again later in 1851, he did not enrol in any of the major studios and was essentially self-taught, being fiercely loyal to his place of origin and supportive of many other provincial centres of art in France. He said in 1887, 'I am a loner, a daydreamer who has been content to remain in his part of the world and look at the sky.' Even so, many artists were attracted to Normandy from the 1850s onwards and Boudin benefited from the contacts he was able to make with Jean-Baptiste-Camille Corot, Jean-François Millet, Constant Troyon, Gustave Courbet, Théodule Ribot and Johan Barthold Jongkind, who all frequented the inn at the Ferme Saint-Siméon above Honfleur with its commanding views of the sea.

Boudin was undoubtedly a marine painter by instinct, but his interests extended well beyond depicting seascapes. For him marine subjects included the comings and goings in ports and harbours (p. 45), as well as the local customs (weddings and religious festivals) of coastal regions such as Normandy and Brittany (p. 44). Any list of places painted by Boudin reveals that he was in fact well travelled even out of France, in spite of his sense of loyalty to the Seine estuary. When combined with his self-discipline and a proclivity for hard work, much of it on a small scale, these wide interests account for the artist's formidable output of over 4,000 paintings and over 7,000 drawings, watercolours and pastels. Part of the reason for Boudin's eventual success, principally owing to the support of the dealer Paul Durand-Ruel, was his recognition (albeit reluctantly) of the importance of Paris, where he worked every winter making paintings from the motifs that he had recorded in his sketchbooks and drawings during the summer. Boudin believed that, 'You don't invent an art all on your own in some corner of the provinces – you need criticism, means of comparison, firm convictions.' These were all to be found in Paris, and he was rewarded with many showings at the Salon.

The artist who is most similar to Boudin is the Dutch-born Jongkind, who was also regarded as a precursor of Impressionism. Both artists were skilful watercolourists, exploring ports and harbours, landscapes and seascapes seen under generous skies with plenty of atmosphere. But Boudin went further than Jongkind in two respects: his preference for beach scenes, which he described as 'a reasonably faithful reproduction of our age', and a remarkable aptitude for pastel, which won the admiration of the poet Charles Baudelaire. Based as he was for most of the year in resorts such as Trouville and Deauville close to Le Havre, Boudin was in a position to observe during the 1860s the growing popularity of such places. This was owing in part to closer links between Paris and the coast brought about by improvements in transport, particularly the railway, and also by the fashion for taking summer holidays by the sea. Adolphe Joanne, the compiler of numerous guidebooks, declared Trouville to be 'Paris, with its qualities, its foibles, and its vices, transported for two or three months to the edge of the ocean'. The medicinal advantages offered by these resorts were not related directly, as they might be today, to exposure to sunshine, but to fresh air and sea bathing. The annual exodus of the privileged from Paris, including members of the court of Napoleon III, transformed what were originally humble fishing villages into holiday resorts. Hotels, villas, casinos and leisure facilities multiplied.

Boudin himself was ultimately ambivalent about such developments, referring to the holidaymakers as 'gilded parasites', even though he benefited financially from depicting such scenes in numerous greatly admired drawings and paintings (p. 43). In these, figures are seen from a discreet distance silhouetted against towering skies and illuminated by the bright light reflected from the sea. The figures huddle together in groups or are widely dispersed across the sand. All are dressed formally with added protection provided by parasols as they stare vacantly out to sea, scan the skies or watch the yachts. Strategically positioned bathing huts help to divide up the compositions, just as dogs and children enliven the scene. What Boudin relishes most, however, is the vibrancy of the spectacle, which he always renders with splashes of bright colour: swaying crinolines, flying hat ribbons, tilting umbrellas intensified by the dangers of a sudden breeze. Retaining the spontaneity of what he first recorded on paper remained the challenge.

If the beach scenes are the work of a puppet master, Boudin's pastels are in marked contrast, being closer in fact to the thunderbolts of Jupiter. The medium is handled with a surprising vigour, and the results make a considerable impact both in terms of the vividness of the colour and the forcefulness of the stroke. This is most evident in the scenes of local fairs and markets (pp. 39 and 42). Even more dramatic are the views of the sky that he made in such numbers at the outset of his career (pp. 40–41). It is possible that Boudin knew of Eugène Delacroix's similar renderings of sky and sea in watercolour and pastel, but what is certain is Baudelaire's reaction to Boudin's efforts. In his review of the Salon of 1859 Baudelaire describes making a visit to the artist's studio in Le Havre and seeing countless examples of 'liquid and aerial enchantments', many of which are specifically inscribed with the date, time of day and wind direction, reminiscent of the cloud studies made by John Constable in the early 1820s. Gradually, Baudelaire is overcome by Boudin's pastels: 'With their fantastic and luminous forms; these ferments of gloom; these immensities of green and pink, suspended and added one upon another; these gaping furnaces; these firmaments of black or purple satin, crumpled, rolled or torn; these horizons in mourning, or streaming with molten metal – in short, all these splendours rose to my brain like a heady drink or like the eloquence of opium.'

  Eugène Boudin

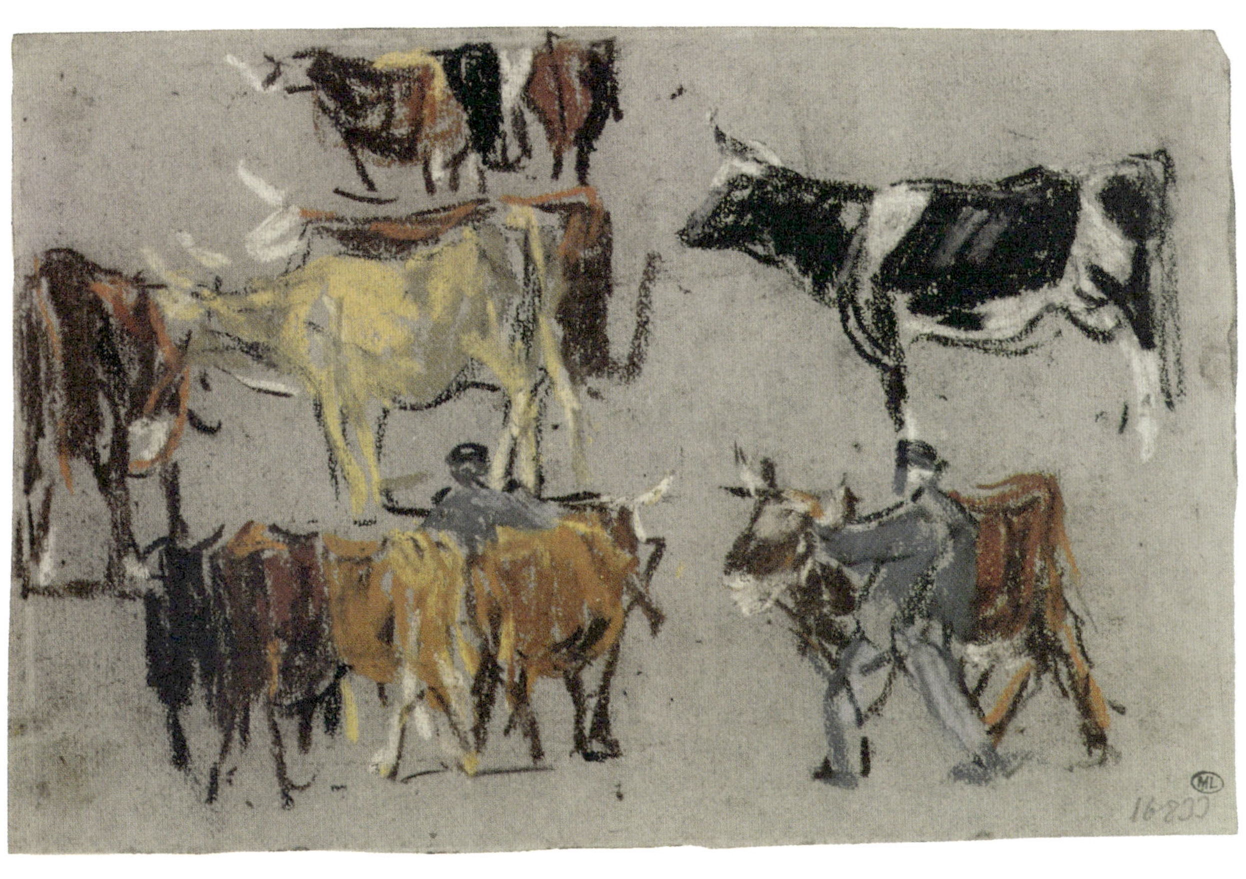

Cattle at a Local Market, c. 1854–60
Pastel on grey paper, 15.1 × 22 cm (5⅞ × 8¾ in.).
MUSÉE DU LOUVRE (COLLECTION MUSÉE D'ORSAY), PARIS

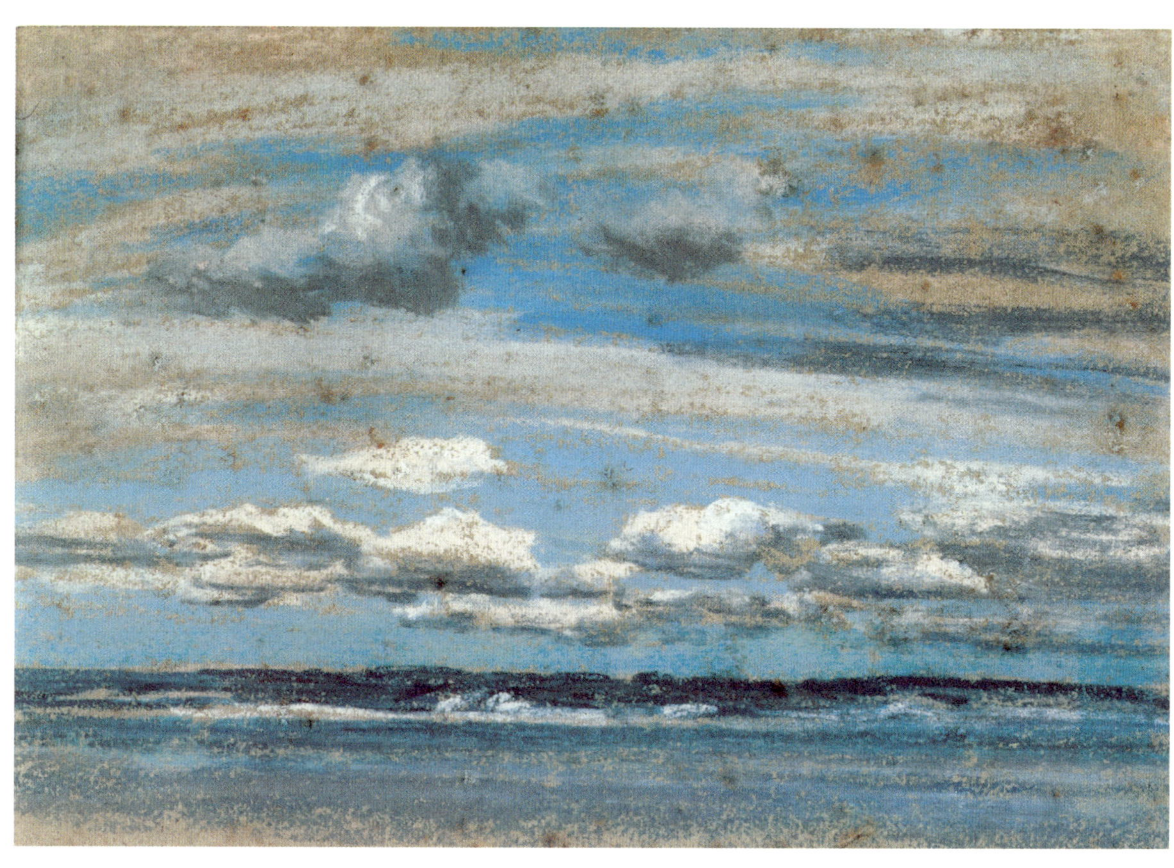

View of the Sky over an Estuary, c. 1854–60
Pastel, 15 × 20 cm (6 × 7⅞ in.).
MUSÉE EUGÈNE BOUDIN, HONFLEUR

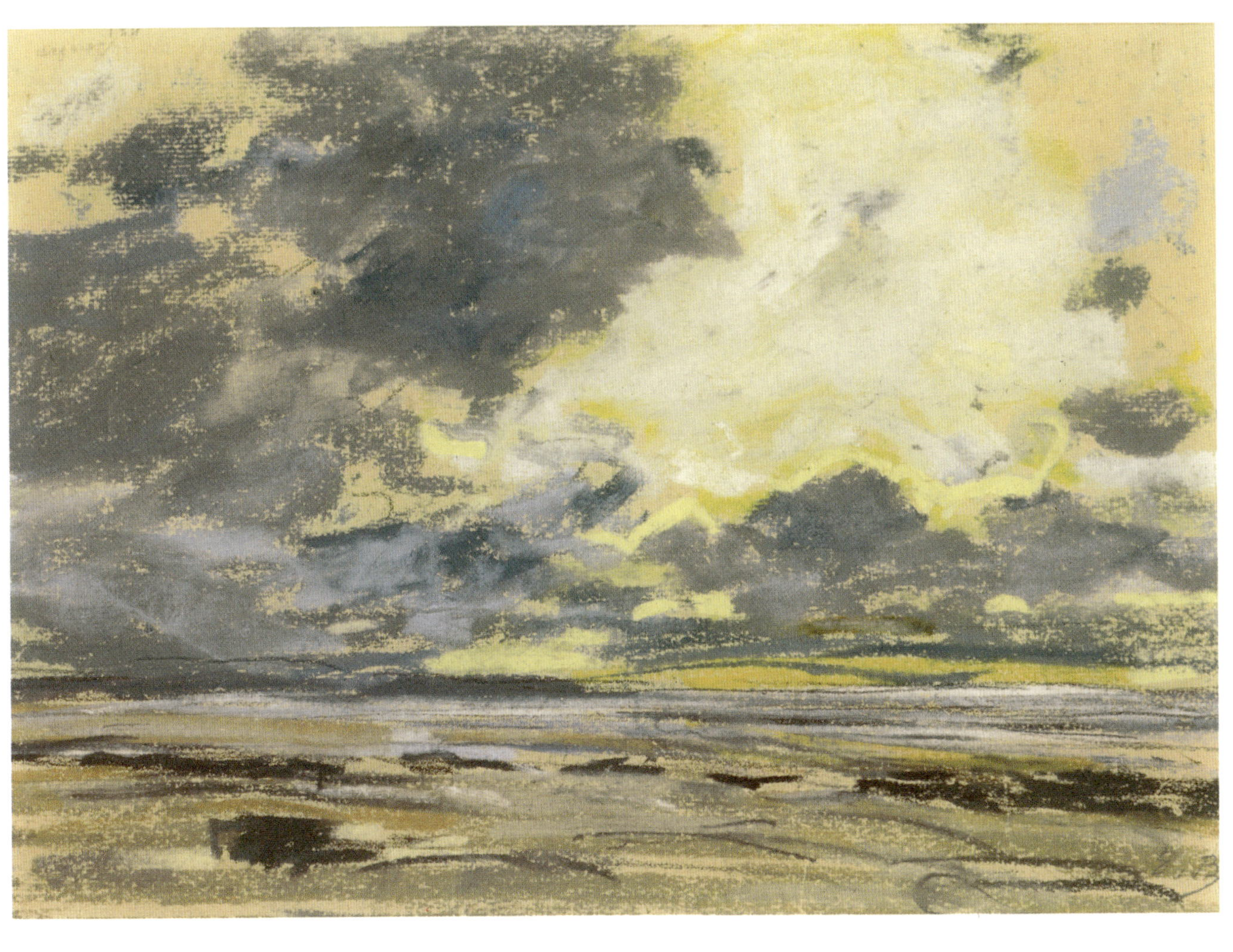

Stormy Sky, c. 1854–60
Pastel, 21.5 × 28.6 cm (8½ × 11¼ in.).
MUSÉE DU LOUVRE (COLLECTION MUSÉE D'ORSAY), PARIS

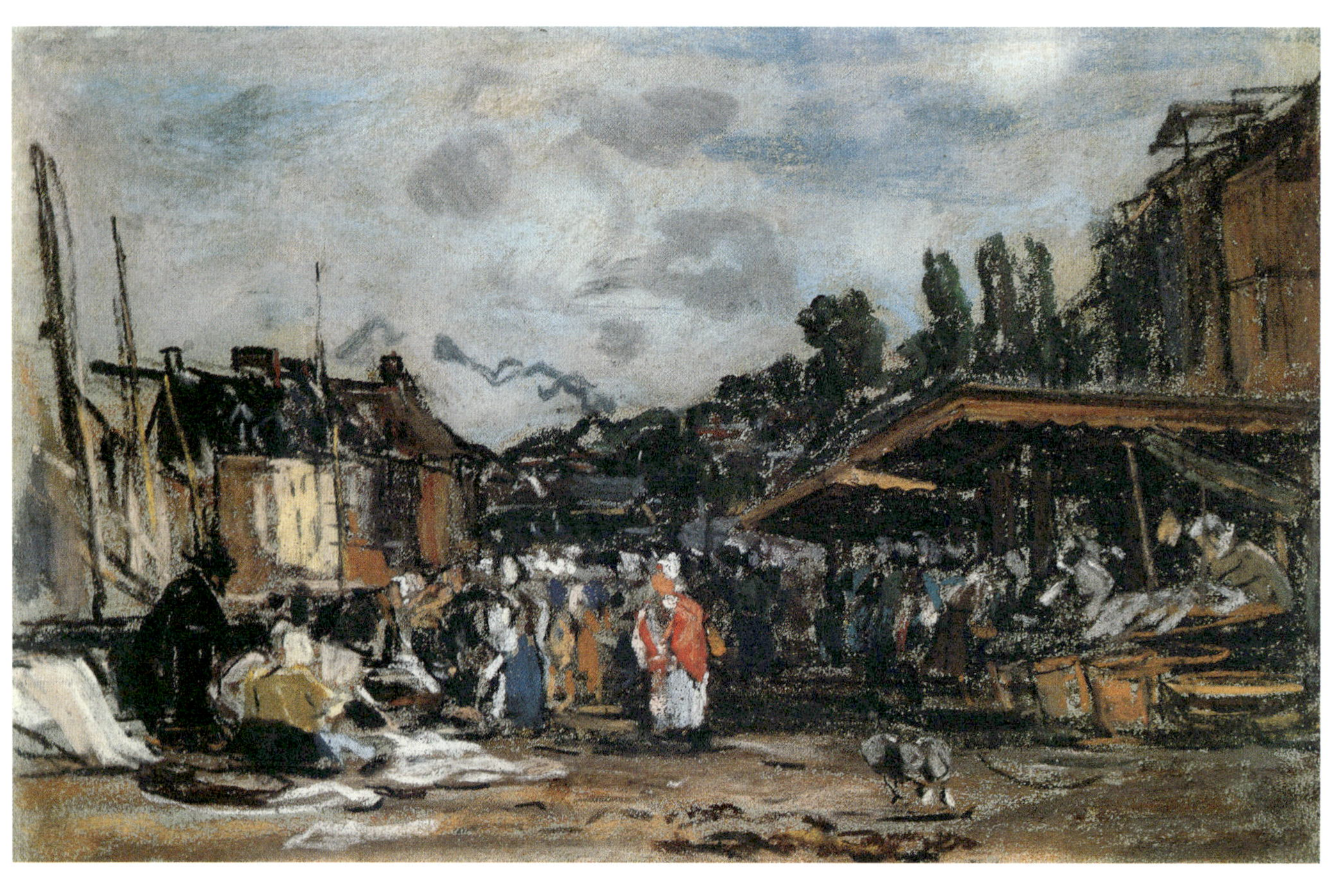

 Eugène Boudin

Fish Market, c. 1859
Pastel on blue-grey paper, 22 × 32 cm (8¾ × 12⅝ in.).
MUSÉE EUGÈNE BOUDIN, HONFLEUR

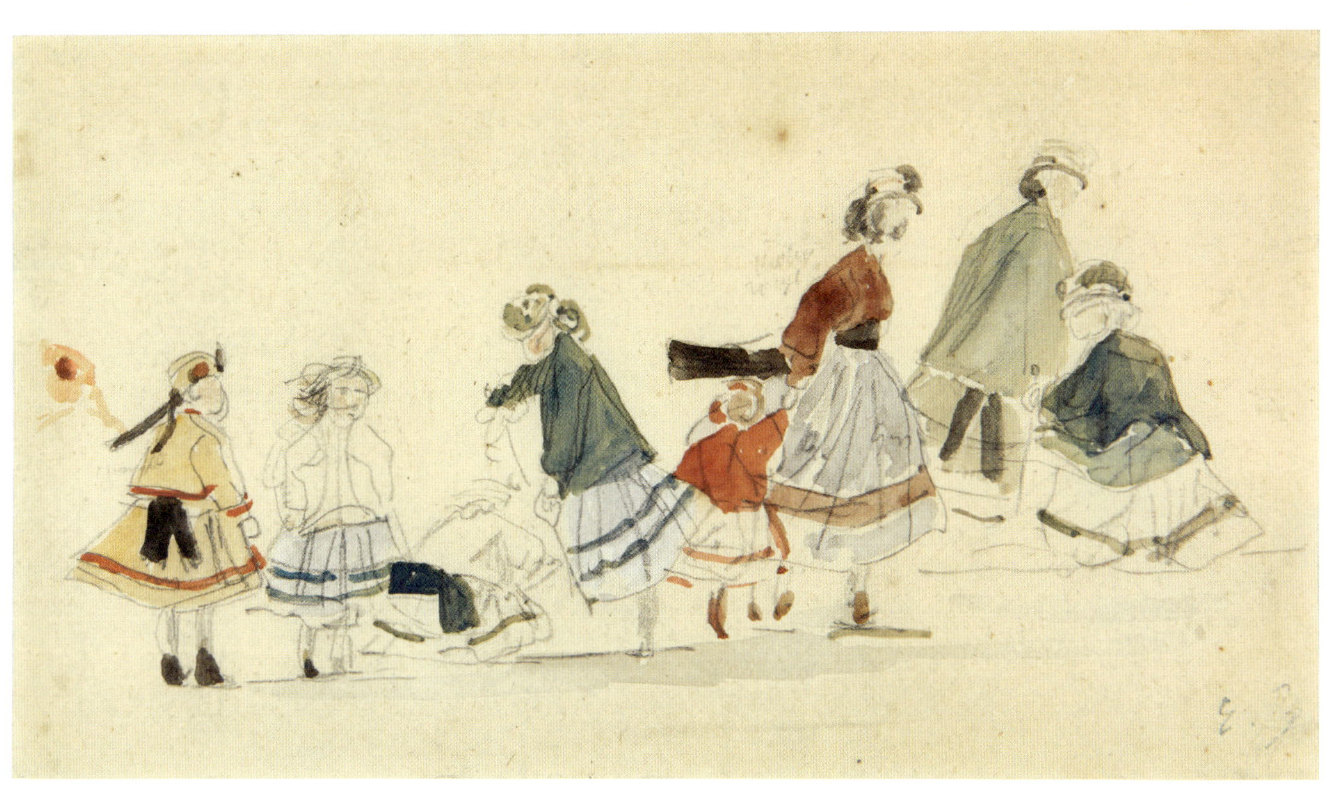

Study of Figures on the Beach, c. 1865–70
Watercolour, 14 × 24 cm (5⅝ × 9½ in.). Artist's stamp.
NEW ART GALLERY WALSALL

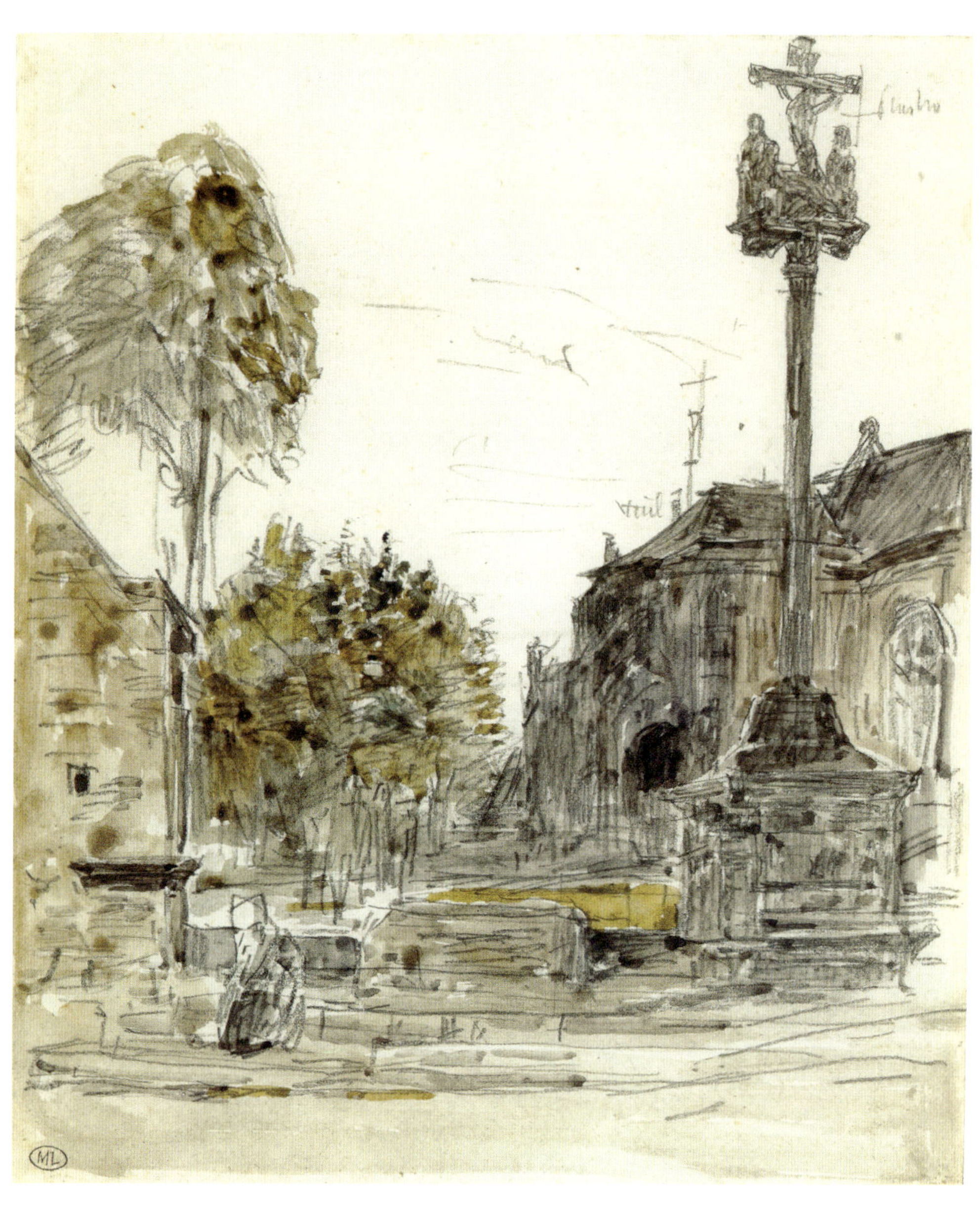

44   *Eugène Boudin*

View of Breton Calvary, c. 1866–67
Pencil and watercolour, 17.8 × 14.7 cm (7⅛ × 5⅞ in.).
MUSÉE DU LOUVRE (COLLECTION MUSÉE D'ORSAY), PARIS

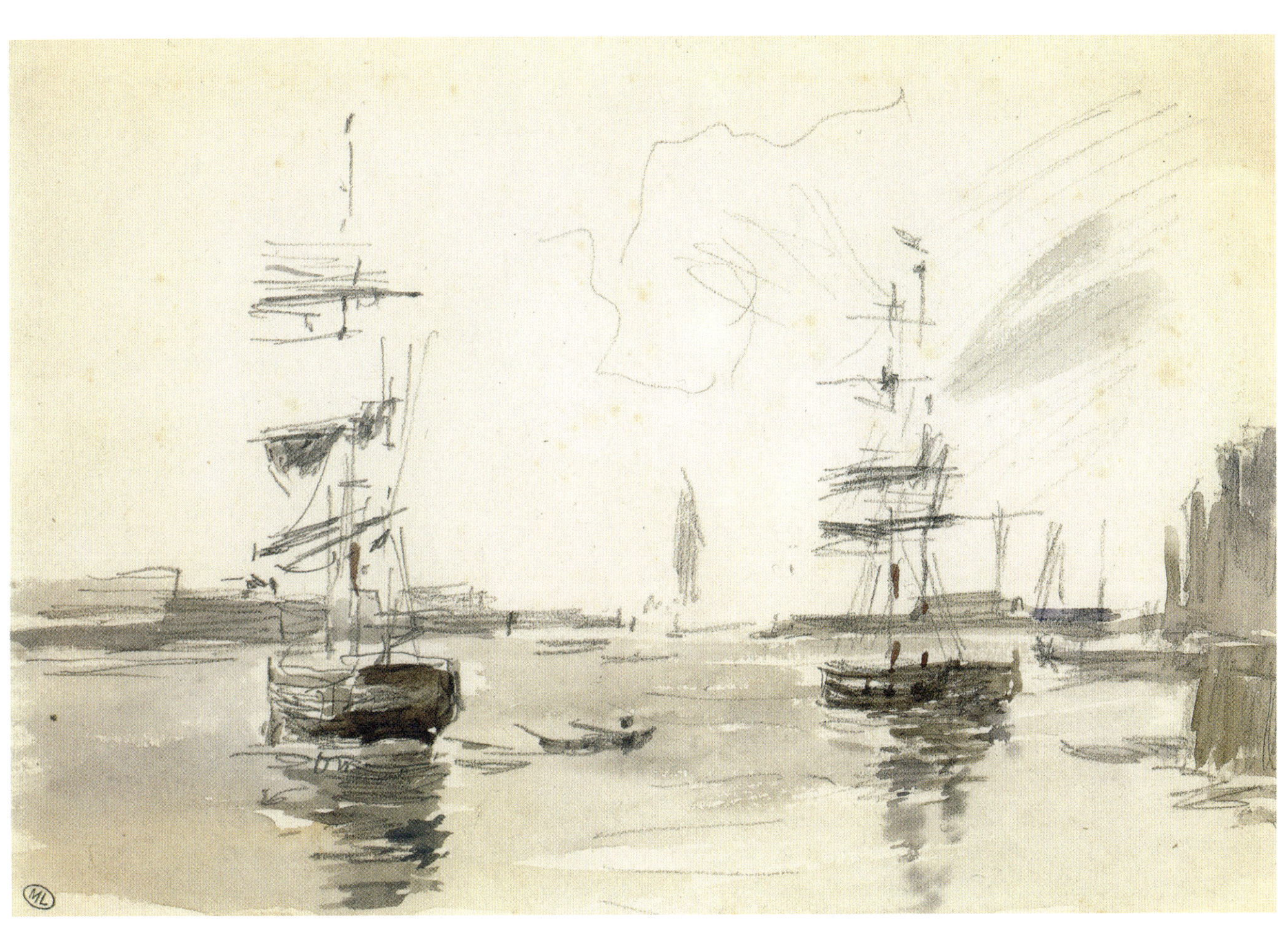

Sailing Ships, c. 1875–80
Pencil and watercolour, 15.5 × 22.6 cm (6⅛ × 9 in.).
Musée du Louvre (Collection Musée d'Orsay), Paris

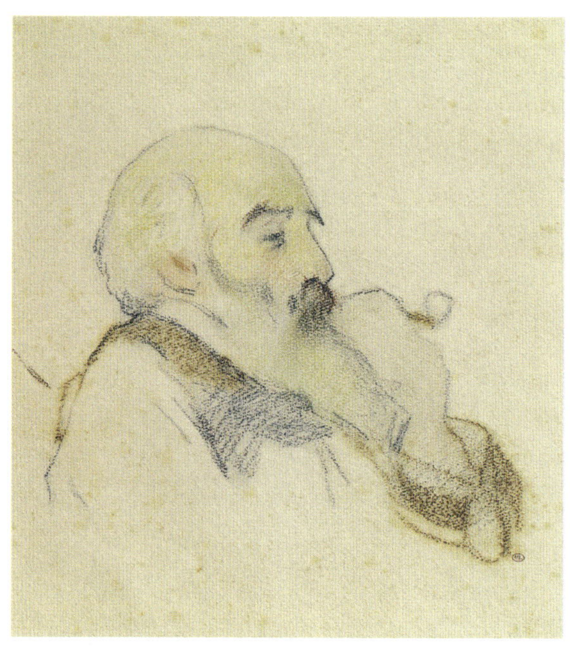

Camille Pissarro
1830–1903

Camille Pissarro is a central figure in the history of Impressionism. He was the only artist to have his work included in all eight of the Impressionist exhibitions held between 1874 and 1886, but he also served as a peacekeeper between the different factions that formed as the movement developed, and encouraged the idea of introducing younger artists to the group. Furthermore, Pissarro was very much a complete artist in the sense that within the context of Impressionism he pursued both urban and rural themes in his work, as well as undertaking both landscape and figure painting. Even so, he himself remarked in a letter of 1895 to his eldest son that he was 'in the rear of Impressionism'.

As a man of steadfast principles, which he often expounded in his correspondence, Pissarro was greatly respected. Cézanne called him 'humble and colossal', while others used biblical terms such as God the Father or Moses – epithets that matched his patriarchal appearance. And Cassatt summarized his influence by saying that, 'He was such a teacher that he could have taught stones to draw correctly.'

Paul Gauguin and Camille Pissarro
Double Portrait of Gauguin by Pissarro: Portrait of Pissarro
by Gauguin (detail), *c.* 1880
Charcoal and coloured pencils, 31.5 × 48.5 cm (12½ × 19⅛ in.).
MUSÉE DU LOUVRE (COLLECTION MUSÉE D'ORSAY), PARIS

The importance of Pissarro stems from the fact that he was a vital link between artists of the mid-century associated with the Barbizon School, such as Jean-Baptiste-Camille Corot, Jean-François Millet and Charles-François Daubigny, and the twentieth-century art of Henri Matisse and Francis Picabia. As well as working alongside Cézanne, he was also a great supporter of the burgeoning talents of Seurat, Signac, Gauguin and Van Gogh, sharing many of their interests in technical matters and for a time also their radical political and social outlook. Indeed, there was hardly an avant-garde artist of consequence who did not consult Pissarro. This was not just on the grounds of his dignified personality, but also because of the sustained quality of his work, which as early as 1866 Emile Zola recognized as possessing 'an extreme concern for truth and accuracy, a rugged and strong will'. Somehow it seems that Pissarro acted as both elder statesman and *enfant terrible* at the same time.

The artist's background was unusual. He was born in the Caribbean on the island of Saint Thomas, one of the Virgin Islands, and at that time a Danish possession. He never officially became a French citizen. The family was Jewish with Portuguese origins and strong French connections. Pissarro's predilection for art manifested itself while he was growing up on Saint Thomas, where he received informal tuition from the Danish artist Fritz Melbye, who instructed him in the rudiments of the European academic tradition. Many drawings survive from this early period of Pissarro's life, two years of which were spent in Venezuela, where he and Melbye set up a studio in Caracas. To a great extent, the strong light and bright colours of the Caribbean were an ideal background for a nascent Impressionist painter, but also, presciently, many of the motifs that he began to explore there anticipated those that he was to pursue in France. *The Bridge at Caracas* (p. 50) demonstrates considerable compositional sophistication, with the artist positioned at a slight distance in the riverbed below. Some figures cross the bridge and others wash clothes in the river. The freedom with which the watercolour is applied for the fronds of the palm tree on the left towering over the bridge indicate the relish with which Pissarro confronted the lush vegetation of the tropics.

On arriving in France for good in 1855, Pissarro was presented with a number of choices, but it was soon clear that he felt a kinship with Barbizon School artists, who were most closely associated with the Forest of Fontainebleau, several miles to the southeast of Paris. In their work they concentrated on landscape and rural life. *Apple Picking* (p. 51) demonstrates the influence of the Barbizon School artists, at the same time as being a good example of Pissarro's innate skill in creating a carefully balanced composition with increasingly confident handling of the softer media, especially in the dense hatching used for the foliage of the trees. The subject was one that particularly appealed to Pissarro, who also ultimately chose to live away from the centre of Paris. He resided at first in small villages along the river Marne and the river Seine where he often, like Monet, Renoir and Sisley, painted scenes of leisure. For many years during the 1870s, after self-imposed exile in London during the Franco-Prussian War and the Paris Commune, he lived in the medieval town of Pontoise, some nineteen miles to the northwest of the capital, which he had already explored to good effect in the late 1860s. Finally, in 1884 he moved further into the country to the small village of Éragny-sur-Epte in Normandy, closer to Rouen than Paris. It was in these rural areas that Pissarro found the subjects that most suited his temperament: fields, orchards, harvests, *jardins potagers* and markets.

He was, however, careful not to eschew Paris altogether as it was the main outlet for his work. Even so, *Boulevard Rochechouart* (p. 52), which was included in the sixth Impressionist exhibition (1882), comes as a surprise, since so many of the other items by him in that exhibition were of rural themes. Viewed slightly from above, the street is seen in winter sunlight evoked by a spectrum of colours – violet, yellow, orange, pink, green, purple. The dark forms of horse-drawn buses and fiacres in the foreground are contrasted with the more bleached effects of the frosted ground, the sides of the buildings and pellucid sky. The composition itself depends on the deep recession emphasized by the avenue of trees framed by the buildings on either side. By such means the artist makes the fugitive seem permanent, and thereafter Pissarro pursued cityscapes of this type, often in series, in Rouen, Paris, Dieppe and Le Havre, which reached a peak in the 1890s.

Although Pissarro was at first regarded as mainly a landscape painter, by the beginning of the 1880s, following the lead of Degas, he began to devise compositions with greater emphasis on the figure. These were predominantly rural scenes of people in the fields either working or at rest, or attending markets. In preparation for these pictures, he drew studies from life in sketchbooks and much larger drawings from posed models, who were often local people rather than professionals. Like *Woman Seen from Behind* (p. 53), the studio drawings are conceived on a monumental scale and seen from unusual angles. Between the strong, reinforced outlines are bravura passages of modelling with highlights in colour chalks. Such powerful drawings were made with specific compositions in mind and were frequently redeployed. This was a practice that Pissarro continued into the 1890s, as with *Two Studies of a Girl* (p. 57), where the same model is seen in two positions on the same sheet. The finished works were not necessarily in oil, but in tempera or gouache, like *The Marketplace, Pontoise* (p. 54 above), which could be produced more easily and thus in commercial terms form part of an increased turnover.

As the Impressionist exhibitions continued, much of the discussion among the artists themselves was devoted to future developments both as regards the content and the style of their work. Younger painters such as Seurat widened the terms of reference by advocating a more scientific approach involving colour theory and a tighter, more controlled technique known as pointillism or divisionism, which was less dependent on spontaneity. Pissarro was sympathetic to such theories in so far as they allowed him to revise his own style at a critical moment, and in the period 1885–90 he produced a number of works in the Neo-Impressionist style. *Pig Market, Saint-Martin Fair, Pontoise* (p. 54 below) is created out of numerous dots made with the pen. Effects of light and areas of tone are suggested by varying clusters of dots. The most remarkable aspect of this style is the restraint required to avoid losing the clarity of the forms or the legibility of the composition.

Pointillism may have been effective in ridding the perceived impurities in Pissarro's style, but it impeded the true expression of his sensations and slowed productivity. Reacting against such restrictions, he increased the output of his watercolours. Most of these were made in and around Eragny-sur-Epte, amounting to a faithful record of the changing seasons, alternating between the crisp chill of winter and the pulsating heat of summer (p. 55).

Of all the Impressionists Pissarro was the most political. He read the works of Pierre-Joseph Proudhon, Prince Pierre Kropotkin and Élisée Reclus and associated himself with journals such as *La Plume, La Révolte* and *Les Temps Nouveaux*. Although professing anarchist views and feeling compelled to go into exile in Belgium in 1894 for three months at the height of anarchist violence in Paris, he believed more realistically in the autonomy of the individual and the need to eliminate social and economic injustices by evolutionary means rather than by revolution. As an illustration of his political beliefs, Pissarro compiled an album of twenty-eight pen-and-ink drawings entitled *Turpitudes Sociales* (1889–90) for his nieces, Esther and Alice Isaacson. The title page (p. 56 above) shows a seated figure of Father Time (in fact a self-portrait) surveying Paris. The sun, representing a new dawn rising over the city, has the word 'Anarchie' inscribed above it, while the Eiffel Tower, newly built for the Universal Exhibition of 1889, tries unsuccessfully to block it out. The drawings comment on the effects of the social iniquities of the Third Republic arising mainly from the pursuit of capitalism. In its energy and exaggeration the style of the drawings is caricatural, and the content is related to illustrations found in contemporary journals.

How far Pissarro's political beliefs, which were well known outside his family, are apparent in his paintings is a moot point. The balance between urban views and rural subjects is certainly not a deliberately calibrated one suggesting that life lived in one place is better than another. Nonetheless, it is apparent that Pissarro's preference was for rural life. *Design for a fan: Female Peasants Placing Pea Sticks in the Ground* (p. 56 below) is a profession of his faith in the virtues of rural labour. The fan-shaped format of the drawing ties in with the desire by the Impressionists to produce work that is more utilitarian, but it is the particular activity that Pissarro relishes. The setting is effulgent, the labour communal, the product mutually beneficial and the action beautifully terpsichorean. As such, it is Pissarro's blueprint for the future of society. Or, as he wrote to his eldest son in April 1890, 'Salvation lies in nature, now more than ever'.

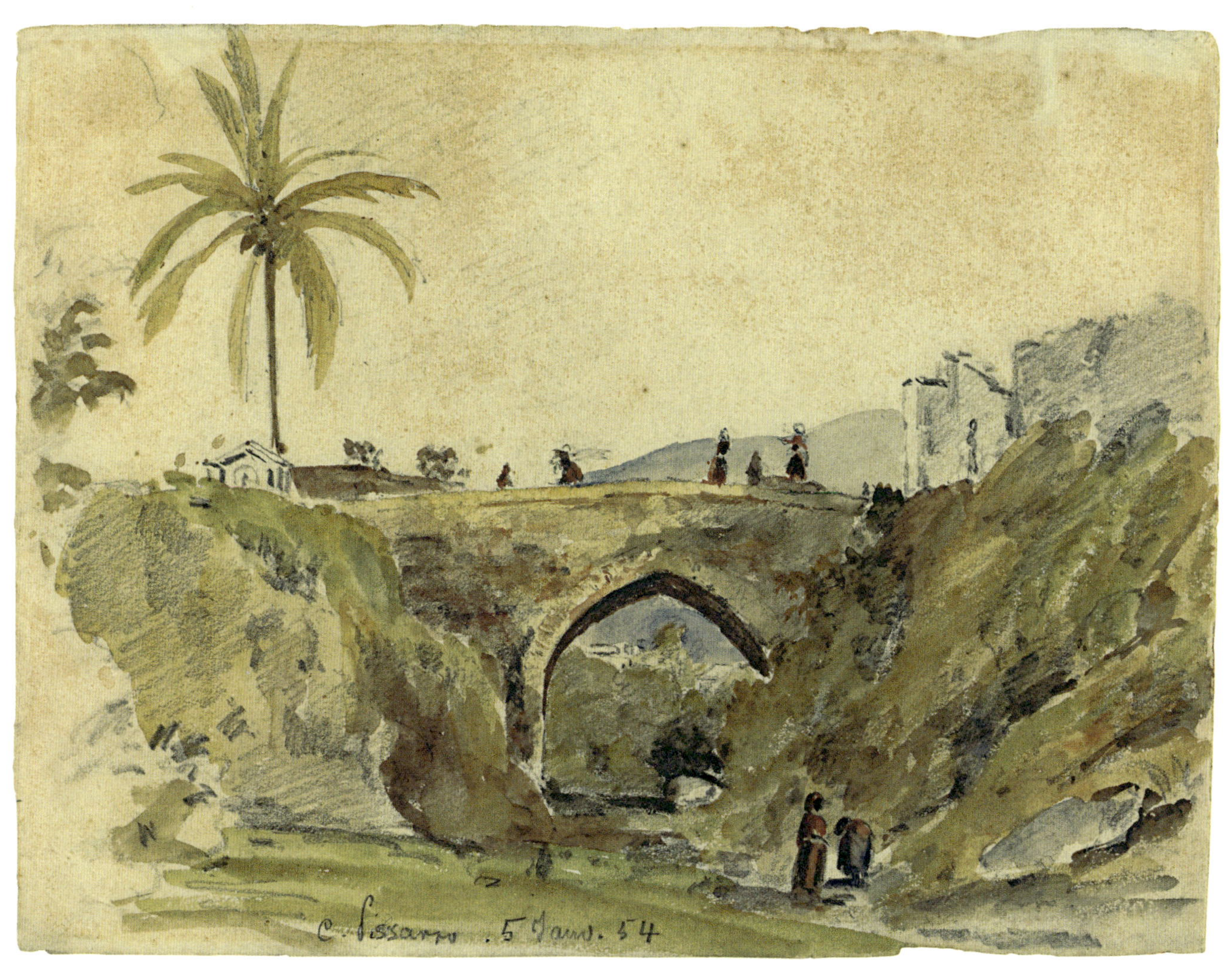

50   *Camille Pissarro*

The Bridge at Caracas, 1854
Watercolour over pencil, 24 × 30.5 cm (9½ × 12 in.).
Signed and dated.
NATIONAL GALLERY OF ART, WASHINGTON, DC

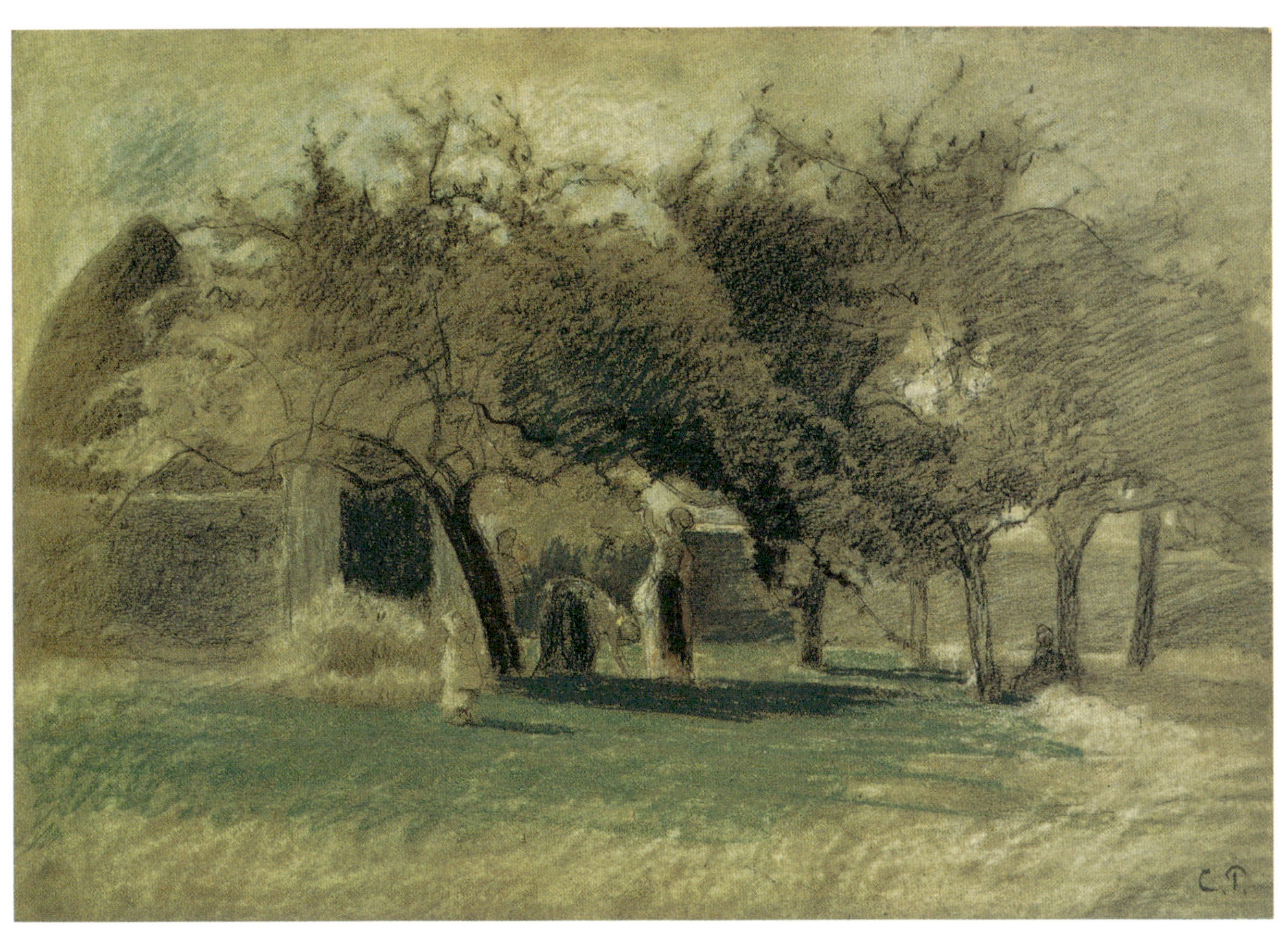

Apple Picking, 1870–75
Pastel with black and white chalk on buff-coloured paper,
34.2 × 49.4 cm (13½ × 19½ in.). Artist's stamp.

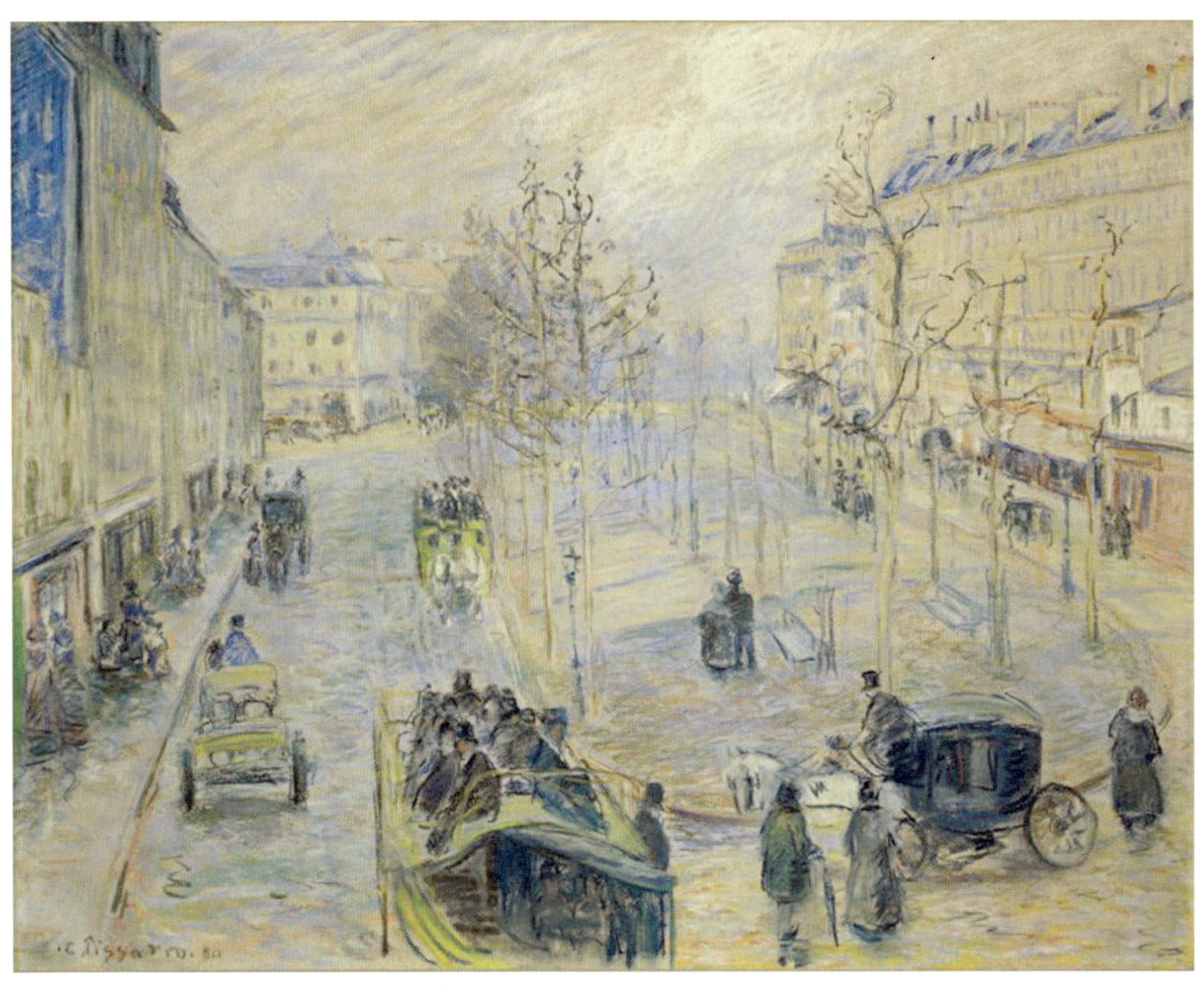

 Camille Pissarro

Boulevard Rochechouart, 1880
Pastel, 59.9 × 73.5 cm (23⅝ × 29 in.). Signed and dated.
STERLING AND FRANCINE CLARK ART INSTITUTE, WILLIAMSTOWN,
MASSACHUSETTS

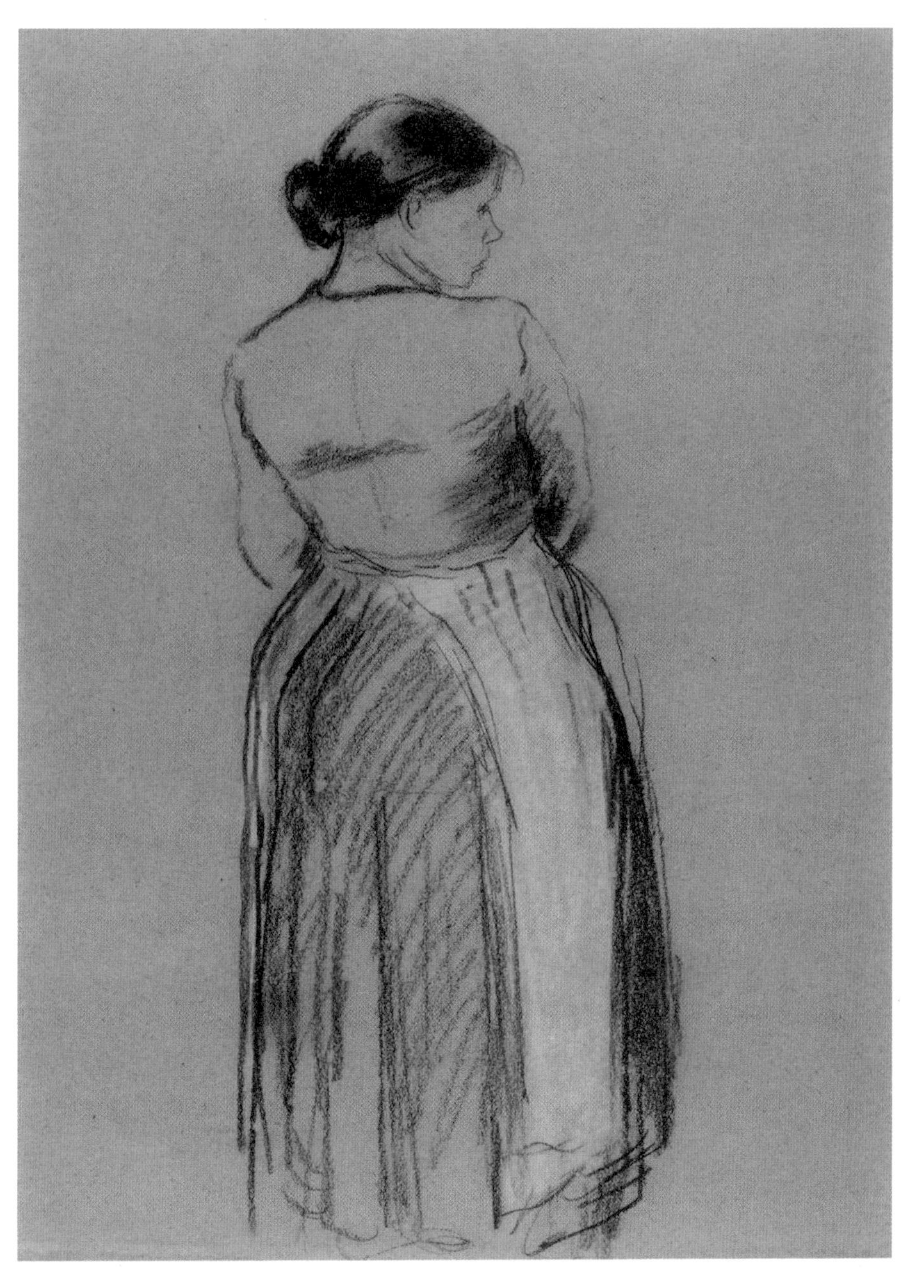

*Woman Seen from Behind; Three-Quarters Length, Head
in Profile to Right, Arms in Front, Wearing an Apron*, 1881
Black, blue and white chalk on grey paper,
44.5 × 31.3 cm (17 ½ × 12 ⅜ in.).
BRITISH MUSEUM, LONDON

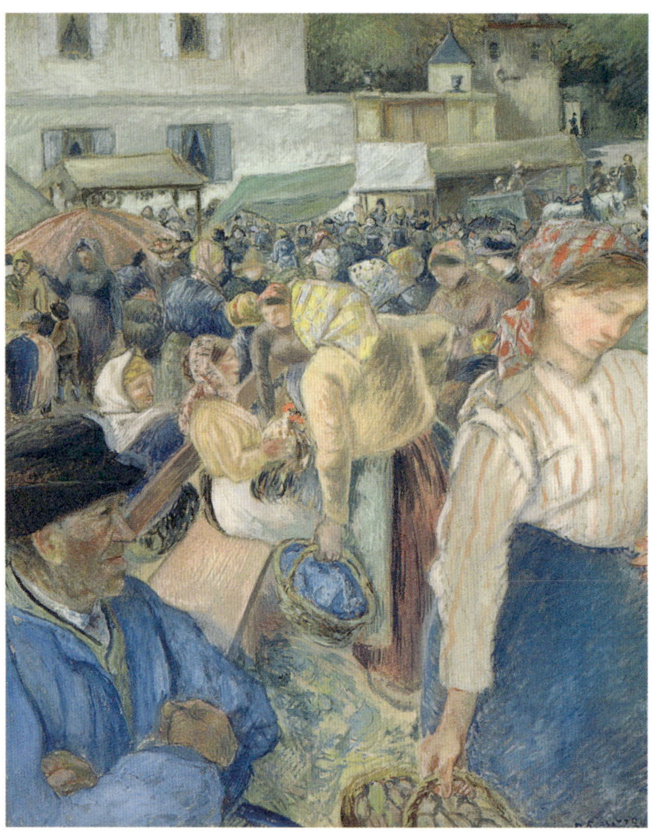

The Marketplace, Pontoise, 1882
Gouache, 80.6 × 64.8 cm (31¾ × 25½ in.).
Signed and dated.
METROPOLITAN MUSEUM OF ART, NEW YORK

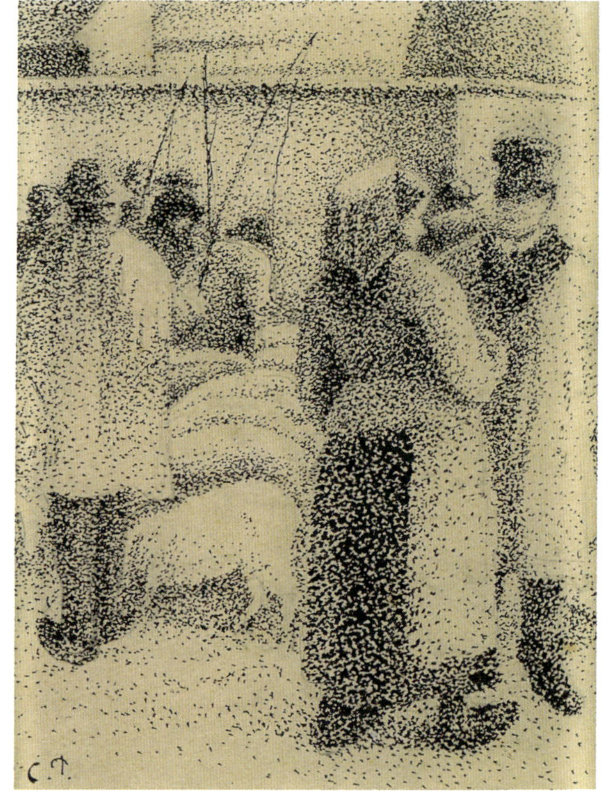

Pig Market, Saint-Martin Fair, Pontoise, 1886
Pen and ink with crayon, 17.5 × 12.7 cm (6⅞ × 5 in.). Signed.
MUSÉE DU LOUVRE (COLLECTION MUSÉE D'ORSAY), PARIS

    Camille Pissarro

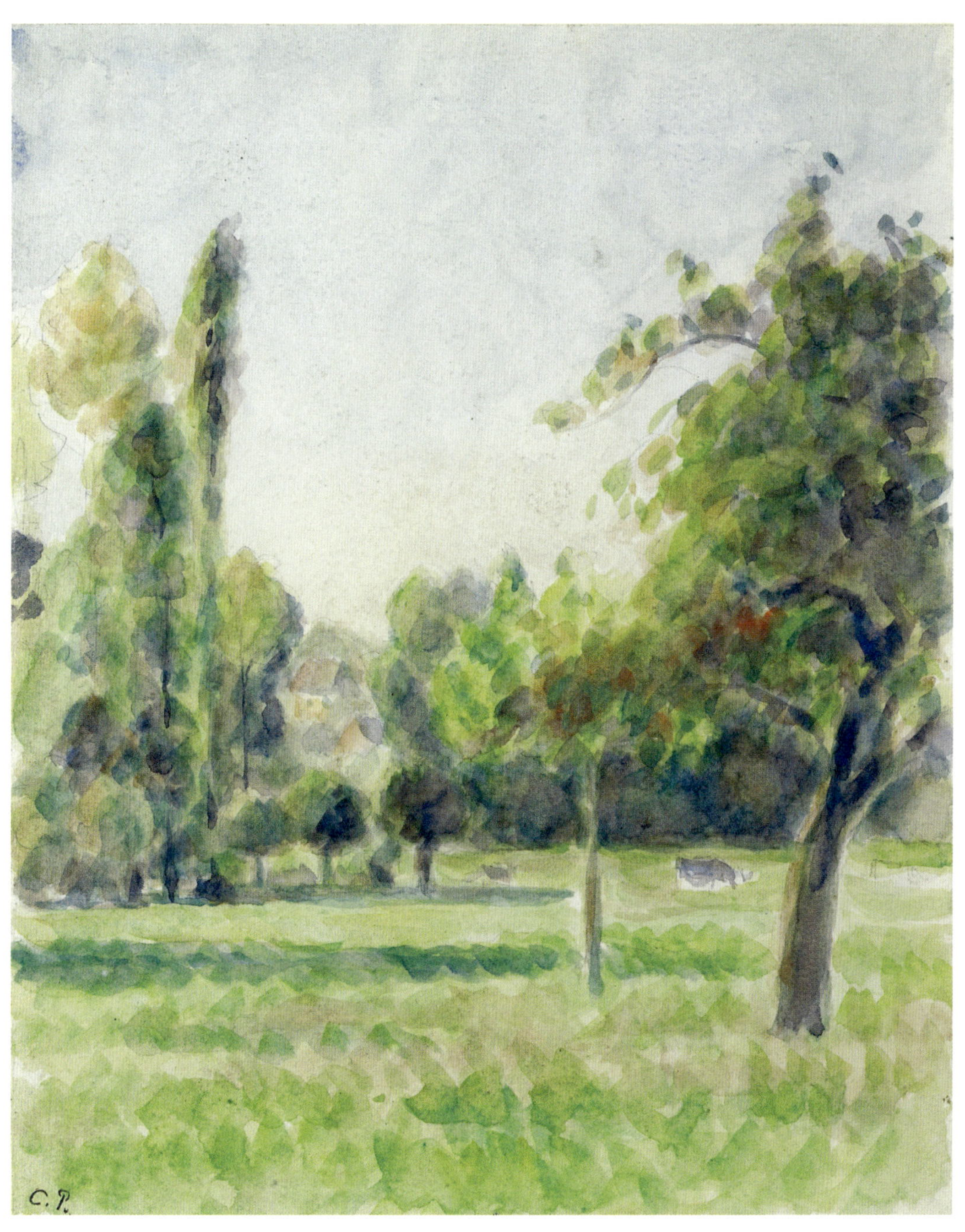

Study of the Orchard of the Artist's House at Eragny-sur-Epte, c. 1890
Watercolour over pencil, 28.3 × 22.5 cm (11⅛ × 8⅞ in.).
Artist's stamp.
ASHMOLEAN MUSEUM, OXFORD

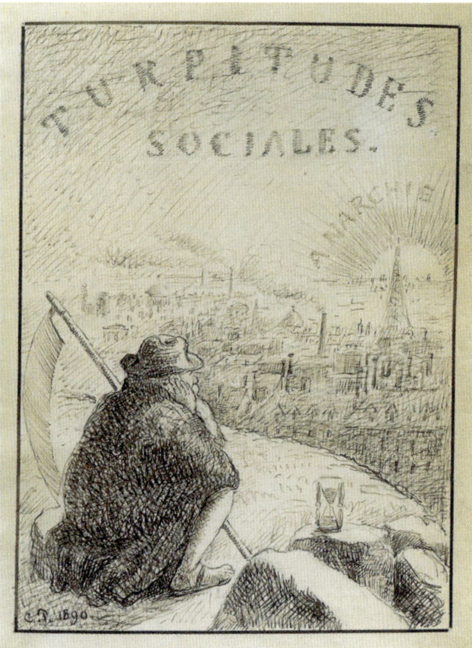

Turpitudes Sociales, 1889–90
Pen and brown ink on glazed paper over traces of pencil,
31.5 × 24.5 cm (12⅜ × 9⅝ in.). Inscribed by the artist
with the title, signed and dated.
COLLECTION OF JEAN BONNA, GENEVA

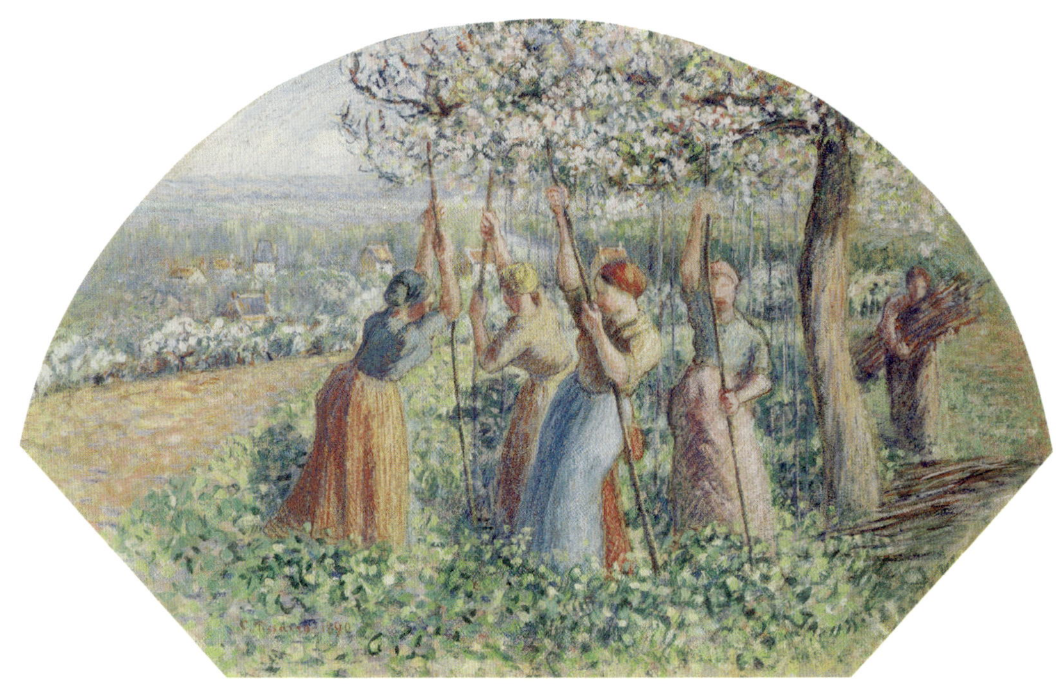

   Camille Pissarro

Design for a fan: Female Peasants Placing Pea Sticks in the Ground, 1890
Gouache with traces of black chalk on brown paper, 40.7 × 64.1 cm
(16 × 25¼ in.). Signed and dated.
ASHMOLEAN MUSEUM, OXFORD

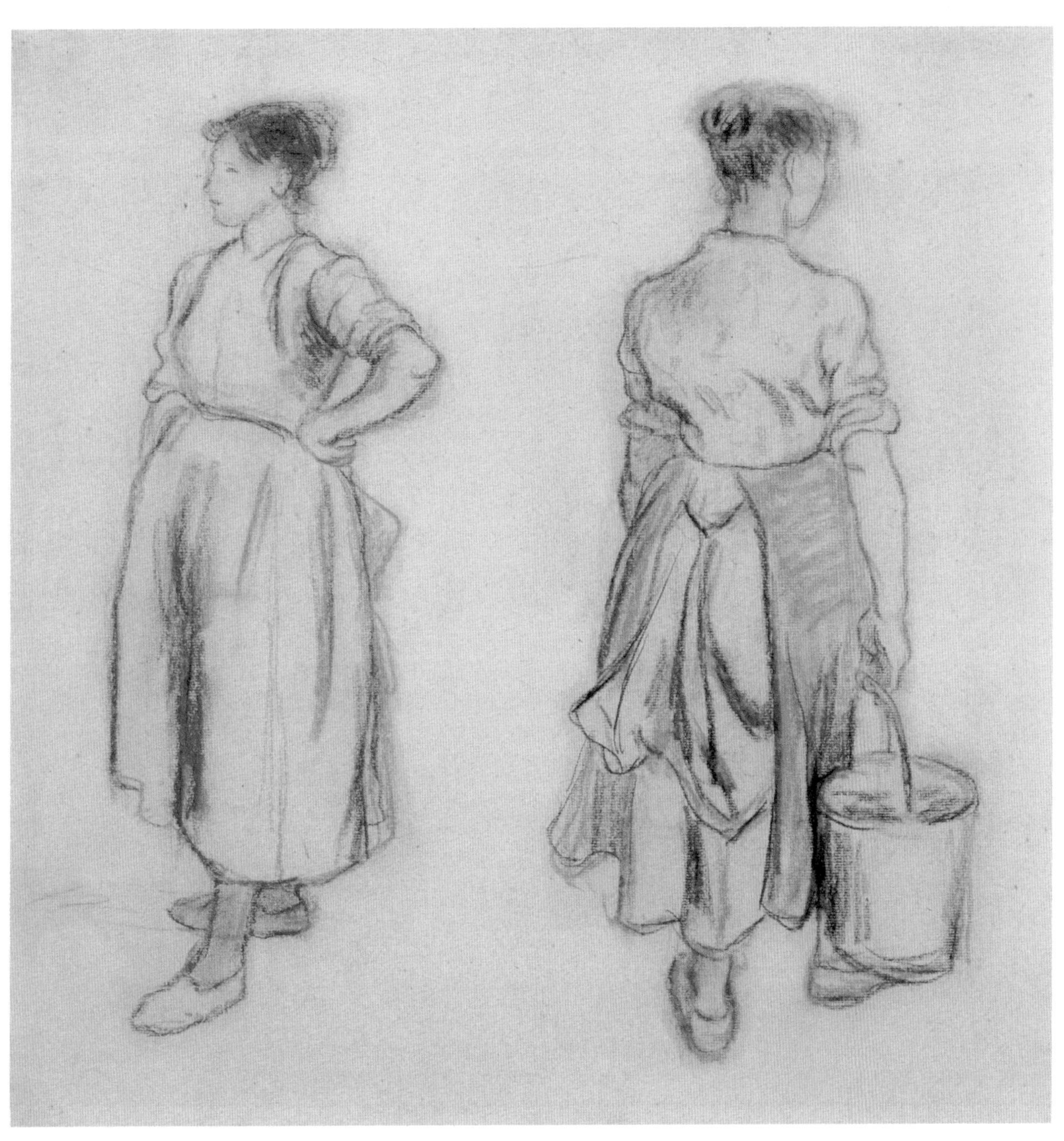

Two Studies of a Girl, c. 1895
Black chalk and pastel on pink paper,
47.6 × 61.8 cm (18¾ × 24⅜ in.).
NATIONAL MUSEUM OF WALES, CARDIFF

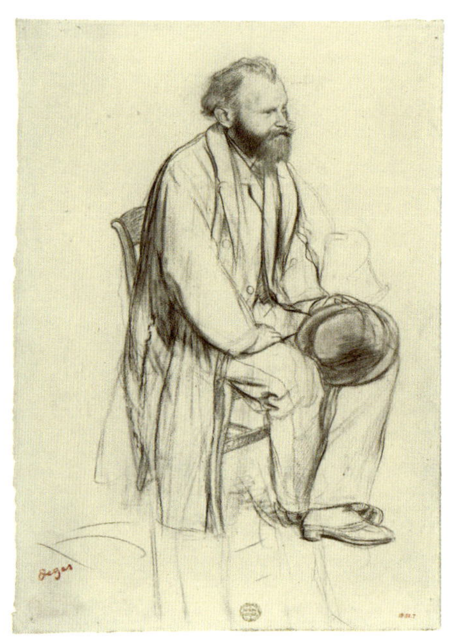

Édouard Manet
1832–1883

The chief characteristic of Édouard Manet's drawn *oeuvre* is its diversity. Wide-ranging in subject (including book illustration) and virtuosic in style, his drawings combine boundless curiosity with technical fluency. As such, they are the counterpart to his paintings, which by tackling contemporary themes and conflating different genres provoked bitter criticism but made a significant breakthrough in art. Such pictures as *Music in the Tuileries Gardens* (1862, National Gallery, London), *Déjeuner sur l'Herbe* (1863, Musée d'Orsay, Paris), *Olympia* (1863, Musée d'Orsay, Paris), *Nana* (1877, Kunsthalle, Hamburg) and *A Bar at the Folies-Bergère* (1881–82, Courtauld Gallery, London) stand at the threshold of modernism.

Both as a man and an artist, Manet presented a paradox. Fortunate in birth and upbringing, he repeatedly sought acceptance for his art in official circles while at the same time being associated in the public mind with the avant-garde. He developed a style that in its directness and commitment he believed to be appropriate for portraying

Edgar Degas
Édouard Manet, Seated, Holding his Hat, c. 1865
Graphite and black chalk, 33.1 × 23 cm (13 × 9 in.).
METROPOLITAN MUSEUM OF ART, NEW YORK

contemporary scenes, yet in doing this intended no discourtesy to tradition. Although he frequented the same bars and cafés as the Impressionists and their apologists, his immaculate dress and refined manners implied that he was somewhat aloof from bohemian circles. In fact, the many portraits of Manet grant him the attributes of the ultimate *flâneur*, who strolls the streets of Paris carefully and disdainfully observing the world from a distance. Even though he was regarded as the honorific leader of the Impressionists, Manet never exhibited with them and to the last remained loyal to the Salon, regardless of so many of his pictures being rejected by successive juries. In addition to influential supporters such as the poets Charles Baudelaire and Stéphane Mallarmé, he had friends in high places and was awarded the Chevalier de la Légion d'honneur the year before his death.

Significant, too, is the fact that Manet chose to live and work in the north of Paris, at first until the mid-1860s in the rapidly changing Batignolles district and then in the adjacent newly developed Quartier de l'Europe close to the Gare Saint-Lazare. The urbanization of this area was part of a masterplan devised by Baron Haussmann and marked the emergence of the modern city from the chrysalis of medieval Paris. The area was fashionable, offering subjects that the artist found sympathetic and to which his uncompromising style could do justice. Here in his apartment in the Rue de Saint-Pétersbourg he held regular soirées, which were attended by leading political and cultural figures who shared his Republican views, and invited patrons, critics and friends to see his pictures in his studio nearby.

When young, Manet was encouraged to pursue a naval career, but on acknowledging his aptitude for art his parents allowed him in 1850 to enrol in the studio of Thomas Couture, where he remained for six years, although not always on good terms with his teacher. Couture was an academic painter whose vast canvas *Romans of the Decadence* (Musée d'Orsay, Paris) had been an enormous success at the Salon of 1847, but it was not the kind of work that Manet was keen to emulate. However, the choice of medium, strong contours and firm modelling of *Seated Woman* (p. 62) reveal the young artist's debt to Couture, while the pose and powerful sense of form indicate a more radical approach to traditional studio practices.

Manet added to his knowledge of art by making numerous copies of works by past masters seen either in Paris or while travelling abroad in the Netherlands, Italy and Spain. Many of these copies (Introduction, fig. 12) are details of compositions and are striking for their specificity and adroitness. Spontaneity and an ability to seize the defining moment became the principal features of Manet's style, just as the straight-forward presentation of the subject in the old masters inspired him in his depiction of the contemporary scene. Manet used the past as a Trojan horse to establish the primacy of modernism. For example, *After the Bath* (p. 63), which is drawn in the traditional medium of red chalk and relates to an etching, is a perfect fusion of the old and the new in so far as the biblical resonances of the subject, recalling the Finding of Moses, Susannah or Bathsheba, have been purloined for an evocation of the everyday.

The selection and handling of media, as well as the variety of purposes for which Manet made drawings, also indicate the originality of his draughtsmanship. Like black or red chalk, pastel was a medium much favoured by French artists in the eighteenth century, but Manet found that its ease of application and vivid colour contrasts suited the tempo and purpose of his art. *Madame Manet on a Blue Couch* (p. 66 above) is a skilfully controlled early pastel in which the artist has exploited the careful manipulation of the cool and warm tones while relishing the piquancy of the blacks accentuating the hat ribbons and the shoes. A private joke is perhaps intended, in that the pose echoes that of the naked Olympia.

Manet's output of pastels increased during his last years as a result of the debilitating effects of tertiary syphilis, which led to the amputation of his left leg at the very end of his life. A one-man exhibition of his work held at the gallery of the journal *La Vie Moderne* in 1880 included fifteen pastels. One of them was *The Beer Drinkers* (p. 67) where the handling is emphatically bolder and looser. The figures are positioned in the front plane sitting close to one another, almost at right angles. The viewer sees both women close up, as though seated at the next table, with the figure on the left in profile and the one on the right dramatically foreshortened. Their physical proximity is emphasized by the diagonal of the raised glass, while the other glass is aligned on the vertical formed with the face of the woman looking down. The composition is a brilliant example of Manet's powers of concision derived from the acuity of his eye and speed of execution.

Most of Manet's pastels, however, are portraits – more of women than men. His portrait *George Moore* (p. 68), of the Irish novelist and memoirist, was done at a single sitting. It is distinguished by the nuanced manipulation of greys and blacks of the clothes and background offset by the lighter tones of the head, although Moore requested changes that Manet refused to make. 'Is it my fault if Moore looks like a squashed egg yolk and if his face is lopsided?', he dismissively remarked. *Mademoiselle Suzette Lemaire* (p. 69), on the other hand, betokens the more sympathetic treatment that Manet reserved for his female friends. The sitter, who was an intimate of Marcel Proust, is presented with a remarkable economy. Her delicate features are set against a pink background, whereas her fichu is seen against the bare canvas and gathered in a knot that suggests a sculpted bust.

Throughout his career Manet was open to experiment. His early dependence on pencil and chalk adhered to the rigid hierarchy imposed by the academic system of teaching, but although he continued to use pencil in his sketchbooks, he had from the early 1860s begun to show a preference for pen and brush used in combination with ink, wash and watercolour. This allowed him to work faster, to experiment more freely, to mix media more readily and to address more expeditiously the fugitive effects that he regarded as the chief characteristic of modern life. *The Spanish Ballet* (p. 64) is a mixed-media drawing in a caricatural style capturing the exuberance of the troupe of famous Spanish dancers who performed in Paris in 1862. As a dedicated Hispanist, Manet was keen to record one of the performances and made this compositional drawing in connection with a painting he asked the dancers to pose for in the studio.

Such compositional drawings are rare in Manet's *oeuvre*. Normally he accumulated a number of ideas on several sheets or in sketchbooks as contributing factors towards a finished composition that he continued to evolve on the canvas, or, if a print, on the metal plate or lithographic stone. *The Rue Mosnier in the Rain* (p. 66 below) depicts the view from Manet's studio on the Rue de Saint-Pétersbourg of one of the smaller new streets (now the Rue de Berne), of which he made three paintings. Here the brush has been freely used over indications in pencil to record the movement on the street below: the swaying of the carriages, the angle of the umbrellas, the shifting light and the reflections on the wet slippery surfaces, all are representative of a world in perpetual motion. The style is influenced by Japanese art and it is not limited to mere description: the speed and energy of execution relay some of the kinetic energy the artist is witnessing.

The Barricade (p. 65) has similar complications. Having served in the National Guard during the Franco-Prussian War when Paris was under siege, Manet also witnessed the bloodshed in 1871 when the Commune was vigorously put down by the Republican government based in Versailles. The starting point for the composition was a tracing he made from his lithograph of *The Execution of the Emperor Maximilian* (1868), which he then updated or refreshed to suit the circumstances of the Commune. Nothing illustrates better Manet's ability to undermine existing hierarchies than his tendency to switch from one medium to another as part of the creative process. The concept of reusing material is also evident in many of his watercolours, which are often traced in the first instance from photographs of his paintings before being worked over in watercolour.

The artist's physical condition began to deteriorate seriously in 1880. He received medical attention and took cures with long periods of rest in the suburbs of Paris – Bellevue, Versailles and Rueil. Now receiving plaudits for his work, he managed to continue painting only with difficulty, including such outstanding works as *A Bar at the Folies-Bergère*, but also, on a smaller scale, magical still lifes of vases of flowers. Apart from the pastels, many of Manet's last drawings are vignettes illustrating letters to friends (pp. 70–71). The letters are very short, inviting people to visit him and asking them not to forget him in his forced absences from the centre of Paris. The sketches demonstrate Manet's eye for detail and, even at a time of great distress, his wit. They are the essence of the man, who once confessed to one of his most well-connected sitters, Mademoiselle Isabelle Lemonnier, 'nothing shocks me, everything amuses me'.

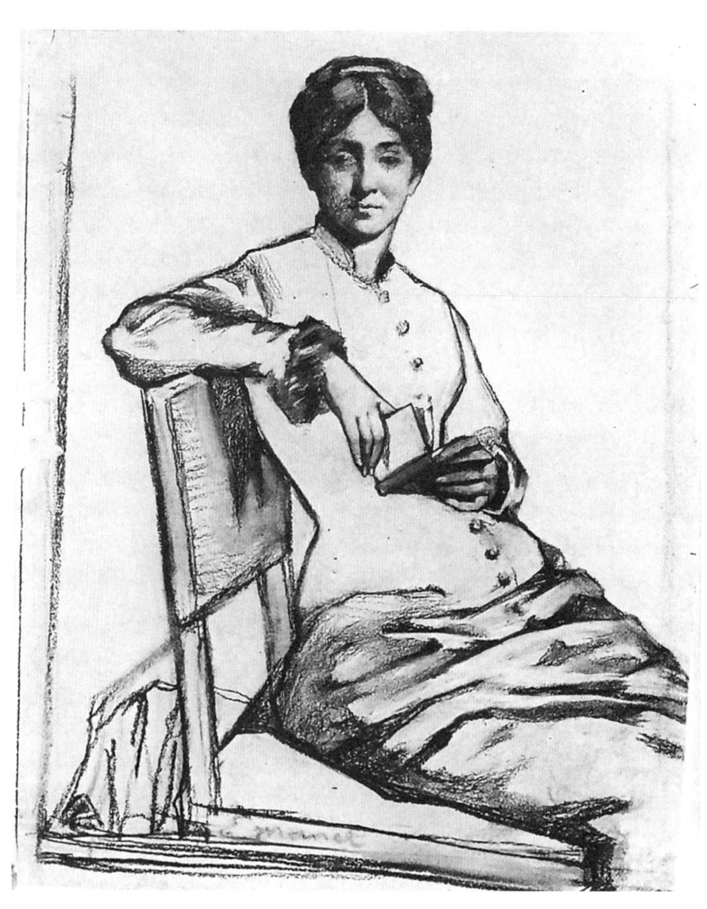

62   *Édouard Manet*

Seated Woman, c. 1859
Charcoal, 54.5 × 41 cm (21½ × 16⅛ in.). Signed.
PRIVATE COLLECTION

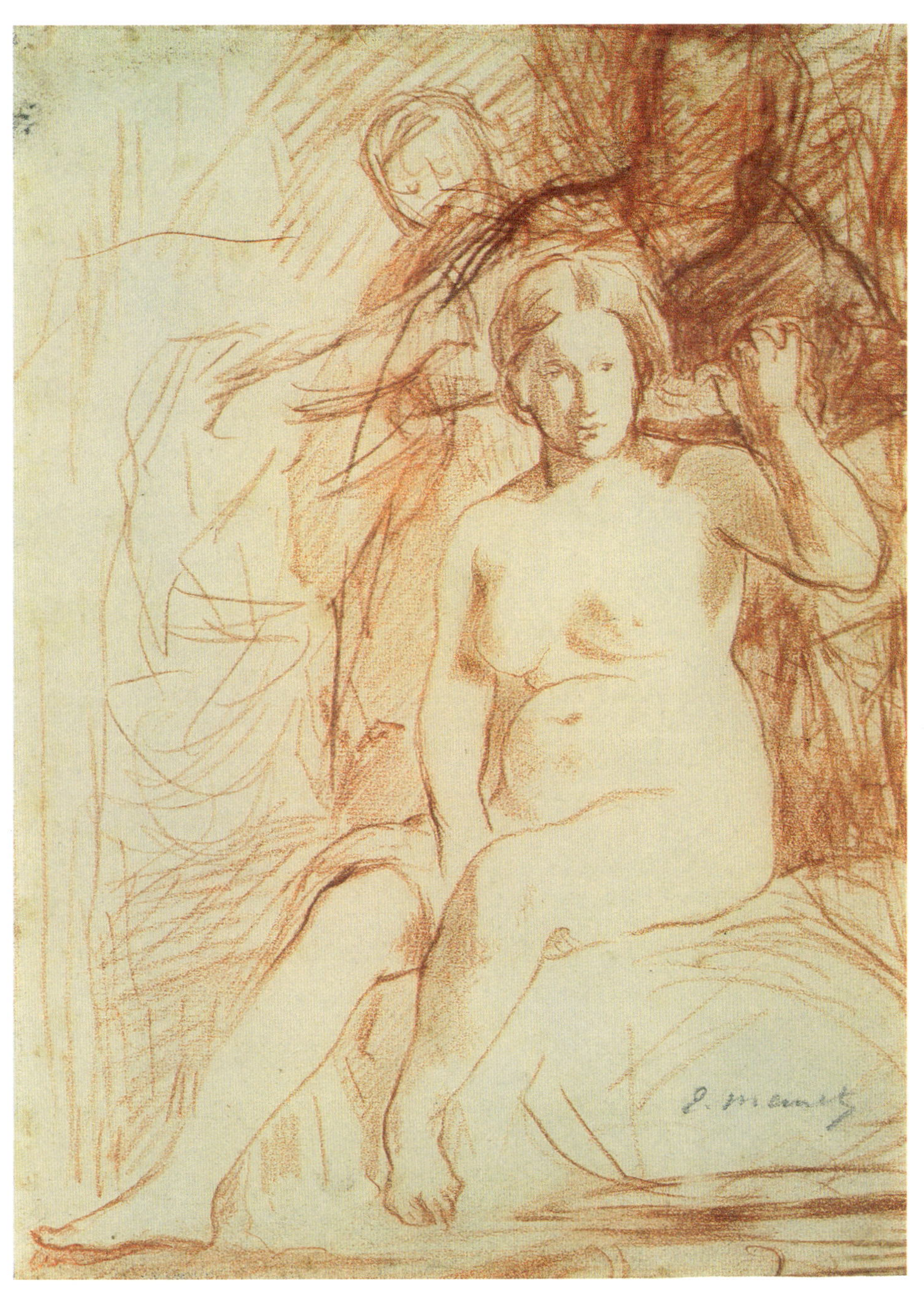

After the Bath, 1860–61
Red chalk with some incising,
28 × 20 cm (11 × 7⅞ in.). Signed.
THE ART INSTITUTE OF CHICAGO

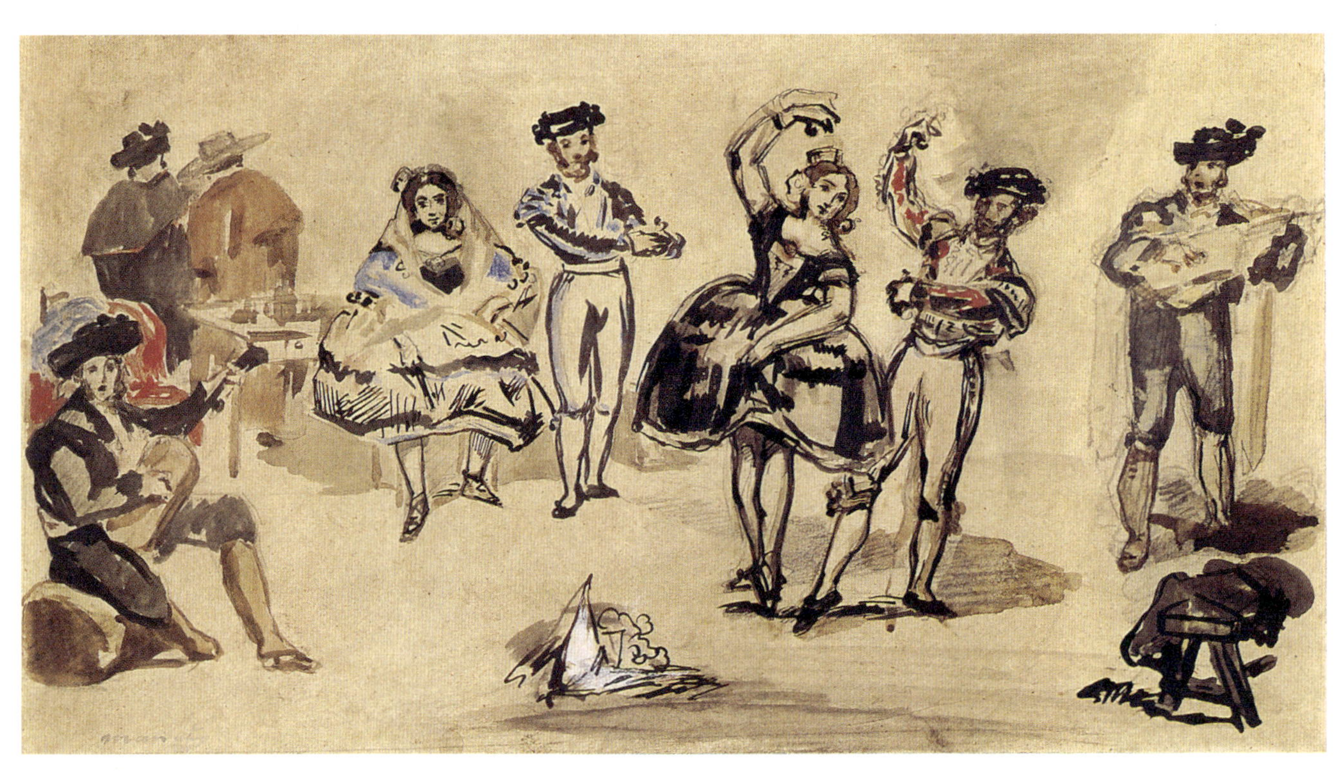

64   *Édouard Manet*

The Spanish Ballet, 1862–63
Pen and ink with wash, watercolour and gouache,
23.3 × 41.5 cm (9⅛ × 16⅜ in.). Signed.
MUSEUM OF FINE ARTS, BUDAPEST

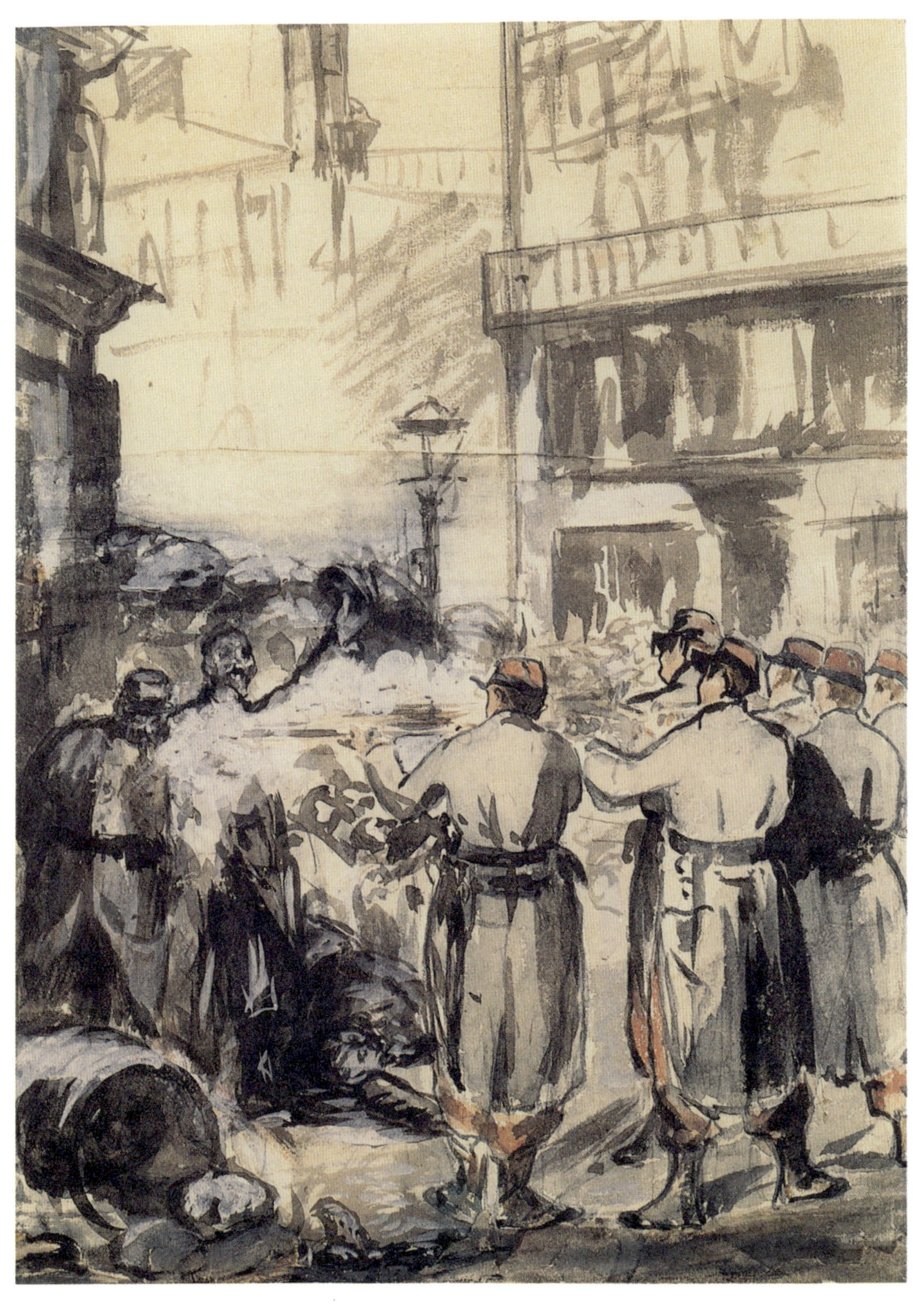

The Barricade, 1871
Watercolour and gouache, 46.2 × 32.5 cm
(18¼ × 12¾ in.). Artist's stamp.
Museum of Fine Arts, Budapest

65

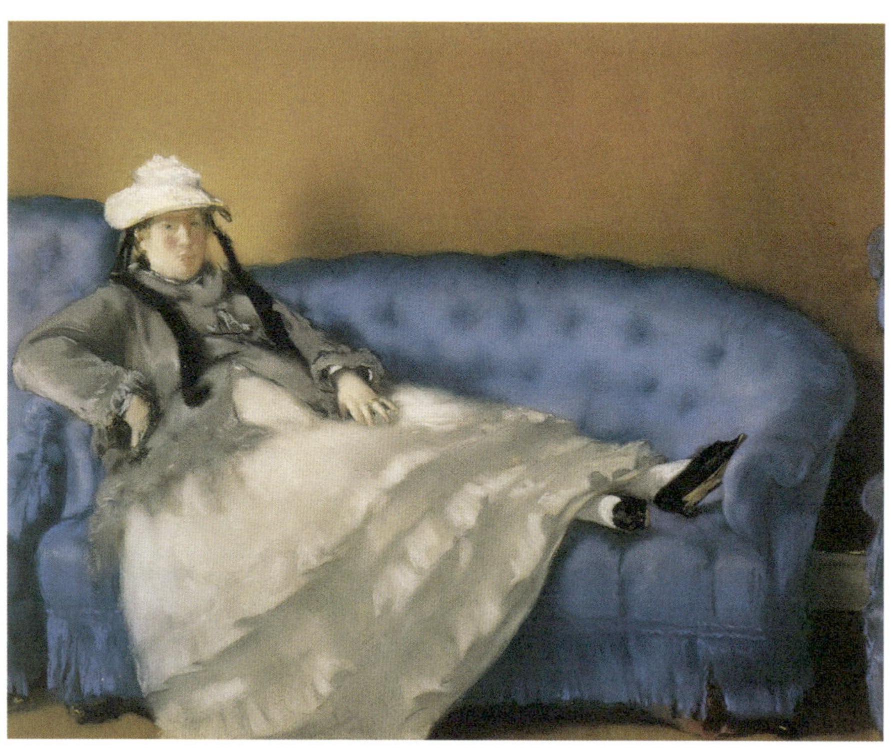

Madame Manet on a Blue Couch, 1874
Pastel, 49 × 60 cm (19¼ × 23⅝ in.). Signed by the artist's wife.
MUSÉE D'ORSAY, PARIS

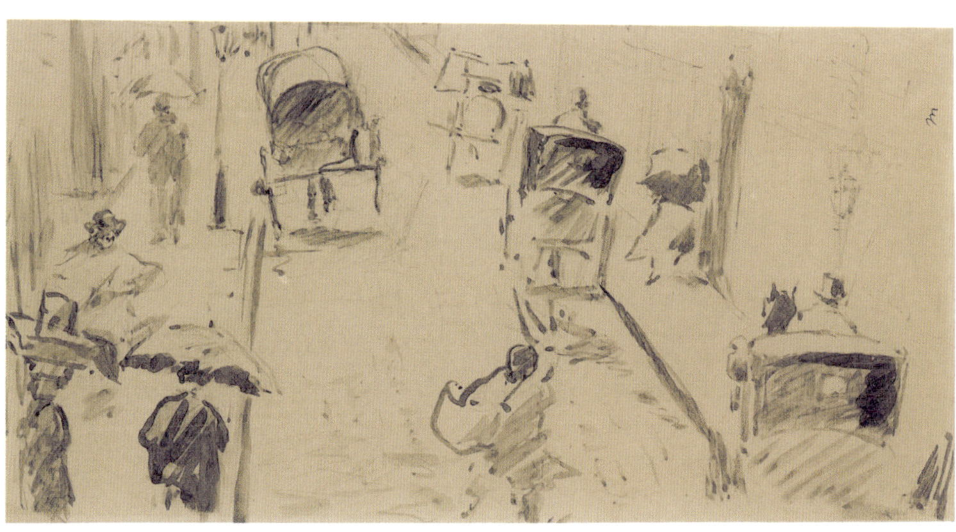

The Rue Mosnier in the Rain, 1878
Brush and lithographic ink over pencil, 19 × 36 cm (7½ × 14⅛ in.).
MUSEUM OF FINE ARTS, BUDAPEST

     Édouard Manet

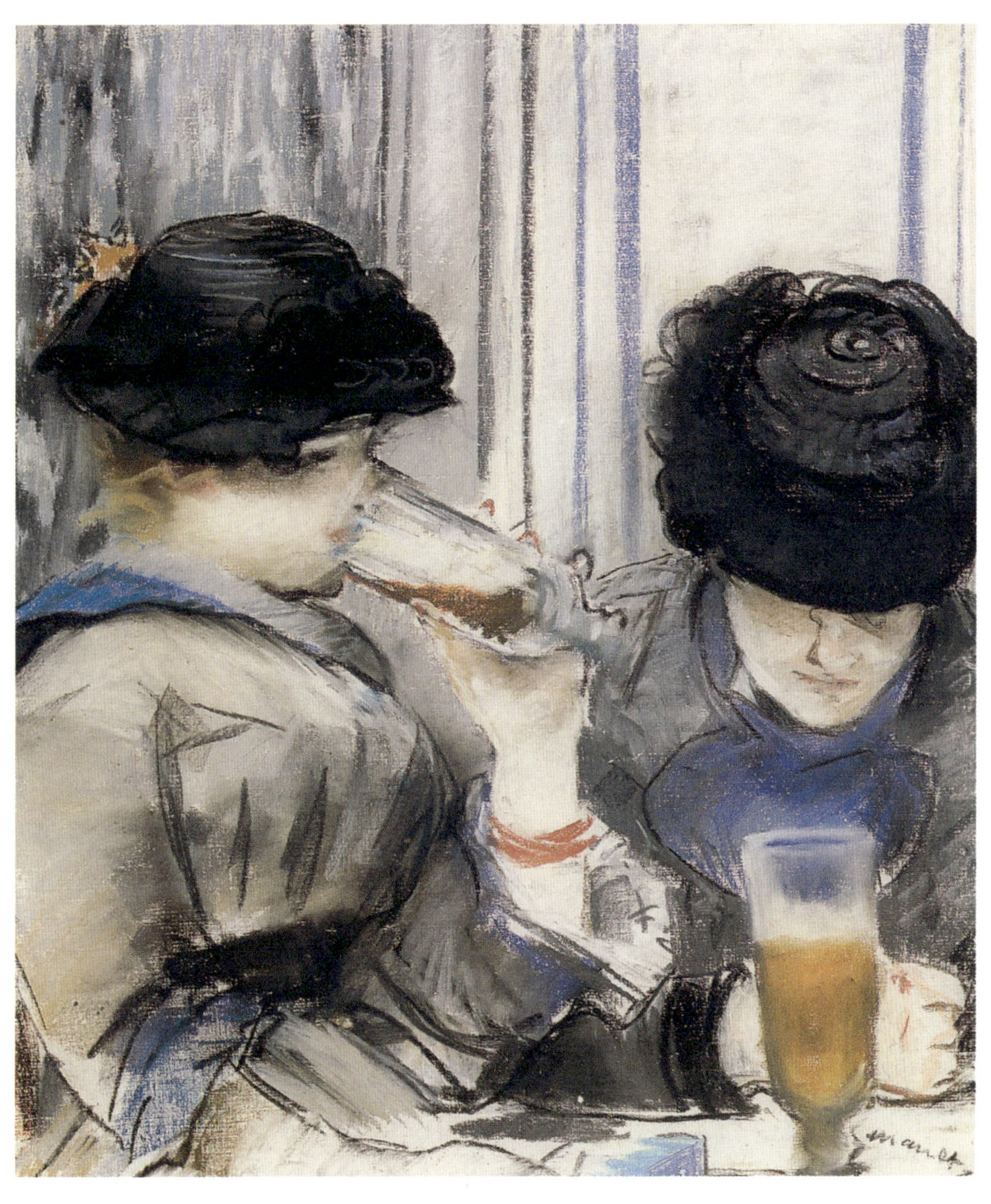

The Beer Drinkers, *c.* 1878–79
Pastel on canvas, 61 × 50.8 cm (24 × 20 in.). Signed.
BURRELL COLLECTION, GLASGOW

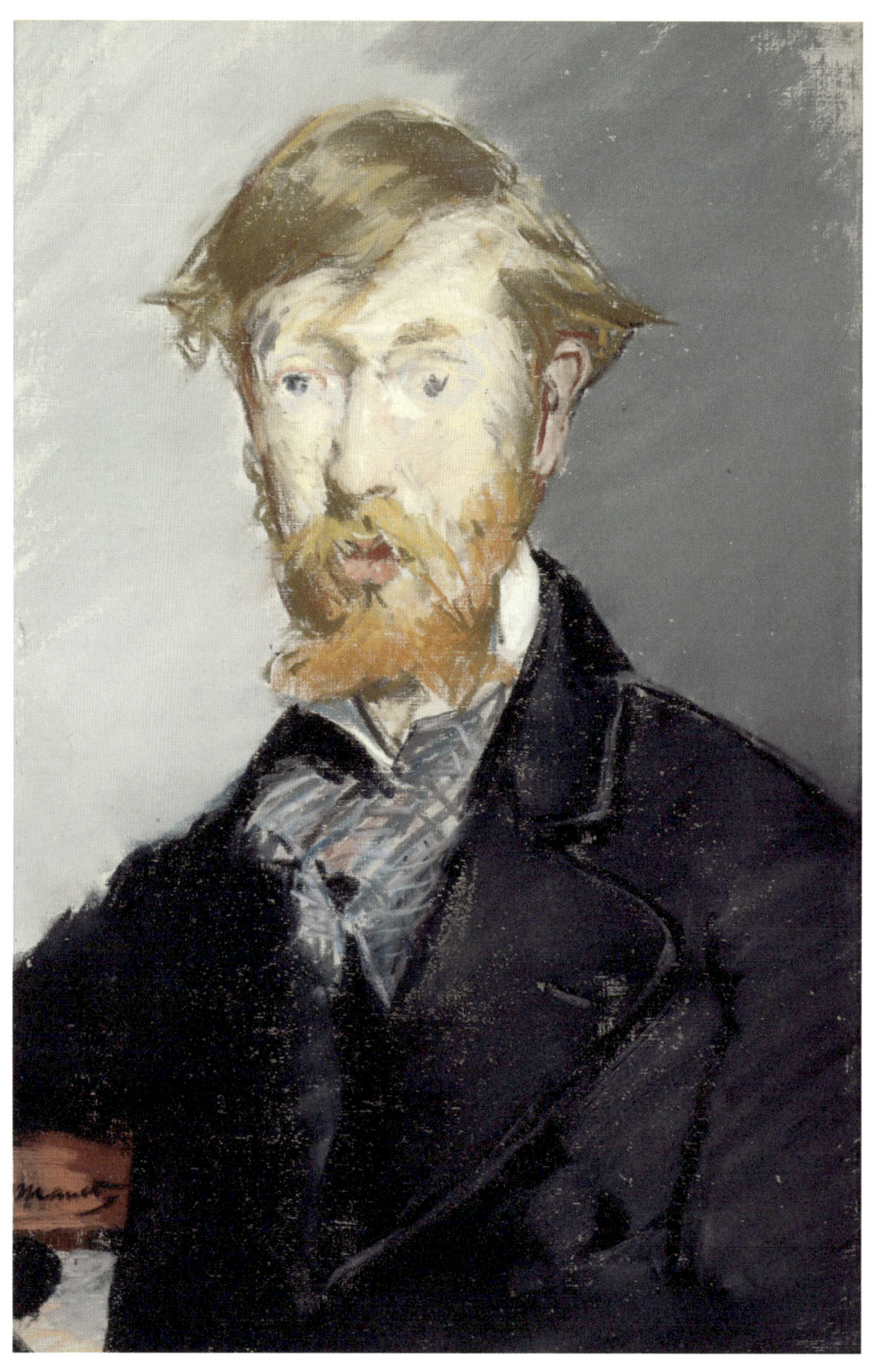

  Édouard Manet

George Moore, 1879
Pastel on canvas, 55.2 × 35.2 cm (21¾ × 13⅞ in.). Signed.
METROPOLITAN MUSEUM OF ART, NEW YORK

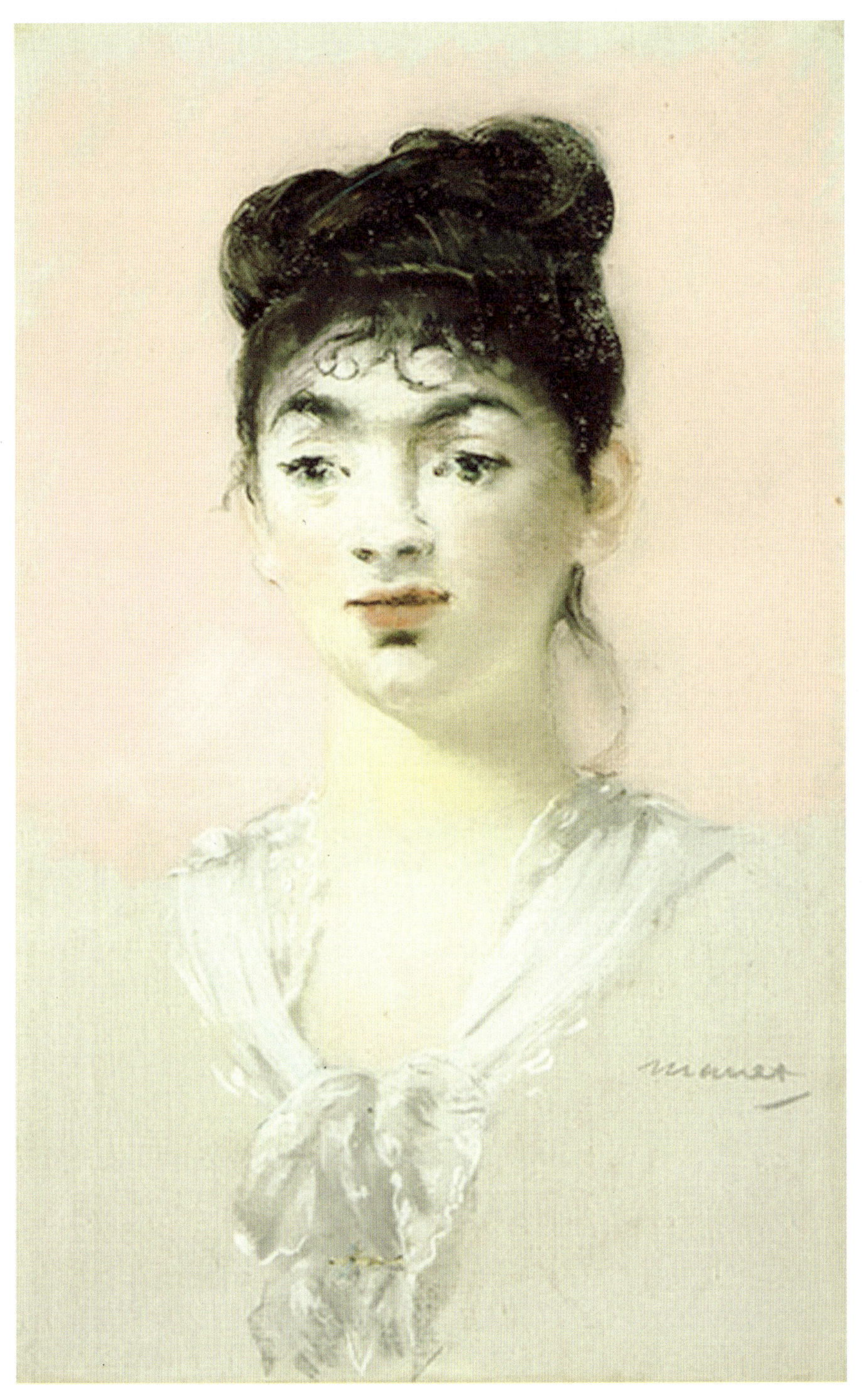

Mademoiselle Suzette Lemaire, c. 1880–81
Pastel on canvas, 53 × 33 cm (20⅞ × 13 in.). Signed.
PRIVATE COLLECTION ON LOAN TO ASHMOLEAN MUSEUM, OXFORD

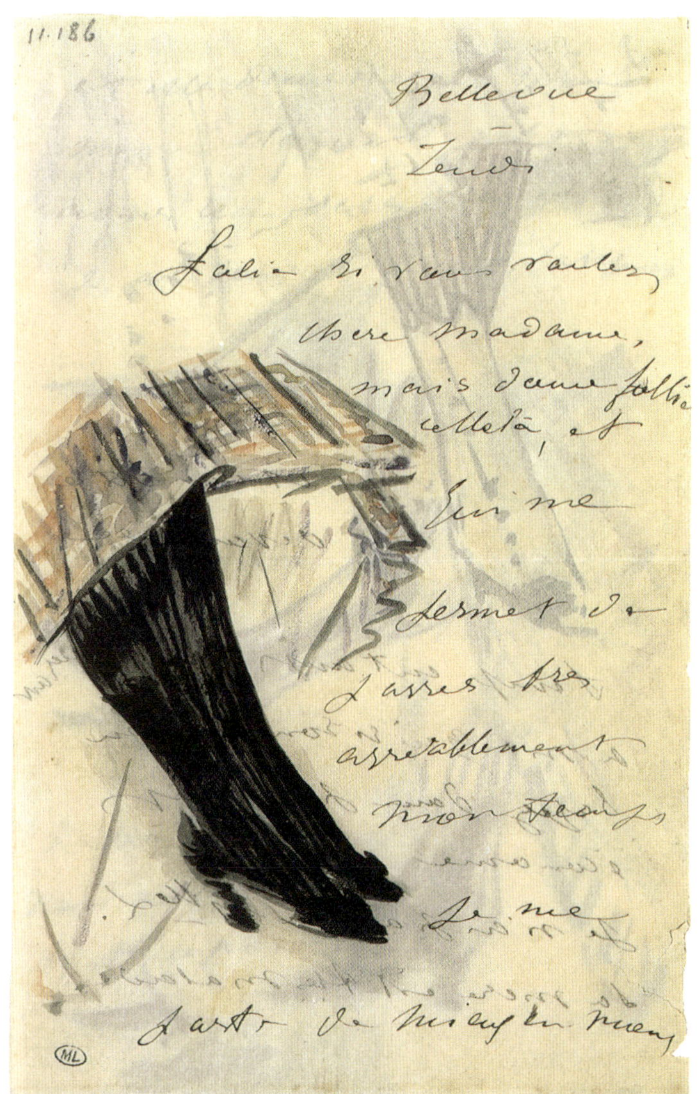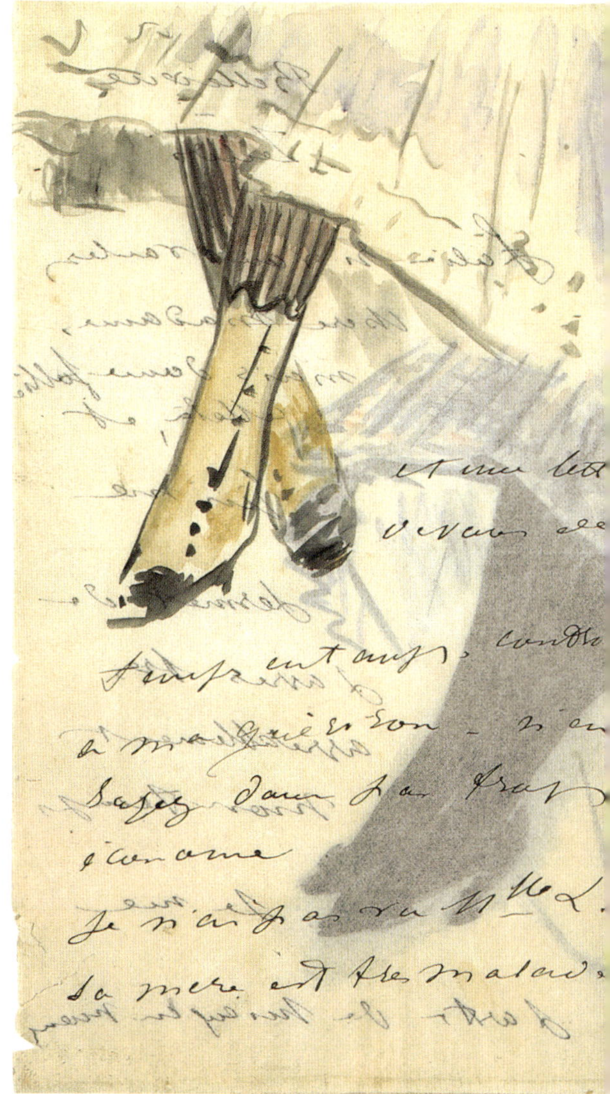

70   *Édouard Manet*   Letter to Mme Jules Guillemet, July–August 1880
Pen and ink with watercolour, 4 sheets, each sheet
20 × 12.5 cm (7⅞ × 4⅞ in.).

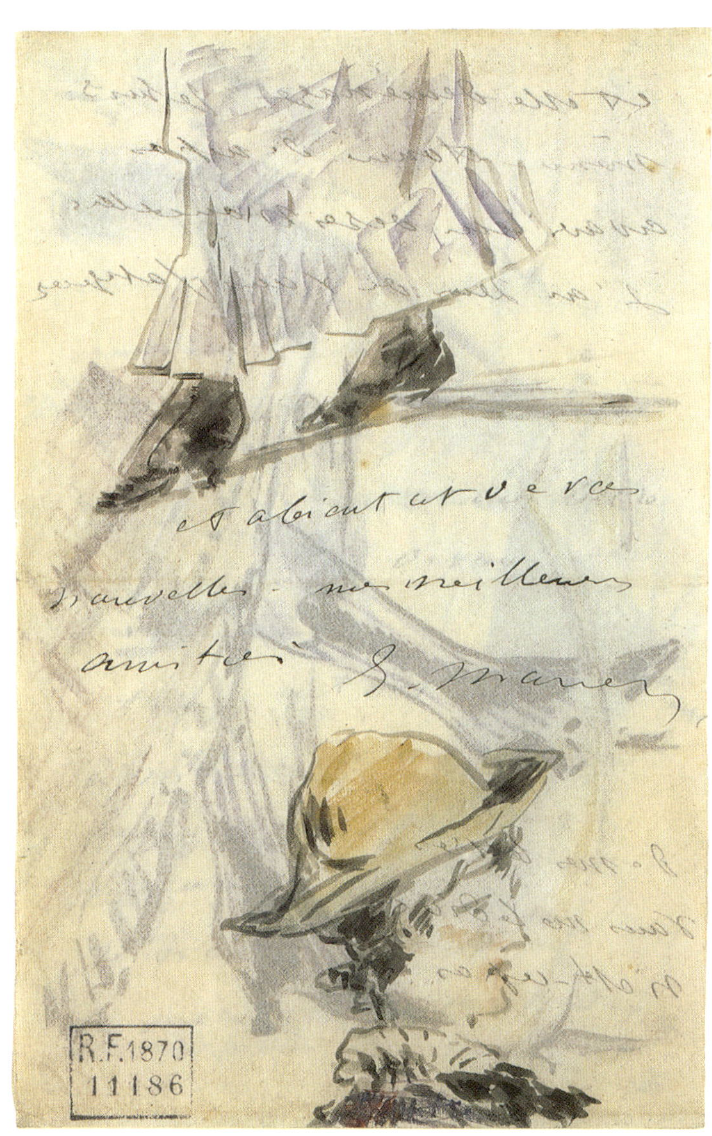

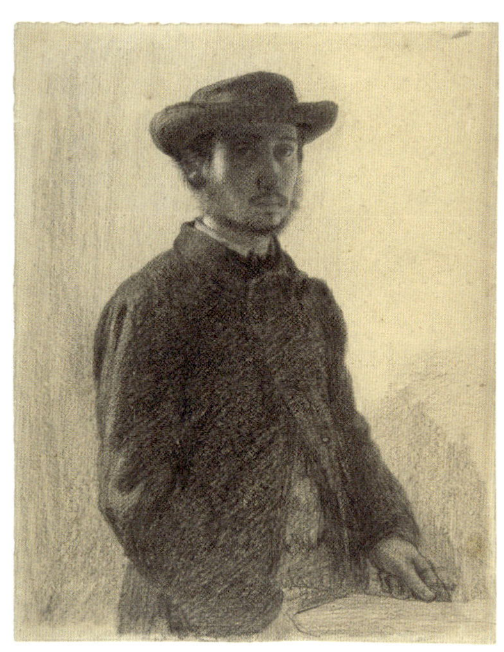

Edgar Degas
1834–1917

Edgar Degas was a prolific draughtsman who throughout his working life felt a compulsion to draw. Although he included drawings in the selection of items he contributed to seven of the eight Impressionist exhibitions, it was only after his death, on the sale of the contents of his studio, that the full extent of his drawn *oeuvre* became apparent.

Drawing formed the basis of Degas's art whatever medium he chose to work in – painting, sculpture or printmaking. This was principally because his main source of inspiration was the human figure. Landscape as a subject was not totally ignored, but it only featured at specific short-lived moments in his life. Degas was quintessentially urban and soon grew bored of nature. As his career progressed he spent an increasing amount of time in the studio, and generally he was more in favour of figurative painters being represented in the Impressionist exhibitions than landscape artists.

For Degas the significance of drawing lay not just in its practical application. Certainly he used it traditionally at the outset, as a method for learning from past masters, and

Edgar Degas
Self-Portrait, 1857
Black crayon touched with white chalk,
29.1 × 23.2 cm (11½ × 9⅛ in.).
METROPOLITAN MUSEUM OF ART, NEW YORK

then quickly realized that it provided an ideal means for recording scenes from contemporary life. But, more significantly, the intensity and frequency with which Degas drew suggests that it was also an exercise in self-discipline with a higher purpose than just a stage in the preparation of a work in a different medium. This implies a moral dimension, which he may have inherited from his mentor, Jean-Auguste-Dominique Ingres.

Any appreciation of Degas's drawings is enhanced by an awareness of the contradictions in his character. Always reactionary in politics, he quickly became anarchic in art, upsetting hierarchies, experimenting with different techniques and embracing new technologies such as photography. 'Art is vice,' he declared, 'you don't marry it legitimately, you ravish it.' Sociable and at ease with a number of friends, many of them young, Degas could also be extraordinarily rude and offensive. Convivial and witty, he never married and later in life became increasingly reclusive, particularly after he began to suffer from photophobia and friends began to predecease him. However dedicated he was to his art and loyal to its traditions, he succeeded at the same time in being innovative, rebellious and subversive. Although basically kind, he was a brilliant raconteur, frequently lacing his bons mots with acerbic and wounding comments, often about fellow artists.

Many of these characteristics translate directly into Degas's art, which is based on a penetrating and intelligent investigation of society comparable in many respects with the novels of contemporary naturalist writers such as Emile Zola and Guy de Maupassant. A keen observer of ballet dancers, cabaret performers, jockeys, milliners, laundresses, ironers and prostitutes, Degas became respectful of the skills of others and the demands made upon them, to the extent that in the wider sense the challenges they faced can be interpreted as a metaphor for the struggles he had in perfecting his own art. In his depiction of everyday modern life, therefore, Degas sought out the heroic amid the mundane and the universal amid the incidental.

The artist was born into a wealthy and cultured family of bankers with Italian connections on his father's side and American ones on his mother's. His decision to become an artist was delayed until 1858, when he registered at the École des Beaux-Arts in Paris. He began to make numerous copies after works by earlier artists (Introduction, fig. 10) and near contemporaries, which are notable for the sophistication with which so many different styles from varying periods are analysed. Copying developed the artist's visual memory and he continued the practice throughout his life. The absorption and distillation of what he saw in the work of his predecessors and contemporaries, when allied to his own visual acuity and highly individual treatment of subject matter, is the essence of Degas's style.

On deciding to distance himself from the École des Beaux-Arts, however, Degas spent a much more fruitful time travelling in Italy in the period 1856–59. New friendships were formed, copying intensified, and life drawings were made in Rome at the

Villa Medici, which was administered by the Académie des Beaux-Arts in Paris. *Two Studies of the Head of a Man* (p. 76) was made from a model and reveals how diligently he could already combine line and tone. The close juxtaposition of the heads on the same sheet anticipates Degas's interest in unusual viewpoints and unexpected conjunctions.

In the light of his admiration for painters such as Ingres and Eugène Delacroix, Degas endeavoured during the 1860s to become a history painter, but failed to have his work exhibited regularly at the official Salon. It was clear that his proclivity was for modern subjects. *Woman Looking through Binoculars* (p. 77) is a figure observed at a racecourse. The medium of *essence* (oil diluted with turpentine applied with a brush) indicates Degas's willingness to experiment with techniques perhaps more suitable for the depiction of contemporary life, just as the subject itself – the viewer being viewed – epitomizes the fleetingness of the everyday. The outline is cursorily laid in, with only the head and hands firmly but delicately modelled. A more traditional technique such as pastel, historically closely associated with portraiture, was also used in a different context by Degas, as when he made a series of early seascapes inspired by a visit to the coast of northern France. The emptiness of the sea and sky in *Marine* (p. 78) is only relieved by the tiny silhouettes of boats on the horizon. The feeling of emptiness and the delicate application of the pastel suggest that the series was done later in the studio and not from life. By the end of the 1860s, therefore, Degas had become an independent-minded artist with novel ideas about content, compositional devices and technical procedures.

One of the principal themes in Degas's *oeuvre* emerged during the 1870s when he began to paint ballet scenes. At first he created complex multi-figured compositions, but during the following decades he concentrated more on showing fewer figures seen from oblique viewpoints, sometimes performing but more often occupying themselves backstage, waiting in the wings or in their dressing rooms. The artist built up a sound working knowledge of classical dance and was given privileged access to classes and rehearsals, where he befriended many of the dancers. The studies made from life were refined in the studio and often quietly redeployed – 'A picture is something that requires as much trickery, malice and vice as the perpetration of a crime', he once announced. The squared-up drawing *Dancer Shown in Position Facing Three-Quarters Front* (p. 79) is of a figure occurring in several of the more elaborate scenes dating from the mid-1870s. The crispness of the lines (even those redrawn) and the sharp accents create the solidity and poise of the figure, counteracted only by the floating quality of the gauze skirt. By contrast, Degas also enjoyed the more popular entertainments at cafés-concerts. For these representations, which were often drawn over monotype prints, he sometimes positioned himself in the audience looking at the performer across the orchestra pit, but on occasion he offers a more daring close-up. *Singer with a Glove* (p. 80), which was included in the fourth Impressionist exhibition (1879), is notable for the wide open mouth and extended hand of the performer, but it also suggests the raucous nature of her act, signalled by the black glove, fur-trimmed costume, red hair and bright lipstick. The use of black contrasts strongly with the coloured stripes in the background and the play of the spotlight on the figure.

Towards the beginning of the 1880s Degas's more elaborate drawings of the ballet were made with softer media: charcoal, pastel, gouache and tempera. *The Dance Examination* (p. 81), which was shown in the fifth Impressionist exhibition (1880), has two young dancers accompanied by chaperones seated behind on a bench. The steep viewpoint, the partial obscuring and cropping of figures, and the emphasis on diagonals create a disorientating spatial effect that is the psychological counterpart of such tense occasions.

Although Degas continued to be sociable and visually curious during the 1880s and 1890s, much of his work was done in the studio. This was partly because of the worsening condition of his photophobia and partly because he was devising more complicated frieze-like compositions. He relied increasingly on models and his memory. Although he did not give up painting entirely, he found charcoal and pastel easier to apply than oil. *At the Milliner's* (p. 82) is typical of a scene that Degas would certainly have witnessed many times, but in terms of the studio the problem he set himself was how to amalgamate genre with still life. Accordingly, the trying on of the hat, which is the true subject, occurs in the middle distance, while greater emphasis is given to the hats on the table in the foreground where the colourful decorations are gloriously depicted with several layers of pastel. Similarly, the horses in *Jockeys in the Rain* (p. 83) twist and turn in one half of the composition while the other is left virtually empty. Degas exercises all his skill on the wet flanks of the horses, the colours of the sodden silks and the streaks of the lashing rain.

One of the peaks of Degas's career was the inclusion in the eighth Impressionist exhibition (1886) of a series of six or seven female nudes in pastel. The subject was a staple of European art, but the artist's intention was to challenge convention by depicting the women in unflattering poses as if in the privacy of their own homes. The images were controversial, but, like the ballet scenes, it was a subject that consumed Degas in his later years. Just as the bathers comb their hair or dry themselves (p. 85), so the ballet dancers glide about on stage (Introduction, fig. 1), or wait in the wings where they stretch, adjust their costumes (p. 84), nurse their feet or recover their breath.

The late pastels of the 1890s onwards are immensely strong both in execution and conception. The figures are on a monumental scale, the surfaces encrusted with layers of colour, the outlines reinforced, the expressions simplified and the movements blurred. Tracing paper is frequently used both as a support and as a method of transference or reversal. Extra strips of paper are boldly added to extend compositions. Degas's studio, normally coated in dust from the vigorous application of pastel, was transformed into a laboratory until his infirmities finally overcame him in 1911–12, five years before his death.

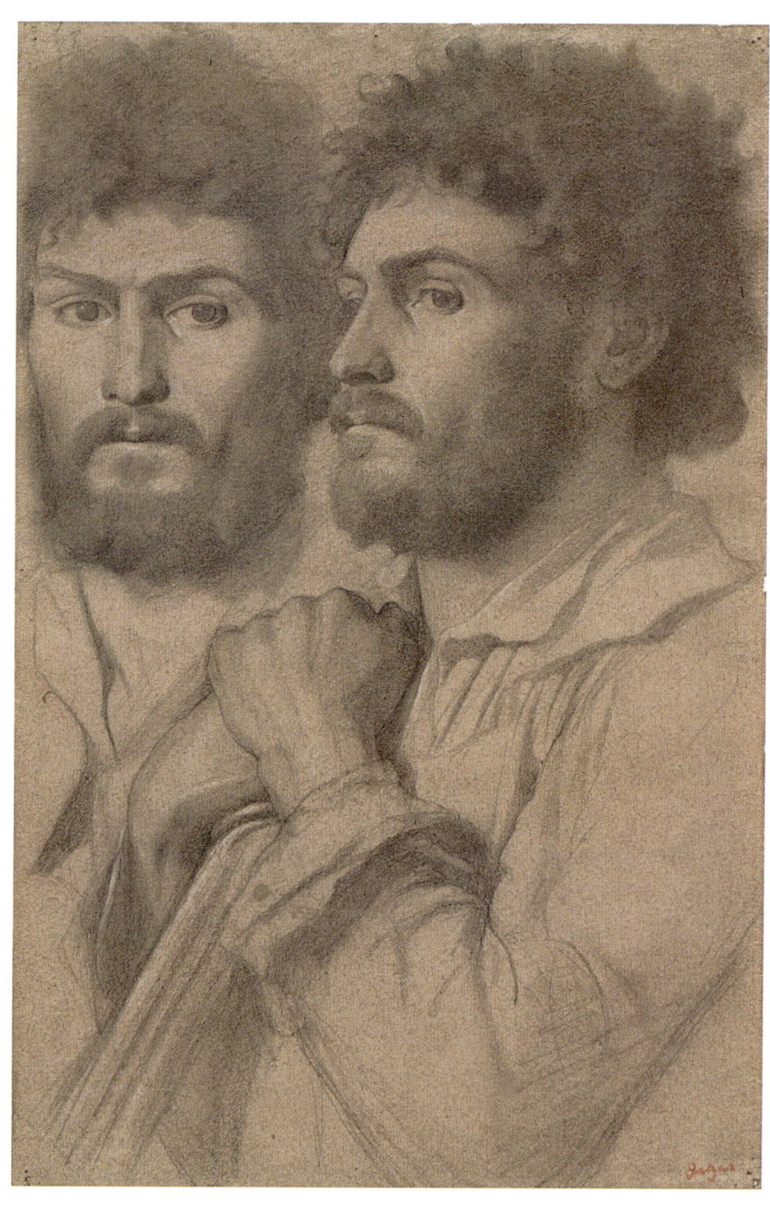

  Edgar Degas

Two Studies of the Head of a Man, c. 1856–57
Pencil heightened with bodycolour on red/brown paper,
44.8 × 22.6 cm (17⅝ × 8⅞ in.). Artist's stamp.
STERLING AND FRANCINE CLARK ART INSTITUTE, WILLIAMSTOWN,
MASSACHUSETTS

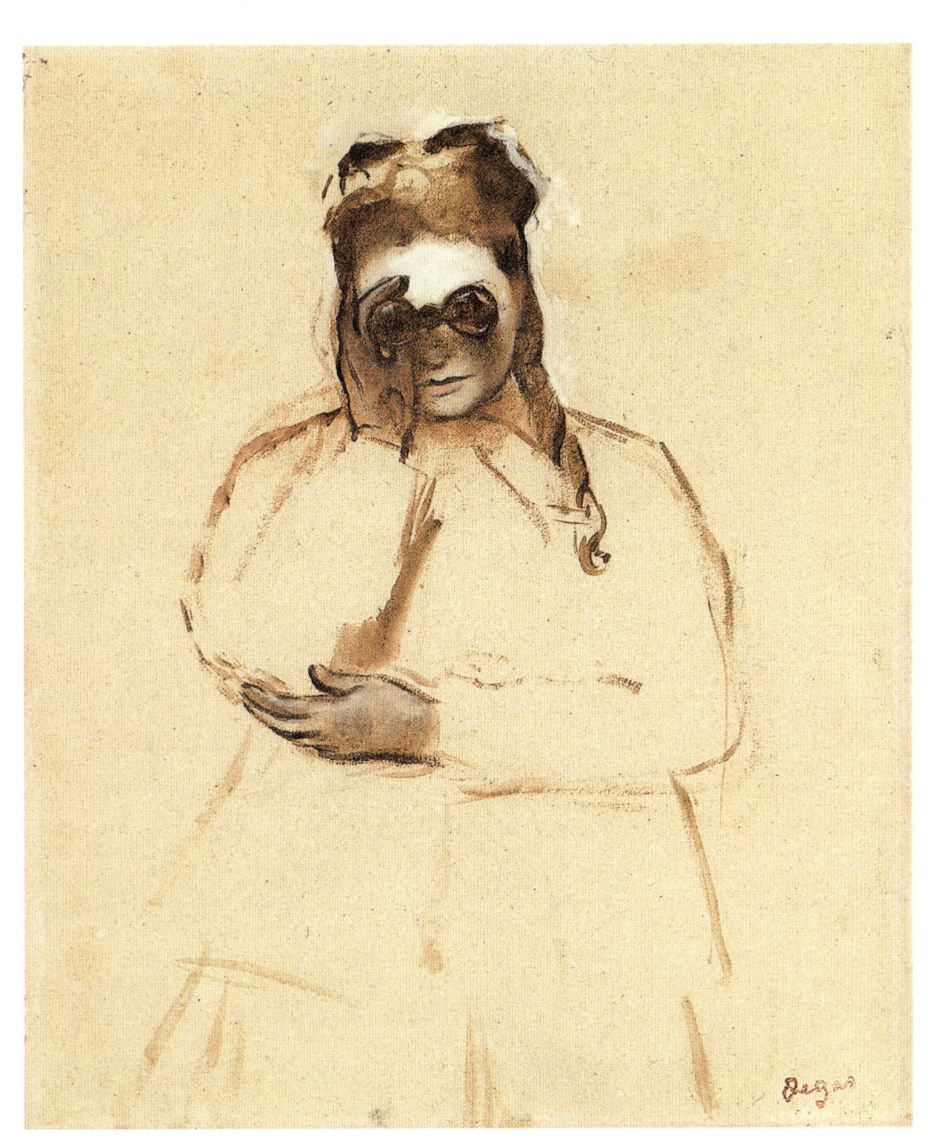

Woman Looking through Binoculars, c. 1866–68   77
Essence on pink paper, 28 × 22.7 cm (11 × 9⅞ in.).
Artist's stamp.
BRITISH MUSEUM, LONDON

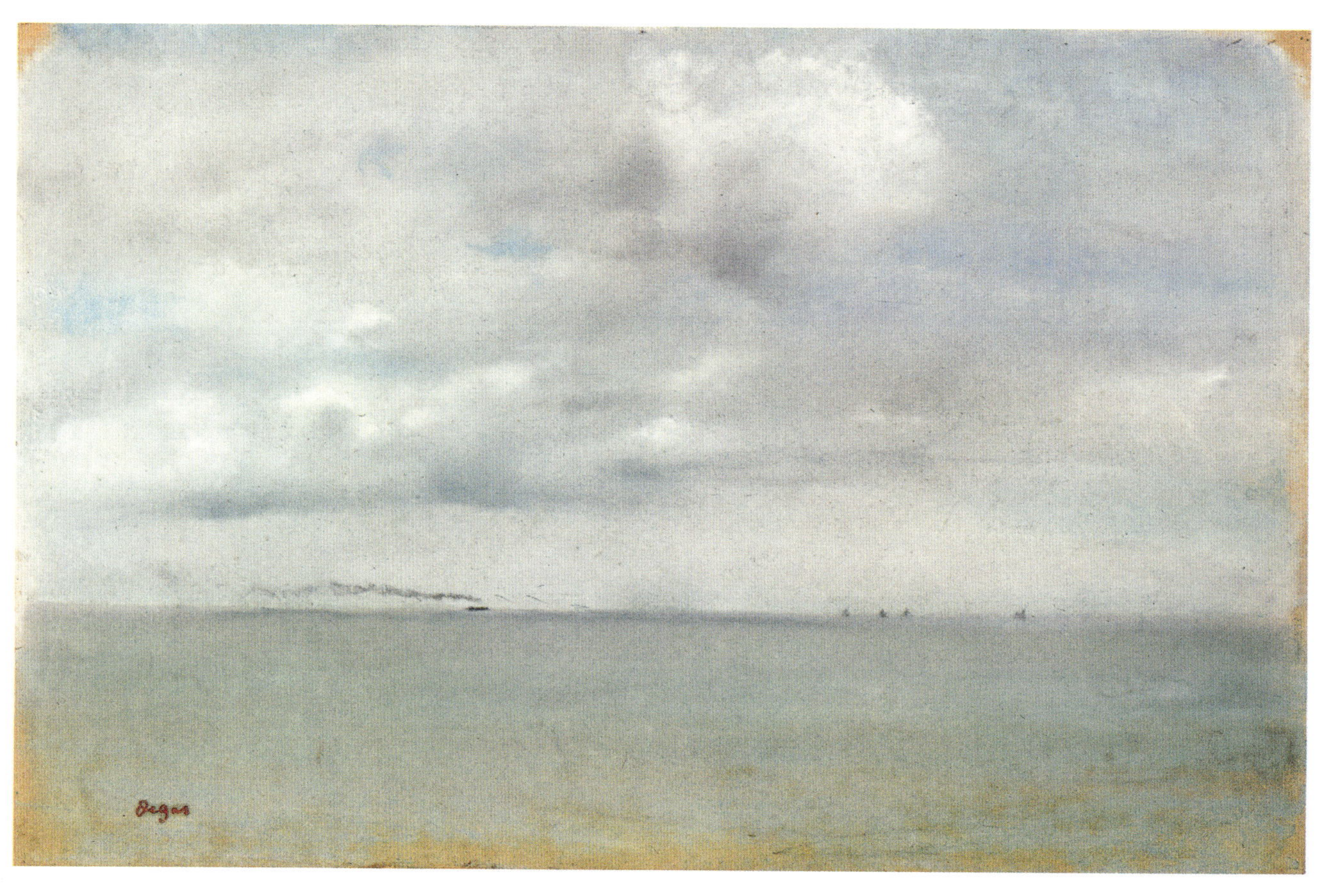

78 *Edgar Degas*

Marine, 1869
Pastel on buff paper, 31.4 × 46.9 cm
(12⅜ × 18½ in.). Artist's stamp.
MUSÉE D'ORSAY, PARIS

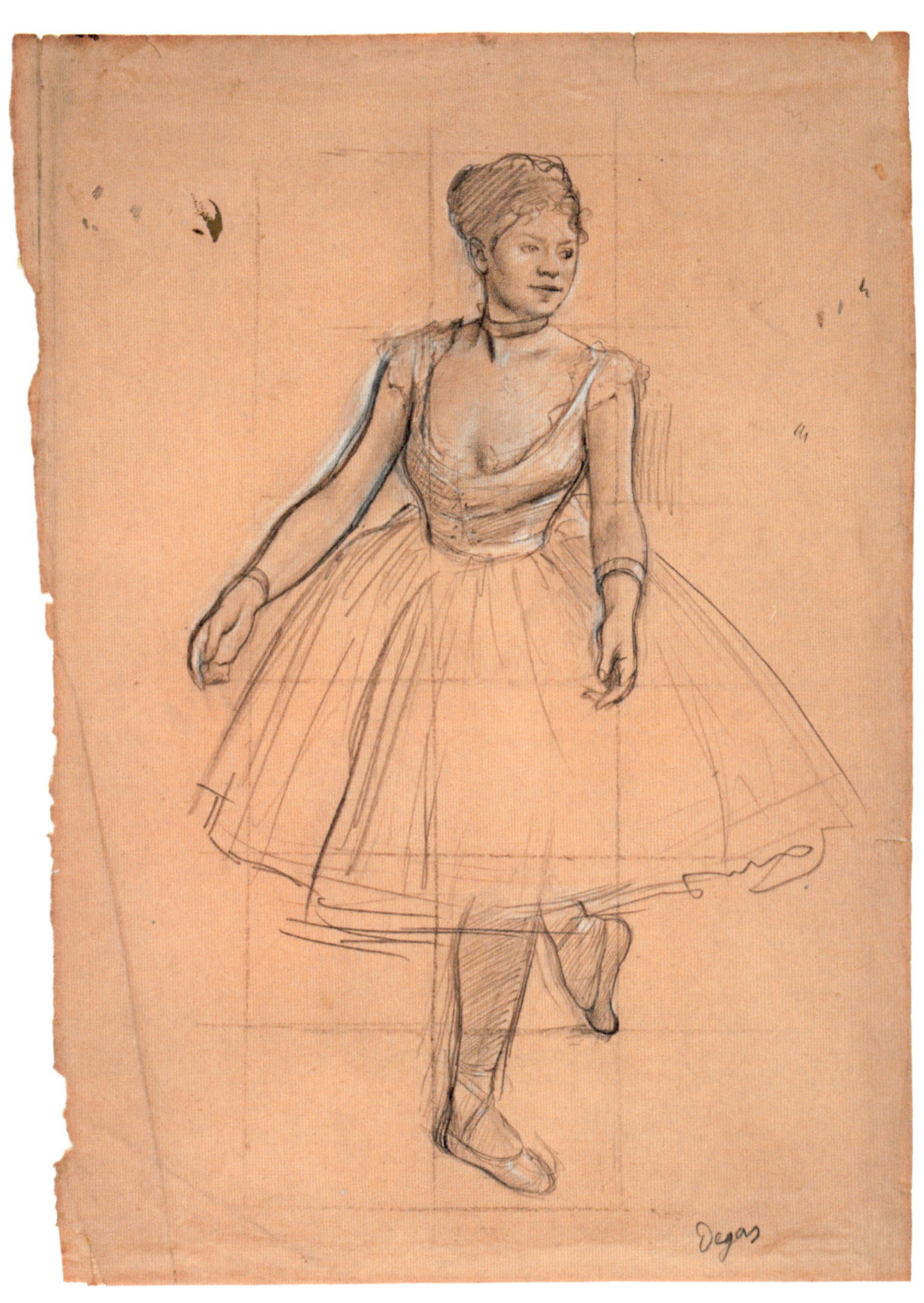

Dancer Shown in Position Facing Three-Quarters Front, c. 1872   79
Pencil and black chalk heightened with white on pink paper,
41 × 27.6 cm (16⅛ × 10⅞ in.), squared. Signed.
HARVARD ART MUSEUMS (FOGG MUSEUM), CAMBRIDGE, MASSACHUSETTS

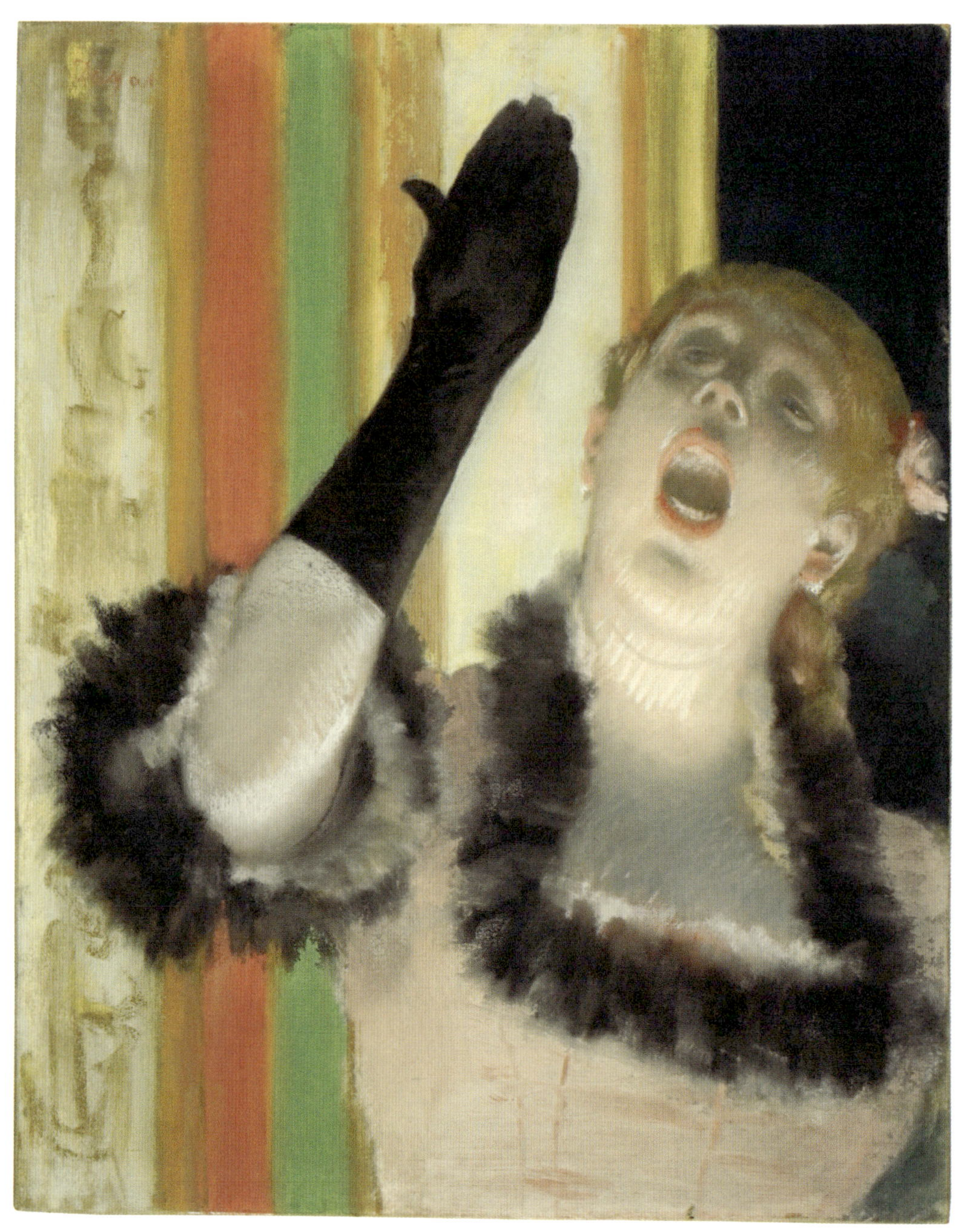

  Edgar Degas

Singer with a Glove, c. 1878
Pastel on canvas, 53.2 × 41 cm (20⅞ × 16⅛ in.). Signed.
HARVARD ART MUSEUMS (FOGG MUSEUM), CAMBRIDGE,
MASSACHUSETTS

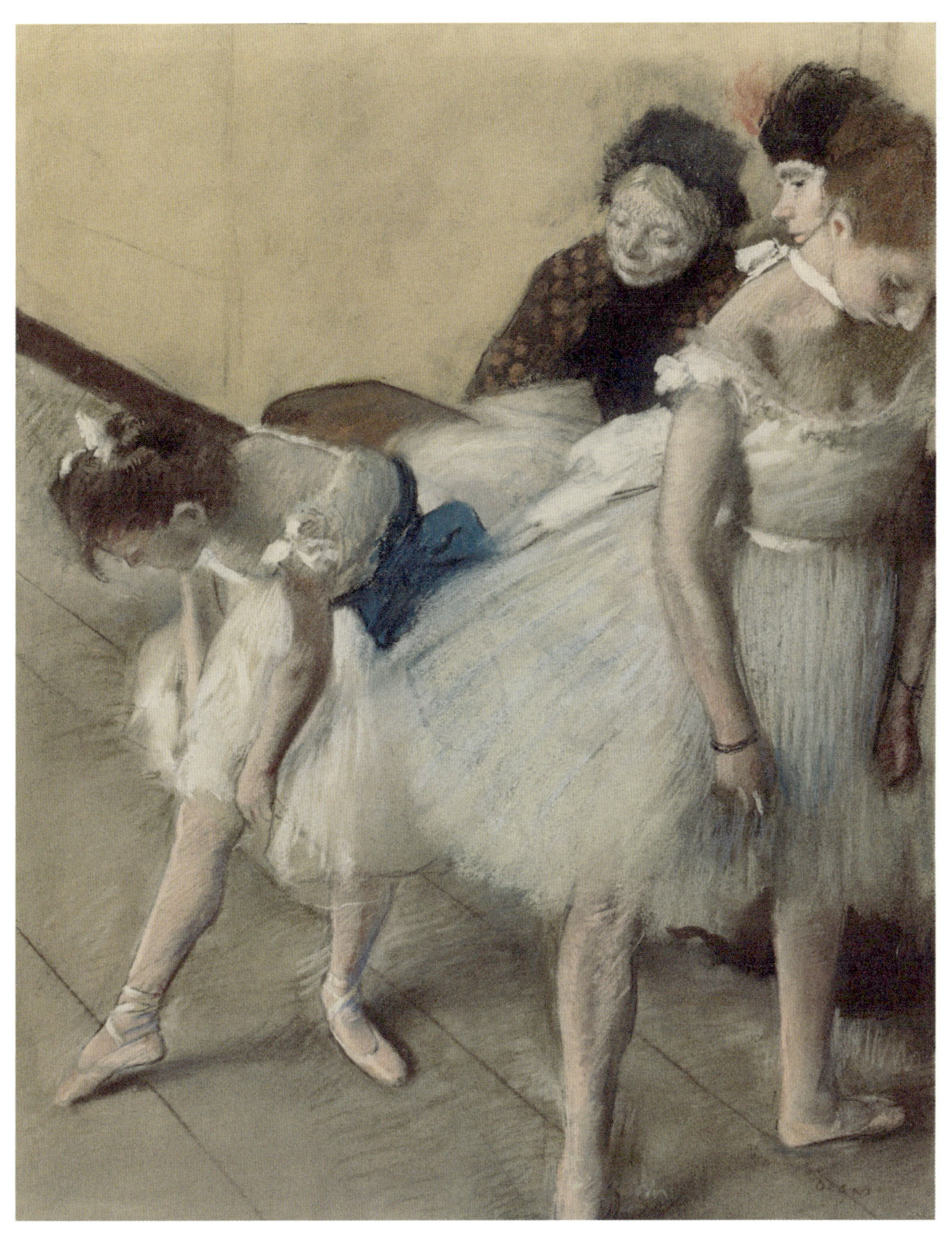

The Dance Examination, c. 1879
Pastel and charcoal, 63.4 × 48.2 cm
(25 × 19 in.). Signed.
DENVER ART MUSEUM

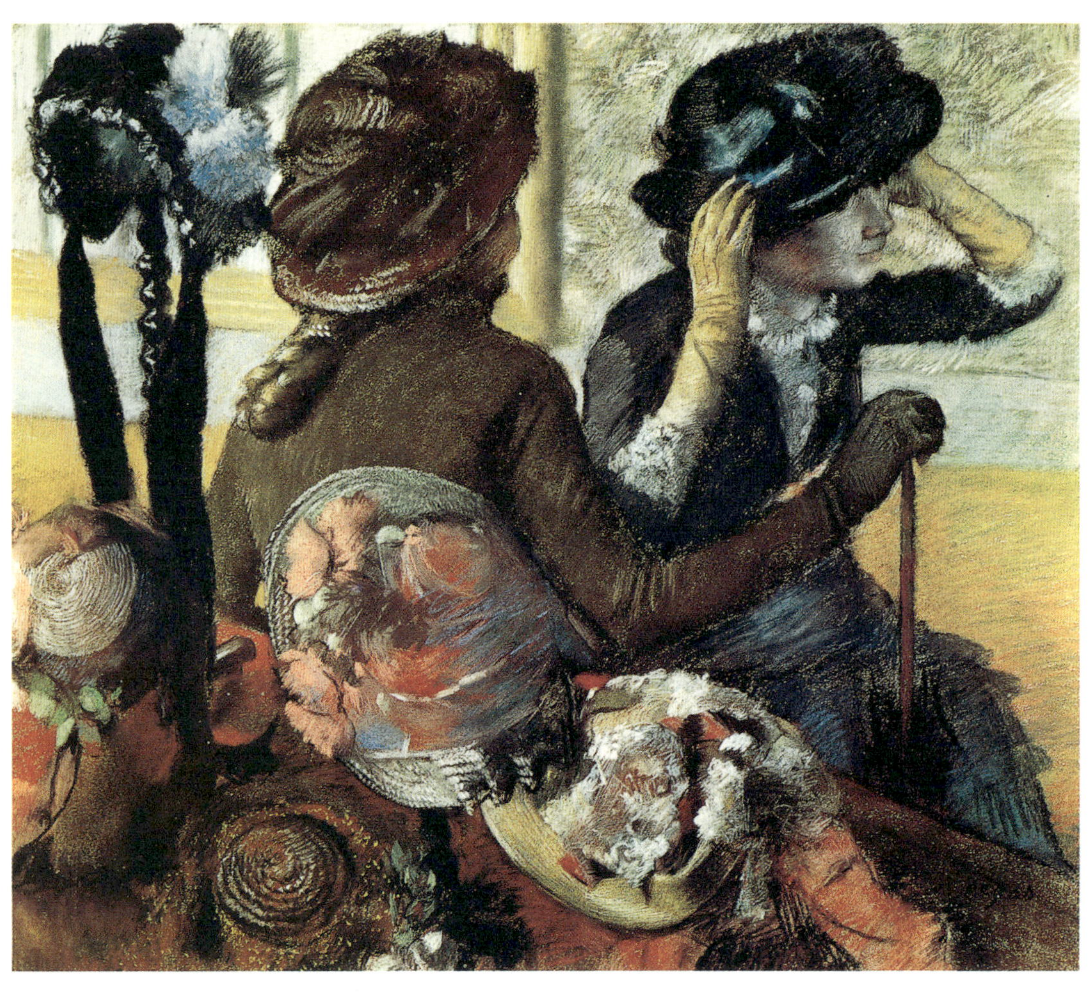

82   *Edgar Degas*

At the Milliner's, 1882
Pastel, 75.5 × 85.5 cm (29¾ × 33⅝ in.). Signed.
THYSSEN-BORNEMISZA MUSEUM, MADRID

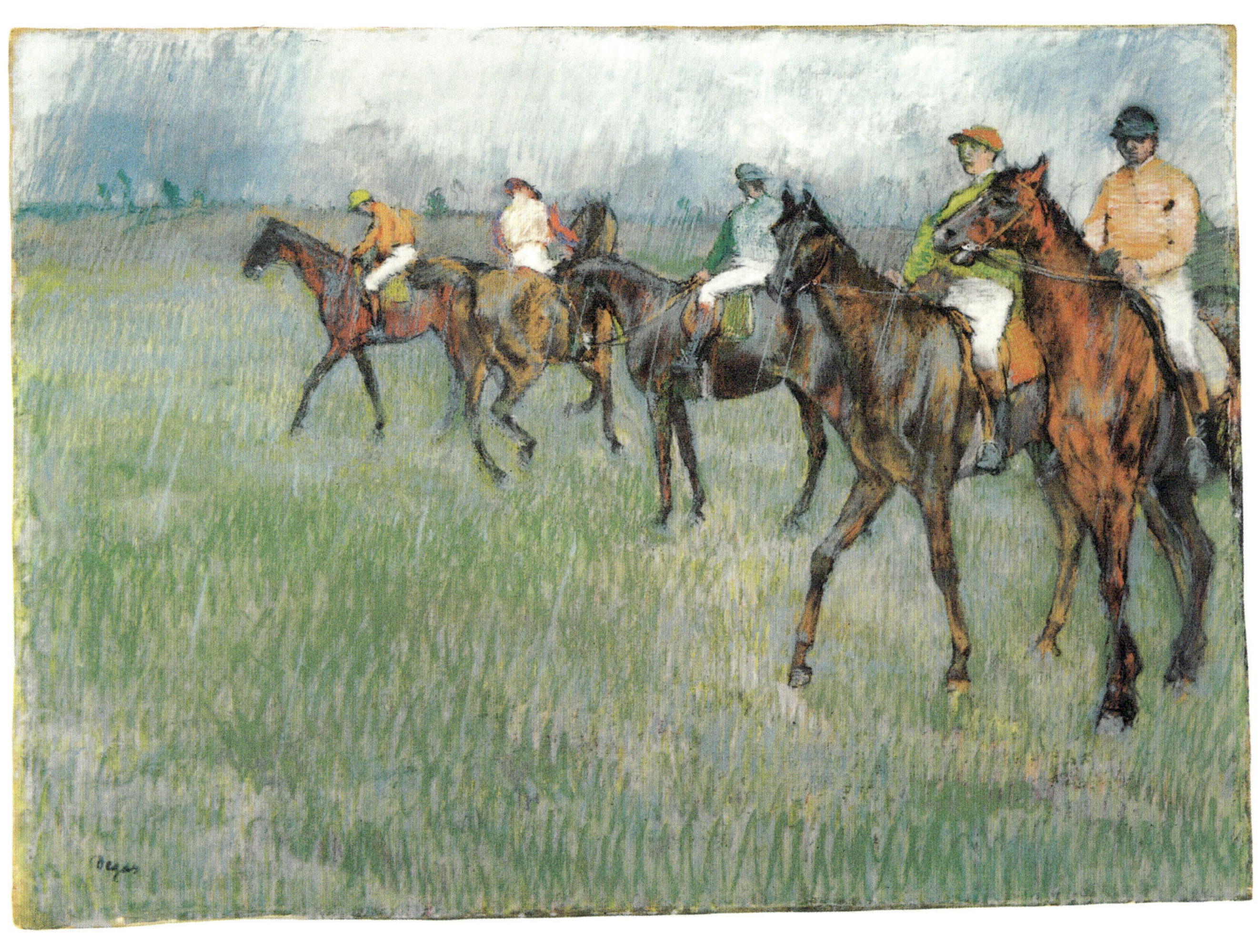

Jockeys in the Rain, c. 1883–86
Pastel, 46.9 × 63.5 cm (18½ × 25 in.). Signed.
BURRELL COLLECTION, GLASGOW

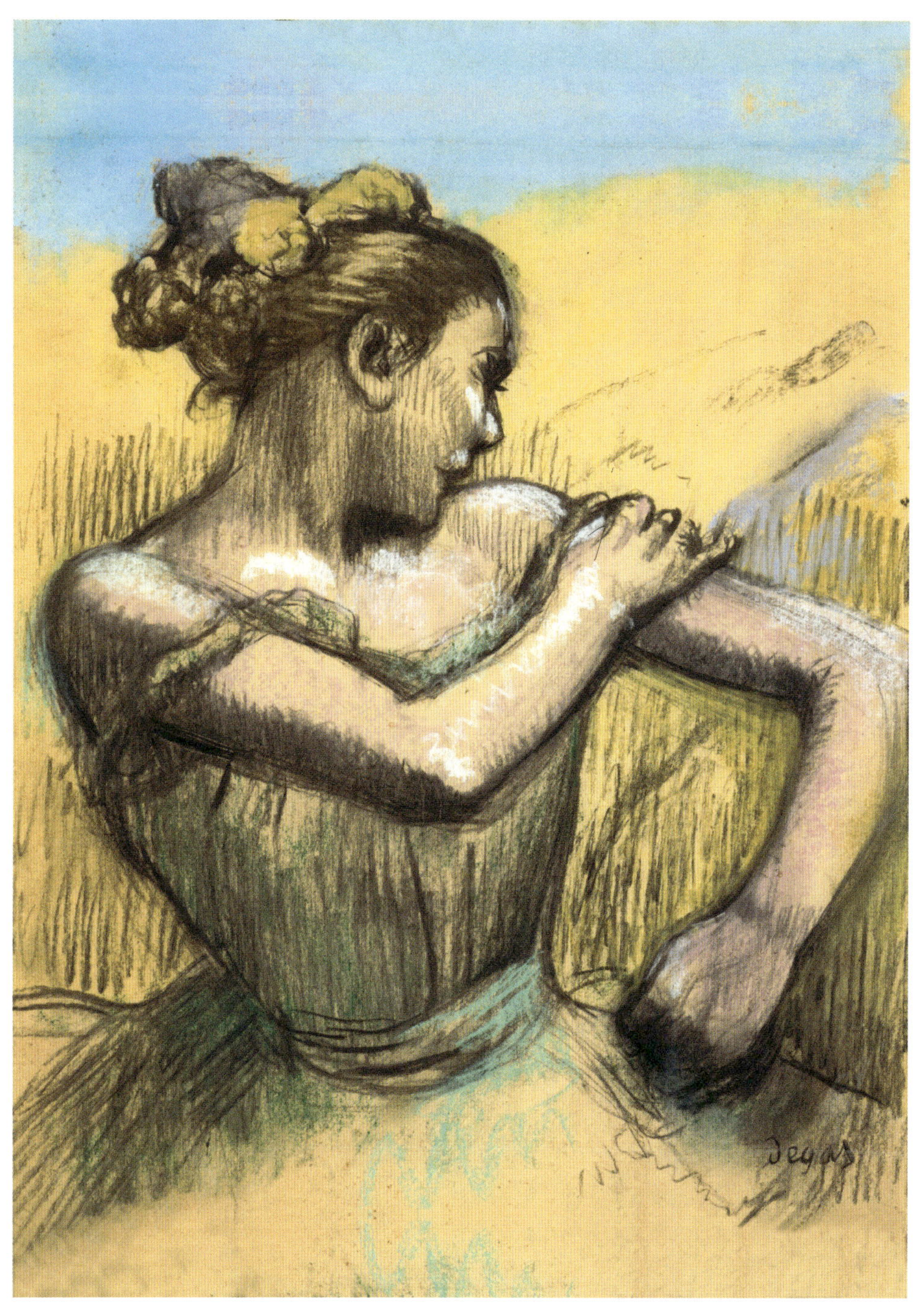

   Edgar Degas

Half-Length Dancer Adjusting her Shoulder Strap, c. 1895–99
Charcoal and pastel on tracing paper, 47.5 × 37 cm
(18¾ × 14½ in.). Signed.
KUNSTHALLE BREMEN

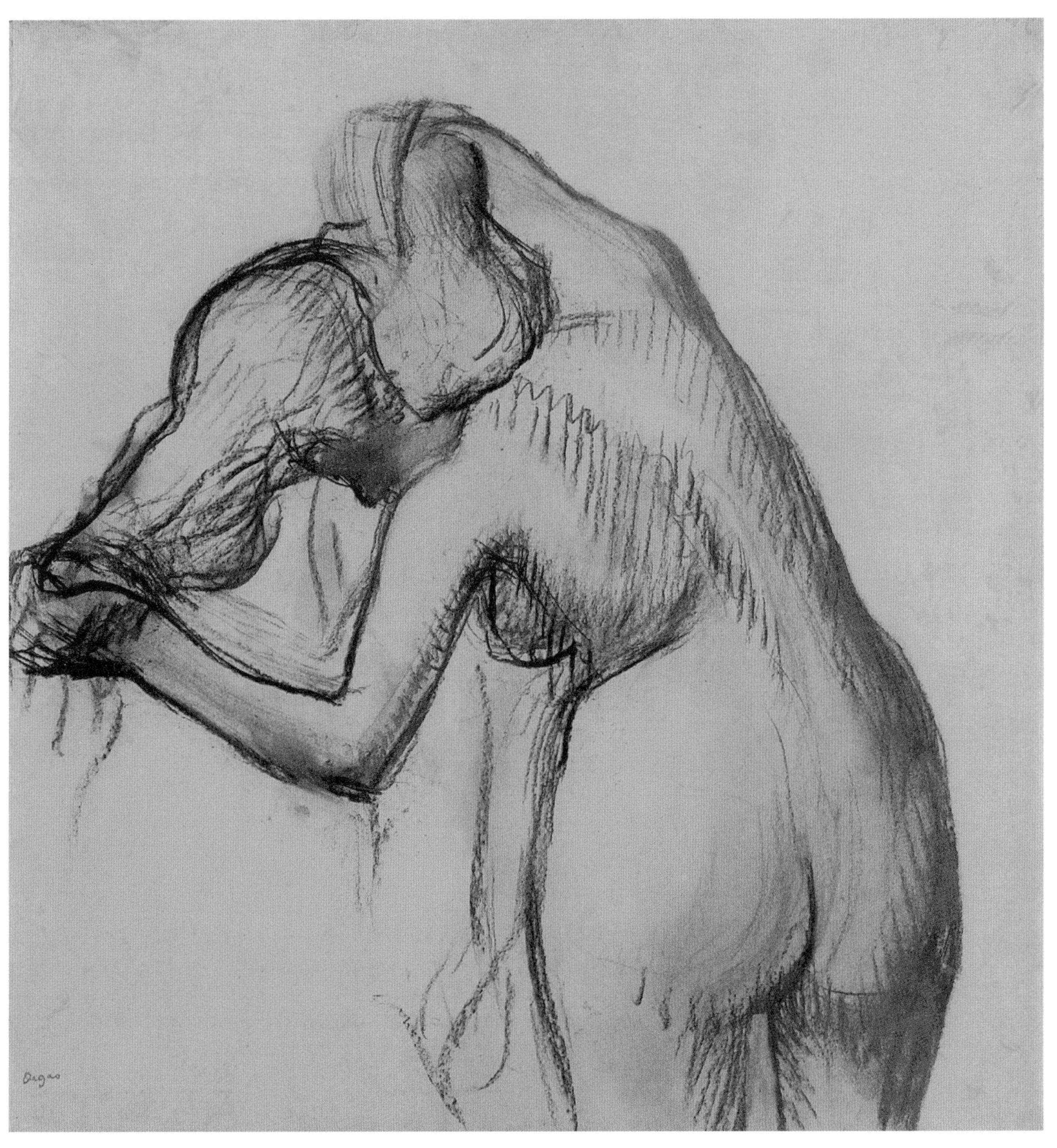

Female Nude Drying her Neck, c. 1900

Charcoal, 79.3 × 76.2 cm (31¼ × 30 in.). Artist's stamp.

KING'S COLLEGE, CAMBRIDGE (KEYNES COLLECTION) ON LOAN TO
THE FITZWILLIAM MUSEUM, CAMBRIDGE

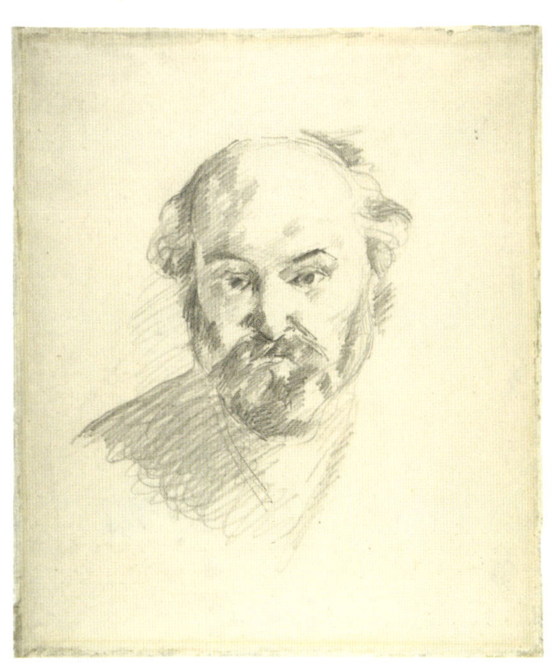

Paul Cézanne
1839–1906

Paul Cézanne's art is essentially about perception and appearance. His stated purpose was to discover a convincing means of recording those sensations he experienced before nature as accurately and faithfully as possible. In many respects he remained an experimental artist throughout his life, never totally satisfied with what he achieved and always conscious of falling short. Yet, as he told the young writer Joachim Gasquet, 'What I want is to be a true classic and rediscover a classic path by means of nature, by sensation'.

Nowhere is Cézanne's personal struggle more evident than in his drawings. Very many of these were made in sketchbooks, some of which have subsequently been dismembered, but during the 1880s when he began to concentrate more on producing watercolours there was a greater emphasis on single sheets that could be exhibited. Indeed, it was the exhibitions of Cézanne's work, particularly the watercolours, mounted by Ambroise Vollard in Paris during the last decade of the artist's life that confirmed his reputation and were described as being revelatory.

Paul Cézanne
Self-Portrait, c. 1880
Pencil, 33 × 27.3 cm (13 × 10¾ in.).
METROPOLITAN MUSEUM OF ART, NEW YORK

Some of Cézanne's drawings lack conviction and decisiveness, or, on other occasions, can appear to be unrefined and incoherent. Yet, undoubtedly, he is a great draughtsman and on close examination his drawings are unquestionably informative, in the same way as his letters and reported conversation address issues that are still of the greatest relevance for artists today. In its totality, Cézanne's drawn *oeuvre* is governed by a rare degree of honesty, as he always worked with deliberation and an overwhelming sense of purpose, which explains why he repeatedly returned to explore the same motifs. It is the accumulation of visual experiences that has resulted in Cézanne's output becoming the seedbed of modern art. It is notable, too, that it was frequently artists who liked to collect his work, not just as a source of momentary inspiration, but more as a touch-stone for continuing study and as a way of measuring their own progress. Cézanne's considerable achievement is that he engaged with problems that led to advances in art. For him the quest was more pertinent than the discovery.

Cézanne was born in Aix-en-Provence and, although he eventually acknowledged the importance of Paris, he remained a man of the south, where the landscape around his birthplace became one of his principal sources of inspiration. His father was a successful hatmaker who became a banker and in 1859 acquired a bastide called the Jas de Bouffan on the outskirts of Aix-en-Provence. Cézanne liked to work there in isolation until its sale in 1899.

The artist's early years were inauspicious even though he formed close friendships with people, including the novelist Emile Zola, who would soon embark on successful careers in their respective fields. Cézanne strongly identified with the Provençal cultural renaissance that was underway by the mid-century and liked to exaggerate his region-alism in speech, dress and manners. His appearance – domed forehead, prominent nose, bushy eyebrows, bulging eyes – as well as his forthright opinions and directness of speech, could be forbidding, but also to some extent misleading, for he was in fact reserved, taciturn and shy. Well versed in both classical and contemporary literature, if he had not been an artist he could easily have become a poet.

Initial training offered by the École Gratuite de Dessin in Aix-en-Provence was easily mastered, but on arriving in Paris at the beginning of the 1860s he failed to secure a place at the prestigious École des Beaux-Arts. As an alternative he attended the Académie Suisse, where he met like-minded artists such as Pissarro and Monet, who were looking for a less regimented approach to artistic training. Live models, for instance, were encouraged to strike less formal, more natural poses, while the artists themselves were allowed to explore unusual viewpoints. *Male Nude* (Introduction, fig. 9), for instance, owes its powerful impact to the bold springing contours and strong, striking chiaroscuro.

To counteract the freedom of the Académie Suisse, Cézanne registered as a copyist in the Musée du Louvre and embarked upon an intense programme of copying from the old masters, a practice that he maintained for the rest of his life (Introduction, fig. II). In this sense Cézanne remained a perpetual student, but his copying was also an exercise in self-discipline. Apart from the Musée du Louvre, Cézanne also favoured the Musée de Sculpture Comparée, which opened in the Palais du Trocadéro in 1882, as well as accumulating a number of illustrated books, journals and reproductions as additional sources for copying. His taste was eclectic and the method of copying was not slavish. It was a process as much of assimilation as divination. 'In my opinion, one does not replace the past, one only adds a new link', he wrote in 1905.

From the time of his arrival in Paris it was clear that Cézanne was an uncompromising artist. His work veered wildly from moments of startling violence to unabashed sensuality, which was reflected both in the choice of subject matter and unsettling style (p. 90). This dichotomy existed in various forms in all departments of his art, and its resolution became the main concern of his working life. There was never any chance that his paintings would be accepted by the Salon on a regular basis and, although close to the Impressionists, he exhibited in only the first (1874) and third (1877) Impressionist exhibitions.

Initially, the problem for Cézanne was to decide what kind of an artist he wanted to be, and it was not until the 1880s and 1890s that he reached maturity in this respect. A steadying influence was provided by Pissarro, with whom he worked on several occasions during the 1870s. Together they examined the landscape around Pontoise and Auvers-sur-Oise to the northwest of Paris, trying to discover its underlying structure in pictorial terms. The benefits of this collaboration are found in such drawings as *Rooftops at L'Estaque* (p. 92) – a place on the Mediterranean coast later important for the Cubists. The buildings in the foreground have been peremptorily outlined in pencil. The dabs of watercolour reinforce the architecture and add in vegetation, but mainly create effects of light and atmosphere. In the upper half, the bay and the mountains beyond are mere whispers.

The many scenes of male and female bathers combine Cézanne's interest in the landscape and the figure. Although not in themselves erotically charged, they can be read as an extension of the artist's sexual fantasies triggered by memories of his youthful exploits in the countryside surrounding Aix-en-Provence. *Four Female Bathers* (p. 91) is a compositional study in which care is taken to relate the figures to the riparian setting as well as to one another in a narrative sense. Redrawn contours and flurries of hatching unify the tight-knit group. So ardently did Cézanne pursue this subject that he created a repertoire of figures such as *Standing Bather Seen from the Back* (p. 94), that could be deployed in any number of different versions. The subtle integration of the figures in the paintings and watercolours of male and female bathers encourages the viewer to read the compositions as relief sculptures. Cézanne persevered with this theme until the very end of his life when, as in *Bathers by a Bridge* (p. 96), he would populate the river Arc to the south of Aix-en-Provence with imaginary figures cooling off in the heat of the day, almost like an episode in classical mythology.

As a portrait painter Cézanne limited himself to depicting his family, friends, dependants or close acquaintances. Sitting for a portrait by him was a demanding experience, and so it is hardly surprising that so many of his portrait drawings are of himself, his wife, Hortense, or their son, Paul, and are confined to sketchbooks. *Madame Cézanne with Hortensias* (p. 93) is a drawing of contrasts – the sensitive pencil work in the right half balanced by the more fulsome watercolour of the bloom in the left half. It is as though the artist is paying joint homage to Jean-Auguste-Dominique Ingres and Eugène Delacroix on the same sheet. There is added charm in that the visual pun on Hortense's name suggests that the drawing might be a love token, revealing the softer side of the artist's character.

Cézanne aimed to provide as much information about his reactions to a subject as succinctly as possible. This determination came to fruition in the late watercolours of still lifes and landscapes. *Armchair* (p. 95) was no doubt part of the furnishings of the Jas de Buffon. The simplicity of such a motif is what may at first have appealed to Cézanne, but he also relishes its complexities: the foreshortening, the play of light and the different textures. Some of the simpler still lifes of fruit incorporate similar challenges, but with the more contrived, almost baroque, compositions the artist excels himself. *Still Life with Blue Pot* (p. 97) and *Three Skulls* (p. 99) are both subjects that Cézanne had attempted as far back as the 1860s. Now, however, there is a sense of fulfilment in the ability to combine such a sophisticated level of spatial organization with a technique of such amplitude that it not only imparts information about form but also instils a feeling of immanence.

Mont Sainte-Victoire, which formed a backdrop to Cézanne's life, is a prominent landmark in Provence and over time it became a personal symbol for him. The mountain, which has historical, cultural and scientific significance for the region, was visible from most of the places where the artist worked during his final years. At first he kept his distance, only occasionally approaching its slopes. The last watercolours depict the view from his studio at Les Lauves (p. 98) and show a wide expanse of receding foreground. The overlaying of pencil and watercolour, as well as the positive use of blank areas of the paper, creates effects of shifting light and shimmering heat. The juxtaposition of patches of colour, which resembles a quilt, was the ultimate form of expression in Cézanne's draughtsmanship. Drawing for him was not a question of line and modelling, but more a matter of contrasting areas of colour. The visual pulses derived from such contrasts became for the artist the only method by which he could represent those sensations that he experienced before nature. Cézanne himself felt that he had failed in this mission, but future generations were not slow to recognize the endless possibilities inherent in his art.

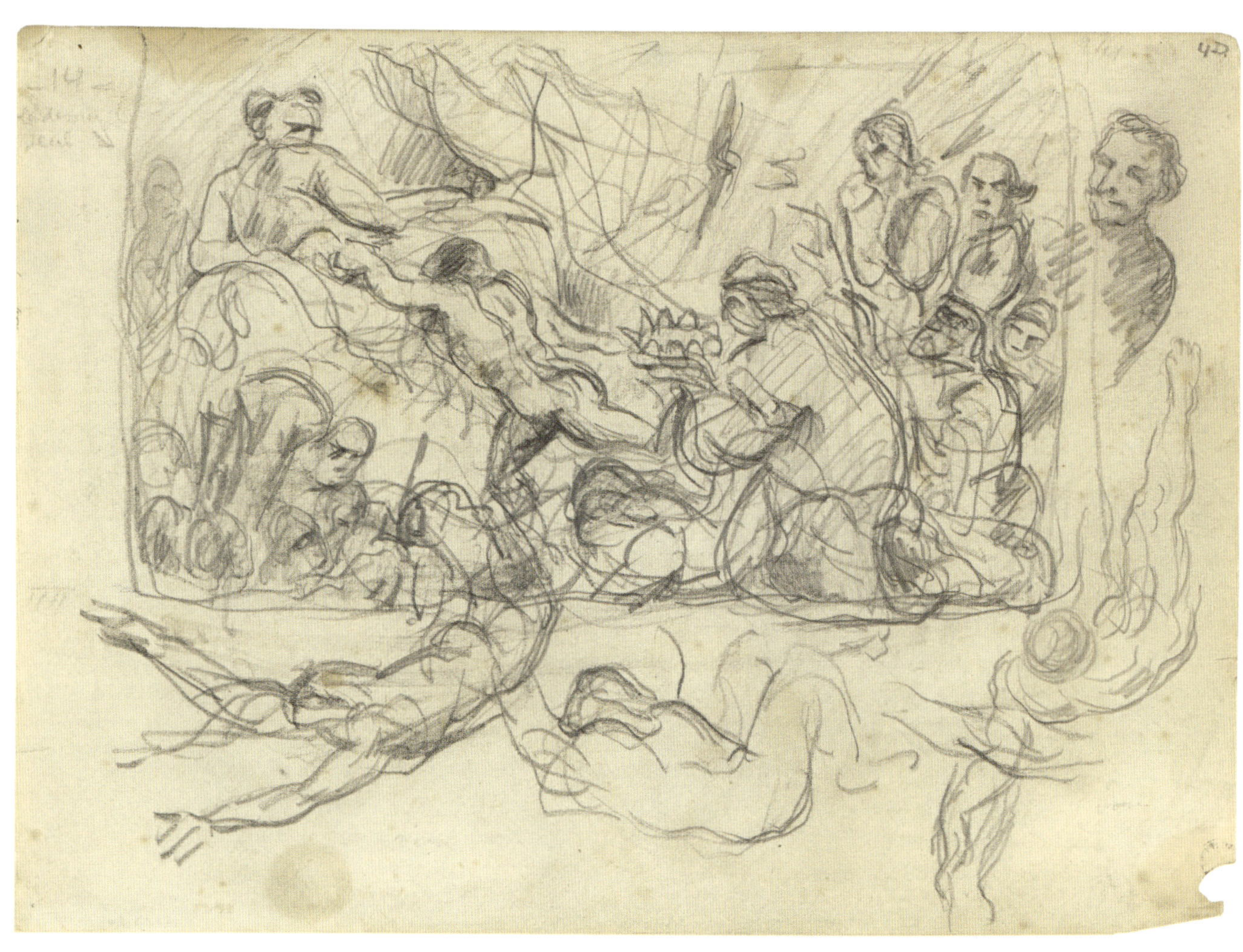

90   *Paul Cézanne*

L'Éternal féminin, c. 1870–75
Pencil and black chalk, 17.7 × 23.6 cm (7 × 9¼ in.).
KUNSTMUSEUM, BASEL

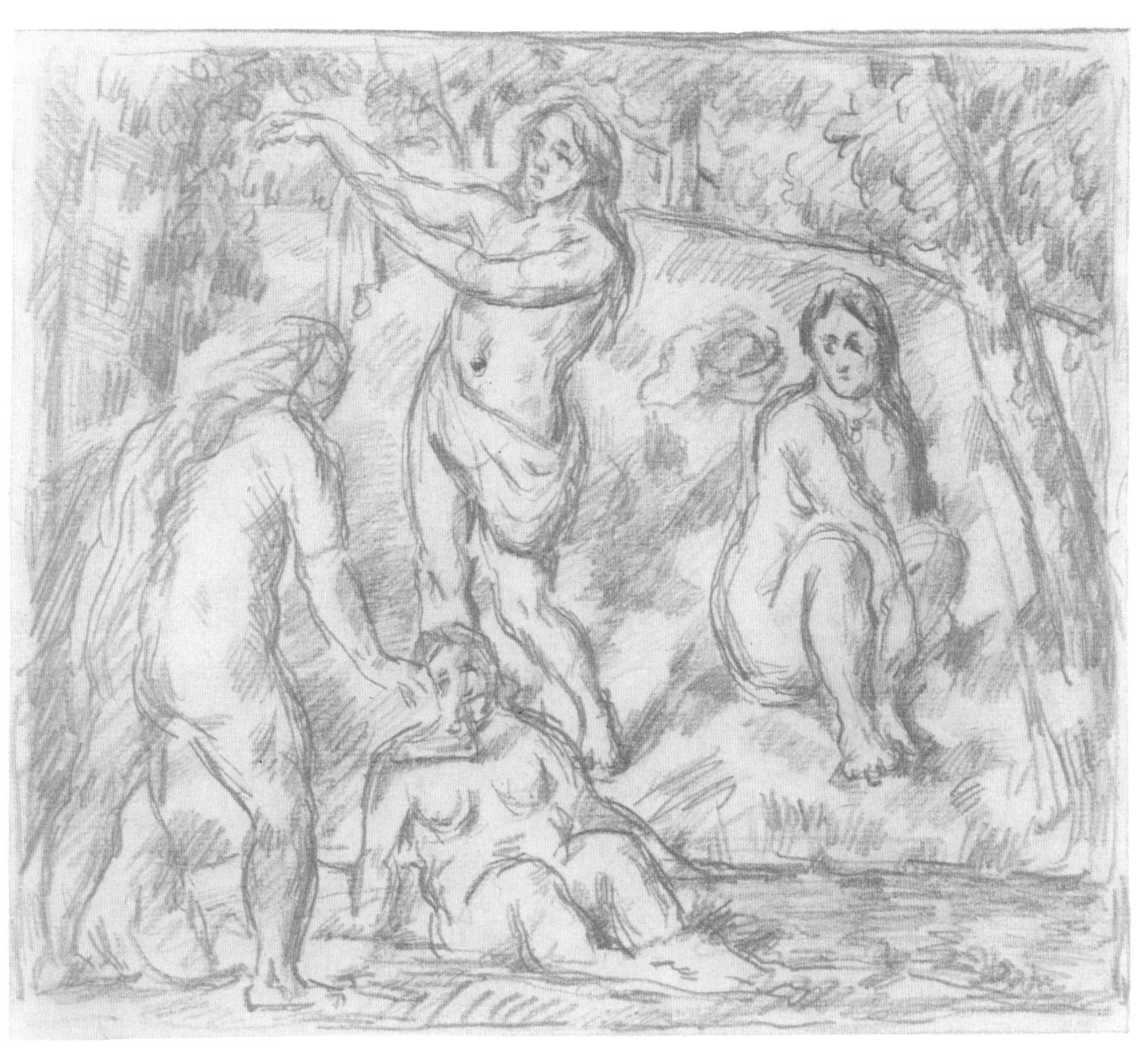

Four Female Bathers, 1879–82

Pencil and black chalk, 20.3 × 22.3 cm (8 × 8¾ in.).

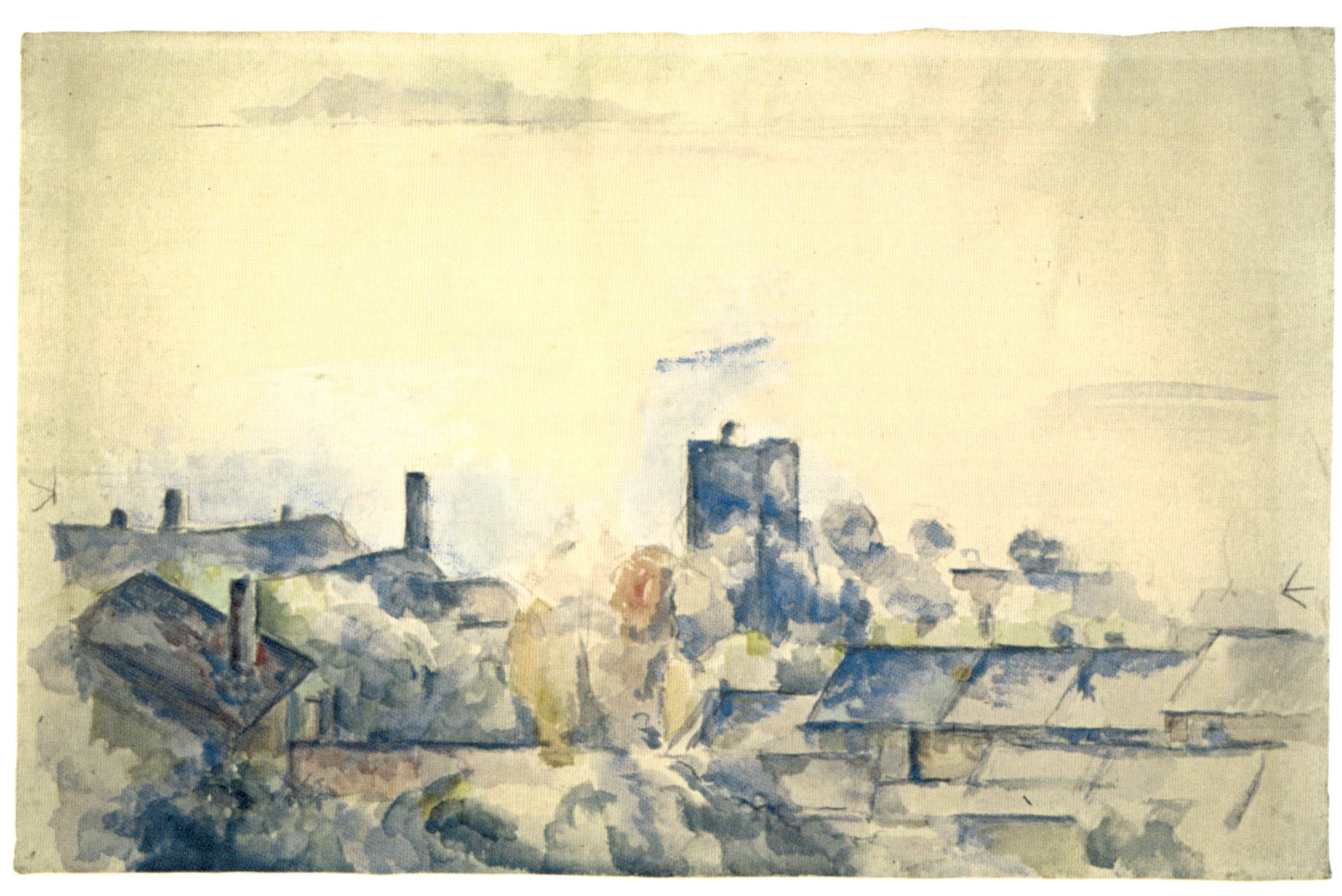

92 *Paul Cézanne*

Rooftops at L'Estaque, 1876–82
Pencil, watercolour and gouache, 30.6 × 47.2 cm
(12½ × 18⅝ in.).
MUSEUM BOIJMANS VAN BEUNINGEN, ROTTERDAM

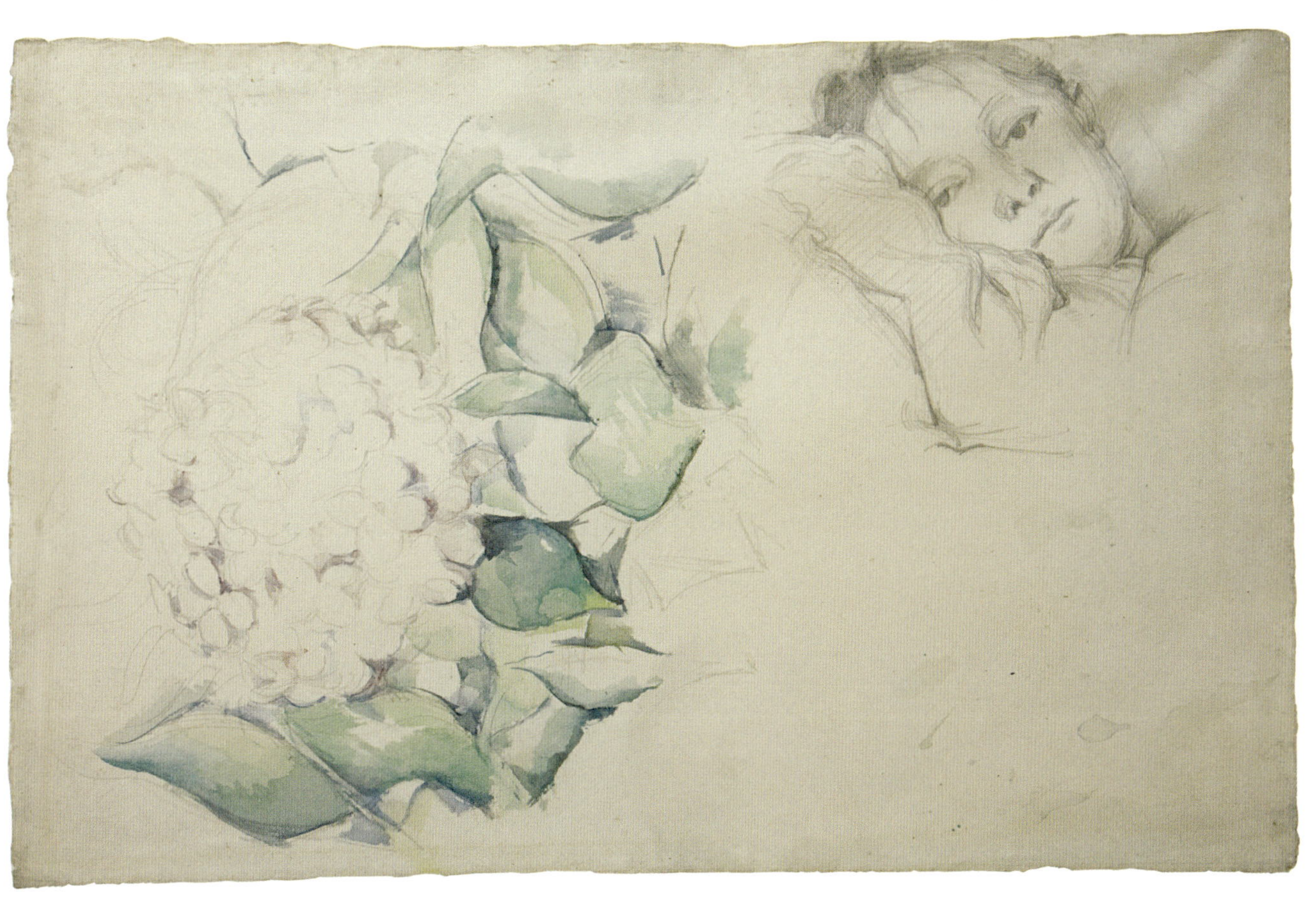

Madame Cézanne with Hortensias, c. 1885
Pencil and watercolour, 30.5 × 46 cm (12 × 18⅛ in.).

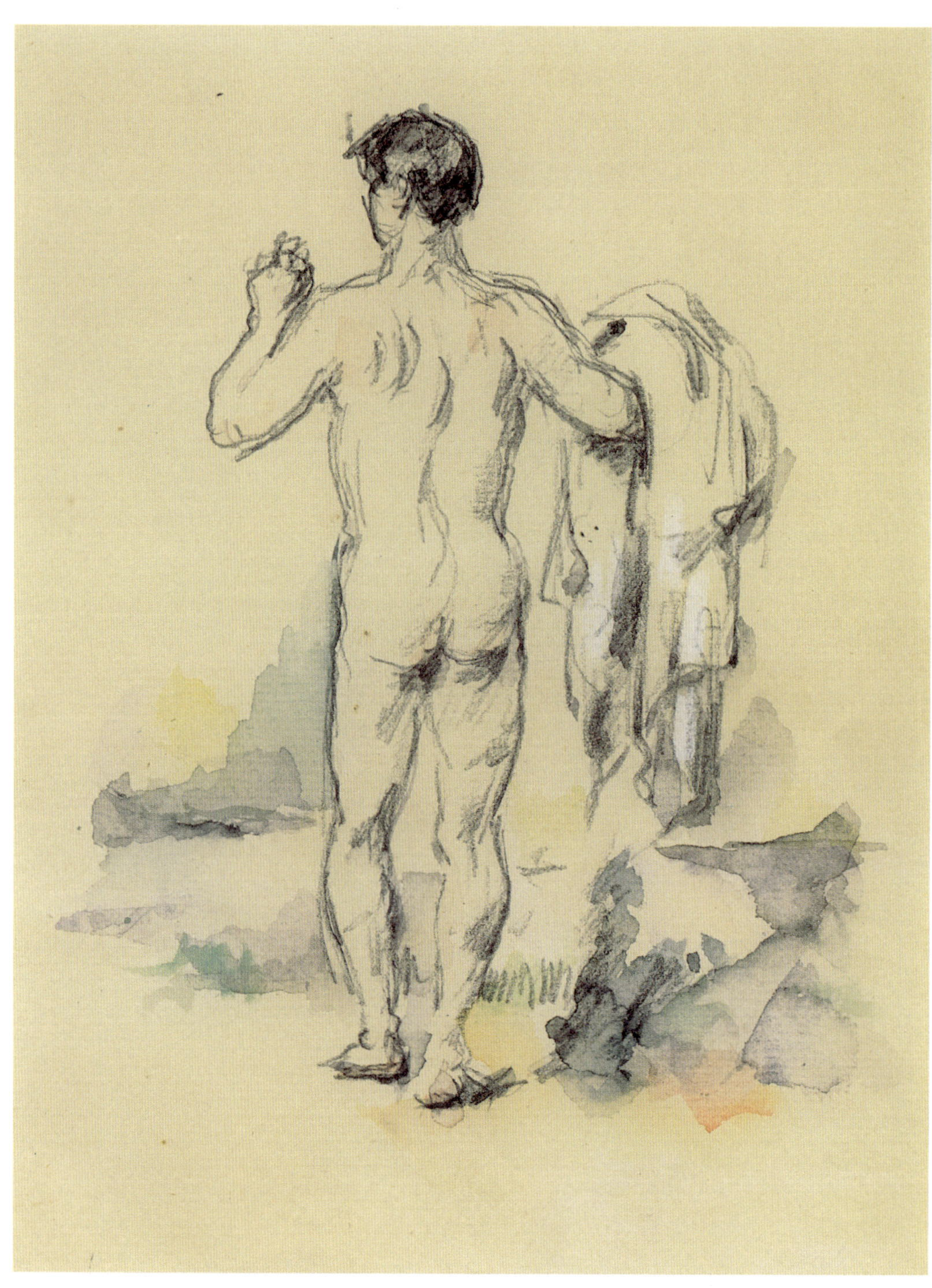

   Paul Cézanne

Standing Bather Seen from the Back, c. 1885
Pencil and watercolour, 22.3 × 17.1 cm (8¾ × 6¾ in.).
WADSWORTH ATHENEUM, HARTFORD, CONNECTICUT

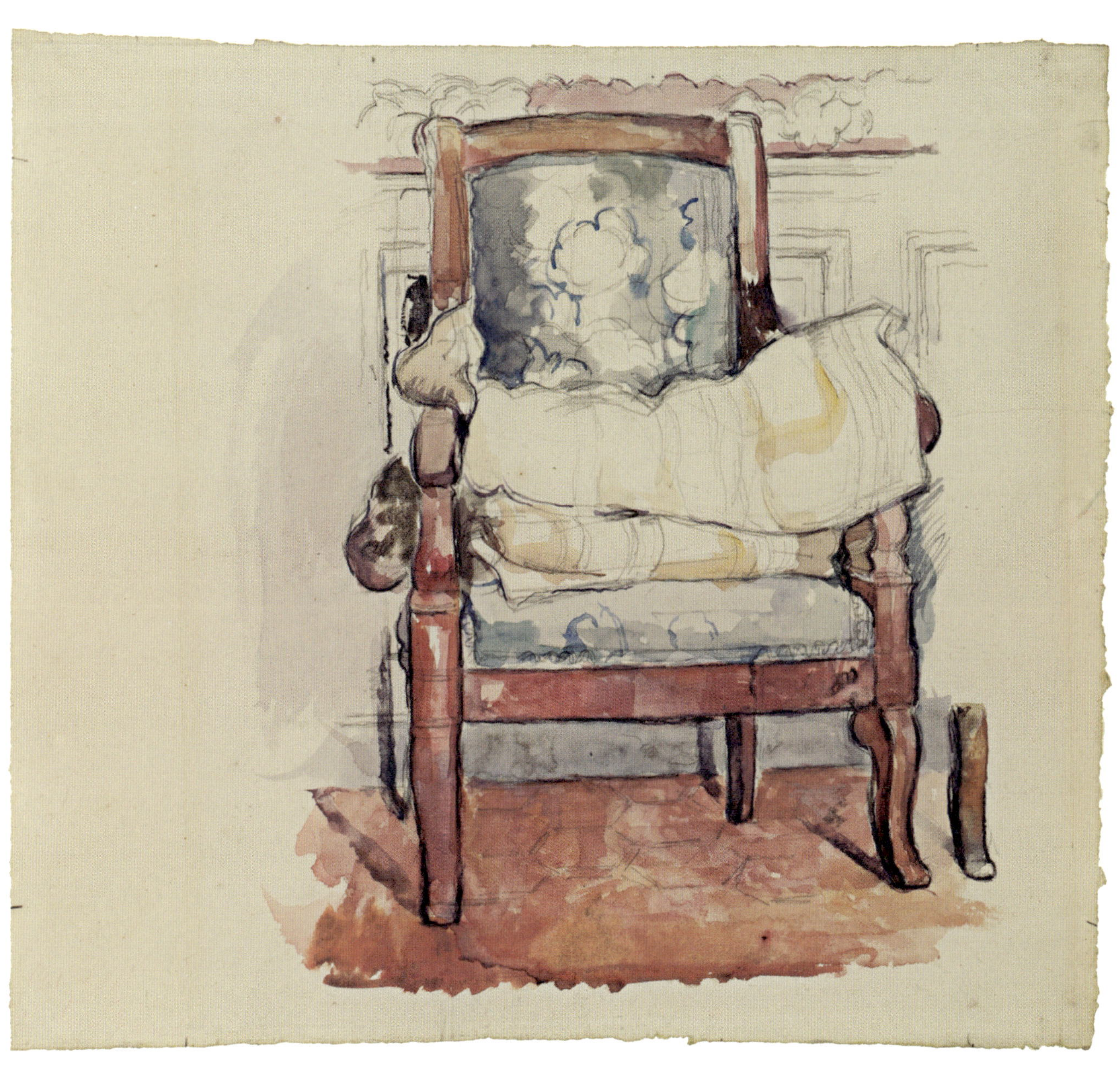

Armchair, c. 1885–90
Pencil and watercolour, 32.2 × 33.8 cm (12⅝ × 13¼ in.).
THE COURTAULD GALLERY, LONDON

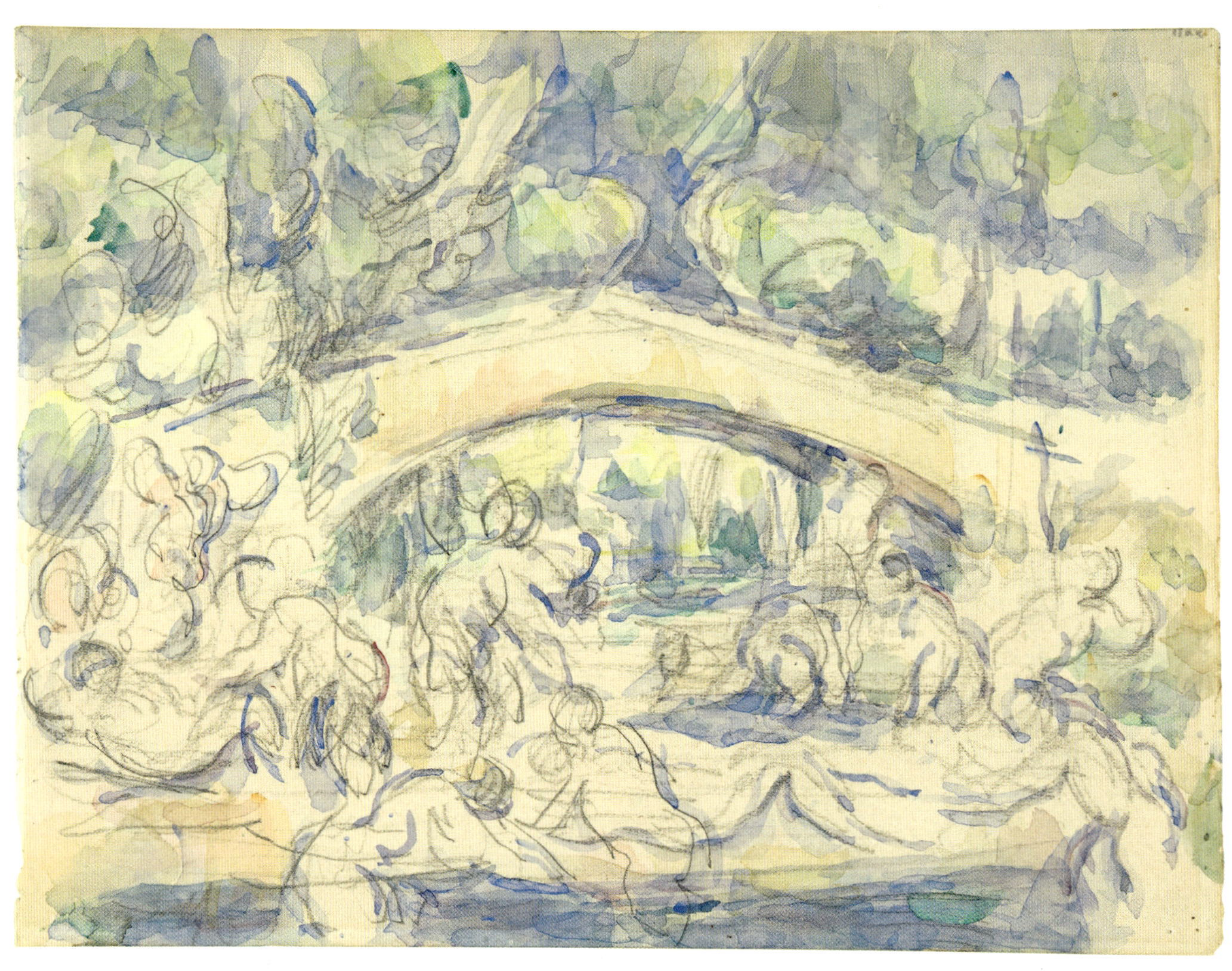

Bathers by a Bridge, 1900–06
Pencil and watercolour, 21 × 27.2 cm (8¼ × 10¾ in.).
METROPOLITAN MUSEUM OF ART, NEW YORK

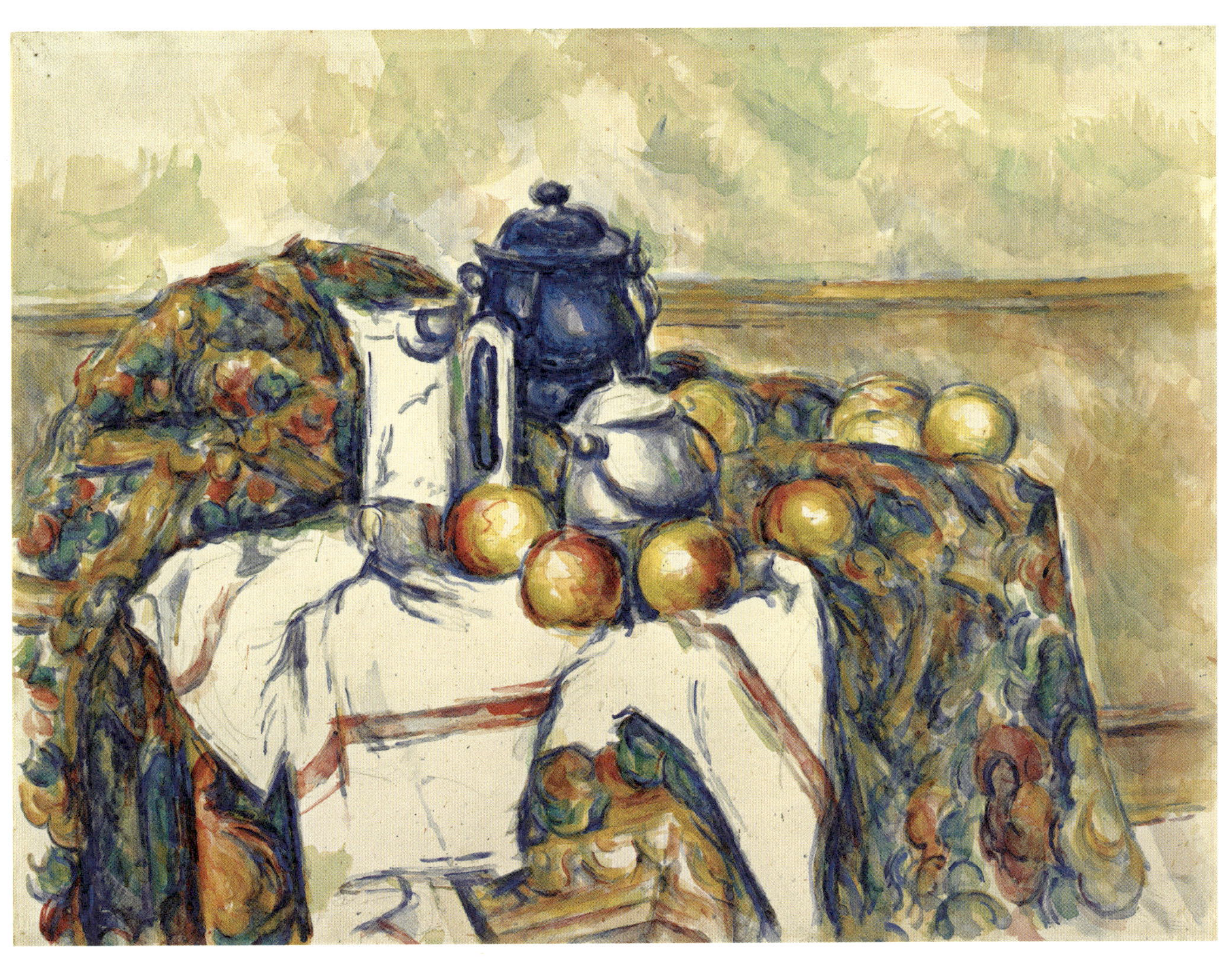

Still Life with Blue Pot, c. 1900–06
Pencil and watercolour, 48.1 × 63.2 cm (18⅞ × 24⅞ in.).
J. PAUL GETTY MUSEUM, LOS ANGELES

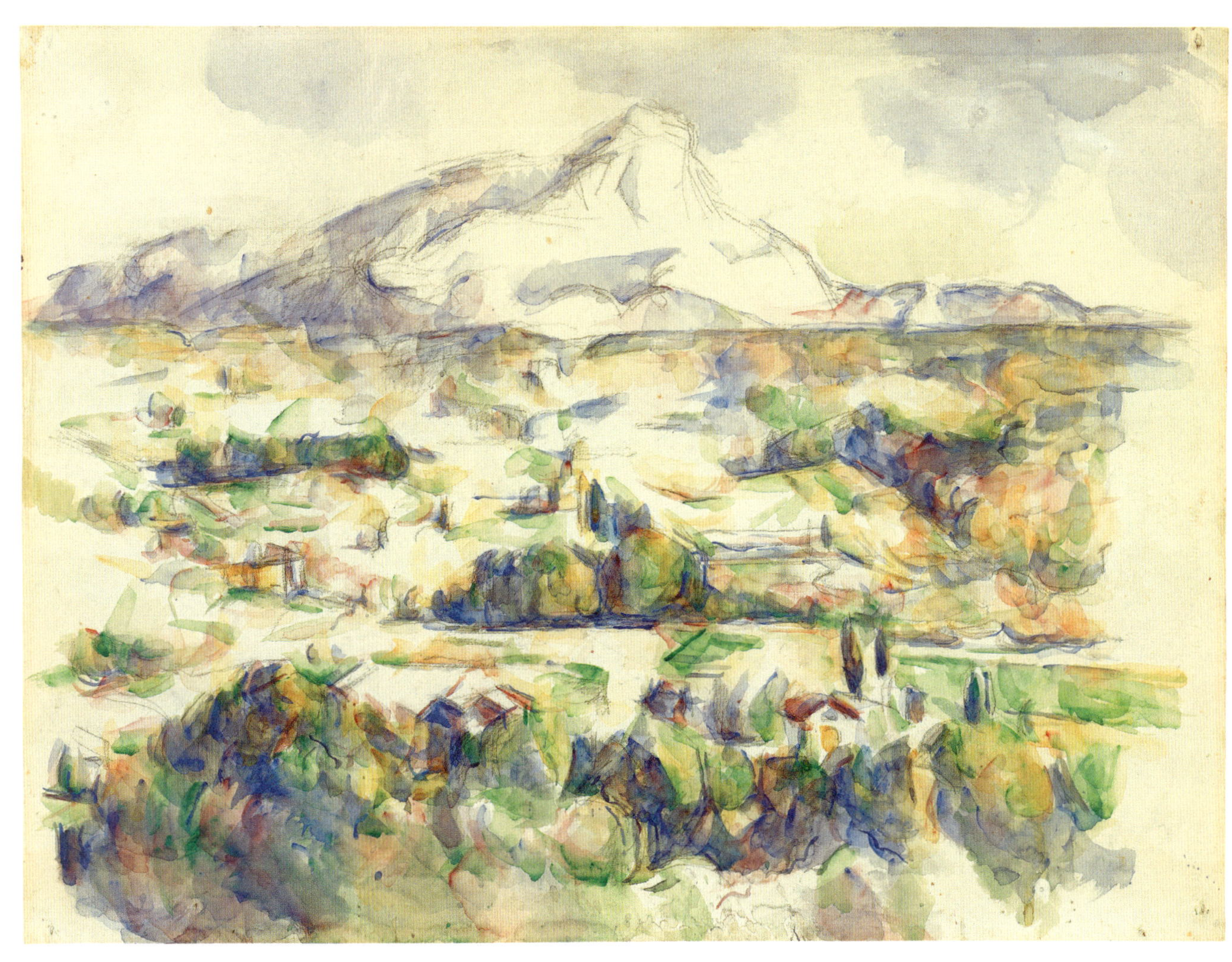

98   *Paul Cézanne*

Mont Sainte-Victoire from Les Lauves, 1902–06
Pencil and watercolour, 48 × 63.2 cm (18⅞ × 25 in.).
OSKAR REINHART COLLECTION 'AM RÖMERHOLZ', WINTERTHUR

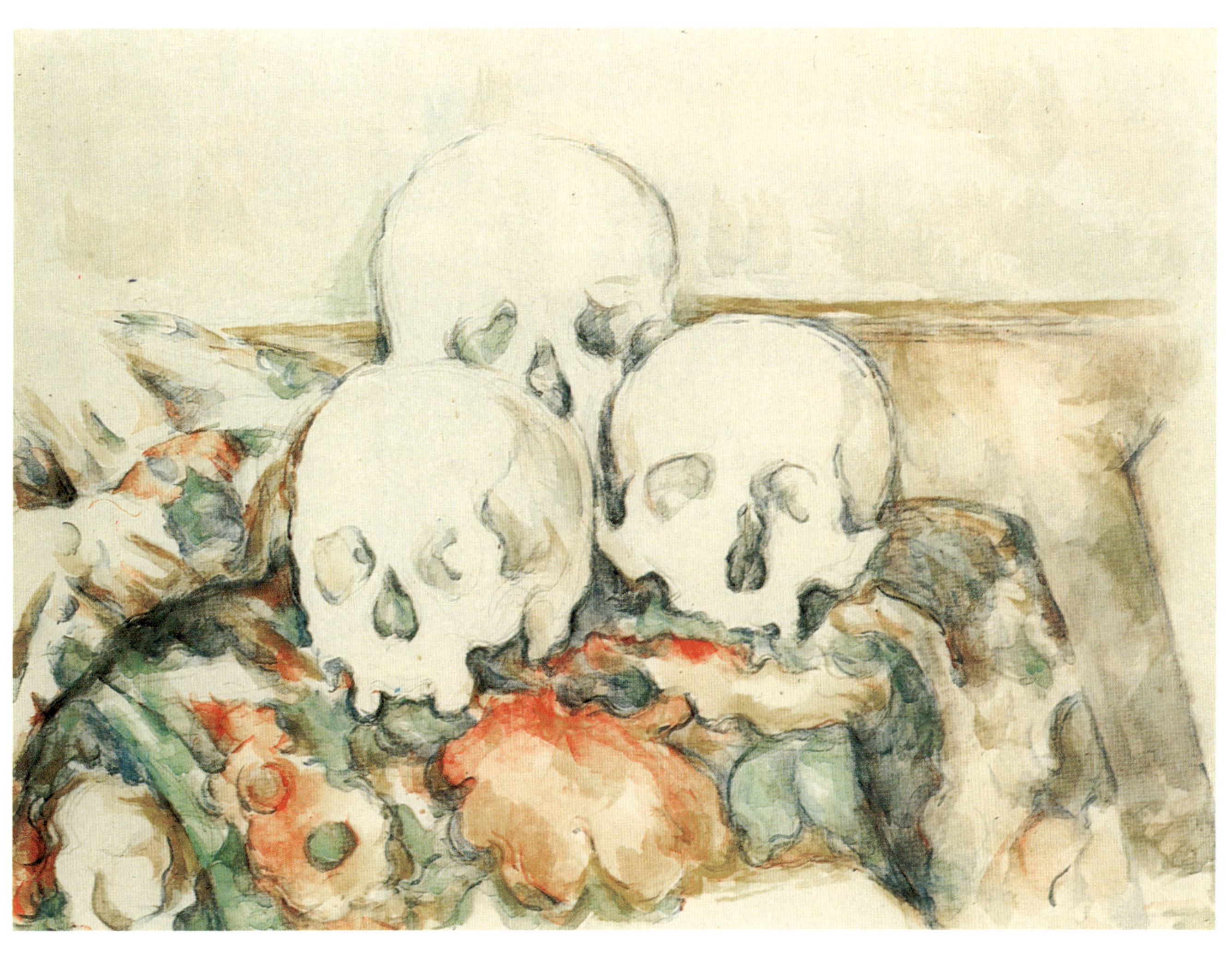

Three Skulls, 1902–06
Pencil and watercolour with touches of gouache,
47.7 × 63.2 cm (18¾ × 24⅞ in.).
THE ART INSTITUTE OF CHICAGO

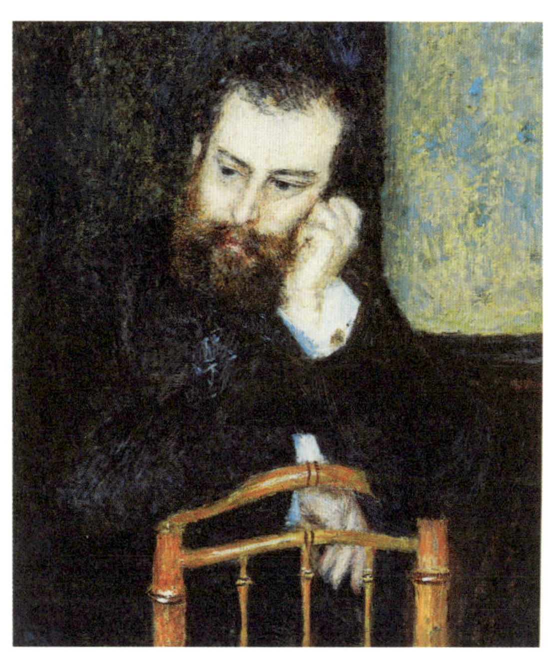

Alfred Sisley

1839–1899

Late in his life Henri Matisse recalled having had a discussion on Impressionism with Pissarro in Paris at the turn of the nineteenth century. Matisse asked, 'What is an impressionist?' To which Pissarro replied, 'An impressionist is a painter who never paints the same picture, who always paints a new picture'. Previously, Pissarro had asserted, 'Cézanne is not an impressionist because all his life he has been painting the same picture'. And so Matisse asked, 'Who is a typical impressionist?' To which Pissarro answered with a single name, 'Sisley'. After some reflection Matisse then opined, 'A Cézanne is a moment of the artist while a Sisley is a moment of nature'. This assessment would have intrigued Pissarro, who in 1895 had written dejectedly to his eldest son, Lucien, that 'like Sisley, I remain in the rear of Impressionism'.

Alfred Sisley was born in Paris into an Anglo-French family and made two unsuccessful attempts to become a naturalized Frenchman. His father ran a textile business with outlets in London and Paris, and it was evident that Sisley was expected to pursue

Auguste Renoir
Alfred Sisley, 1876
Oil on canvas, 66.4 × 54.2 cm (26⅛ × 21⅜ in.).
THE ART INSTITUTE OF CHICAGO

a career in commerce. Instead he became an artist, entering the studio of the Swiss painter Charles Gleyre, where in quick succession he met Renoir, Frédéric Bazille and Monet, with whom he went on painting expeditions to the Forest of Fontainebleau.

At an early stage in life Sisley had a predilection for landscape art and rapidly absorbed the influence of the Barbizon School painters, particularly Jean-Baptiste-Camille Corot. Later he told Adolphe Tavernier, who was one of the few critics who had a profound understanding of Sisley's work and spoke at the artist's funeral, 'Which painters do I like? To confine myself to contemporaries: Delacroix, Corot, Millet, Rousseau, Courbet, our masters. All those who loved nature and felt it deeply…'. If Sisley's decision to become an artist created friction with his father, then his relationship with a florist, Eugènie Lescouezec, by whom he had two children, Pierre (born 1867) (p. 104) and Jeanne (born 1869), worsened the situation. Only in 1897, while on a visit to Wales, were these two children legitimized when he also finally married Eugènie in a quiet ceremony in Cardiff town hall.

During the late 1860s and early 1870s, working alongside Renoir, Monet and Pissarro, Sisley helped to develop the Impressionist style. These artists shared an interest in depicting scenes from contemporary life in compositions that seemed spontaneous, although they were in fact often contrived, using vibrant colours and free brushwork. Sisley was particularly skilful at capturing the effects of nature, as the poet Stéphane Mallarmé wrote in 1876: 'Sisley seizes the passing moments of the day; watches the fugitive cloud and seems to paint it in flight; on his canvass [*sic*] the live air moves and the leaves yet thrill and tremble…space and light are one, and the breeze stirring the foliage prevents it from becoming an opaque mass, too heavy for such an impression of mobility and light.'

Sisley exhibited in four of the eight Impressionist exhibitions – the first (1874), second (1876), third (1877) and seventh (1882). He missed the fourth exhibition (1879) owing to the difficulties he was experiencing in selling his work and uncertainty over how he might develop his style – anxieties that he shared with other Impressionists. Throughout his life Sisley suffered from crippling financial difficulties. A number of patrons and dealers made it possible for him to continue painting: for example, the opera singer Jean-Baptiste Faure supported a trip to London in 1874 and the industrialist François Depeaux made the visit to Wales in 1897 possible. Yet the fact remains that during his lifetime Sisley was an unrewarded artist: his work generated limited interest among a small number of collectors, and critical acclaim was granted for the most part towards the end of his life only by younger writers – Tavernier, Gustave Geffroy and Octave Mirbeau.

The zeal that Sisley brought to the birth of Impressionism, and displayed in occasional moments of astounding compositional brilliance (*The Machine at Marly*, 1873, Ny Carlsberg Glyptotek, Copenhagen; *Under the Bridge at Hampton Court*, 1874,

Kunstmuseum Winterthur; *The Aqueduct at Marly*, 1874, Toledo Museum of Art, Ohio), gradually evaporated, although he continued to produce work of the highest quality. The truth is that the combination of Sisley's personal reticence and his elegiac style of painting meant that his work could easily be overlooked. His skills were more readily admired by his fellow artists than by the public: compositional assurance, eye for detail and delicacy of touch were applied equally to panoramic views, quiet corners, arching skies, trembling leaves, sharp frosts, flowing water, ground covered in snow and warm sunlight.

Having started out in Paris, Sisley retreated slowly further and further from the capital. First he lived in the more distant suburbs along the banks of the river Seine to the southwest of Paris – Louveciennes, Marly-le-Roi, Sèvres – but in 1880 he moved out to the area around Moret-sur-Loing, well to the southeast of Paris, close to the Forest of Fontainebleau. In effect Sisley had come full circle, but, more importantly, in all the places that he resided he was confronting history. In Louveciennes, Marly-le-Roi and Sèvres it was the royal court of Louis XIV at the nearby Château of Versailles and the Château of Marly; in Moret-sur-Loing it was medieval France. In the first set of locations, Sisley chose to negate history by superimposing modern aspects on the landscape, thereby draining it of its historical significance, whereas in Moret-sur-Loing he did the opposite by emphasizing the Gothic heritage, singling out the church of Notre-Dame, the gateway and the bridge to the extent that modernity is almost lost in the shadow of the past. Such contrasting approaches to subject matter suggest that Sisley is perhaps not the straightforward painter as has often been assumed.

The artist's drawings certainly present a challenge. It is not clear how often he drew or for what purpose. The surviving works on paper are varied in quality and lack consistency. Some of the compositional drawings may not be preparatory at all, but, rather, made as visual records of paintings. An exception may be made for those studies of the coastline in south Wales and Langland Bay where Sisley was only too pleased to explore new motifs in the open air (p. 109 below). The only surviving sketchbook, now in the Musée du Louvre, dating from the early 1880s, is a *livre de raison* in the tradition of the *Liber Veritatis* kept by Claude.

The emergence over the years of a number of examples suggests that pastel may have been Sisley's preferred medium. Certainly as ill-health began to dominate his life he appreciated the advantage of a medium that was not so arduous to use and that could increase his output for exhibitions while also providing dealers with stock. Some of his pithier studies (p. 109 above) may well have been made in preparation for these particular pastels (p. 108).

In many of the places that Sisley lived his method was to map out the territory by recording it from different viewpoints. He began this process in Louveciennes and Marly-le-Roi and continued it at Hampton Court, Saint-Mammès at the confluence of the rivers Seine and Loing, Moret-sur-Loing and south Wales. Occasionally, the artist would concentrate on a single motif such as the church of Notre-Dame in Moret-sur-Loing and, inspired by Monet, create a group of works (not strictly speaking a series) by viewing the building from various positions, at different times of day under changing weather conditions and effects of light.

During the winter of 1888, while living at Veneux-Nadon (now Veneux-les-Sablons), Sisley made at least eight pastels of the view through a window of his house, which was near the station. This group of pastels, which he referred to as a 'suite', were included under the generic title of '*La Gare de Moret*' in an exhibition organized by Paul Durand-Ruel in the summer after they were made (pp. 105–07). The pastels are similarly composed in horizontal bands – the front garden of the artist's house in the immediate foreground, the road beyond the wall of the house, the railway line and sheds on the other side of the road and the wintry sky above. The only important verticals are formed by the bare trees. The writer Félix Fénéon described these pastels as 'singularly expressive and unique' while also hinting at their bleak atmosphere. Like Van Gogh, Sisley's highly individual skill as an artist was to lift the mundane and the banal on to the level of the universal and numinous. This is precisely what he achieves in these pastels.

By the late 1880s Sisley's health had begun to decline. His output dropped and his mood swings increased as he became more and more reclusive at Moret-sur-Loing. Eugènie died of cancer of the tongue in October 1898 and three months later the artist himself died of cancer of the throat.

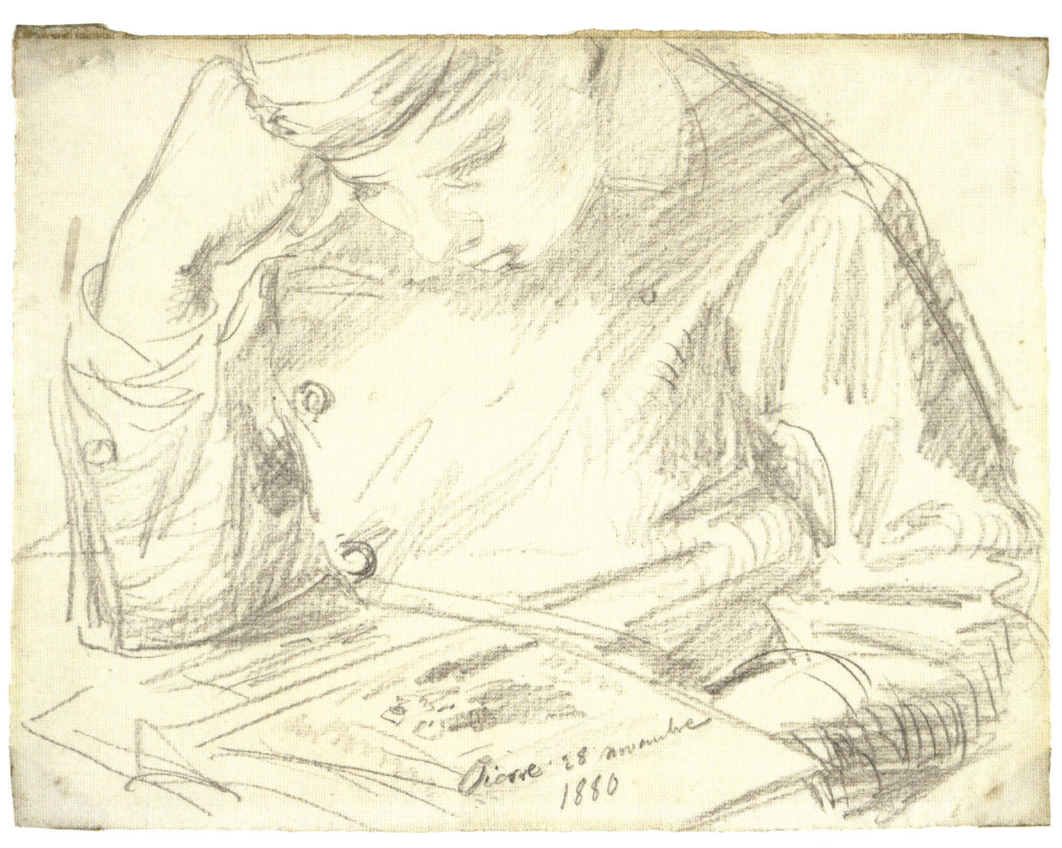

104   *Alfred Sisley*

The Artist's Son, Pierre, 1880
Black chalk, 23 × 31 cm (9 × 12¼ in.). Inscribed and dated.
THE NEW ART GALLERY WALSALL

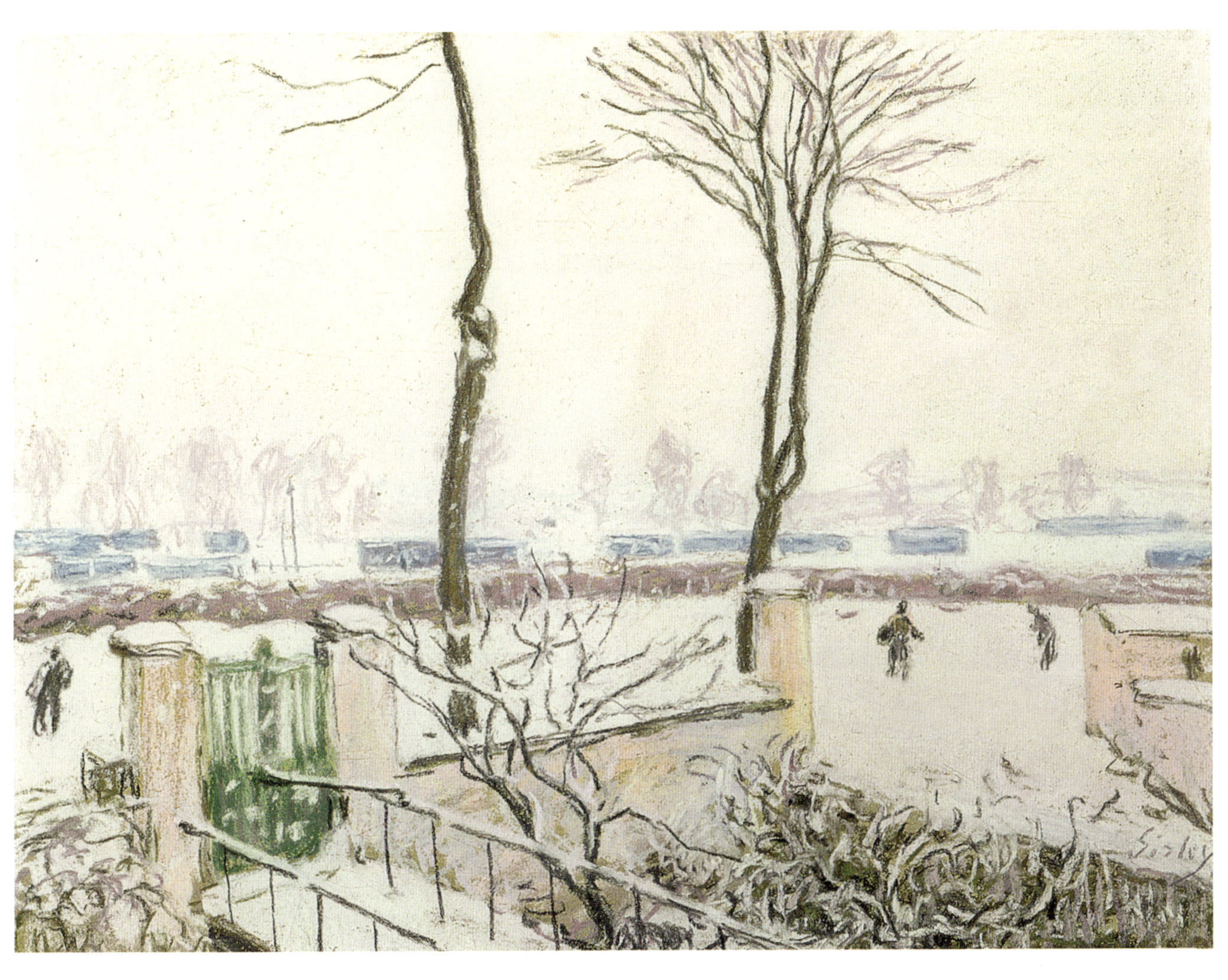

Approach to the Railway Station in Winter, Moret-sur-Loing, 1888
Pastel, 38.4 × 46 cm (15⅛ × 18⅛ in.). Signed.
CINCINNATI ART MUSEUM

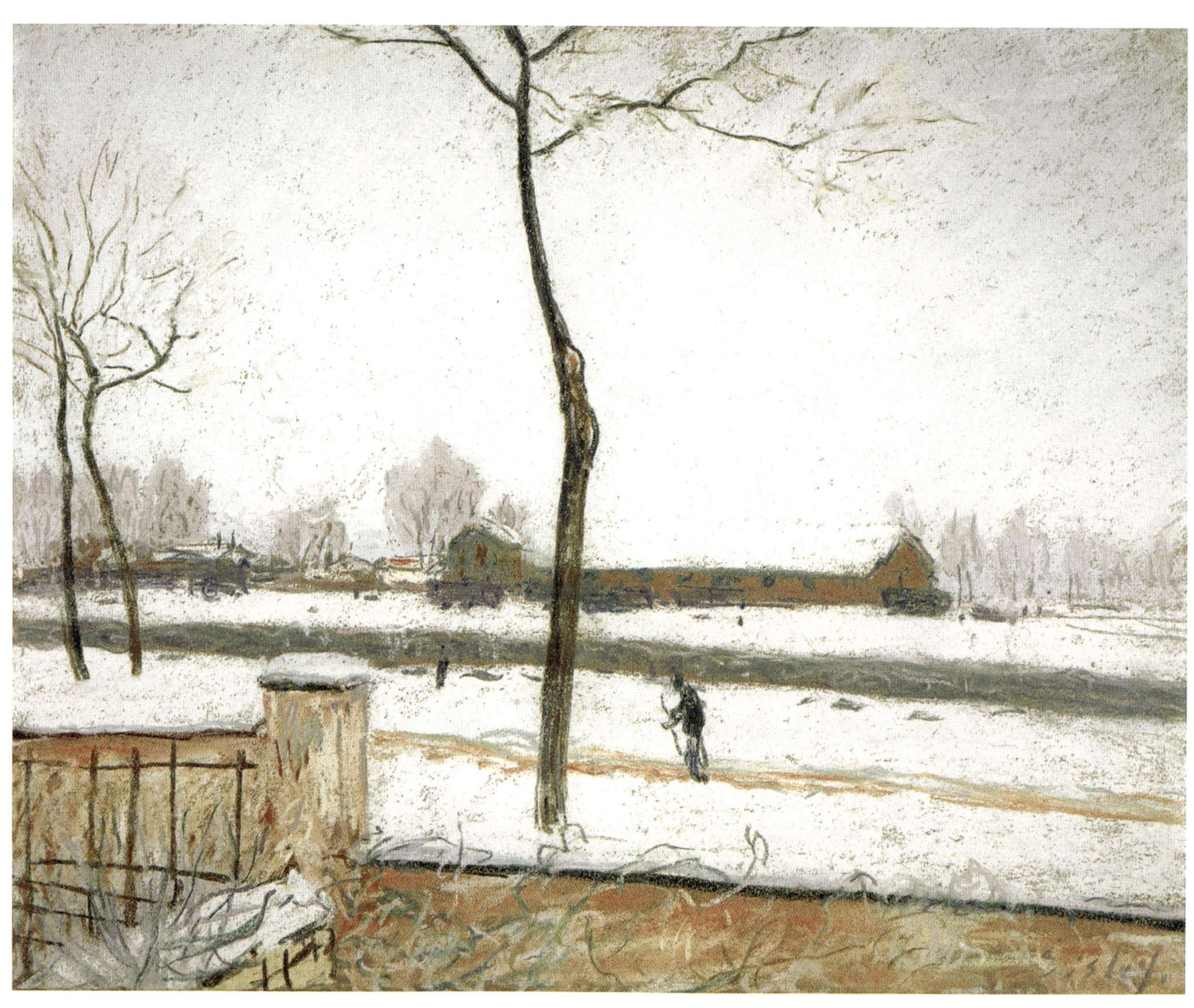

 Alfred Sisley

Snow Scene, Moret-sur-Loing Railway Station, 1888
Pastel, 45.7 × 54.6 cm (18 × 21½ in.). Signed.
NATIONAL GALLERY OF SCOTLAND, EDINBURGH

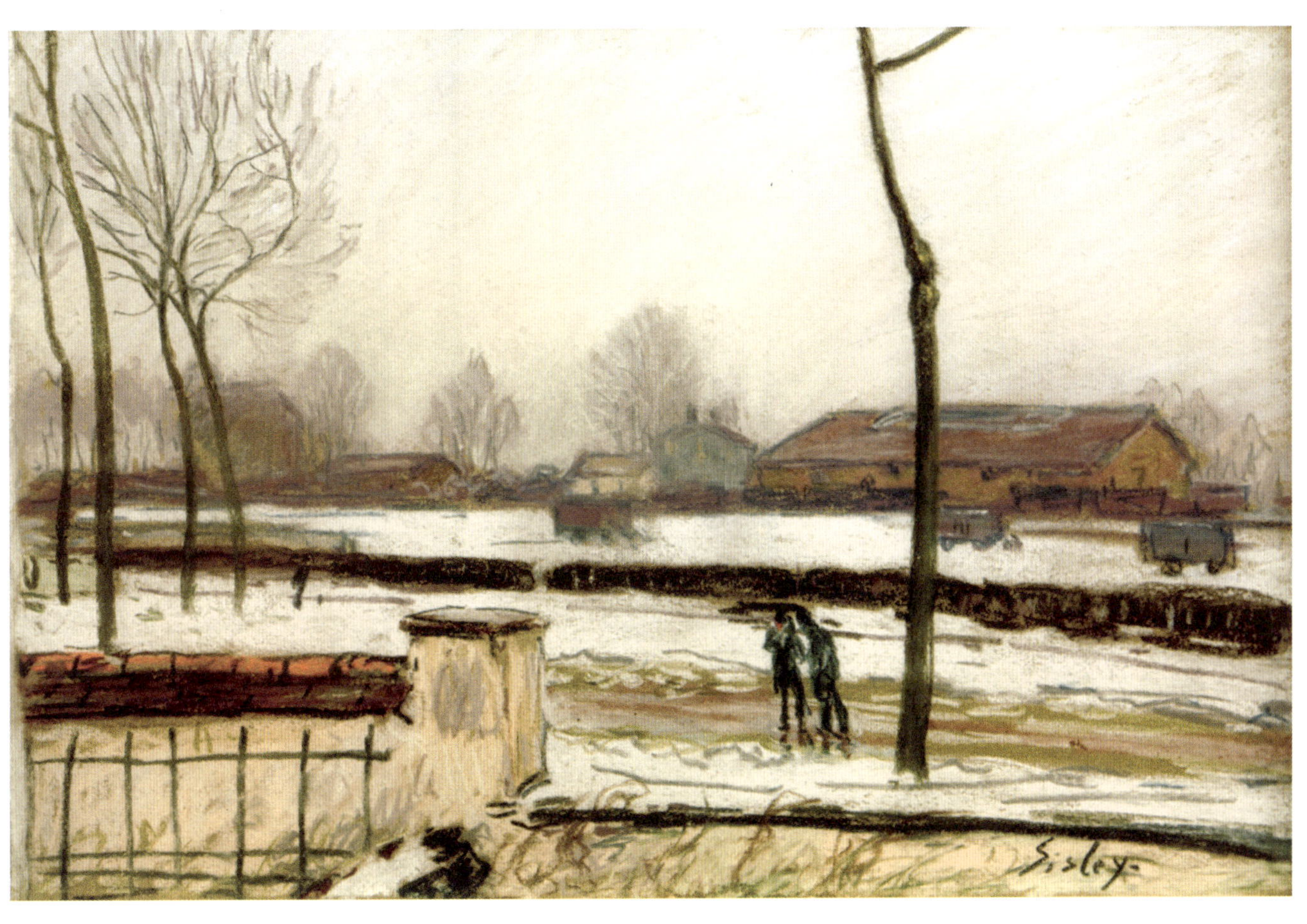

Winter Landscape, Moret-sur-Loing, 1888
Pastel, 38 × 55.4 cm (15 × 21¾ in.). Signed.
VON DER HEYDT MUSEUM, WUPPERTAL

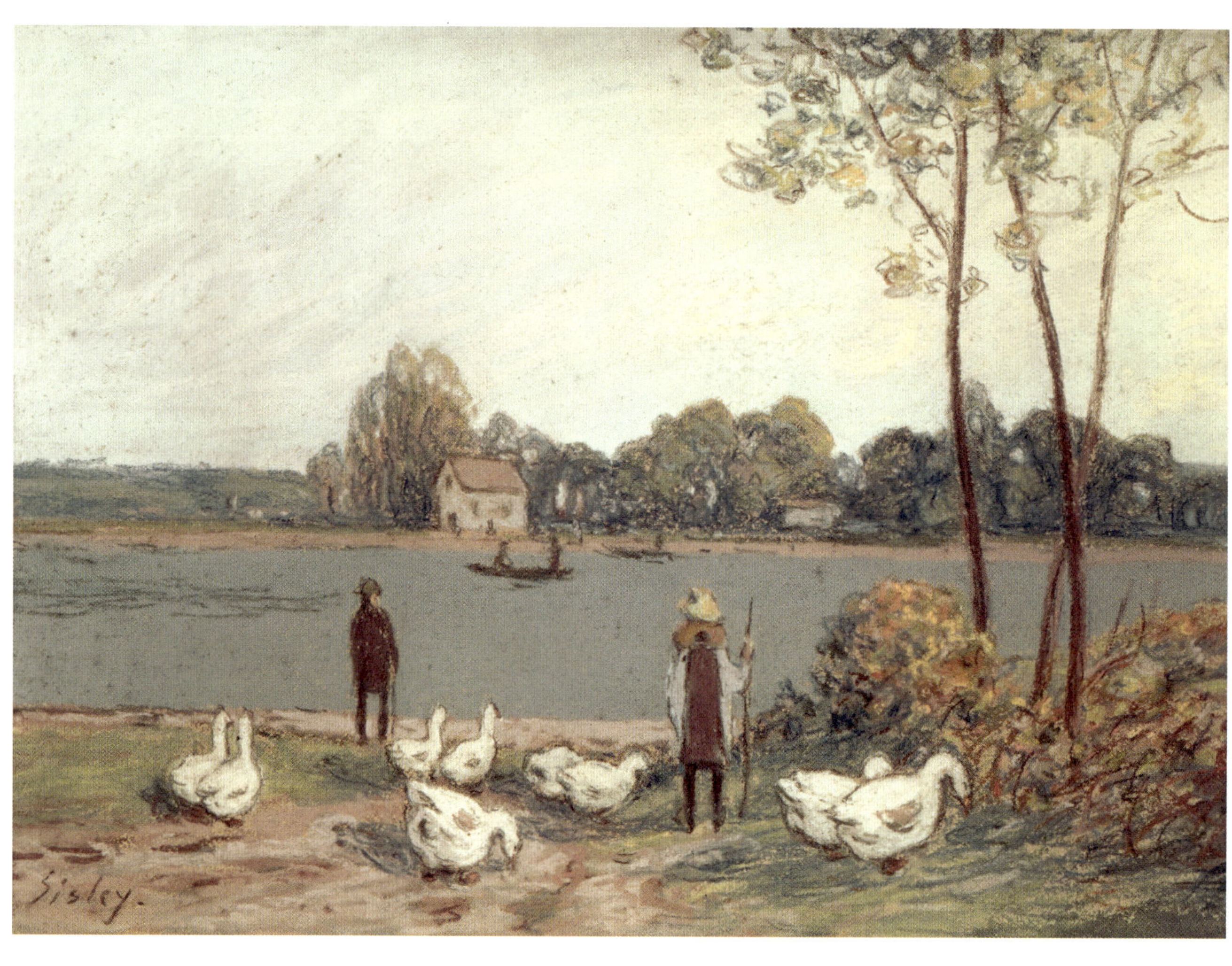

108 *Alfred Sisley*

By the River Loing, c. 1896
Pastel, 30 × 40.5 cm (11¾ × 15⅞ in.). Signed.
MUSÉE DES BEAUX-ARTS, ROUEN

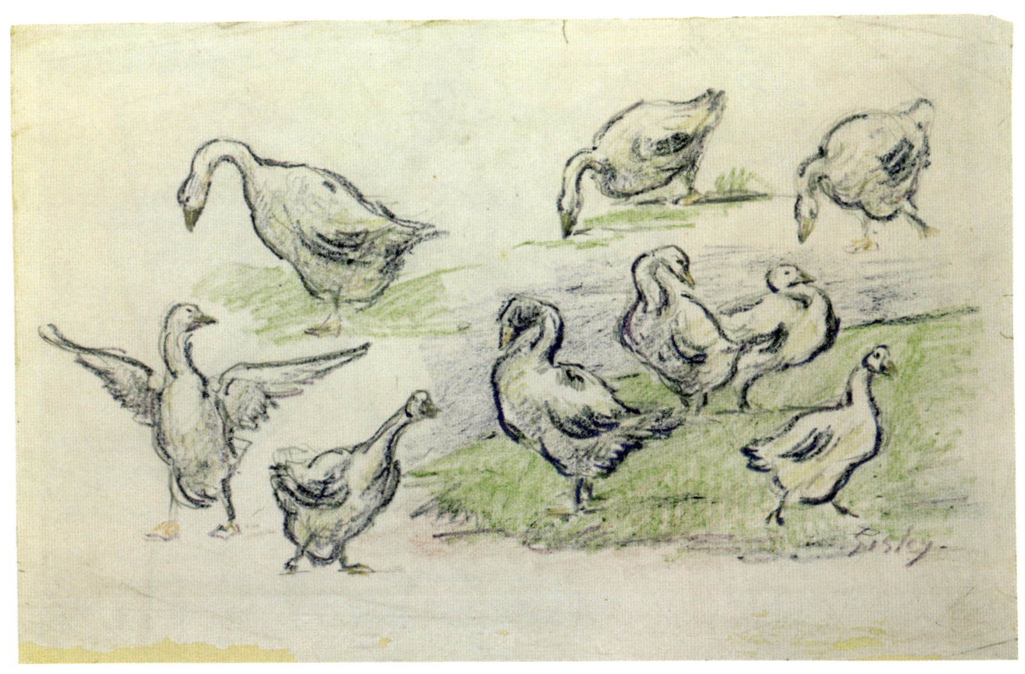

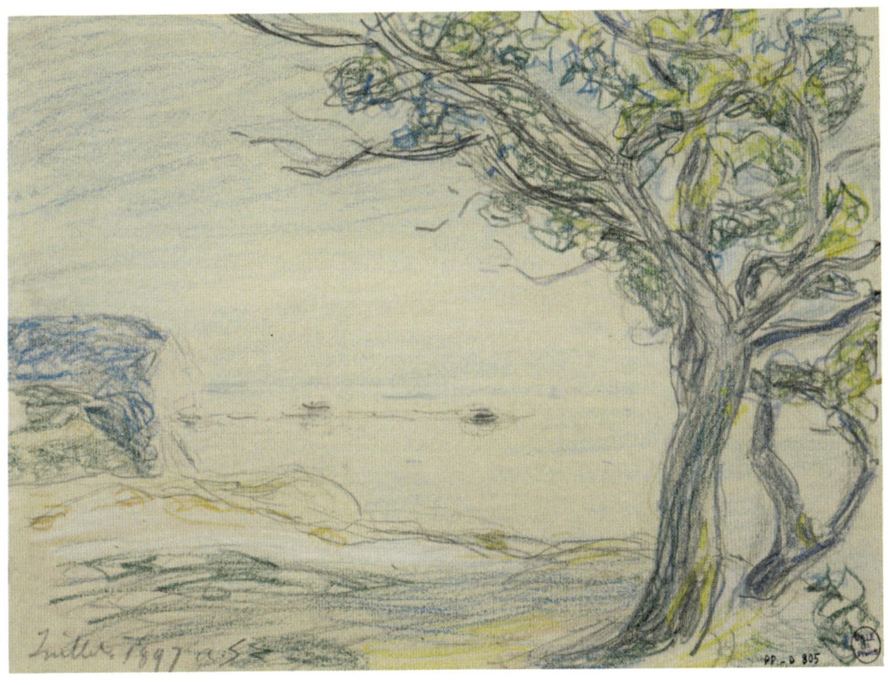

Geese, c. 1896
Pastel, 19.8 × 30.8 cm (7¾ × 12⅛ in.). Signed.
MUSEUM OF FINE ARTS, BUDAPEST

Trees on the Shore, July 1897
Coloured crayons, 16 × 21 cm (6¼ × 8¼ in.).
Signed and dated.
PETIT PALAIS, MUSÉE DES BEAUX-ARTS DE LA VILLE DE PARIS

109

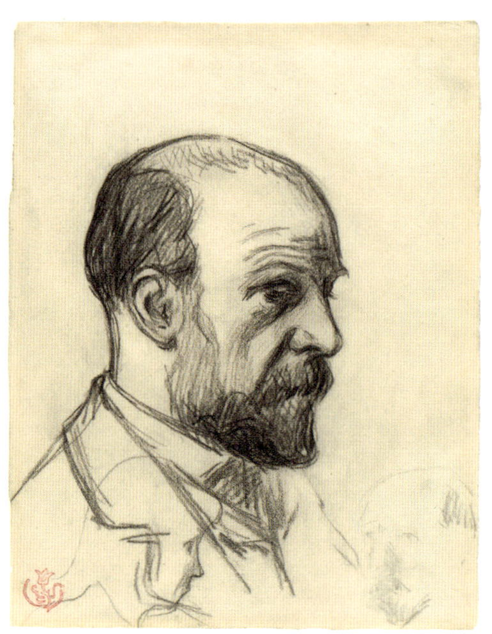

Odilon Redon
1840–1916

A painting by Maurice Denis dated 1900 and now in the collection of the Musée d'Orsay in Paris shows a group gathered around an easel on which is displayed a picture, *Still Life with Compotier*, by Cézanne dating from 1879–80 and formerly owned by Gauguin. This *Homage to Cézanne* was intended as an acknowledgement of the new developments in art, which the younger generation saw as the result of the advances made by Cézanne.

The setting is the gallery of Ambroise Vollard, who stands behind the easel as though fearful for the fate of the picture that is the subject of examination. Most of the figures are positioned behind or in line with the picture, but in front of it to the left is Redon, who stands calmly cleaning his spectacles while listening to the more animated Paul Sérusier on the right, who appears to be leading the discussion. Redon is depicted as a tall, heavily built, broad-shouldered man with a high forehead and a beard. He has a commanding air, stoops slightly and is dressed more formally than his younger companions, thereby exuding a certain gravitas.

Emile Schuffenecker
Portrait of Odilon Redon, c. 1891
Fabricated black chalk, 31 × 54.2 cm (12⅛ × 9⅜ in.).
METROPOLITAN MUSEUM OF ART, NEW YORK

It was not unusual for Redon to set himself apart in the way that is clearly indicated by Denis in his *Homage to Cézanne*, and it was said of him that he had 'an aptitude for silence'. The inclusion of Redon in the eighth and last Impressionist exhibition in 1886, when he exhibited a number of charcoal drawings, which were shown in a corridor, puzzled the more intelligent critics and dumbfounded most of them. The seventh Impressionist exhibition had been held four years before, in 1882, and the organization of the subsequent one proved to be acrimonious, particularly as regards the choice of location and the selection of participants. The wide range of styles and types of art revealed the tensions that had already been well rehearsed on earlier occasions but were now exacerbated by the presence of the younger Neo-Impressionists, represented by Seurat and Signac. But, in Redon's case, it was not the style of his drawings that caused comment so much as their content, which tended on the whole to be regarded as Symbolist.

The artist was born in Bordeaux. His father had accumulated wealth in America in Louisiana; his mother was Creole. Redon's upbringing was lonely and was spent in isolation at the family property at Peyrelebade in Médoc on the Atlantic coast. The low horizons of the barren, mournful landscape of this region haunted Redon for the rest of his life and are reflected in many of his landscapes (p. 115). The sale of Peyrelebade in 1897 affected him deeply, but he continued to return to the area each summer, renting a villa at St-Georges-de-Didonne near Royan. The emptiness of the landscape remained a vital source and fuelled his imagination.

Redon showed an aptitude for drawing at a young age, but was slow to embark on his career, not beginning to exhibit his work until over forty years of age. His family wanted him to be an architect, but he failed to gain the necessary qualifications in Paris and so in 1864 he entered the studio of the successful Salon painter Jean-Léon Gérôme, where once more he did not thrive. It was apparent that Redon was nurturing an independent spirit, and his formative influences were in fact nearer to home in Bordeaux where the older, decidedly eccentric artist, Rodolphe Bresdin, was living during the late 1860s. Bresdin's prints and drawings, often of epic struggles involving numerous figures, depicted on a minute scale, have a visionary quality evoking comparisons with Jacques Callot and Francisco de Goya. At this same stage Redon met the botanist Armand Clavaud, later Curator of the Botanical Gardens in Bordeaux, who introduced him to scientific and philosophical publications, as well as to the works of Gustave Flaubert, Charles Baudelaire and Edgar Allan Poe, in addition to Eastern literature and religion.

Both Bresdin and Clavaud encouraged Redon to use his imagination, but he was also conscious of the more mainstream elements in the French artistic tradition. He venerated all the multifarious aspects of Eugène Delacroix's art, singling out the ceiling painting in the Galerie d'Apollon in the Palais du Louvre and writing a remarkable account of following the great artist home one night after a reception and watching him 'walking the pavements with the delicacy of a cat'. Redon also admired the various styles in Jean-Baptiste-Camille Corot's work and accepted the older artist's suggestion that he should combine the observed with the unobserved. Many of Redon's drawn studies, as opposed to his finished drawings, are, like Corot's, sparse and economical in treatment with carefully nuanced passages of shading (p. 114).

Given the emphasis that Redon placed on the imagination, it is not surprising that he was critical of the Impressionists. 'True parasites of the object,' he wrote, 'they have cultivated an art which is uniquely rooted in the visual world, and have closed their eyes to that which is beyond…'. By contrast, Redon described his own originality as 'putting the logic of the visible at the service of the invisible'. Put another way, the direction of Redon's art was from the external to the internal. He was careful not to associate himself with any identifiable art movement and, although he wrote about art, he was not a theorist.

Redon made numerous paintings, but it is in the quantity of drawings and prints that his highly individual approach to subject matter and materials is most evident. The finished works on paper are autonomous and fall broadly into two complementary categories: the charcoal drawings, which the artist referred to as his *'noirs'*, dating from the 1870s onwards (pp. 116–20), and the pastels, which he began to make during the 1890s in celebration of his conversion to colour (pp. 121–23).

It was after fighting in the Franco-Prussian War of 1870–71 that Redon began to make his charcoal drawings, and when they did not sell he was encouraged by Henri Fantin-Latour to print them as lithographs and publish them in albums as a way of promoting his work. Accordingly, several such albums were published between 1879 and 1899, gradually extending the artist's reputation, particularly with writers in France, such as Joris-Karl Huysmans and Stéphane Mallarmé, and also in Belgium, Germany and the Netherlands. Many of Redon's early supporters in the 1870s attended the Salon of Madame de Rayssac in Paris, the wife of the poet Saint-Cyr de Rayssac who died aged thirty-six in 1874. Exhibitions of the *'noirs'* were first held at private venues such as the offices of journals (*La Vie Moderne* and *Le Gaulois*), but at intervals from 1884 the dealers Paul Durand-Ruel and Vollard began to take an interest. These kinds of exhibitions were supplemented by submissions to the Société des Artistes Indépendants and the Salon d'Automne, as well as by invitations to exhibit in Brussels with the Les Vingt avant-garde group. These occasions brought mounting critical attention, not all of it laudatory or sympathetic. Nonetheless, many of his friends – musicians and poets – hung Redon's drawings on their walls.

The strange, phantasmagoric, sometimes impenetrable images created by Redon were often based on human body parts, the vegetable kingdom or the animal world. Their appeal was in the first instance limited, but the technical skill was unmistakable.

Redon treated black as a colour in its own right, calling it 'the most essential colour'. Using his charcoal on tinted papers, he could manipulate the surface not only by the pressure of the hand, but also by more invasive ways that resulted in varying textures, sometimes of a three-dimensional quality. It is in his technical abilities that Redon's art can be seen to be very earthbound and, tempting though it is, he preferred that his images, even those of mythological or religious origin, were not interpreted symbolically or even personally. He regretted the need for specific titles. 'My drawings inspire… They determine nothing. They please in the same way as music in the ambiguous world of indeterminacy.' This is perhaps why the pleasure derived from Redon's '*noirs*' is essentially a lingering one like a dying chord, which, considering the artist was a gifted musician, is perhaps what he intended.

During the 1890s Redon's art changed course as he began to favour pastel over charcoal. He started by adding highlights to his '*noirs*' and then transposed many of those compositions into full-bodied pastels. As with his earlier works, Redon covered the whole sheet of paper, which, when combined with the intensity of the colours, grants these works considerable power. From 1900 he devoted himself totally to pastel and was by this means able to build a reputation whose influence can be seen in artists as diverse as Henri Matisse, Pablo Picasso and Marcel Duchamp. At the same time and in accordance with his growing popularity, Redon extended his repertoire beyond the phantasmagoric and the oneiric to themes arising from mythological and biblical sources, as well as still life and portraiture (p. 121). To modern eyes the beauty of these pastels suggests a spiritual dimension, and it is true that Redon was conscious of the Catholic Revival in France at the end of the nineteenth century. For example, the boats that appear in the '*noir*' *Guardian Spirit of the Waters* (p. 116) and the pastel *Flower Clouds* (p. 122) might be a reference to the voyage of life, which is subject to hidden dangers and might require safeguards. Nonetheless, Redon professed only to be 'wedded to colour' and concerned to push the medium to its limits. The radiance of these pastels that glow like stained-glass windows at one minute (p. 122) or quiver like precious metalwork at another (p. 123), appealed to a wider audience than that for the '*noirs*'. It is as though Redon was abandoning the inhospitable world of Pieter Bruegel the Elder or Hieronymus Bosch for the comforts of a Proustian salon.

The undeniably decorative quality of the later pastels made after 1900 was admired by Redon's wealthier or more committed patrons – Robert de Domecy, Gustave Fayet, Arthur Fontaine, André Bonger – who gave the artist special commissions. Even these larger, more formal works retained the spell that characterizes the whole of Redon's *oeuvre*. As he stated in a letter of 21 July 1898 to André Mellerio, 'The only aim of my art is to produce within the spectator a sort of diffuse but powerful affinity with the obscure world of the indeterminate, and to predispose him to thought.'

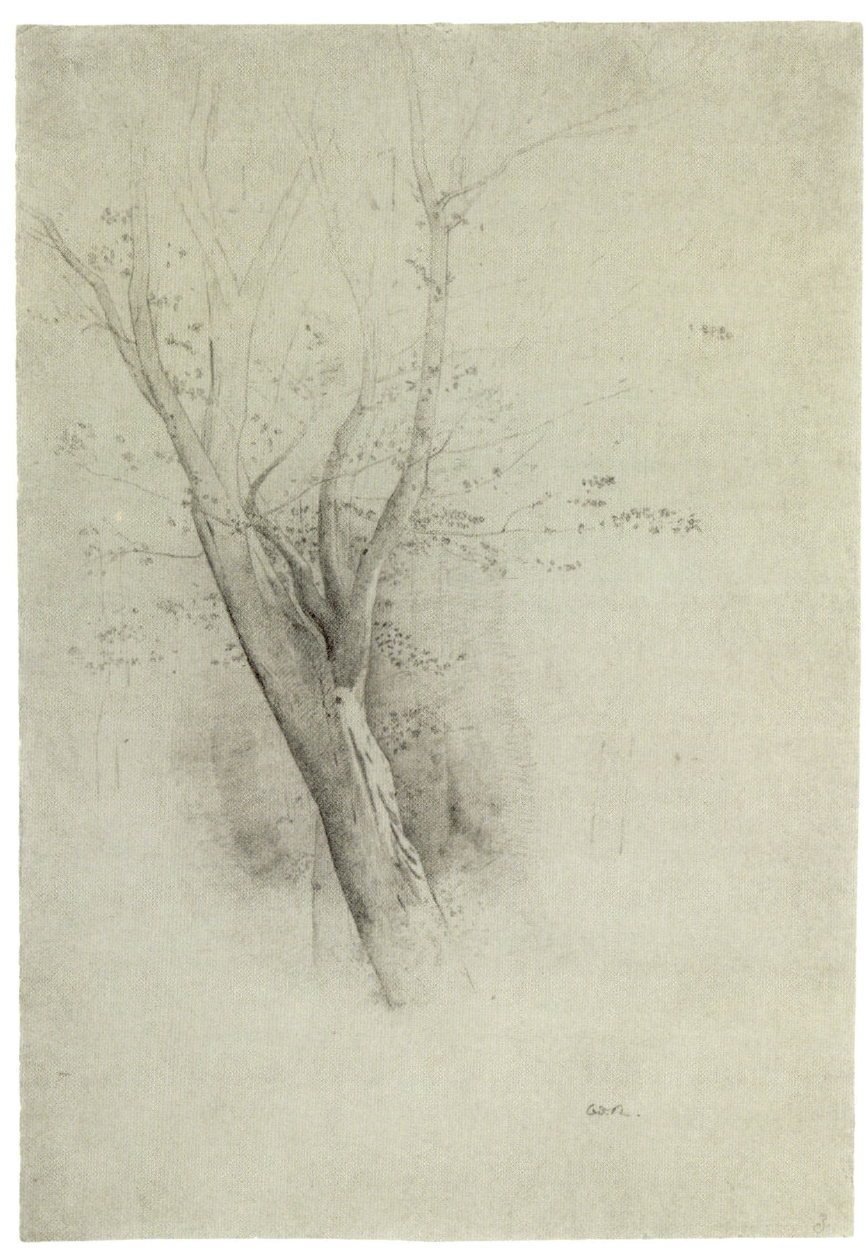

  Odilon Redon

Trees, 1865–68
Pencil on blue-green paper,
42.5 × 29.5 cm (16¾ × 11⅝ in.). Signed.
MUSEUM OF MODERN ART, NEW YORK

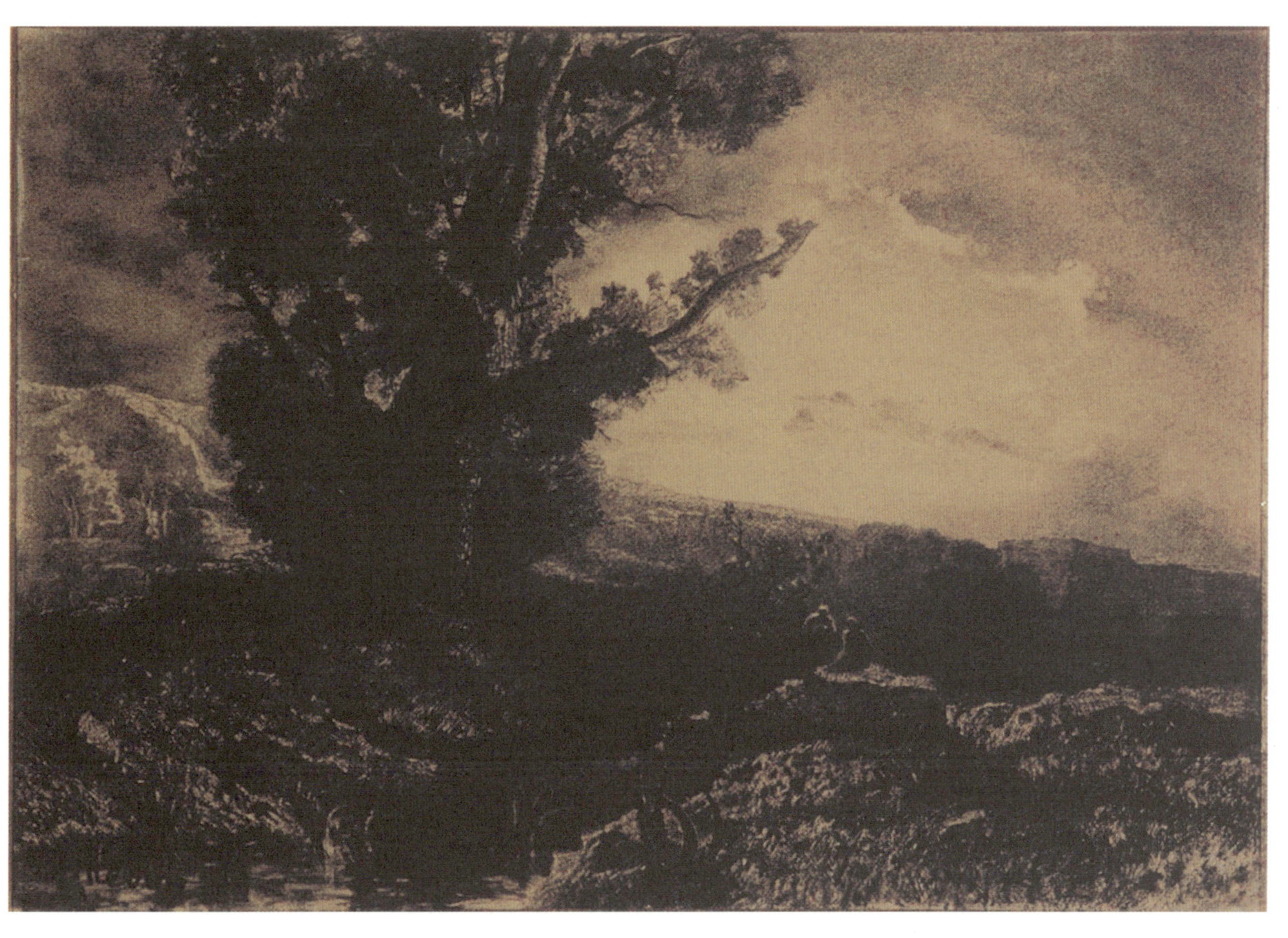

Landscape, 1868
Various charcoals, black chalk and conté crayon,
53.6 × 75.5 cm (21⅛ × 29¾ in.). Signed and dated.
THE ART INSTITUTE OF CHICAGO

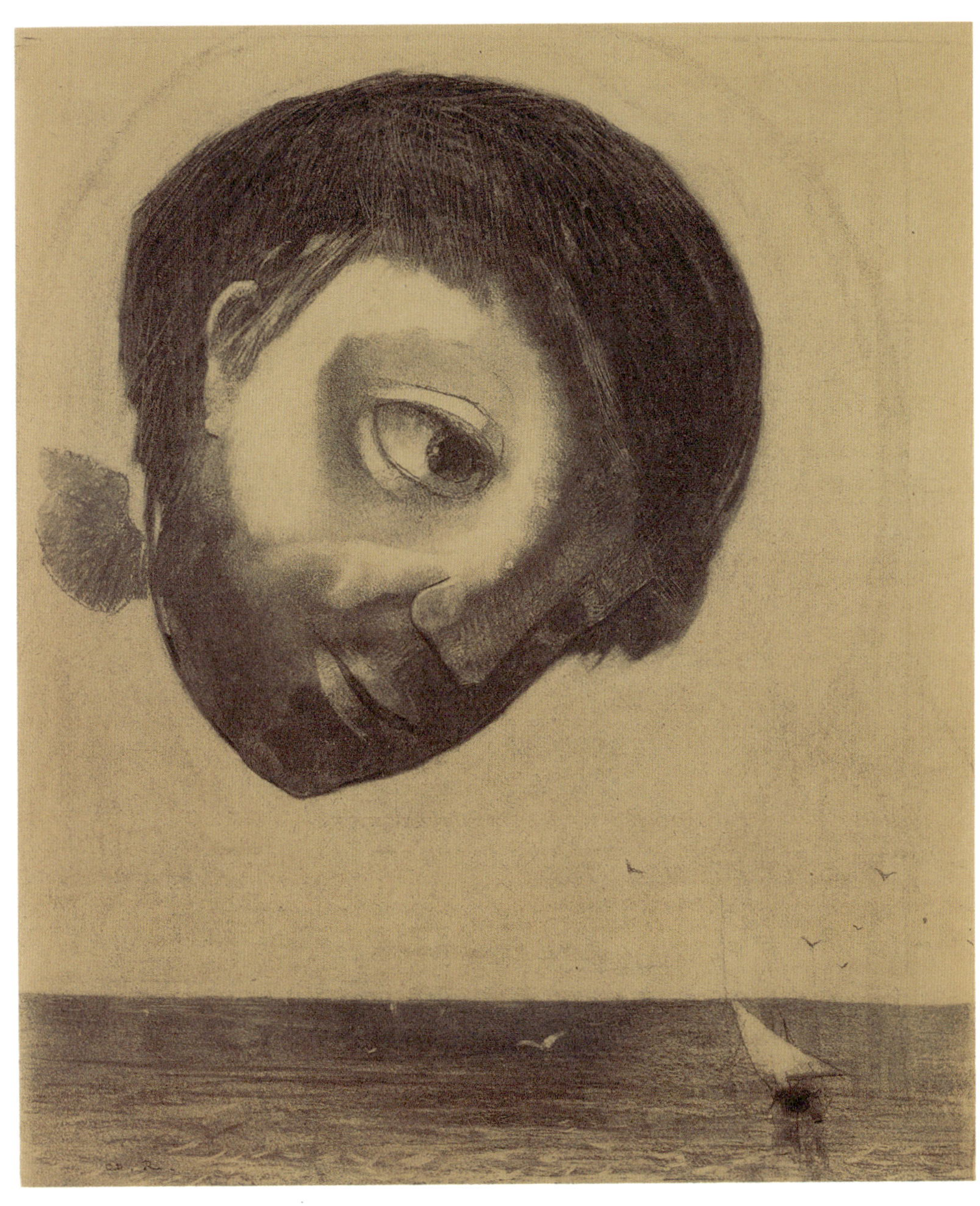

116 *Odilon Redon*

Guardian Spirit of the Waters, 1878
Various charcoals with touches of black chalk,
46.6 × 37.6 cm (18⅜ × 14¾ in.). Signed.
THE ART INSTITUTE OF CHICAGO

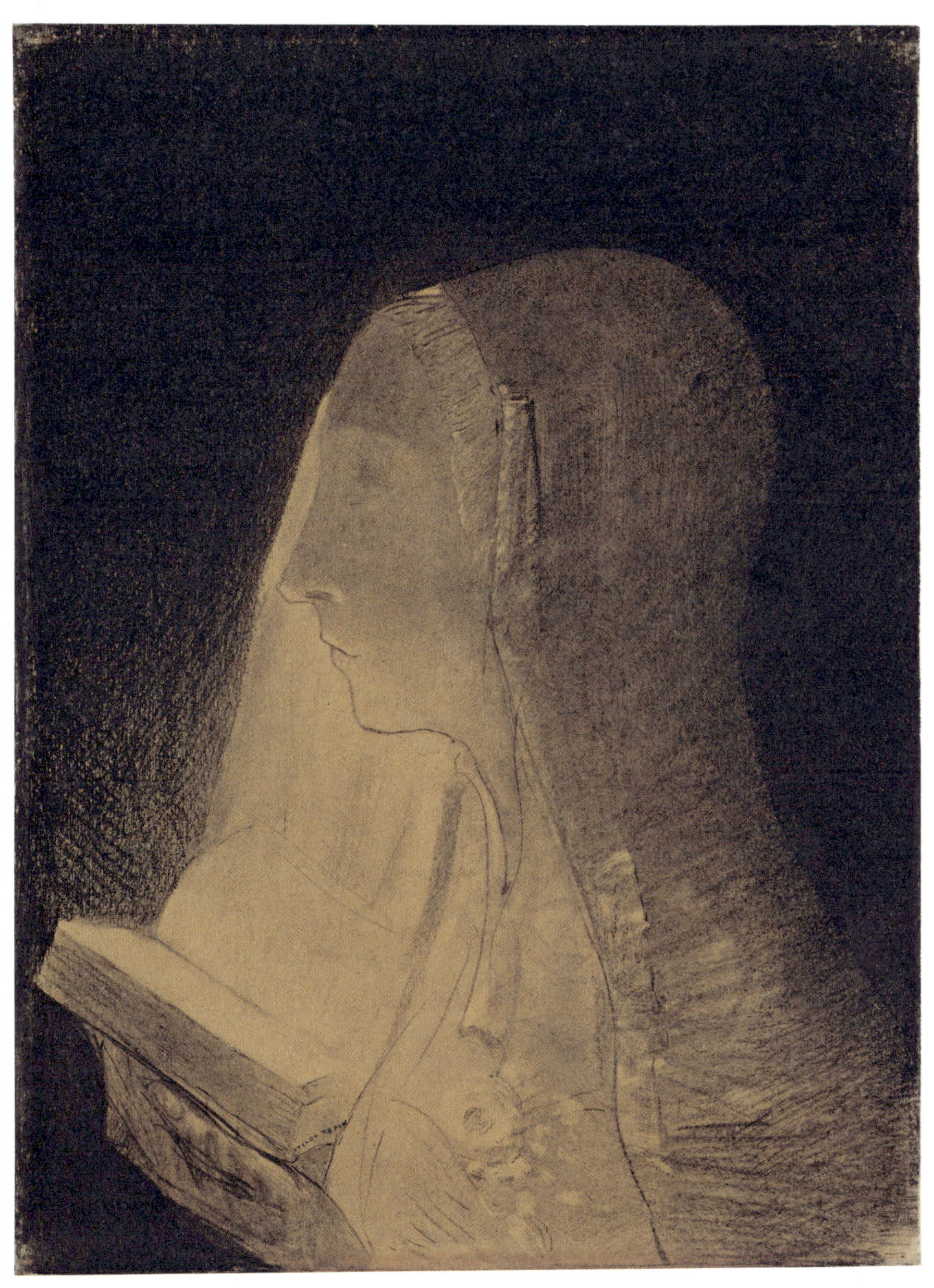

The Book of Light, 1893
Charcoal on tan paper, 52.2 × 37.5 cm
(20½ × 14¾ in.). Signed.
NATIONAL GALLERY OF ART, WASHINGTON, DC

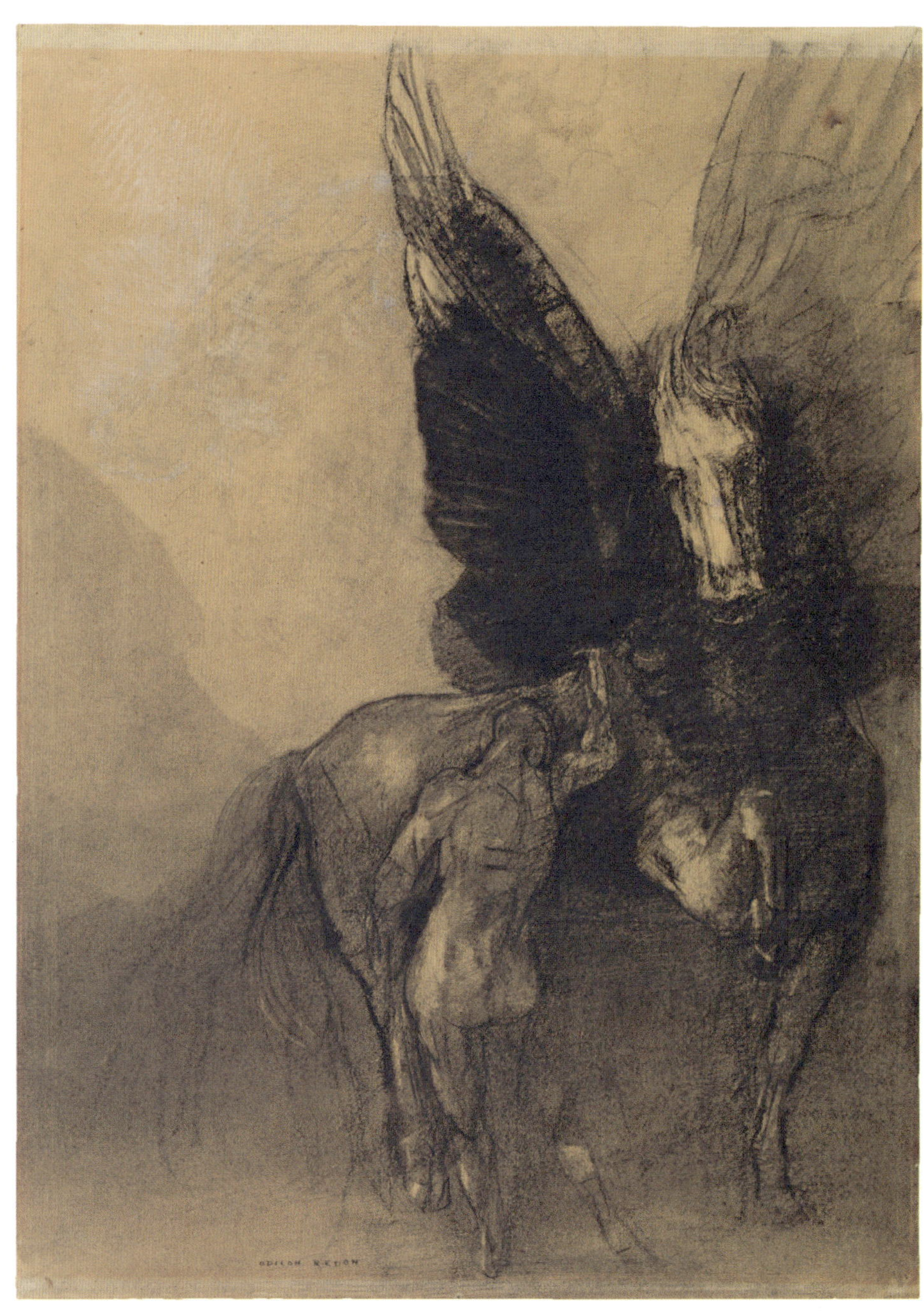

118   *Odilon Redon*

Pegasus and Bellerophon, c. 1888
Charcoal, white chalk and conté crayon,
53.7 × 36.1 cm (21⅛ × 14¼ in.). Signed.
METROPOLITAN MUSEUM OF ART, NEW YORK

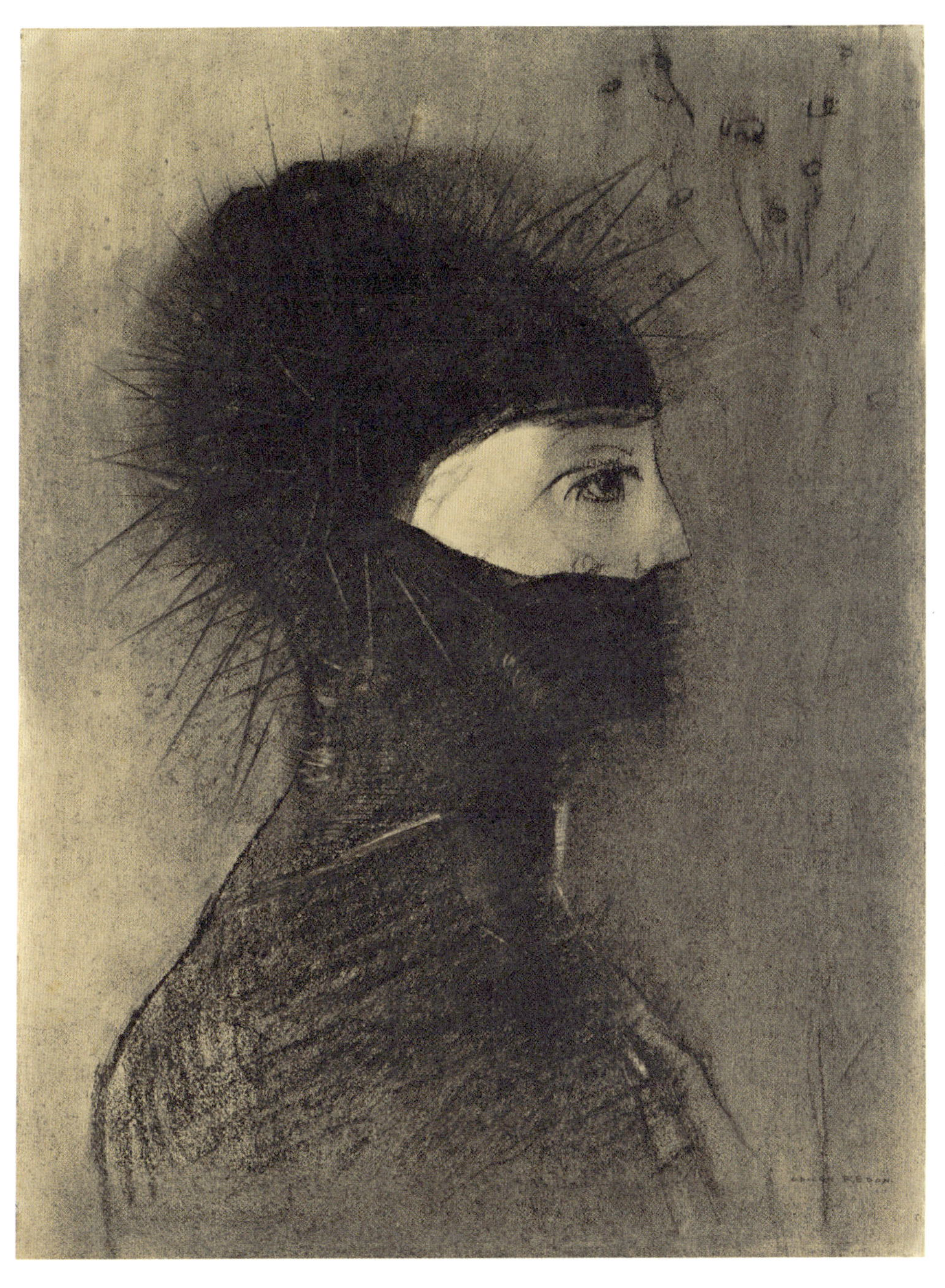

Armour, 1891
Charcoal and conté crayon,
50.7 × 36.8 cm (20 × 14½ in.). Signed.
METROPOLITAN MUSEUM OF ART, NEW YORK

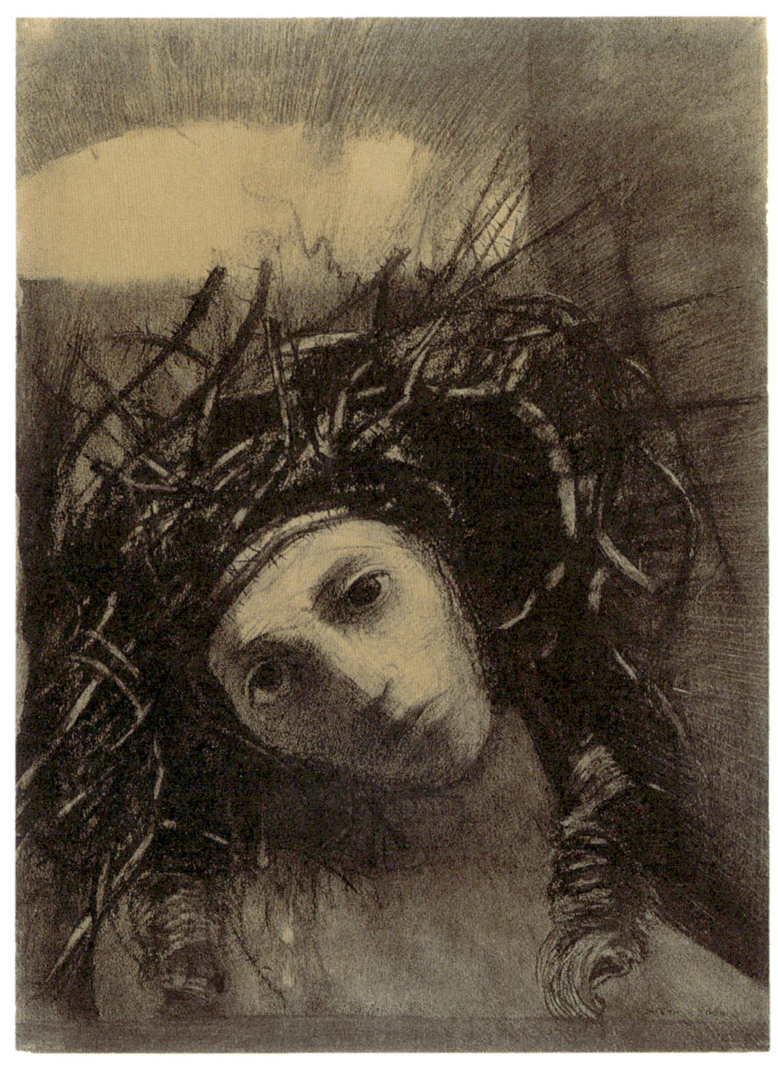

120   *Odilon Redon*

Christ Crowned with Thorns, 1895
Charcoal, black pastel and black crayon, stumping,
erasing, and incising on tan wove paper toned gold,
52.2 × 37.9 cm (20½ × 14⅞ in.). Signed.
BRITISH MUSEUM, LONDON

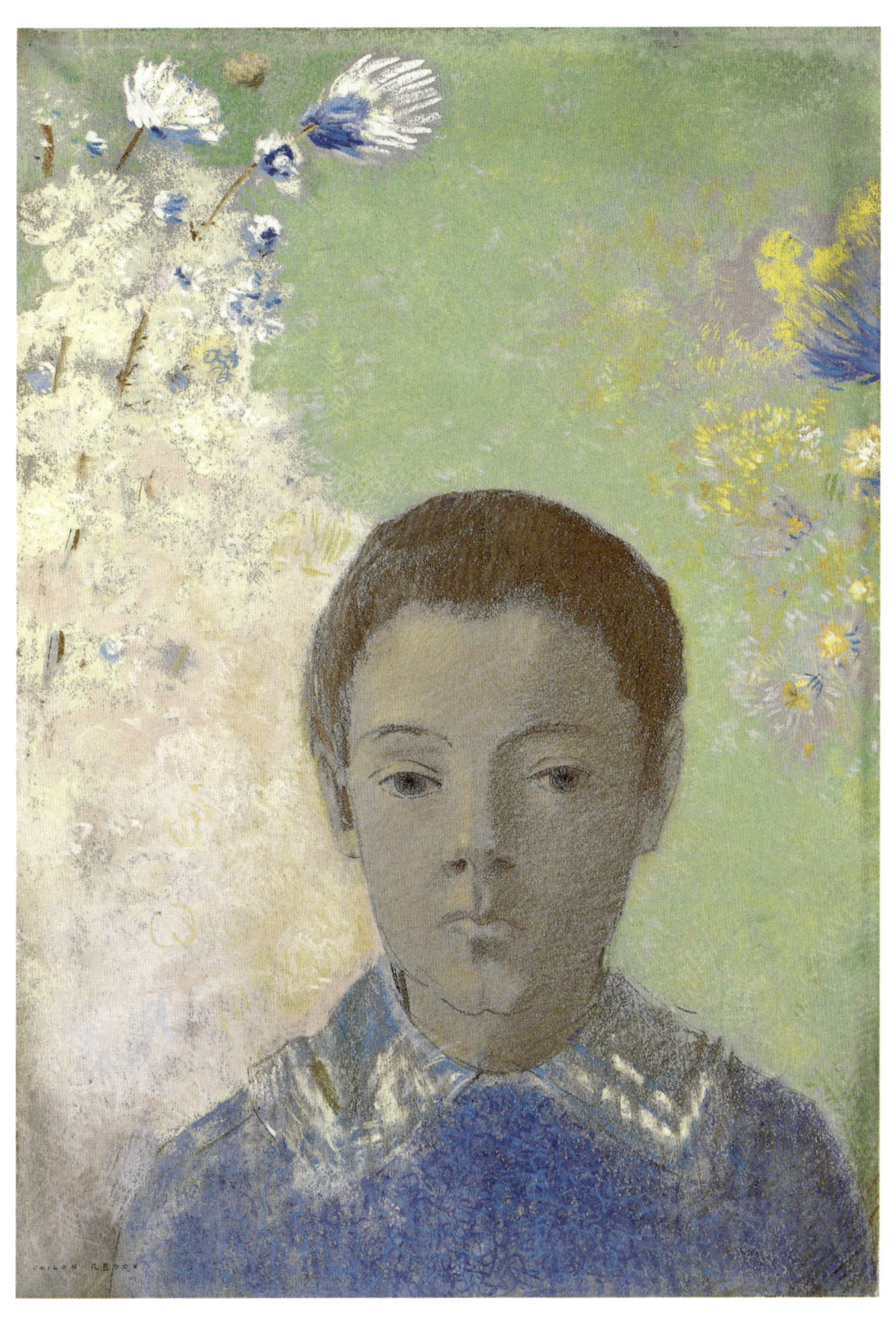

Portrait of Ari Redon, c. 1898
Pastel on pale blue paper, 44.8 × 30.8 cm
(17⅝ × 12⅛ in.). Signed.
THE ART INSTITUTE OF CHICAGO

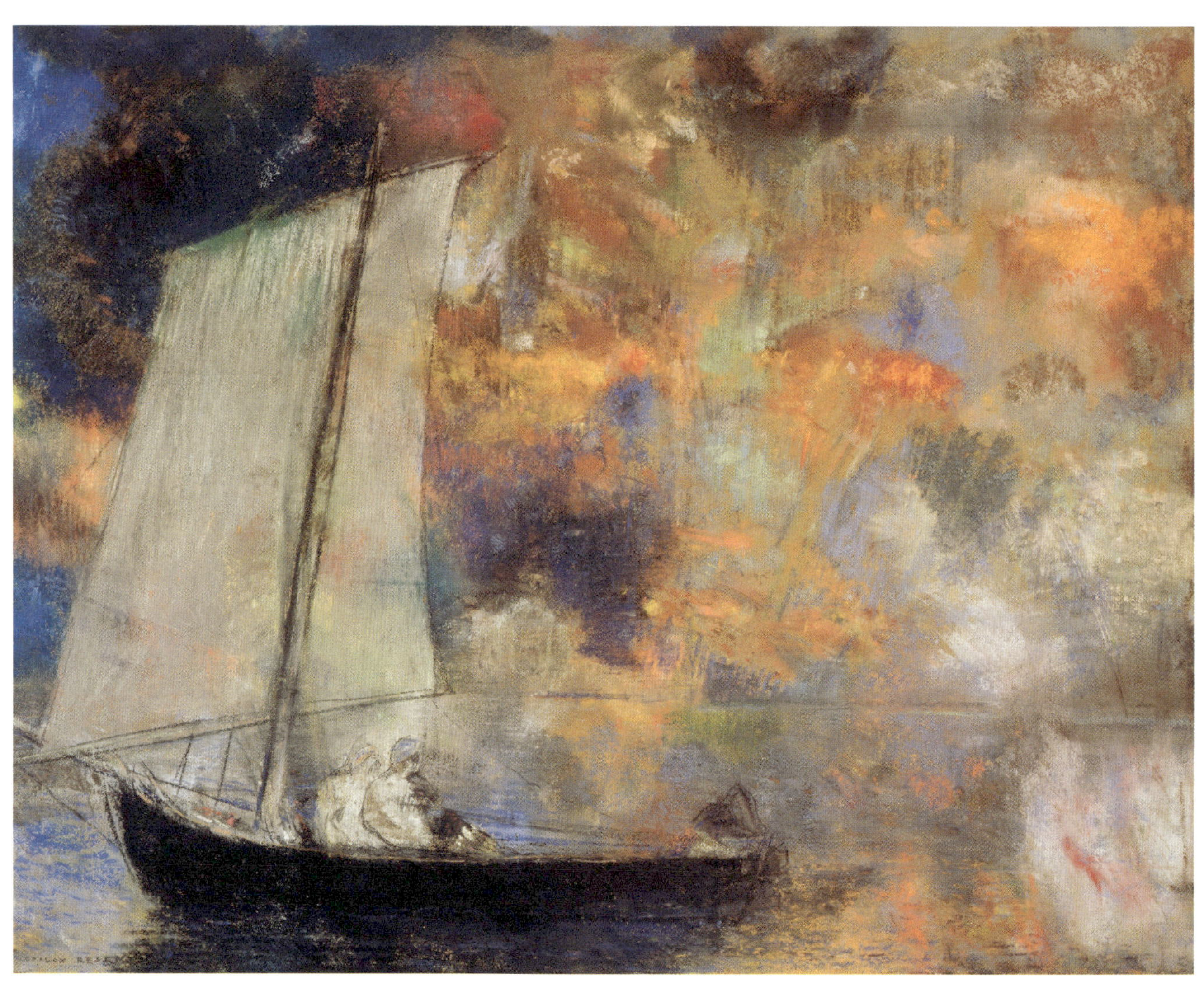

122   *Odilon Redon*

Flower Clouds, c. 1903
Pastel with brushwork on blue-grey paper mounted
on cardboard, 44.5 × 54.2 cm (17 ½ × 21 ⅜ in.). Signed.
THE ART INSTITUTE OF CHICAGO

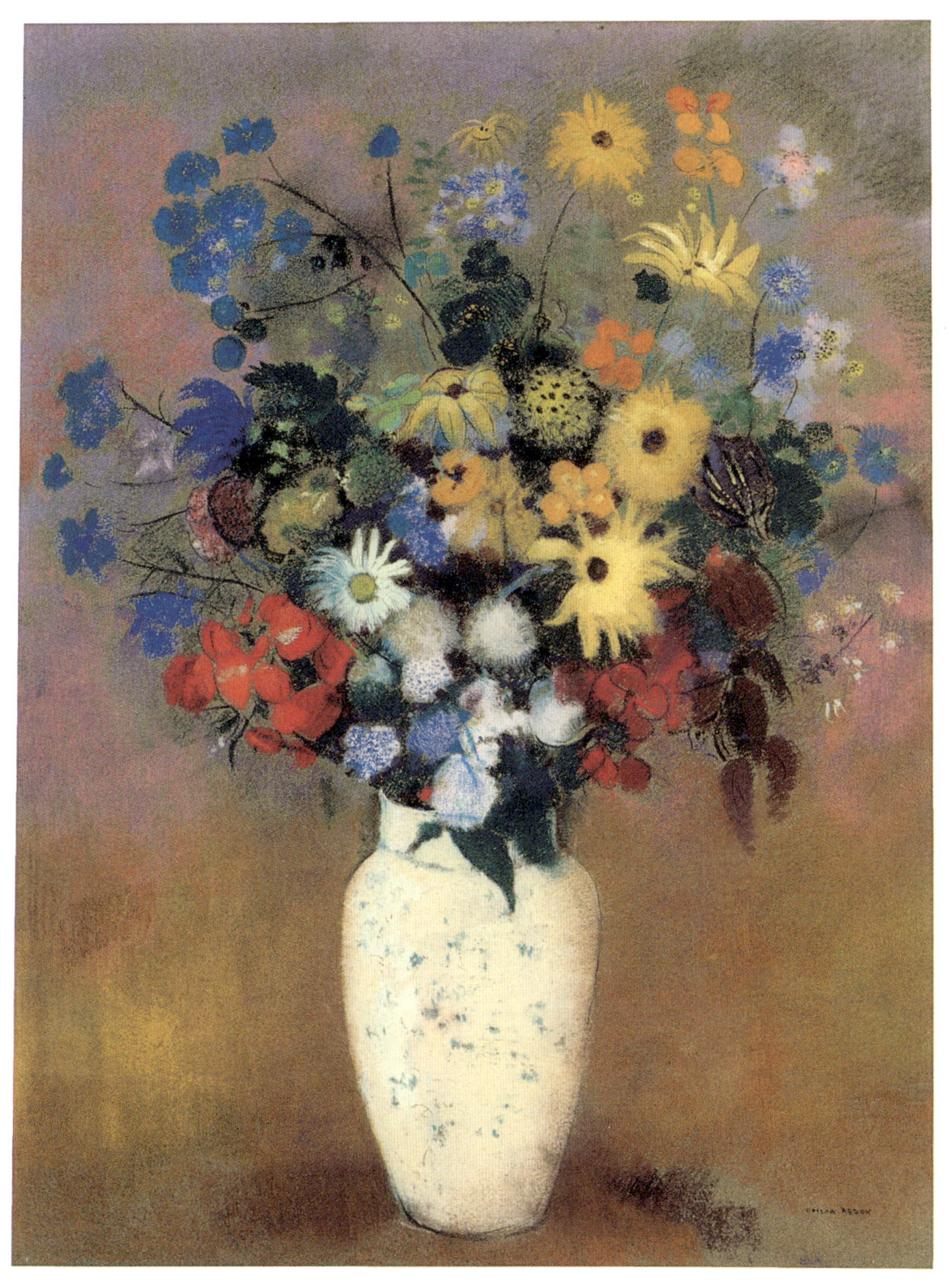

Vase of Flowers, c. 1912–14
Pastel and pencil on coloured paper,
73 × 53.7 cm (28¾ × 21⅛ in.). Signed.
MUSEUM OF MODERN ART, NEW YORK

123

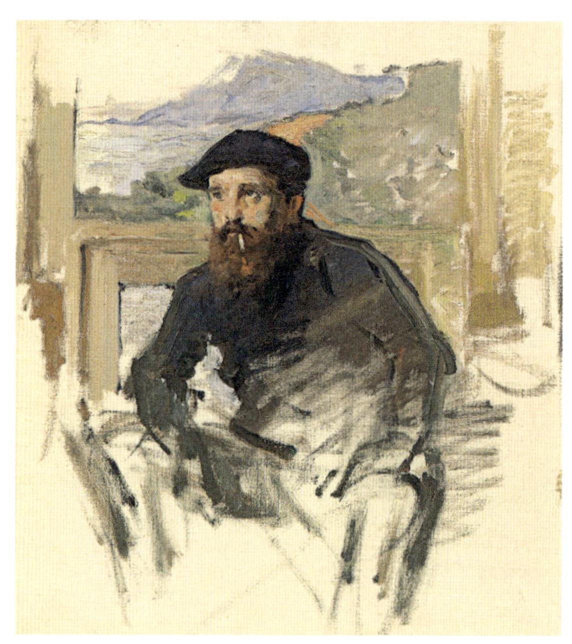

Claude Monet
1840–1926

For many years it was thought that Claude Monet had little or no interest in drawings and did not even regard them as part of his working practices. Paintings by Renoir (*Monet Painting in his Garden at Argenteuil*, 1873, Wadsworth Atheneum, Hartford) and Manet (*Monet in his Studio Boat*, 1874, Bayerische Staatsgemäldesammlungen, Munich) are among several works that were thought to represent the ideal conditions under which the artist liked to paint. This involved him in the direct observation of nature before painting spontaneously onto the canvas, seemingly without any intermediary stages. Such widely recognized visual evidence does in fact extend to the very end of Monet's long life and should not, or indeed cannot, be contradicted. Nonetheless, other factors now need to be taken into account.

A considered reassessment of Monet's drawings shows that he was by no means an intermittent or irregular draughtsman. Sketchbooks and independent drawings dating from all stages of his life reveal that Monet's approach to the art of drawing was

Claude Monet
Self-Portrait in his Atelier, 1884
Oil on canvas, 85 × 55 cm (33½ × 21⅝ in.).
MUSÉE MARMOTTAN MONET, PARIS

instinctual. Furthermore, close analysis of this material shows that in many instances such drawings were made in connection with individual finished paintings or those done in series.

Monet began drawing at a young age, having been encouraged to do so from 1851 while at school in Le Havre, relying heavily on published drawing manuals to learn about the various types of media and techniques. Crucial at this stage was the presence of Boudin, who provided essential guidance and encouragement. It is Boudin's connections with artists of the Barbizon School, for instance, that inspired the young Monet to become a landscape painter. At first, though, in order to have an income, Monet exhibited and sold caricatures in Le Havre. Some of these were copied from *portraits-charges* by established caricaturists, but many were of Monet's own devising, such as that believed to be of the animal painter Jules Didier (p. 128). The most striking of these caricatures are on a large scale and are signed *O. Monet* (his full Christian names being Oscar-Claude). The humour derives from the exaggerated size of the heads in relation to the rest of the body, which in a political context gave the image an extra edge. Monet made over fifty of these caricatures.

During the 1860s Monet's development was dictated by the contacts he made in Paris, to which he gravitated in 1859 determined to pursue a career in art. Attendance at the Académie Suisse in 1860 was followed after military service by a year (1862–63) in the studio of the Swiss history painter Charles Gleyre, where he worked alongside Renoir, Ludovic-Napoléon Lepic, Sisley and Frédéric Bazille. Of these artists Monet was closest at this moment to Bazille, who was from Montpellier but who was killed in 1870 during the Franco-Prussian War. In such company, during the early 1860s Monet's skills as a landscape draughtsman improved noticeably. Inspired by the views presented by the coastline around Le Havre and motivated by the examples of Boudin and Johan Barthold Jongkind, he proved himself to be adept in the use of black chalk and pastel. *Sunset at Sea* (p. 129 above) compares favourably with Boudin's pastels and foreshadows Degas's seascapes of 1869, whereas the monochromatic *Cliffs and Sea, Sainte-Adresse* (p. 129 below), which is dominated by the strongly silhouetted cliff top on the left and the different types of vessel on the right, heralds the masterly sea views undertaken at Sainte-Adresse in 1867. What is evident in both the paintings and the drawings of the 1860s, particularly in the placing of the strong horizontals created by the horizons and the awareness of recession, is the speed with which Monet matures. There is an impressive confidence in technique and economy of means, exuding a surprisingly strong inner conviction.

Except on very few occasions, this self-assurance, both personal and technical, would remain with Monet for the rest of his life. The pastel *Etretat, The Needle Rock and Porte d'Aval*, made *c.* 1885 (p. 134), however, does reveal a more private side to Monet. The subject is the dramatic outcrop close to Fécamp to the north of Le Havre, which here is seen vertiginously from the cliff-top. The penumbrous tones demonstrate Monet's sophisticated appreciation for the range of pastel. Yet, although he did make many paintings of this famous landmark over the years, often showing it in sparkling sunshine, there is by contrast in this pastel a feeling of desolation. The motif lacks any sign of human activity and the time of day is not clear.

At the same time as he was exploring the possibilities of the various techniques of drawing, Monet was advancing his compositional procedures, which at the outset, after his training in Gleyre's studio, were traditional. During the mid-1860s Monet's purpose was to achieve success at the Salon, but, inspired by Manet, his preference for modern subject matter matched by an appropriately advanced style of painting meant that his submissions were often rejected. *Luncheon on the Grass* is a massive work developed in 1865–66, but never fully realized. Only two large fragments survive (both in the Musée d'Orsay, Paris), but the planned composition is known through a preparatory drawing (p. 130) and an oil study (Pushkin State Museum, Moscow). The setting is Chailly in the Forest of Fontainebleau and the drawing was clearly made at an early stage, since considerable changes are recorded in the oil study. Bazille and Monet's mistress, Camille Doncieux, posed as models, and a study of the latter alone shows a blending of line and tone, which emphasizes the folds of the elegantly embroidered day dress, reflecting the artist's familiarity with illustrations found in fashion magazines (p. 131).

From the beginning of the 1870s, however, Monet departed from conventional preparatory methods and began to rely more on ideas recorded in his sketchbooks. Apart from three early sketchbooks dating from the 1850s, the eight surviving ones in the Musée Marmottan Monet in Paris are relevant for the second and more expansive part of Monet's career. There is nothing consistent in the deployment of these eight sketchbooks: the dates vary within each one, the orientation and grouping of the drawings on the pages are random and there is little stylistic unity. Some accumulate a surprising amount of detail given the available space (p. 132), while others are so stenographic as to be difficult to interpret (p. 135 below). The fact is that the content of the sketchbooks represents Monet's eye at work instantaneously recording motifs, either compositionally as a whole or in part, as he prospects for subjects to paint. They were not made for presentation or sale, but retained for reference in connection with possible future use, as evidenced by the framing lines sometimes implied by the edges of the paper or peremptorily drawn on the page. The overall style is notational, just as the main preoccupation is with the juxtaposition of forms as opposed to light or colour, which Monet preferred to resolve as he worked on the canvas itself. By no means all the drawings made in the sketchbooks were developed further and so, in addition to stylistic considerations, they add to the general context of Monet's art.

At the other extreme are those relatively few finished drawings Monet made specifically for the reproduction of his paintings in art journals. This was a way of promoting his work, but it was also a technical challenge to translate the effects of an original painting purely in black and white. In previous centuries this was a task performed by specialists and so for Monet it was a demanding exercise. He had to exercise his drawing skills on textured paper resembling scraper board (known as Gillot), which could be drawn on directly and also scratched to produce highlights. *View of Rouen* (p. 133) is based on a painting of 1872 (Private collection) chosen for exhibition at Paul Durand-Ruel's gallery in 1883. A few changes of emphasis between the painting and the drawing are discernible, but on the whole Monet succeeds in replicating the silvery and violet tones of the original, as well as the numerous reflections in the water. The drawing was duly made into a print to illustrate a review of the exhibition in *Gazette des Beaux-Arts* written by Alfred de Lostalot.

Wherever he went, or whenever he undertook protracted visits, Monet made an extensive investigation of his surroundings. He acted like a surveyor, or a mining engineer, examining topographical landmarks and natural features with equal intensity. The viewer today sees places in proximity to Paris such as Argenteuil, Vétheuil or Giverny through Monet's eyes and encounters important landmarks in more distant places such as Rouen, London or Venice recorded with the same degree of commitment. Similarly, Monet concentrated on features of the landscape – the cliffs of the coast of Normandy, haystacks in fields or rows of poplar trees – possibly intending such imagery to represent the regeneration of France after the disaster of the Franco-Prussian War. There had always been a tendency in Monet's work to create in series, as in the pictures of the Gare Saint-Lazare in Paris, but the subjection of so many motifs to such close scrutiny over a period of time and in changing light enabled him to develop and sustain this practice while working at the height of his powers. When exhibited, each of these series made a considerable impact, and they are important for the development of modern painting.

One such opportunity arose in London in January 1901 while on his third visit of long duration to the city. When his painting materials were delayed by customs Monet had to resort to using pastels (p. 135 above). Overlooking the river Thames from his room in the Savoy Hotel, he returned to the motifs that he had singled out on his two earlier visits: the view upstream towards Charing Cross Bridge and in the opposite direction the view downstream to Waterloo Bridge. The twenty-six pastels resulting from this short burst of activity make an interesting comparison with the paintings of the same subjects. The softer medium enhances the alchemical effects produced by the commingling of air and water. Solid forms are clearly defined one minute and shrouded the next. Behind Charing Cross Bridge Monet depicts smoking chimneys, which no doubt helped to create the fogs and miasma that blighted London at the turn of the century. But, for Emile Zola, the fogs on the Thames created a *'pays de rêve'*, and no doubt Monet, too, as a painter, like James Abbott McNeill Whistler, relished the spectral beauties that so often lay before them.

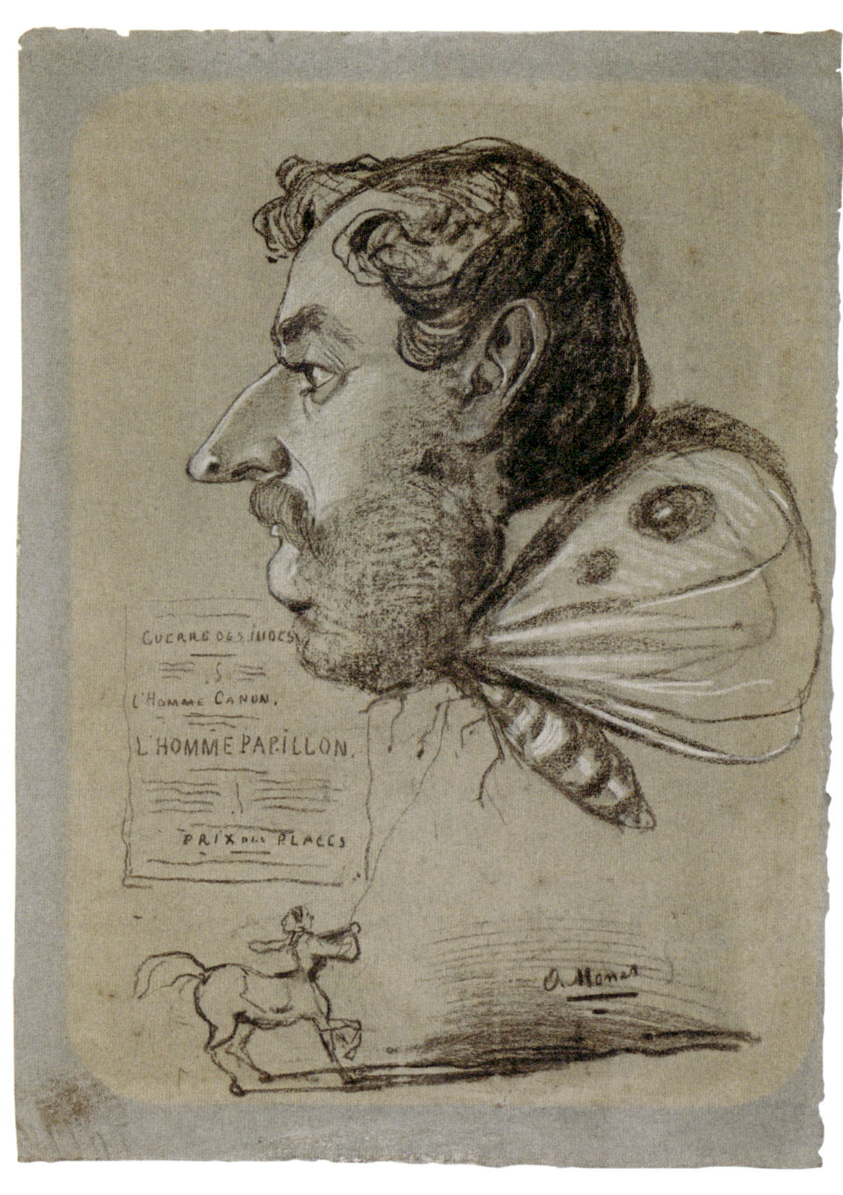

128 *Claude Monet*

Caricature of Jules Didier, c. 1858
Charcoal heightened with white chalk on blue paper
(discoloured to light brown), 61.6 × 43.6 cm
(24¼ × 17⅛ in.). Signed.
THE ART INSTITUTE OF CHICAGO

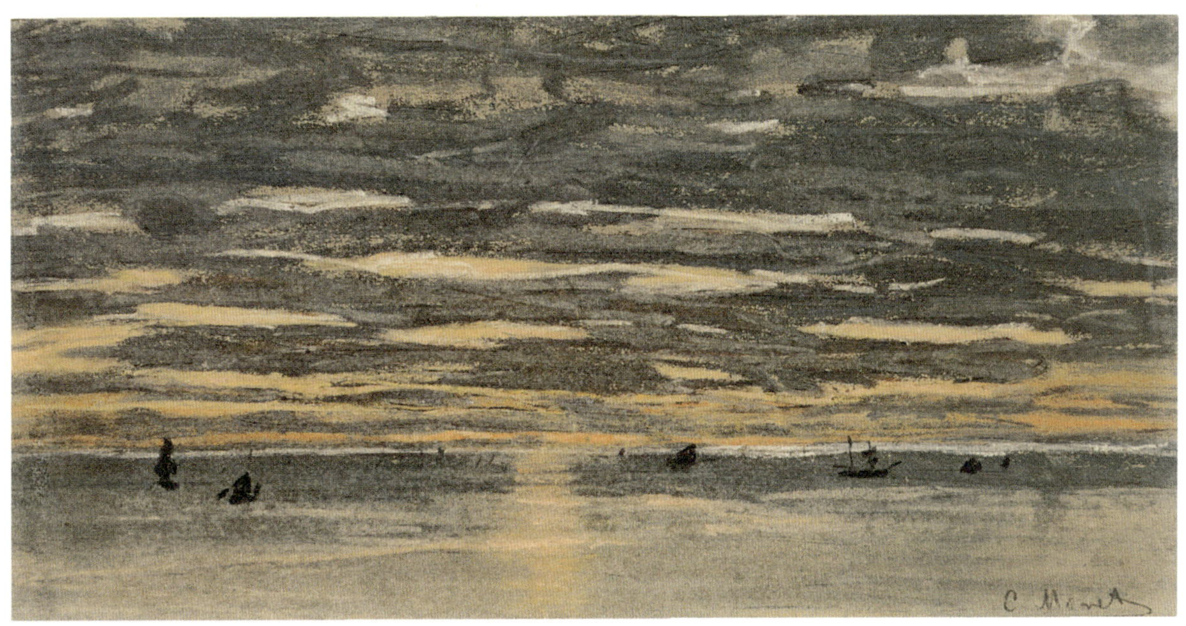

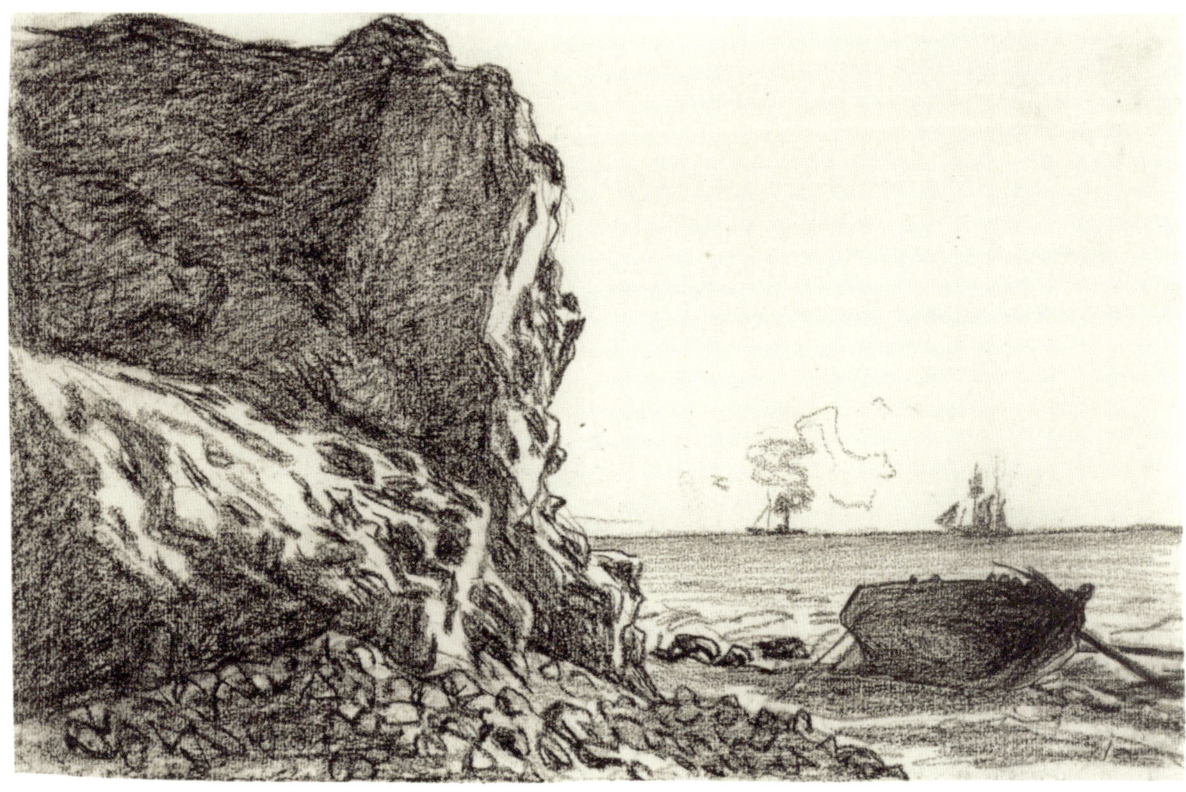

<table>
<tr>
<td>

Sunset at Sea, c. 1862–64
Pastel and gouache on buff-coloured paper,
17.3 × 33 cm (6¾ × 13 in.). Signed.
ASHMOLEAN MUSEUM, OXFORD

</td>
<td>

Cliffs and Sea, Sainte-Adresse, c. 1864
Black chalk on off-white paper,
20.6 × 31.4 cm (8⅛ × 12⅜ in.).
THE ART INSTITUTE OF CHICAGO

</td>
<td>

129

</td>
</tr>
</table>

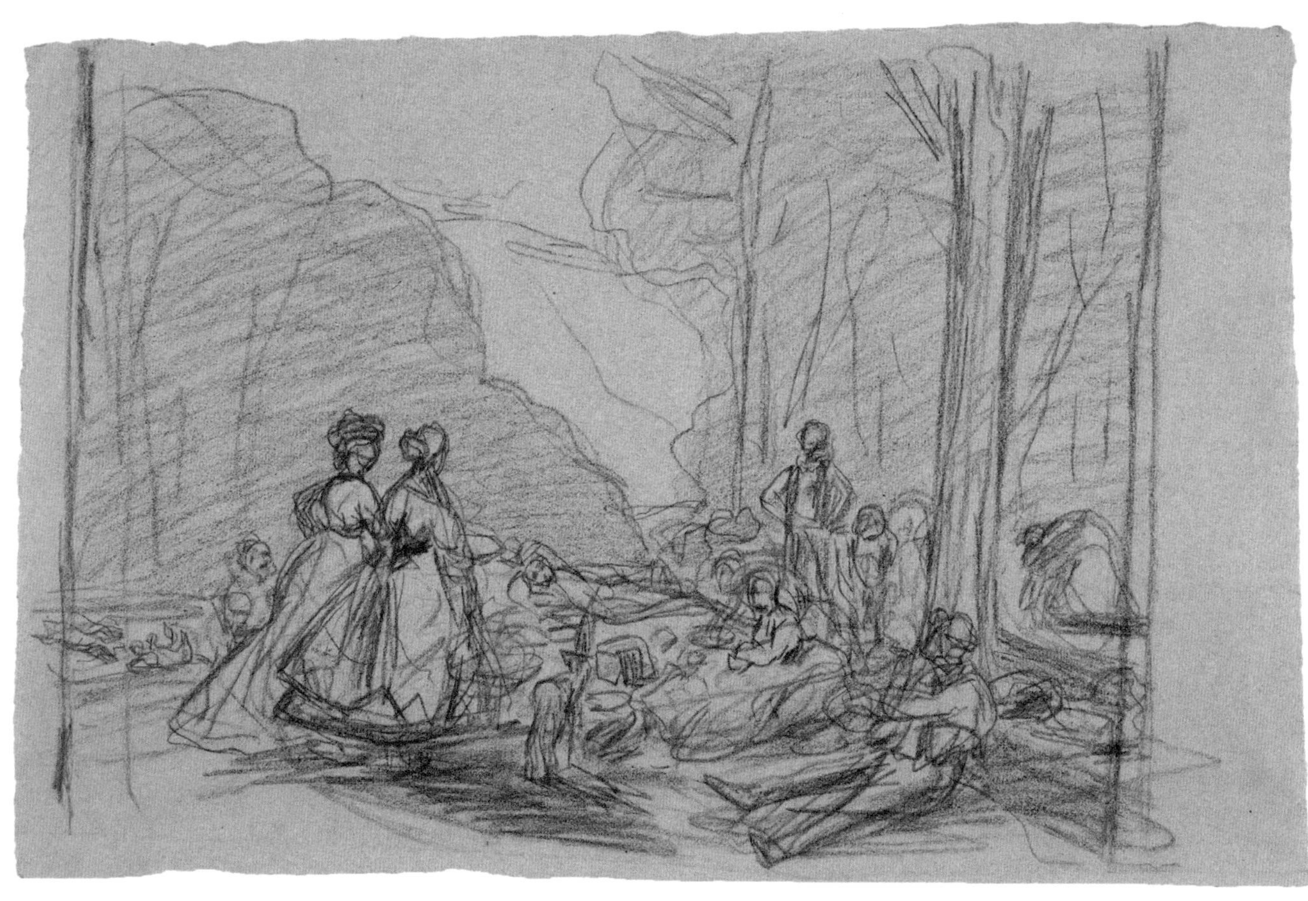

130　　*Claude Monet*

Luncheon on the Grass, c. 1865
Black chalk on blue paper, 30.5 × 46.8 cm (12 × 18⅜ in.).
NATIONAL GALLERY OF ART, WASHINGTON, DC

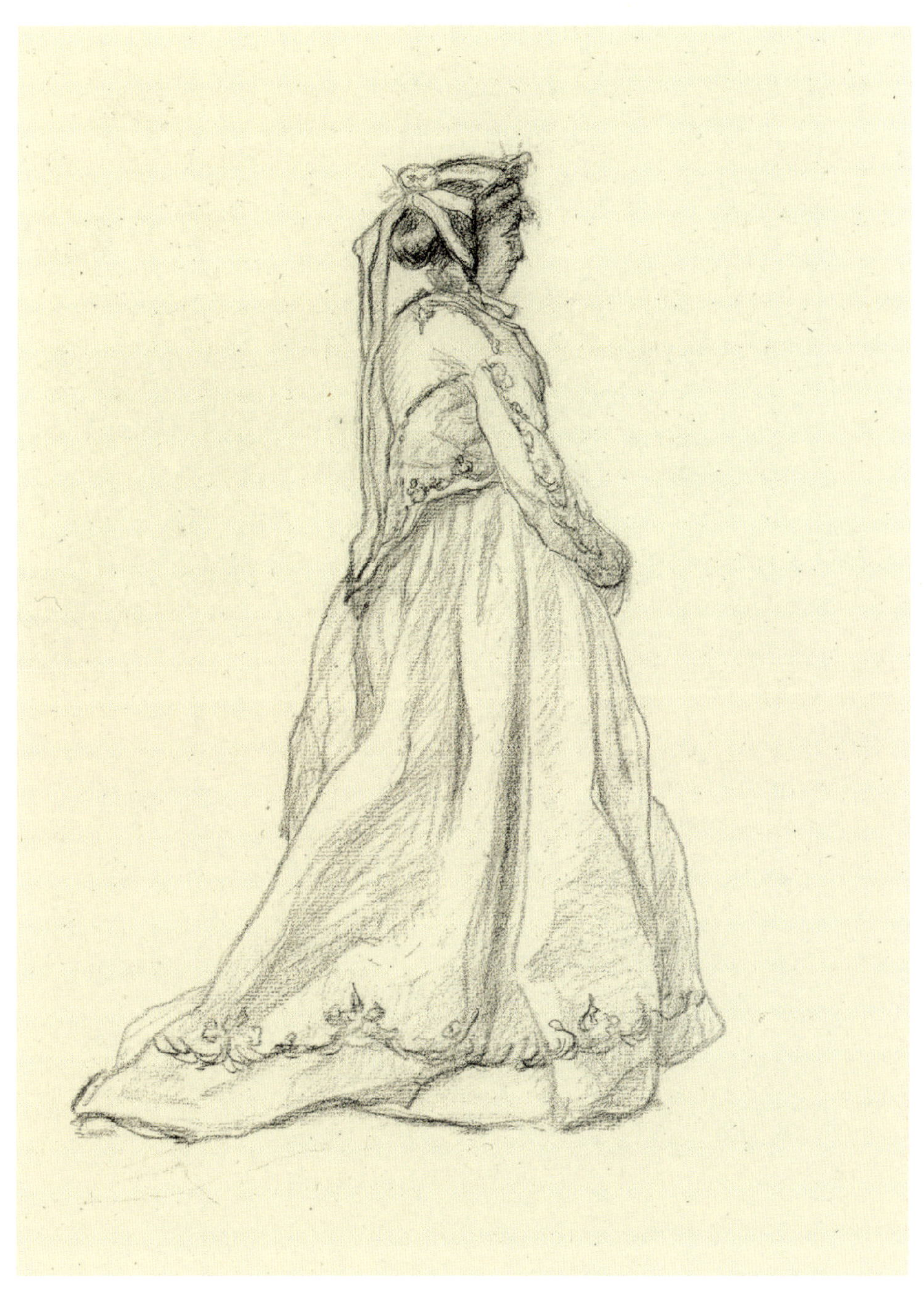

Figure of a Woman (Camille Doncieux), c. 1865
Black chalk, 47.2 × 31.5 cm (18⅝ × 12⅜ in.).
PRIVATE COLLECTION

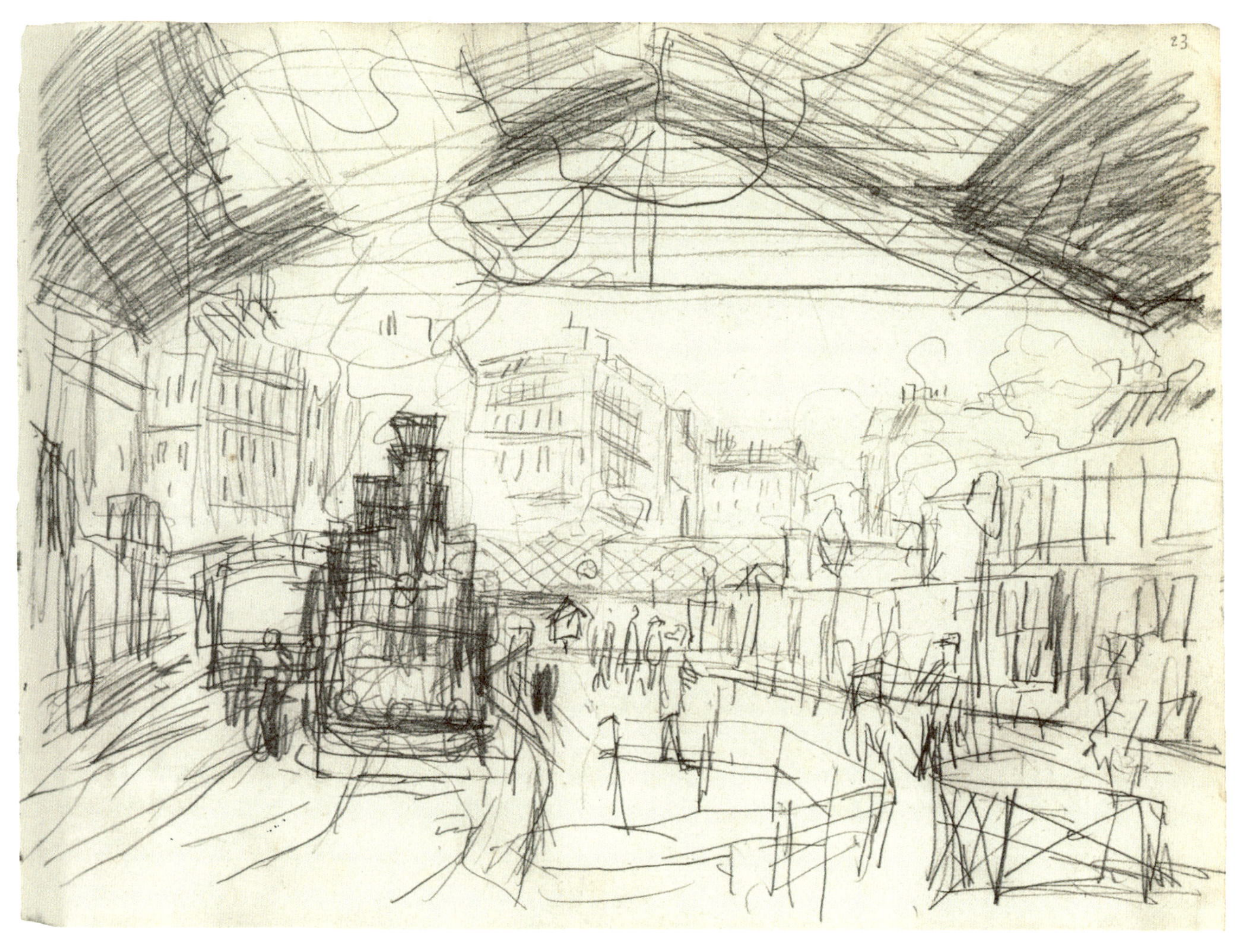

132 *Claude Monet*

The Gare Saint-Lazare (Suburban Lines), 1877
Pencil, 25.5 × 34 cm (10 × 13⅜ in.). Sketchbook 1, fol. 23v.
MUSÉE MARMOTTAN MONET, PARIS

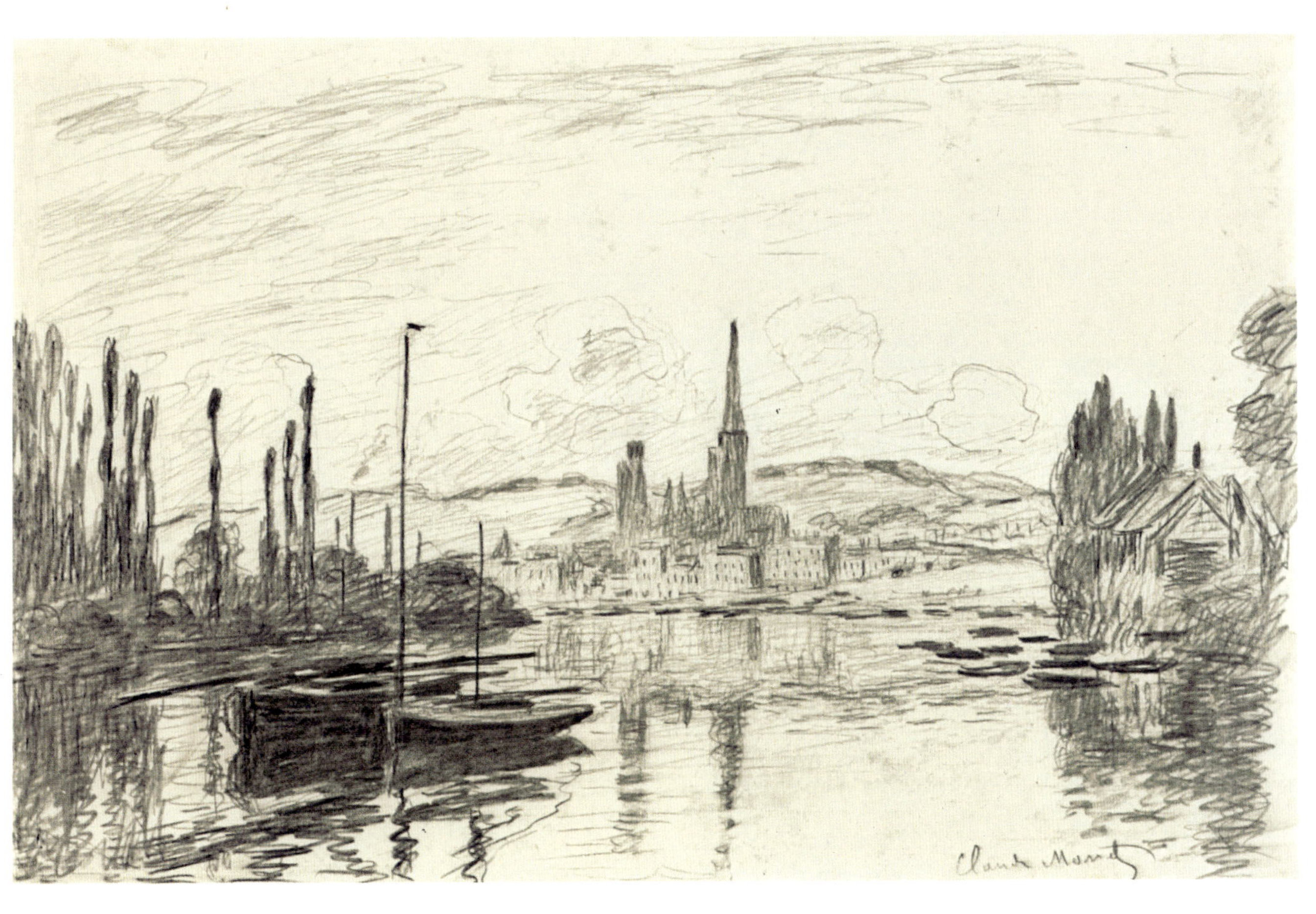

View of Rouen, 1883
Black crayon and scratchwork on Gillot paper,
31.2 × 47.5 cm (12⅜ × 18¾ in.). Signed.

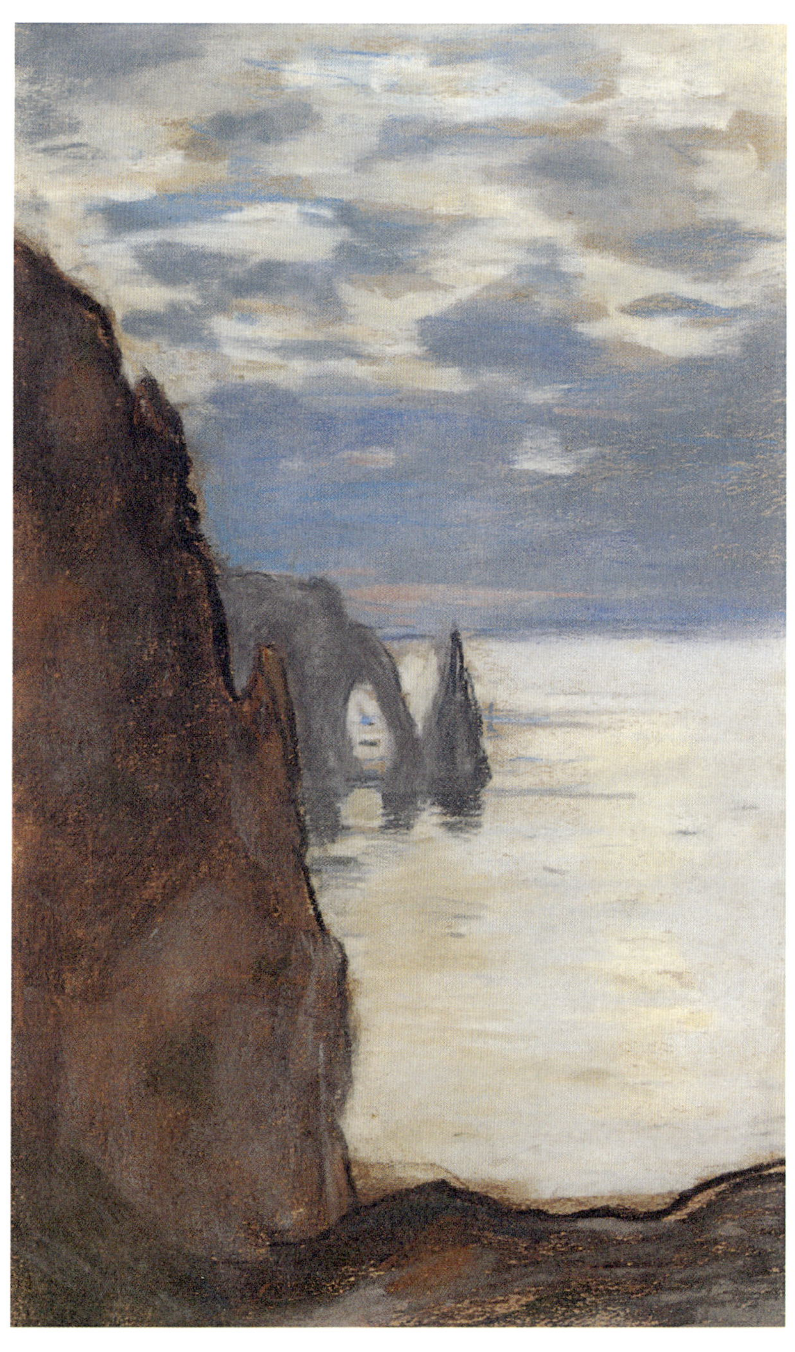

134   *Claude Monet*

Etretat, the Needle Rock and Porte d'Aval, the Cap d'Antifer
(Cliffs at Etretat), c. 1885
Pastel, 39 × 23 cm (15⅜ × 9 in.).
SCOTTISH NATIONAL GALLERY OF MODERN ART, EDINBURGH

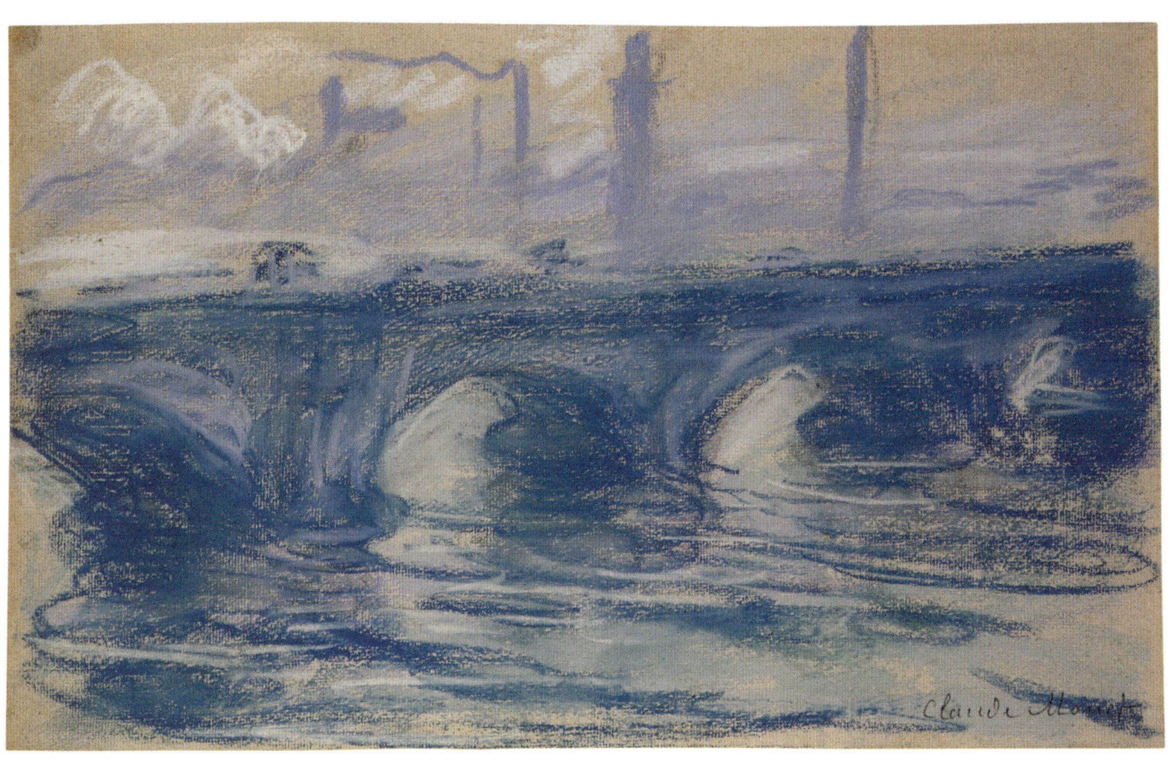

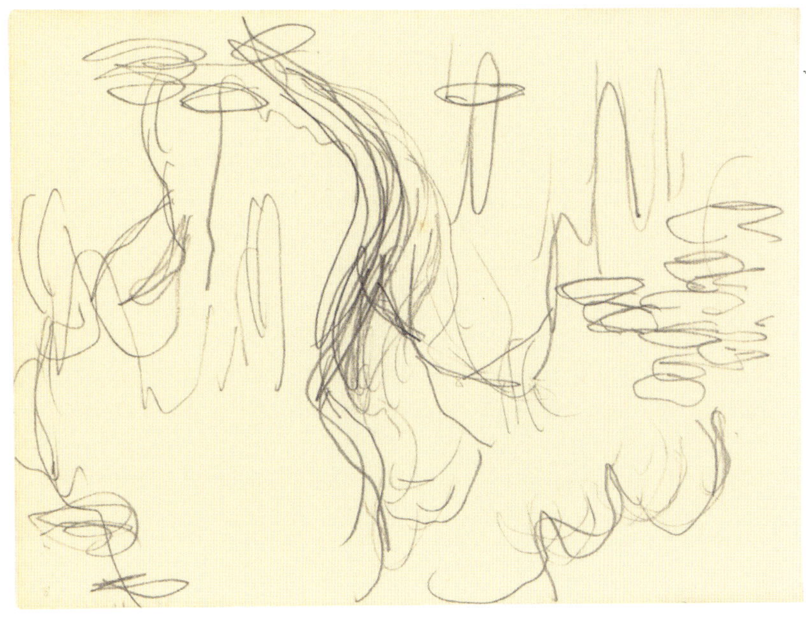

Waterloo Bridge, London, 1901
Pastel on beige paper, 31.3 × 48.5 cm
(12⅜ × 19⅛ in.). Signed.
MUSÉE D'ORSAY, PARIS

Water Lilies, c. 1914–19
Pencil, 23.5 × 31.5 cm (9¼ × 12⅜ in.).
Sketchbook 6, fol. 8v.
MUSÉE MARMOTTAN MONET, PARIS

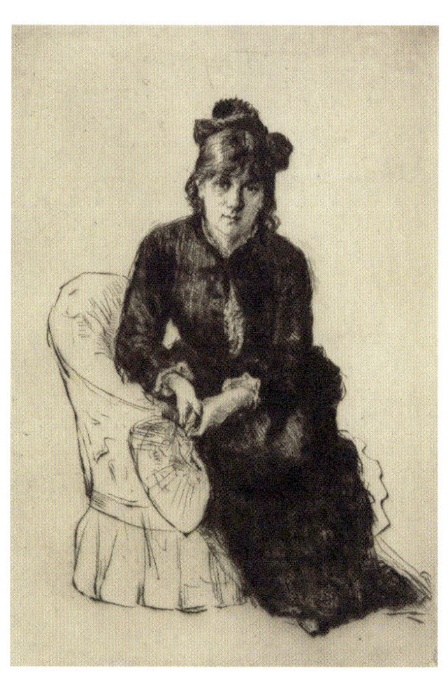

Berthe Morisot
1841–1895

The death of Berthe Morisot from complications arising from influenza in March 1895 aged fifty-four deprived Impressionism of one of its leading exponents. She was much mourned. As Pissarro wrote to his eldest son, Lucien, 'You can hardly conceive how surprised we all were and how moved, too, by the disappearance of this distinguished woman, who had such a splendid feminine talent and brought honour to our Impressionist group which is vanishing – like all things. Poor Mme Morisot, the public hardly knows her'. A year later a comprehensive memorial exhibition of paintings (174), pastels (54), watercolours (69), drawings (67) and sculptures (3) was held at Paul Durand-Ruel's gallery in Paris. This was organized and hung (not without disagreements) by Degas, Renoir, Monet and the poet Stéphane Mallarmé, all of whom greatly admired Morisot's work. The artist had been represented liberally in seven of the eight Impressionist exhibitions held between 1874 and 1886, only absenting herself from the seventh in 1879 owing to the birth the previous year of her daughter, Julie, which had prevented her from preparing enough items to display.

Marcellin Desboutin
Berthe Morisot, 1876
Drypoint, 26 × 17.5 cm (10¼ × 6⅞ in.).
BIBLIOTHÈQUE NATIONALE DE FRANCE, PARIS

It was, however, not only Morisot's role as an artist that resulted in her playing such a central role in Impressionism. She participated in the discussions about the selection of artists and their works, as well as helping with the financing of the exhibitions. Her personal circumstances were also advantageous; having posed for Manet on numerous occasions during the late 1860s and early 1870s, she married the artist's brother, Eugène, in 1874. Their weekly soirées, which were attended by artists and writers, proved to be one of the focal points in Paris for the discussion of avant-garde ideas. A flavour of such events survives in Morisot's correspondence and notebooks, as well as in her daughter's diary entries (published in book form with the title *Growing Up with the Impressionists*). The very personal nature of much of this primary evidence was carried forward into the next generation when Julie, having been cared for by her guardian Mallarmé, married Ernest Rouart, the son of Henri, a friend of Degas, who exhibited several times with the Impressionists. The occasion was in fact a double wedding, since Julie's cousin, Jeannie Gobillard, with whom she had lived after her mother's death, married the poet Paul Valéry at the same ceremony in 1900.

Morisot was fortunate in having been born into a wealthy family keen to promote the arts. Her father, a senior civil servant, encouraged his three daughters in particular (there was one son) to become artists and to this end erected a studio for them in his garden. From 1857 Morisot was given private lessons by Joseph Guichard, a former pupil of Jean-Auguste-Dominique Ingres, before being befriended by Jean-Baptiste-Camille Corot, who passed her on to one of his own students, Achille Oudinot. Through these connections Morisot was introduced to many other artists: Pierre Puvis de Chavannes, Honoré Daumier, Charles-François Daubigny, Henri Fantin-Latour and Alfred Stevens. Morisot's early proficiency as an artist was such that her works were accepted regularly at the Salon between 1863 and 1874, when she became more closely associated with the Impressionists. Her elder sisters, Yves and Edma, who were also talented, had in the meantime chosen not to pursue careers as artists. Yves was married to Théodore Gobillard in 1866 and Edma to Adolphe Pontillon in 1869.

Morisot was very much a Parisian. Her parents had moved to the capital in 1852 and lived in the prosperous and still quite rural *arrondissement* of Passy on the west side of the city, close to the Bois de Boulogne, but with good transport connections with the centre. This is the area where, after she married, Morisot herself settled and remained for the rest of her life, living in considerable style. Two of her finest early Impressionist paintings incorporate panoramic views of Paris, as if attesting to her affiliation: *View of Paris Seen from the Trocadéro* of 1871–72 (Santa Barbara Museum of Art) and *On the Balcony* of 1872 (Private collection). A detailed preparatory study for *On the Balcony* (p. 140) shows Yves Gobillard with her daughter, Paule, looking out from what is probably the balcony of the Morisot family home in Passy across the river Seine towards the dome of Les Invalides on the Left Bank. The artist, however, did not restrict herself to urban scenes; at various stages during her career, she painted landscapes and sea-scapes in the suburbs of Paris and further west along the banks of the river Seine, as well as travelling to Normandy, Brittany, the Channel Islands, the Isle of Wight and the south of France, often continuing to work while on vacation with members of her family. Travel abroad (Spain, Belgium, the Netherlands, Italy) was also undertaken until 1892 when her husband died.

Morisot was as committed to watercolours and pastels as to painting in oils. The most striking aspect of her output is indeed the stylistic unity she achieves in all three media, which is best characterized as sketchy owing to the thinness and speed of her application. The critics regarded her technique as having a lack of finish, but it is perhaps more fairly described as an economy of means. Paul Mantz, a reviewer of the third Impressionist exhibition (1877), referred to her as the 'only one Impressionist in the group' with 'an honest eye' and a 'skilled hand', adding, 'Never does Mademoiselle Morisot finish a painting, a pastel or a watercolour. It is as if she were composing prefaces to books she will never write.'

The remarkable fluidity and nimbleness of the brushwork in Morisot's watercolours are such that the image only just coheres in time before it slithers off the paper altogether. The loose brushstrokes in *Carriage in the Bois de Boulogne* (p. 141) are used to suggest the speed of the vehicle under the trees, while the greater restraint in *On the Clifftop* (p. 143) implies the loftier, more precipitous aspects of the location. Technical adjustments of this type also demonstrate Morisot's sophisticated approach to solving compositional issues through her choice of medium.

It is likely that Morisot was introduced to pastel by Léon Riesener, who was a cousin of Eugène Delacroix, and a family friend. Many of her pastels were made for exhibition. *Portrait of Madame Pontillon* (p. 142) – the artist's sister Edma – was included in the first Impressionist exhibition (1874). The pose could well have been inspired by early portraits by Degas, but the contrast between the monumentality of the figure shrouded in a black garment and the patterned fabrics dominating the light-filled space reveals why Morisot was so admired by her contemporaries. Similarly, in *Daydreaming* (p. 144), which was shown at the third Impressionist exhibition (1877), the figure is seen in a room lit *contre-jour* and so has an almost ethereal presence. The sitter has a languid air as she holds her fan and the mood is one of reverie or even melancholy, as is so often the case in Morisot's interiors with young women. The strength of such scenes, however, is their feeling of domestic intimacy, which the artist creates by the use of familiar furnishings and by bringing considerable psychological insight into bourgeois family existence in late nineteenth-century France.

Like Renoir, around 1880 Morisot began to concern herself with the problem of how to develop the Impressionist style and produce compositions that appeared to be less ephemeral. This involved her in refining her style by re-examining works by old masters such as Peter Paul Rubens and François Boucher, among others. The preparation of her pictures became more elaborate and greater prominence was given to the human figure in the compositions. The subject matter itself was less concerned with realism or the contemporary and inclined more towards the decorative or symbolic.

This process is underway, for example, in the pastel *Paule Gobillard Drawing* (p. 145 above), which was shown at the eighth Impressionist exhibition (1886) and could almost be interpreted as an allegory. It may have been made in connection with the picture *Paule Gobillard Painting* of 1886–87 (Musée Marmottan Monet, Paris). The toddler by her mother's side in *On the Balcony* (p. 140) is now shown at work sketching, presumably copying, in a room with a nude female statuette on a pedestal. The vibrancy of Morisot's strokes with the pastel echoes the movements of her niece's own hand, while the silhouetting of the figure dominating the foreground emphasizes the confidence that the artist herself now places in her treatment of the human form. This continues to be the case in the studies for *Before the Mirror* of 1891 (Private collection), which emulates the colour print entitled *The Coiffure* by Mary Cassatt of the same date.

Another theme that links Morisot and her friend Cassatt at this time is fruit-picking. Morisot, for example, painted *Picking Oranges* in 1889 (Private collection) and *The Cherry Tree* in 1891 (Collection of Bruce and Robbi Toll). These pictures were preceded by studies of figures working amid the branches of trees (p. 145 below), which are notable for their lyricism in spite of the difficulty of having to fit the figure in between the tracery of the branches. It is as well to remember that the central panel of Cassatt's mural *Modern Woman*, decorating the Woman's Building at the World's Columbian Exposition held in Chicago in 1893, was a fruit-picking scene. The subject, therefore, had a certain symbolic significance, as well as providing an arcadian context. Settings of this type appealed to artists with Symbolist tendencies, such as Puvis de Chavannes and the young Nabis painter Maurice Denis, who strove to find antidotes to the naturalist themes pursued earlier in the century. In this way, Morisot contributed to both Impressionism and Post-Impressionism.

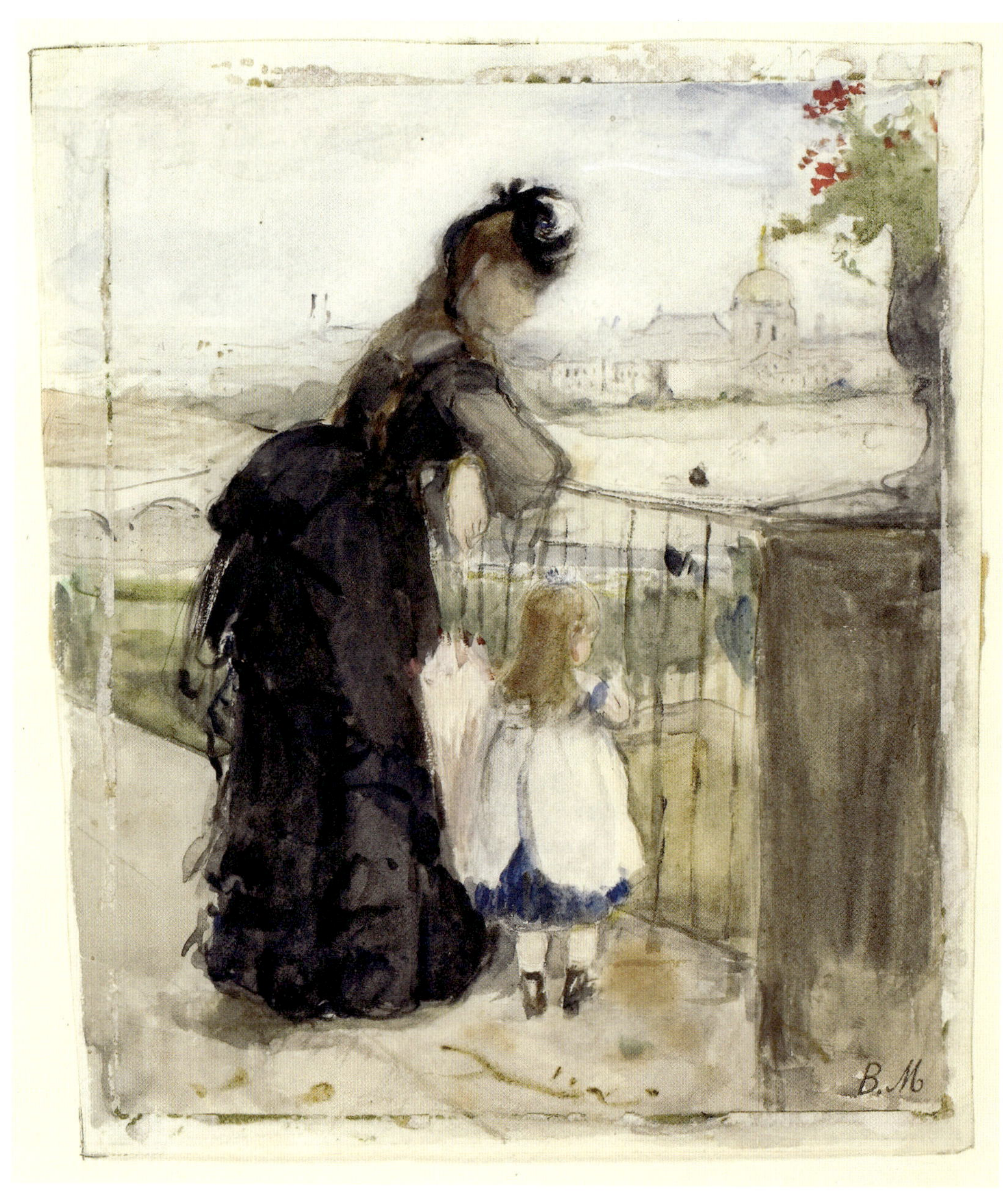

140   *Berthe Morisot*

On the Balcony, 1871–72
Watercolour with touches of gouache over pencil on off-white
paper, 20.6 × 17.3 cm (8⅛ × 6¾ in.). Artist's stamp.
THE ART INSTITUTE OF CHICAGO

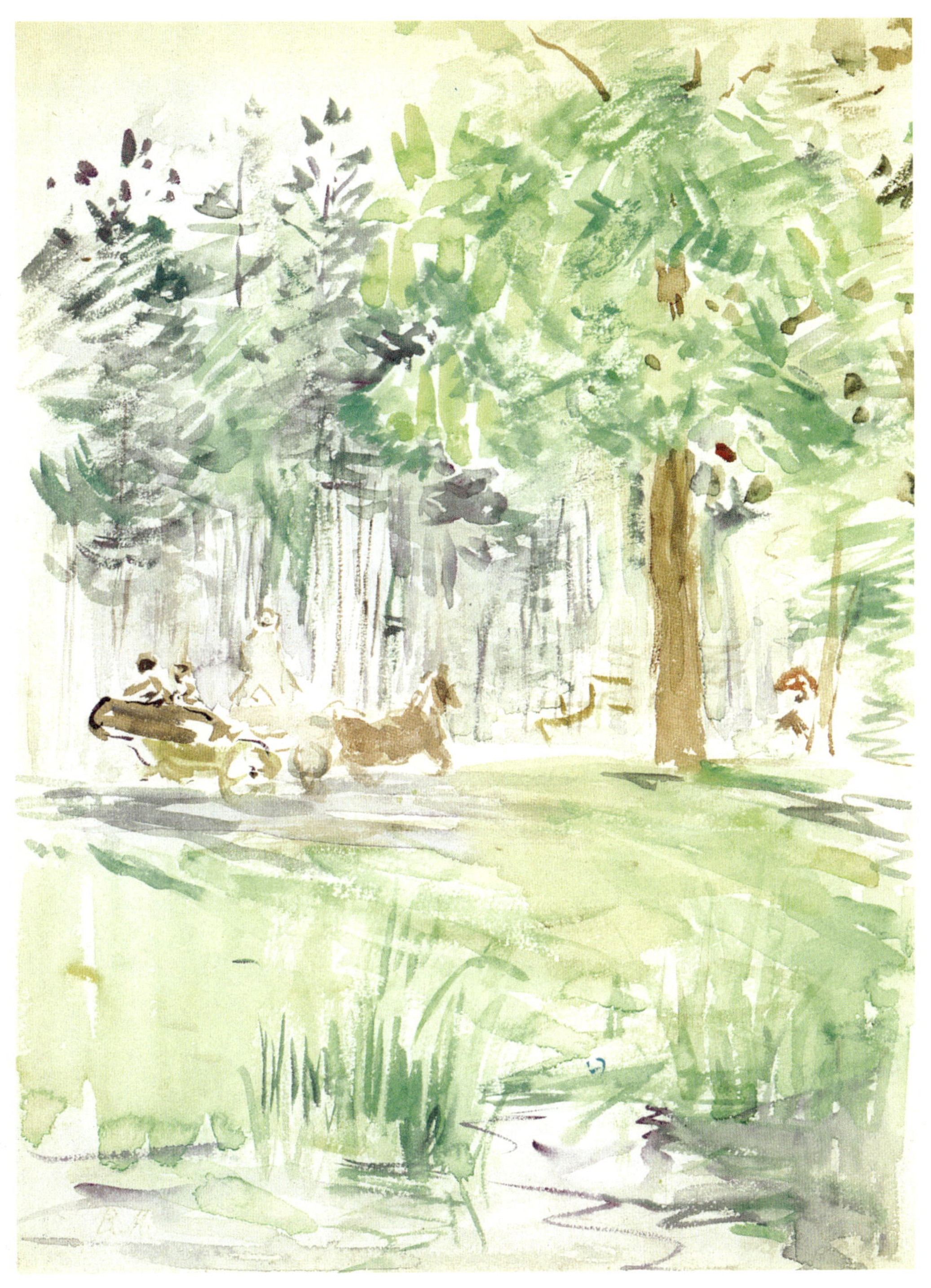

Carriage in the Bois de Boulogne, c. 1874 or later
Watercolour, 28.4 × 20.4 cm (11¼ × 8 in.).
Inscribed with title on verso with artist's stamp.
ASHMOLEAN MUSEUM, OXFORD

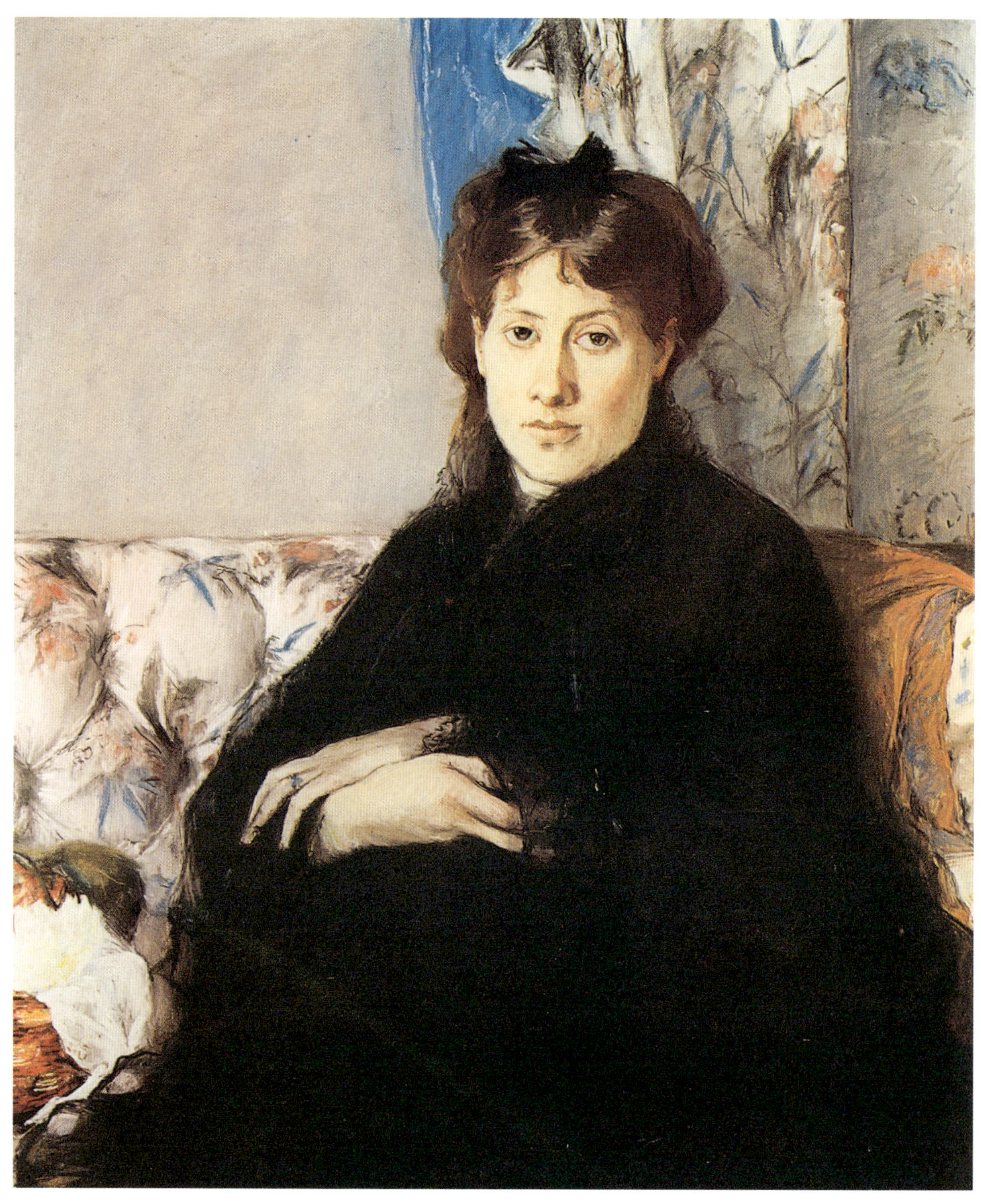

Berthe Morisot

Portrait of Madame Pontillon, 1871
Pastel, 80 × 64.5 cm (31½ × 25⅜ in.).
MUSÉE DU LOUVRE (COLLECTION MUSÉE D'ORSAY), PARIS

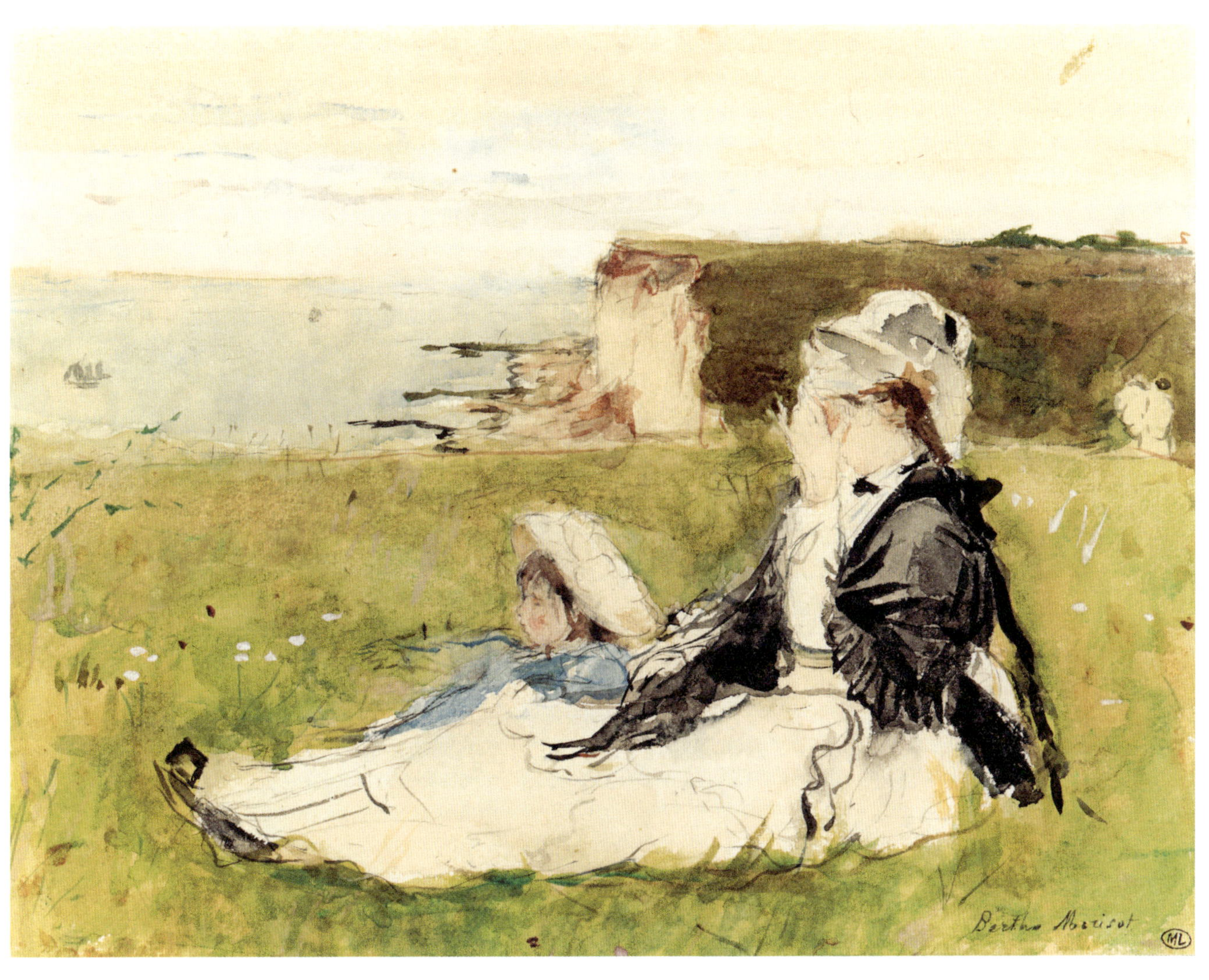

On the Clifftop, c. 1873
Watercolour, 18 × 23 cm (7 × 9 in.). Signed.
MUSÉE DU LOUVRE (COLLECTION MUSÉE D'ORSAY), PARIS

143

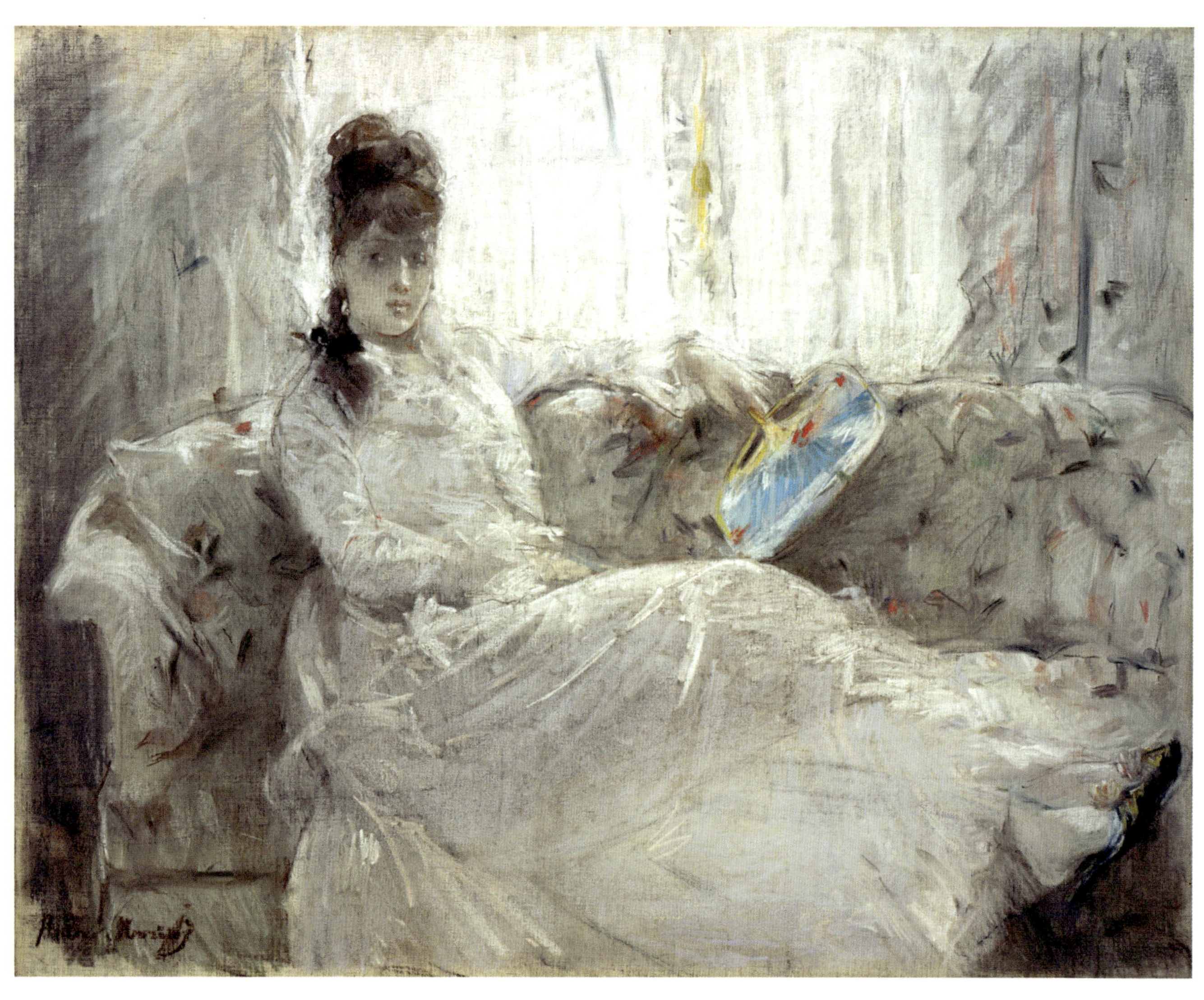

Berthe Morisot

Daydreaming, 1877
Pastel on canvas, 50.2 × 61 cm (19¾ × 24 in.). Signed.
NELSON-ATKINS MUSEUM OF ART, KANSAS CITY, MISSOURI

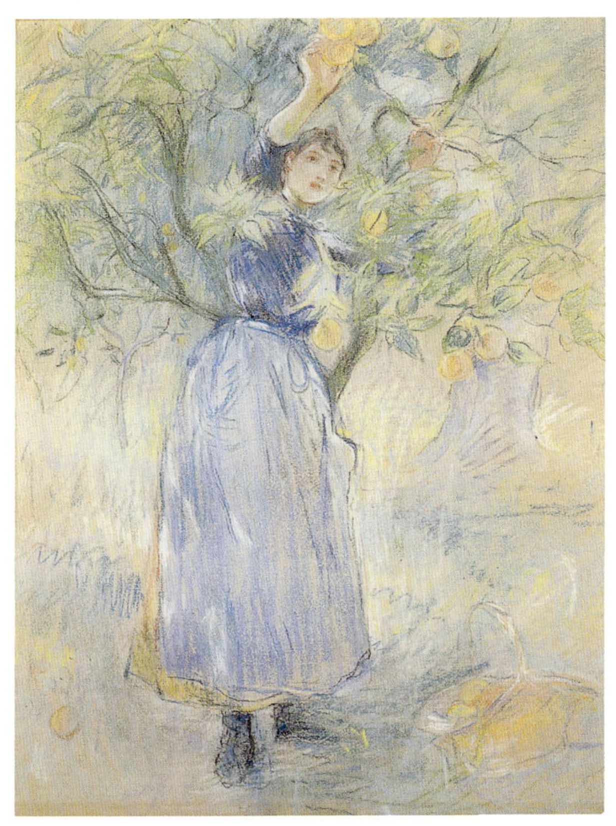

Study for 'Picking Oranges', 1891
Pastel, 61 × 46 cm (24 × 18⅛ in.).
MUSÉE D'ART ET D'HISTOIRE DE PROVENCE, GRASSE

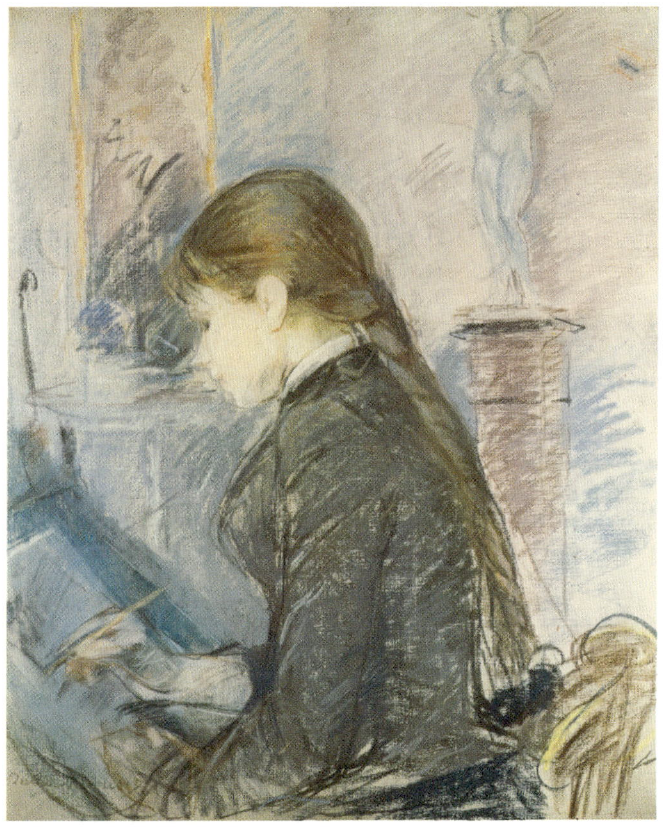

Paule Gobillard Drawing, 1886
Pastel on canvas, 73 × 60 cm (28¾ × 23⅝ in.).
MONTE CARLO ART S.A.

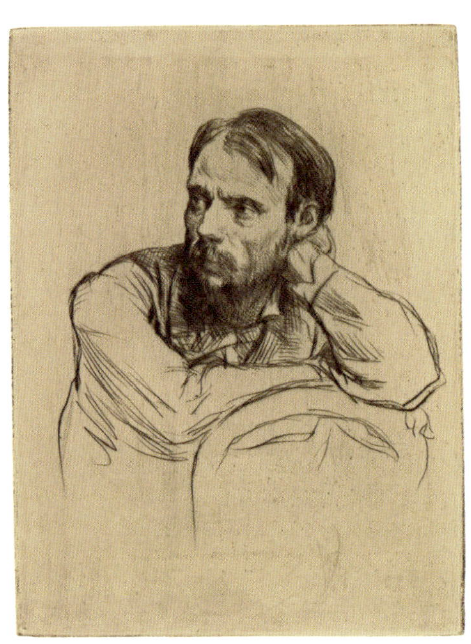

Pierre-Auguste Renoir
1841–1919

Pierre-Auguste Renoir had the uncanny habit of painting a number of pictures that, over time, have in general estimation come to be regarded as the quintessence of Impressionism. An example of this phenomenon is *Luncheon of the Boating Party* of 1880–81 (The Phillips Collection, Washington, DC), an ambitious, multi-figure composition depicting the upstairs terrace of the Restaurant Fournaise on an island in the river Seine at Chatou, to the west of Paris. This area was one of the increasingly popular suburbs of the capital where city dwellers sought relaxation at weekends. Chatou itself was particularly favoured by oarsmen. The painting positively breathes contentment, with young people in the open air enjoying one another's company after refreshing themselves with good food and wine. The critic Octave Mirbeau wrote in 1913 that 'Renoir may be the only great painter who has never painted a sad picture'.

The style of *Luncheon of the Boating Party* is as beguiling as its content. A dappled light flickers across the figures and the still life of bottles, glasses and fruit on the table.

Marcellin Desboutin
Pierre-Auguste Renoir, 1877
Drypoint, 16.3 × 11.7 cm (6⅜ × 4⅝ in.).
BIBLIOTHÈQUE NATIONALE DE FRANCE, PARIS

The glowing colours are scattered across the surface as though applied by an aspergill. It is a complex painting seemingly undertaken by an artist at the height of his powers, and yet it dates from a time when both the future of Impressionism was uncertain and the artist himself was questioning the basis of his own style. Such ambivalence was highly characteristic of Renoir, who, even though he enjoyed company and feared isolation, was fickle, hesitant, indecisive and unpredictable, often causing great anguish and frustration among his many friends.

Renoir's personality was to a large extent determined by his upbringing. His father was a tailor in Limoges and his mother a former assistant to a dressmaker. The family was poor, and the younger painter Jacques-Emile Blanche records that Renoir 'spoke like a working-class labourer with a rasping guttural Parisian accent'. Financial pressures meant that the artist was at first apprenticed at a young age to a porcelain-painting firm in Paris where he worked until 1858. Soon afterwards, he joined the studio of Charles Gleyre, where he met Monet, Sisley and Frédéric Bazille, before entering the orbit of Manet.

Partly to achieve financial security, Renoir remained cautious throughout his life about what kind of pictures he made and where he exhibited them. He chose his friends carefully and cultivated his patrons, dealers and collectors with a sense of purpose. The result was that during the 1880s, with his reputation established in America, as well as in Europe, he was in fact finally free of financial worries so that he could travel at will and eventually own houses in the village of Essoyes, south of Troyes in the Aube, which was the birthplace of his wife Aline Charigot, and an estate at Cagnes on the Côte d'Azur.

Yet, in spite of all Renoir's deliberations and equivocations, he was at the same time an avant-garde artist. After all, it was he who in 1869, together with Monet, embarked upon the earliest demonstration of the Impressionist style when they painted at the fashionable open-air restaurant and bathing establishment known as La Grenouillère on the Île de Croissy, near Bougival on the river Seine, also to the west of Paris. And it was Renoir, rather than any of his confrères, who was appointed the executor of Gustave Caillebotte's will in 1894, giving him the responsibility of persuading the French government to accept a collection of such importance that it now forms one of the foundation stones of the state's holdings of Impressionist art displayed in the Musée d'Orsay.

Equally important was Renoir's concern to develop his own style beyond Impressionism in order to endow it with a greater sense of permanence. A visit to Italy in 1880–82, where he saw Pompeian frescos in Naples and works by Raphael in Rome, inspired him to concentrate more on the human form. This led to those paintings of female bathers in which he declared, 'I have ended up by only seeing the broad harmonies without any longer preoccupying myself with the small details which dim the sunlight rather than illuminating it.' The subject of female bathers remained a feature of Renoir's later work dating from after 1900, when he was increasingly crippled by rheumatoid arthritis without hope of cure. The progress of the illness is vividly portrayed in photographs and on film showing the emaciated artist in various wheelchairs, with the brushes attached to his hand with bandages and special provision made for the supply and control of his materials. The brushstrokes were now by necessity looser and freer and the forms somewhat inflated. Pictures such as *The Judgement of Paris* of 1913 (Hiroshima Museum of Art) or *The Great Bathers* of 1919 (Musée d'Orsay, Paris) are not always fully appreciated today, but they won the respect of Pierre Bonnard, Henri Matisse and Pablo Picasso.

As a draughtsman Renoir was remarkably varied. His range extends from vignettes and doodles reminiscent of his work as a porcelain painter through groups of preparatory studies and illustrations for books and journals to landscapes and finished portraits. Owing to his training, his approach was essentially artisanal, paying close attention to the processes of art, and it is significant that in 1911 he wrote a preface for a reissue of Cennino Cennini's manual, *The Book of Art* (c. 1390). It is also notable that Renoir was particularly adept in the use of eighteenth-century techniques such as pastel and sanguine, in addition to watercolour. Ultimately, he regarded the purpose of painting as decorative in both public and private contexts, which is why he sought in his work for the perfect balance between form and colour.

Three portraits demonstrate Renoir's superb handling of pastel. The soft, deft rendering of the hair, facial features and flesh tones of *Head of a Young Woman with Red Hair* of c. 1876–78 (p. 150) contrasts strongly with the almost wild abandon of *Paul Cézanne* of 1880 (p. 156), while the more fulsome treatment of *The Two Sisters* of c. 1889 (p. 157), with its close harmonies of red, black and orange placed against a blue background, is more typical of the portraits made for the artist's wealthier patrons. Unsurprisingly, Renoir frequently exhibited his pastels, beginning in 1879 with a group shown on the premises of the journal *La Vie Moderne*, which was owned by one of his main patrons, Georges Charpentier.

Preparatory studies by Renoir for his finished paintings reveal a wide range of techniques. The drawing for *Acrobats at the Cirque Fernando (Francisca and Angelina Wartenberg)* (p. 151) was made spontaneously *in situ* and the finished painting now in the Art Institute of Chicago has several refinements, such as the omission of the clown in the lower right corner and the positioning of the two girls closer to the centre of the composition.

Renoir's emphasis on the figure, following his visit to Italy, prompted his exploration of the theme of dancing couples – virtually his final attempt at a subject of urban or suburban recreation. Of the three pictures, all dated 1883, *Dance in the City* and *Dance in the Country* (both Musée d'Orsay, Paris) were conceived as pendants, whereas the third, *Dance at Bougival* (Museum of Fine Arts, Boston), is slightly larger in format.

The study (p. 153) for *Dance in the Country*, with Paul Lhote and Aline Charigot as the models, is not so much about the pose as the swaying motion of the dancers. The fluidity of the drawing is enhanced by the use of the brush in the final stages, reinforcing outlines and making corrections.

The acknowledged masterpiece of the mid-1880s is *The Great Bathers, an Experiment in Decorative Painting* of 1887 (Philadelphia Museum of Art) for which there are as many as twenty preparatory drawings. No other composition by Renoir was as carefully planned, and it took him several years to execute. It was not the large scale of the work so much as the significance that the artist attached to it. Having seen works by Raphael in Italy, Renoir was keen to establish his credentials as a classical artist and specifically as a French one. The sources for the picture include the sculptor François Girardon, François Boucher, Jean-Auguste-Dominque Ingres and Pierre Puvis de Chavannes, but the drawings prove the extent to which Renoir made the subject his own. *Two Nude Women* (p. 154) explores the interconnecting poses of the figures reclining on the bank in the left foreground, filling the left half of the composition. The even more refined study, *Splashing Figure* (p. 155), relates to the more playful figure in the water in the foreground in the right half. Morisot saw a group of these preparatory drawings in Renoir's studio in January 1886 and wrote in her diary, 'He is a draughtsman of the first order: it would be interesting to show all these preparatory drawings for a painting, to the public, which greatly imagines that the Impressionists work in a very casual way. I do not think it possible to go further in the rendering of form.'

Morisot is surely correct in her judgement, but Renoir could be surprisingly uneven owing in part to over-production and in part to his physical incapacities. His handling of chalk, however, is one of the high points of French nineteenth-century draughtsmanship, matching the tradition of Jean-Antoine Watteau, Boucher, Jean-Honoré Fragonard and Jean-Baptiste Greuze. *Young Woman with a Muff* (p. 152) exhibits the finesse and delicacy with which Renoir could handle the softer media. The habit of silhouetting the figure against a prepared white ground not only brings her closer to the viewer but also suggests the cold against which she protects herself. On the other hand, *The Snack (La Collation)* (p. 159) is a harvesting scene dating from ten or so years later. The figures are more statuesque and the handling rougher, owing in some respects to the progression of Renoir's arthritis. But there is a pleasure for the artist and viewer alike in the rich tactile quality of the finish. It should be no surprise that Picasso owned a drawing of this type, albeit one on a larger scale. The bravura technique and sympathetic treatment of *Coiffure* (Musée Picasso, Paris) of 1900–01 not only challenges Degas but at the same time must have been a source of inspiration – if not of veneration – for Picasso, who was no doubt aware of Renoir's figures during his own neoclassical phase at the beginning of the 1920s, after the birth of Cubism.

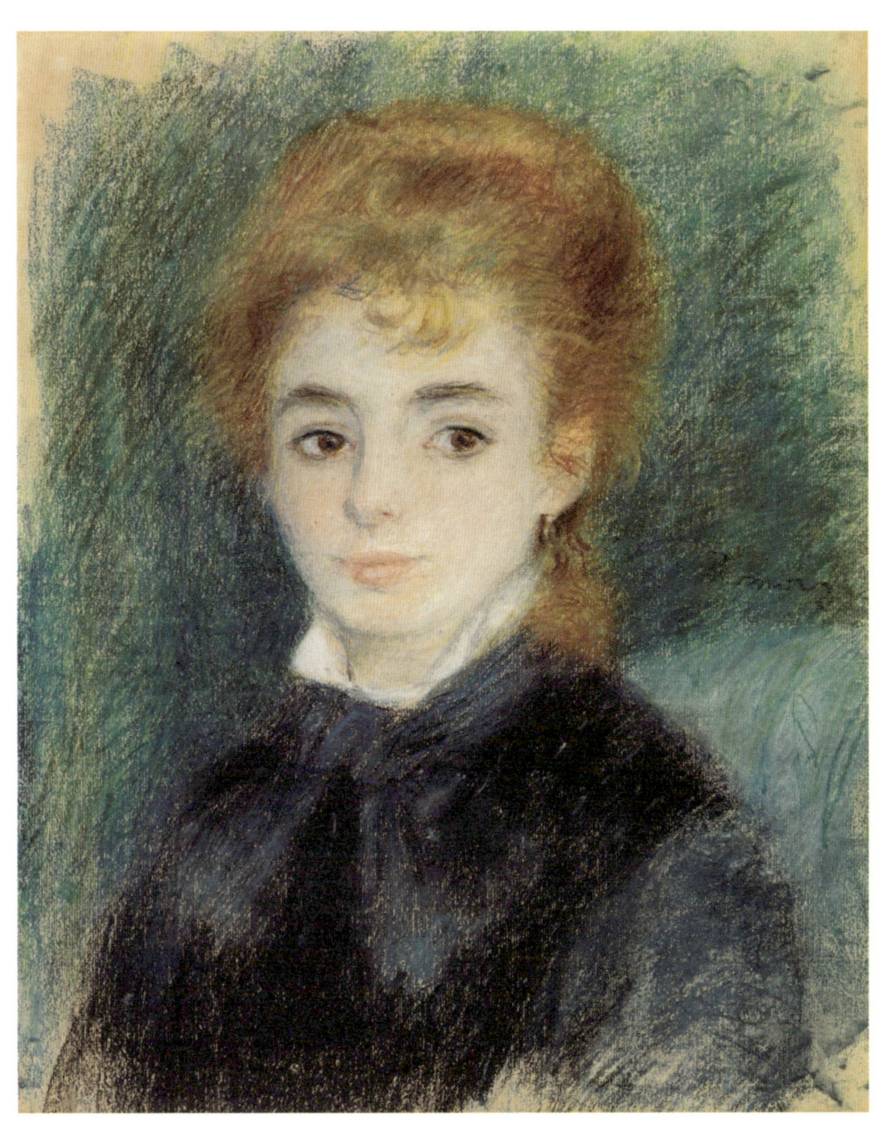

 Pierre Auguste Renoir   *Head of a Young Woman with Red Hair*, c. 1876–78
Pastel, 50.8 × 40 cm (20 × 15¾ in.). Signed.
BURRELL COLLECTION, GLASGOW

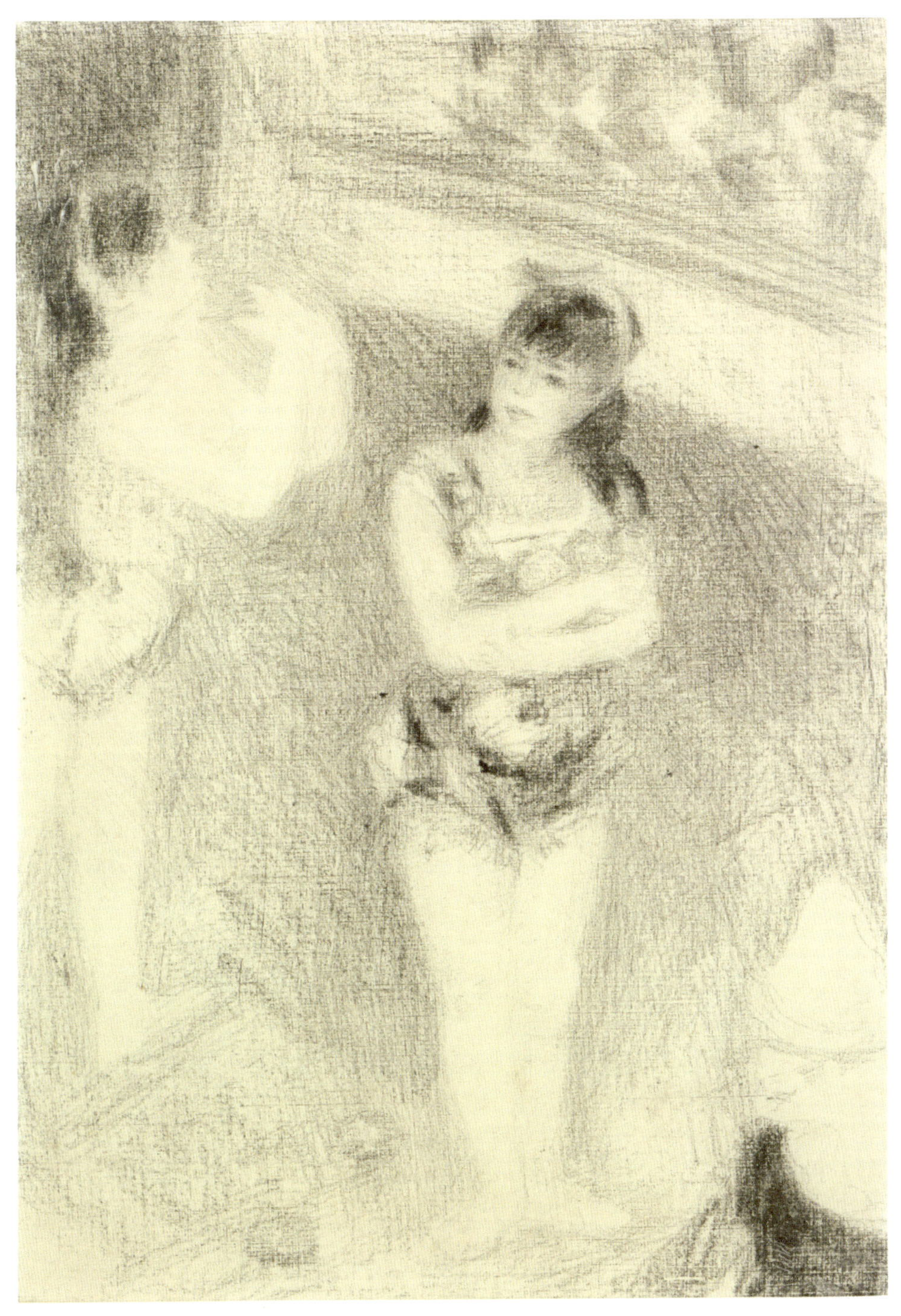

Study of Two Circus Girls (Francisca and Angelina Wartenberg), c. 1879
Black chalk on linen-faced paper, 31.8 × 22.5 cm (12½ × 8⅞ in.).
PRIVATE COLLECTION

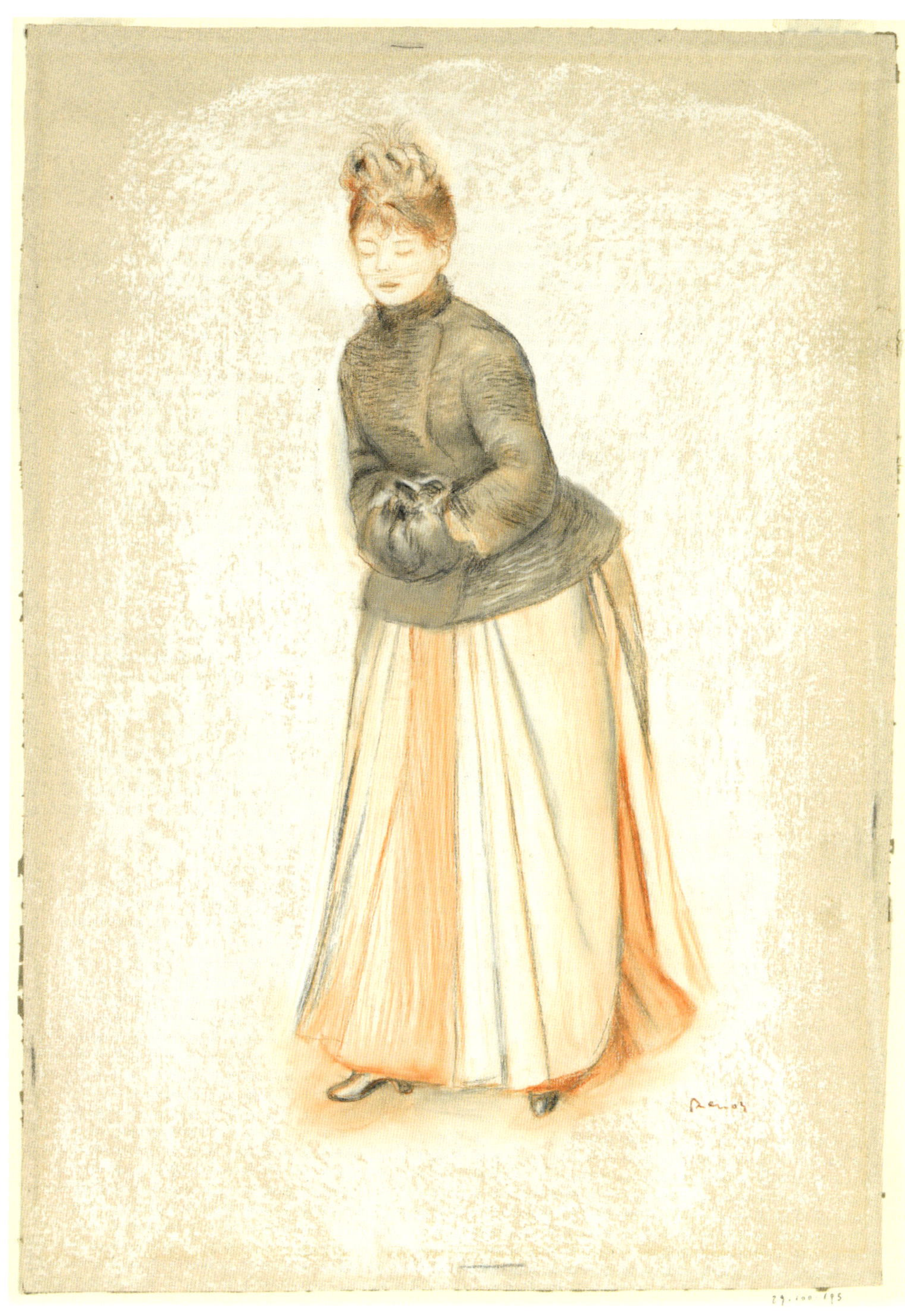

   Pierre-Auguste Renoir   *Young Woman with a Muff,* 1880–81
Pastel, 52.7 × 36.2 cm (20¾ × 14¼ in.). Signed.
METROPOLITAN MUSEUM OF ART, NEW YORK

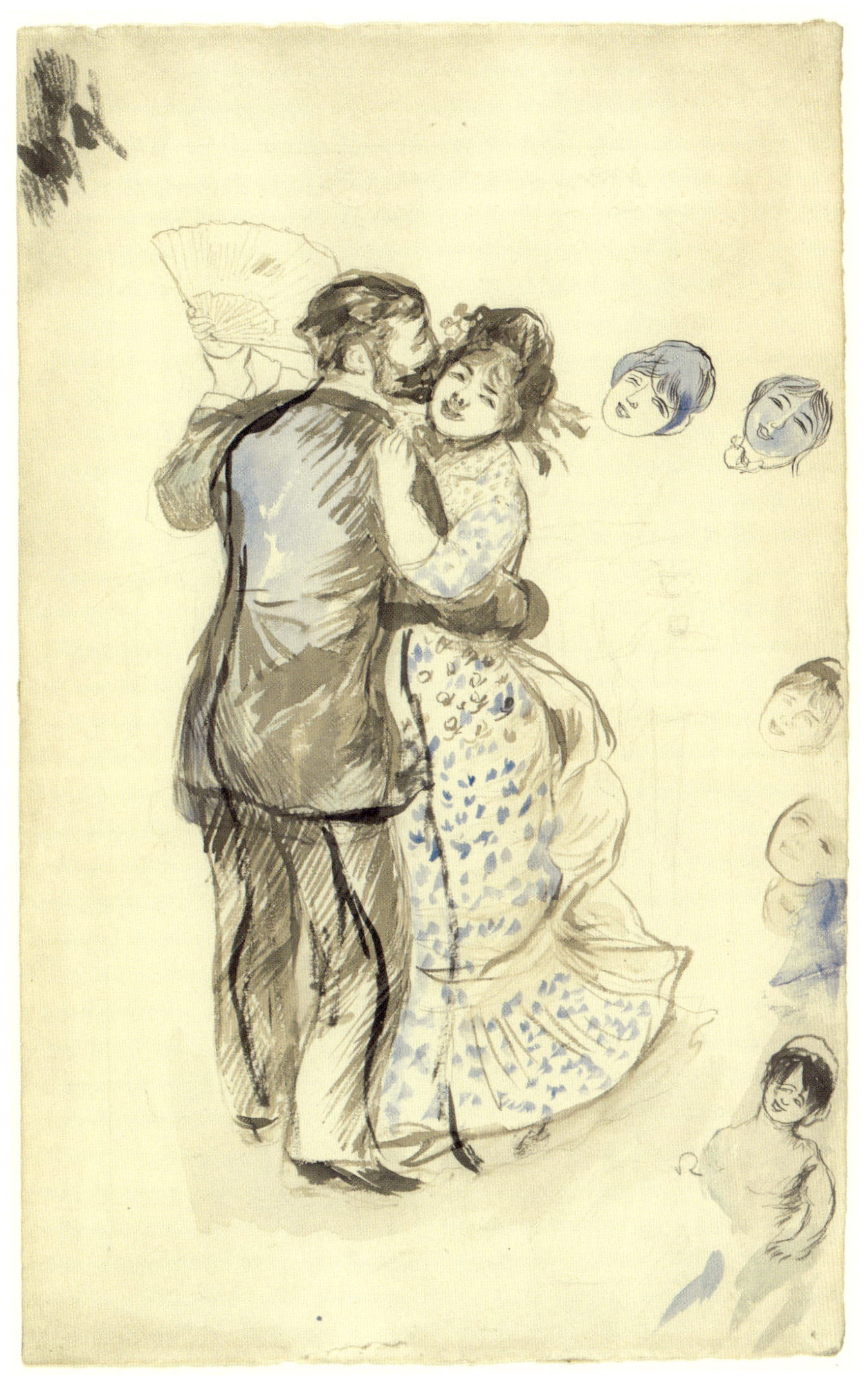

Study for 'The Dance in the Country', 1883
Brush and brown, blue and black wash over black chalk
or pencil, 49.5 × 30.5 cm (19½ × 12 in.).
YALE UNIVERSITY ART GALLERY, NEW HAVEN, CONNECTICUT

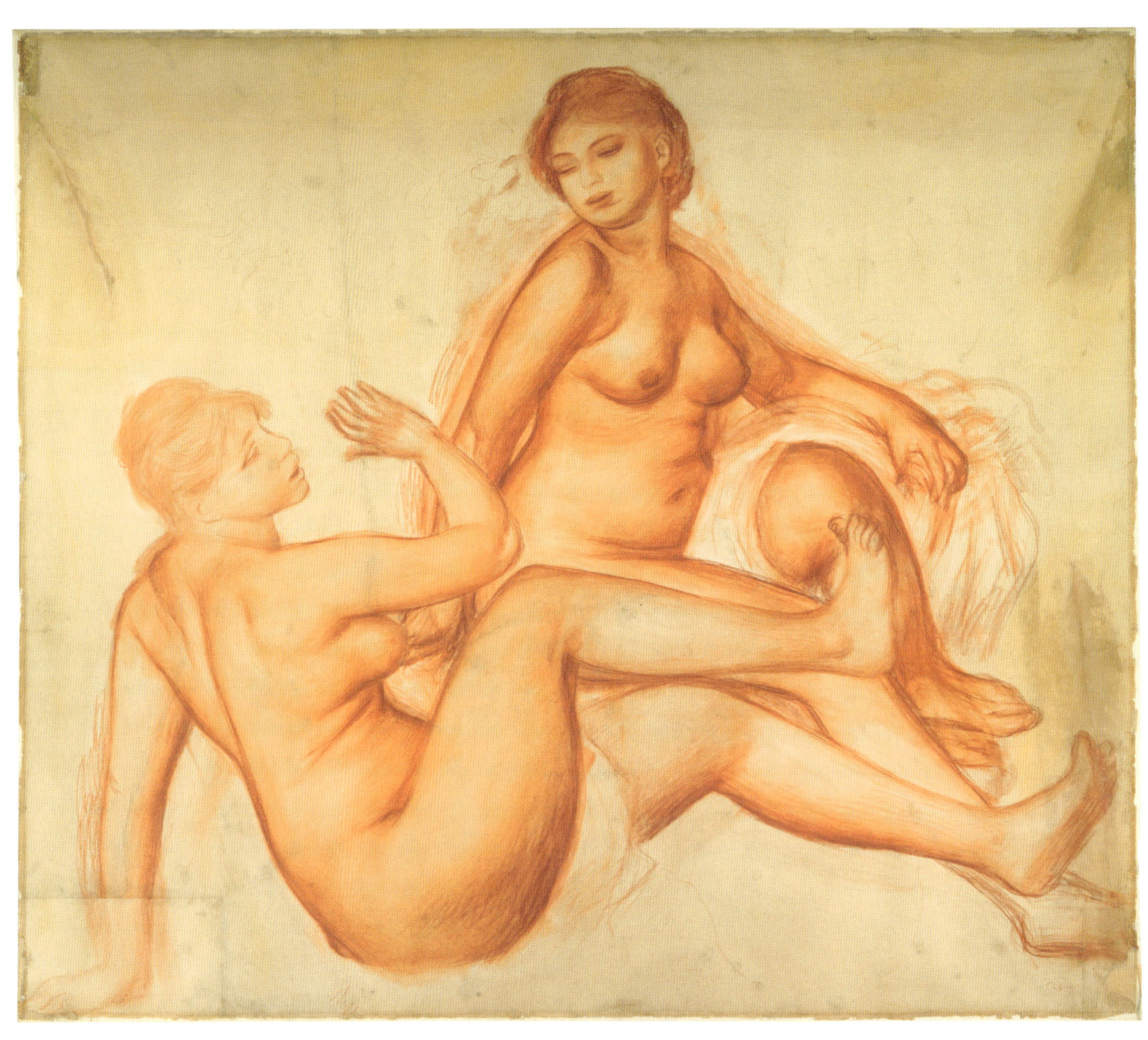

154   *Pierre-Auguste Renoir*   *Two Nude Women, Study for 'The Great Bathers'*, c. 1884–87
Red and white chalk on buff paper, 110.6 × 124.7 cm
(43½ × 49⅛ in.). Signed.
HARVARD ART MUSEUMS (FOGG MUSEUM), CAMBRIDGE, MASSACHUSETTS

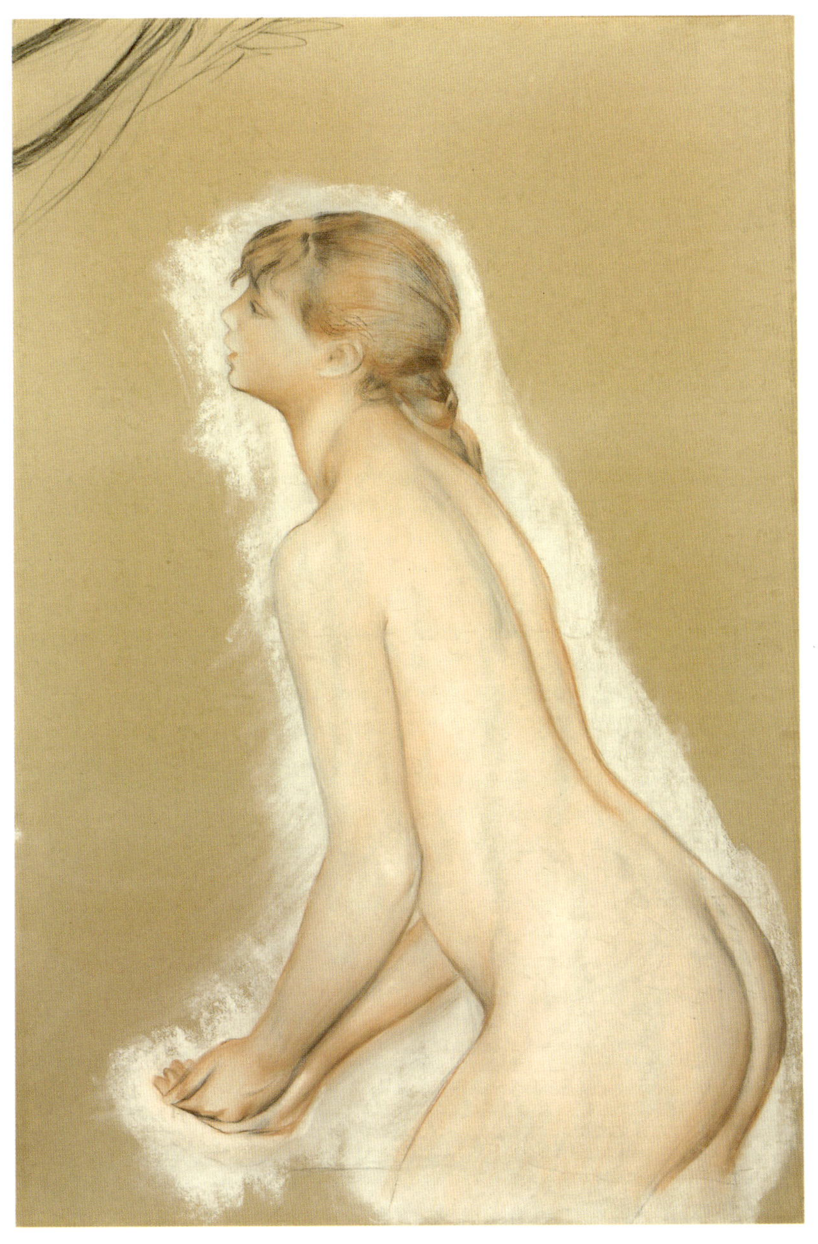

Splashing Figure, Study for 'The Great Bathers', c. 1884–87
Conté crayon, red, white and black chalk on buff-coloured
paper mounted on canvas, 98.9 × 63.5 cm (38 × 25 in.).
THE ART INSTITUTE OF CHICAGO

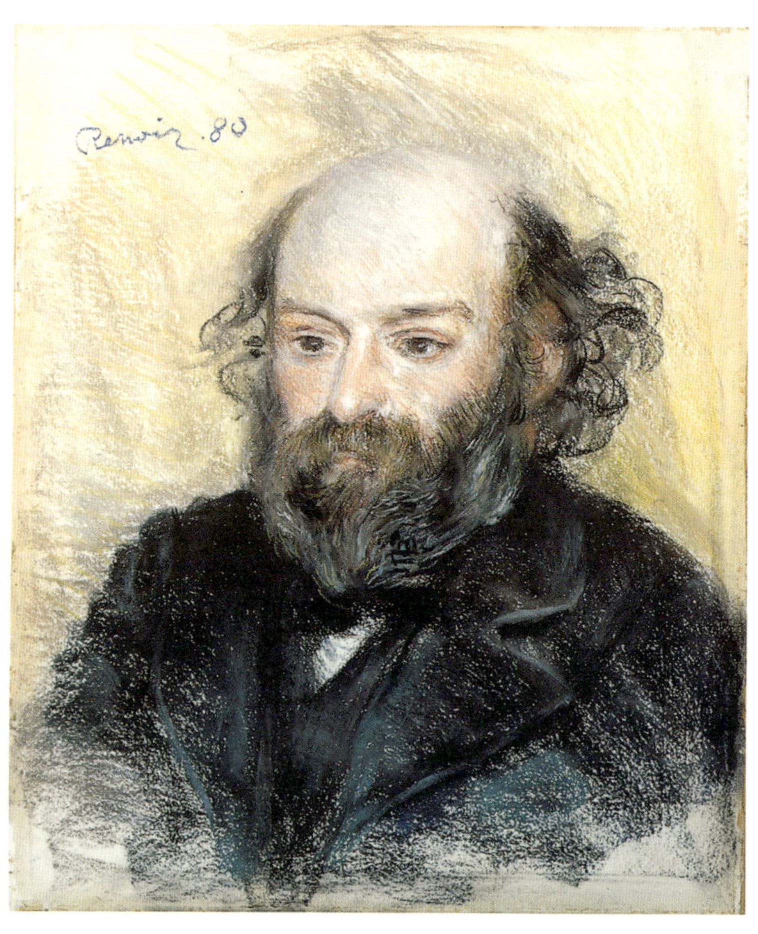

156 *Pierre-Auguste Renoir*

Paul Cézanne, 1880
Pastel, 53.5 × 44.4 cm (21 × 17½ in.). Signed and dated.
PRIVATE COLLECTION

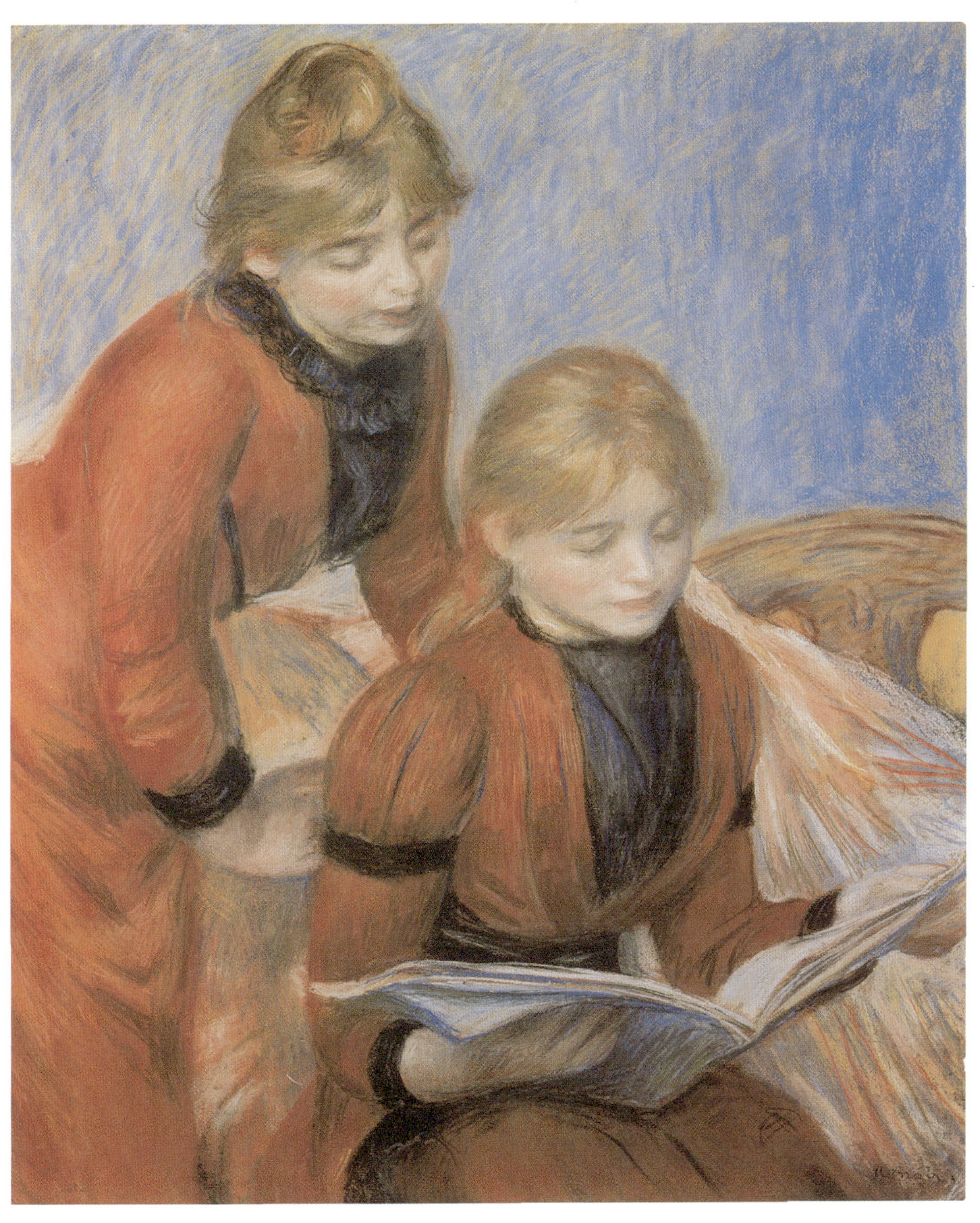

The Two Sisters, c. 1889
Pastel on grey paper, 79 × 63.5 cm (31⅛ × 25 in.). Signed.
Bristol Museum & Art Gallery

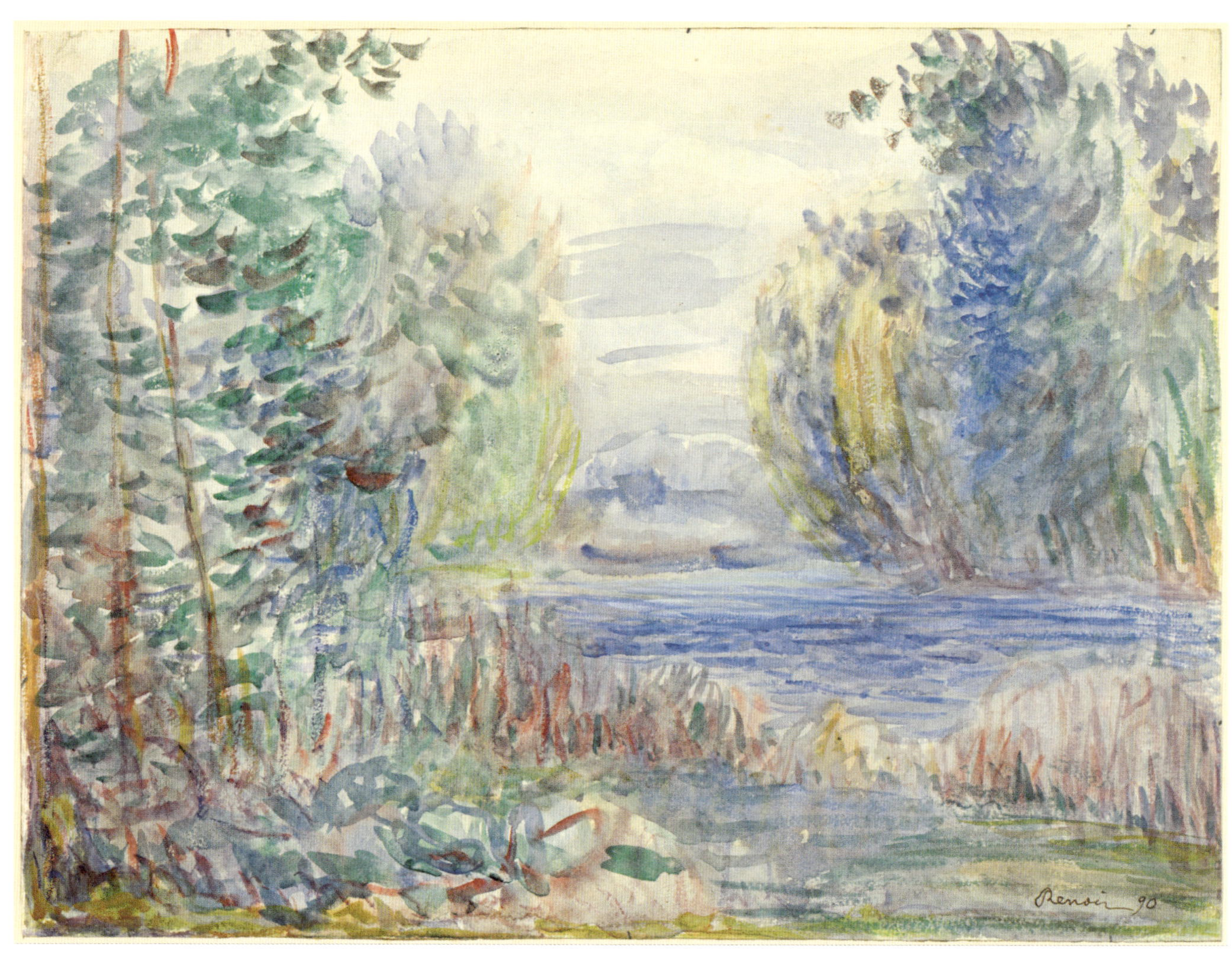

 Pierre-Auguste Renoir

River Landscape, 1890
Watercolour, 25.4 × 33.8 cm (10 × 13⅜ in.).
Signed and dated.
ALBERTINA, VIENNA

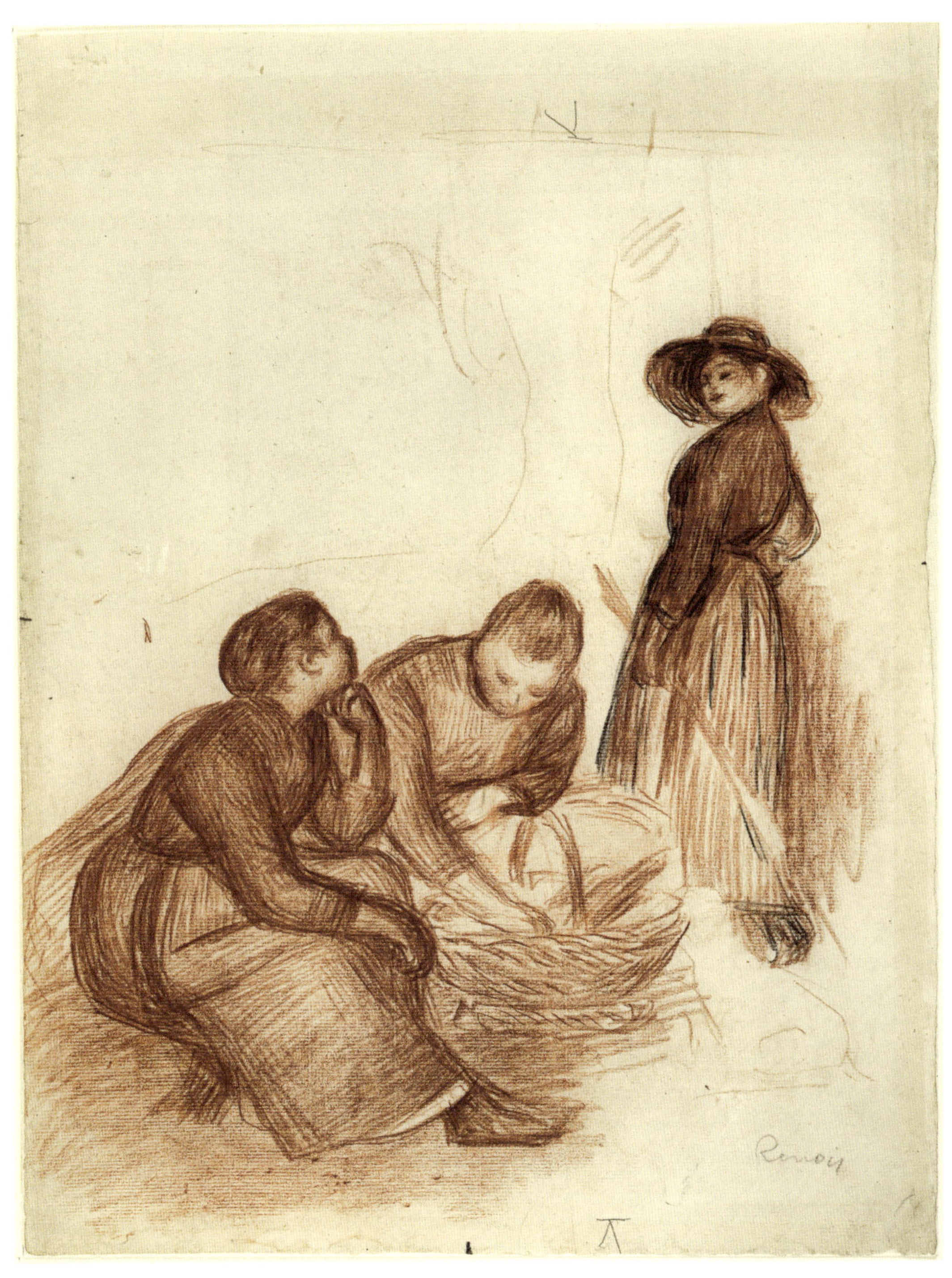

The Snack (La Collation), c. 1895
Red and black chalk, 42.3 × 31.5 cm (16⅝ × 12⅜ in.). Signed.
FITZWILLIAM MUSEUM, CAMBRIDGE

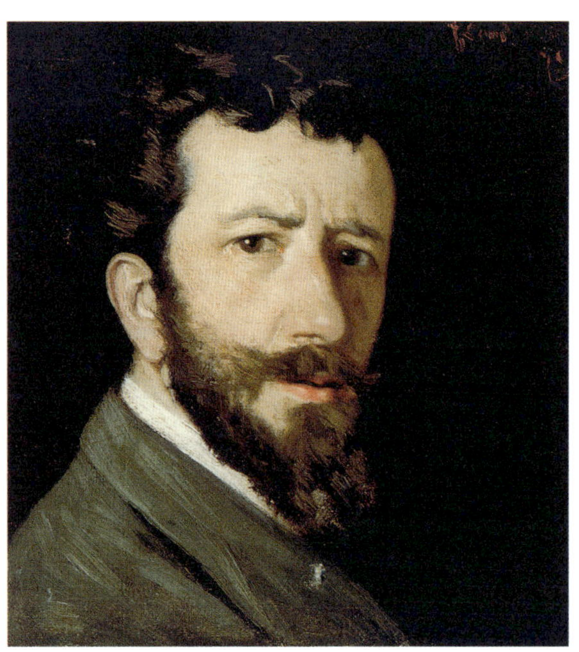

Federico Zandomeneghi
1841–1917

For Federico Zandomeneghi, 1874 was a pivotal year. It was when he decided to leave Italy and move to Paris. After exhibiting at four of the Impressionist exhibitions (1879, 1880, 1881 and 1886), he spent the rest of his life in the city. Although Venetian by birth, from 1862 he had established himself as a painter in Florence, where he had frequented the Caffè Michelangiolo, the gathering place for the group of artists known as the Macchiaioli.

The Macchiaioli made a similar stance against the official academies of art in Italy to that which the Impressionists were to make slightly later in France. Their name was derived from the word '*macchia*', meaning 'splash' or 'patch', referring to their type of brushstroke. They advocated a direct approach to nature, preferring to paint out of doors in a loose style recording the effects of light and colour more accurately than conventional teaching allowed, and choosing interior scenes based on everyday life as opposed to historical, religious or mythological sources. There was also an element of social realism in works by the Macchiaioli, since they readily identified with the

Federico Zandomeneghi
Self-Portrait, 1875
Oil on canvas, 35.5 × 31.5 cm (14 × 12⅜ in.).
ISTITUTO MATTEUCCI, VIAREGGIO

ideals of the Risorgimento, the movement striving for independence from the Austro-Hungarian empire, which they hoped might lead to the reunification of Italy. Many of the Macchiaioli, including Zandomeneghi in 1860, took part in the Risorgimento campaigns and painted scenes based on the hardships and deprivations suffered by the impoverished population of an occupied country. Of these artists, he was closest at this stage of his life to Giovanni Fattori, Telemaco Signorini, Silvestro Lega and the short-lived Giuseppe Abbati.

Several of the paintings executed by Zandomeneghi after he arrived in Paris reflect his origins as a Macchiaioli artist, even though he was quick to absorb Impressionist influences: for example, *Place d'Anvers* (Galleria d'Arte Moderna Ricci Oddi, Piacenza), which was shown at the sixth Impressionist exhibition (1880). Zandomeneghi had been preceded in his move to Paris by several other Italian artists, including the Neapolitan Giuseppe de Nittis, who had five paintings included in the first Impressionist exhibition (1874). During the mid-1870s de Nittis, like Zandomeneghi later, began using pastel on a regular basis, mostly depicting social occasions, such as the spectacular *At the Racetrack in Auteuil* of 1881 (Galleria Nazionale d'Arte Moderna, Rome).

In one sense, on coming to Paris Zandomeneghi was exchanging the Caffè Michelangioli for the Café de la Nouvelle-Athènes on the Place Pigalle and spurning his Italian heritage. His immediate Venetian forebears were sculptors whose finest achievement was the large monument to Titian in the church of S. Maria Gloriosa dei Frari. His training as a painter, thereby breaking with the family tradition, was divided between the Accademia di Belle Arti, first in Venice and then in Milan. The Impressionist who gave most support to the Italian artists who went to Paris was Degas, and interestingly both he and Zandomeneghi made portraits of the Italian critic and collector Diego Martelli, who supported the Macchiaioli and also took an interest in the Impressionists. Martelli inherited a villa at Castiglioncello on the Tuscan coast where many of the Macchiaioli liked to paint. He made several visits to Paris during the 1860s and 1870s when he became an admirer of the painters of the Barbizon School.

Encouraged by Zandomeneghi, it was while in Paris in 1878–79 that Martelli became enthusiastic about the Impressionists, meeting Degas and adding works by Pissarro to his collection. The loosely painted portrait by Degas now in Edinburgh (National Gallery of Scotland) was included in the fourth Impressionist exhibition (1879) and shows Martelli occupying a Savonarola chair in a room dominated by a work desk in the right half of the composition and a sofa pushed up against the back wall. The high viewpoint dramatically foreshortens the short-legged figure who sits with his arms crossed, somewhat resembling a curled-up hedgehog. By contrast, Zandomeneghi's portrait of Martelli, which was also shown at the fourth Impressionist exhibition, is more sympathetic (Galleria d'Arte Moderna, Florence). The figure is seated in a chair before a fireplace positioned almost parallel to the picture plane. The head is turned towards the viewer as though in greeting or in discussion. He wears a skull cap and strokes his beard: he looks amiable as opposed to defensive. The artist lavishes great care over the still-life objects on the mantelpiece where the sitter's pipe has been carefully placed, as well as on the watch chain and finger ring that he wears. The tonal values are carefully unified, which gives the white highlights of the cuff, collar and porcelain dish greater prominence.

The stylistic virtues apparent in Zandomeneghi's *Portrait of Diego Martelli* are found in abundance in his pastels. There can be little doubt that it was Degas, and possibly also de Nittis, who encouraged him to use pastel and it became his preferred medium, certainly from the 1890s onwards. Many of the subjects that he chose are related to those undertaken by Degas, but the treatment is totally different and not without its stylistic idiosyncrasies. Zandomeneghi made pastels for exhibition or for sale through his dealer, Paul Durand-Ruel, and in this he had some success. Even so, he needed to supplement his income by making illustrations for fashion magazines.

Zandomeneghi's pastels are highly finished and, as might be expected of an artist of Venetian origin, rich in tone and saturated in colour. The theme of women at their toilette often produces some surprising results. *Female Nude at the Mirror* (p. 164) feels like an invasion of privacy, not in the way in which Degas seizes such moments, but more because of the seclusion of the setting, which enfolds and protects the vulnerable figure. There is a quickening of rhythm in *Woman Drying Herself* as the seated figure bends to dry her legs (p. 168). The diagonal of the towel stretched across the body emphasizes the action of rubbing. The nude figure is offset by the colours of the furnishings, which are intensified by the glow from the fire. *Waking Up* is a more expansive composition where the overall tone and the light coming through the curtains at the back suggest the start of the day (p. 167). The contrast between the languorous figure stretching in the chair and the bustling maid peering into the cupboard is heightened by the distribution of the verticals across the surface. There is humour, too, in the way the faces of the two protagonists are half-obscured – a lesson learnt from Degas's method of cutting figures off at the edges of his compositions. On comparison, *By the Fireplace* and *The Pearl* are full of atmosphere, but somewhat moribund (pp. 166 and 169). This is partly due to a softer palette and partly to the more suffused handling of the pastel. There was always a danger – depending perhaps on the commission – that Zandomeneghi's pastels might tip towards the sentimental.

Sharpness of observation and execution were often present when the artist left the domestic environment and pursued his models in public places. *Young Woman with Blue Glove* is a figure that he may have seen at the theatre (p. 165). The young woman is seen from the back with the head tilted in three-quarters profile. The dark background sets off the paleness of the exposed flesh that is as luminous as marble. The overall velvety texture of the pastel, however, matches the materials of the evening dress and the promi-nently proffered glove, emphasizing the gesture that completes the compositional circle.

At the Theatre is more elaborate, with the viewer positioned in semi-darkness at the back of the box (below). It has a compositional device that Degas and Renoir explored. The eye is forced to move round the silhouetted heads of the two women in the foreground in order to peer at the performance on the stage. In effect, *At the Theatre* can be read as a metaphor for Impressionism as a whole – the artist espying the world from an advantageous viewpoint for the purpose of revealing it with the utmost conviction. The problem here is that Zandomeneghi, who died three months after Degas, was intent upon doing this long after avant-garde art had moved on to face other challenges.

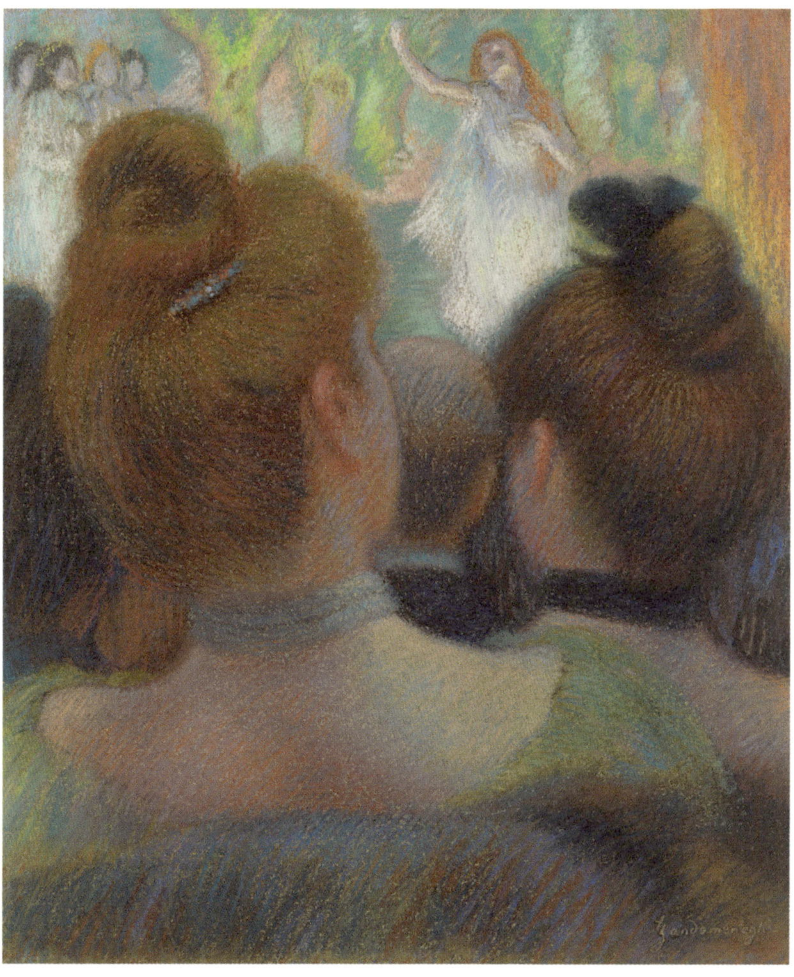

At the Theatre, c. 1895
Pastel, 45.7 × 35.6 cm (18 × 14 in.). Signed.
Private collection

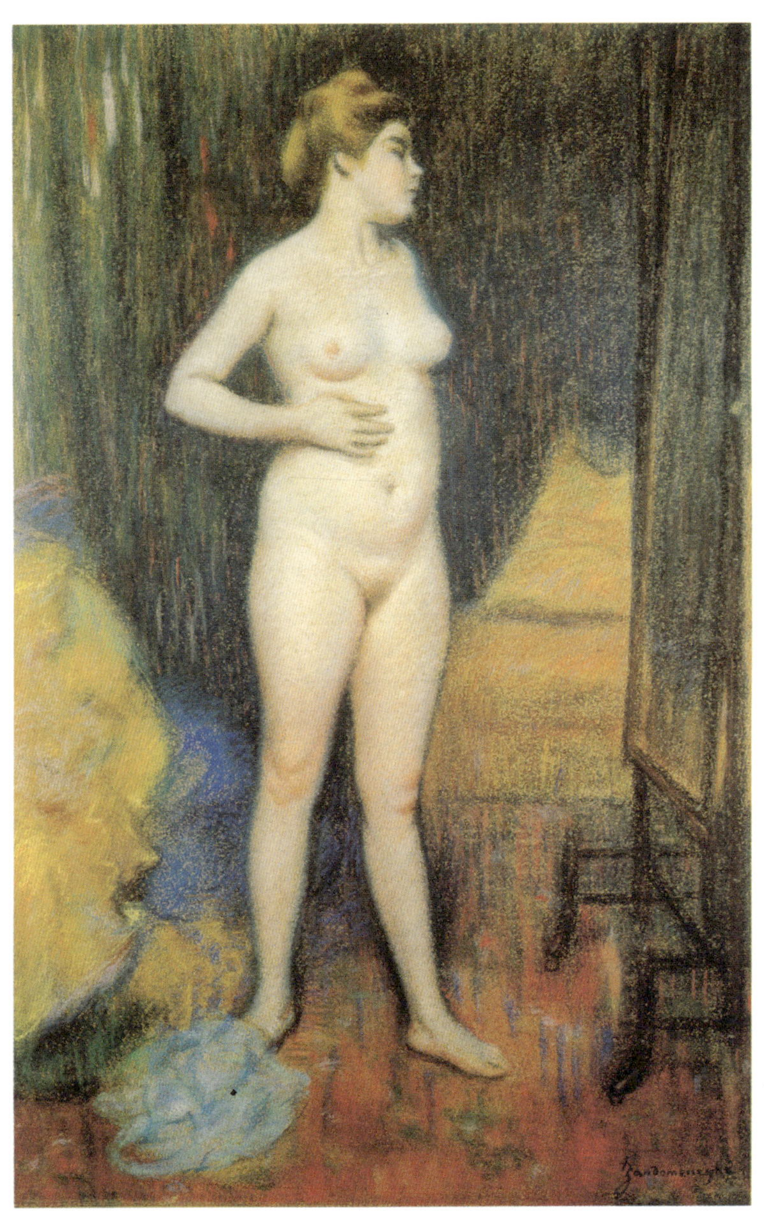

   Federico Zandomeneghi

Female Nude at the Mirror, c. 1893–1900
Pastel, 70 × 40 cm (27½ × 15¾ in.). Signed.
PRIVATE COLLECTION

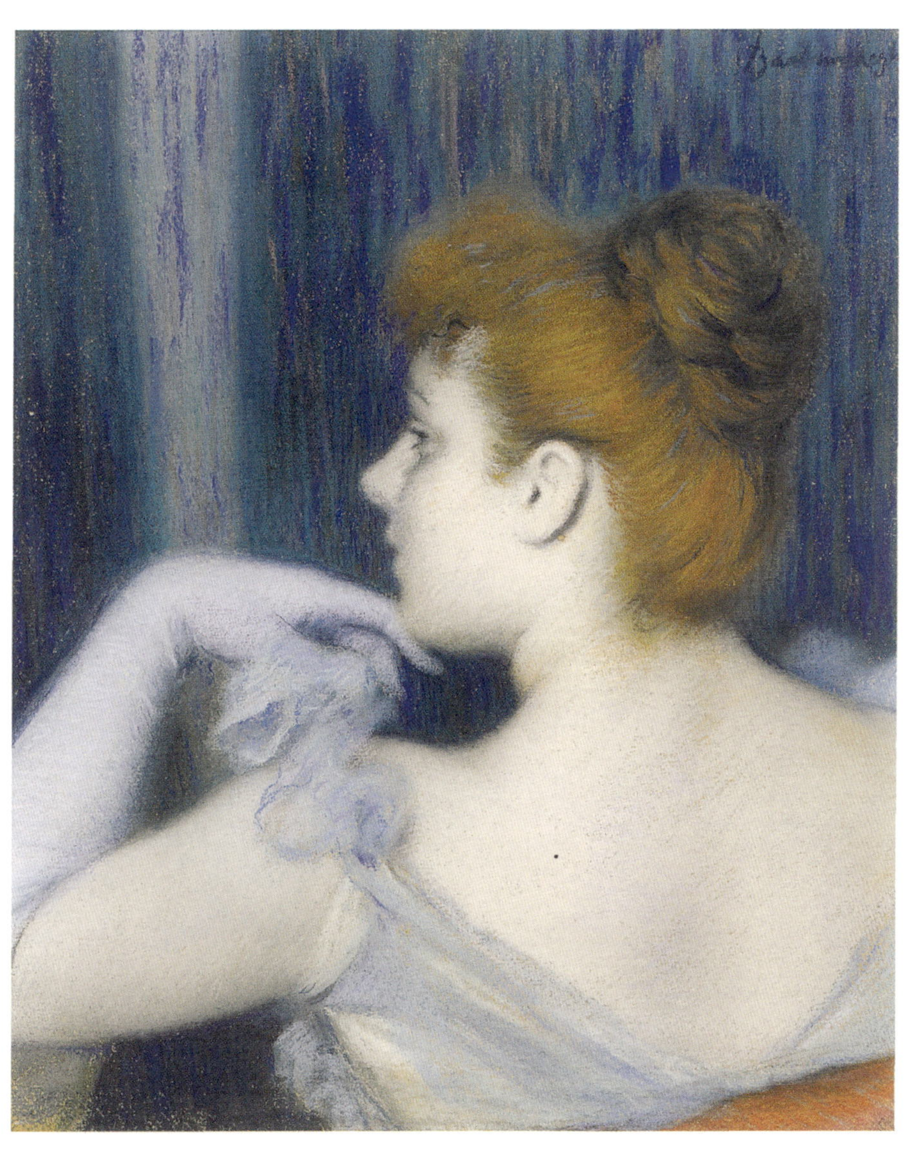

Young Woman with Blue Glove, c. 1895–96
Pastel, 46 × 38 cm (18⅛ × 15 in.). Signed.

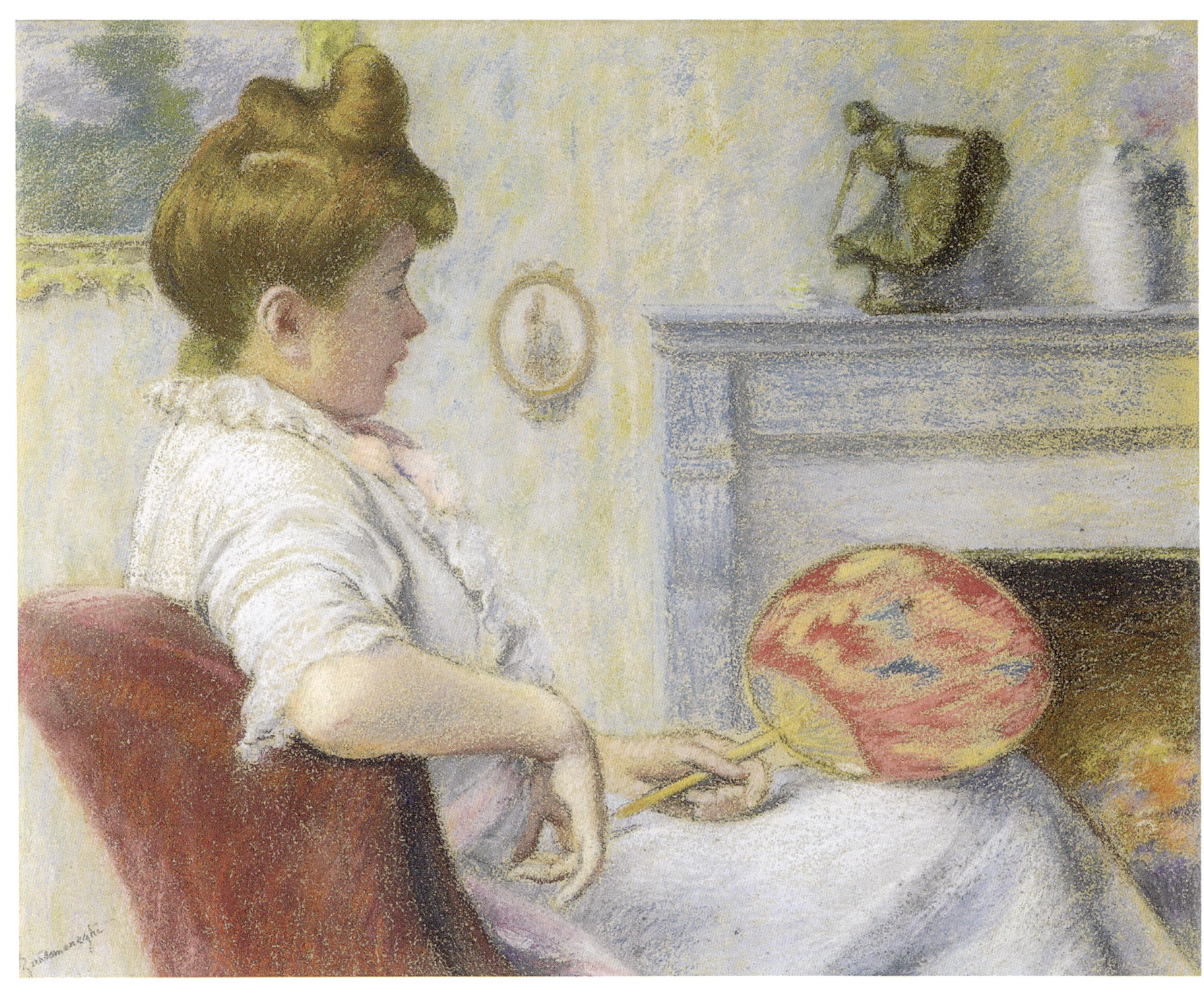

  Federico Zandomeneghi

By the Fireplace, c. 1894
Pastel, 49 × 60 cm (19¼ × 23⅝ in.).
Signed.
PRIVATE COLLECTION

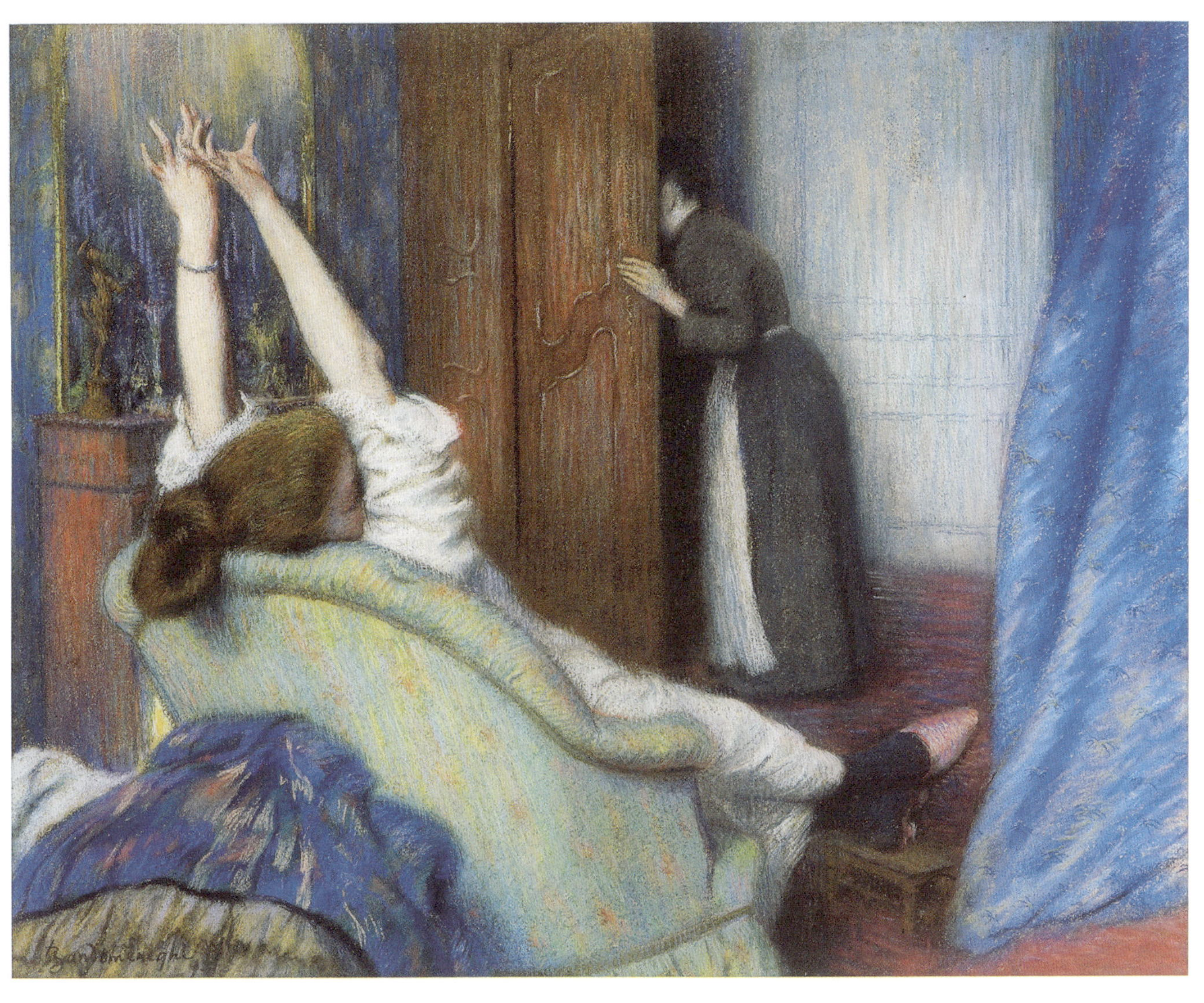

Waking Up, 1895
Pastel mounted on board, 60 × 72 cm
(23⅝ × 28⅜ in.). Signed.
PALAZZO DEL TE, MANTUA

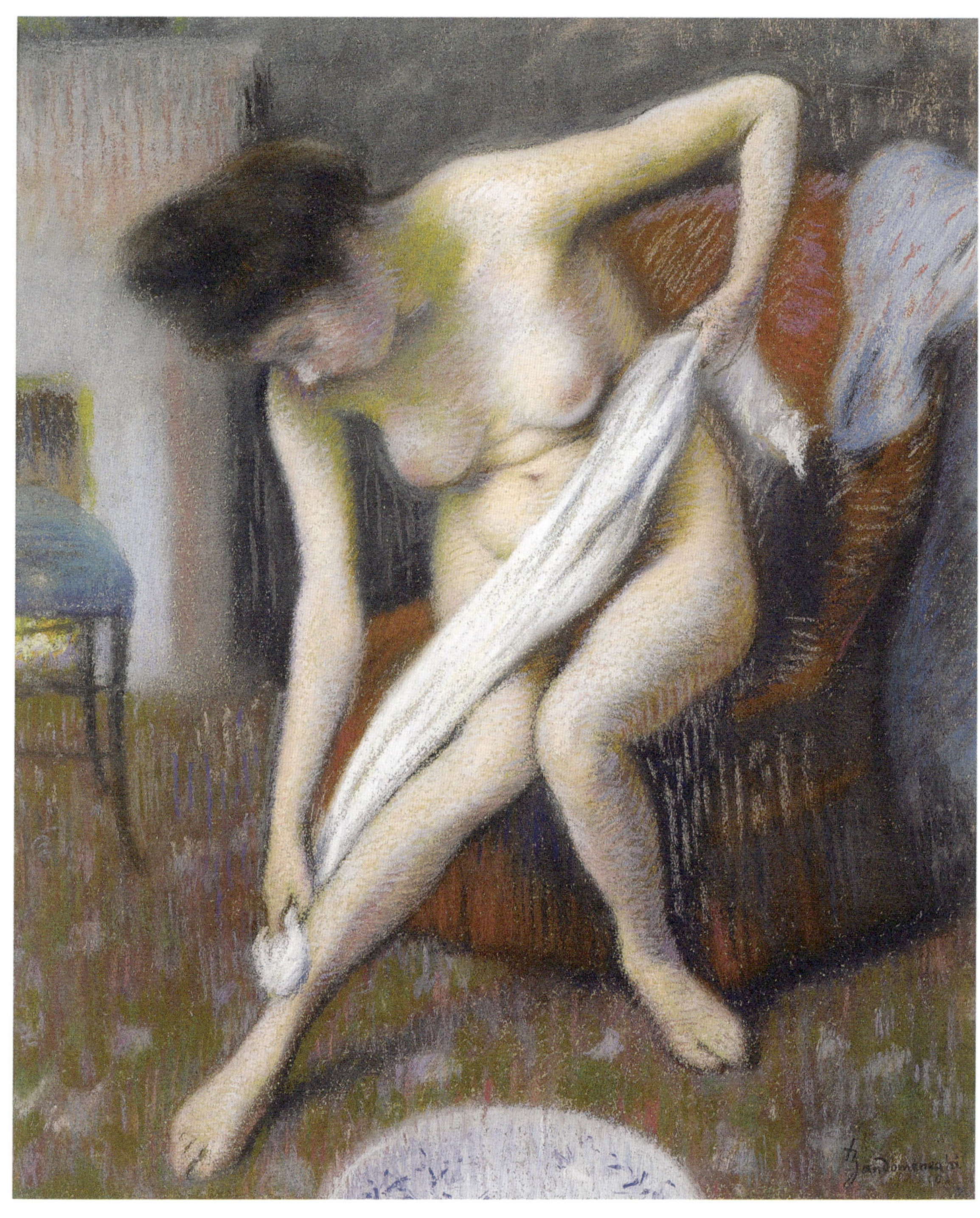

168   *Federico Zandomeneghi*

Woman Drying Herself, c. 1896–98
Pastel, 45 × 37 cm (17¾ × 14½ in.). Signed.
PRIVATE COLLECTION

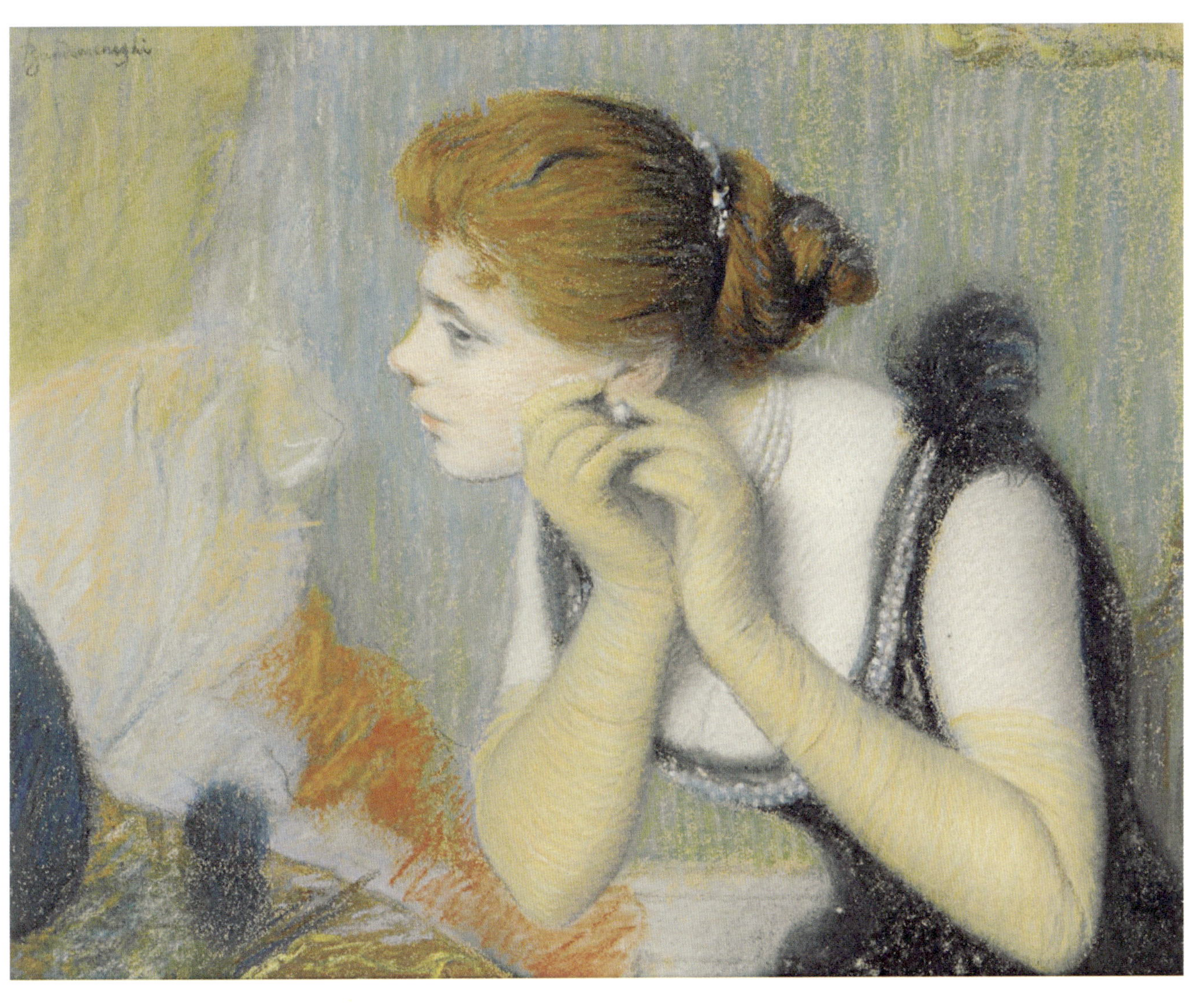

The Pearl, c. 1893
Pastel, 35 × 44 (13¾ × 17⅜ in.). Signed.
PRIVATE COLLECTION

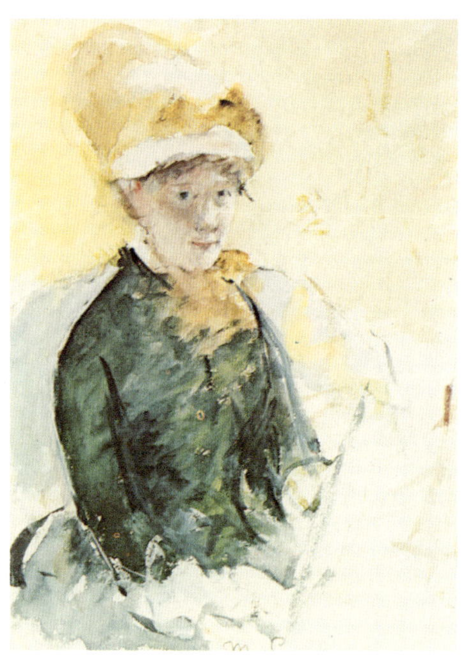

Mary Cassatt
1844–1926

Two prints by Degas made at the end of the 1870s provide considerable insight into Mary Cassatt's character as a person and an artist. Both compositions show two figures in different galleries in the Musée du Louvre, then called the Etruscan Gallery and the Paintings Gallery (possibly the Grande Galerie) respectively. The seated figure consulting her guidebook is in both instances almost certainly the artist's elder sister, Lydia. The standing figure seen from the back has a striking silhouette and is totally absorbed in looking at the art, ignoring her companion. This figure is Mary Cassatt, fashionably but distinctively dressed in a *robe de promenade* comprising a tubular skirt and a jacket with a cuirasse bodice, a shawl collar, a large hat and a furled umbrella. Fashion and its accessories were an important element in Degas's depiction of modern life, and in Cassatt he recognized the perfect model. Her somewhat individual way of dressing and her striking pose signify her essential characteristics – modish, independent, vibrant, opinionated, confident.

Mary Cassatt
Self-Portrait, c. 1880
Watercolour, 33 × 24.4 cm (13 × 9⅝ in.).
NATIONAL PORTRAIT GALLERY, SMITHSONIAN INSTITUTION, WASHINGTON, DC

Degas had seen a portrait by Cassatt at the Salon of 1874 and identified her to a fellow artist as 'someone who feels as I do'. The *Portrait of the Artist* of 1878 (p. 174) in watercolour and gouache is a good indication of the affinity between the two artists, which is apparent here in the nonchalant pose and the serpentine curve of the body. Degas duly recruited Cassatt to exhibit with the Impressionists and she contributed to the fourth (1879) (pp. 175 and 176), fifth (1880), sixth (1881) and eighth (1886) exhibitions. By doing this, Degas was strengthening the representation of figurative painters among the Impressionists in preference to the landscapists.

Cassatt, however, was never a pupil of Degas, or indeed profoundly influenced by him. Even though she had a forceful personality, like most people she often found Degas intimidating. They were essentially kindred spirits, and their professional relationship was founded on mutual respect. This was most evident in their interest in printmaking. The Impressionists had ceased to be satisfied by traditional printing methods and, as in other areas of their art, experimented freely with different techniques. They were also prepared to exhibit impressions of the early states of their prints as works of art in their own right, sometimes in series. This enthusiasm led to the formation of the Société des Peintres-Graveurs Français in 1889 by Félix Bracquemond and Henri Guérard (the husband of Eva Gonzalès), which held two exhibitions at Paul Durand-Ruel's gallery, helping to foster a revival in printmaking during the 1890s. Shortly after first meeting Cassatt, Degas began to plan the launch of a journal called *Le Jour et la Nuit* for which they, together with Bracquemond, Pissarro and Raffaëlli, were to make prints. Partly owing to Degas's procrastination, the journal was never officially published, although some of the work done in preparation was shown at the fifth Impressionist exhibition.

Success at printmaking led to Cassatt embarking with Degas and Pissarro on experimenting with printing in colour. The culmination of this project for Cassatt was the inclusion of a suite of ten colour prints, depicting scenes from the life of a modern woman, at her first retrospective exhibition organized by Durand-Ruel in 1891. *The Coiffure* (p. 177) is a preparatory drawing for the last image in the sequence. Inspired by prints by the Japanese artist Kitagawa Utamaro, which she had seen at an exhibition organized by Siegfried Bing at the École des Beaux-Arts in 1890, this particular set of prints is central to any evaluation of Cassatt's art, demonstrating the strength of her drawing, her skill in obtaining delicate tones and the empathetic nature of her subject matter.

Cassatt was born in Allegheny City, a suburb of Pittsburgh in Pennsylvania. She had an elder sister and three brothers. An indication of her affluent background is supplied by the fact that her father took the family to travel in Europe between 1851 and 1855 and that her elder brother became a Vice-President of the Pennsylvania Railway. Determined to become an artist, Cassatt enrolled in the Pennsylvania Academy of Fine Arts in 1860, where she was guided by John Sartain, who specialized in printmaking.

The lure of Europe, however, proved too much and in 1865 she moved to Paris where with characteristic vitality she studied in the studios of several artists – Jean-Léon Gérôme, Charles Chaplin, Thomas Couture, Pierre-Édouard Frère and Paul Constant Soyer. Her progress was such that one of her paintings was accepted at the Salon of 1868. The outbreak of the Franco-Prussian War in 1870 slowed the advance of her career, and she returned to America for the duration. On settling back in Europe, Cassatt moved between Italy, Spain and Belgium, spending several months in each country visiting museums, making copies and meeting other artists. In many respects Cassatt was almost overqualified as an artist by the time she returned to Paris, and her individuality was for a time suppressed by her desire for success at the Salon. Released from this dilemma by her friendship with the Impressionists, which began in the mid-1870s, she later declared of this moment, 'I already knew who were my true masters. I admired Manet, Courbet and Degas. I hated conventional art. I began to live.'

By that time, however, several members of her family had decided to join her in Paris, where they all eventually occupied a large, lavishly furnished apartment and a château at Beaufresne near Mesnil-Théribus in the Oise valley north of the capital. The frenetic activity that had gathered momentum during the 1880s and 1890s began to slow in the new century, with less emphasis on printmaking. The style of the paintings and pastels became freer, with more open drawing and stronger colours. Following the death of her parents during the first half of the 1890s, Cassatt's chances to travel again recurred. A visit to America in 1898 was followed by a trip to Egypt in 1910–11. However, she suffered from a growing fear of blindness that a series of cataract operations in 1915 did little to relieve. And the loss of all her siblings by 1911 led to an increasing sense of loneliness that was only offset by her new role as an advisor and facilitator to plutocratic American collectors. She was particularly close to Mrs Henry Havemeyer, but also served Mrs Potter Palmer, James Stillman, the Whittemores and the Sears in the same capacity. Cassatt's activities in this sphere helped to bring about the spectacular holdings of Impressionist art in America today. During the First World War Cassatt took refuge in Switzerland, but afterwards presided as the chatelaine of Beaufresne, where she died.

Cassatt's debut at the fourth Impressionist exhibition was well judged and the critics were generous in their praise. The modernity of her subject matter and style is immediately apparent in the paintings and pastels she submitted. The *Portrait of Moïse Dreyfus* (p. 175) is one of the very few male portraits she made outside her immediate family. It is notable for its stable composition based on a pyramid, with the seated figure placed low down in the picture space, contained within an armchair before a blank wall. The sitter's body is positioned at an angle, but his head looks directly at the viewer and is given greater emphasis by being seen against the empty background. Cassatt often resorted to pyramidal compositions in later years as a way of filling the picture space, with the figures shown prominently in the foreground, giving the whole a sense of amplitude.

In the Loge (p. 176) was one of several such treatments that Cassatt included in the fourth exhibition, all of which stand comparison with similar works by Renoir and Degas. The handling of the pastel evokes the fugitive effects of artificial lighting in an interior setting, while the blurring of the balconies in the background suggests the distance across the open space. The fan is more than an accessory and is employed as a pictorial device obscuring the view of the auditorium, as well as protecting the anonymity of the young woman situated within the privacy of her loge. As in works by Degas, there is skilful play upon the theme of who exactly is viewing whom and for what purpose.

Although in 1892 Cassatt was commissioned to paint a large mural for the Woman's Building at the World's Columbian Exposition in Chicago and chose for her subject *Modern Woman* (presumed destroyed), her most sustained exploration of the domestic scene, both formal and informal, occurred in her paintings and pastels. Many of these works are devoted to mothers tending their children in the nursery or at play both inside and outdoors, and there are moments of striking intimacy in them (pp. 178–82). It is no exaggeration to say that Cassatt's depiction of the mother-and-child theme is unsurpassed in nineteenth- and twentieth-century art. The gestures she used of embracing, caressing and touching have their origins in religious iconography stretching back to the thirteenth century, but what is so movingly represented in Cassatt's paintings and pastels is the potential warmth in all humanity. She combines the squirming movements of Leonardo da Vinci's holy children with the calm assurance of Raphael's or Giovanni Bellini's and the reflective confidence of Sassoferrato's. The viewer is persuaded of the boldness of Cassatt's images in part because she thrusts the figures forwards right up to the picture plane, but there is also a purity in the drawing and a resonance in the colouring that make an immediate impact. There is no need for mediation or special interpretation: you see what you see. And this is certainly the case with her portraits of children on their own (p. 183).

One critic who immediately saw what Cassatt was trying to achieve was Joris-Karl Huysmans, whose bizarre lifestyle was far removed from the artist's own. He wrote in *L'Art Moderne* (1883) that she is 'an artist who owes nothing any longer to anyone, an artist totally spontaneous and personal...It is a miracle how in these subjects...Miss Cassatt has known the way to escape from sentimentality on which most...foundered. For the first time...I have seen family life painted with distinction...[and with] a penetrating feeling of intimacy.'

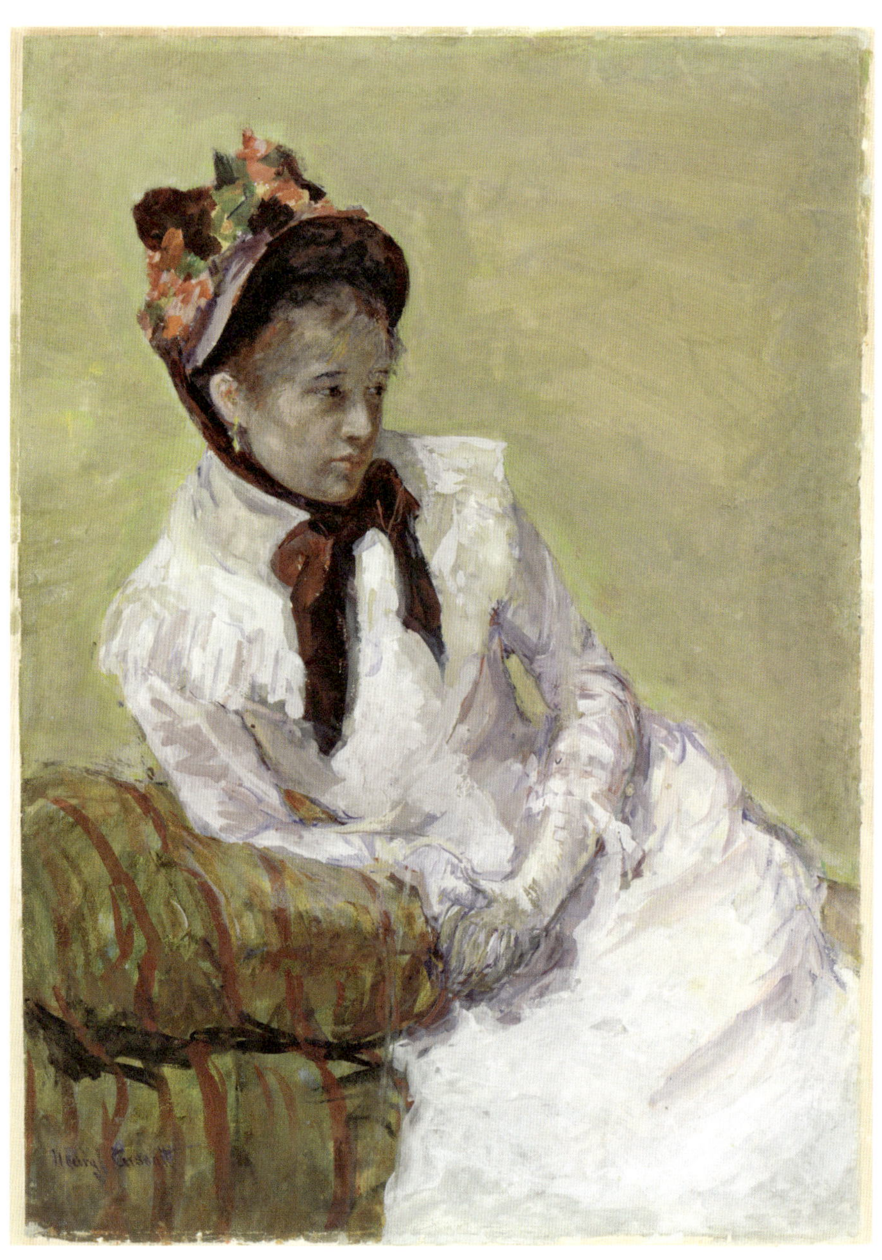

174 *Mary Cassatt*

Portrait of the Artist, 1878
Watercolour and gouache, 60 × 41.1 cm (23⅝ × 16⅛ in.).
METROPOLITAN MUSEUM OF ART, NEW YORK

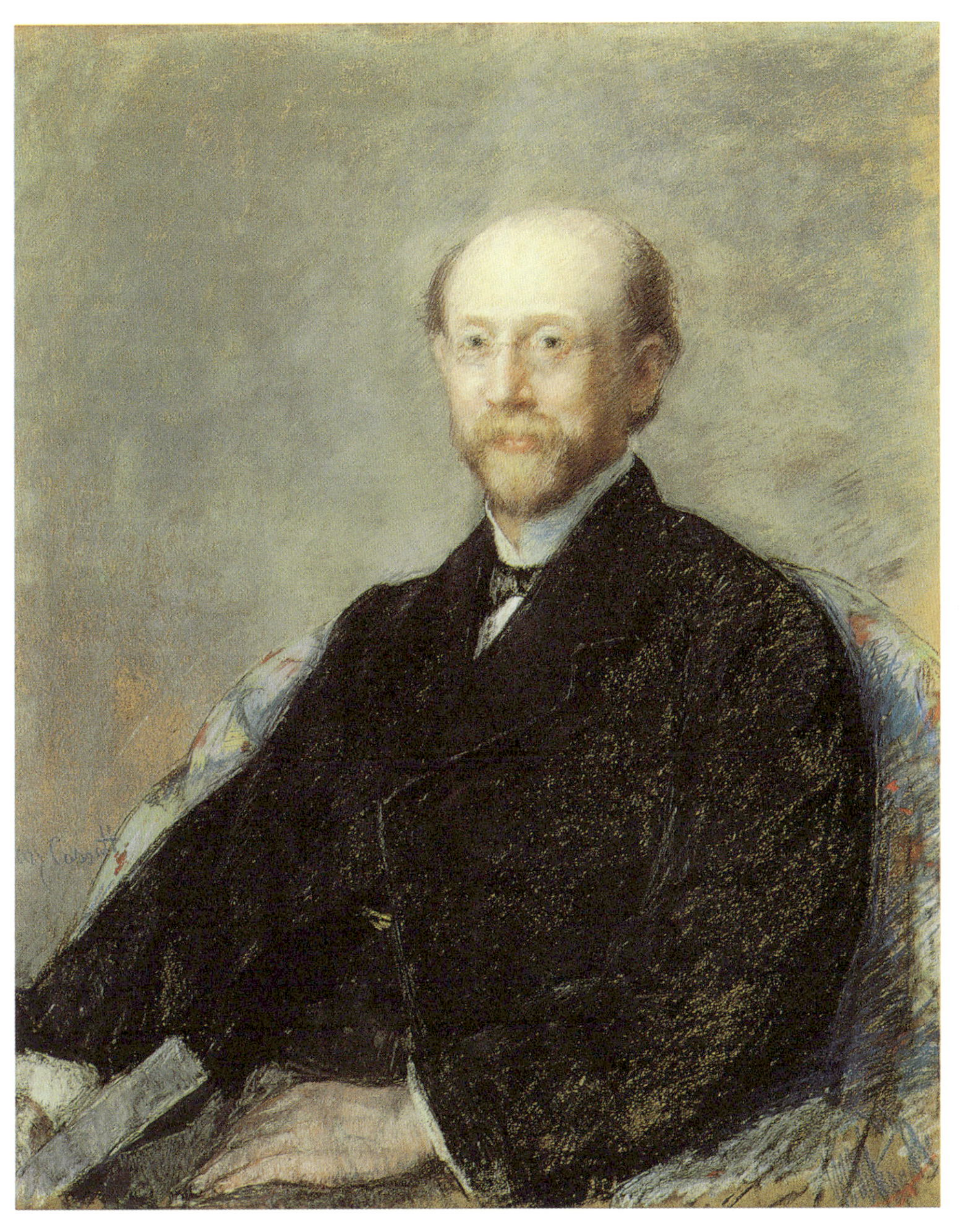

Portrait of Moïse Dreyfus, 1879
Pastel on buff-coloured paper, 81.2 × 65.2 cm (32 × 25⅝ in.).
PETIT PALAIS, MUSÉE DES BEAUX-ARTS DE LA VILLE DE PARIS

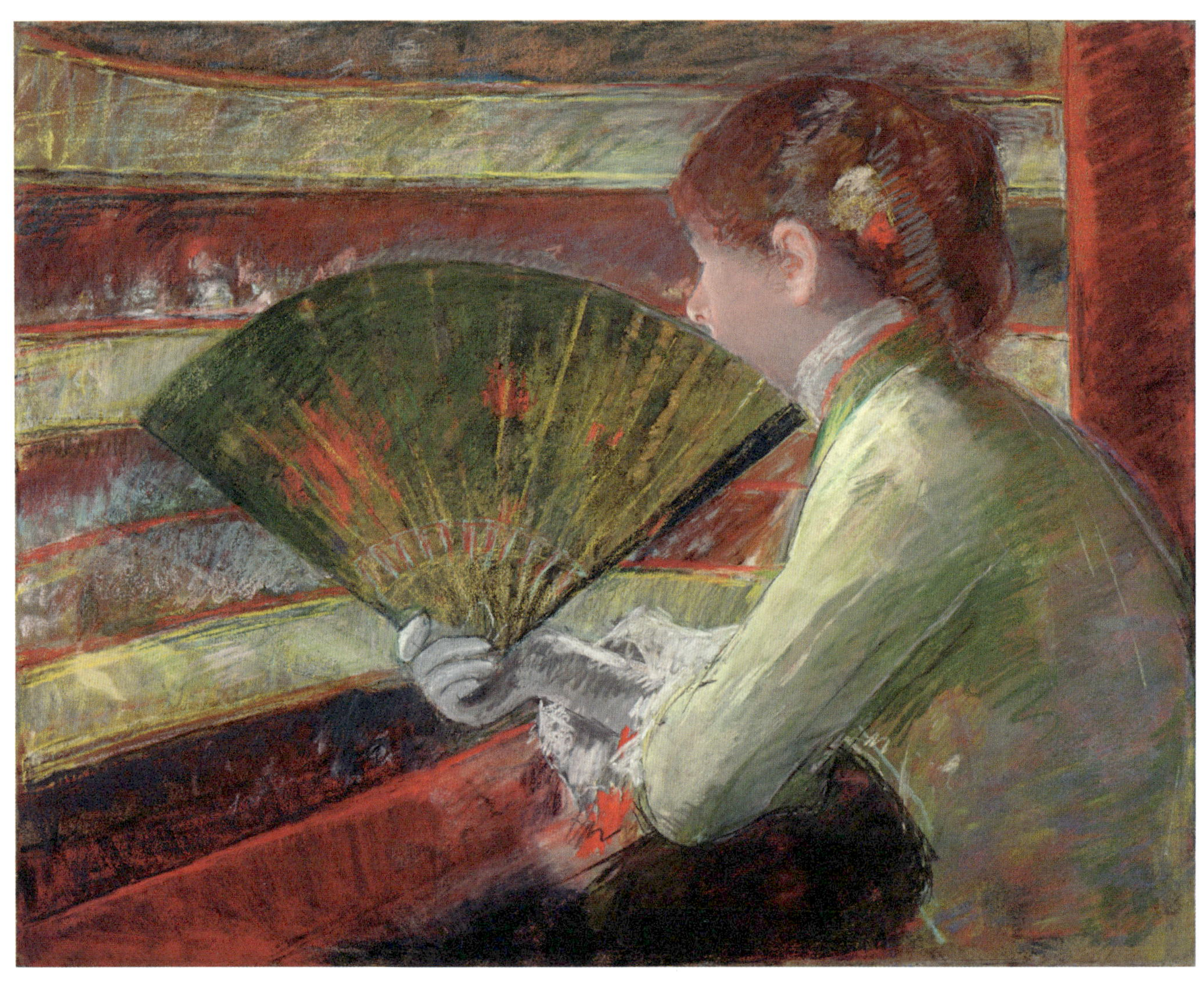

  Mary Cassatt

In the Loge, 1879
Pastel and gold metallic paint on canvas,
65.1 × 81.3 cm (25⅝ × 32 in.).
PHILADELPHIA MUSEUM OF ART

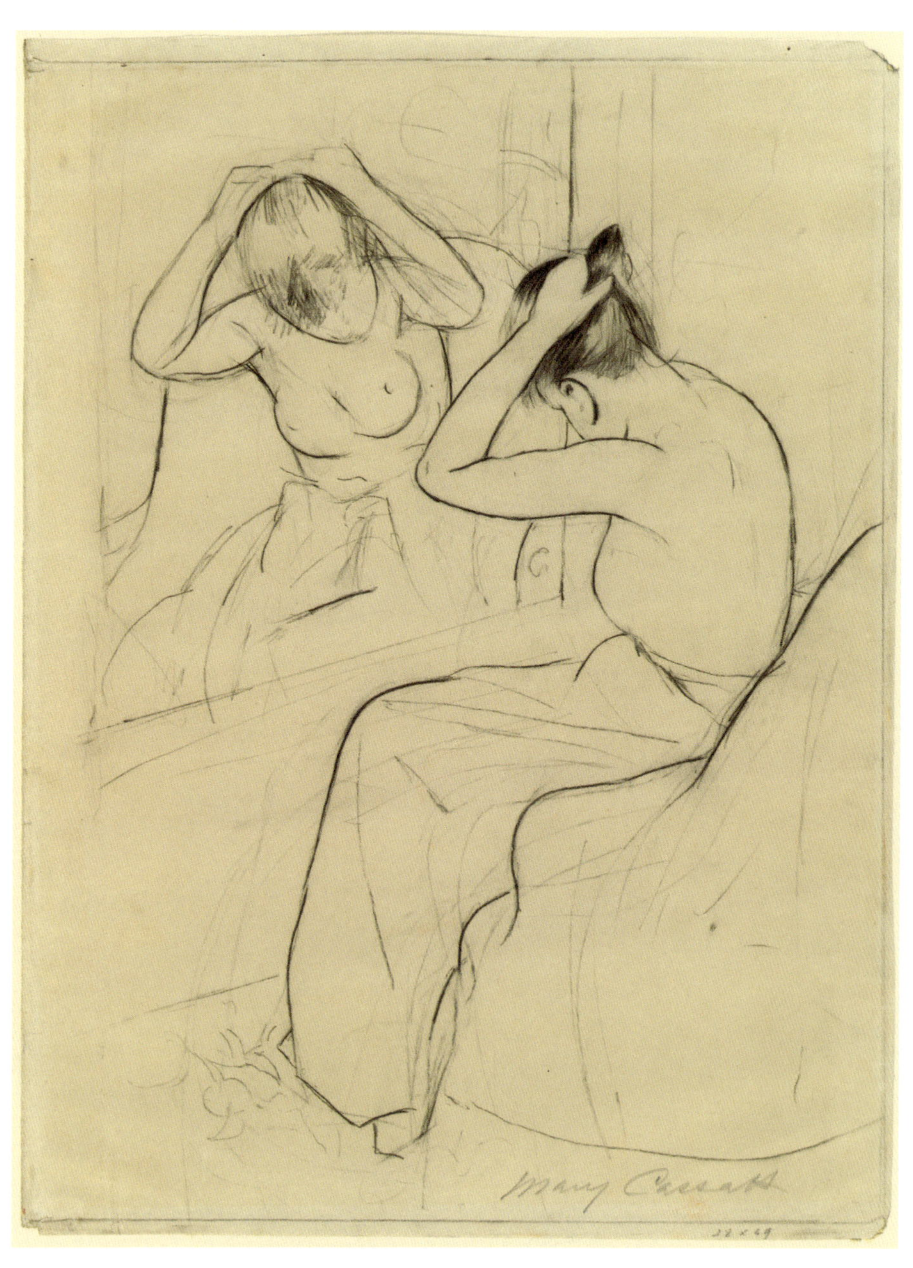

The Coiffure, 1891
Black crayon and pencil,
38.3 × 27.7 cm (15 × 10⅞ in.). Signed.
NATIONAL GALLERY OF ART, WASHINGTON, DC

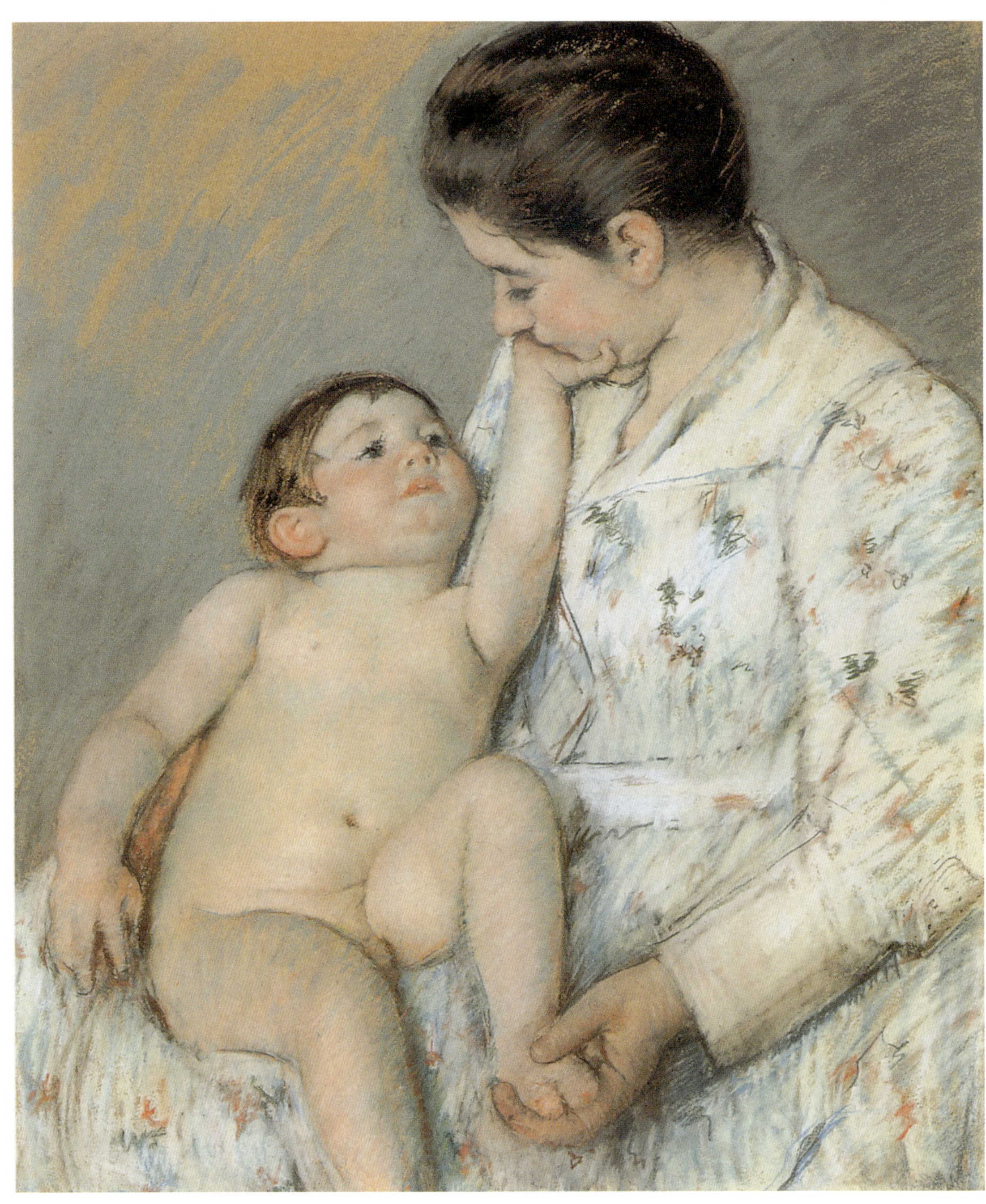

   Mary Cassatt

Baby's First Caress, c. 1890
Pastel, 76.2 × 61 cm (30 × 24 in.).
NEW BRITAIN MUSEUM OF AMERICAN ART, CONNECTICUT

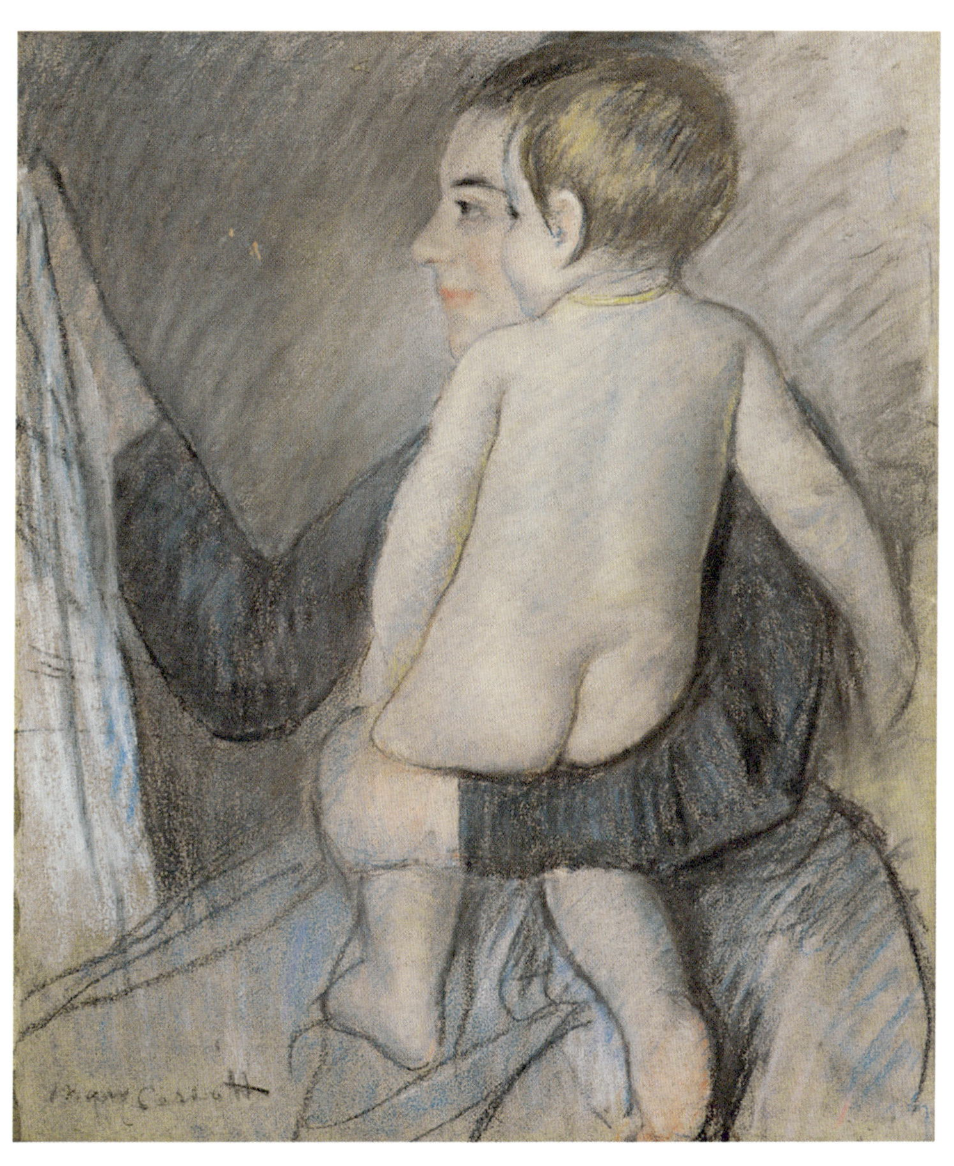

At the Window, 1889
Pastel and charcoal on grey paper,
74.5 × 62.5 cm (29⅜ × 24⅝ in.). Signed.
Musée d'Orsay, Paris

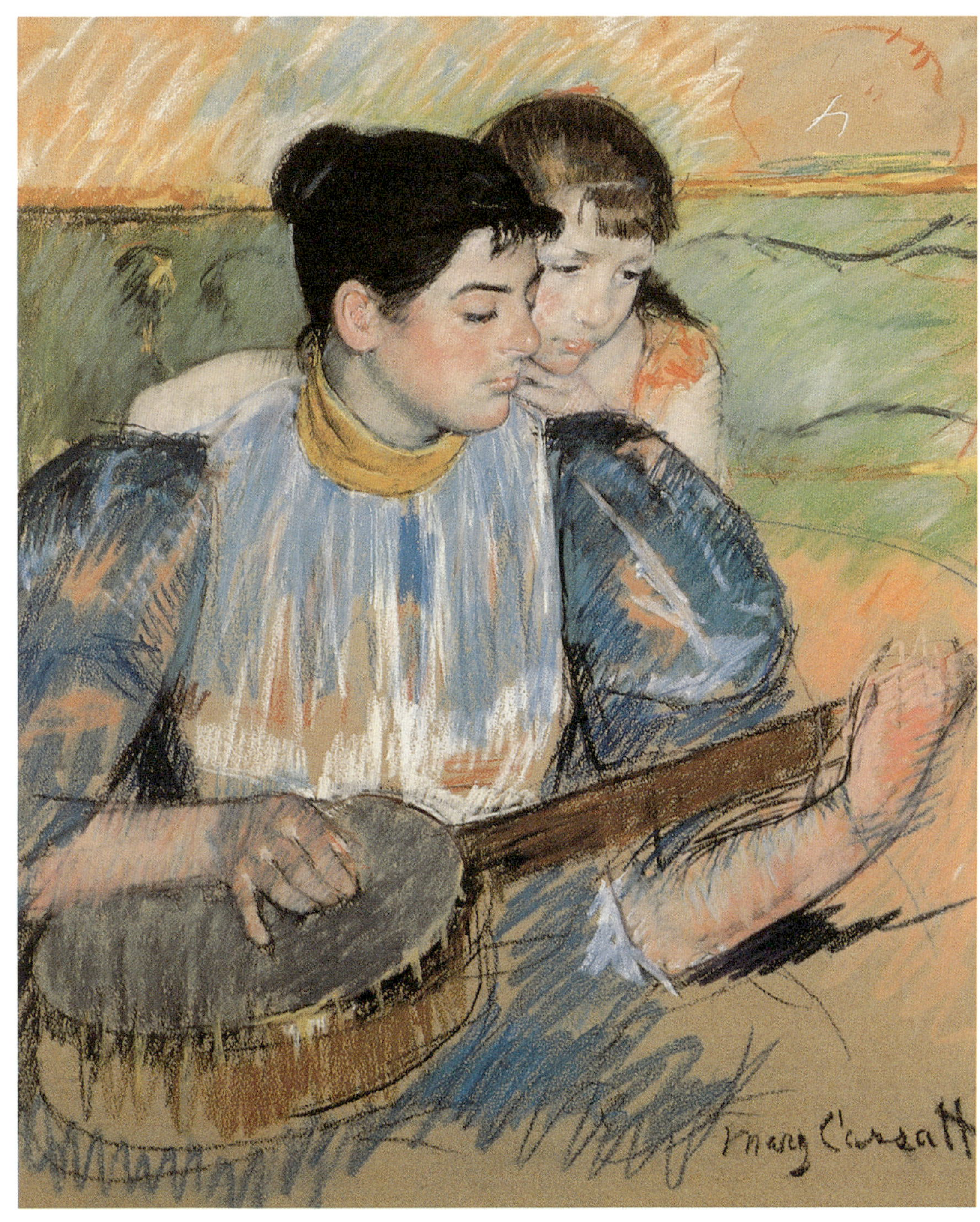

180   *Mary Cassatt*

The Banjo Lesson, c. 1894
Pastel over oiled pastel on tan wove paper,
71.1 × 57.2 cm (28 × 22½ in.). Signed.
VIRGINIA MUSEUM OF FINE ARTS, RICHMOND

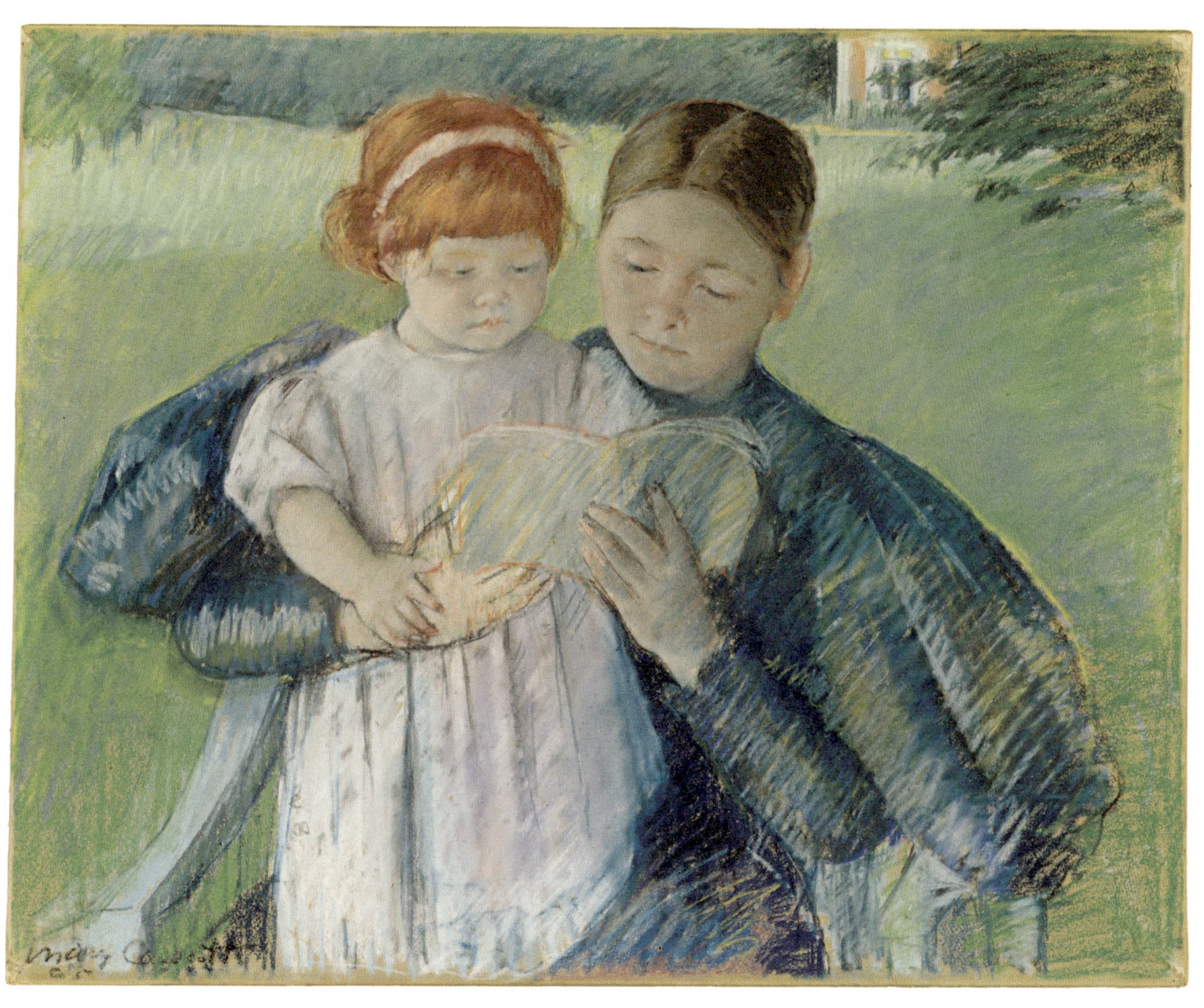

Nurse Reading to a Little Girl, 1895
Pastel on paper mounted on canvas,
60 × 73 cm (23⅝ × 28¾ in.). Signed.
METROPOLITAN MUSEUM OF ART, NEW YORK

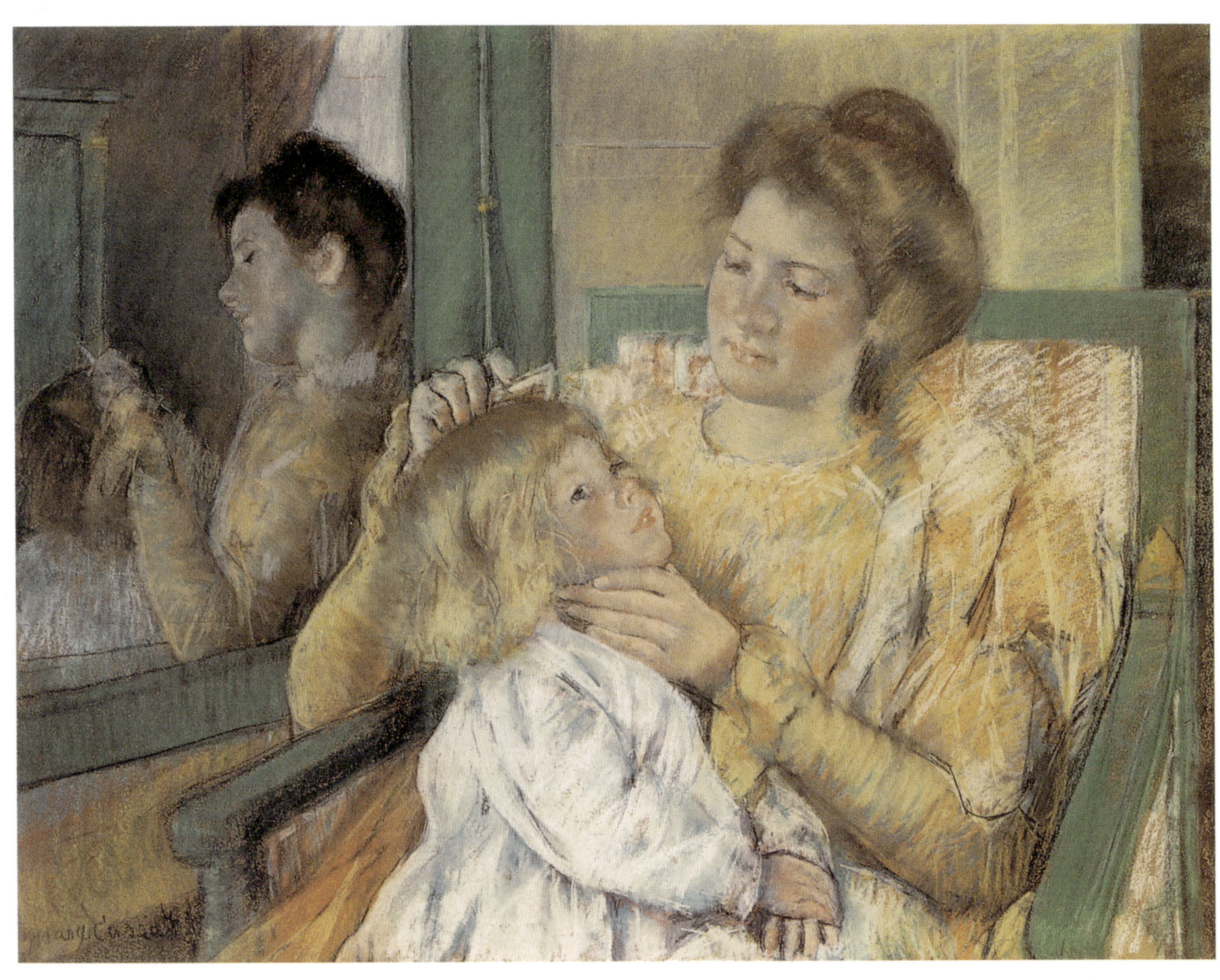

  Mary Cassatt

Mother Combing her Child's Hair, c. 1901
Pastel on grey paper, 64.1 × 80.3 cm (25¼ × 31⅝ in.). Signed.
BROOKLYN MUSEUM, NEW YORK

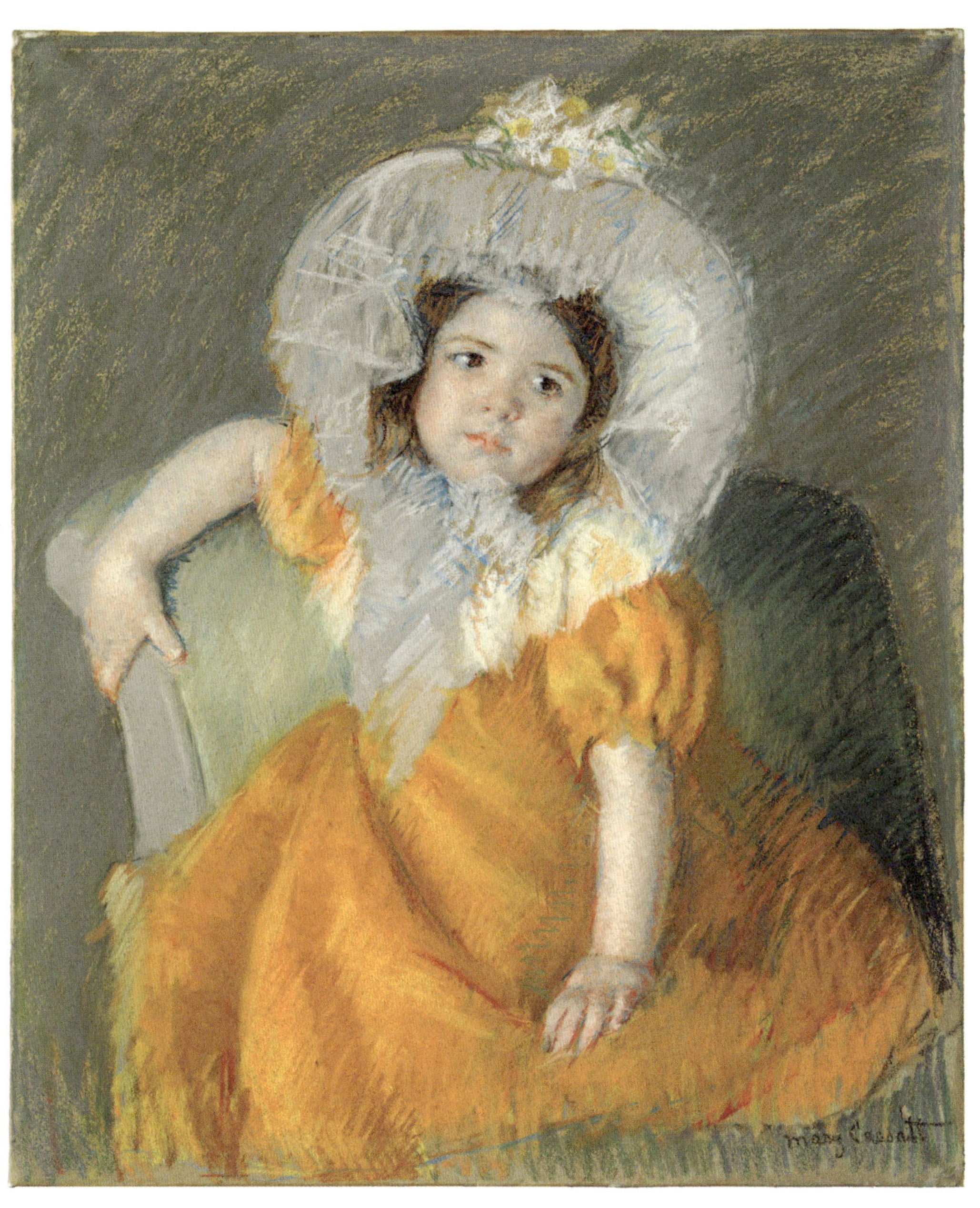

Margot in Orange Dress, 1902
Pastel on paper mounted on canvas,
72.4 × 59.4 cm (28½ × 23⅜ in.). Signed.
METROPOLITAN MUSEUM OF ART, NEW YORK

183

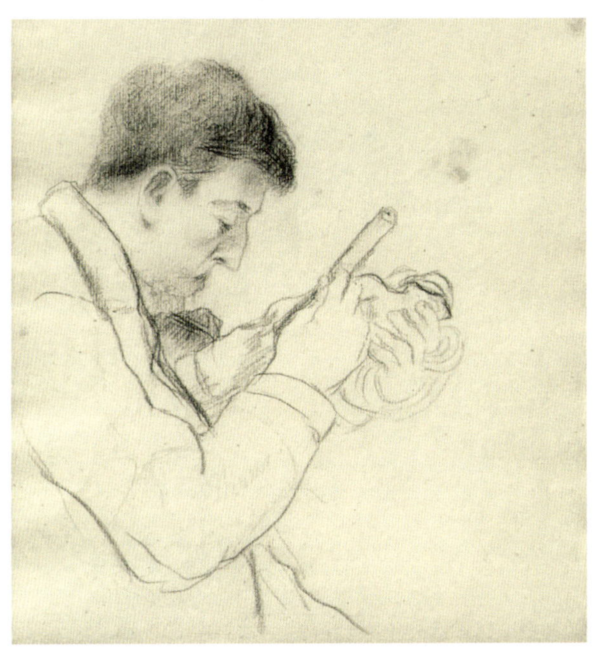

Paul Gauguin
1848–1903

Anyone looking at Paul Gauguin's work has to learn to disentangle myth from reality. The artist himself, sometimes deliberately, tended to distort the truth, and his nomadic spirit may well have been a search for his own identity as well as a way of enriching his art. For, although born in Paris, Gauguin's early years were unsettled. Part of his child-hood was spent in Peru, and after schooling in France he served for six years (1865–71) at sea before beginning a career in the financial world as a stockbroker, which he pursued until 1882. Both Gauguin's parents died before his coming of age, but he was fortunate in that one of his guardians, Gustave Arosa, was a successful businessman who had an important collection of nineteenth-century French art, including many works by the Impressionists. Gustave's brother, Achille, formed a similar collection and also had a wide range of contacts in the business and art worlds. Whether it was the collections formed by the Arosa brothers (Gustave's was sold at auction in 1878 and Achille's in 1891) that ignited Gauguin's interest in art is not known, but they certainly encouraged it.

Camille Pissarro
Gauguin Carving 'Strolling Woman', 1880
Black chalk, 29.5 × 23.3 cm (11⅝ × 9¼ in.).
NATIONALMUSEUM, STOCKHOLM

Marriage to a Danish woman, Mette Gad, in 1873 meant that Gauguin needed to start thinking about his future. Increasingly, he chose art over business. By the time of his marriage he had begun to paint as an amateur and subsequently one of his paintings was accepted for exhibition at the Salon of 1876. Two years later, he began to form his personal collection of Impressionist art, which he used first of all as a source of reference for his own painting and then as a hedge against financial disaster.

Essentially, Gauguin was self-taught and throughout his life guarded his independence jealously. This is perhaps best demonstrated by the number of times he turned his back on Paris, preferring to find his inspiration in places further and further from the capital: Brittany (1886, 1888–90 and 1894), followed by French possessions overseas – Martinique (1887) and islands in the southern Pacific Ocean (Tahiti in 1891–93 and 1895–1901 and the Marquesas in 1901–03). Fortunately, Gauguin's abilities were recognized by Pissarro, Degas and indirectly by Cézanne. With such support he was invited to participate in five of the Impressionist exhibitions, beginning with the fourth in 1879. Although he was a late starter, it is not true to say that Gauguin was a slow developer since as an autodidact he felt no allegiance to any single style or theory and therefore followed his own course.

Gauguin was, however, attentive to tradition. No copies of works by old masters from his hand are known, but he travelled everywhere with a portfolio of prints, photographs and reproductions of art of all periods, schools and countries. A certain dualism therefore exists in his art, because, although deliberately seeking and confronting new subject matter, he often presented such material in symbolist terms based on religious or mythological iconography. To that extent, Gauguin did not so much transform art as refresh it. His criticism of the Impressionists was that their work lacked imagination: it was not sufficient to copy nature. As he wrote to Emile Schuffenecker in 1888, 'Art is an abstraction; extract it from nature while dreaming in front of it and pay more attention to the act of creation than to the result.' The closely related Cloisonnist and Synthetist styles that Gauguin began to use in Brittany sought unity and clarity of composition, achieved with strong contours and clear patches of colour that resulted in works left open to interpretation by the viewer.

Combative in spirit, egotistical by nature and bombastic in manner, Gauguin's ambition was unrestrained. This involved him in a degree of self-sacrifice: the break-up of his family and estrangement from his five children by Mette; constant financial difficulties leading to a shortage of basic art materials and personal neglect; and over-dependence on others often complicated by slow communications when in distant places. In addition, there were periods of illness and self-doubt, particularly during his final years in the South Seas. In fear of being misunderstood or misinterpreted, Gauguin wrote, or started to write, a number of apologias that are a mix of autobiography, art theory, history and anthropology. However, his proselytizing and self-promotion often led to disagreements and embarrassments. Many of those who had supported him at the outset were often ignored or contradicted. Pissarro, for example, had already concluded by 1891 that Gauguin was not a 'prophet' but a 'schemer'. Undoubtedly, though, what Gauguin did establish was artistic freedom: subject, style, treatment and materials should be the artist's choice alone and not dictated or influenced by any set of existing rules.

Gauguin was a complete artist. He was not only a painter, but also a sculptor, ceramicist, wood-carver and printmaker, who, owing to unusual circumstances, was occasionally obliged to initiate new ways of making art. His working methods did not recognize any hierarchical division between painting, drawing and printmaking, just as in the painting process itself he fused drawing and colour. Gauguin relished the enigmatic and he enjoyed exploiting techniques that were ambivalent, such as mono-types, transfer drawings and collage. The pastel *The Sculptor Aubé and his Son, Emile* (p. 188) signals Gauguin's independent approach to art. Mounted as a diptych, the two figures ignore one another and may not even share the same space since they seem to be placed on different levels. The only unifying factor is the ceramic vase on the workbench in the foreground. Paul Aubé was a sculptor, who also fashioned figurines for ceramic vases, as indeed did Gauguin himself.

Brittany was the first of the alternative locations explored by Gauguin, where to begin with he worked at Pont-Aven and later at Le Pouldu. *Breton Girl* (p. 189 above) is a study used initially for the painting *Four Breton Women Chatting* of 1886 (Bayerische Staatsgemäldesammlungen, Munich) and then on a vase (Musées Royaux d'Art et d'Histoire, Brussels). The influence of both Degas and Pissarro is evident in this back view of a figure standing with hands on hips, and even though the face is hidden the pose is full of character. On the other hand, *Young Breton Bather* (p. 189 below), which was used for a painting of the same title dating from 1888 (Kunsthalle, Hamburg), at first sight resembles an academic study. But, in fact, the strong outlines in the lower half of the body denote the Synthetist style that Gauguin had fully evolved by 1890. Similar heavily defined outlines are found in *Head of a Martinique Girl* (p. 190) and particularly in the drawing of Mme Ginoux (p. 191) for the painting *At the Café* (Pushkin State Museum of Fine Arts, Moscow) executed in Arles in 1888. The former shows Gauguin's respect for Eugène Delacroix and the latter for Raphael: both sheets were known to Van Gogh, who had invited Gauguin to share a studio with him in Arles during the autumn of 1888.

Gauguin may have had a mercurial personality, likening himself on many occa-sions to a savage, but he was a slow and methodical worker who liked to absorb the landscape and atmosphere of a place by recording myriad motifs in sketchbooks, ready for future use. During his two stays on Tahiti, the artist was determined to become fully integrated by intermingling with the people and becoming conversant with their history and customs, as well as experiencing the beauties of the tropical landscape. He did this with mixed success. Just as Brittany was beginning to be exploited by tourism, so Tahiti and the Marquesas Islands had already been exposed to colonialism for many years. Gauguin was not unaware of this situation, and ironically in both cases he may be described as a participant in the process of change, but this did not stop him finding both the landscape and the people in such places full of inspiration.

Crouching Tahitian Woman (p. 192 above) forms part of the preparatory process for the painting *Nafea faaipoipo (When Will You Marry?)* of 1892 (Private collection). The self-contained figure with its firm curvilinear outlines and carefully blocked-in areas of colour was repeated in several other compositions. The fan (p. 192 below) with the folds visible, indicating that it was intended for use rather than decoration, is based on the painting *Arearea (Joyousness)* of 1892 (Musée d'Orsay, Paris) and was probably made in France between Gauguin's two Tahitian periods. The scene may represent a festival, with worshippers visiting a shrine in the background. The title is reflected in the lyrical style: arabesque lines and bright colours with an unusual emphasis on white in the foreground. The flatness of the figures demonstrates Gauguin's knowledge of Assyrian and Egyptian art.

The two watercolours *Pape Moe (Mysterious Water)* (p. 193) and *Te Arii Vahine (The Queen of Beauty)* (p. 194) are related to paintings dating from 1893 and 1896 respectively. For the first, although Gauguin had witnessed a similar scene himself when he came across a girl drinking from a stream of water before diving into a pool below and disappearing, he actually based the composition on a photograph by Charles Spitz. The second renders a Tahitian subject in terms of classical iconography refracted through works by Lucas Cranach the Younger and Manet's *Olympia*. It is perhaps more likely that these watercolours were made after the paintings as opposed to being preparatory. As independent works, they reveal Gauguin's preference for applying his watercolours sparingly and in a fairly dry state, leaving the paper to provide the luminosity.

There are many studies of the heads of Tahitian women dating from Gauguin's final years. *Tahitian Faces (Frontal View and Profiles)* (p. 195) is one of the finest and was made in connection with a painting, *Two Tahitian Women,* of 1899 (Metropolitan Museum of Art, New York) where the central figure confronts the viewer holding a tray with an offering of flower petals or fruit. The three heads in the drawing are in all likelihood the same person, who is the dominant figure in the picture, but the *mise-en-page* is reminiscent of a *Three Ages of Man*. This study is notable for its directness and does not underplay the heavy, almost sculptural, features typical of Tahitian women in Gauguin's art. The charcoal has been gently applied, with only some of the outlines being redrawn, and limited areas of accented shading. The whiteness of the paper makes the face seem almost ghostly, but without any loss to the sense of majesty. As such, the image imparts something of the hypnotic beauty that Gauguin found in the people of the islands of the South Seas, to whom he was totally committed by the end of his life and among whom he died.

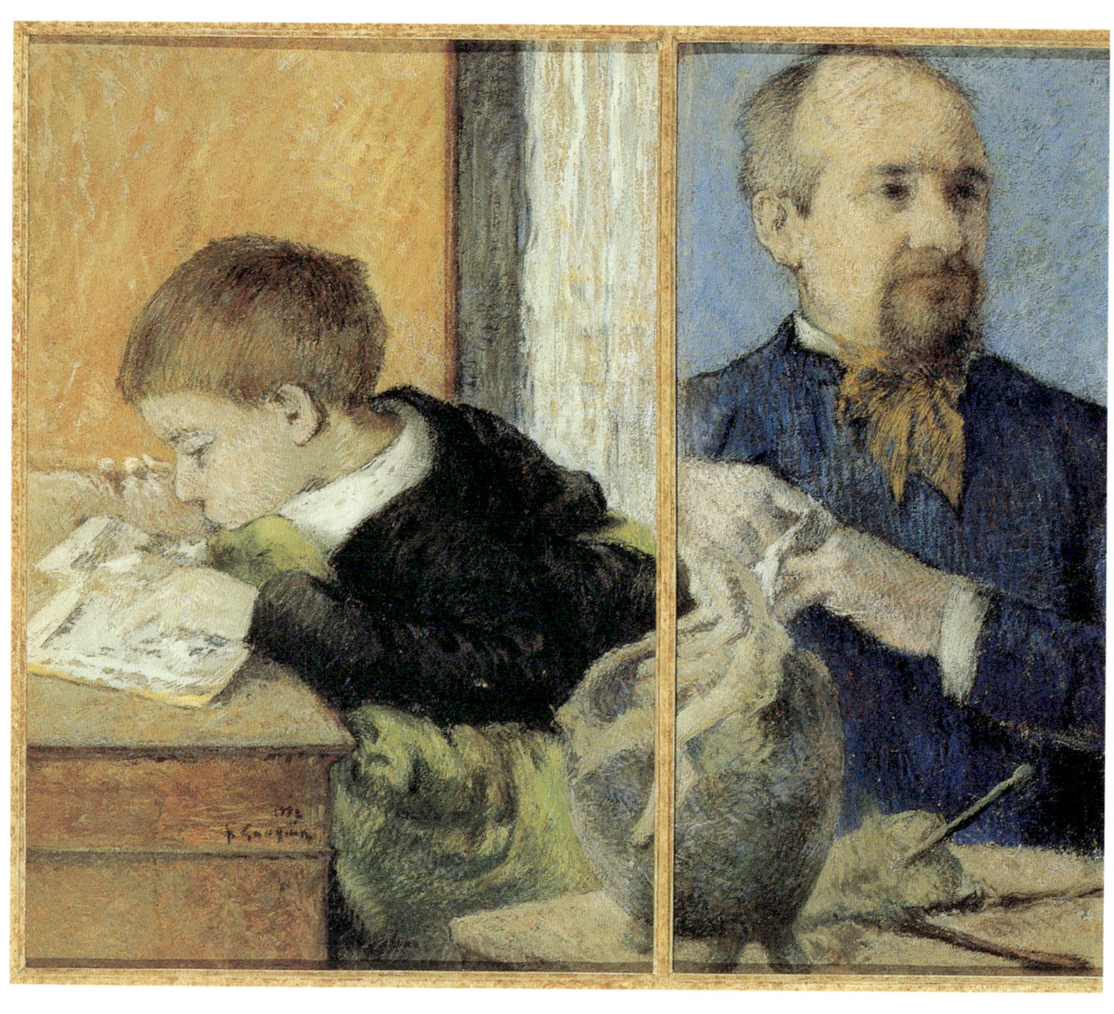

    Paul Gauguin

The Sculptor Aubé and his Son, Emile, 1882
Pastel on grey paper mounted on card,
53.8 × 72.8 cm (22⅛ × 28⅝ in.). Signed and dated.
PETIT PALAIS, MUSÉE DES BEAUX-ARTS DE LA VILLE DE PARIS

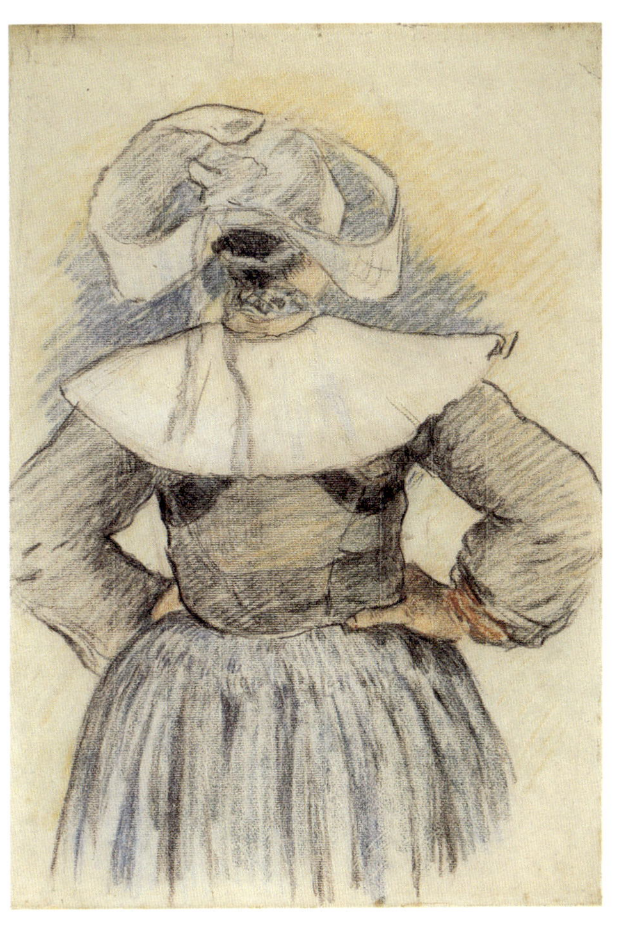

Breton Girl, 1886
Charcoal and pastel, 48 × 32 cm (18⅞ × 12⅝ in.).
BURRELL COLLECTION, GLASGOW

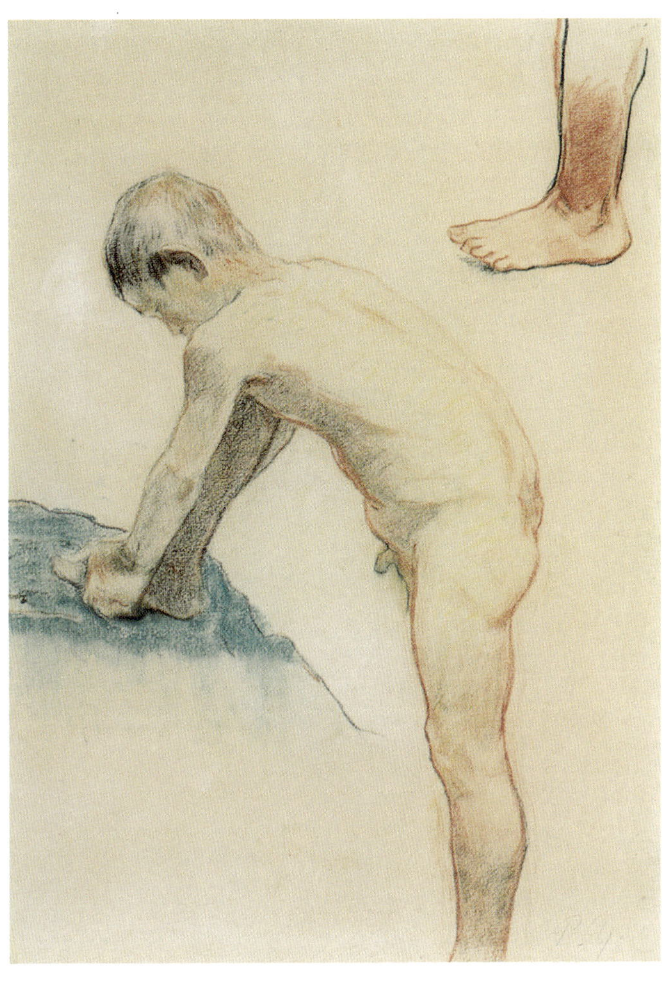

Young Breton Bather, 1888
Red chalk, pastel and charcoal,
59.5 × 41.5 cm (23⅜ × 16⅜ in.), squared.
MUSÉE DU LOUVRE (COLLECTION MUSÉE D'ORSAY), PARIS

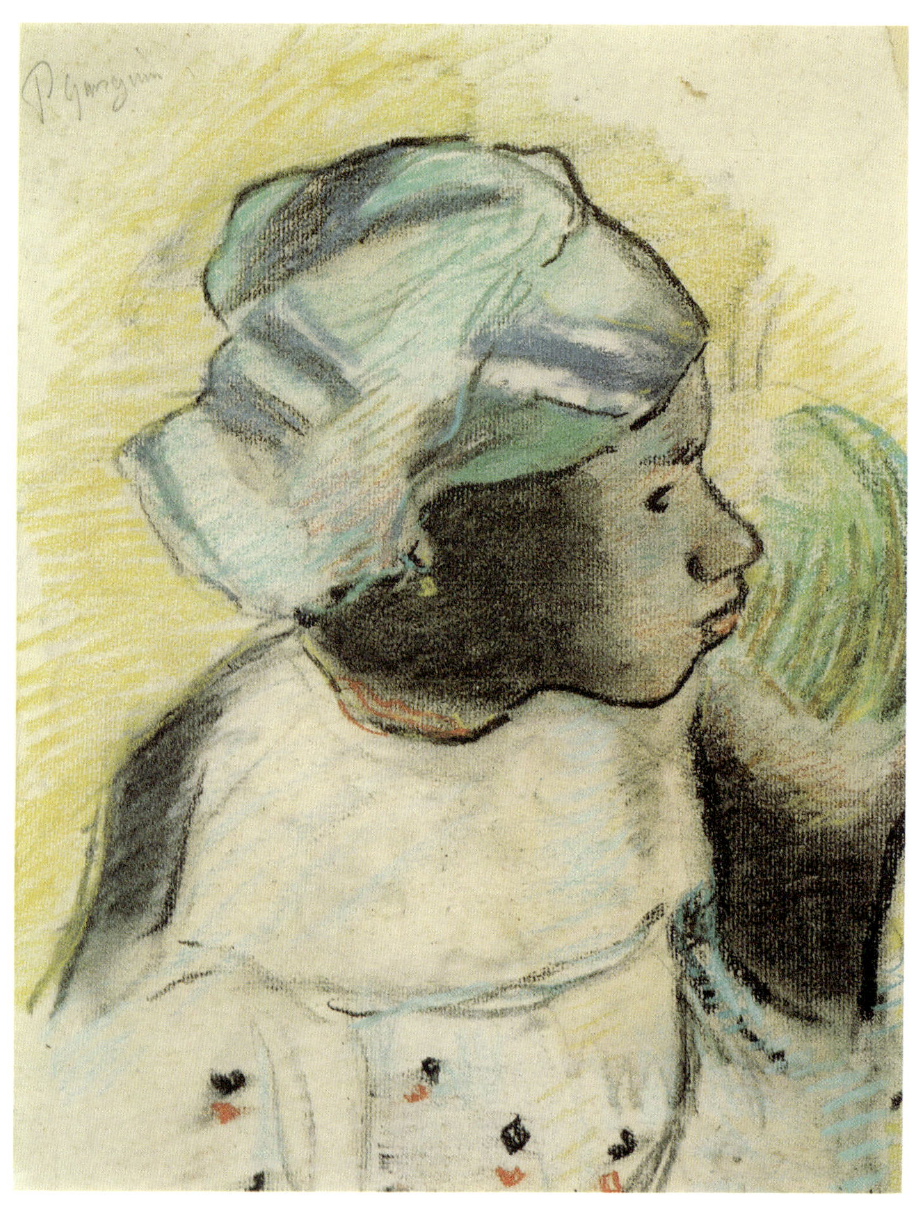

190   *Paul Gauguin*

Head of a Martinique Girl, 1887
Pastel, 36 × 27 cm (14⅛ × 10⅝ in.). Signed.
VAN GOGH MUSEUM, AMSTERDAM

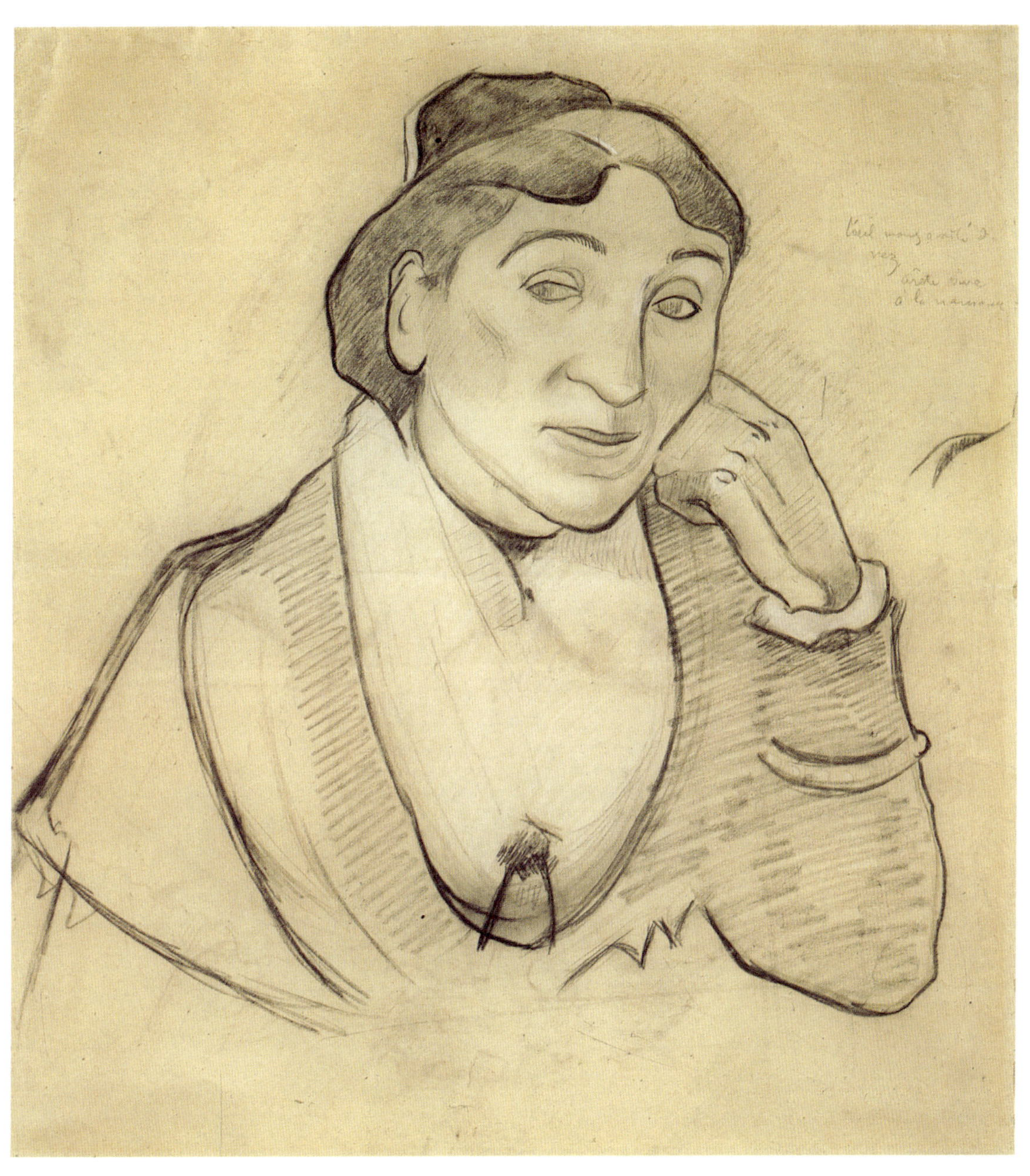

The Arlésienne (Mme Ginoux), 1888
Charcoal and pastel heightened with white chalk
on beige paper, 56.1 × 49.2 cm (22⅛ × 19⅜ in.).
THE FINE ARTS MUSEUMS, SAN FRANCISCO

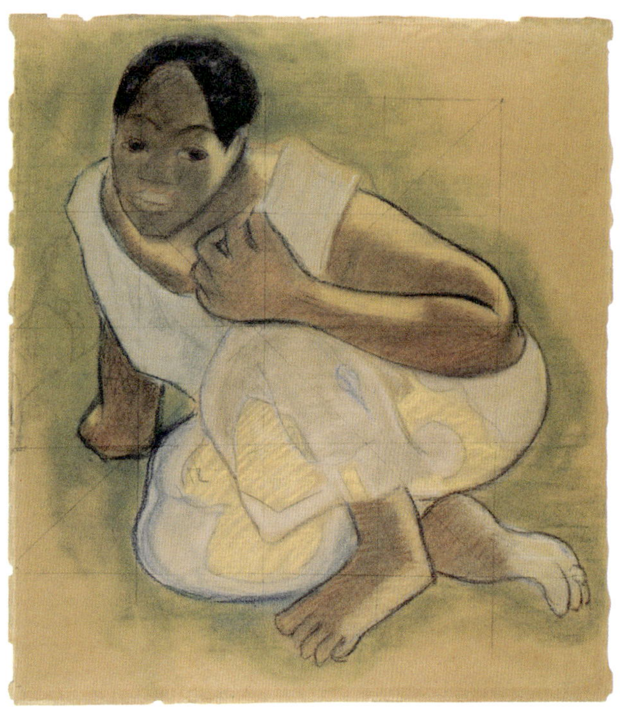

Crouching Tahitian Woman, 1892
Pastel and charcoal with stumping,
55.5 × 48 cm (21⅞ × 18⅞ in.), squared.
THE ART INSTITUTE OF CHICAGO

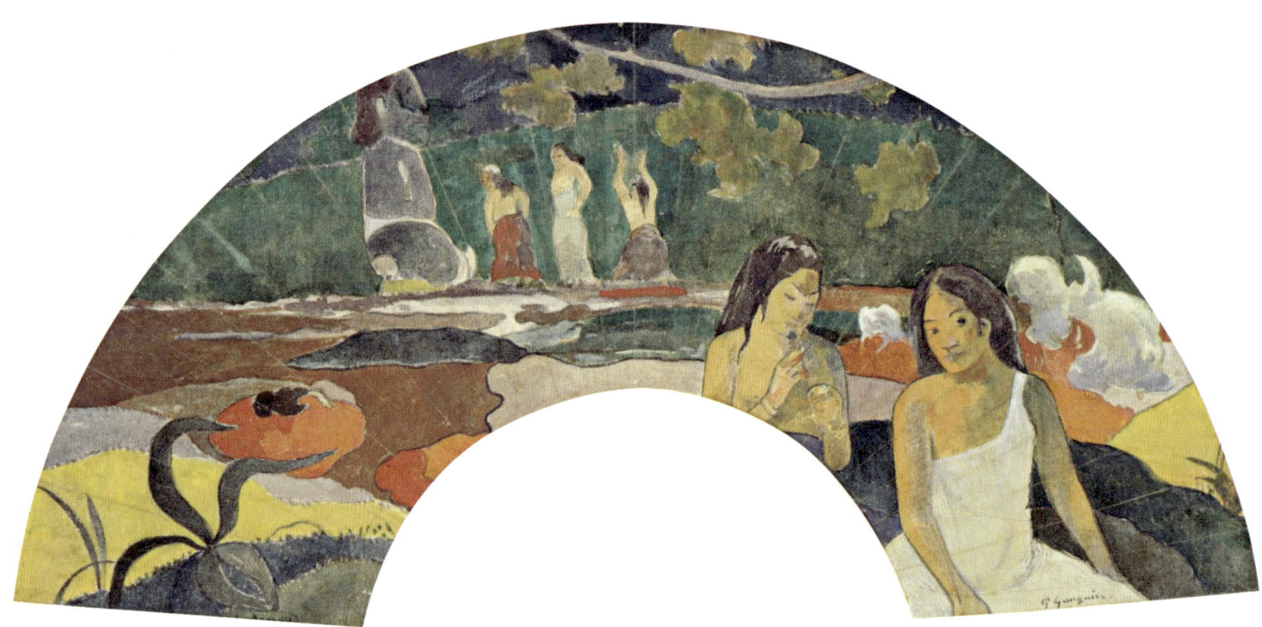

  Paul Gauguin

Fan Decorated with Motifs from Arearea (Joyousness), c. 1894–95
Watercolour and gouache over pencil on linen, 28.6 × 58.4 cm
(11¼ × 23 in.). Signed.
HOUSTON MUSEUM OF FINE ARTS

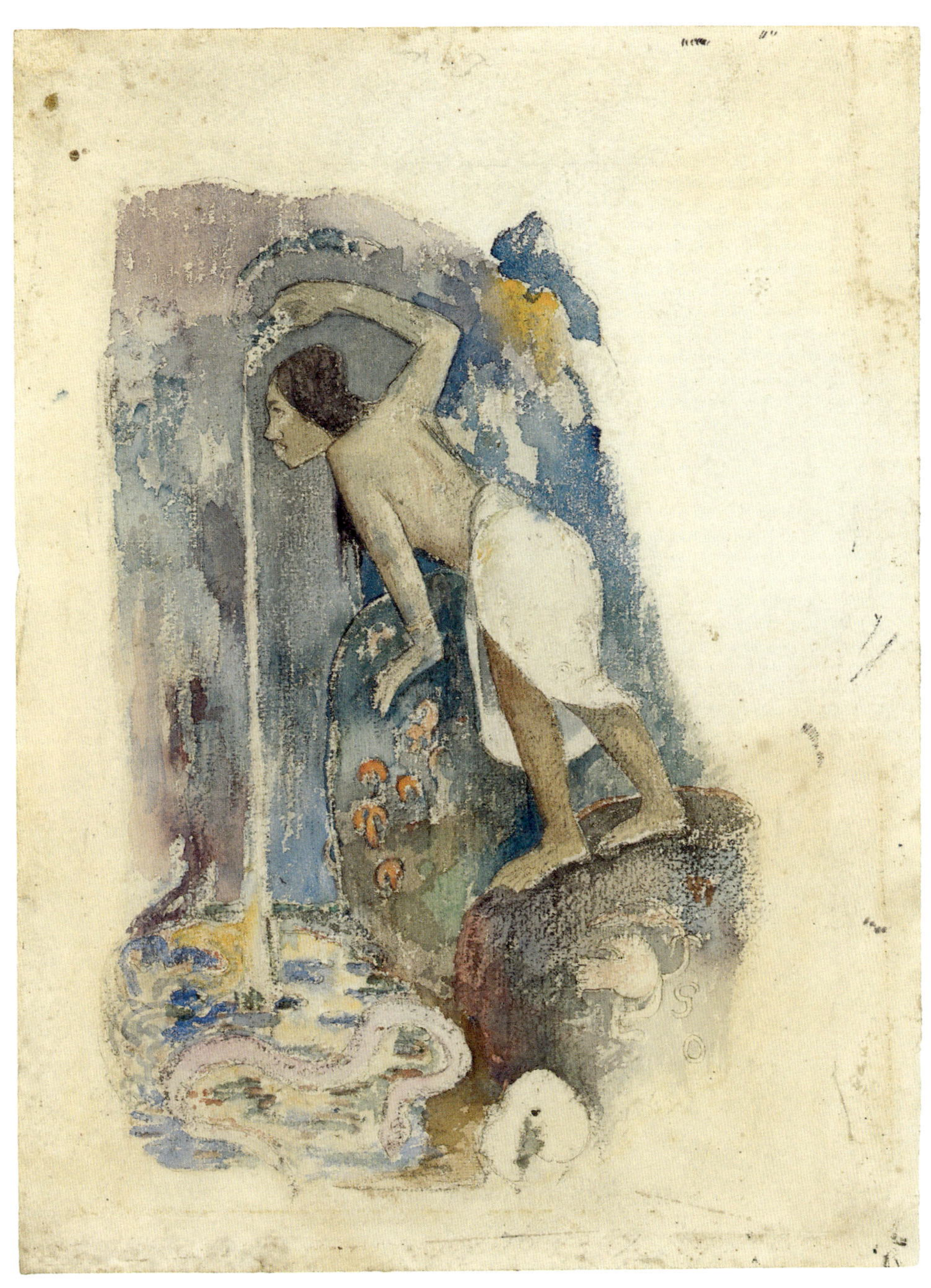

Pape Moe (Mysterious Water), 1893
Watercolour and black chalk with pen and ink,
35.4 × 25.5 cm (13⅞ × 10 in.). Signed.
THE ART INSTITUTE OF CHICAGO

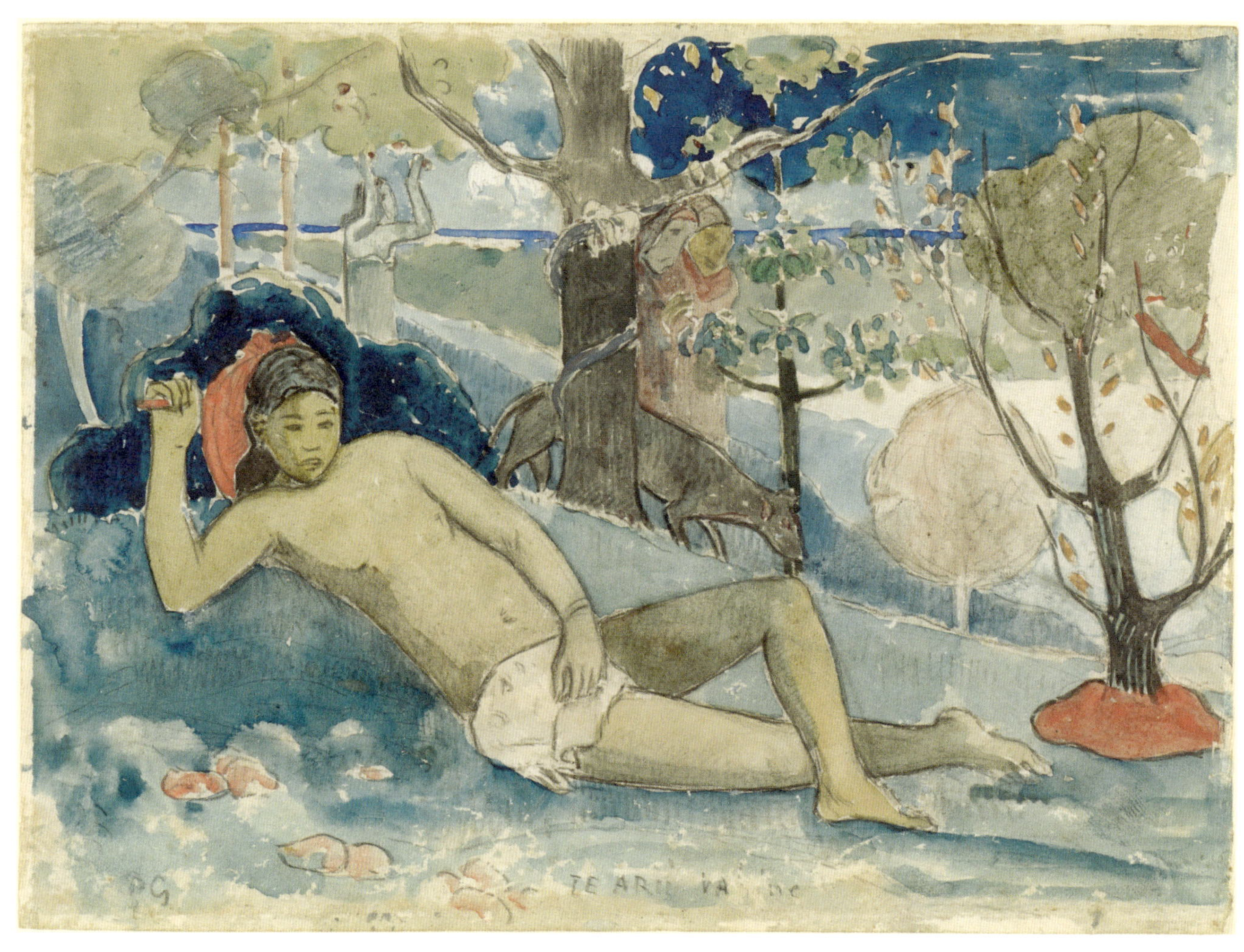

194   *Paul Gauguin*   *Te Arii Vahine (The Queen of Beauty)*, c. 1896–97
Watercolour over black chalk, 17.6 × 23.5 cm (6⅞ × 9¼ in.).
PIERPONT MORGAN LIBRARY, NEW YORK

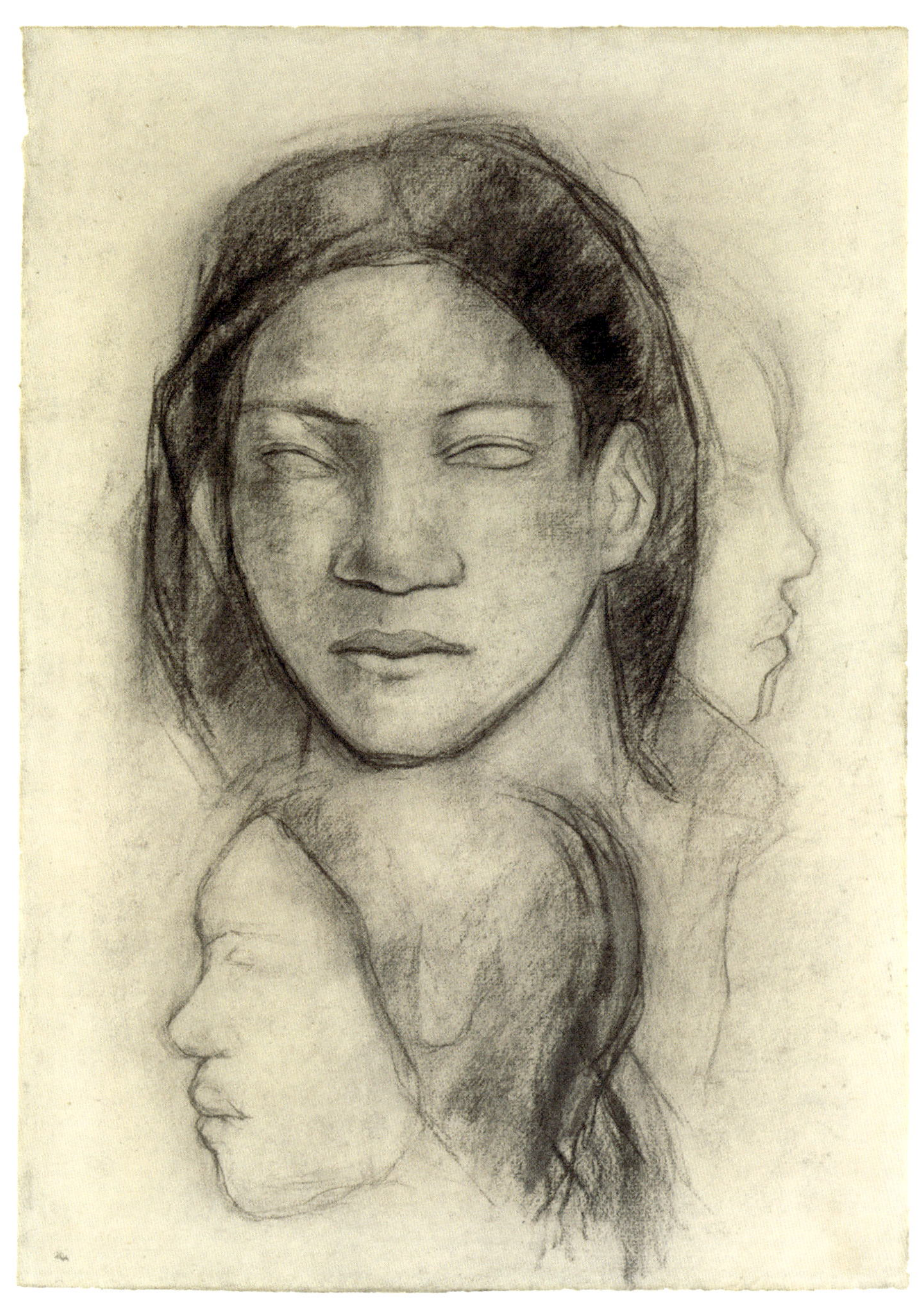

Tahitian Faces (Frontal View and Profiles), c. 1899
Charcoal, 41 × 31.1 cm (16⅛ × 12¼ in.).
METROPOLITAN MUSEUM OF ART, NEW YORK

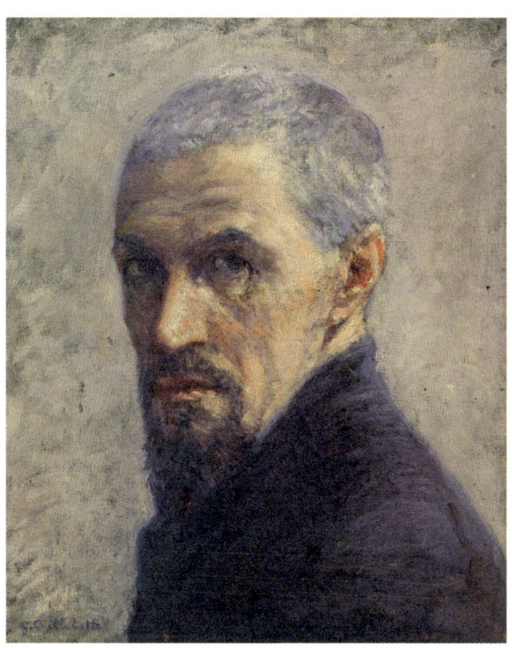

Gustave Caillebotte
1848–1894

Painting was only one of many diverse interests for Gustave Caillebotte. He was enthusiastic about different aspects of boating – sailing, rowing, canoeing – and designed his own yachts; he was a keen horticulturalist who specialized in cultivating orchids; and he was a serious philatelist whose collection forms the basis of the holdings in the British Library. Caillebotte shared these interests with his youngest brother, Martial, who was a gifted musician.

Nonetheless, and even though proper recognition has been slow in coming, Caillebotte's contribution to Impressionism was immense, both as a painter and as a collector. The collection formed by him from the mid-1870s was comprised mainly of works by the Impressionists, which he certainly bought in the first instance for their quality but also as a way of helping his artist friends financially. The importance he attached to his growing collection was established early when in 1876 in a draft of his will he declared his intention of leaving his pictures to the French state, specifically

Gustave Caillebotte
Self-Portrait, 1892
Oil on canvas, 40 × 32 cm (15¾ × 12⅝ in.). Signed.
MUSÉE D'ORSAY, PARIS

for display in the Musée du Luxembourg in Paris, where contemporary art was then shown, and ultimately on the walls of the Musée du Louvre. Since Impressionist art was essentially avant-garde and would not normally have been acceptable to the authorities of the Musée du Luxembourg, this was an inflammatory move by Caillebotte and even his Impressionist colleagues had their doubts about his judgment. And, indeed, after his death in 1894 at the age of forty-six, the executors of the will, Martial Caillebotte and Renoir, did not find it easy to persuade the curator of the Musée du Luxembourg, Léonce Bénédite, to honour the will on behalf of the French state.

At the time of Caillebotte's death the collection amounted to about sixty items, with many of the artists represented by several works. The Musée du Luxembourg had limited space and also a rule stipulating that only a maximum of three works by any one artist could be shown at a time. After protracted negotiations, which included the Impressionists themselves, the French state was persuaded by Bénédite in 1896 to accept a total of forty works. The decision enhanced the reputation of the Impressionists and today Caillebotte's bequest forms the nucleus of the Impressionist pictures in the Musée d'Orsay. Other collectors – in particular, Étienne Moreau-Nélaton, Comte Isaac de Camondo, Auguste Pellerin and Antonin Personnaz – were encouraged by Caillebotte's bequest and decided to donate their collections in turn.

Family wealth was the reason why Caillebotte could pursue his many and varied interests. His father's entrepreneurial skills and investments led to the possession of a country estate at Yerres to the southeast of Paris and a house in the Rue Miromesnil, situated in a part of the city newly constructed by Baron Haussmann close to the Gare Saint-Lazare and the Pont de l'Europe. Both these places and their immediate surroundings featured on many occasions in paintings by Caillebotte during the first half of the 1870s. The properties, however, were closely associated with his parents, and eventually he decided to sell them. In 1879, together with Martial, he purchased an apartment on the Boulevard Haussmann and the following year a property at Petit-Gennevilliers in a suburb to the west of Paris, on the more fashionable bank of the river Seine opposite Argenteuil, which happened to be the headquarters of the Cercle de la Voile, who organized yachting in France.

Caillebotte was educated at the prestigious Lycée Louis-le-Grand and subsequently qualified as a lawyer, as well as doing military service during the Franco-Prussian War of 1870–71. Then, encouraged by the Italian artist Giuseppe de Nittis, who knew many of the Impressionists, he frequented the studio of the Salon painter Léon Bonnat, and in 1873 gained a place at the École des Beaux-Arts. *Naked Woman on a Sofa* (p. 199), a highly finished pastel and no doubt intended for exhibition at the Salon, is an accomplished exercise in the academic tradition using a limited palette. The tonal qualities reveal a mastery of the medium, but unusual are the proximity of the model, the viewpoint and the pose. Direct and unequivocal representation of contemporary subject matter was to become the hallmark of Caillebotte's style, far removed from the historical, religious or allegorical themes that might have been expected from someone emerging from the École des Beaux-Arts.

The artist's association with the Impressionists came about through his likely connection with Degas and the people around him. No doubt Degas sympathized with Caillebotte's preference for urban subjects and his distinctive treatment of spatial intervals, which made his art seem so independent and modern. He was duly included in five (1876, 1877, 1879, 1880, 1882) of the eight Impressionist exhibitions, as well as playing a crucial role in organizing and financing them. His works mirrored the diversity of his interests, encompassing urban themes, landscapes, riverscapes, seascapes and still life. To each of these categories he brought a fresh and original eye, so that among the Impressionists his art stands out as a true marriage of realism and modernism. The exceptional quality of his work was only briefly acknowledged during his lifetime, and after the retrospective exhibition held at Paul Durand-Ruel's gallery in June 1894, Caillebotte disappeared from critical view until the acquisition in 1964 of the enormous canvas *Paris Street: Rainy Weather* (1877) by the Art Institute of Chicago, which in part triggered the reassessment of the artist.

Caillebotte confronted whatever he saw in the street, in his apartment, on the river or in the garden head-on and without flinching, however difficult or novel the motif. This accounts for the steep viewpoints, plunging perspectives, unusual angles and striking close-ups that characterize so many of his pictures. One writer has likened the effect of looking at works by Caillebotte to a meeting of 'the worlds of Uccello and Jacques Tati' (p. 202).

Much of the fascination of Caillebotte's work derives not only from the novelty of the subject matter, but also from the iconographic innovations found there. Some of his pictures (for example, *The Floor Scrapers* of 1878 [Musée d'Orsay, Paris], or *The House Painters* of 1877 [Private collection]) must have seemed highly daring, whereas others (such as *Young Man at his Window* of 1875 [Private collection] or *Man at his Bath* of 1884 [Museum of Fine Arts, Boston]) must have impressed by their sheer ingenuity. Caillebotte's originality is reflected in his drawings. He prepared many of his compositions meticulously with numerous studies of the principal figures (pp. 200 and 201) and also of the perspective and the setting, as though he was designing a stage set. In essence, Caillebotte did not so much compose his paintings as plot them like an engineer.

The more finished of Caillebotte's drawings sometimes surprise. The sudden emptiness of *The Wall of the Vegetable Garden, Yerres* (p. 203) is unsettling, while the juxtaposition in *Portrait of Madame X* (p. 205) between the actual sitter in the foreground and the painted portrait on the easel behind raises the question of the relationship between the two, particularly since the woman is wearing clothes for outdoors although seated inside. The severe cropping of the two figures is also startling, as is the play between the spatial depth of the room being depicted and the flatness of the real and putative pictorial surfaces.

Humour occasionally arises. The crumpled figure in the study for the painting *At the Café* of 1880 (Musée des Beaux-Arts, Rouen) looks as though he is steadying himself after perhaps having had too much to drink (p. 204). The pose calls to mind Edmond Duranty's observation in *La Nouvelle Peinture* (1876) of the need for the artist's pencil to be 'infused with the essence of life', even suggesting that, 'Hands kept in pockets can be eloquent'.

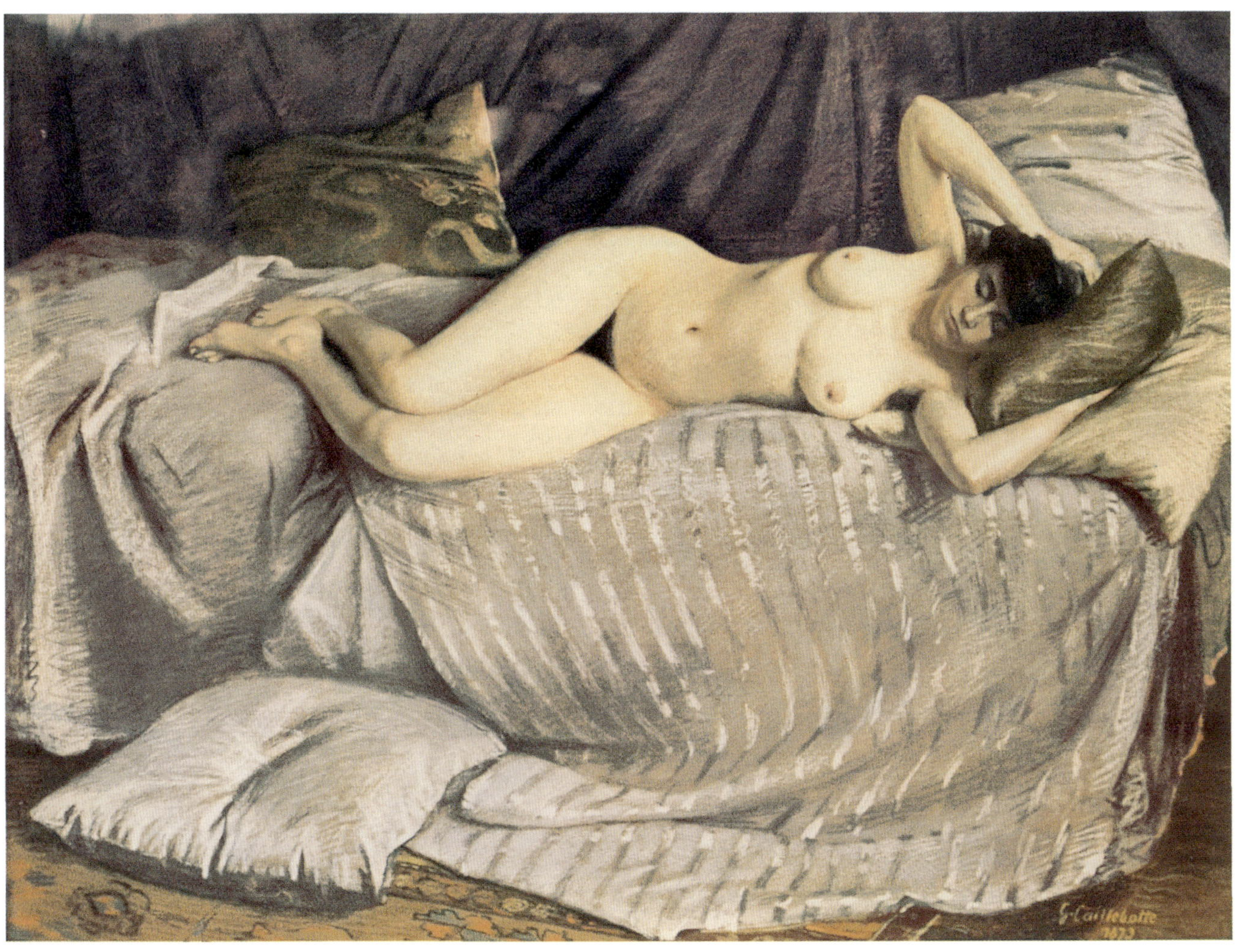

Naked Woman on a Sofa, 1873
Pastel, 87 × 113 cm (34¼ × 44½ in.). Signed.
IRIS AND GERALD CANTOR, NEW YORK

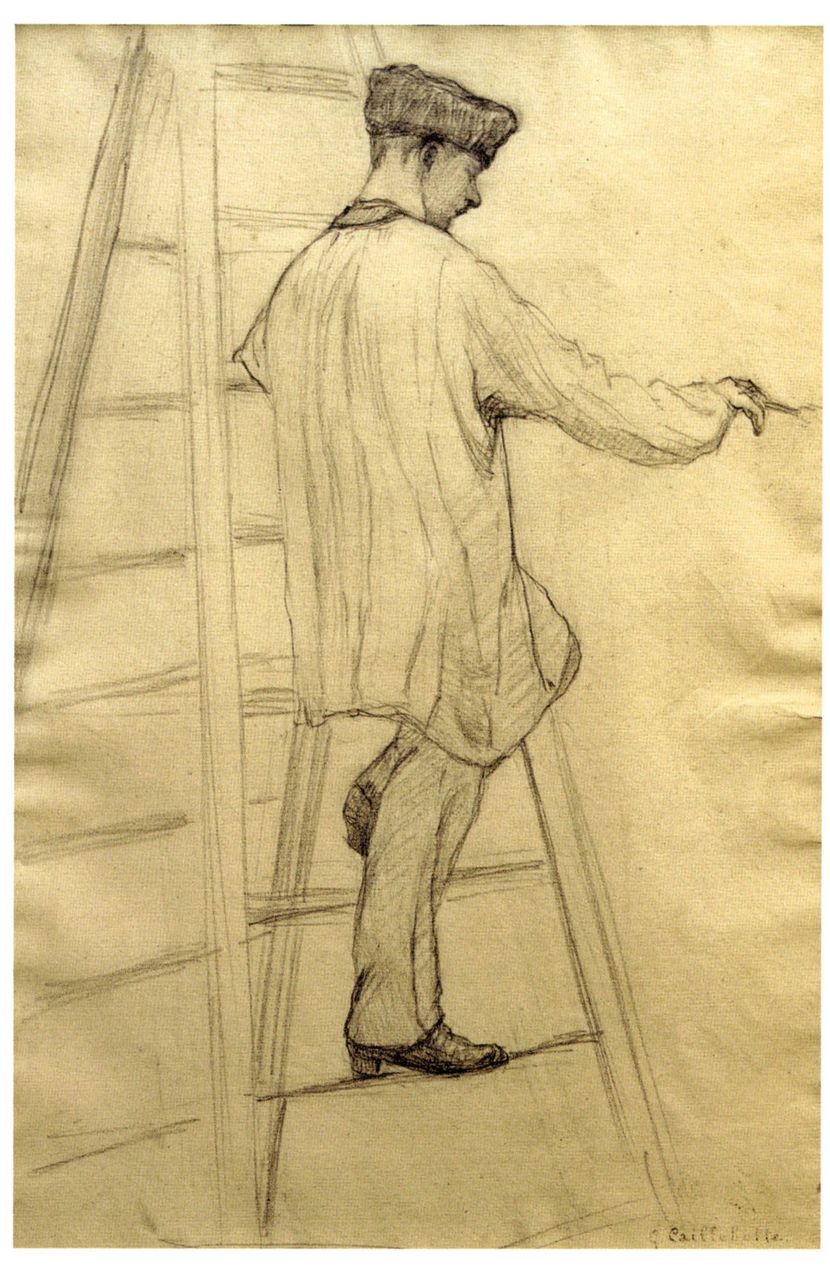

 Gustave Caillebotte

Study for 'House Painters', 1877
Pencil and charcoal, 48 × 30.8 cm (18⅞ × 12⅛ in.). Signed.
PRIVATE COLLECTION

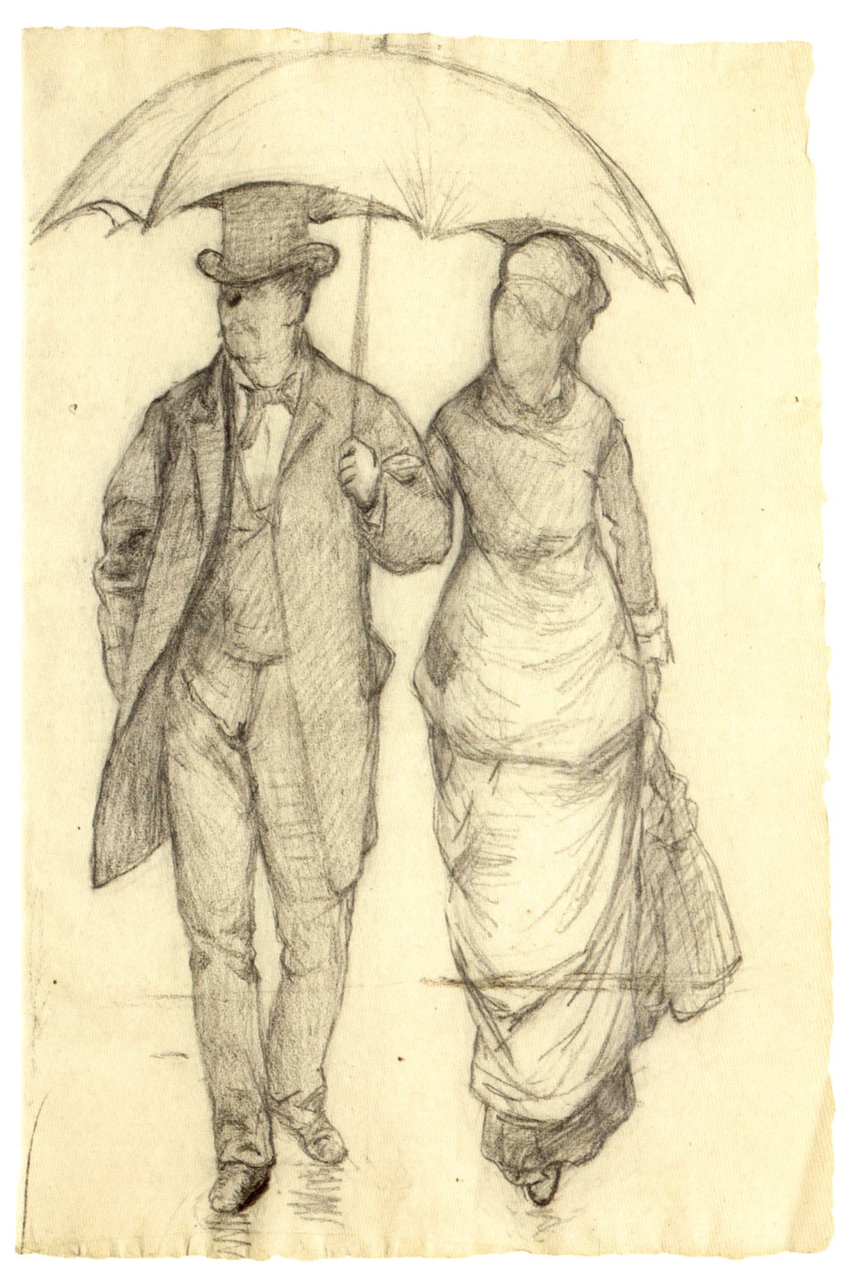

Study for 'Paris Street: Rainy Day', 1877
Pencil and charcoal, 47 × 30.9 cm (18½ × 12⅛ in.).

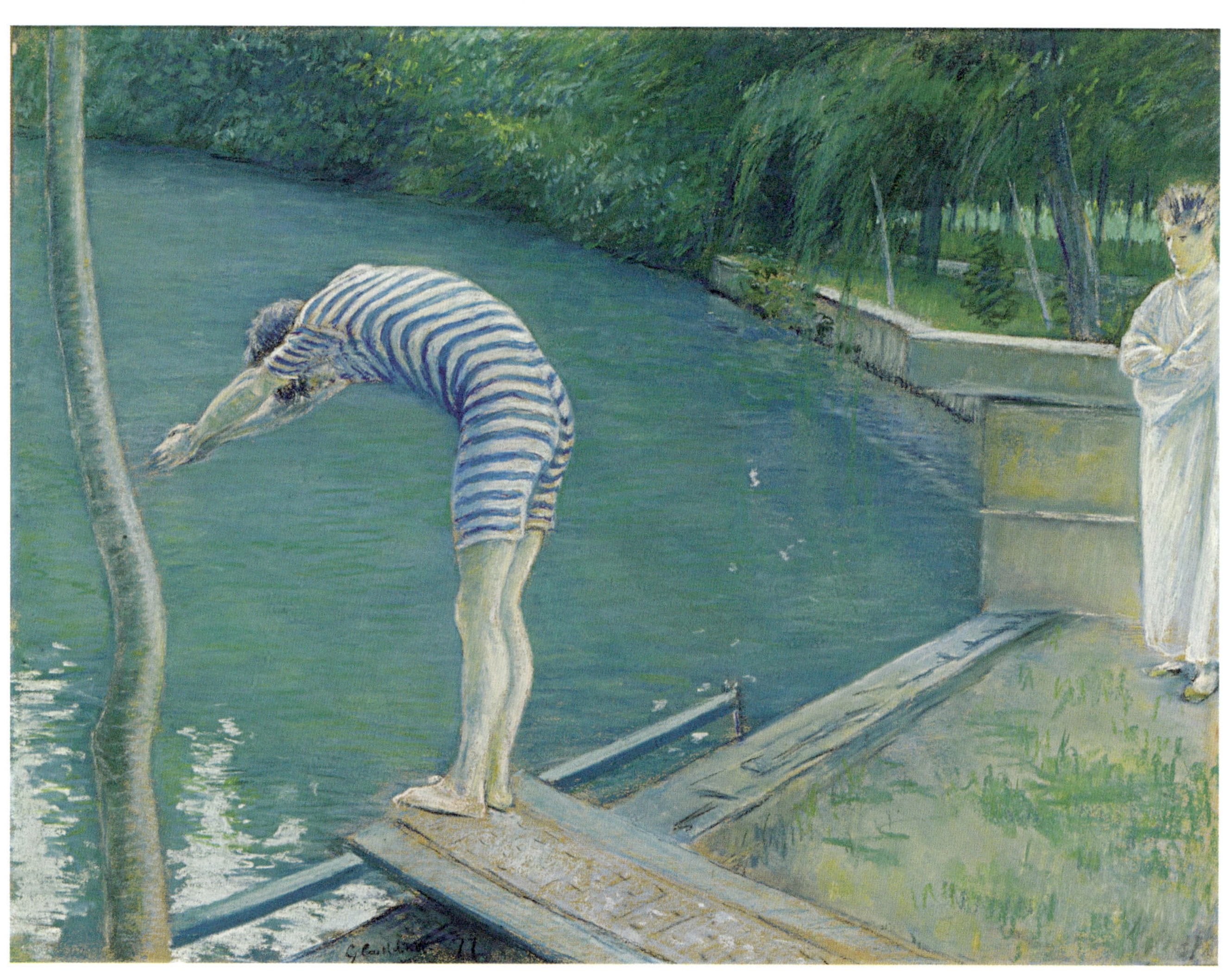

202 *Gustave Caillebotte*

The Swimmer, 1877
Pastel, 75 × 95 cm (29½ × 37⅜ in.). Signed and dated.
MUSÉE D'ORSAY, PARIS

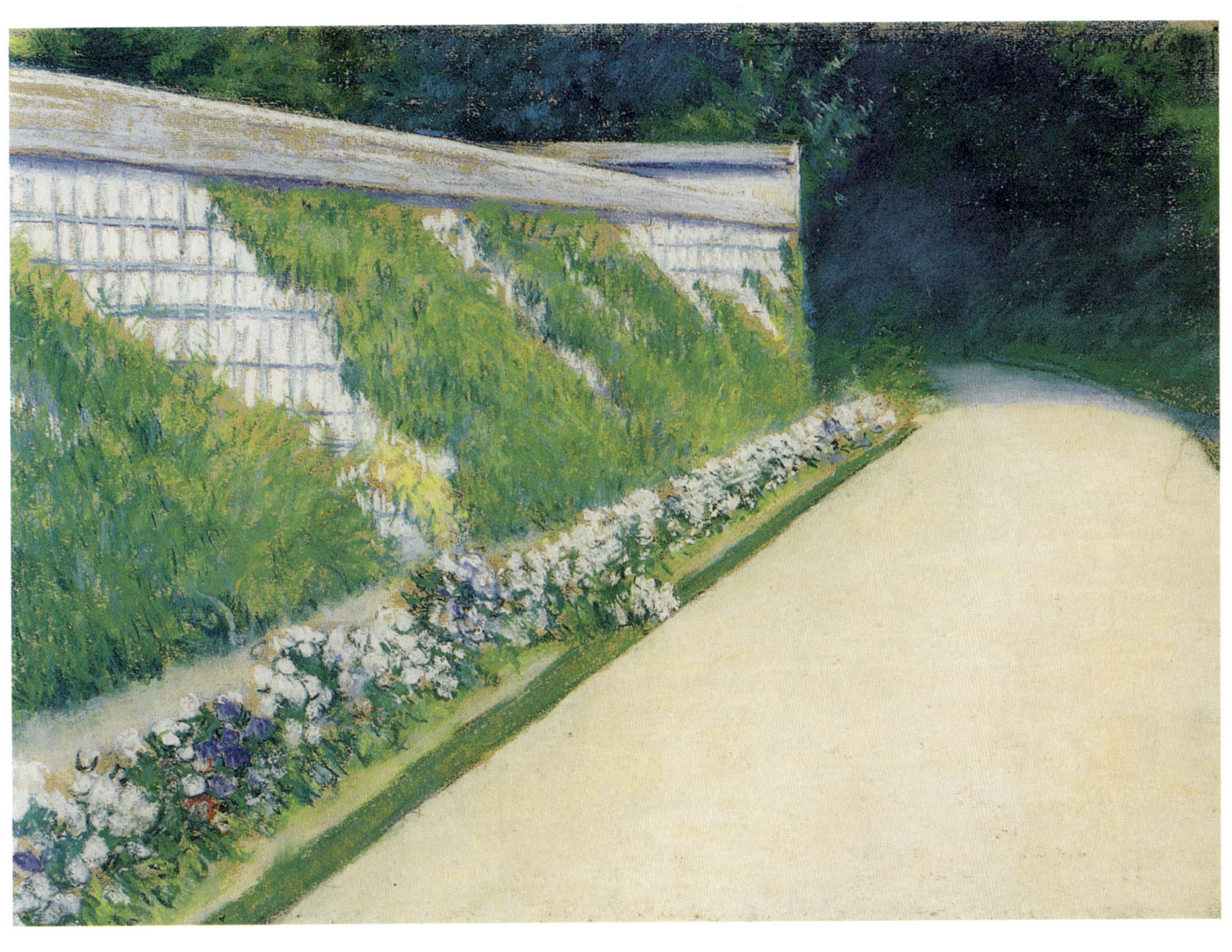

The Wall of the Vegetable Garden, Yerres, 1877
Pastel, 43.5 × 58.5 cm (17⅛ × 23 in.). Signed and dated.
PRIVATE COLLECTION

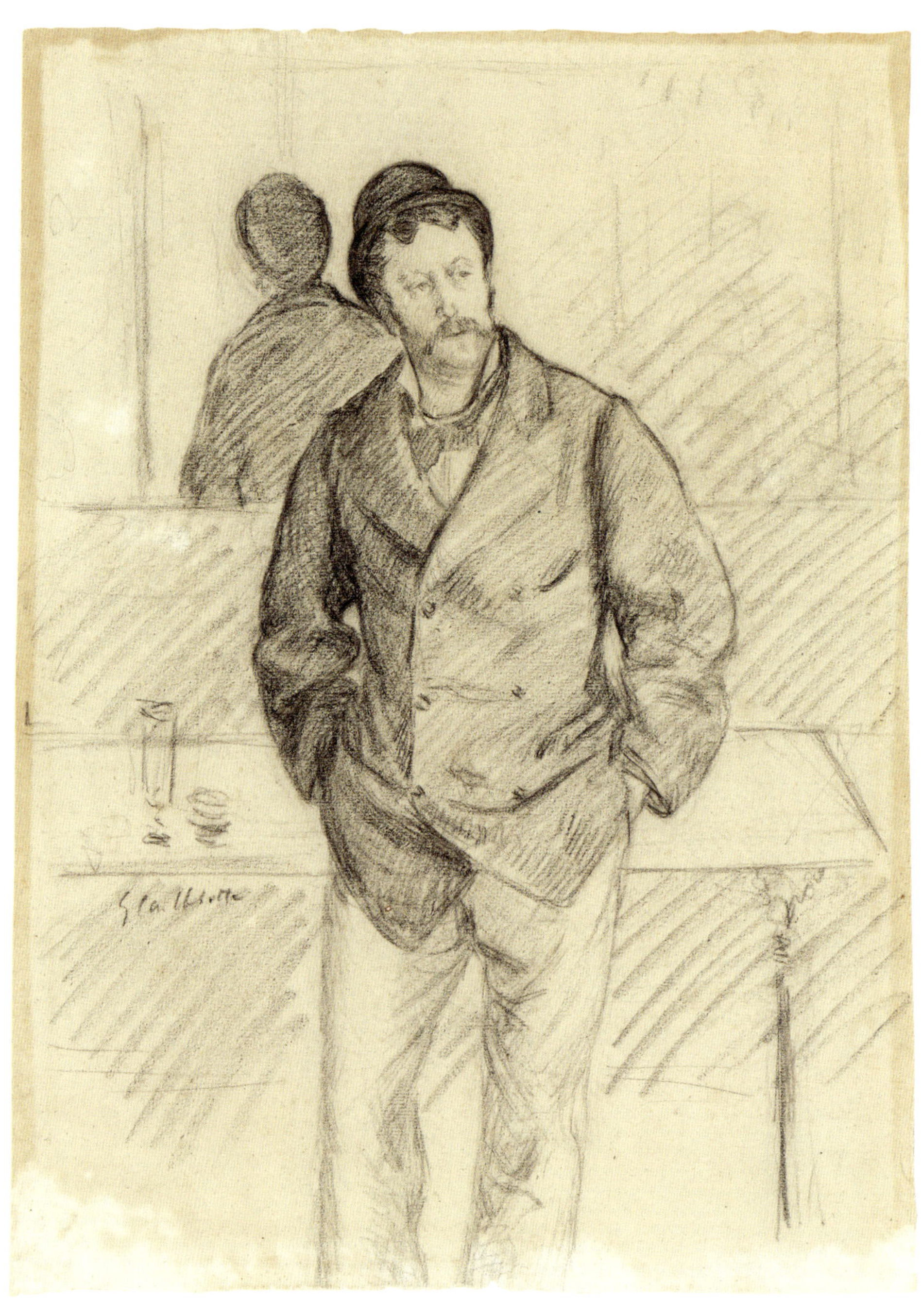

204   *Gustave Caillebotte*

Study for 'At the Café', c. 1880
Black chalk, 44.7 × 31.7 cm (17⅝ × 12½ in.). Signed.
YALE UNIVERSITY ART GALLERY, NEW HAVEN, CONNECTICUT

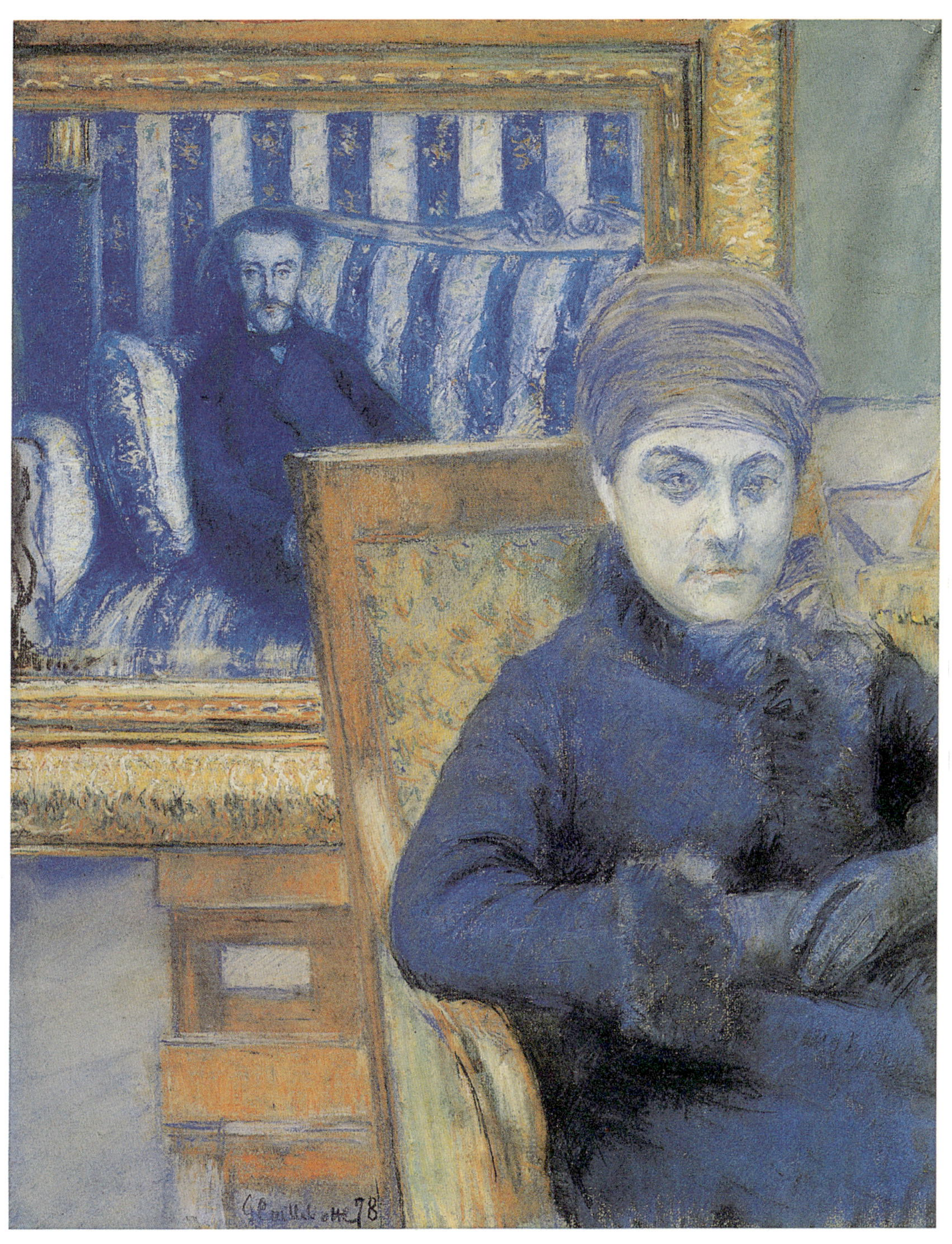

Portrait of Madame X, 1878
Pastel, 63 × 50 cm (24¾ × 19¾ in.). Signed and dated.
MUSÉE FABRE, MONTPELLIER

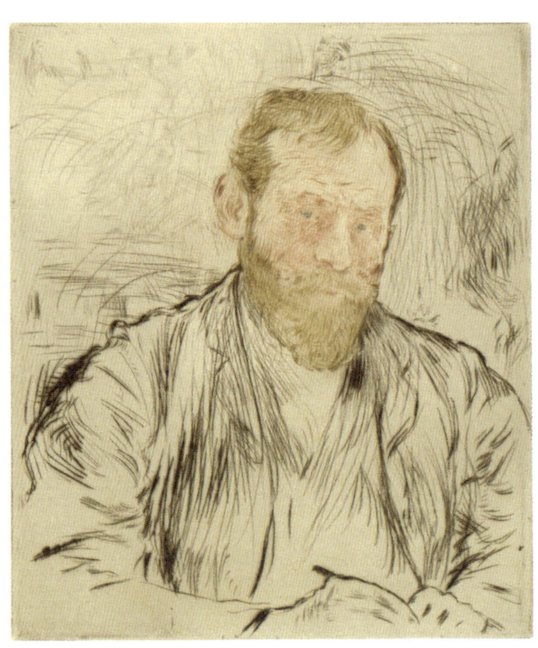

Jean-François Raffaëlli
1850–1924

Jean-François Raffaëlli participated in the fifth (1880) and sixth (1881) Impressionist exhibitions. On both occasions he had the distinction of exhibiting far more works than any of the other contributors. Several critics, however, challenged the idea that he was included among the Impressionists at all. Albert Wolff was the most outspoken, stating categorically in 1880 that Raffaëlli's 'tightly wrought art has nothing to do with the formless rapid sketches of the ladies and gentlemen of Impressionism. Why the hell did Raffaëlli join this enterprise?'

Although the subject matter of Raffaëlli's work was undeniably modern, its manner seemed conservative, with a degree of finish and attention to detail more suitable to the Salon than an avant-garde group exhibition. Like other Impressionists, Raffaëlli had already, while still young, achieved some success at the Salon, but he was a convincing and powerful figurative painter, which appealed to Degas, who was one of the principal organizers of both the fifth and sixth exhibitions. The lack of direction that

Jean-François Raffaëlli
Self-Portrait, 1893
Drypoint, 18.9 × 15.7 cm (7½ × 6⅛ in.).
Metropolitan Museum of Art, New York

the Impressionists experienced during the late 1870s and early 1880s may well have been counterbalanced by the inclusion of an artist such as Raffaëlli, whose work could be described as modern while appearing to be traditional. Consequently, its ambiguity proved to be its strength and his work was on the whole well received. Even the usually uncharitable Wolff, who actually lent two works by the artist from his own collection, unsurprisingly wrote about the quality of Raffaëlli's output and encouraged others to buy the work while the prices were still low:

> *Like Millet he is the painter of the humble. What the great master did for the fields, Raffaëlli begins to do for the modest people of Paris. He shows them as they are, more often than not stupefied by life's hardships.*

Raffaëlli was a proficient artist in several media – painter, draughtsman, pastellist, sculptor, printmaker and illustrator. He also evolved theories about the practice and purpose of art, which he published in essays, propounded in lectures and demonstrated in his finest works, dating from the late 1870s and 1880s. For the portrayal of modern life, he argued, the artist should seek an objectivity that could only be found as the result of a proper scientific analysis of the relevant social milieu. At the heart of this was what he termed '*caractère*', which he regarded as 'man's distinctive trait' formed as a result of the interaction between the individual and natural phenomena. These views reflected current positivist philosophy and the new discipline of sociology developed in parallel with naturalist writers such as Emile Zola, the Goncourt brothers, Joris-Karl Huysmans and Guy de Maupassant. It is significant that among the works shown by Degas at the sixth Impressionist exhibition were two pastels entitled *Physionomie de criminel*. The novelty of Raffaëlli's contribution to this debate is the particular section of society that he chose to subject to a sustained and objective examination.

The first part of the artist's upbringing was comfortable. His father manufactured silk dyes, but when the business collapsed Raffaëlli was forced to undertake a series of jobs (including dentist's receptionist) while slowly discovering an interest in art on regular visits to the Musée du Louvre and the Musée du Luxembourg. Without any formal training, he had a landscape painting accepted at the Salon of 1870, but when in 1871, after serving in the Franco-Prussian War, he enrolled in the classes of Jean-Léon Gérôme at the École des Beaux-Arts he failed to flourish and left after only three months. Still uncertain as to what kind of painter he wanted to be and not winning acceptance at the Salon on a regular basis, Raffaëlli experimented briefly with history painting and orientalism. Yet a painting entitled *The Family of Jean-le-Boiteux, Peasants from Plougasnou* (Musée d'Orsay, Paris), made on a visit to Brittany in 1876 and shown at the Salon the following year, introduced Raffaëlli to a theme that inspired his best work, which gained considerable respect from critics and fellow artists in both France and Belgium.

Coinciding with his decision to move into the suburbs to the northwest of Paris was Raffaëlli's interest in observing the lives of the disenfranchised urban poor living at the margins of society. During the 1880s he concentrated on depicting the *déclassés* in oil and pastel, putting into practice his ideas about physiognomy and characterization. His success with such pictures at the Impressionist exhibitions of the early 1880s seems not to have been matched at the Salon, and so in 1884 he hired premises on the Avenue de l'Opéra and mounted to huge success his own one-man exhibition of one hundred and fifty-five works divided into two groups: '*Portraits-Types de Gens du Bas Peuple*' and '*Portraits-Types de Petits Bourgeois*'. It was a defining move by such an independent artist and provided him with an opportunity to explain his views on art and society. But the singularity of his vision could not be sustained beyond the 1880s and during the next decade he returned to live in the centre of Paris. For the rest of his life, which included two visits to America in 1895 and 1899, Raffaëlli reverted to less challenging subjects that appealed to a wider audience and ensured sales – scenes of the Parisian streets (p. 214) and entertainments (p. 215) supplemented by views of the French countryside and harbours.

The northwest suburb of Paris that Raffaëlli went to live in at the end of the 1870s was Asnières, which was famous for its association with weekend pleasures such as sailing. But on the other side of the river Seine were the more industrialized suburbs of Clichy and Levallois, dominated by factories and shanty buildings and crisscrossed by railway lines and telegraph poles. This wasteland formed the landscape background of Raffaëlli's pictures of the 1880s (p. 209). It is an area described by the writer Octave Mirbeau in 1889 as 'no longer city and which is not yet countryside, where nothing ends and nothing begins, where people [are] the flotsam of social misfortune: circumscribed bourgeois existences, shady businesses, nocturnal loiterings, proletarian debasement'. The people depicted by Raffaëlli in these depressing panoramas often, but not always, have identifiable occupations. Blacksmiths (p. 210), ragpickers, roadmen (p. 211), vegetable sellers of various kinds, tinkers and vagabonds stumble through the landscape; others, higher up the social scale, dressed in their *habits noirs*, drink beer or absinthe in soulless cafés (p. 212). Such depictions anticipate the world that would be explored by the twentieth-century playwright Samuel Beckett. The figures plead their case in the court of humanity.

Raffaëlli's compositional method is clear-cut. He places the figures prominently in the foreground and sets them on a monumental scale, silhouetted against an open background often beset with a smoking factory chimney. The format is usually vertical and only occasionally square. The paintings are thinly executed in light tones, whereas the medium of the pastels (of which he made his own more oily variety) and the drawings is thickly applied and dark in tone. In all cases, as contemporary critics readily acknowledged, the quality of the drawing was high, particularly in its attention to detail.

Although Raffaëlli's originality as 'the poet of the Parisian suburbs' was acknowledged, he was in fact working within a recognized tradition. The representation of 'types' usually associated with urban life was a standard subject for many seventeenth- and eighteenth-century artists. These compilations, incorporating crafts, occupations, pastimes and domestic chores, were often published in book form with titles such as *Les Cris de Paris*. The expansion of printing techniques in the nineteenth century led to a multiplication of these titles, including the nine-volume *Les Français Peints par Eux-mêmes* (1839–42), which many painters (François Bonvin, Théodule Ribot and Manet among them) almost certainly knew. Indeed, Raffaëlli himself helped to extend this tradition by contributing to *Les Types de Paris* of 1889 with a preface by Wolff. This does not detract from the significance of Raffaëlli's depictions of the *déclassés* whose lives he so carefully observed in the suburbs during the 1880s. Critics could compare him with seventeenth-century artists such as Adriaen and Isaac van Ostade (Jules Claretie) or the Le Nain brothers (Huysmans), but the impact that his images made was because, as Edmond Duranty maintained in his *La Nouvelle Peinture* (1876), he showed 'the special characteristics of the modern individual – in his clothing, in social situations, at home, or on the street' (p. 213).

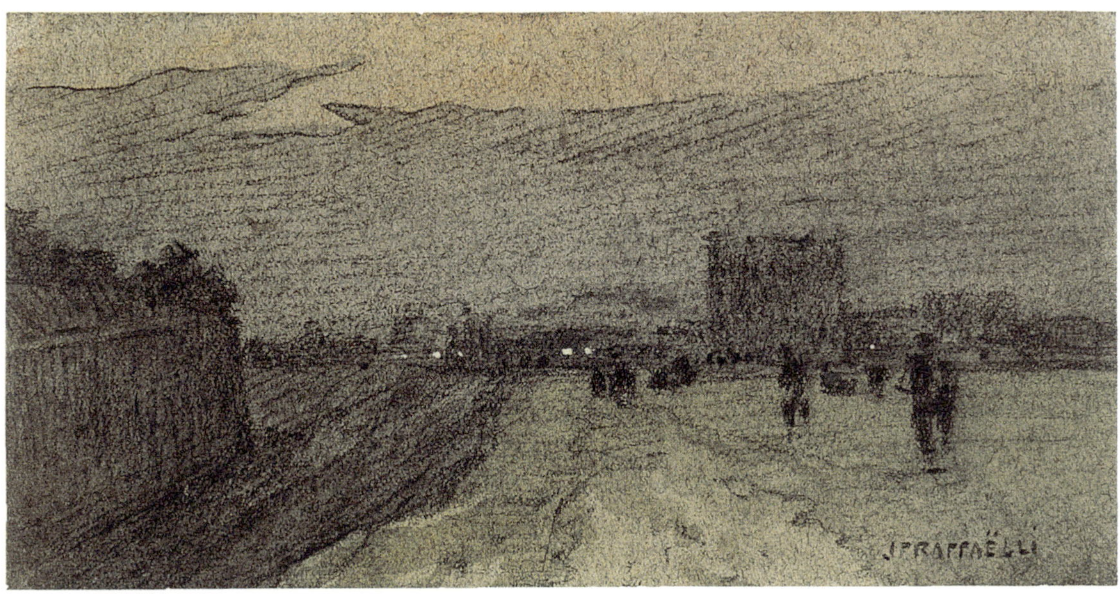

Landscape with Road Approaching the City, c. 1880–85
Charcoal, chalk and wash heightened with gouache on blue-grey
paper mounted on card, 8.3 × 15.8 cm (3¼ × 6¼ in.). Signed.
METROPOLITAN MUSEUM OF ART, NEW YORK

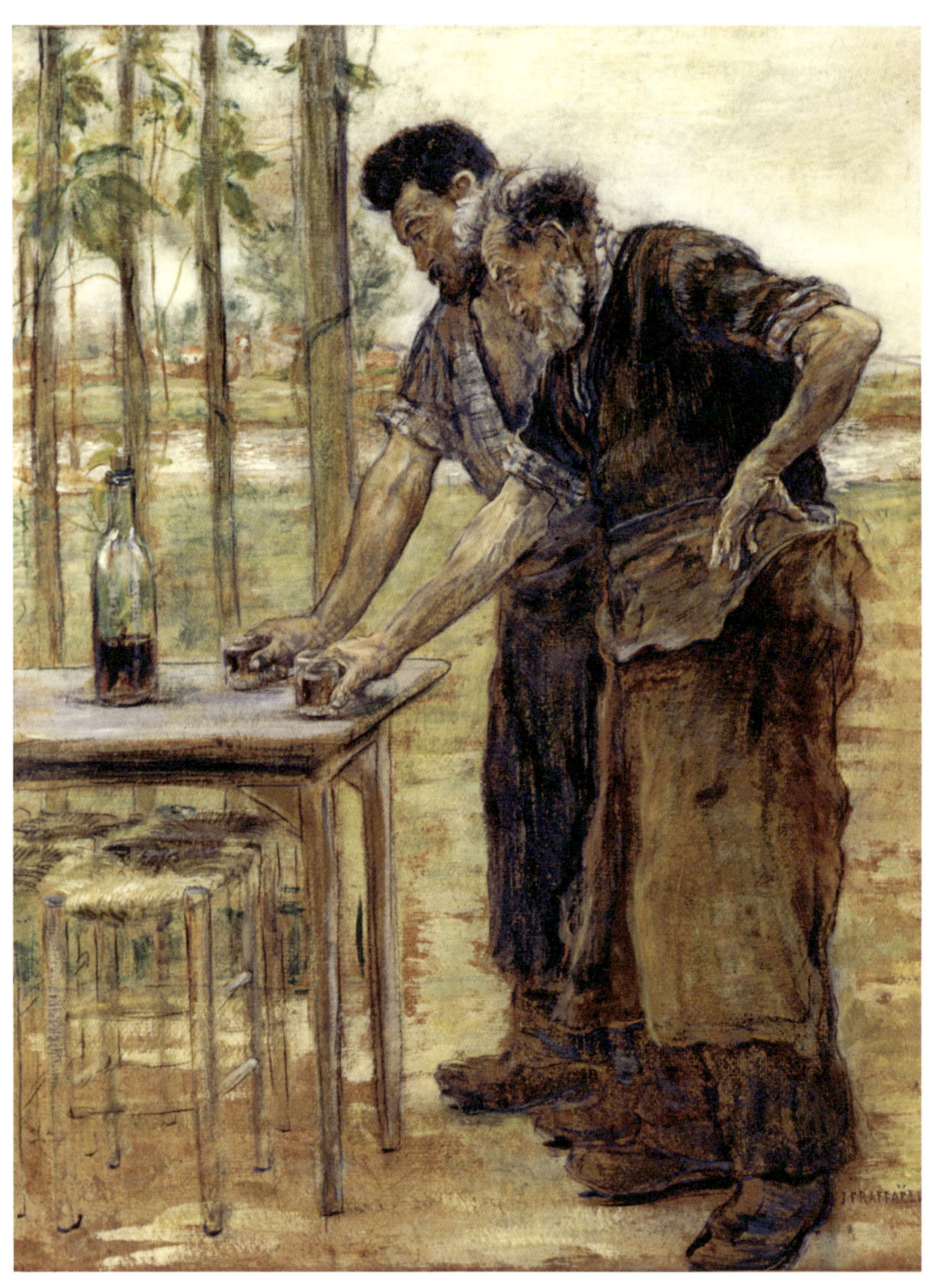

210 *Jean François Raffaëlli*

Blacksmiths Drinking, c. 1885
Coloured chalks heightened with oil on cardboard laid
on panel, 77 × 57 cm (30⅜ × 22⅜ in.). Signed.
MUSÉE DE LA CHARTREUSE, DOUAI

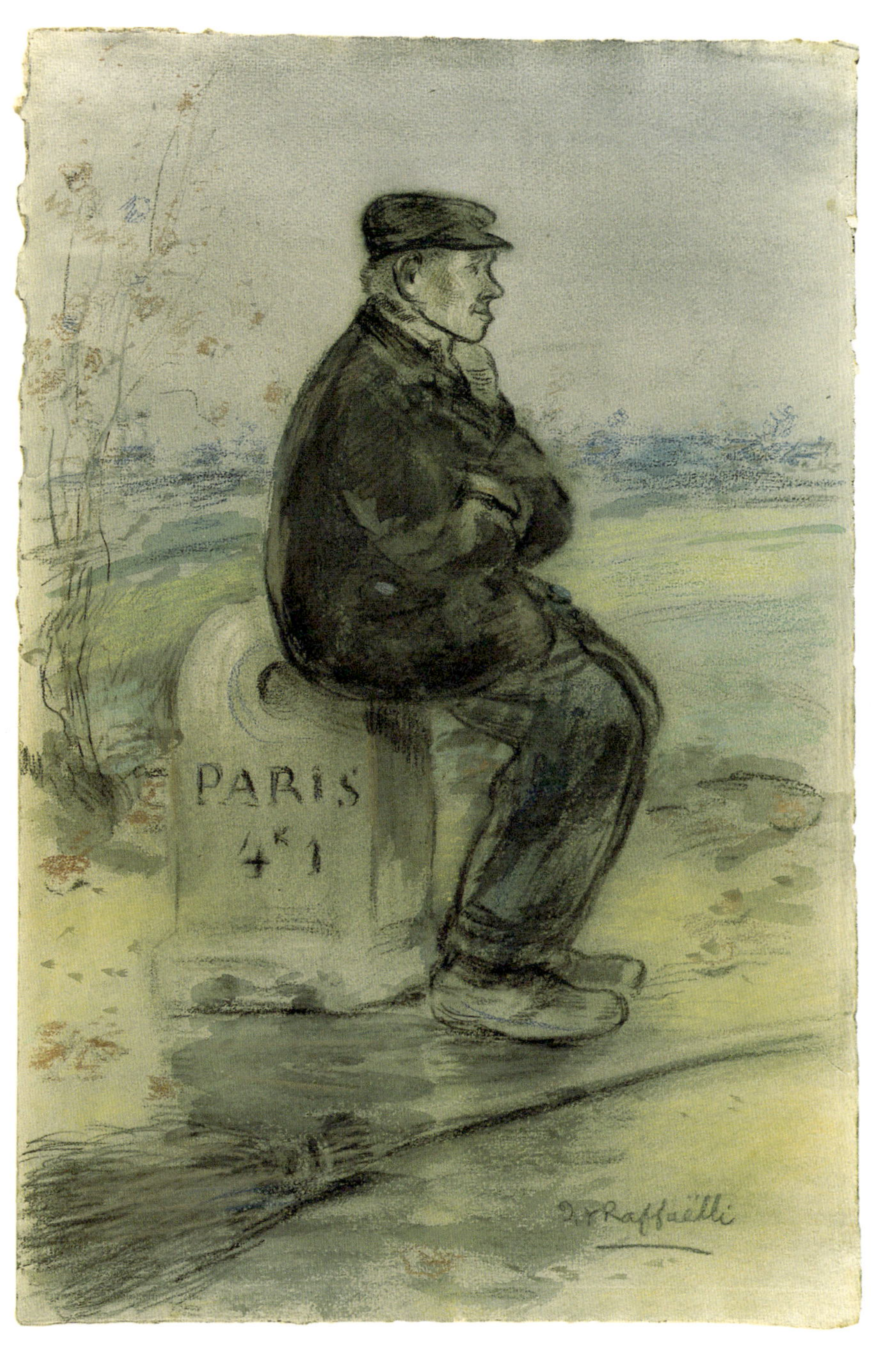

Roadman, Paris 4 k. 1., c. 1881
Watercolour, pastel, pencil, 48.3 × 31.4 cm (19 × 12⅜ in.). Signed.
LANDESGALERIE, NIEDERSÄCHSISCHES LANDESMUSEUM, HANNOVER

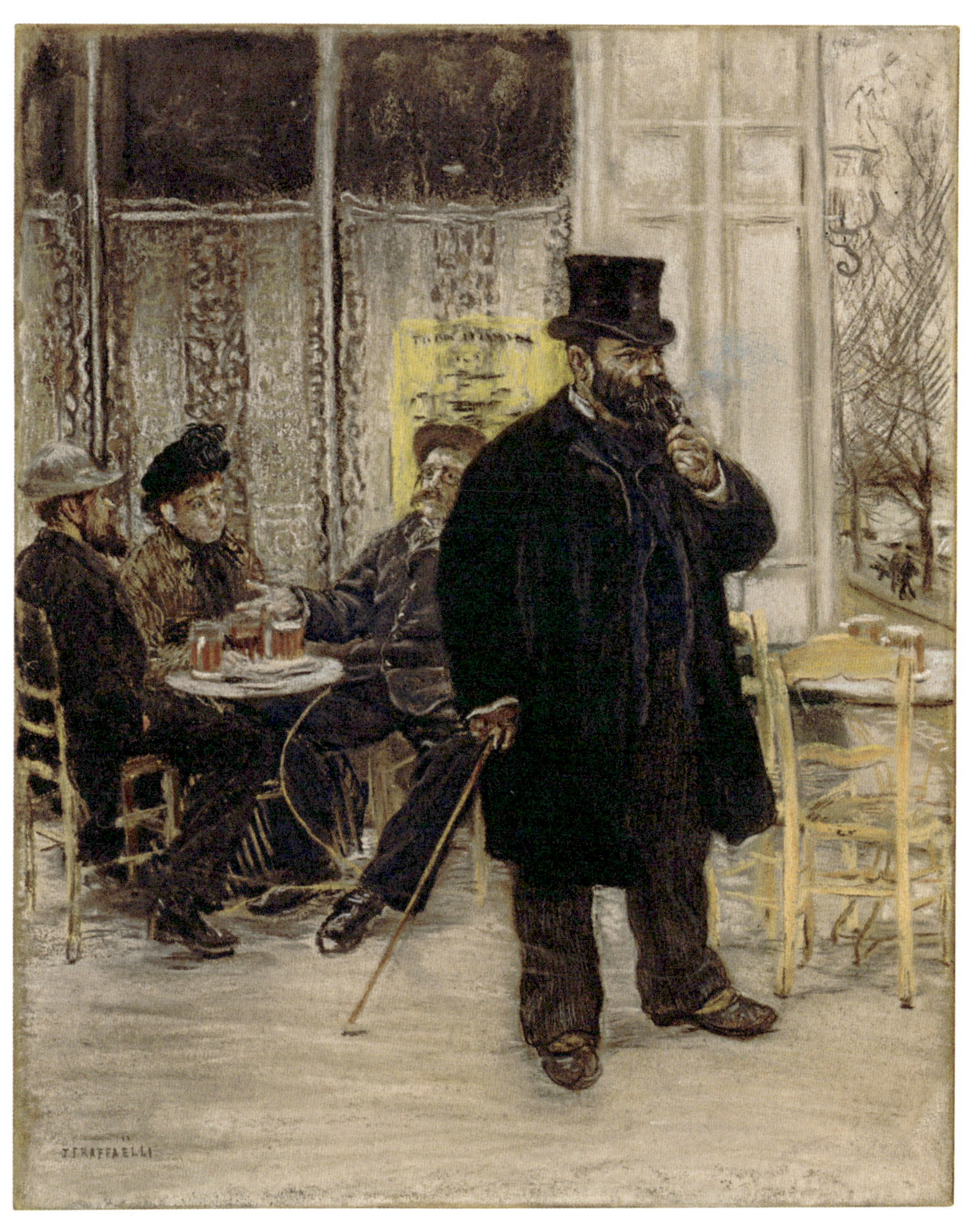

212   *Jean-François Raffaëlli*   *Bohemians at the Café*, c. 1885
Pastel on paper laid on canvas,
55.5 × 44 cm (21⅞ × 17⅜ in.). Signed.
MUSÉE DES BEAUX-ARTS, BORDEAUX

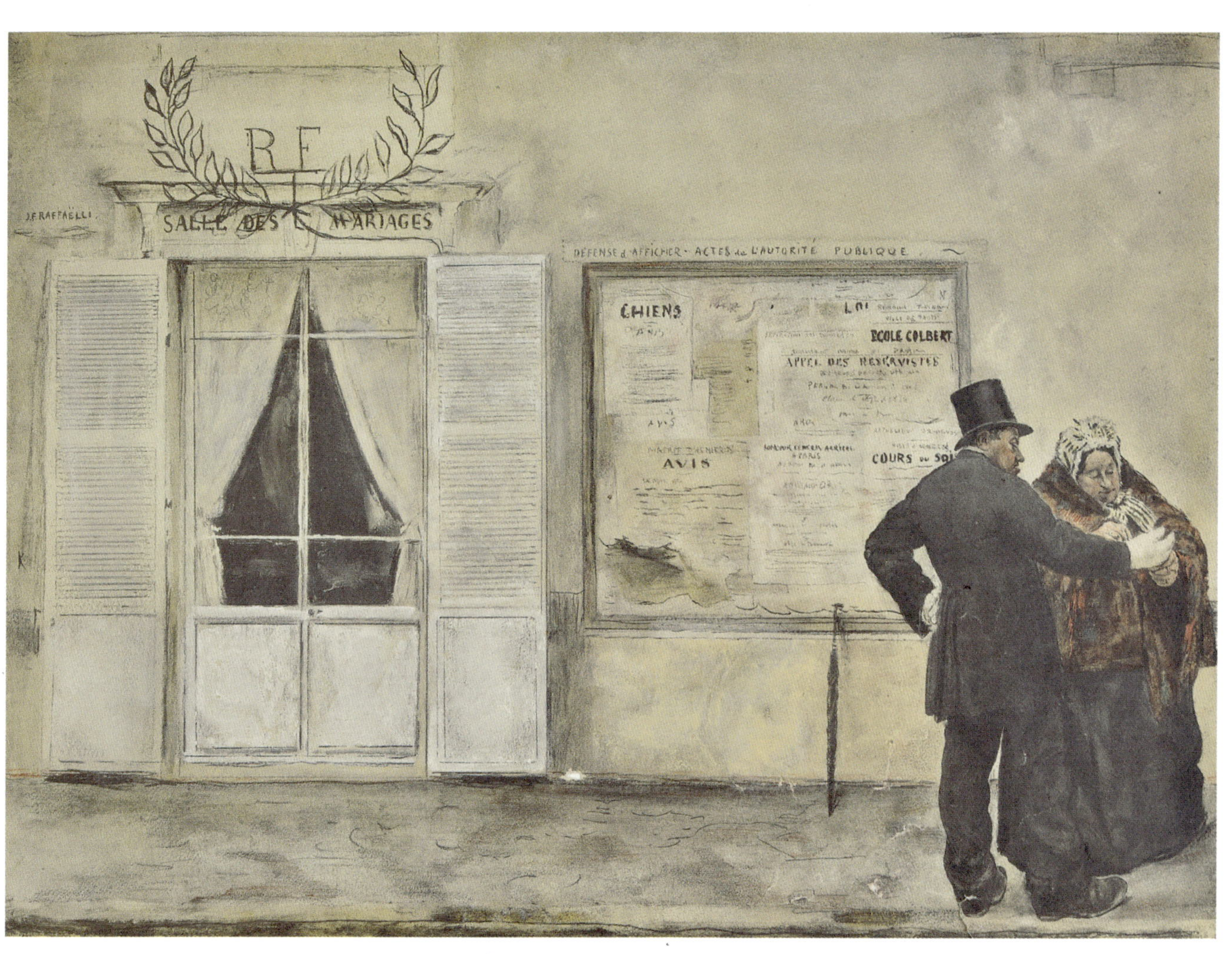

In Front of the Town Hall, c. 1890
Coloured chalks and white bodycolour,
42 × 56 cm (16½ × 22 in.). Signed.
PRIVATE COLLECTION

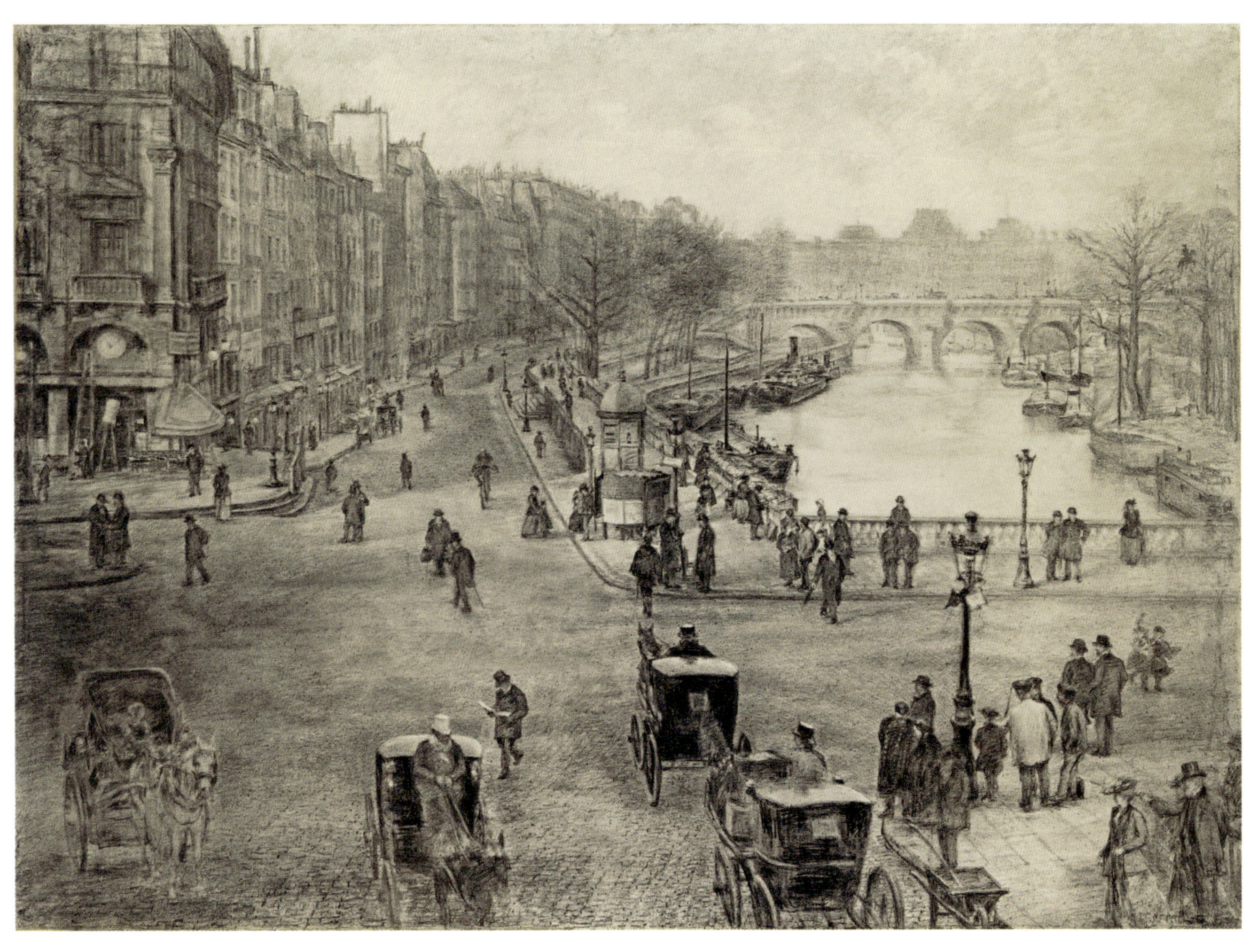

214   *Jean François Raffaëlli*

*Paris, The Place Saint Michel with the Quai des Grands
Augustins and the Saint Michel Bridge, c.* 1900
Charcoal on buff paper laid on canvas,
94.6 x 127.3 cm (37¼ x 50⅛ in.). Signed.
PRIVATE COLLECTION

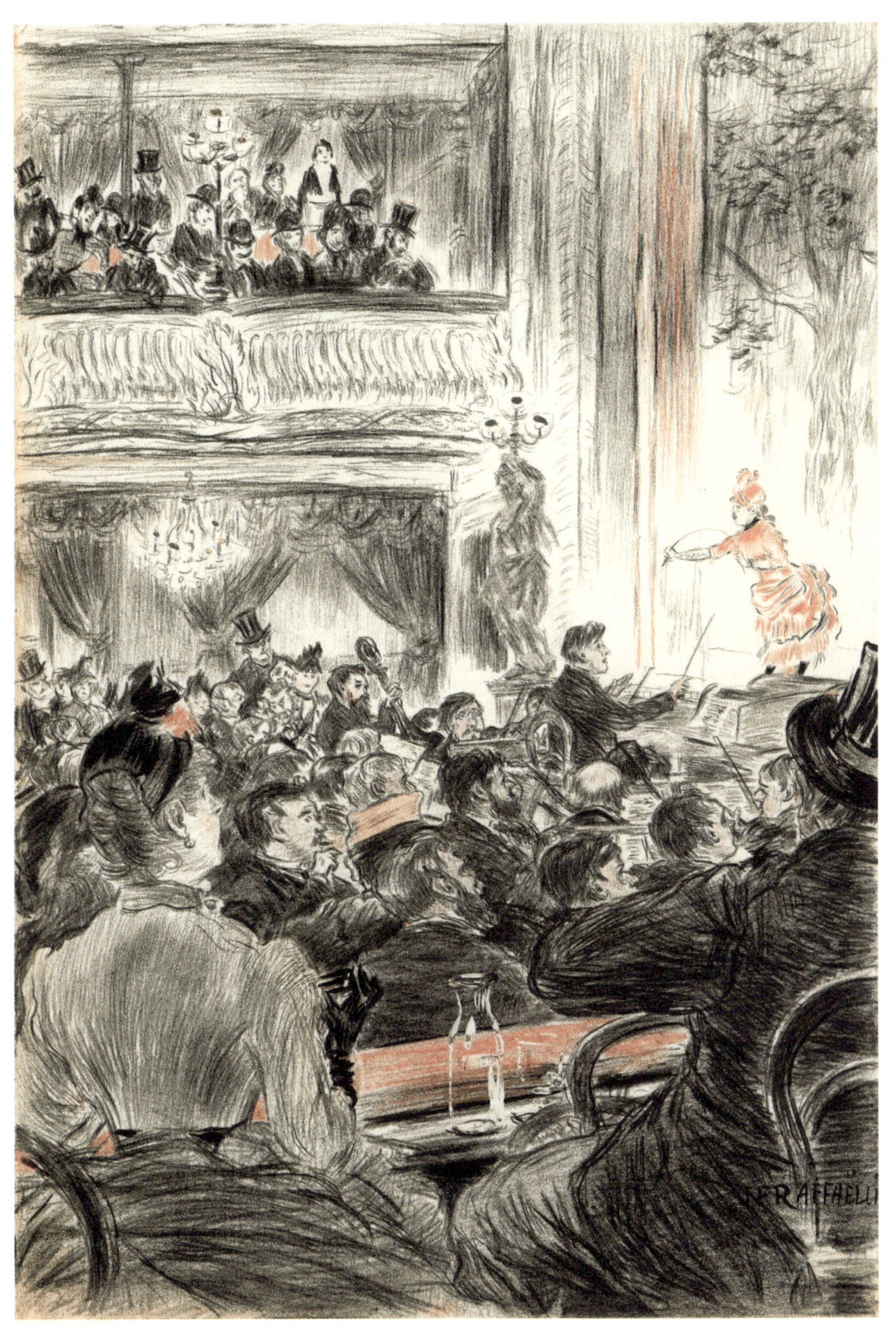

Café-concert at La Scala, Paris, c. 1886
Charcoal, ink, red chalk and gouache,
44.5 × 29.5 cm (17½ × 11⅝ in.). Signed.
PRIVATE COLLECTION

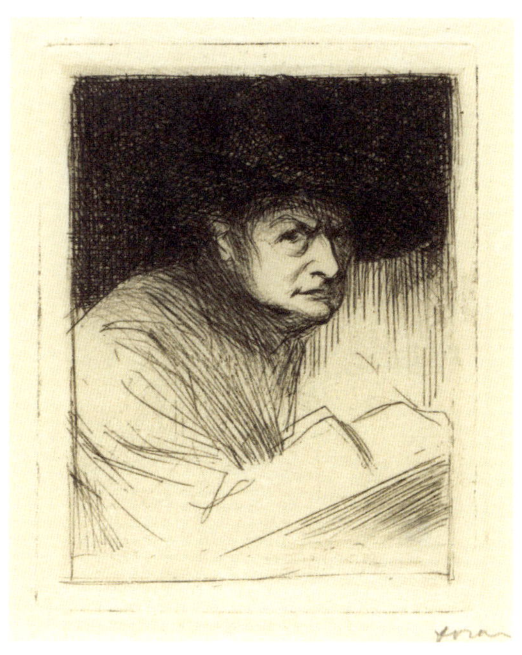

Jean-Louis Forain
1852–1931

For an artist who lived for so long at the centre of the art world, an outline of Jean-Louis Forain's career is surprisingly uncomplicated. Born in Reims, he studied for a short time at the École des Beaux-Arts during the late 1860s under Jean-Léon Gérôme and then in the studio of the sculptor Jean-Baptiste Carpeaux. Shortly afterwards, however, he began to move in avant-garde circles, becoming friends with Manet and Degas, as well as with the poets Paul Verlaine and Arthur Rimbaud. Recognizing the still-young Forain's ability as a figurative painter, Degas invited him to participate in four of the Impressionist exhibitions (1879, 1880, 1881, 1886). His subject matter was based, in parallel with Degas, on scenes from contemporary life, although they were often given a more deliberately political emphasis, which from the 1890s became increasingly reactionary. Forain chose not to alter his style in the light of any of the Post-Impressionist developments that emerged during the 1880s and he continued to show his work at the Salon. The long period of activity after the turn of the century was dominated by paintings

Jean-Louis Forain
Self-Portrait, 1912
Etching, 13.9 × 10.3 cm (5½ × 4 in.) (plate). Signed.
NATIONAL GALLERY OF ART, WASHINGTON, DC

dealing with themes concerning religion, the law and the First World War, in which he participated. These late works reflect his virulent anti-Semitism, extreme nationalism and ultraconservative Catholicism.

By instinct a humourist, Forain created pictures that fascinate viewers because they raise questions to which they will never know the answers. Will the funambulist in *The Tight-Rope Walker* of *c.* 1880 (The Art Institute of Chicago) fall into the crowd? Will the two figures in *Place de la Concorde* of 1884 (Private collection), who are social opposites, come to blows? Will the man and his dog posed so precariously on the plank jutting out from the quayside in *The Fisherman* of 1884 (Southampton City Art Gallery) keep their balance or fall into the water? Such imponderables are not just the result of compositional tricks, but are also due to the artist's varied treatment of the figures and wide range of facial expressions, both of which are even more pronounced in his drawings.

Forain was one of the great caricaturists of the nineteenth century, at a time when such drawings were highly regarded as an art form and of some social significance. The critic most supportive of the art was the poet Charles Baudelaire, who published two articles on the subject in the 1850s. Of those exponents he discussed, it is Honoré Daumier who is described as 'one of the most important men…in the whole of modern art…who each morning keeps the populace of our city amused, a man who supplies the daily needs of public gaiety and provides its sustenance'. Forain admired Daumier, while he himself influenced Toulouse-Lautrec, whose family he knew.

The Impressionists paid particular attention to the art of caricature. Pissarro, for example, was overjoyed by his purchase in Rouen in 1884 of a copy of *Histoire de la Caricature Moderne* (1865) by Champfleury (Jules François Félix Husson), with its many illustrations. The figures in paintings by the Impressionists depended strongly on this rapid and exaggerated manner of drawing that not only promised a more truthful rendition of life but also allowed greater insight into the foibles and idiosyncrasies of humanity. The skill required to capture such quiddities was defined by Baudelaire as 'the logic of a *savant* transported into a light and fugitive art, which is pitted against the very mobility of life'. That Forain for one possessed this skill is demonstrated in his paintings, pen-and-ink drawings, watercolours and pastels.

The spread of caricature was due in large part to technical developments, which led to dramatic increases in the launch and circulation of newspapers, journals and printed ephemera. New methods of reproduction, such as photo-relief, photogravure and gillotage, and new inventions such as the rotary press could be used for printing colour illustrations in high numbers, as well as for the production of posters. Ongoing educational reforms in France led to greater literacy and a sense of purpose in the publication of daily newspapers, whose readership amounted to many millions by the turn of the century. Just as the press relied on scandals, gossip and sensationalism for sales, so places of popular entertainment (cafés-concerts and dance halls) in Montmartre and cultural institutions (theatres, the opera, art galleries) published their own journals to promote performances or exhibitions. Similarly, political groups launched supporting literature in order to draw attention to their causes and to influence the course of events.

Such activities were boosted by the relaxation of the censorship laws in July 1881, which had been imposed on the press in 1835. And this proliferation of printed material was carefully calibrated to appeal to different sections of society. The political injustices of the Third Republic, as well as its social ills, could now be fully exposed, and artists such as Forain who had the requisite skills were in demand. Many of the illustrated journals had small circulations and were often short-lived, but for several avant-garde artists such work was a financial and professional boon. Forain was among those who contributed to a host of new journals – *Le Courrier Français*, *L'Echo de Paris*, *Figaro Illustré*, *La Plume*, *Le Rire*, *La Vie Parisienne*, and *Psst...!*. He even founded his own journal, *Le Fifre* (with Adolphe Willette), and published a series of his drawings in book form (*La Comédie Parisienne* of 1892).

Forain had little difficulty – perhaps considerable pleasure – in puncturing the social hypocrisy of the Third Republic. Like Degas, he had a caustic wit, but he exercised it more through anecdote and narrative than in single defining statements. Apart from isolating the corruption, pretentiousness and outmoded conventions of bourgeois society, he also liked to explore particular social predicaments. *The Client* (p. 219), which dates from 1878 but was shown in the fifth Impressionist exhibition two years later, is a subject that aligns Forain with Degas and Toulouse-Lautrec in the treatment of brothel scenes. Women are shown lining up for inspection by a patron. He sits passively on the right in his *habit noir* with a mirror above him while the semi-naked women parade in front of him, skimpily clad in gartered stockings, gowns and hairbands. They twist and turn, using their gowns like capes in order to attract his attention. Forain liberally splashes the white highlights throughout so that the gowns resemble sparklers. The composition is arranged deliberately to recall the Judgement of Paris, and the woman on the left of the main group wears a cross at her neck – both references meant satirically.

A Box at the Opéra (p. 221) is a tight-knit composition on a vertical axis. The penumbral interior is offset by the bright highlights of the formal garments. Forain heightens the air of theatricality by making the woman lean forward out of her box to hold a conversation with one of the standing men. For *In the Wings* (p. 220) the contrast is between the white of the dancers' tutus and the men's evening dress, which may also be interpreted as references to good and evil. The pert expressions of the young dancers differ markedly from the threatening ursine physiognomy of the men.

The Actress's Dressing Room (p. 222) and *After the Ball: The Reveller* (p. 223) illustrate the aftermath of events. The actress, who looks out of the composition, changes out of her costume attended by her dresser, who is being engaged in conversation by an admirer or potential suitor. Forain bathes the principal figure in bright light while the business being conducted behind her is shadowy.

The artist was a close friend of the novelist and critic Joris-Karl Huysmans, who reviewed the sixth Impressionist exhibition (1881) at which *The Actress's Dressing Room* (p. 222) was shown. In his review Huysmans argues that no one medium has priority over another:

> *The truth is that today, each of the techniques of painting corresponds more directly to one of the various sides of contemporary life. Watercolour has a spontaneity, a freshness, a vibrant sparkle unattainable with oil…And pastel has a beauty, softness, like a freedom of delicacy and a dying grace that neither watercolour nor oil could reach. It is simply a matter for a painter to choose among these different methods the one that seems best suited to the subject matter he wants to treat.*

The full range of Forain as a pastellist is evident in *At the Evening Party: Woman in White with a Fan* (p. 224) and *Woman Smelling Flowers* (p. 225), which was included in the last Impressionist exhibition (1886). The former is drawn in a brisk tense manner, while the latter is 'like the pollen of a lily or the dust from a butterfly's wing' – the words used by the critic Paul Desjardins to describe the art of pastel.

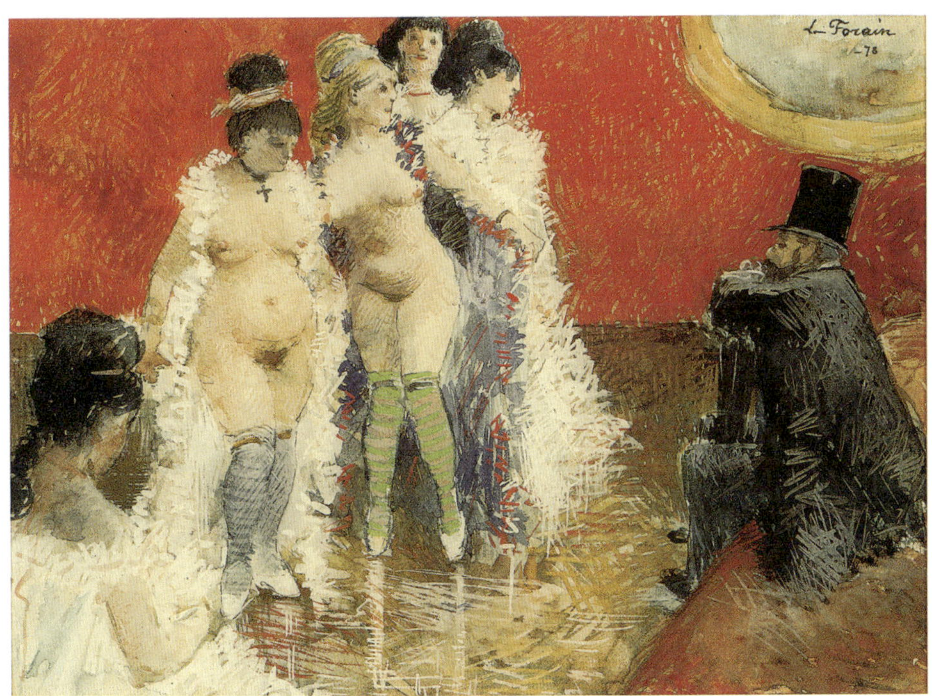

The Client, 1878
Pencil, watercolour and gouache, 24.7 × 32.8 cm
(9¾ × 12⅞ in.). Signed and dated.
DIXON GALLERY AND GARDENS, MEMPHIS, TENNESSEE

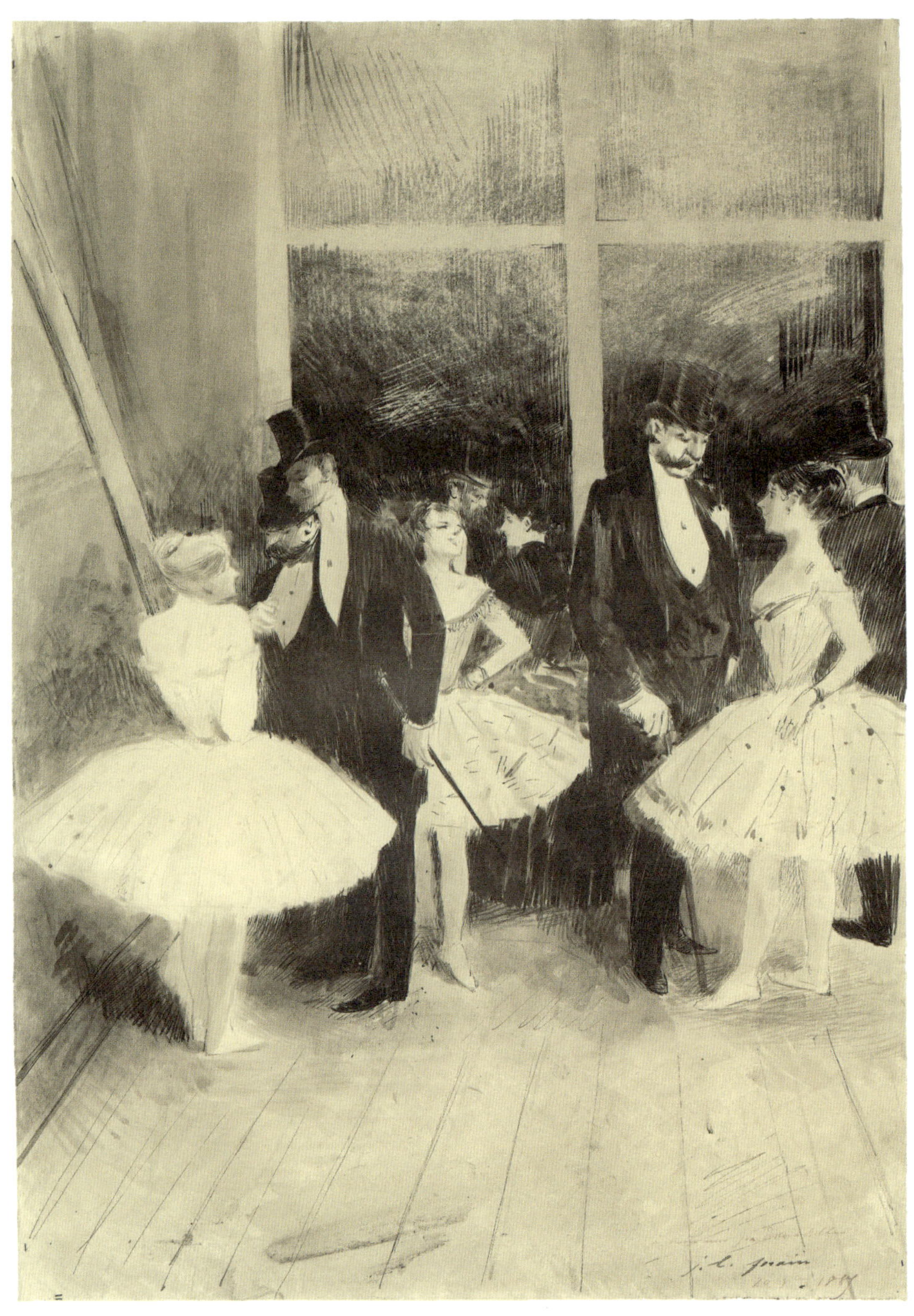

 Jean-Louis Forain

In the Wings, 1889
Ink and wash, 45.7 × 31.4 cm (18 × 12⅜ in.). Signed.
BOSTON PUBLIC LIBRARY, MASSACHUSETTS

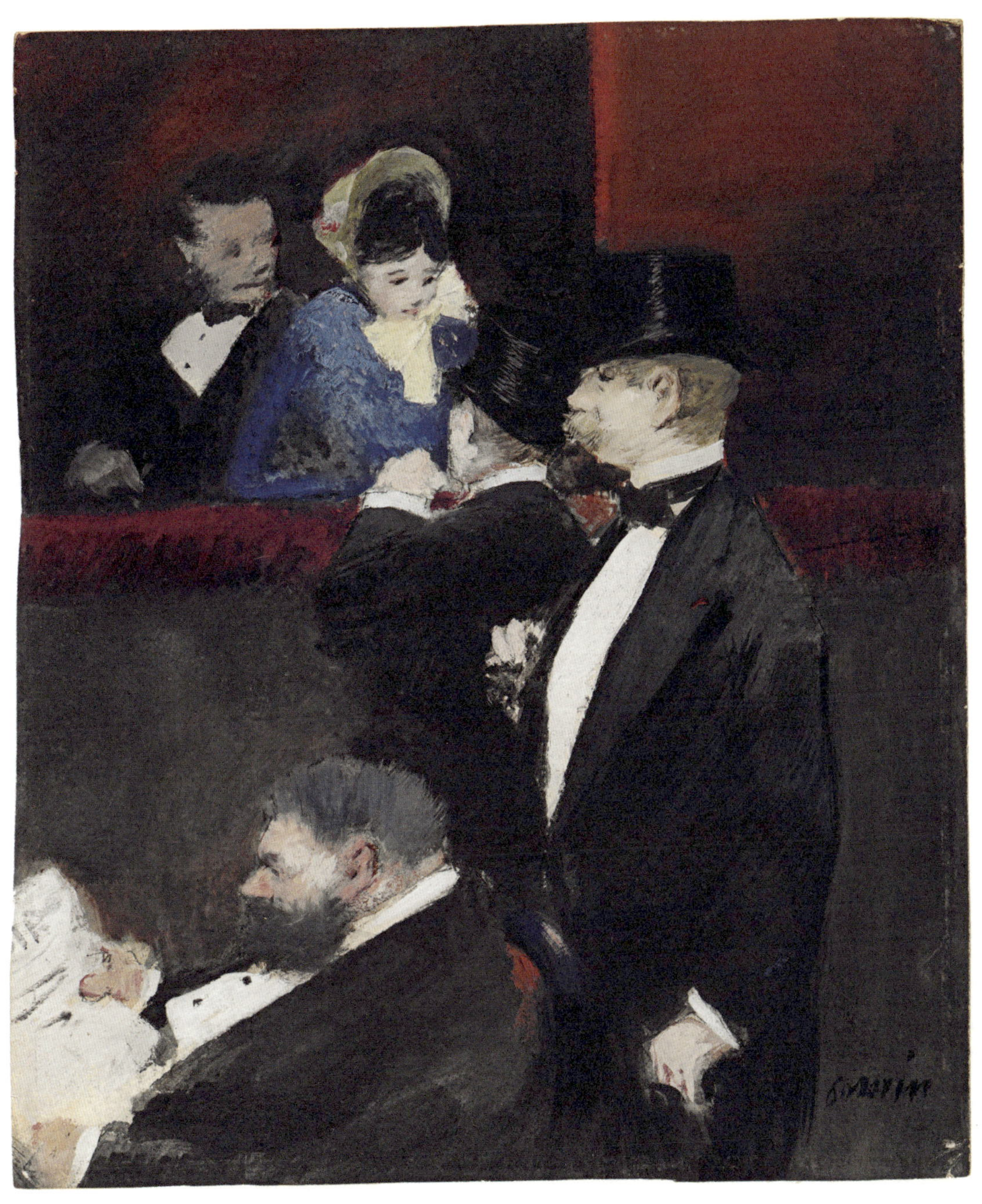

A Box at the Opéra, c. 1880
Gouache and oil on board, 28.9 × 23.7 cm
(11⅜ × 9⅜ in.). Signed.
HARVARD ART MUSEUMS (FOGG MUSEUM), CAMBRIDGE, MASSACHUSETTS

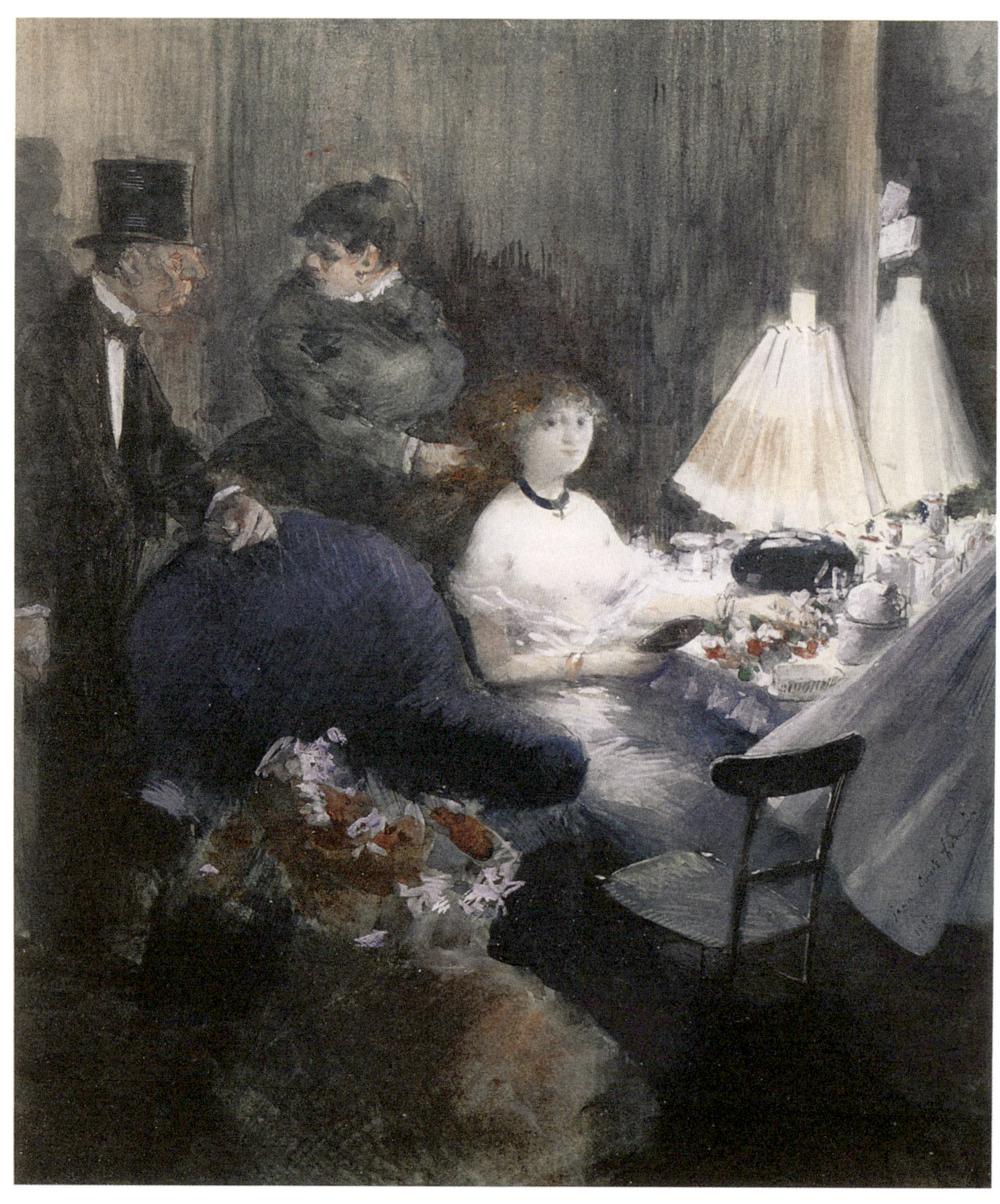

  Jean-Louis Forain

The Actress's Dressing Room, 1880
Watercolour heightened with gouache,
28 × 23 cm (11 × 9 in.). Signed and dated.
PRIVATE COLLECTION

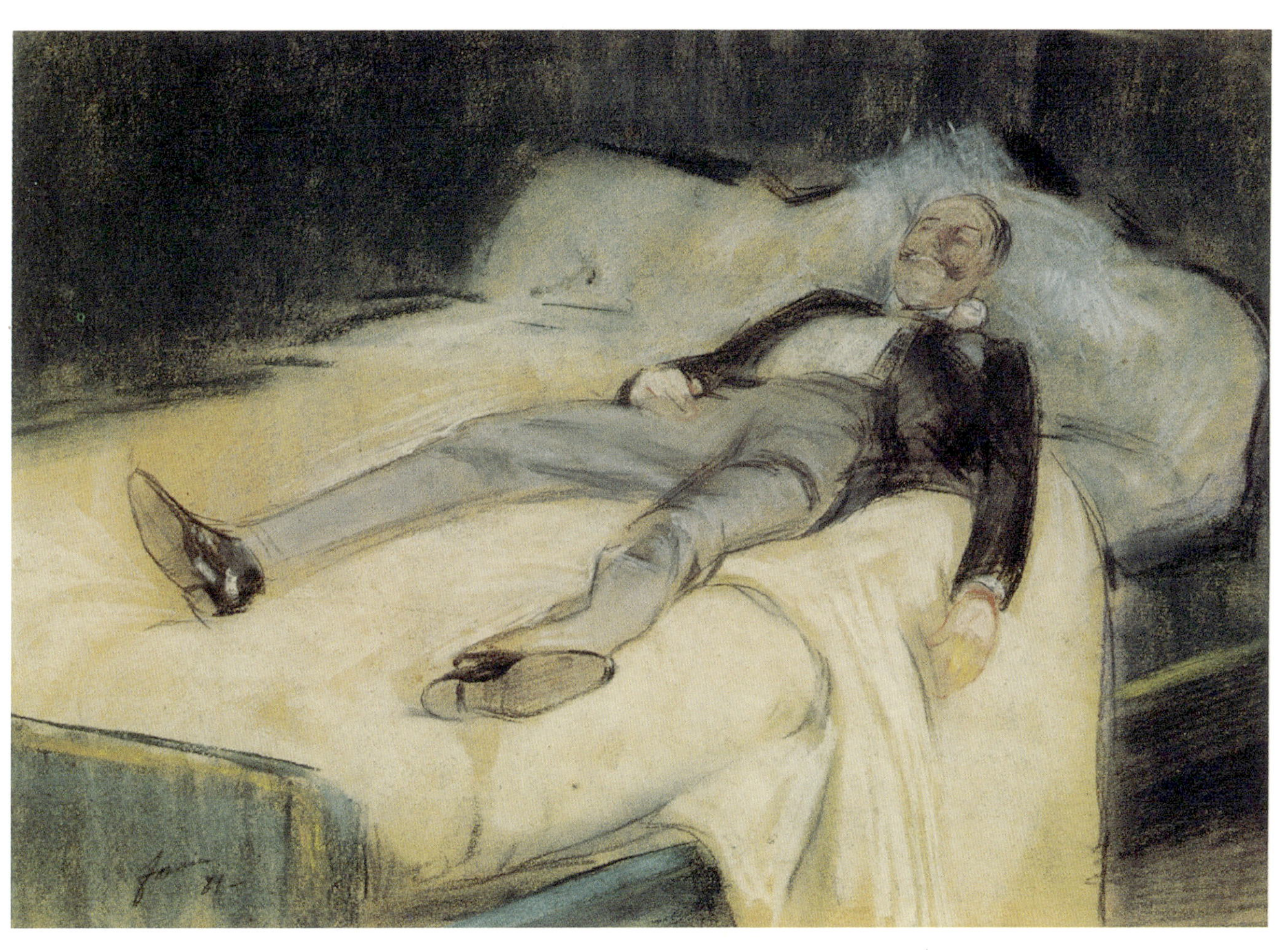

After the Ball: The Reveller, 1882
31.1 × 47 cm (12¼ × 18½ in.). Signed and dated.
DIXON GALLERY AND GARDENS, MEMPHIS, TENNESSEE

224   *Jean-Louis Forain*   *At the Evening Party: Woman in White with a Fan*, 1883–84
Pastel, 55.2 × 45.7 cm (21¾ × 18 in.). Signed.
NORTON SIMON MUSEUM, PASADENA

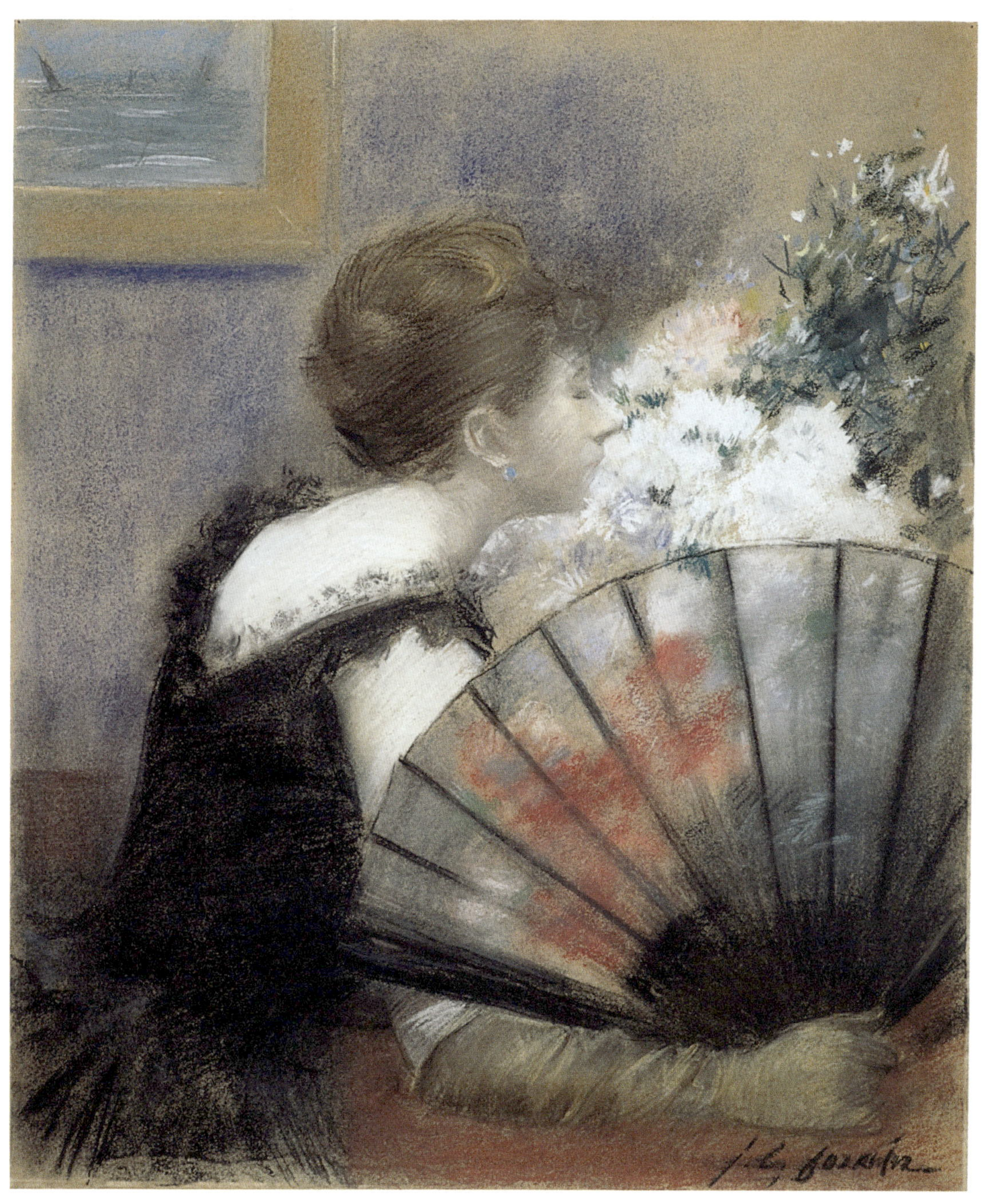

Woman Smelling Flowers, 1883
Pastel, 88.9 × 78.7 cm (35 × 31 in.). Signed.
DIXON GALLERY AND GARDENS, MEMPHIS, TENNESSEE

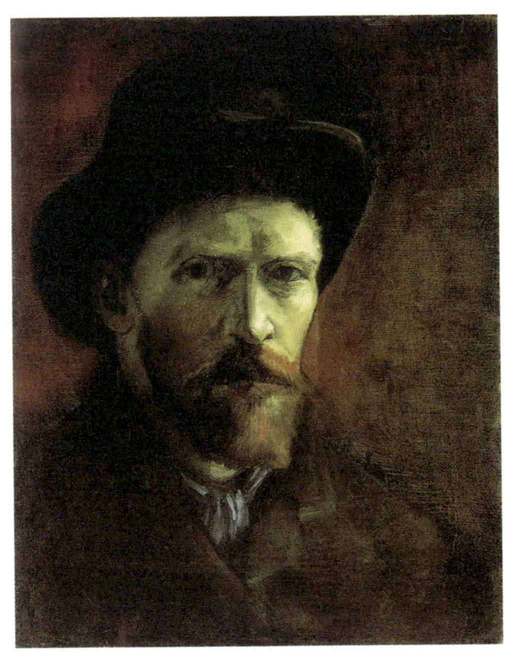

Vincent van Gogh
1853–1890

Drawings by Vincent van Gogh are plentiful and date from each phase of his working life, which was intense, short and dramatic. He only decided to become an artist in 1880 at the age of twenty-seven and died a decade later, leaving behind an extensive *oeuvre* of paintings and drawings, which is complemented by his voluminous correspondence. The letters were written mainly to his brother Theo, who was four years younger, but also to other family members and fellow artists. The connection between life and art in Van Gogh's work is close, and consequently through his letters more is known about his personal aspirations and difficulties, as well as his technical concerns and procedures, than for any other painter.

The son of a pastor in the Dutch Reformed Church, Van Gogh was born in Brabant, a province in the south of the Netherlands. After leaving school in 1869 there was uncertainty as to what career he might pursue, and he ended up following a number of leads in quick succession. He was immediately apprenticed to an art dealer, which ended

Vincent van Gogh
Self-Portrait with Felt Hat, 1886–87
Oil on canvas, 41.5 × 32.5 cm (16⅜ × 12¾ in.).
VAN GOGH MUSEUM, AMSTERDAM

in 1875, whereupon he spent a year teaching in England at Ramsgate and Isleworth. On returning to the continent in 1877, he started to work in a bookshop in Dordrecht before studying theology in Amsterdam, but this too was unsatisfactory and he set about gaining practical experience as a lay preacher and evangelist in the Netherlands and Belgium. Although identifying closely with the urban and rural poor, among whom he chose to live in considerable hardship, Van Gogh finally became disillusioned with religion and sought to find alternative ways of redressing the injustices of the world. Ultimately, he realized that the best and only means of achieving this end was through art, which he then pursued with the same fanaticism as he had taken up the cause of the dispossessed. Such fanaticism was a constant in Van Gogh's life: it could produce great art, but at the same time it brought on psychological crises that often required medical treatment, and eventually resulted in self-harming and finally in the artist taking his own life.

Van Gogh always found it difficult to conform. Outwardly this manifested itself in forms of dress, displays of unruly manners and patterns of irregular behaviour, but inwardly there was immense mental turmoil leading to self-doubt and endless self-examination, prompted by feelings of inadequacy. His aim was nothing more than to improve the condition of mankind. However grandiose that might seem, it was sincere, and Van Gogh was in fact well qualified intellectually to undertake it. A gift for languages was supplemented by his wide reading, which helped him to formulate his social and ethical ideals. The problem in 1880 was how to translate those ideals into the visual form that he had, after much thought, chosen as his main mode of expression. Even before becoming an artist, he frequently visited museums and was an avid collector of prints. Once committed, therefore, he was fairly conversant with art in general.

Not surprisingly, the subjects of Van Gogh's early work were the landscape and people of his homeland. Although advised by the artists Anthon van Rappard and Anton Mauve, and in receipt of commissions for his drawings from a family member, Van Gogh virtually taught himself to draw and to paint. He had recourse to standard manuals by Charles Bargue and Armand Cassagne, which were in wide circulation, but he was also inspired by the illustrations published in such journals as *The Graphic* and *The Illustrated London News* that he had first encountered in England and collected subsequently. Progress at first was uneven, but it was swift and relentless. Once started, it is as though Van Gogh never stopped drawing, and his output comprises not just studies but also *répétitions* made for friends, as well as illustrations in his letters to keep Theo and others up to date with his progress.

As with his paintings, there is nothing diffident about Van Gogh's drawings. For landscapes he nearly always covered the whole sheet, and the figure studies are normally vigorously modelled. The use of traditional media is also unusually elaborate and challenging: a preference for opaque rather than transparent watercolours, for natural chalks rather than manufactured ones, for alternative types of pen and pencil, and for invasive procedures involving dilution, stumping and scratching out. Any description of the media found in Van Gogh's drawings is often very elaborate. Partly this is because a large proportion of them were made for sale and highly finished, although his expectations were never fulfilled in this respect.

Road in Etten (p. 230) is one of many drawings revealing Van Gogh's love of the changing perspectives and shifting light of the Dutch landscape, which never dimmed even when he was working in the south of France. Roads feature strongly throughout Van Gogh's work and probably came to have a symbolic significance, marking man's passage through life. *Road in Etten* is perhaps a more mundane exercise in perspective, which the artist found difficult, often resorting to a special frame that he used in front of the motif. No doubt as he was making this drawing he was aware of the rich tradition of seventeenth-century Dutch landscape painting, but the presence of the figure sweeping the road indicates the artist's interest in the relationship between man and his natural surroundings.

Figure drawing presented Van Gogh with problems, which he acknowledged, even though he recognized its importance and asserted at the outset that he preferred it to landscape drawing. *Sien Sewing* (p. 231) is an early example where the handling is stiff and the features wooden. On the other hand, the profile is striking and the modelling strong. The sitter was a former prostitute with whom the artist lived in 1882–83 in an attempt to help her and her child.

Both *The Kingfisher* (p. 232) and *Peasant Woman Gleaning* (p. 233) indicate the rapid advance in Van Gogh's style. The filigree pen work and delicate use of white highlighting are expertly done in the landscape, but so too is the treatment of the light behind the church and the moist atmosphere rising from the sunken pond. The inspiration for this drawing was a poem by Jules Breton entitled *Autumn*. Breton was a popular painter of rural scenes, who Van Gogh admired. *Peasant Woman Gleaning* is one of a series of studies made at Nuenen, where his parents were then living and where his father died. All are notable for their monumentality. Such drawings are indebted to the Barbizon artist Jean-François Millet, but the proximity of the figure viewed from above and the varied hatched strokes are singular.

Van Gogh made two attempts to improve his credentials: firstly by attending the Academy of Fine Arts at Antwerp for a short period in 1885 and then, after moving to Paris the following year, in the studio of Fernand Cormon (Introduction, fig. 7), where he met Toulouse-Lautrec, Emile Bernard, Louis Anquetin and John Russell. Previously having only known paintings by The Hague School of artists, the Impressionists and the Neo-Impressionists were a revelation and made an immediate impact, as did the Japanese woodblock prints that he now started to collect. Van Gogh's Paris drawings, many of which were made in Montmartre, reflect this sudden advance in his art in their mixed technique and colour range (p. 234).

After two years in Paris, Van Gogh travelled south in early 1888 to Provence, where he settled in Arles and was joined several months later by Gauguin. He had hoped to found an artists' colony in the south, but his mental frailty and corrosive relationship with Gauguin resulted in his eventually being committed to the asylum of Saint-Paul-de-Mausole at nearby Saint-Rémy in May 1889. Nonetheless, many of Van Gogh's finest drawings were made in Arles. The scale and confidence of these drawings signal a sudden release in the artist's creative energy. The emphasis now is more on pen and ink than on watercolour. Specially cut reed pens and quill pens are given prominence over standard metal nib pens, chalk or pencil. If Van Gogh was determined to rival Rembrandt, it is in these drawings that he succeeded.

View of Arles (p. 235) is still carefully composed, but with a wider range of strokes, each governed by the pressure of the hand or the flow of ink. It is the diversity and quantity of marks that plots the feeling of recession across the fields to the town in the distance. *Souvenir of Saintes-Maries on the Mediterranean* (p. 236) was a Damascene moment when Van Gogh realized that he no longer needed to use traditional perspective. As a result, his style became more impulsive and buoyant. *The Country on the Banks of the Rhône Viewed from Montmajour* (p. 237) demonstrates a remarkable skill in giving due attention to individual parts of a panoramic landscape without losing sense of the whole. The variations of touch in the assembled strokes, dashes, dots and squiggles may suggest a *horror vacui*, but they also represent the heat and colour of Provence. The degree of empathy is such that the viewer not only sees with Van Gogh's eyes but also feels as he feels. In such works there is human activity and signs of modernity, but they are subservient to the variety and fecundity of nature. The paper virtually crawls with life as though covered by a plague of insects.

The brush drawings done in the asylum at Saint-Rémy and afterwards at Auvers-sur-Oise, a village to the northwest of Paris, near Pontoise, where Van Gogh was looked after by the sympathetic Dr Paul Gachet, are bolder. They match the final paintings in their flowing rhythms, but they are also the determined efforts of an artist under immense mental strain. There seems no escape from the *Corridor in the Asylum* (p. 238), which echoes to the clamour of the inpatients.

Auvers-sur-Oise was a release both emotionally and artistically. It also had associations with Pissarro and Cézanne. Van Gogh responds eloquently (p. 239) to the gentle riparian landscape, but it was here that he died and is buried. His brother Theo, who throughout had shown such concern for his brother, helped him financially and cared for him emotionally, died only three months later. Both are now buried side by side in the local cemetery at Auvers-sur-Oise.

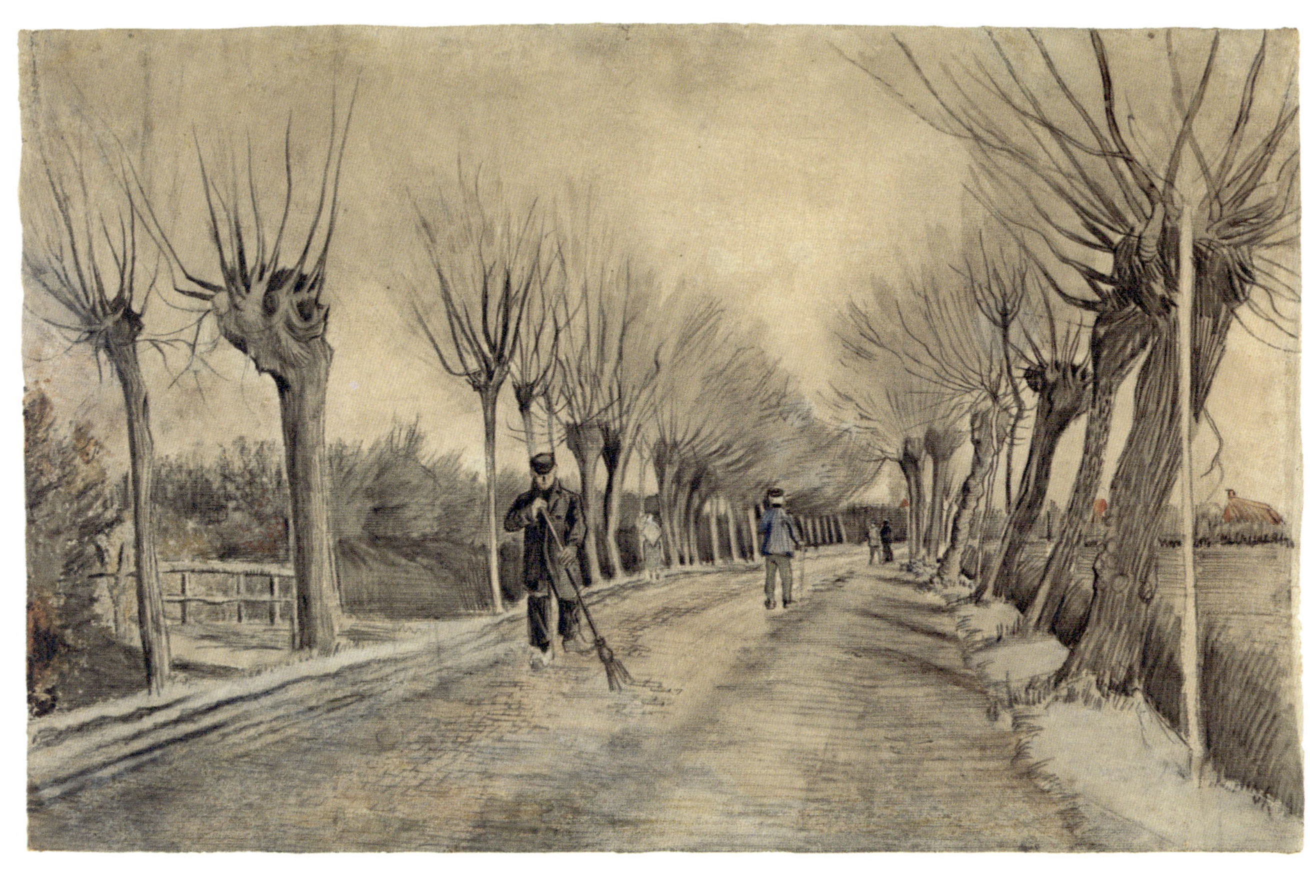

  Vincent van Gogh

Road in Etten, October 1881
Pen and brown ink under-drawing, chalk, pencil,
pastel, watercolour, 39.4 × 57.8 cm (15½ × 22¾ in.).
METROPOLITAN MUSEUM OF ART, NEW YORK

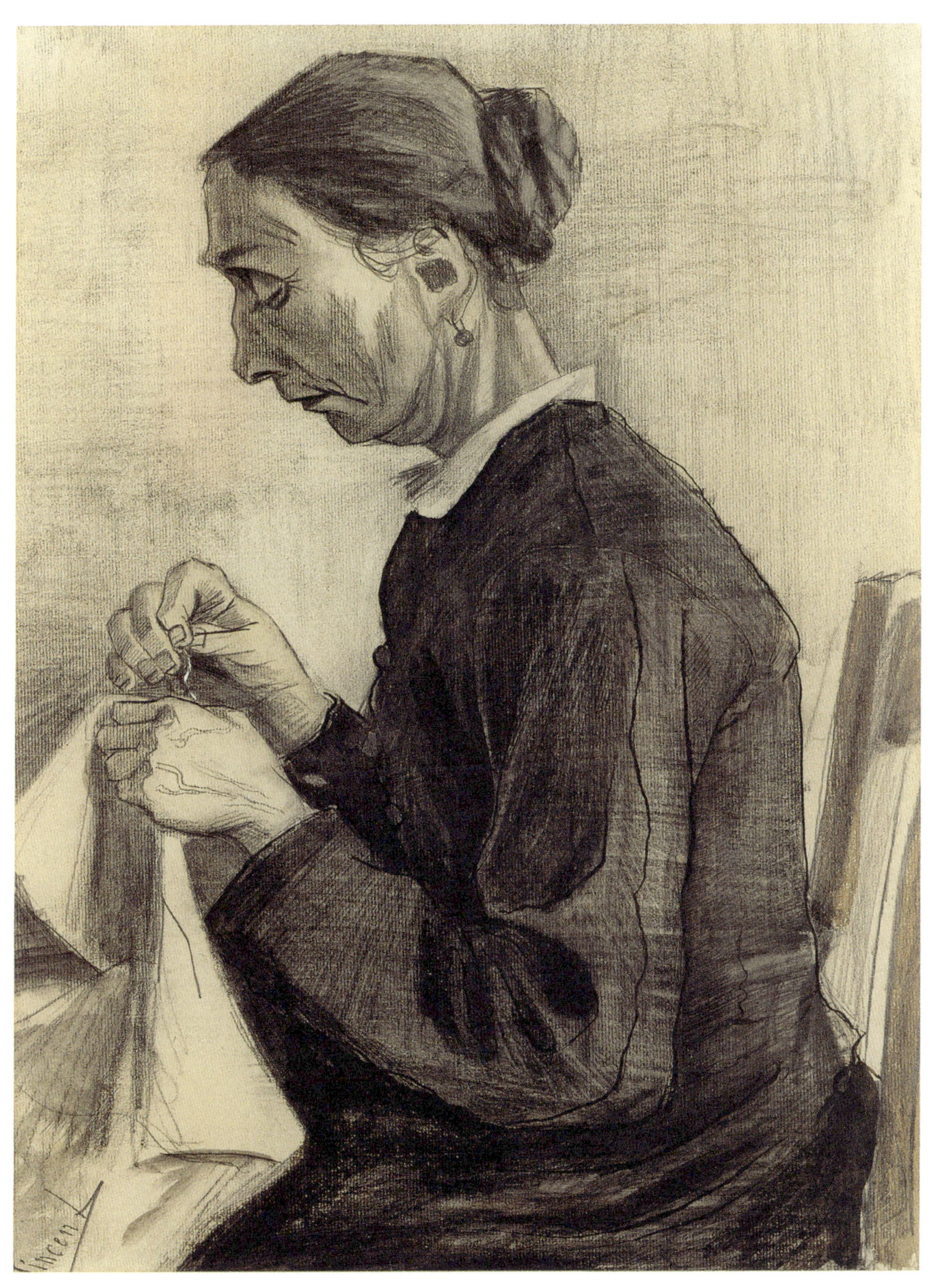

Sien Sewing, April–May 1882
Pencil, black chalk, pen and brush in black
ink and grey wash heightened with white,
53.2 × 37.6 cm (20⅞ × 14¾ in.). Signed.
MUSEUM BOIJMANS VAN BEUNINGEN, ROTTERDAM

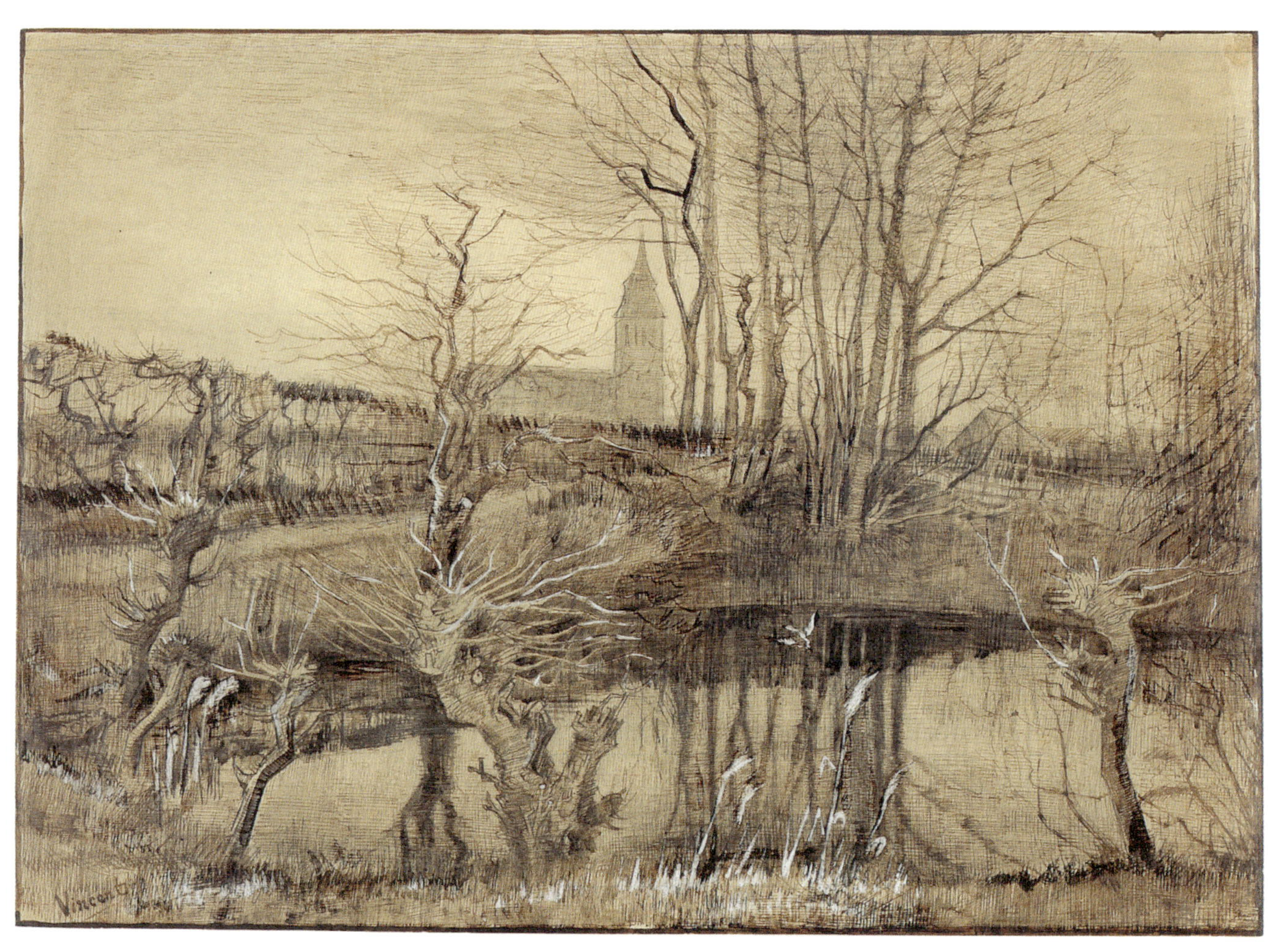

232   *Vincent van Gogh*

The Kingfisher, March 1884
Pen, brush and ink, pencil heightened with white,
40.2 × 54.2 cm (15⅞ × 21⅜ in.). Signed.

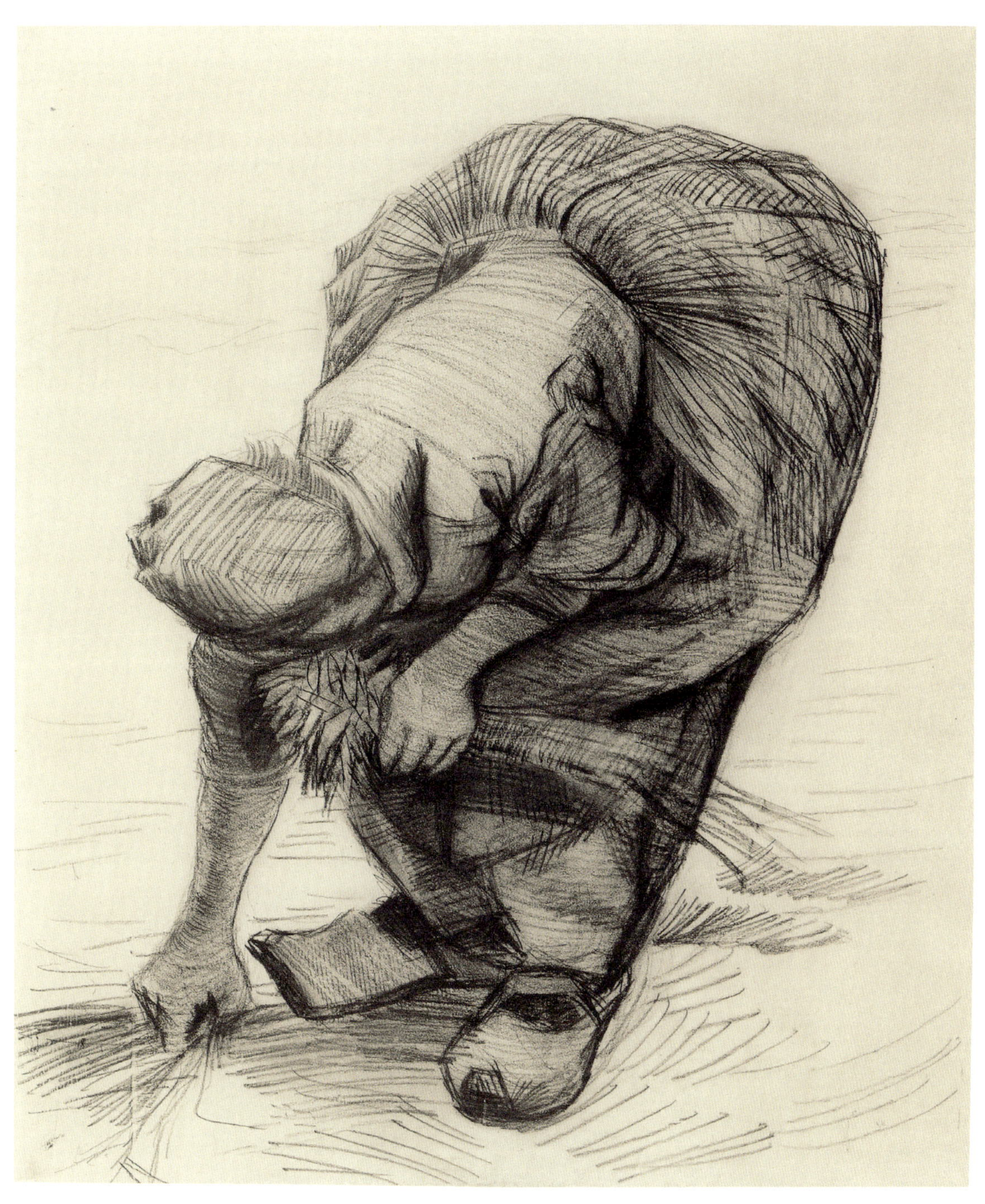

Peasant Woman Gleaning, July–September 1885
Black chalk, 51.4 × 41.5 cm (20¼ × 16⅜ in.).
MUSEUM FOLKWANG, ESSEN

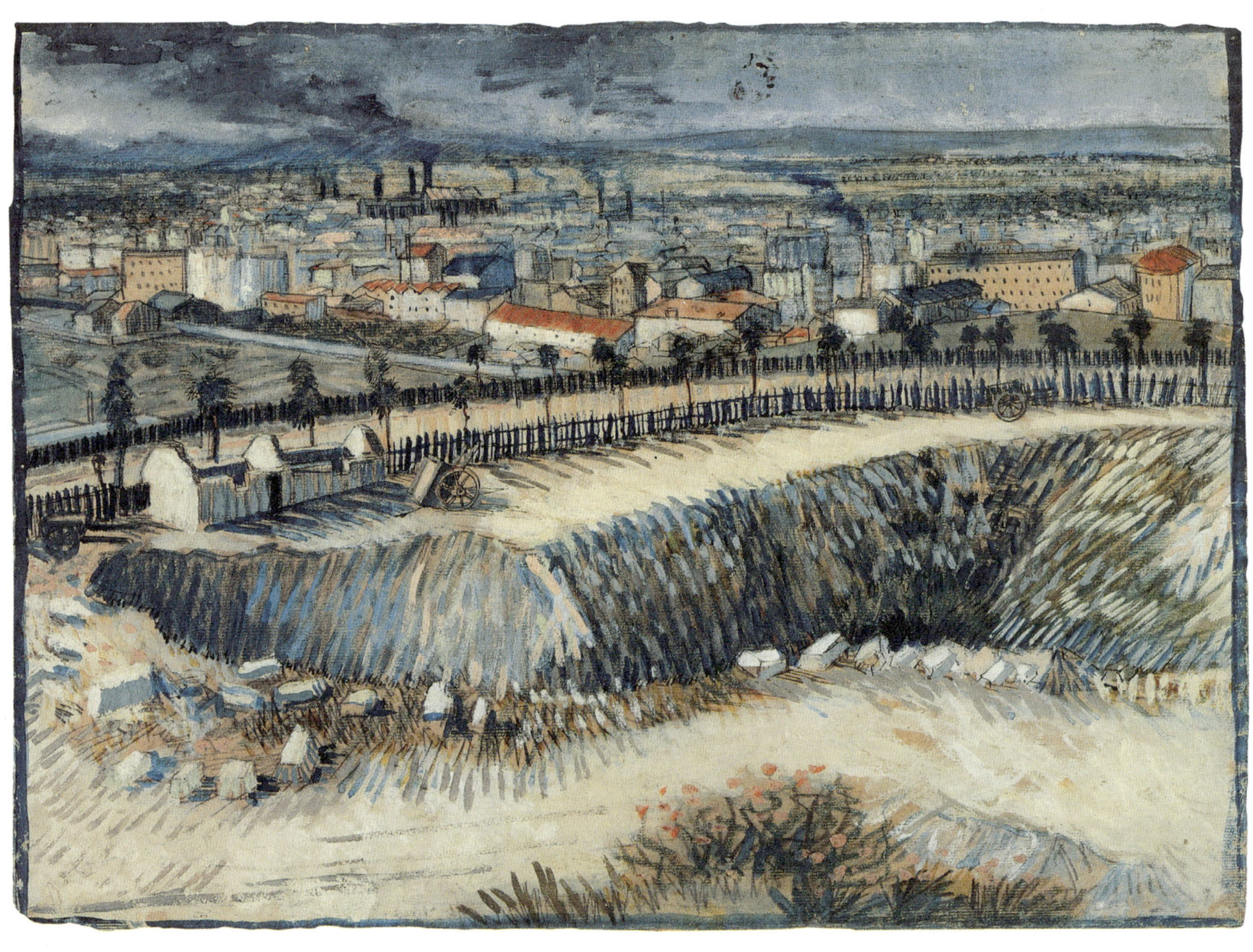

234   *Vincent van Gogh*

View from Montmartre, June–September 1887
Watercolour, gouache, chalk, pencil with pen and ink,
39.5 × 53.5 cm (15½ × 21 in.).
STEDELIJK MUSEUM, AMSTERDAM

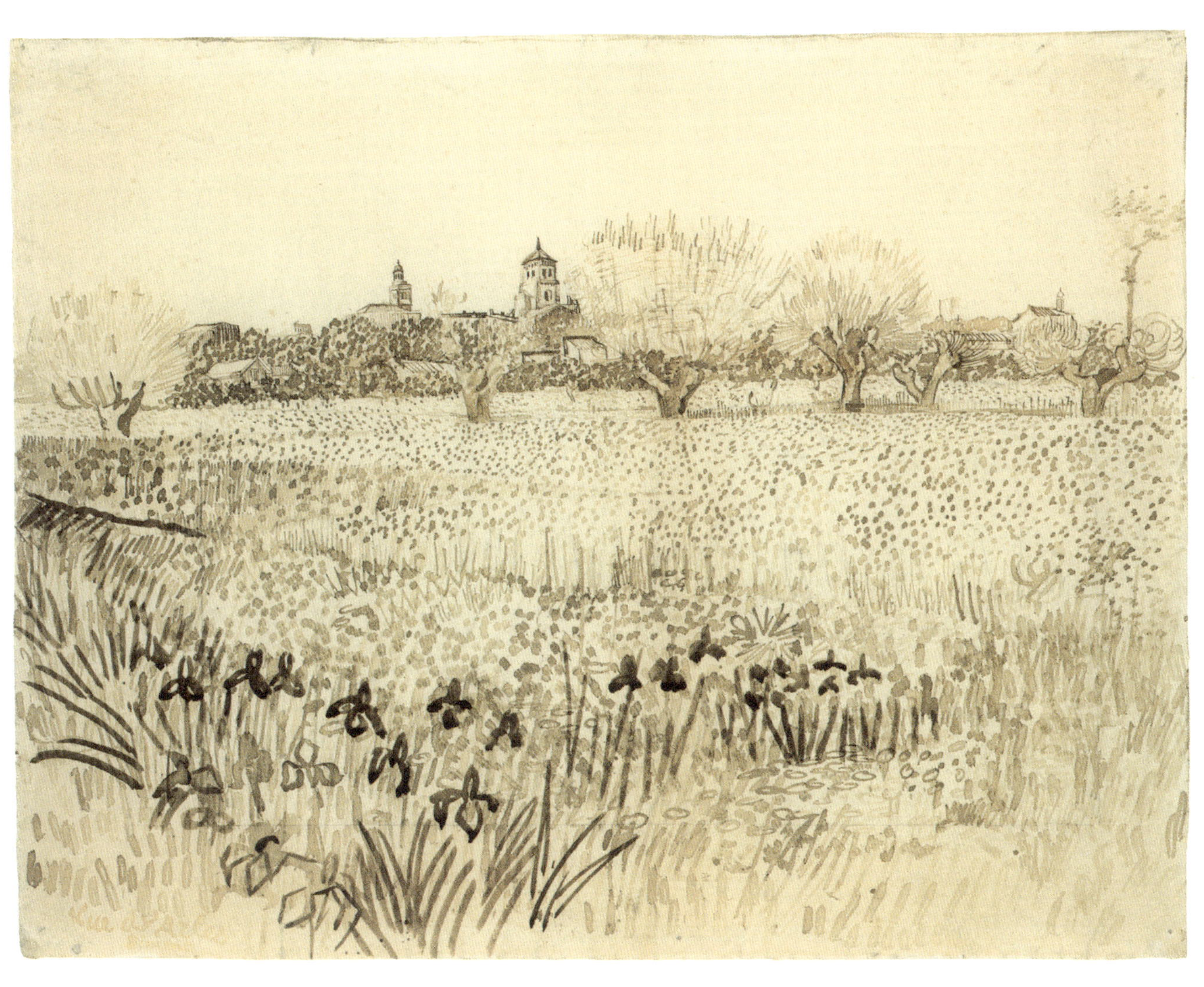

View of Arles, May 1888
Reed pen, ink and wash over pencil,
43.2 × 54.6 cm (17 × 21½ in.).
RHODE ISLAND SCHOOL OF DESIGN MUSEUM, PROVIDENCE

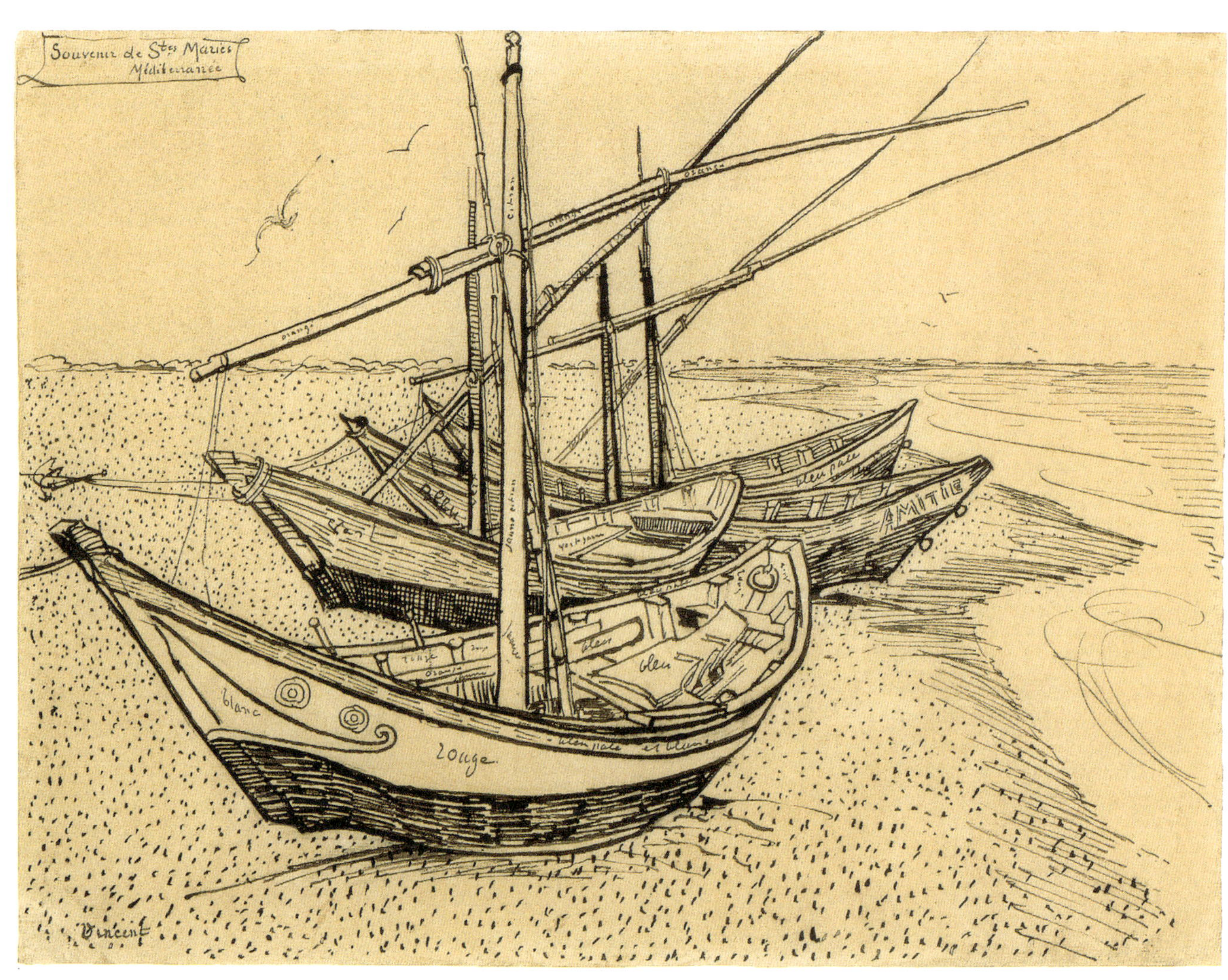

  Vincent van Gogh

*Souvenir of Saintes-Maries on the Mediterranean: Boats
on the Beach, Saintes-Maries-de-la-Mer, c. 4 June 1888*
Reed pen and ink over pencil, 39.5 × 53.3 cm (15½ × 21 in.).
Inscribed with the title and signed.
PRIVATE COLLECTION

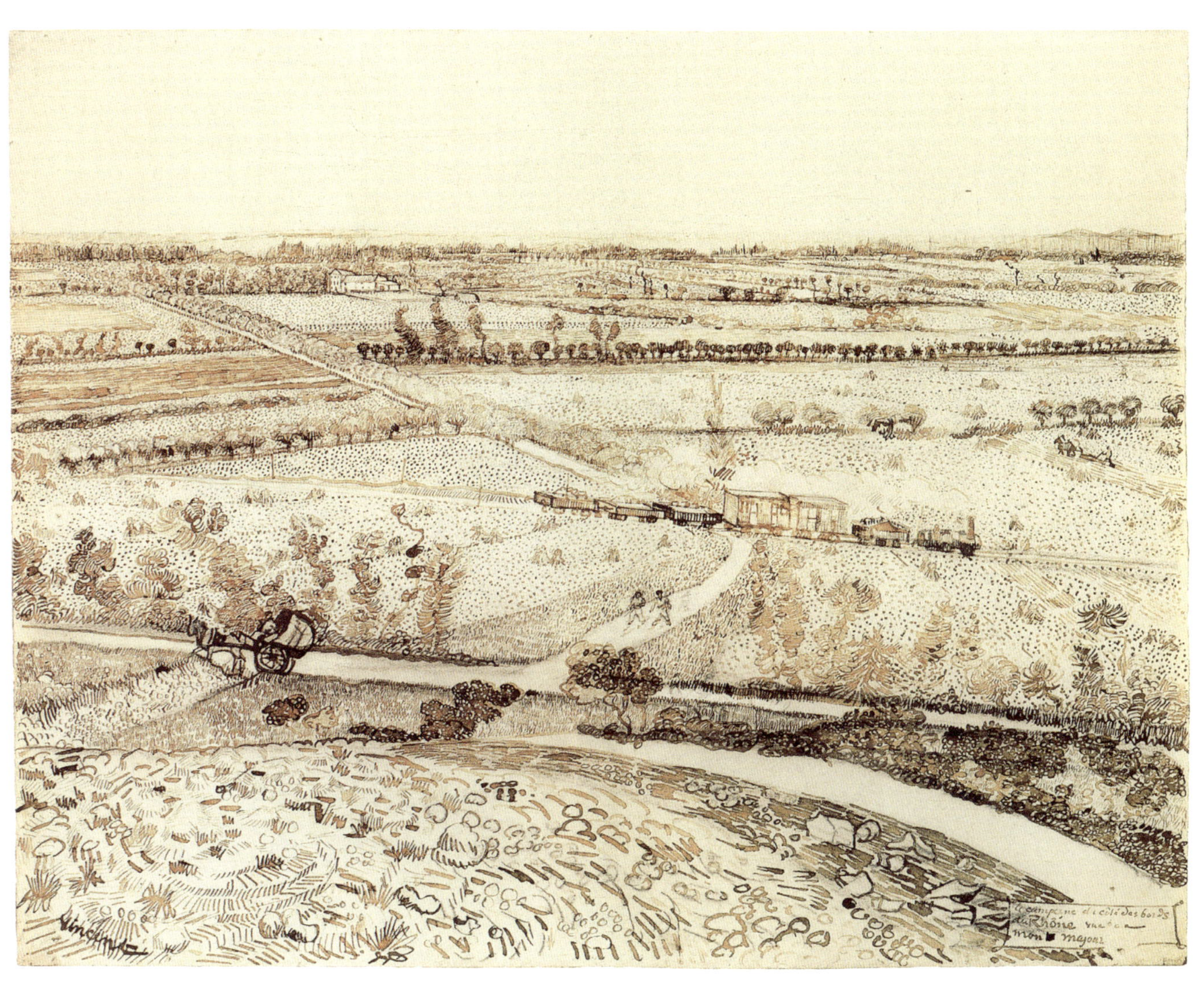

The Country on the Banks of the Rhône Viewed
from Montmajour, 6–12 July 1888
Reed pen, quill, and ink over black chalk and pencil,
48.7 × 60.7 cm (19⅛ × 23⅞ in.). Signed.
BRITISH MUSEUM, LONDON

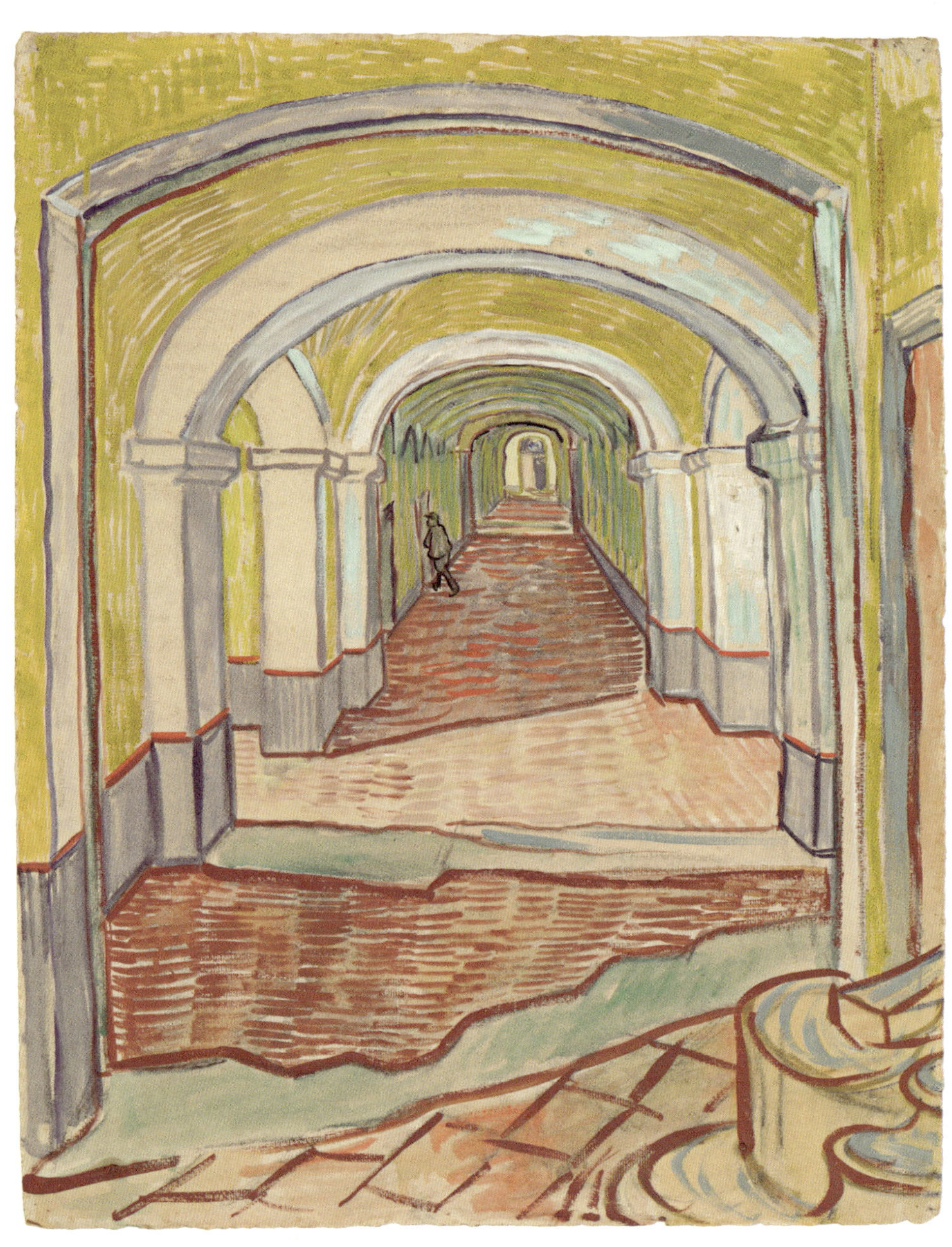

238   *Vincent van Gogh*

Corridor in the Asylum, September 1889
Brush and oils, black chalk on pink paper,
65.1 × 49.1 cm (25⅝ × 19⅜ in.).
Metropolitan Museum of Art, New York

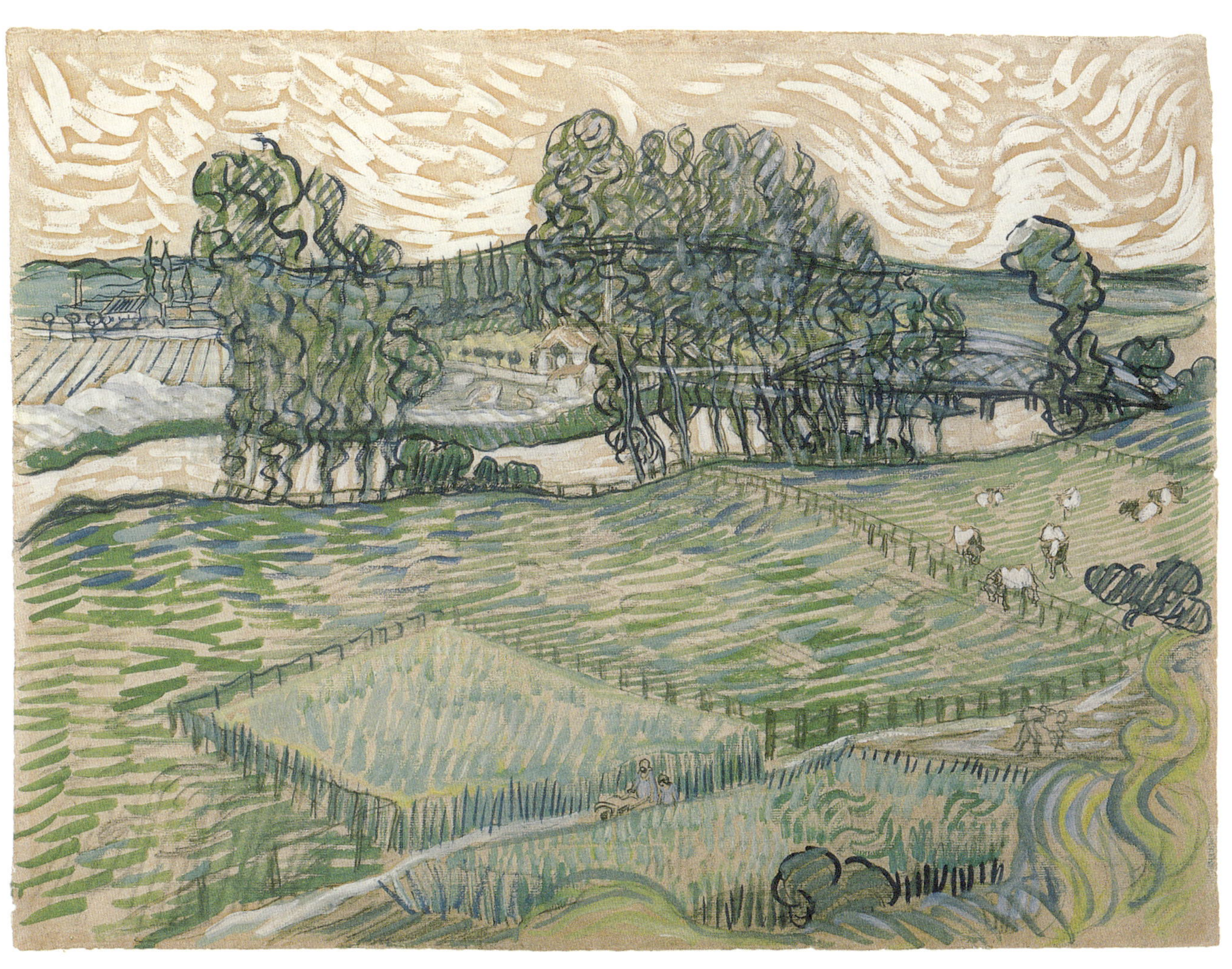

The Oise at Auvers, late May–early June 1890
Brush, opaque watercolour, and oils, pen and ink,
pencil on pink paper, 47.3 × 62.9 cm (18⅝ × 24¾ in.).
TATE, LONDON

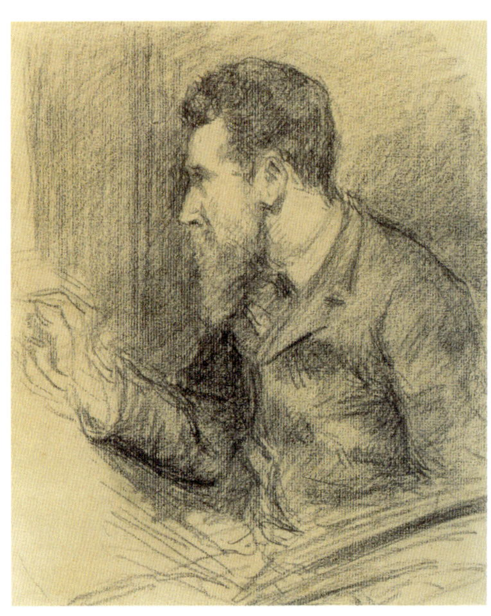

Georges Seurat
1859–1891

Georges Seurat died prematurely aged thirty-one, possibly of diphtheria, but during his short life he initiated and refined new ways of painting and drawing, now designated as Neo-Impressionism. This avant-garde movement aimed to develop Impressionism to a more advanced stage. Although works by Seurat and Signac were included in the eighth Impressionist exhibition (1886), the main outlets for the Neo-Impressionists were the Société des Artistes Indépendants in Paris and Les Vingt in Brussels.

Seurat's painting style – known as pointillism or divisionism – was aimed at overcoming the randomness of Impressionism, characterized by free improvised brushwork and arbitrary selection of colour. The younger generation advocated a more scientific approach to painting and drawing. The starting point for Seurat's theories was the omnium gatherum of Charles Blanc's *Grammaire des Arts du Dessin* (1867), but this popular text was supplemented by the close study of the latest research into aesthetics and colour harmonies conducted by Michel-Eugène Chevreul, Ogden Rood and Charles Henry. Inspired by such publications, he slowly evolved a style that put

Maximilien Luce
Georges Seurat, 1890
Conté crayon, 29.6 × 22.5 cm (11⅝ × 8⅞ in.).
PRIVATE COLLECTION

greater emphasis on compositional unity, arising from more controlled handling, a clearer sense of form through drawing and a profounder understanding of colour. On this basis, Seurat always sought to create an ensemble, which is why his work, however avant-garde in outlook, remained firmly within the classical tradition. It may be that Seurat's intellectual proclivities and disciplined application of ideas gave his art a certain detachment, but, as his drawings show as much as his paintings, his style conceals a passionate engagement with contemporary life. The overall description of Seurat's Neo-Impressionist style as pointillist or divisionist is in fact too narrow and ultimately misleading. While for a short time he did limit his brushstroke to the dot, on close inspection there is in his oeuvre a far greater variety of brushwork than is generally admitted, and not only in the oil sketches.

A similar observation could be made about Seurat's drawings, which are essentially tonal in style and tenebrist in effect. He was a prolific draughtsman and immensely proud of his works on paper, which from the early 1880s he produced in great number in a highly finished form ready for exhibition or sale. His preferred medium was conté crayon and there are only a handful of drawings in other media. Conté crayon is harder and greasier than charcoal or chalk and therefore less friable. The choice of support was crucial, and Seurat elected to use a type of 'Ingres' paper called Michallet, which is a milk-coloured laid paper of the highest quality, with pronounced ridges on the surface and often a clearly visible watermark (p. 253). The tonal effects vary as a result of the pressure applied by the artist as the conté crayon is dragged across the surface where its deposit remains only on the raised ridges, with the sunken furrows left untouched. The interaction between the medium and the paper is such that the drawings can have a three-dimensional appearance. This technique was not discovered by Seurat and one or two of his contemporaries had previously exhibited items in a tenebrist style, but it is Seurat who brought this type of drawing to its highest level of sophistication. Prints by Rembrandt and Francisco de Goya were sources of inspiration, as, nearer to his own time, was the Barbizon painter Jean-François Millet.

Seurat was born into a comfortable bourgeois family and was not troubled by financial concerns. Although he came to enjoy the company of his fellow artists and writers, he was prickly, distant and reserved in character, which made him difficult to befriend. Much admired for his professionalism and his dedication to art, he was at the same time deeply conscious of his achievements, for which he was always anxiously determined to obtain due credit. Seurat was extremely well read and as conversant with the naturalist novels of Emile Zola and the Goncourt brothers as with the Symbolist poets Félix Fénéon, Paul Adam, Gustave Kahn and Emile Verhaeren, who were his friends and also wrote art criticism. The extent to which he guarded his privacy is illustrated by the fact that neither his parents, nor it seems his friends, knew of the existence of his mistress, Madeleine Knobloch, by whom he had a son.

The artist was trained in the academic tradition, at first at a local municipal school of drawing in Paris, culminating in one year of study (1878–79) at the École des Beaux-Arts under Henri Lehmann – a former pupil of Jean-Auguste-Dominique Ingres. He proved himself to be an accomplished copyist after the antique (Introduction, fig. 6) and of works by artists such as Raphael, Holbein the Younger, Nicolas Poussin and Ingres. During one year (1879–80) of military service he relied on sketchbooks to record glimpses of everyday life. *Woman on a Bench* (p. 244) was drawn at about this time and reveals Seurat's proclivity for intricately constructed compositions, with the figure carefully placed against the wooden bars of the bench. Although the outlines of the woman are still discernible, the rapidly drawn hatched areas have an experimental air, flattening the form while also dividing it into different segments.

Seurat was quick to realize the potential of tonal drawing, and at the start of the 1880s he began to make independent sheets of that type in considerable numbers. By the time of *Woman Sewing* (p. 245) he has dispensed with outlines and depends solely on tonal relationships. The lighter tones belie the sitter's form, which is seen against a darker background. The highlights are generated by the more restricted areas of paper left blank. A typical touch is the treatment of the hat, which emphasizes the bowed head of the faceless figure concentrating on her sewing. *The Gleaner* (p. 246), by contrast, is a towering dark form looming against the sky. The looser strokes overlaying the foreground suggest the activity of gleaning. Indeed, one of the artist's greatest skills in these first independent drawings is his ability to match his style to the subject, which became particularly important in the context of creating a series of urban and rural 'types'.

A similar sophistication is apparent in the landscape and cityscape motifs that Seurat began to explore in these early tonal drawings. *Place de la Concorde, Winter* (p. 247) has a melancholy air. The dark fountain on the left and the fiacre moving out of sight on the right emerge from the gloom, forming a strong horizontal axis. The spatial intervals of the empty snowy foreground and middle distance are marked out by lamp posts. It is an image steeped in atmosphere, realized on a poetic level.

Seurat's principal subjects during the 1880s, however, were not found in the centre of Paris, but in the suburbs that were growing on the northwest side of the city. Many oil sketches and drawings were made in preparation for the two large-scale pictures, *Bathers at Asnières* of 1884 (National Gallery, London) and *A Sunday on the Island of La Grande-Jatte* of 1884–86 (The Art Institute of Chicago), which are essentially modern versions of allegories by Pierre Puvis de Chavannes. In these paintings, set in locations that were near enough to the city for people to commute to work but at the same time in the throes of being industrialized, Seurat explored the interaction between different sections of society as they relax on the banks of the river Seine. *Seated Youth* (p. 248), who appears prominently in the *Bathers*, is treated as a nude, although in the finished work he wears shorts as well as his hat. The changes in the gradation of tones are barely perceptible as the light plays over the body. Although seen in profile, the boy's character is suggested by the slumped shoulders and the cheerless expression. *Landscape with a Dog* (p. 249) is a compositional study for *A Sunday on the Island of La Grande-Jatte* in which Seurat examines the area where he will situate his figures, whose presence is anticipated by the dog. What is in essence a gentle *sous-bois* scene reminiscent of Jean-Baptiste-Camille Corot is only disturbed by the activity on the river in the background. All is calm before the invasion of the happy weekenders.

During his final years there is a greater diversity in Seurat's art. *Circus Sideshow* of 1887–88 (Metropolitan Museum of Art, New York) and *The Circus* of 1891 (Musée d'Orsay, Paris) are well-rehearsed themes in French nineteenth-century art, while *Models* of 1886–88 (Barnes Foundation, Philadelphia) is a re-examination of his own academic training. *Trombonist: Study for 'Circus Sideshow'* (p. 250) is a night scene with the tall figure of the trombonist silhouetted against a brightly lit interior. His task is to catch the attention of the passing crowds and encourage them to come and watch the circus acts about to take place inside. The horizontal emphasis of the composition establishes a sense of recession while also increasing the isolation of the trombonist. The various café-concerts that Seurat attended were another attraction where he could examine the interaction between different sections of society and also observe the efforts of performers trying to hold an audience's attention. There is humour in *At the Concert Européen* (p. 251), with the row of heads in the foreground partially blocking the view of the stage.

Almost every summer from 1885 Seurat escaped from Paris to visit the coast of the English Channel, where he painted a number of marine subjects. These views of the sea and the seaports where he stayed are in several ways the summation of Seurat's work. The carefully constructed compositions, the quiet gradations of colour and the subtle modulation of light bring these pictures close to the Aesthetic Movement, while the subject matter has elements of Symbolism. Not many related drawings are known, but *The Lighthouse at Honfleur* (p. 252) has an ethereal quality enhanced by the fact that at the end of the nineteenth century a sailing boat was often interpreted as representing the passage from this world to the next. Similarly, *Anaïs Faivre Haumonté on her Death-Bed* (p. 253), which is an unusually personal drawing for Seurat, showing his close relative hovering between life and death, highlights the religious connotations of the scene with the flickering candlelight on the private altar on the other side of the bed.

Seurat is an artist who appeals to modern sensibilities. The abstract and symbolist tendencies in his work and the trouble he took over the process of his art are now all seen as aspects that anticipate modern art. Significantly, the many drawings that were left after his death were eagerly collected by his writer friends and fellow artists including Pissarro, Signac, Pierre Bonnard, Henri Matisse and Pablo Picasso.

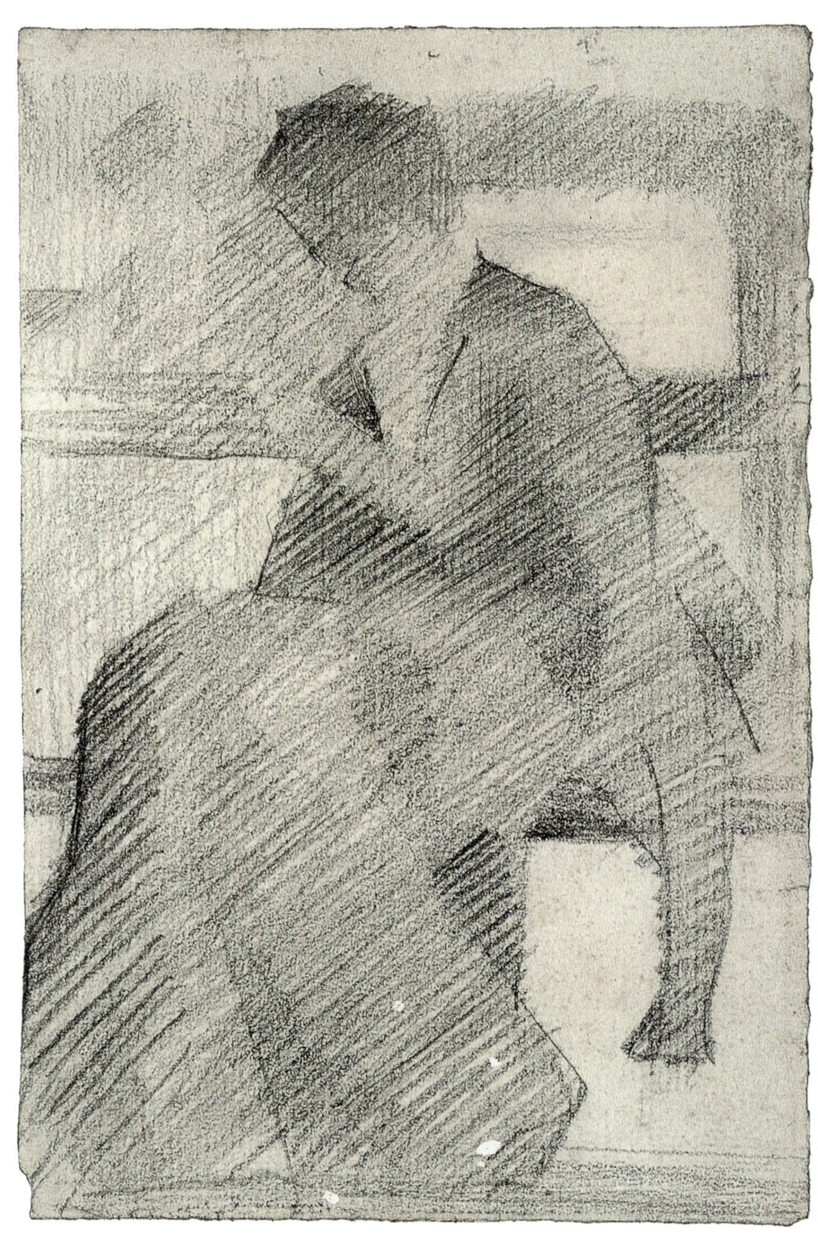

244   *Georges Seurat*

Woman on a Bench, 1880–81
Pencil, 16.5 × 10.4 cm (6½ × 4⅛ in.).
SAINSBURY CENTRE FOR VISUAL ARTS, UEA, NORWICH

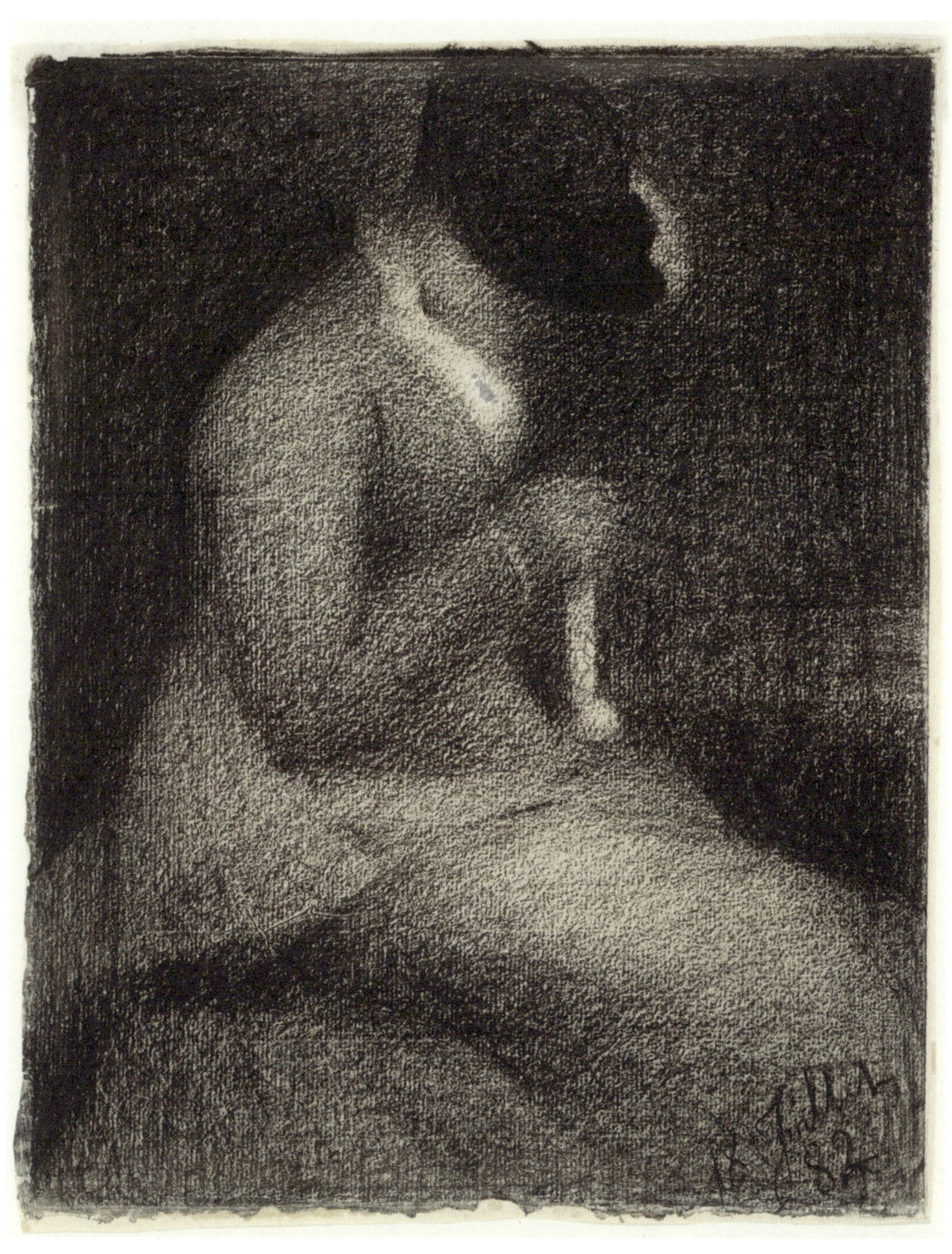

Woman Sewing, 1882
Conté crayon, 32.2 × 24.5 cm (12⅝ × 9⅝ in.).
HARVARD ART MUSEUMS (FOGG MUSEUM), CAMBRIDGE, MASSACHUSETTS

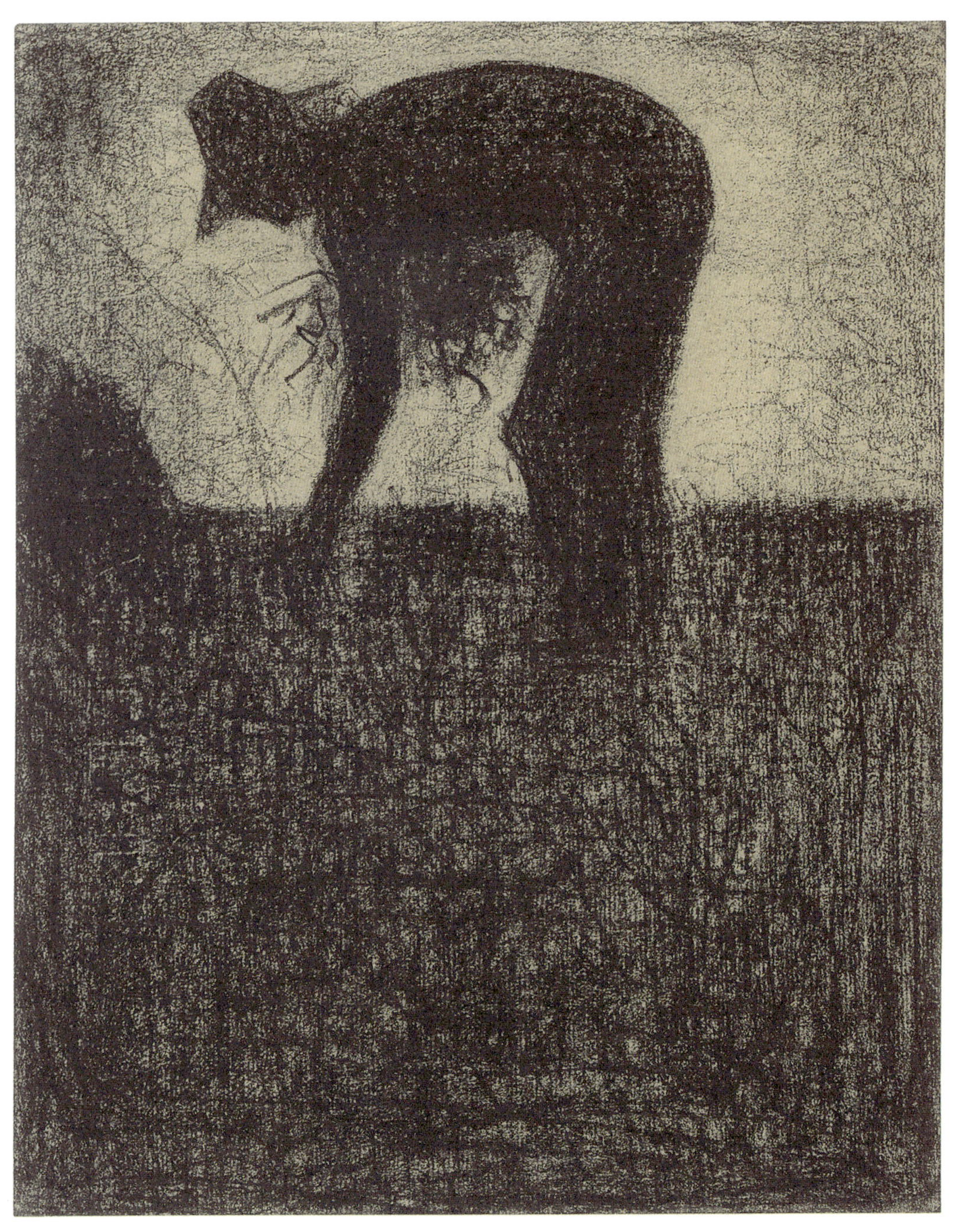

 Georges Seurat

The Gleaner, c. 1883
Conté crayon, 31.4 × 23.7 cm (12⅜ × 9⅜ in.).
BRITISH MUSEUM, LONDON

Place de la Concorde, Winter, c. 1882–83
Conté crayon, 23.2 × 30.7 cm (9⅛ × 12⅛ in.).
SOLOMON R. GUGGENHEIM MUSEUM, NEW YORK

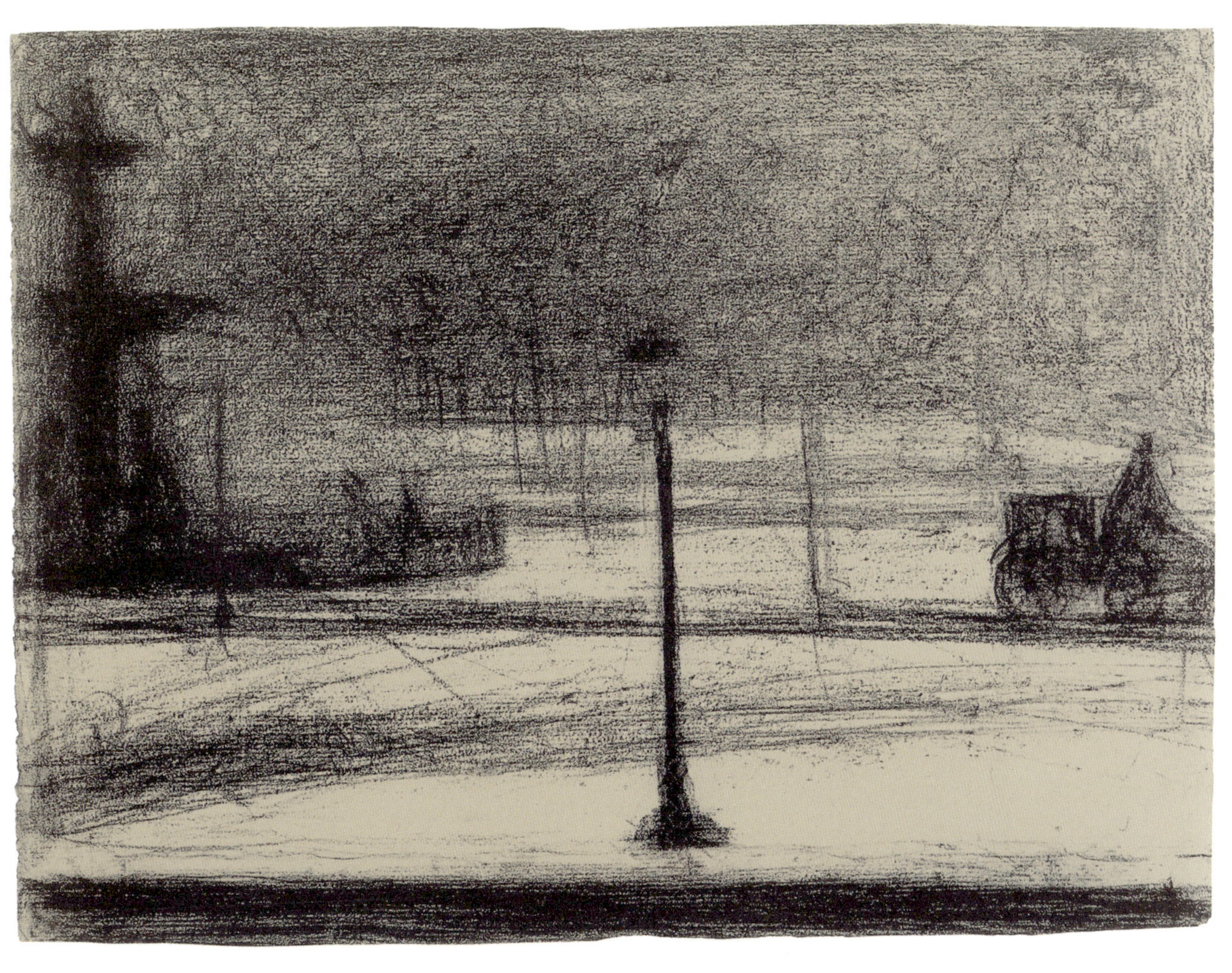

247

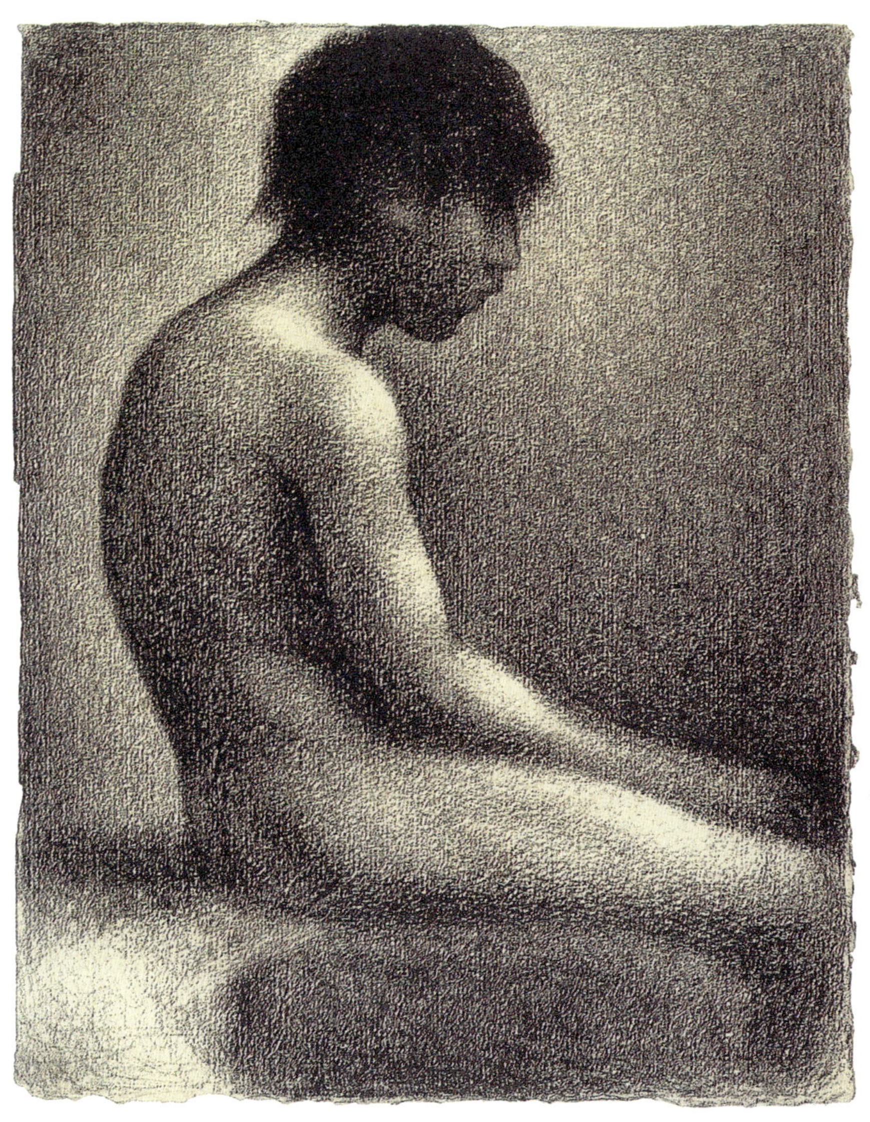

    Georges Seurat

Seated Youth, Study for 'Bathers', 1883
Conté crayon, 31.7 × 24.7 cm (12½ × 9½ in.).
NATIONAL GALLERY OF SCOTLAND, EDINBURGH

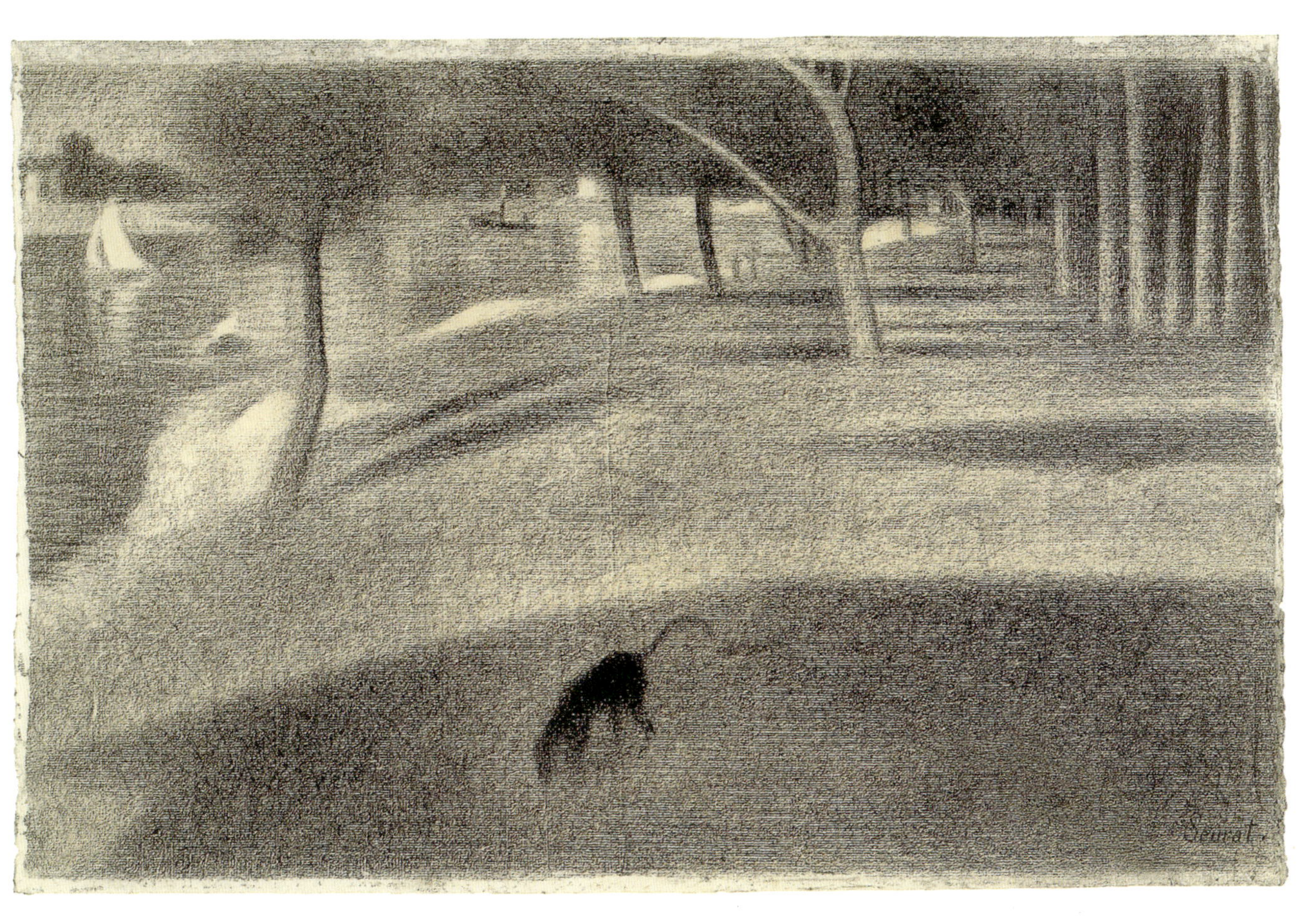

Landscape with a Dog, Study for 'La Grande Jatte', 1884
Conté crayon, 42.5 × 62.8 cm (16¾ × 24¾ in.).
BRITISH MUSEUM, LONDON

249

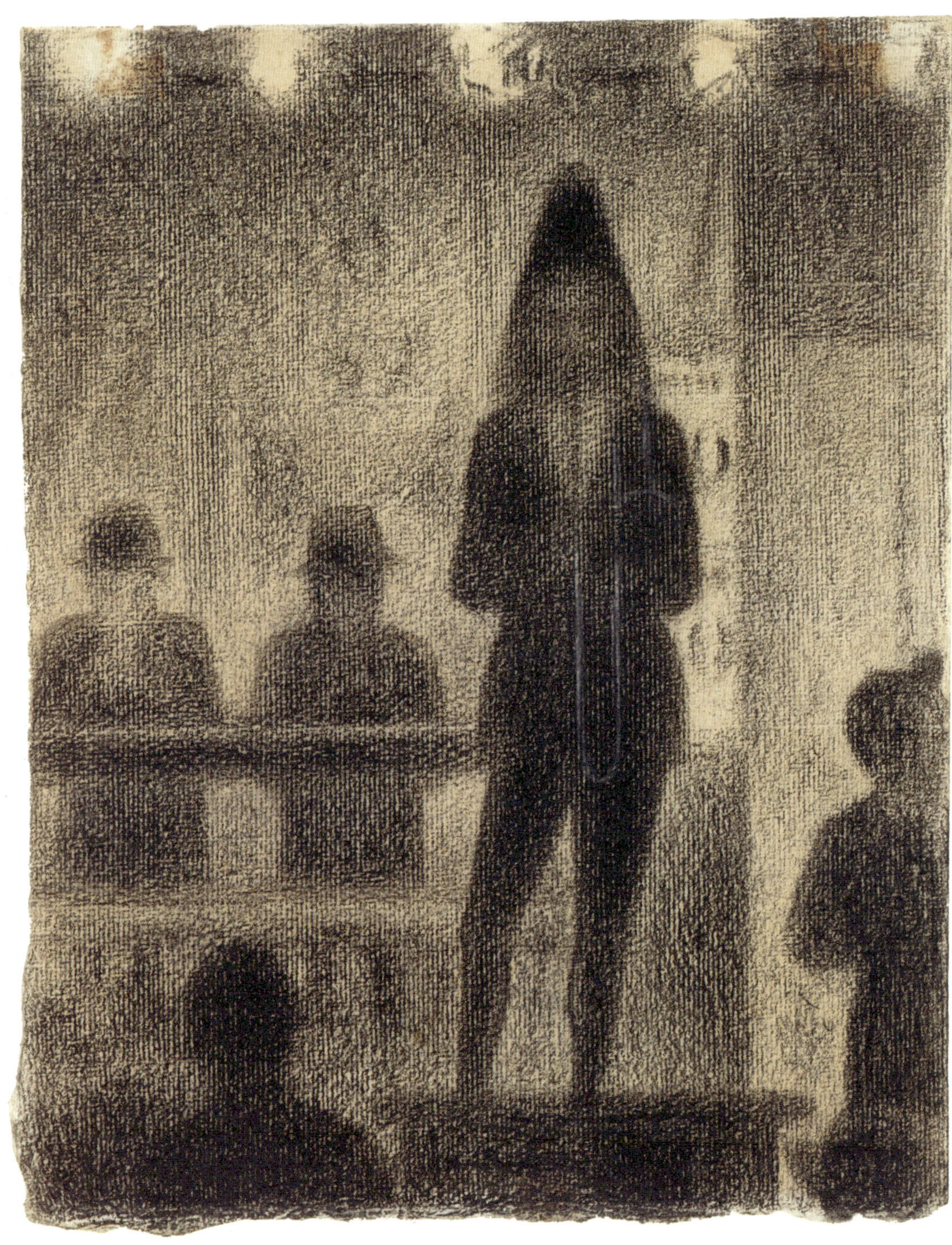

250 *Georges Seurat*

Trombonist, Study for 'Circus Side Show', c. 1887
Conté crayon heightened with white chalk,
31.1 × 23.8 cm (12¼ × 9⅜ in.).
PHILADELPHIA MUSEUM OF ART

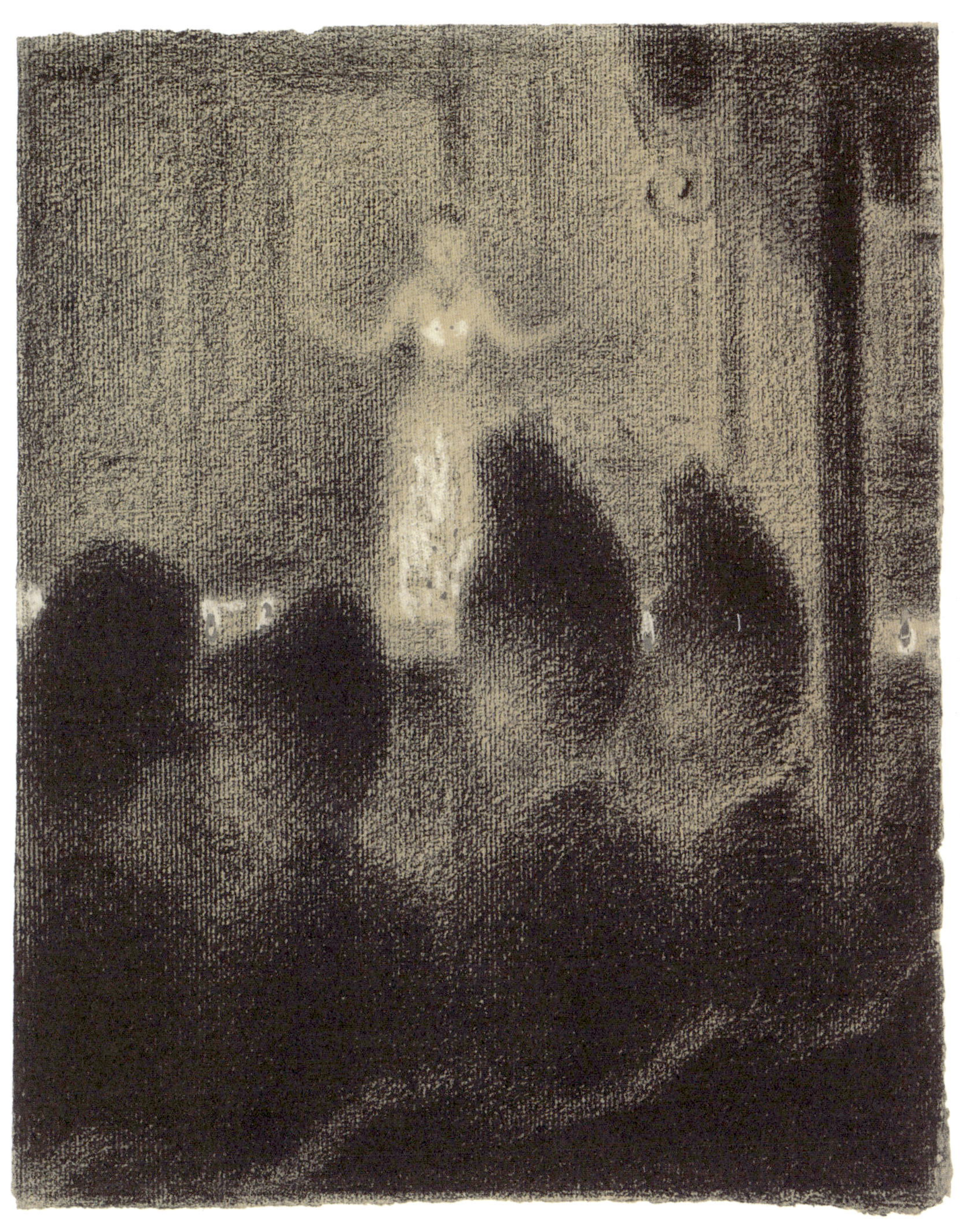

At the Concert Européen, c. 1887–88
Conté crayon and gouache,
31.1 × 23.8 cm (12¼ × 9⅜ in.).
MUSEUM OF MODERN ART, NEW YORK

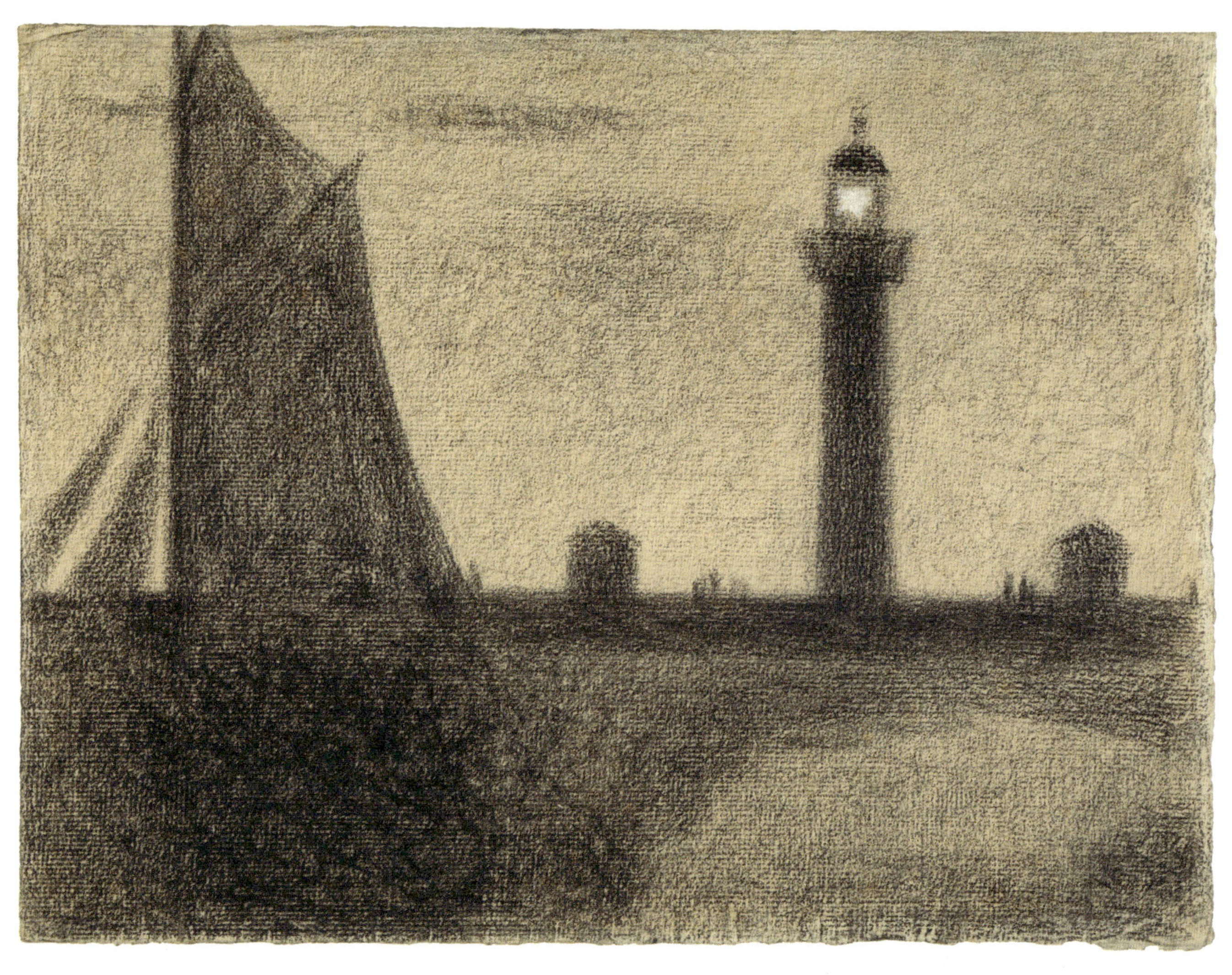

252   *Georges Seurat*

The Lighthouse at Honfleur, 1886
Conté crayon heightened with gouache,
24.1 × 30.8 cm (9½ × 12⅛ in.).
METROPOLITAN MUSEUM OF ART, NEW YORK

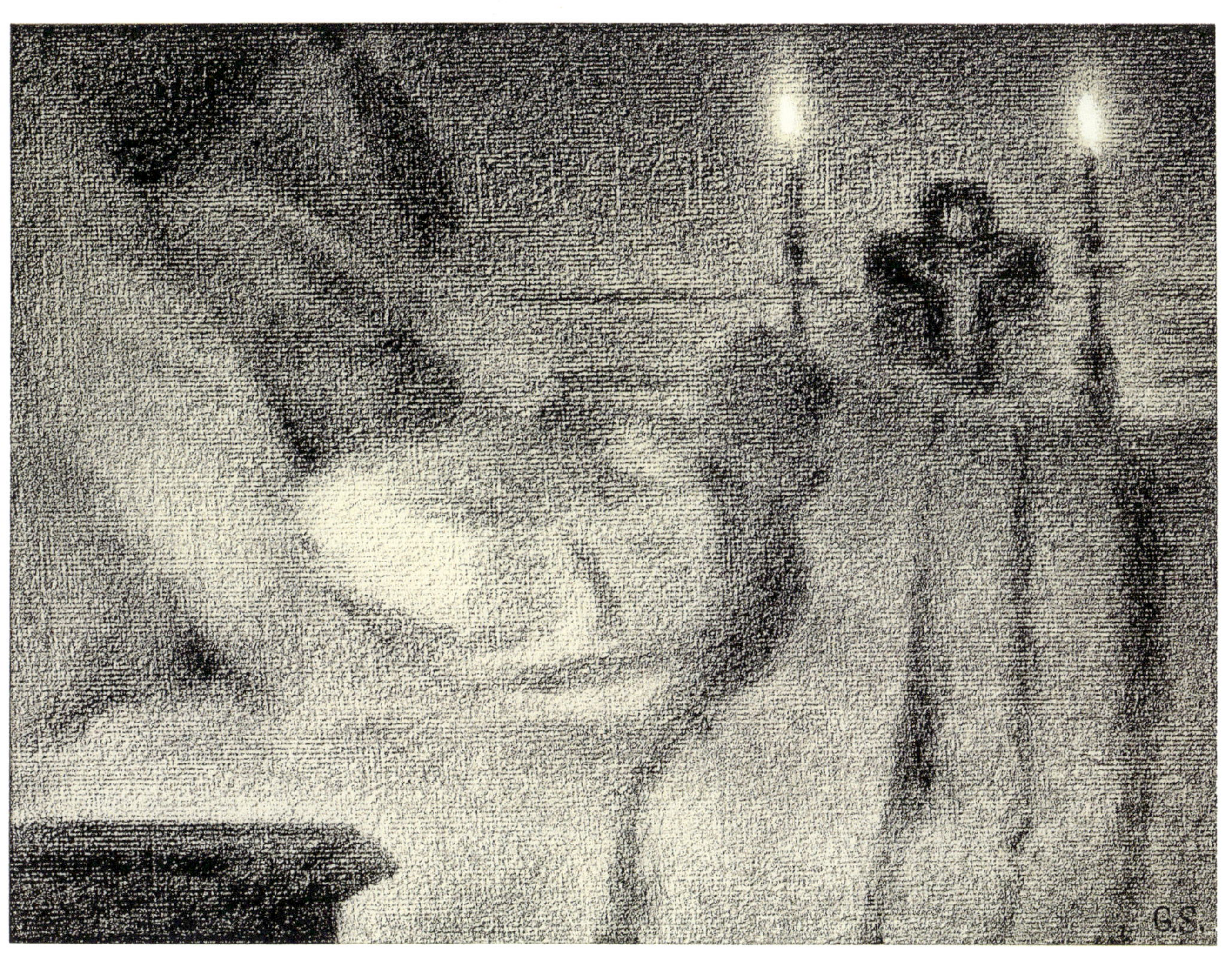

Anaïs Faivre Haumonté on her Death-Bed, 1887
Conté crayon heightened with white chalk, 23 × 33 cm (9 × 13 in.).

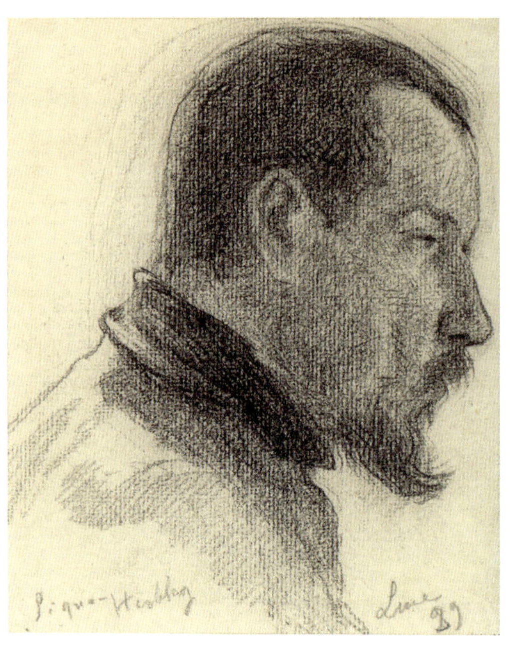

Paul Signac
1863–1935

The eighth and last Impressionist exhibition (1886) demonstrated irrevocably how divided this group of avant-garde artists had now become. Preliminary discussions underlined the stylistic and practical differences that had always existed but had finally reached a point where they were undermining any sense of unity. The ever-compliant Pissarro argued successfully for the inclusion of the younger artists Seurat and Paul Signac, who were working in the fully developed pointillist style known as Neo-Impressionism, of which he himself was temporarily an exponent. But he had to agree that the works by the Neo-Impressionists would be shown in a separate room – a space that was dominated by Seurat's monumental *A Sunday on the Island of La Grande-Jatte*. Signac contributed eighteen items, including the painting *Passage du Puits-Bertin, Clichy* (present whereabouts unknown), which is recorded in a drawing made in connection with an illustration published in the journal *La Vie Moderne* in February 1887 (p. 259). The drawing is almost certainly the artist's first experiment in ink using the divisionist style.

Maximilien Luce
Paul Signac, 1889
Conté crayon, 19 × 15.9 cm (7½ × 6¼ in.). Signed and dated.

Signac was born in Paris. His father was a saddler and harness maker. The artist later said, 'My family wanted me to be an architect, but I preferred to draw on the banks of the Seine rather than in a studio at the École des Beaux-Arts' (p. 258). In fact, Signac was self-taught, inspired principally by examining works by Armand Guillaumin and Monet. His own important collection of art, which was not far below those of Caillebotte and Degas in importance, was formed so that he could have such works on hand for consultation.

Owing to his multifarious interests and his ebullient and gregarious personality, Signac moved easily among literary and artistic circles, forming friendships that would last a lifetime. In May 1884, his meeting with Seurat would prove to be particularly significant, leading to the formation of the Société des Artistes Indépendants, which would become the focus of Post-Impressionism, holding annual exhibitions well into the twentieth century, in which Signac always had a leading role. The meeting with Seurat led to the creation of the pointillist style, which was based on a close examination of scientific theories about colour and light. Seurat regarded himself as the founder of this new style of working, but his reserved manner and jealous personality contrasted strongly with Signac's more worldly and spirited outlook.

On the sudden death of Seurat in 1891, at the age of thirty-one, Signac became the chief spokesman and chronicler of Neo-Impressionism, although the style had by then been overtaken by future developments, beginning with the Nabis and the Fauves. His book *D'Eugène Delacroix au Néo-impressionnisme* (1899, reissued 1910 and 1921) stands as an official account of Neo-Impressionism, notwithstanding that it is more about the history of colour and was intended to complement the writings of leading critics such as Félix Fénéon, to whom he was very close.

The strength of Signac as an artist lies in the wide range of his interests, which in turn made him such a loved and admired figure in late nineteenth- and twentieth-century art. The portrait drawing of him done by Seurat for the cover of *Les Hommes d'Aujourd'hui* (May 1890), with an accompanying text by Fénéon, gives no indication of Signac the artist. Dressed formally in top hat, buttoned cape and cane, he is outwardly the epitome of a bourgeois gentleman. It is a surprising portrayal of a man who formed a vital personal link between the artists of mid-century France and the emerging talents of the early twentieth century.

There were, however, many sides to Signac. Although he enjoyed fencing, his main passion outside painting was sailing, as an early vigorous tenebrist drawing, probably done at Petit-Gennevilliers on the river Seine opposite Argenteuil, makes plain (p. 258). He owned over thirty craft, and there are two superb paintings of him on the water: *Signac on his Boat* of 1896 by Théo van Rysselberghe (Private collection) and *Signac and Friends on his Boat* of 1924–25 by Pierre Bonnard (Kunsthaus, Zurich). Signac frequently sailed off the coast of France, but in 1892 he took his yacht, *Olympia* (named after Manet's picture), south to Bordeaux and down the river Garonne as far as Toulouse, where he followed the Canal du Midi to the Mediterranean port of Sète. The voyage ended in his discovery of Saint-Tropez, which was at that time more easily approached by sea (p. 260). Signac established Saint-Tropez as an alternative base to Paris and returned there regularly, encouraging such artists as Charles Camoin, Albert Marquet and Henri Matisse to explore the plentiful motifs offered by the bright sunlight of the Côte d'Azur. On arriving, he declared, 'There is enough material to work on for the rest of my days. Happiness – that is what I have just discovered.'

Signac was also a bibliophile, being an omnivorous reader with an extensive library. He took a close interest in the published and unpublished writings of Stendhal and, like other Neo-Impressionists, admired the works of John Ruskin, especially *The Elements of Drawing* (1856). When his enthusiasm for watercolour was at its height, he wrote a monograph on the Dutch artist Johan Barthold Jongkind (1927) – an artist with whom several of the Impressionists felt a particular kinship.

Allied to Signac's love of books was his zeal in exploring new ideas. Like several avant-garde artists (Pissarro *père et fils* and Maximilien Luce) and writers (Fénéon and Verhaeren), from the late 1880s he adopted the views of anarchist philosophers such as Pierre-Joseph Proudhon, Prince Pierre Kropotkin, Élisée Reclus and Jean Grave, the editor of *La Révolte* and *Les Temps Nouveaux*. An anarchist painter, Signac wrote, is 'the one who struggles with his entire being against official and bourgeois conventions, without concern for wealth and reward, but with a personal contribution'. Politically, the anarchist movement in France was at its most active during the 1890s, but the aim of correcting social evils and creating a fairer and more equitable society was as much an issue as the right of artists to choose the style most appropriate for an expression of their ideals in public. They did this at exhibitions organized by such bodies as the Société des Artistes Indépendants in Paris or Les Vingt and the Salon de la Libre Esthétique in Brussels.

Signac's political beliefs are unambiguously represented in two canvases: *In the Time of Harmony* of 1893–95 (Mairie de Montreuil) and *The Wrecker* of 1896 (Musée des Beaux-Arts, Nancy); he made a copy in pen and ink of the former (p. 261 above), and a lithograph of the latter was published in *Les Temps Nouveaux*. The artist remained politically aware for the rest of his life, publishing articles, embracing pacifism during the First World War, making a stand against Fascism and being suspicious of Communism.

Although an intrepid traveller throughout France, Signac also visited Britain, the Netherlands, Belgium and Italy. As a respecter of tradition, he made copies in numerous museums and it was in part his study of the watercolours of J. M. W. Turner that encouraged him to work more in that medium. Earlier drawings, made while Seurat was still alive, were in black and white (p. 258), but following Pissarro's example he began to favour watercolour over oil and insisted that his works on paper should be given equal status in exhibitions with his paintings. Signac liked working outdoors, and for this purpose watercolour was preferable to oil and suited his restless temperament. Stylistically, too, the contrived process of pointillism denied him spontaneity and resulted in compositions that were too static or decorative, whereas with watercolour he needed to work quickly and with precision.

The style of Signac's watercolours is not a denial of Neo-Impressionism, but, rather, an exciting coda to it. At first, during the late 1890s, he used the medium in conjunction with pen and ink in a manner reminiscent of Van Gogh (p. 261 below). For what are in effect preparatory cartoons for pictures, Signac continued to use ink but applied it with a brush, giving the drawings a lyrical quality that was sometimes missing from the finished work (p. 262). Soon after the beginning of the twentieth century this phase passed, when a more free-flowing style dominated by broken strokes of pure colour without layering was adopted. His aim was to achieve on paper the appearance of 'strewn flowers'. For still-life subjects in homage to Cézanne, Signac combined pencil with watercolour. Where Cézanne analyses forms to the extent that they seem immanent, as though frozen in time forever, Signac's still lifes appear pulsating and vibrant (p. 263).

The high point of Signac's later years was the series of approximately one hundred watercolours known as the *Ports of France*, made between 1929 and 1931 with the support of Gaston Lévy, the co-founder of the retail store Monoprix and a keen collector. A similar project had been undertaken in the eighteenth century by Joseph Vernet, but for Signac, who had already been depicting harbours for some time, it was a way to emulate the topographical achievements of Turner and Jongkind. The *Ports of France* was a singular undertaking and anticipated in earlier drawings (p. 262). The demands of the medium, and, indeed, of the topographical tradition in which he was working, suited Signac's peripatetic nature. As a sailor he relished capturing the reflective qualities of water or the changing effects of wind and light, just as his skill as a fencer allowed him to manipulate his brushes with the utmost speed and dexterity.

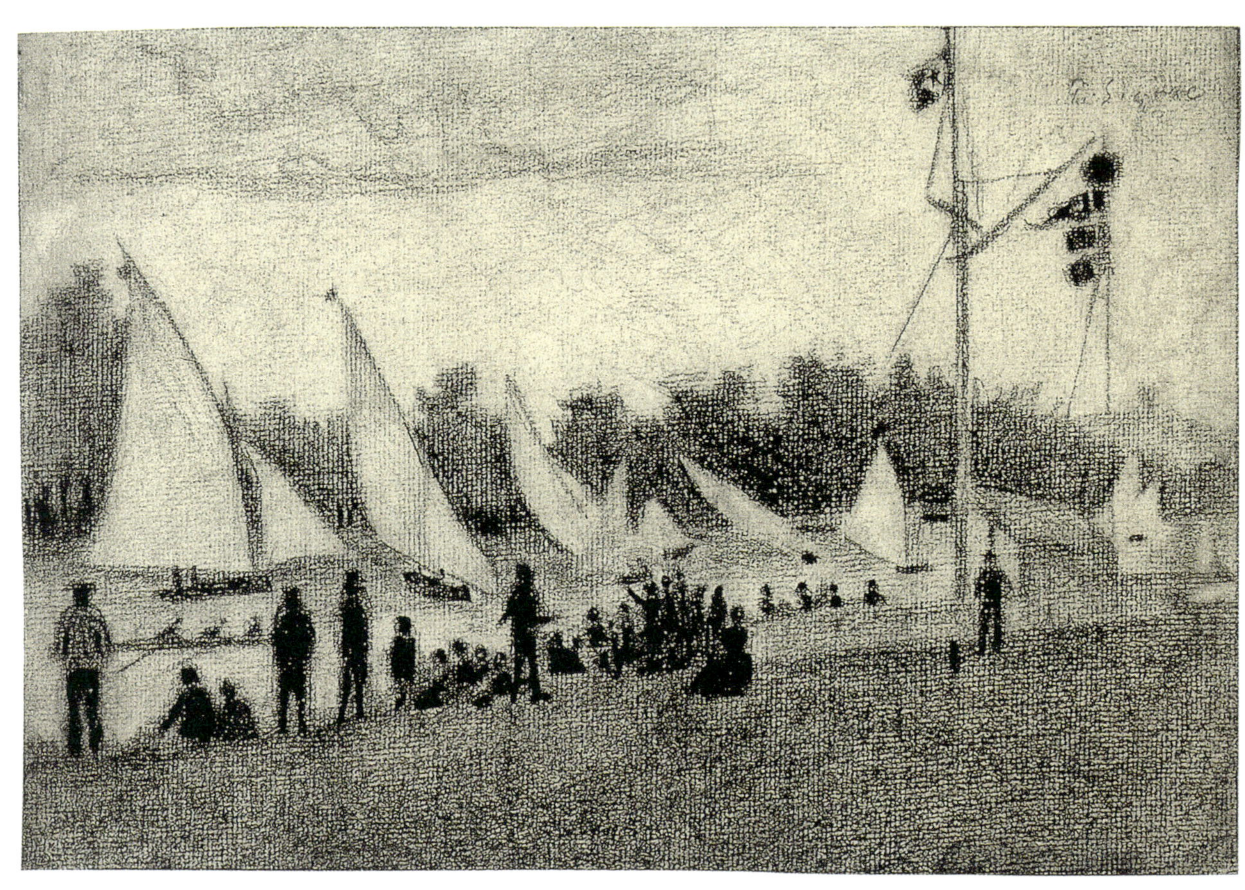

258   *Paul Signac*   *Regatta on the River Seine, c. 1885–86*
Conté crayon, 21.7 × 31.2 cm (8½ × 12¼ in.). Signed and dated.
MUSÉE DU LOUVRE (COLLECTION MUSÉE D'ORSAY), PARIS

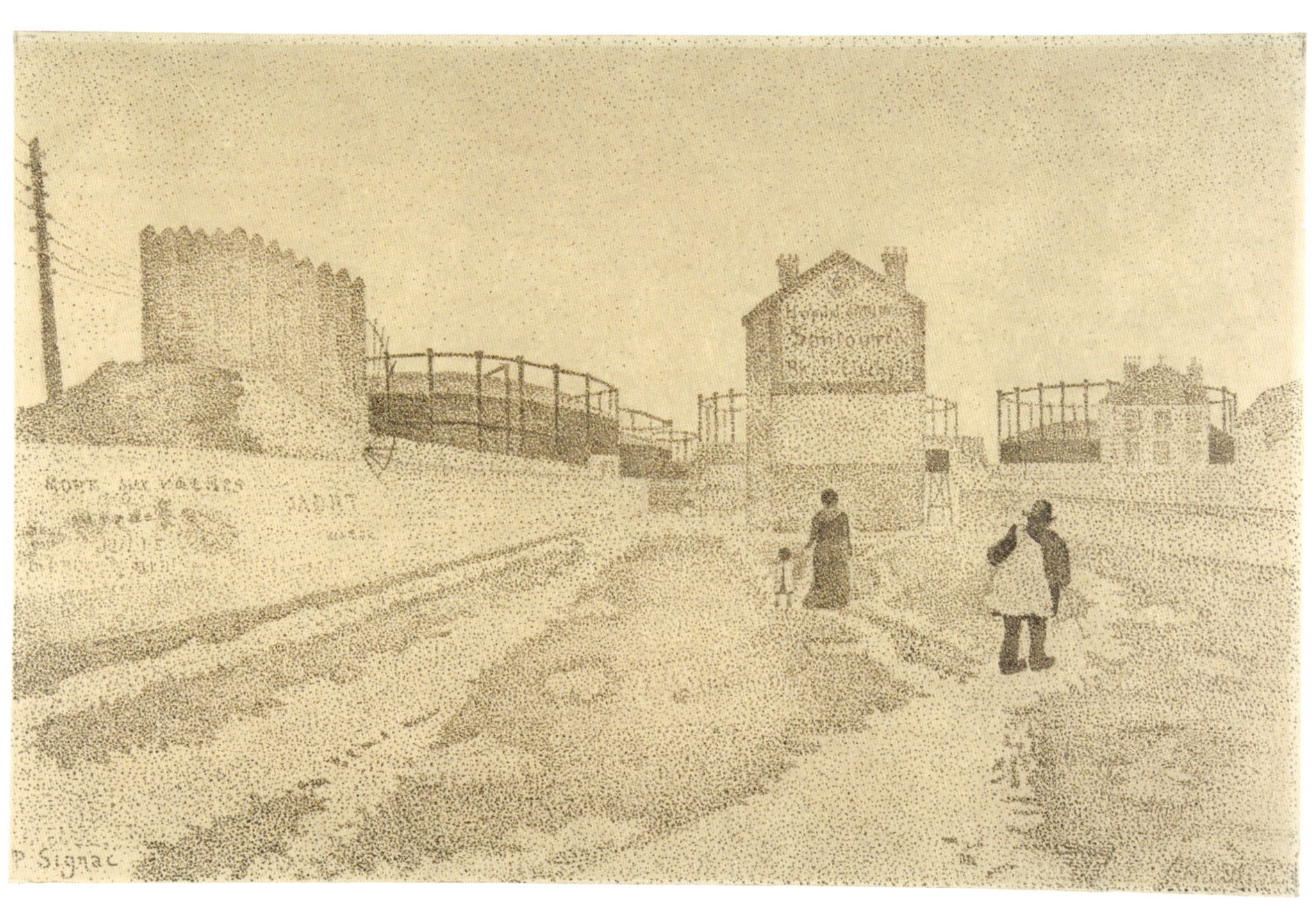

Passage du Puits-Bertin, Clichy, 1886
Pen and ink over pencil on paper mounted on cardboard,
24.5 × 36.6 cm (9⅝ × 14⅜ in.). Signed.
METROPOLITAN MUSEUM OF ART, NEW YORK

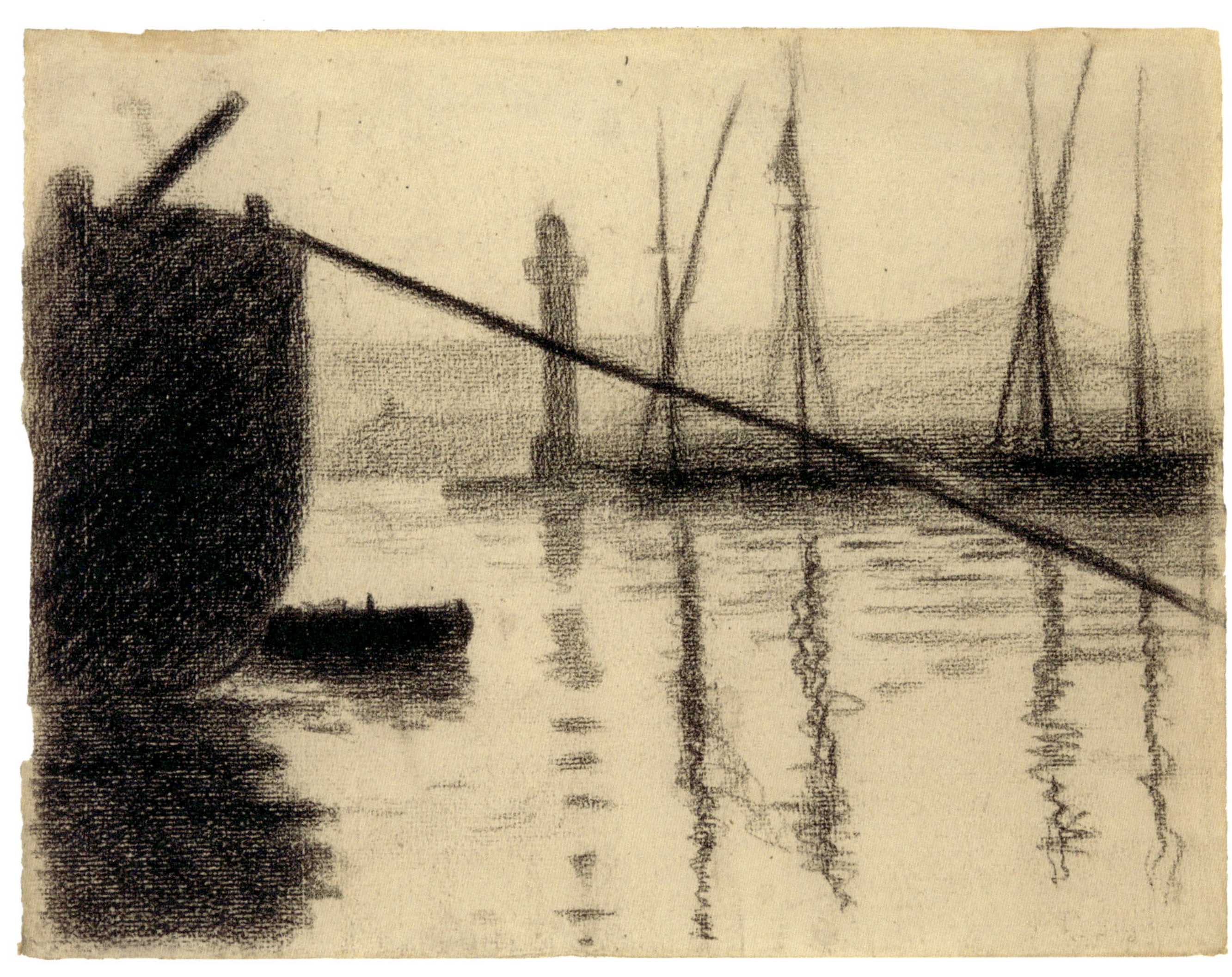

260   *Paul Signac*

Saint-Tropez: The Jetty in the Shipyard, 1892
Conté crayon, 23.5 × 30.2 cm (9¼ × 11⅞ in.).
COLLECTION TRITON FOUNDATION, THE NETHERLANDS

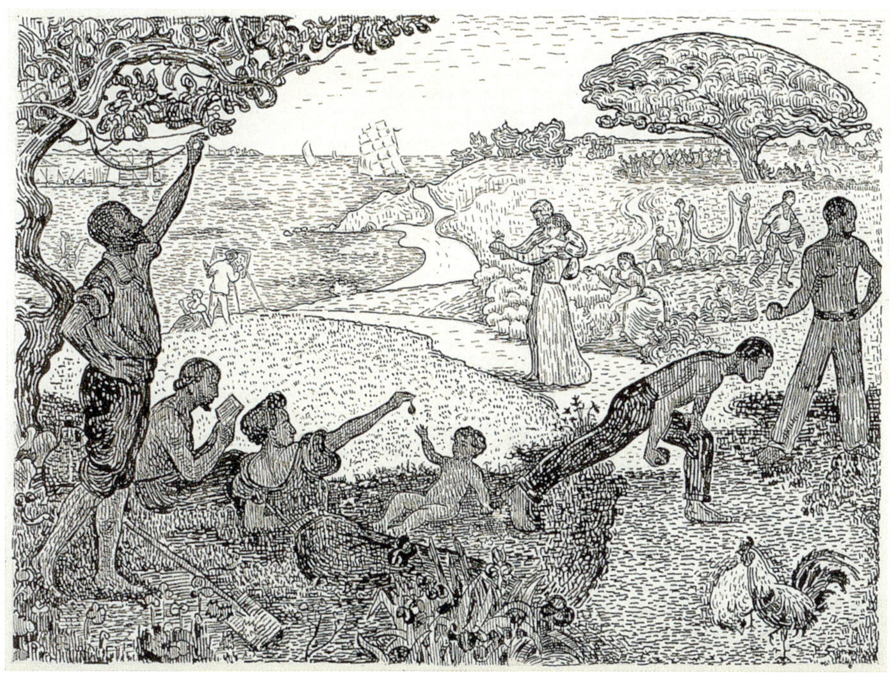

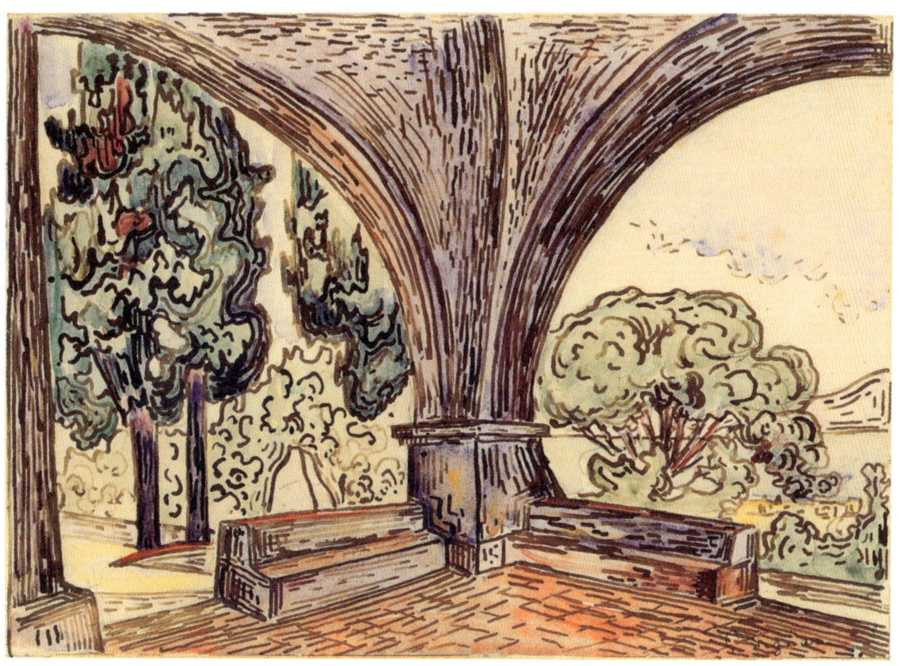

In the Time of Harmony, 1895–96
Pen and ink over pencil,
50 × 61.7 cm (19¾ × 34¼ in.).

PRIVATE COLLECTION

The Chapel of St Anne, Saint-Tropez, c. 1895
Watercolour with pen and ink,
21 × 28.5 cm (8¼ × 11¼ in.). Signed.

ARKANSAS ARTS CENTER, LITTLE ROCK, ARKANSAS

261

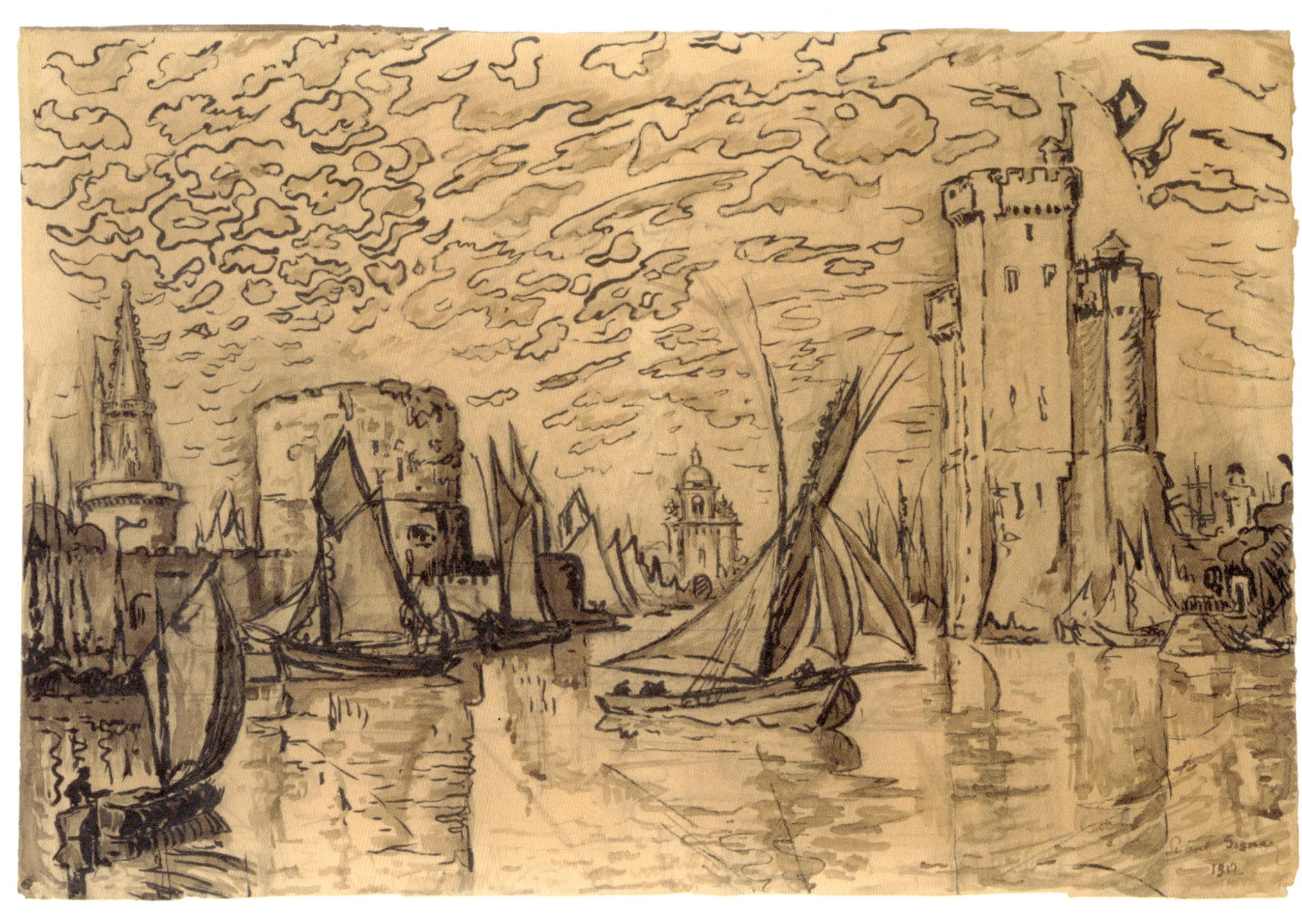

     Paul Signac

La Rochelle, 1912
Brush with ink and wash over pencil and charcoal
70 × 100 cm (27½ × 39⅜ in.). Signed.
METROPOLITAN MUSEUM OF ART, NEW YORK

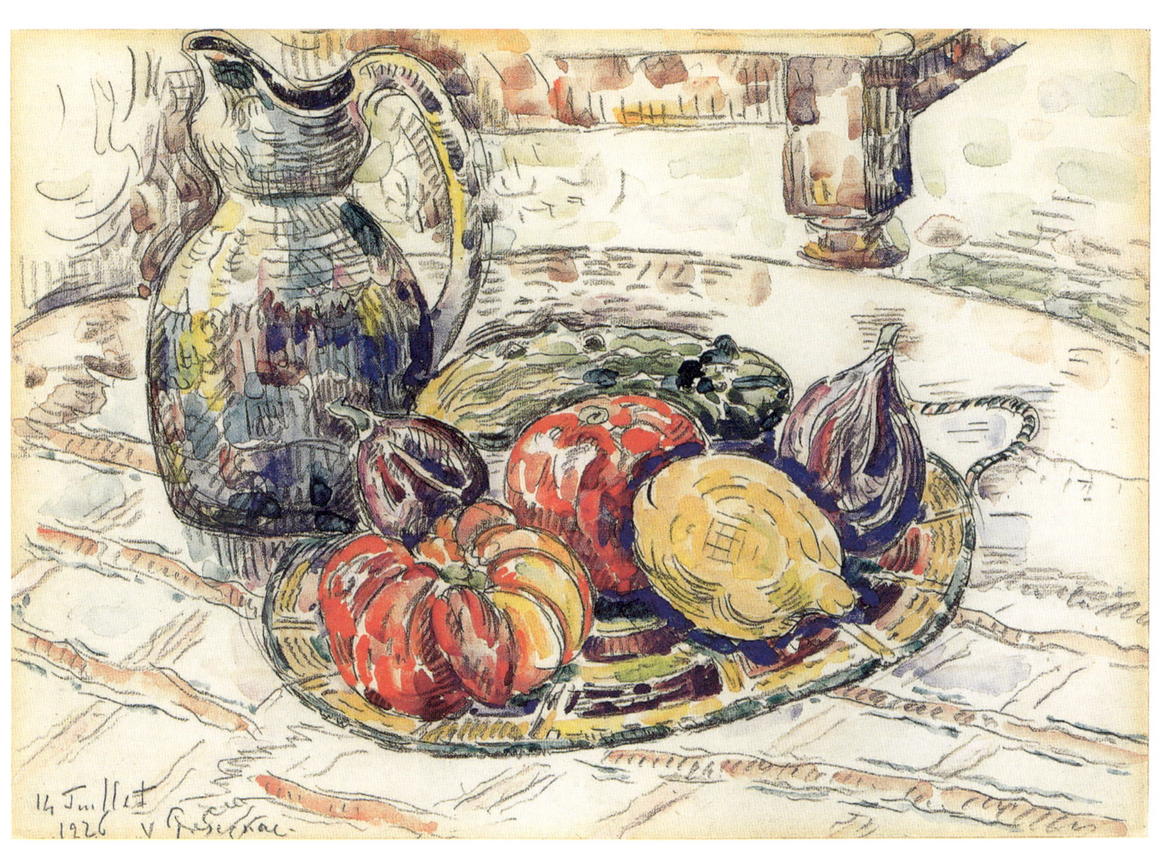

Still Life with Fruit, 1926
Watercolour and pencil, 30.4 × 42.2 cm
(12 × 16⅝ in.). Signed and dated.
ARKANSAS ARTS CENTER, LITTLE ROCK, ARKANSAS

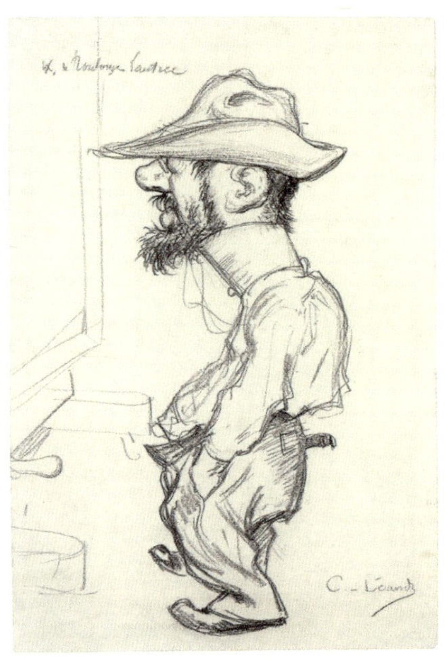

Henri de Toulouse-Lautrec
1864–1901

Assessing the life and art of Henri de Toulouse-Lautrec is like examining different sides of the same coin. The scion of a long-standing aristocratic family with extensive property in the Midi and Gironde as well as rented apartments in Paris, the artist became in time more closely associated with the bohemian activities pursued in the *quartier* of Montmartre, located on a slope north of the centre of Paris. Correspondingly, having begun as a painter of sporting scenes and animal pictures, he eventually became an assiduous recorder of urban decadence and human depravity in a city that was then the centre of the art world and the focus of *la belle époque*. This dramatic shift in choice of subject is also reflected in the transformation of Toulouse-Lautrec's style from its academic beginnings through naturalism to an avant-garde position that extended well beyond Impressionism to embrace Symbolism and Art Nouveau, while also pointing the way to Expressionism. His career is testament to the competing aesthetic interests at play in France during the 1880s and 1890s.

Charles Lucien Léandre
Henri de Toulouse-Lautrec, c. 1896–97
Pencil, 47.3 × 31.4 cm (18⅝ × 12⅜ in.).
THE JANE VOORHEES ZIMMERLI ART MUSEUM, RUTGERS, THE STATE
UNIVERSITY OF NEW JERSEY

Toulouse-Lautrec's greatest significance as an innovator is that he ignored the distinction between 'high' and 'low' art. He did this not just in the content of his *oeuvre* or his inventive use of materials and techniques, but also by forming alliances with commercial ventures and discovering new outlets for his work. This development is most evident in his printmaking and especially in his posters, which he began to design in 1891. The novelty and impact of Toulouse-Lautrec's posters at the end of the nineteenth century was such that as an art form the poster became elevated in status. Posters were acknowledged to be the 'frescoes of the poor', and their display likened to the 'salon of the street' – descriptions with political overtones.

Determining factors in Toulouse-Lautrec's life, and ones that were possibly also relevant for his art, were his appearance and personality. Probably as the result of a bone disorder, he was well below average height, with short legs, but with a fully developed upper body. Contemporary descriptions of his unusual appearance and physical difficulties are unflattering. Toulouse-Lautrec, however, compensated for these setbacks in several ways: hard work, humour, play-acting (he was frequently photographed in masquerade costumes), outlandish extrovert behaviour and total immersion from the mid-1880s in the mixed society of Montmartre, where aristocrats, politicians and businessmen crossed paths with artists, entertainers, prostitutes and shop assistants – all in the pursuit of pleasure and escape. One of the consequences of Toulouse-Lautrec's own somewhat dissolute lifestyle was that his health deteriorated steadily during the 1890s and he died aged thirty-six. But he was immensely prolific, and his art may well have gained an edge from what seems to have been a self-destructive urge in his character. In a moving letter written in the immediate aftermath of his son's death, Count Alphonse de Toulouse-Lautrec wrote of 'the terrible ending of a miserable destiny'.

The British artist William Rothenstein wrote of Toulouse-Lautrec that 'Human weakness lay naked and unprotected before his eyes'. And, indeed, Toulouse-Lautrec's principal legacy is an almost comprehensive evocation of the dance halls, café-concerts, brothels, bars, restaurants and circus entertainment that made Montmartre a place of such vitality in *fin-de-siècle* Paris.

Like other artists, Toulouse-Lautrec made paintings in oil and drawings on paper, but a large proportion of his output is a hybrid. These are the works executed from the late 1880s in the technique of *peinture à l'essence* (oil paint diluted with turpentine), frequently with cardboard as the support (p. 271). This medium was easier to apply and dried quickly as it soaked into the support with a matt finish. It prompted Toulouse-Lautrec to develop a more linear style, relying on multiple striations, or cross-hatching, as the principal form of modelling. Degrees of finish varied considerably so that it is not always obvious what is a completed work and what is a preparatory study. Notable, too, irrespective of whether the support is canvas or cardboard, is the fact that the underdrawing for a composition, which is often strengthened or reintroduced later in the process, is given equal prominence with the brushstrokes so that painting and drawing are perfectly fused. Both play an equal part in the creative act. Furthermore, Toulouse-Lautrec's palette was generally rather subdued or muted so that the appearance of his paintings tends to have as much emphasis on line as colour.

Toulouse-Lautrec was introduced to painting by a family friend, a deaf-mute artist, René Princeteau, who specialized in sporting subjects. The habit of drawing increased as a result of the long periods of convalescence that he experienced while young, and anticipates his predilection for illustration and the development of his caricatural style that underpins all his art. After it was accepted by his family that he wished to be a full-time artist, Toulouse-Lautrec moved in 1882 to Paris, hoping to gain admission to the École des Beaux-Arts. For this purpose, he entered the studio classes offered first by Léon Bonnat and then by Fernand Cormon, who interpreted the system of academic training quite freely. The poses adopted by the models for life drawing were more relaxed than was then usual (Introduction, fig. 8). A preparatory study (p. 268) for an early portrait of his painter friend Gustave-Lucien Dennery shows Toulouse-Lautrec searching for an informal pose within conventional terms. The upper half of the body is adroitly but not wholly convincingly executed, with skilful use made of stumping in the shadowed areas, but there is greater hesitation in the foreshortening of the legs where the outlines are more obviously redrawn.

In the end, Toulouse-Lautrec did not attend the École des Beaux-Arts, but at Cormon's studio he did meet a number of younger artists who also found the more liberal atmosphere congenial: Van Gogh, Emile Bernard and Louis Anquetin. The portrait of Van Gogh (p. 270) in pastel reveals Toulouse-Lautrec's own independent spirit. The medium is applied in a very animated way, with a wide range of short strokes covering the whole sheet. The intensity of the sitter is captured by his pose, leaning forward over the table, and by the artist's choice of complementary colours.

Toulouse-Lautrec began to make a living out of his art by undertaking illustrations for several journals while still attending Cormon's atelier. The drawings he made in the mid-1880s for publication in *Le Courrier Français* and *Le Mirliton* not only introduced him to Montmartre, but also encouraged him to observe the social scene, as well as to analyse and classify people according to type. In the study for *The Laundress* (p. 269), one of four illustrations accompanying an article by Emile Michelet entitled 'L'Été à Paris' in *Paris Illustré* in July 1888, the sense of movement and the disposition of the body carrying a heavy basket are convincingly portrayed, while the varied handling of the charcoal, notably in the skirt, reveals a growing confidence. Laundresses, who were often seen in the streets carrying heavy loads in all weathers, were considered easy targets for bourgeois male sexual predators.

The poster *Moulin Rouge: La Goulue* of 1891, which was Toulouse-Lautrec's first lithograph, was an instant success. Previous exponents of poster art, such as Jules Chéret, had failed to produce the same visual impact. The main characteristics of

Toulouse-Lautrec's posters are present in the preparatory cartoon for *Moulin Rouge: La Goulue* (p. 272): a bold composition, arresting perspective, clear text, emphasis on the chief protagonists and an indication of the kind of entertainment on offer together with a sense of place. Japanese woodblock prints and shadow plays performed at café-concerts were two of Toulouse-Lautrec's sources, but of vital importance was the identification of the principal figures by their most recognizable features. La Goulue was famous for her high-kicking cancan, during which she often removed the men's top hats with her whirling leg. Similarly, Valentin le Désossé, silhouetted in the foreground, was double-jointed, as his stage name and indeed his pose suggest.

It was because of Toulouse-Lautrec's compelling representation of the most popular performers that they became celebrities. Extended coverage, for example, was given to the *diseuse* Yvette Guilbert in an album of sixteen lithographs published in 1894. A tall, slim woman, her trademarks were a green satin dress and black gloves (p. 273).

The artist also formed close relationships with the prostitutes who worked in Montmartre. The scenes are of the utmost intimacy: waiting for clients, medical inspections, dressing (p. 274), undressing and moments of affection between the women. Unlike Degas, Toulouse-Lautrec treats the figures as individuals and manages to combine objectivity with subjectivity by presenting the images in close-up while remaining aloof. The summation of the brothel scenes is the album of eleven lithographs entitled *Elles* of 1896, for which some of the studies are in red chalk (p. 275).

Another attraction was the circus, and particularly the Cirque Fernando. When in 1899 his health broke down owing to alcoholism, the artist was admitted to a clinic at Neuilly in the suburbs of Paris. Keen to be discharged, he sought to demonstrate his recovery by producing a series of drawings of circus scenes (p. 276). These are deftly drawn, almost certainly from memory. They have a whimsical delicacy, but with their sudden changes in scale, elongated twisting forms and strongly cast shadows they also have a hallucinatory quality. The performers seem to be rehearsing, since the seats are empty, which perhaps reflects Toulouse-Lautrec's state of mind while he was in the clinic and missing the conviviality of Montmartre.

Having resumed drinking, Toulouse-Lautrec spent most of the final painful year of his life in Bordeaux, where he attended performances of the opera. At the Théâtre-Français he saw a revival of Jacques Offenbach's light-hearted *La Belle Hélène*, which had been first performed in Paris in the year of the artist's birth. A parody of the Trojan Wars, the opera appealed to Toulouse-Lautrec's sense of humour, as did the matronly appearance of Mathilde Cocyle, who sang the part of Helen (p. 277). Playful to the last, Toulouse-Lautrec uses elegance of line to portray the brightly lit figure, emphasizing her high coiffure, ample bosom and revealing costume. But it is the stage gesture that is so memorable, with the arms raised like the wings of a butterfly either in salutation or in farewell.

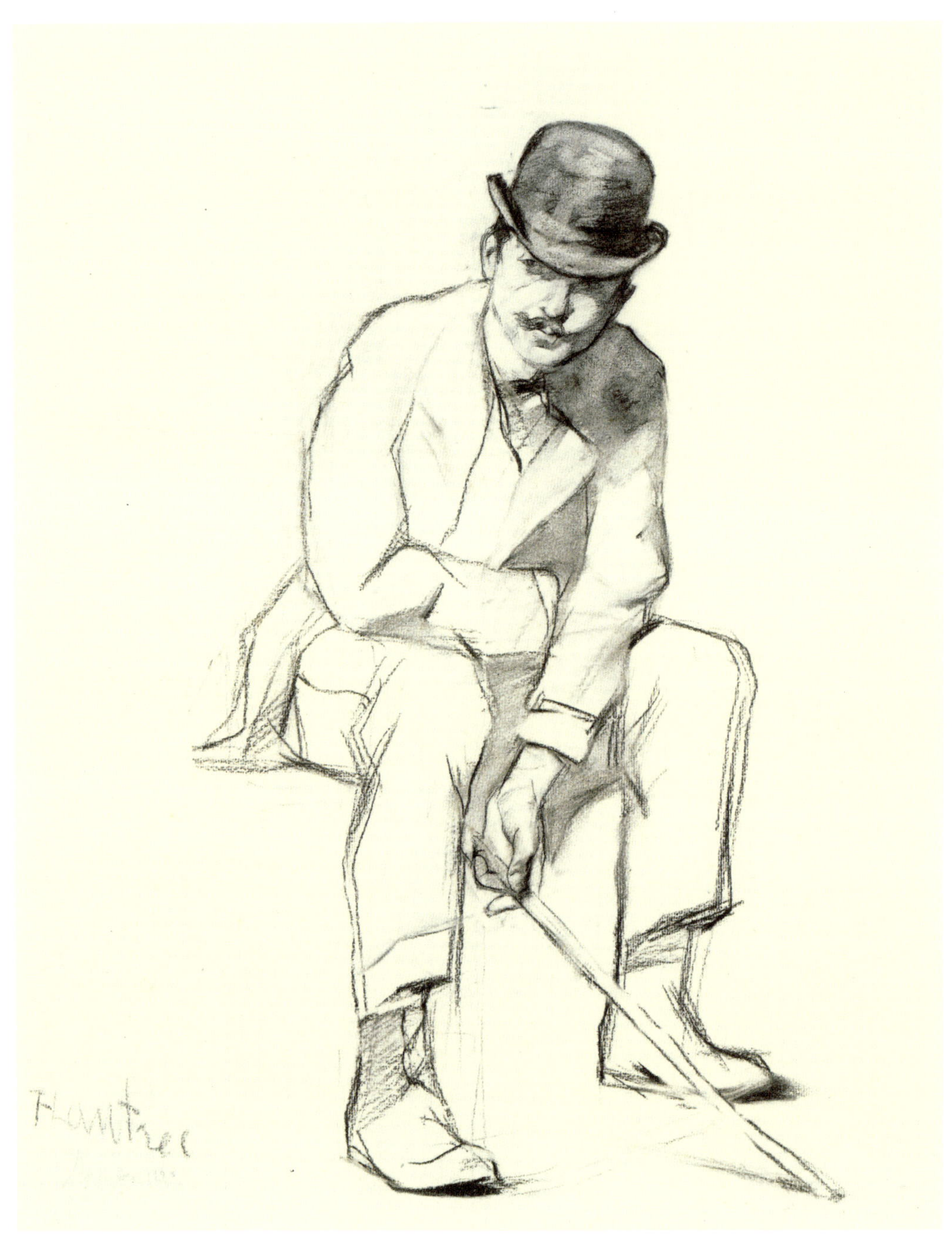

268   *Henri de Toulouse-Lautrec*

Portrait of Gustave-Lucien Dennery, 1883
Charcoal, 61.6 × 47 cm (24¼ × 18½ in.). Signed.
PHILADELPHIA MUSEUM OF ART

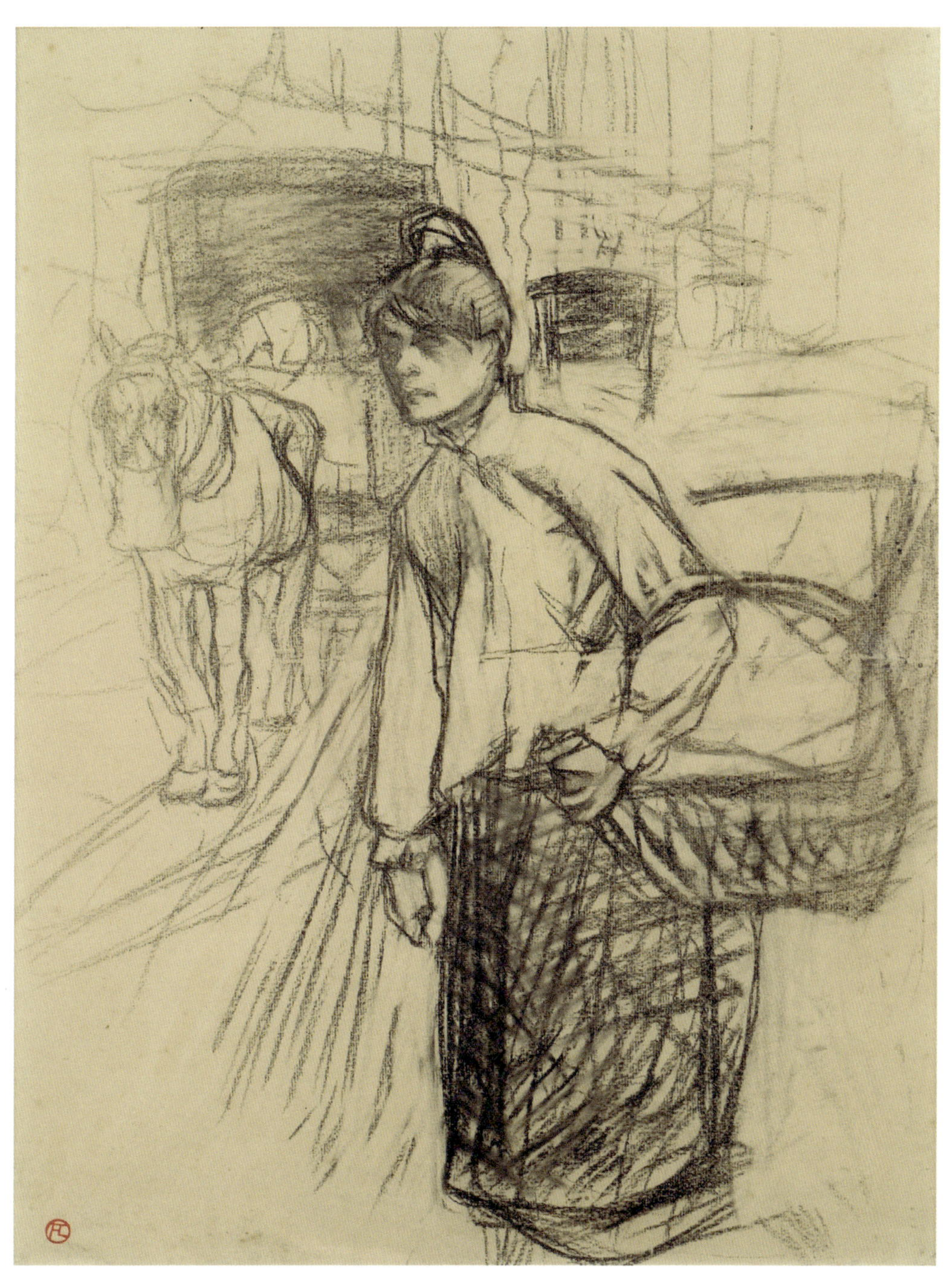

Study for 'The Laundress', 1888
Charcoal, 65 × 50 cm (25⅝ × 19¾ in.). Artist's stamp.
MUSÉE TOULOUSE-LAUTREC, ALBI

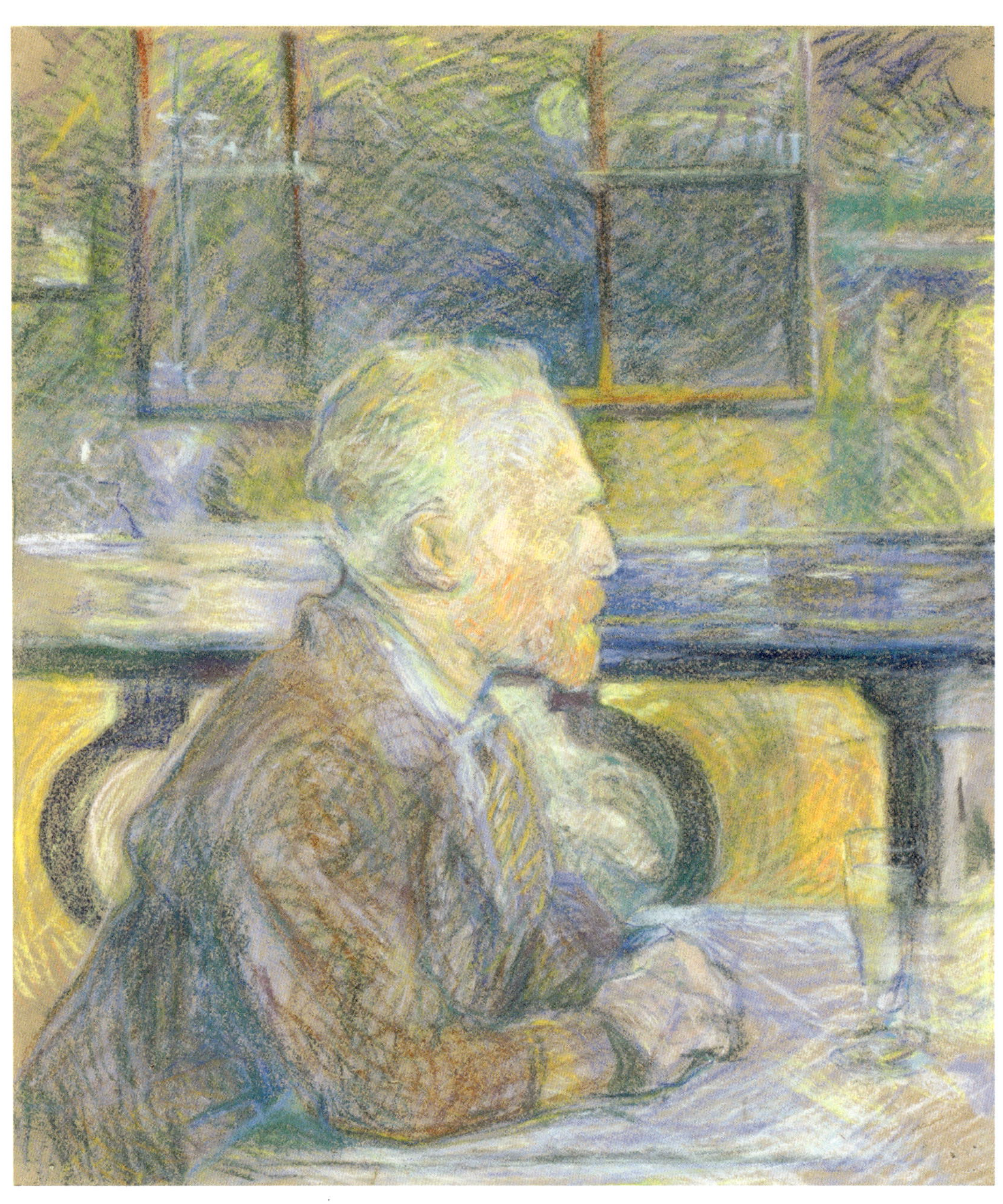

270   *Henri de Toulouse-Lautrec*

Vincent van Gogh, 1887
Coloured chalks on cardboard,
57 × 46 cm (22⅜ × 18⅛ in.).
VAN GOGH MUSEUM, AMSTERDAM

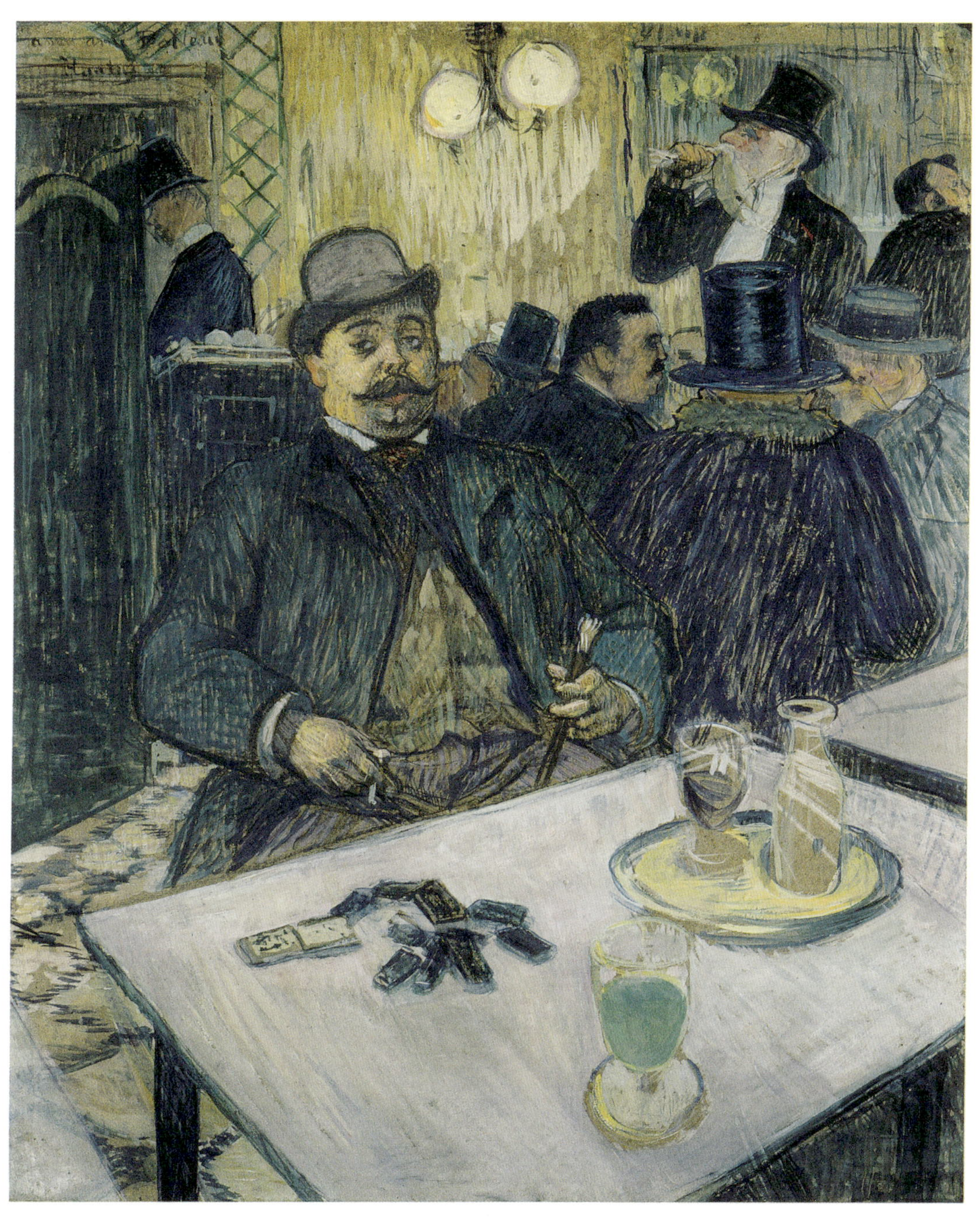

Monsieur Boileau at the Café, c. 1893
Essence on cardboard, 80 × 65 cm
(31½ × 25⅝ in.). Signed.
CLEVELAND MUSEUM OF ART

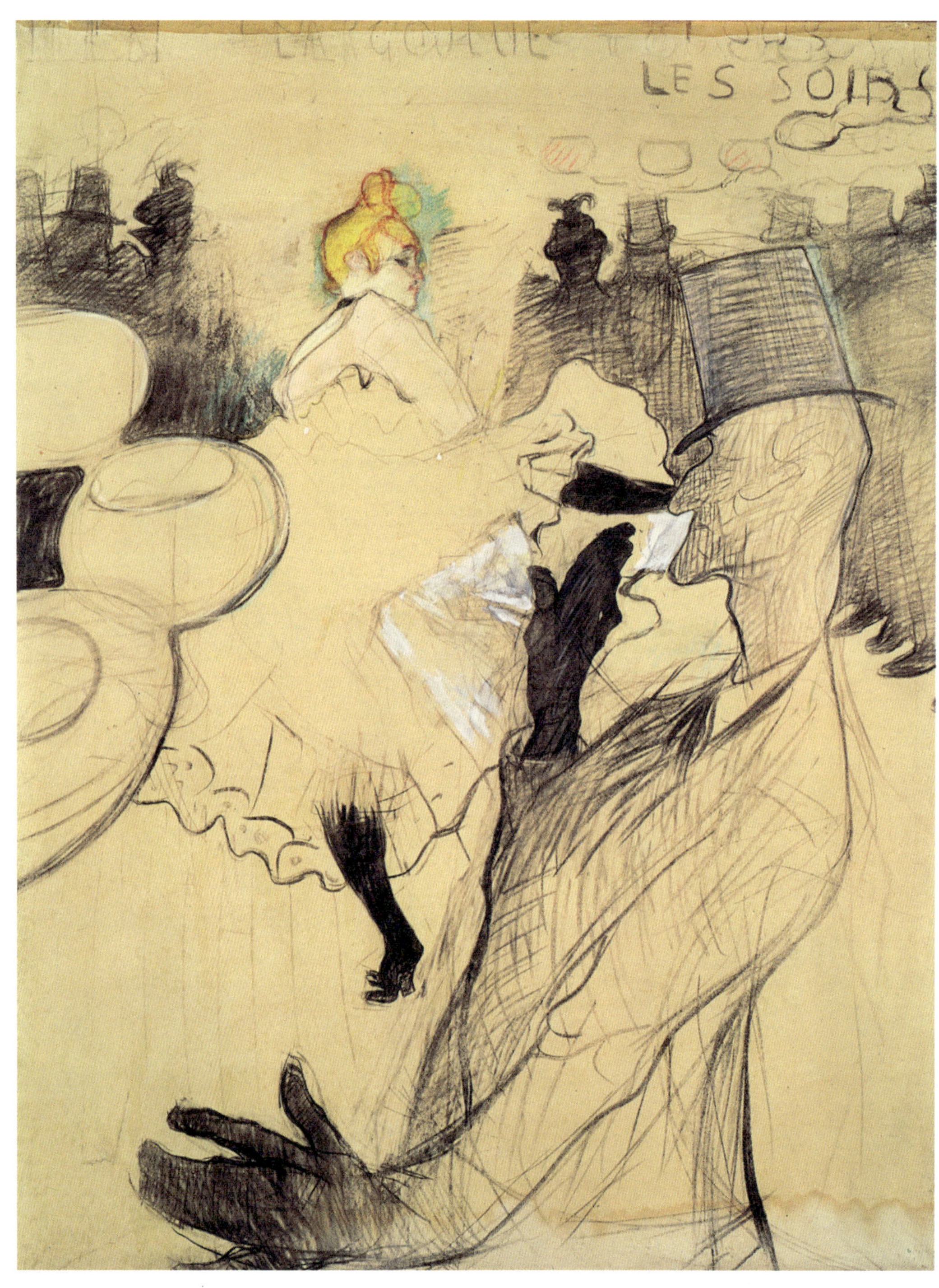

 Henri de Toulouse-Lautrec

Study for 'Moulin-Rouge–La Goulue', 1891
Charcoal, pastel, wash and oil on paper laid on canvas,
154 × 118 cm (60⅝ × 46½ in.).
MUSÉE TOULOUSE-LAUTREC, ALBI

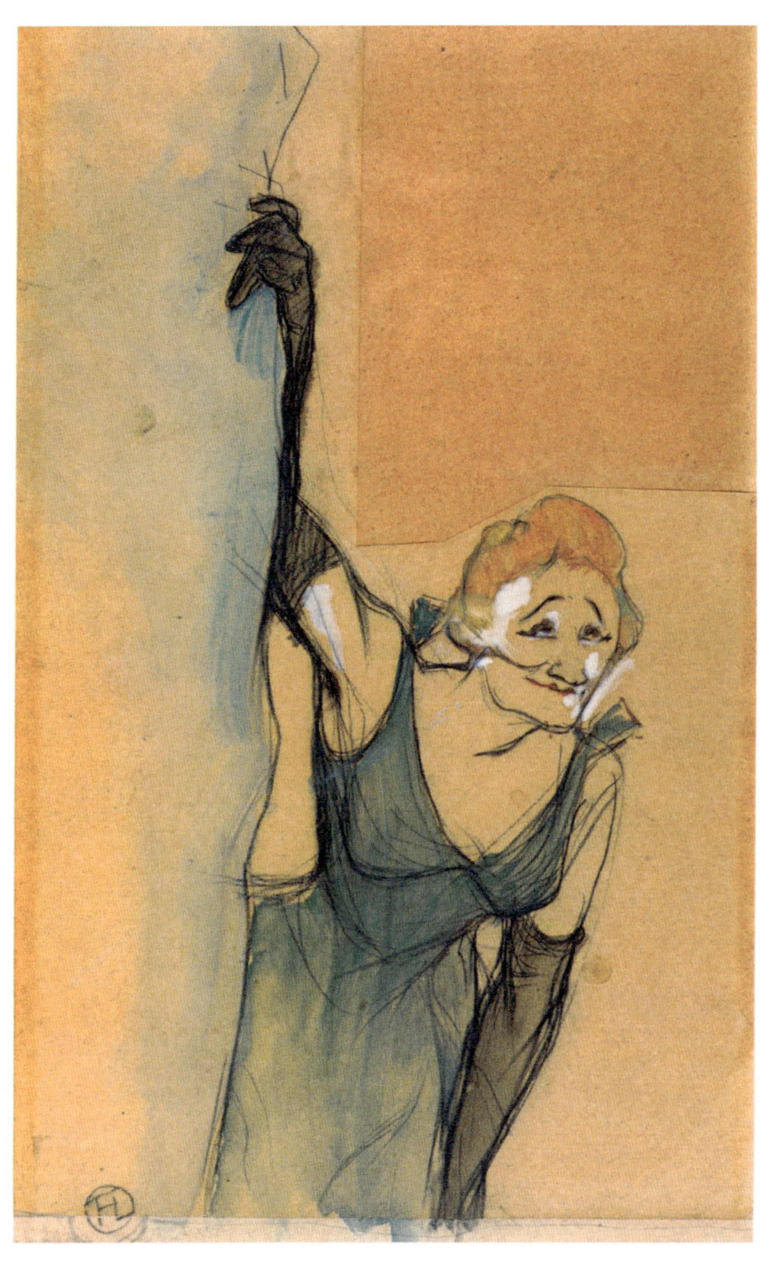

Yvette Guilbert Taking a Curtain Call, 1894
Crayon, watercolour and oil on tracing paper mounted
on cardboard, 41.7 × 24.5 cm (16⅜ × 9½ in.). Signed.
RHODE ISLAND SCHOOL OF DESIGN MUSEUM, PROVIDENCE

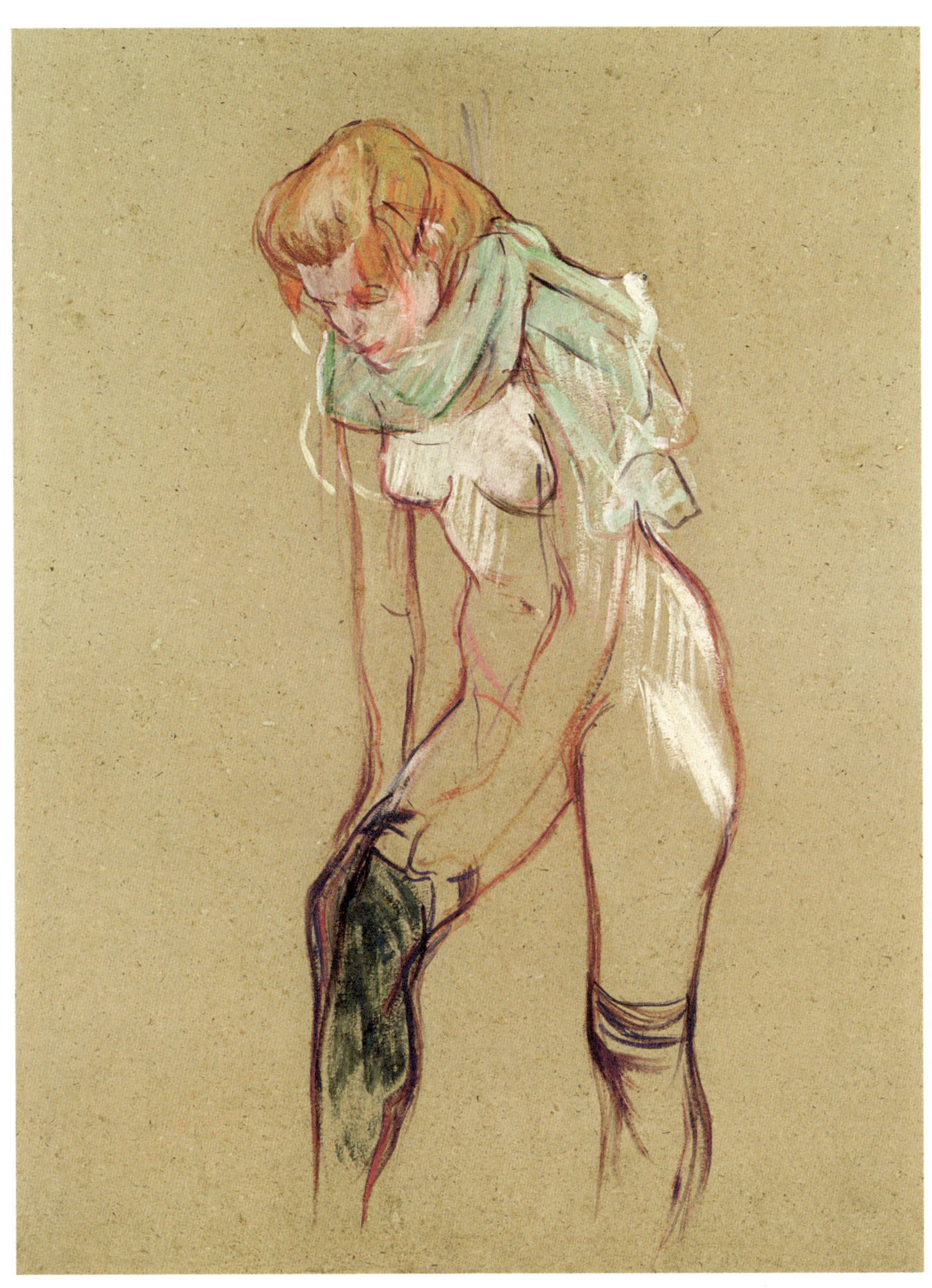

 Henri de Toulouse-Lautrec

Study for 'Woman Pulling on her Stocking', c. 1894
Essence on board, 80 × 60 cm (31½ × 23⅝ in.).
MUSÉE TOULOUSE-LAUTREC, ALBI

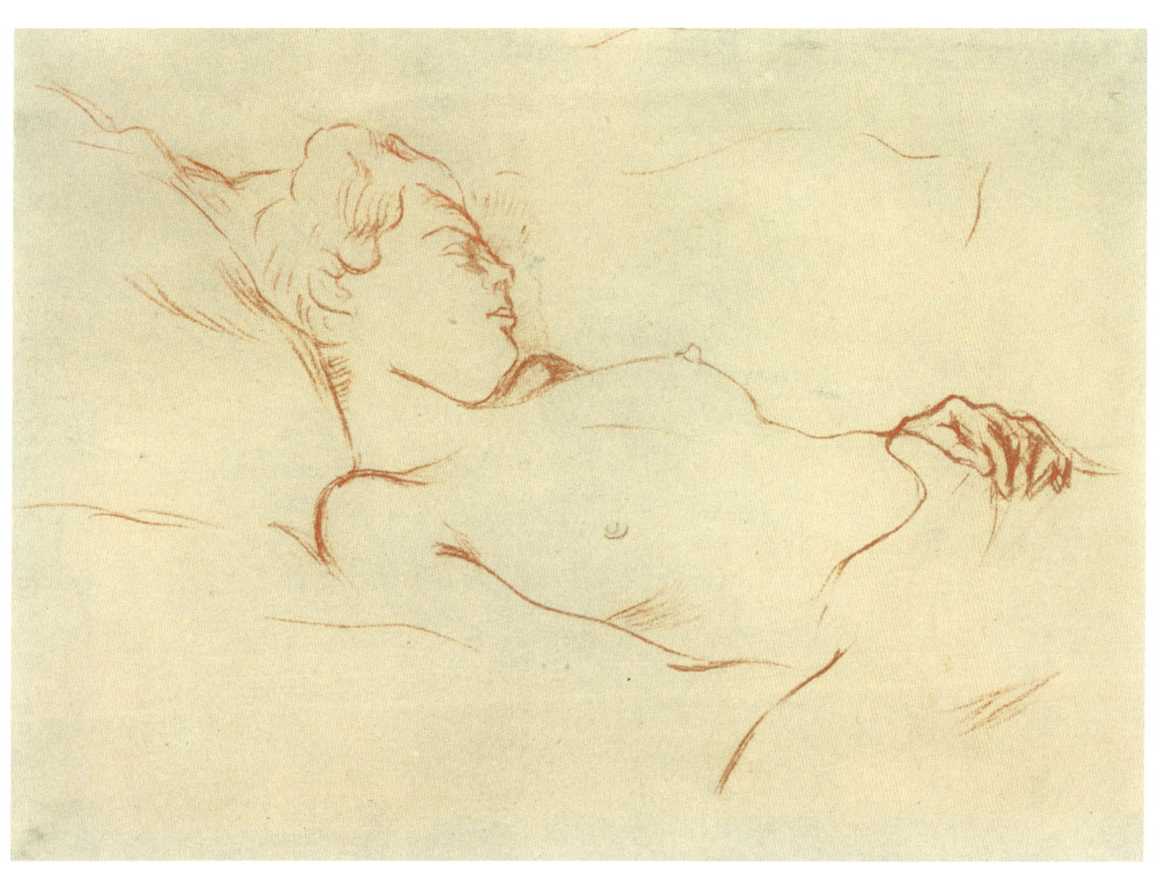

Study for 'Sleep', 1896
Red chalk on tracing paper, 20.3 × 26.6 cm (8 × 10½ in.).
MUSEUM BOIJMANS VAN BEUNINGEN, ROTTERDAM

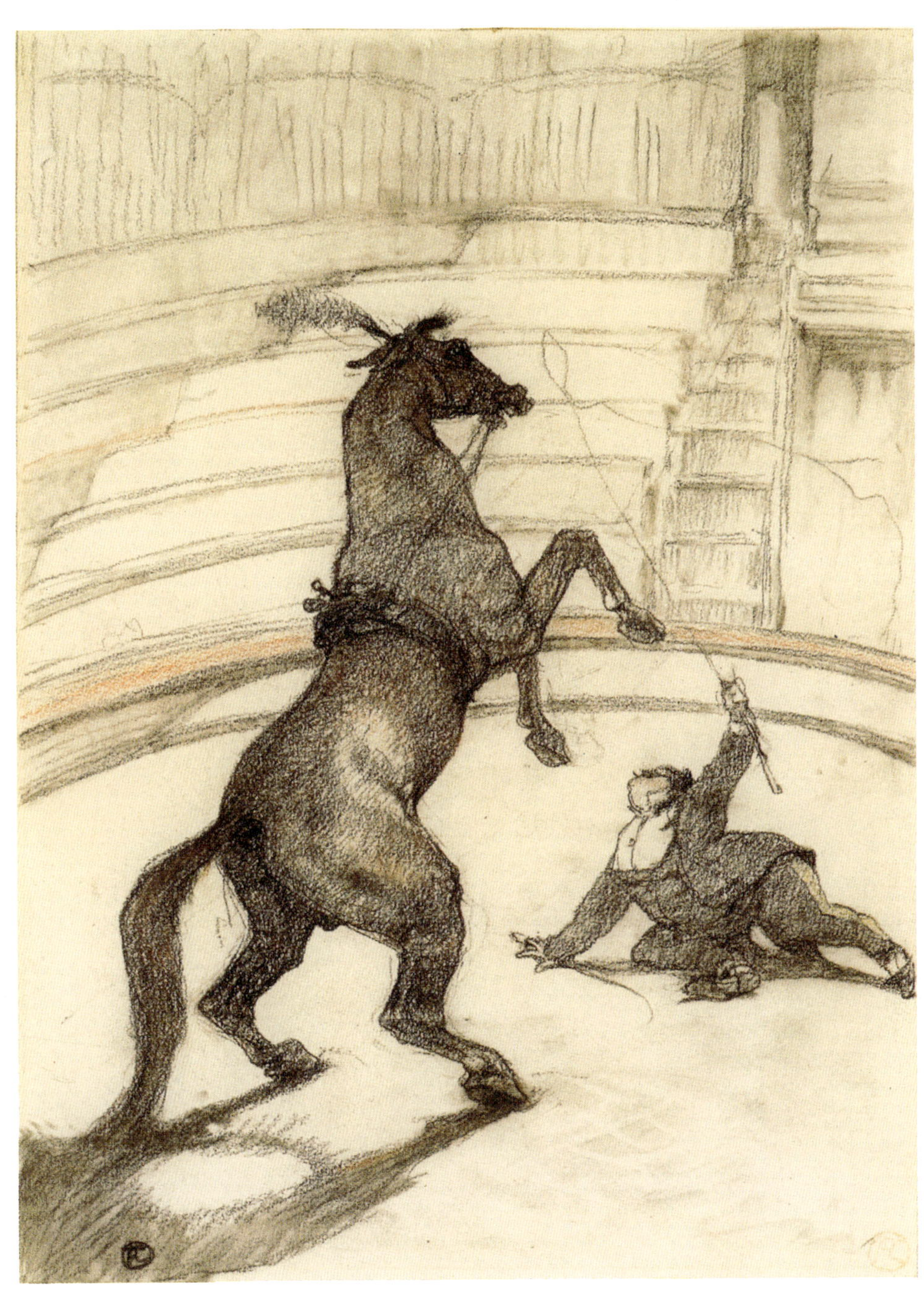

Henri de Toulouse-Lautrec

At the Circus – Performing Horse, 1899
Black chalk and coloured pencils,
35.7 × 25 cm (14⅛ × 10 in.). Artist's stamp.
THE FINE ARTS MUSEUMS, SAN FRANCISCO

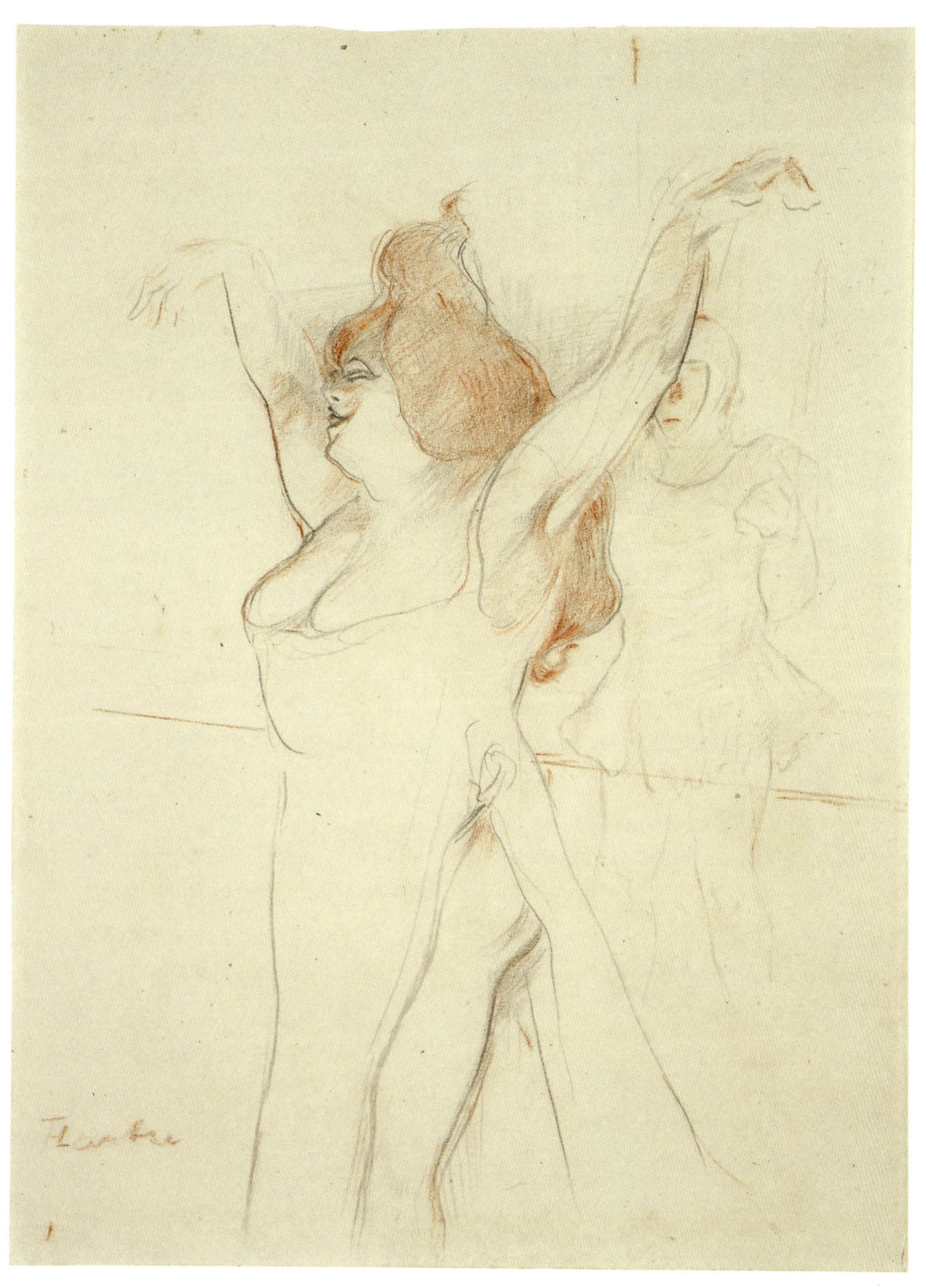

Mademoiselle Cocyle as Helen of Troy in La Belle Hélène, 1900
Pencil, black crayon and red chalk heightened with white chalk,
35.1 × 25.4 cm (13¾ × 10 in.). Signed.
THE ART INSTITUTE OF CHICAGO

Bibliography

The literature on drawings by Impressionist and Post-Impressionist artists is sporadic. Individual catalogues raisonnés, monographs and exhibition catalogues often include drawings, but usually without due consideration being given to the actual role of drawing in the artist's *oeuvre*. The titles given below, therefore, are limited to those publications relating specifically to the principal argument of this book and are further restricted to those that were of particular use to the author.

General

Adler, Kathleen, *Unknown Impressionists*, Oxford, 1988

Aymonino, Adriano and Anne Varick Lauder (eds), *Drawn from the Antique: Artists and the Classical Ideal*, exh. cat., Teylers Museum, Haarlem and Sir John Soane's Museum, London, 2015

Berson, Ruth (ed.), *The New Painting. Impressionism 1874–1886. Documentation*, 2 vols, Fine Arts Museum of San Francisco, 1996

Burns, Thea and Philippe Saunier, *The Art of the Pastel*, New York and London, 2015

DeWitte, Debra J., 'Drawings on View in State-funded Venues and Artists' Societies in Paris, 1860–90', *Master Drawings*, 55:2 (2017), pp. 225–48

Dunn, Ashely E., *Delacroix Drawings: The Karen B. Cohen Collection*, exh. cat., Metropolitan Museum of Art, New York, 2018

Ekelhart, Christine and Christopher Lloyd, *Impressionism: Pastels Watercolors Drawings*, exh. cat., Milwaukee Art Museum and Albertina, Vienna; Milwaukee, 2011, and Vienna and Cologne, 2012

The Essence of Line: French Drawings from Ingres to Degas, exh. cat., Baltimore Museum of Art, Walters Art Museum, Baltimore, Birmingham Museum of Art and Tacoma Art Museum, 2005

Hendrix, Lee (ed.), *Noir: The Romance of Black in 19th-Century French Drawings and Prints*, exh. cat., The J. Paul Getty Museum, Los Angeles, 2016

Herbert, Robert L., *Impressionism: Art, Leisure, and Parisian Society*, New Haven and London, 1988

Impressionists on Paper: Degas to Toulouse-Lautrec, exh. cat., Royal Academy of Arts, London, 2023

Lloyd, Christopher and Richard Thomson, *Impressionist Drawings from British Public and Private Collections*, exh. cat., Ashmolean Museum, Oxford, Manchester City Art Gallery, Burrell Collection, Glasgow; Oxford, 1986

Petherbridge, Deanna, *The Primacy of Drawing: Histories and Theories of Practice*, New Haven and London, 2010

Pfeiffer, Ingrid and Max Hollein (eds), *Women Impressionists*, exh. cat., Schirn Kunsthalle Frankfurt and Fine Arts Museums of San Francisco, 2008

Shapiro, Barbara Stern (ed.), *Pleasures of Paris: Daumier to Picasso*, exh. cat., Museum of Fine Arts Boston and IBM Gallery of Science and Art, New York, 1991

Tonkovich, Jennifer (ed.), *Drawn to Greatness: Master Drawings from the Thaw Collection*, exh. cat., The Morgan Library and Museum, New York, and Clark Art Institute, Williamstown, 2017

Wadley, Nicholas, *Impressionist and Post-Impressionist Drawing*, London, 1991

Ward, Martha, 'Impressionist Installations and Private Exhibitions', *Art Bulletin*, 73 (1991), pp. 599–622

Weisberg, Gabriel P. (ed.), *The Realist Tradition: French Painting and Drawing 1830–1900*, Cleveland Museum of Art, Brooklyn Museum, New York, St Louis Art Museum and Glasgow Art Gallery and Museum Kelvingrove, 1980

Eugène Boudin

Gottlieb, Carla, 'Boudin's Drawings', *Master Drawings*, 6:4 (1968), pp. 395–404

Hamilton, Vivien, *Boudin at Trouville*, exh. cat., Burrell Collection, Glasgow, and Courtauld Institute Galleries, London, 1992

Manoeuvre, Laurent, *Eugène Boudin: Dessins*, Paris, 2001

Rapetti, Rodolphe, *Eugène Boudin: Dessins Inédits*, exh. cat., *Les Dossiers du Musée d'Orsay* 14, Paris, 1987

Camille Pissarro

Brettell, Richard and Christopher Lloyd, *A Catalogue of Drawings by Camille Pissarro in the Ashmolean Museum, Oxford*, Oxford, 1980

Thomson, Richard, 'Drawings by Camille Pissarro in Manchester Public Collections', *Master Drawings*, 18:3 (1980), pp. 257–63

Édouard Manet

Leiris, Alain de, *The Drawings of Édouard Manet*, Berkeley and Los Angeles, 1969

Edgar Degas

Boggs, Jean Sutherland and Anne Maheux, *Degas Pastels*, London and New York, 1992

Fowle, Frances, *Discovering Degas: Collecting in the Time of William Burrell*, exh. cat., The Burrell Collection, Glasgow, 2024

Kendall, Richard, *Degas: Beyond Impressionism*, exh. cat., National Gallery, London, and The Art Institute of Chicago, 1996–97

Lloyd, Christopher, *Edgar Degas: Drawings and Pastels*, London, 2014

Reff, Theodore, *The Notebooks of Edgar Degas: A Catalogue of the Thirty-Eight Notebooks in the Bibliothèque Nationale and Other Collections*, 2 vols, Oxford, 1976

Paul Cézanne

Chappuis, Adrien, *The Drawings of Paul Cézanne*, 2 vols, London and Greenwich, Connecticut, 1973 [to be read in conjunction with the article by Karsten Schubert, 'Cézanne, Chappuis and the limits of connoisseurship', *Burlington Magazine*, 148 (2006), pp. 612–20]

Haldemann, Anita (ed.), *The Hidden Cézanne: From Sketchbook to Canvas*, exh. cat., Kunstmuseum Basel; Munich, London, New York, 2017

Lloyd, Christopher, *Paul Cézanne: Drawings and Watercolours*, London, 2015

Rewald, John, *Paul Cézanne: The Watercolours. A Catalogue Raisonné*, London and Boston, 1983

Simms, Matthew, *Cézanne's Watercolours: Between Drawing and Painting*, New Haven and London, 2008

Alfred Sisley

Shone, Richard, *Sisley*, London, 1992

Odilon Redon

Druick, Douglas W. (ed.), *Odilon Redon: Prince of Dreams 1840–1916*, exh. cat., The Art Institute of Chicago, Van Gogh Museum, Amsterdam, and Royal Academy of Arts, London, 1994

Claude Monet

Ganz, James A. and Richard Kendall, *The Unknown Monet: Pastels and Drawings*, exh. cat., Sterling and

Francine Clark Art Institute, Williamstown, and Royal Academy of Arts, London, 2007

Berthe Morisot

Adler, Kathleen and Tamar Garb, *Berthe Morisot*, Oxford and Ithaca, New York, 1987

Berthe Morisot 1841–1895, exh. cat., Palais des Beaux-Arts, Lille, and Fondation Pierre Gianadda, Martigny; Paris, 2002

Stuckey, Charles F. and William P. Scott (eds), *Berthe Morisot, Impressionist*, exh. cat., National Gallery of Art, Washington, Kimbell Art Museum, Fort Worth, and Mount Holyoke College Art Museum; New York, 1987

Pierre-Auguste Renoir

House, John, 'Renoir's "Baigneuses" of 1887 and the politics of escapism', *Burlington Magazine*, 134 (1992), pp. 578–85

Rewald, John, *Renoir: Drawings*, New York, 1946

Riopelle, Christophe, 'Renoir: The Great Bathers', *Bulletin Philadelphia Museum of Art*, 86:367–368 (1990)

Federico Zandomeneghi

Piceni, Enrico, *Zandomeneghi*, Milan, 1967

Mary Cassatt

Barter, Judith A. (ed.), *Mary Cassatt: Modern Woman*, exh. cat., The Art Institute of Chicago, Museum of Fine Arts, Boston, and National Gallery of Art, Washington; New York, 1998

Paul Gauguin

Brettel, Richard, Françoise Cachin, Claire Frèches-Thory and Charles F. Stuckey, *The Art of Paul Gauguin*, exh. cat., National Gallery of Art, Washington, The Art Institute of Chicago, Grand Palais, Paris, 1988

Ives, Colta and Susan Alyson Stein (eds), *The Lure of the Exotic: Gauguin in New York Collections*, exh. cat., Metropolitan Museum of Art, New York; New Haven and London, 2002

Pickvance, Ronald, *The Drawings of Gauguin*, London and New York, 1970

Gustave Caillebotte

Chardeau, Jean, *Les Dessins de Caillebotte*, Paris, 1989

Lloyd, Christopher, 'An Unknown Sketchbook by Gustave Caillebotte', *Master Drawings*, 26:2 (1988), pp. 107–17

Varnedoe, Kirk, *Gustave Caillebotte*, New Haven and London, 1987

Jean-François Raffaëlli

Weisberg, Gabriel P. (ed.), *The Realist Tradition; French Painting and Drawing 1830–1900*, Cleveland Museum of Art, Brooklyn Museum, New York, St Louis Art Museum, and Glasgow Art Gallery and Museum Kelvingrove, 1980, pp. 229–30

Jean-Louis Forain

Browse, Lillian, *Forain: The Painter 1852–1931*, London, 1978

Jean-Louis Forain, Artist, Realist, Humanist, exh. cat., International Exhibitions Foundation, Washington, DC, 1982–83

Jean-Louis Forain (1852–1931): 'La Comédie Parisienne', exh. cat., Musée des Beaux-Arts de la Ville de Paris (Petit Palais) and Dixon Gallery and Gardens, Memphis, 2011

Reff, Theodore and Florence Valdès-Forain, *Jean-Louis Forain: The Impressionist Years. The Dixon Gallery and Gardens Collection*, exh. cat., Van Gogh Museum, Amsterdam, The Burrell Collection, Glasgow, Fondation de l'Hermitage, Lausanne, and Galerie Hopkins-Thomas, Paris, 1995–96

Vincent van Gogh

Cachin, Françoise and Bogomila Welsh-Ovcharov, *Van Gogh à Paris*, exh. cat., Musée d'Orsay, Paris, 1988

Dumas, Ann, Leo Jansen, Hans Luijten and Nienke Bakker, *The Real Van Gogh: The Artist and His Letters*, exh. cat., Royal Academy of Arts, London, 2010

Ives, Colta, Susan Alyson Stein, Sjraar van Heugten and Marije Vellekoop, *Vincent Van Gogh: The Drawings*, exh. cat., Van Gogh Museum, Amsterdam, and Metropolitan Museum of Art, New York, 2005

Lloyd, Christopher, *The Drawings of Vincent Van Gogh*, London, 2023

Georges Seurat

Broude, Norma, 'The Influence of Rembrandt Reproductions on Seurat's Drawing Style: A Methodological Note', *Gazette des Beaux-Arts*, Pér. 6, 88 (1976), pp. 155–60

Cachin, Françoise, Robert Herbert, Anne Distel and Gary Tinterow, *Seurat*, exh. cat., Grand Palais, Paris and Metropolitan Museum of Art, New York, 1991

Hauptman, Jodi (ed.), *Georges Seurat: The Drawings*, exh. cat., Museum of Modern Art, New York, 2007

Herbert, Robert L., *Seurat's Drawings*, London and New York, 1962

Thomson, Richard, *Seurat*, Oxford, 1985

Paul Signac

Ferretti-Bocquillon, Marina, Anne Distel, John Leighton and Susan Alyson Stein, *Signac, 1863–1935*, exh. cat., Galeries Nationales du Grand Palais, Paris, Van Gogh Museum, Amsterdam, and Metropolitan Museum of Art, New York, 2001

Henri de Toulouse Lautrec

Frèches-Thory, Claire, Anne Roquebert and Richard Thomson, *Toulouse-Lautrec*, exh. cat., Hayward Gallery, London, and Grand Palais, Paris, 1991

Murray, Gale B., *Toulouse-Lautrec: The Formative Years, 1878–1891*, Oxford, 1991

Thomson, Richard, Philip Dennis Cate and Mary Weaver Chapin, *Toulouse-Lautrec and Montmartre*, exh. cat., National Gallery of Art, Washington, and The Art Institute of Chicago, 2005

Picture credits

akg-images **107, 200**; Albertina, Vienna **158**; Albi, Musée Toulouse-Lautrec, inv. 2578-D 33 **17, 269**; Amsterdam, Stedelijk Museum **234**; Amsterdam, Van Gogh Museum **16r, 190, 232, 270**; Arkansas, The Dyke Collection **254**; Baltimore Museum of Art **23l**; Basel, Kuntsmuseum **19l**, Kupferstichkabinett **90**; Berlin, Kupferstichkabinett, Staatliche Museen zu Berlin **13**; Boston, Museum of Fine Arts **29**; Boston Public Library, Albert H. Wiggin Collection **220**; Bremen, Kunsthalle **84**; Bridgeman Images **46, 108, 109t, 124, 150, 272, 274**; Bristol Museum & Art Gallery **157**; Brooklyn Museum **182**; Budapest, Museum of Fine Arts **65, 65, 66b, 123**; Cambridge, Fitzwilliam Museum Frontispiece (University of Cambridge, Bridgeman Images), **18l, 28l** (University of Cambridge, Bridgeman Images); Cambridge, King's College, Keynes Collection **85**; Cambridge, MA, Harvard Art Museums/ Fogg Museum **21** (Bequest of Meta and Paul J. Sachs, 1965.294. Photo Imaging Department President and Fellows of Harvard College), **79** (Bequest of Meta and Paul J. Sachs, 1965.263 Photo Imaging Department President and Fellows of Harvard College), **80** (Bequest from the Collection of Maurice Wertheim, Class of 1906, 1951.68. Photo Imaging Department © President and Fellows of Harvard College), **154** (Bequest from the Collection of Maurice Wertheim, Class of 1906, 1951.77. Photo Imaging Department President and Fellows of Harvard College), **221** (Bequest of Annie Swan Coburn, 1934.32. Photo Imaging Department President and Fellows of Harvard College), **245** (Bequest of Grenville L. Winthrop, 1943.919. Photo Imaging Department President and Fellows of Harvard College); Cardiff, National Museum of Wales **57**; Chicago, Art Institute of Chicago **12, 34, 63, 99, 100, 116, 121, 122, 128, 129b, 140, 155, 192t, 193, 277**; © 2019 Art Institute of Chicago/Art Resource, NY/Scala, Florence **115**; Photo © Christie's Images/Bridgeman Images **201, 214, 260**; Cincinnati Art Museum **105**; Cleveland Museum of Art, **271**; Denver Art Museum **81**; Detroit Institute of Arts **36**; Maria DeWitt Jesup Fund, 1951; acquired from The Museum of Modern Art, Lillie P. Bliss, 55.21.2 96; © Douai, Musée de la Chartreuse. Photo Hugo Martaens **210**; Edinburgh, National Gallery of Scotland **106, 248**; Essen, Museum Folkwang **233**; Mary Evans/Diomedia **28r**; Geneva, Collection of Jean Bonna **56t**; Glasgow, Burrell Collection **30** (Gifted by Sir William and Lady Burrell to the City of Glasgow, 1944. Bridgeman Images), **67, 83, 189l**; Grasse, France, Musée d'Art et d'Histoire de Provence **145l**; Hannover, Landesmuseum/Artohek **211**; Hartford, CT, Wadsworth Atheneum **94**; Heritage Image Partnership Ltd/Alamy Stock Photo **18r, 169**; Heritage Images/Ashmolean Museum/Diomedia **55**; Honfleur, Musée Eugène Boudin **40, 42**; Houston Museum of Fine Arts **192b**; Kansas City, MO, Nelson-Atkins Museum of Art **144**; Little Rock, AR, Arkansas Arts Center **261b, 263**; London, British Museum **15r, 53, 77, 120, 237, 246, 249**; London, The Courtauld Gallery **15l, 95**; London, Photo Lefevre Fine Art Ltd./ Bridgeman Images **151**; London, Tate **239**; Los Angeles, J. Paul Getty Museum **97**; Madrid, Thyssen-Bornemisza Museum **82**; Mantua, Palazzo del Te **167, 168**; Memphis, TN, Dixon Gallery and Gardens **219, 223, 225**; Monte Carlo Art S.A **145r**; Montpelier, Musée Fabre **205**; New Britain Museum of American Art **32, 178**; New Haven, CT, Yale University Art Gallery **153, 204**; New York, Iris and Gerald Cantor **199**; New York, Solomon R. Guggenheim Museum **247**; New York, Metropolitan Museum of Art **23r** (Rogers Fund, 1937, 37.165.93), **26** (Rogers Fund, 1926, 26.169.2.), **58** (Rogers Fund, 1918, 19.51.7), **68** (H. O. Havemeyer Collection, Bequest of Mrs H. O. Havemeyer, 1929, 29.100.55), **72** (Bequest of Walter C. Baker, 1971, 1972.118.207), **86** (Bequest of Walter C. Baker, 1971, 1972.118.198), **110** (Gift of Roberta J. M. Olson and Alexander B. V. Johnson, 2016, 2016.765.2), **118** (Robert Lehman Collection, 1975, 1975.1.686), **119** (Harris Brisbane Dick Fund, 1948. 48.10.1), **152** (H. O. Havemeyer Collection, Bequest of Mrs H. O. Havemeyer, 1929, 29.100.195), **174** (Bequest of Edith H. Proskauer, 1975, 1975.319.1), **181** (Gift of Mrs Hope Williams Read, 1962, 62.72), **183** (From the Collection of James Stillman, Gift of Dr Ernest G. Stillman, 1922, 22.16.25), **195** (Purchase, The Annenberg Foundation Gift, 1996, 1996.418), **206** (Rogers Fund, 1922, 22.82.1-17), **209** (Robert Lehman Collection, 1975, 1975.1.683), **230** (Robert Lehman Collection, 1975, 1975.1.774), **238** (Metropolitan Museum of Art, New York. Bequest of Abby Aldrich Rockefeller, 1948, 48.190.2), **252** (Robert Lehman Collection, 1975, 1975.1.705), **259** (Harris Brisbane Dick Fund, 1948, 48.10.4), **262** (Robert Lehman Collection, 1975, 1975.1.720); New York, Museum of Modern Art **114, 251**; New York, Pierpont Morgan Library **194**; Norwich, Sainsbury Centre for Visual Arts, UEA **244**; Oxford, Ashmolean Museum **56b, 129t, 141**; Paris, Bibliothèque Nationale de France **136, 146**; Paris, Musée du Louvre **39, 41, 44, 45, 54r, 66t, 70, 70–71, 71, 189r, 253, 258**; Paris, Musée Marmottan Monet **132, 135b**; Paris, Musée d'Orsay **78, 135t, 142, 179, 196, 202**; Paris, Petit Palais, Musée des Beaux-Arts de la Ville de Paris **175, 188**; Paris, Photo RMN-Grand Palais **19r** (Musée d'Orsay)/Michèle Bellot), **22** (Musée du Louvre)/Michel Urtado), **33** (Agence Bulloz), **143** (Musée d'Orsay)/Tony Querrec), **212** (A. Danvers); Pasadena, Norton Simon Museum **224**; Philadelphia Museum of Art **176** (Gift of Mrs Sargent McKean, 1950-52-1), **250** (The Henry P. McIlhenny Collection in memory of Frances P. McIlhenny, 1986-26-31), **268** (The Henry P. McIlhenny Collection in memory of Frances P. McIlhenny, 1986-26-33); The Picture Art Collection/Alamy Stock Photo **69**; Pictures Now/Alamy Stock Photo **226**; Providence, Rhode Island School of Design Museum **235, 273**; Private collections **7, 16l, 54l, 62, 93, 131, 156, 163, 164, 165, 166, 203, 222, 236, 248, 261t**; Richmond, Virginia Museum of Fine Arts **180**; Roger-Viollet/TopFoto **109b**; Rotterdam, Museum Boijmans Van Beuningen **91, 92, 231, 275**; Rutgers, The Jane Voorhees Zimmerli Art Museum, The State University of New Jersey, Herbert D. and Ruth Schimmel Museum Library Fund **264**; San Francisco, The Fine Arts Museum **276**; Stockholm, Nationalmuseum **184**; Viareggio, Italy, Istituto Matteucci **160**; Walsall, Courtesy The New Art Gallery. Photo Sallie Magnante **43, 104**; Washington, DC, National Gallery of Art **50** (collection of Mr and Mrs Paul Mellon), **117** (Wildenstein vol. 1, no. 194, Rosenwald Collection, 1951.16.64), **130** (collection of Mr and Mrs Paul Mellon, 1995.47.60), **177** (Rosenwald Collection, 1948.11.50), **216** (Rosenwald Collection, 1943.3.3825); Washington, DC, National Portrait Gallery, Smithsonian Institution **170**; Westimage/Art Digital Studio © Sotheby's **215**; Williamstown (MA), Sterling and Francine Clark Art Institute **52, 76, 133**; Dominic Winter Auctioneers **213**; Winterthur, Oskar Reinhart Collection 'Am Römerholz' **98**; York Art Gallery **51**.

Acknowledgments

I am grateful to Richard Brettell for the reference to the article in *Master Drawings* by Debra DeWitte cited in the Introduction. Dennis Cate gallantly and kindly came to my rescue over drawings by Jean-François Raffaëlli. My wife, Frances, once again solved problems arising from my inadequacies with technology and also helped with the proofreading.

As on previous occasions, I owe a huge debt to Julia MacKenzie at Thames & Hudson for her editorial work, and for the present publication also to her colleagues Giovanni Forti, the picture researcher; Sarah Praill, the book's designer; and Susanna Ingram, who oversaw the printing and production. Their encouragement and application at all stages have been very much appreciated.

About the author

Christopher Lloyd worked in the Department of Western Art of the Ashmolean Museum in Oxford from 1968 to 1988, combining curatorial duties with teaching. During that time he was appointed by Harvard University to a Fellowship at Villa I Tatti in Florence and was Visiting Research Curator of Early Italian Painting at the Art Institute of Chicago. He was appointed Surveyor of The Queen's Pictures in the British Royal Collection in 1988 and retired from that post in 2005. His publications include monographs on painters, catalogues of museum collections and surveys of the Royal Collection, as well as *Edgar Degas: Drawings and Pastels* and *Paul Cézanne: Drawings and Watercolours*.